G. v. Bochmann   D. K. Probst (Eds.)

Computer Aided Verification

Fourth International Workshop, CAV '92
Montreal, Canada, June 29 - July 1, 1992
Proceedings

Springer-Verlag

Berlin Heidelberg New York
London Paris Tokyo
Hong Kong Barcelona
Budapest

Volume Editors

Gregor von Bochmann
Departement d'IRO, Université de Montreal
P. O. Box 6128, Station A, Montreal, Quebec, H3C 3J7, Canada

David Karl Probst
Department of Computer Science, Concordia University
1455 de Maisonneuve West, Montreal, Quebec, H3G 1M8, Canada

CR Subject Classification (1991): F.3, D.2.4, B.7, C.2.2

ISBN 3-540-56496-9 Springer-Verlag Berlin Heidelberg New York
ISBN 0-387-56496-9 Springer-Verlag New York Berlin Heidelberg

Typesetting: Camera ready by author/editor
45/3140-543210 - Printed on acid-free paper

Preface

This is the Proceedings of the Fourth Workshop on Computer-Aided Verification (CAV '92), held in Montreal, June 29 - July 1, 1992. The objective of this series of workshops is to bring together researchers and practitioners interested in the development and use of methods, tools and theories for the computer-aided verification of concurrent systems. The workshops provide an opportunity for comparing various verification methods and practical tools that can be used to assist the applications designer. Emphasis is placed on new research results and the application of existing results to real verification problems.

Of the 75 papers that were submitted, 31 were accepted for presentation. Leslie Lamport gave the invited talk on hierarchical structure in proofs. Amir Pnueli was the banquet speaker. There were sessions devoted to Reduction Techniques, Proof Checking, Symbolic Verification, Timing Verification, Partial-Order Approaches, Case Studies, Model and Proof Checking, and Other Approaches.

Financial support was provided by Concordia University, Computer Research Institute of Montreal (CRIM), Bell Northern Research (BNR), the IDACOM-NSERC-CWARC Industrial Research Chair on Communication Protocols, the Institut National de la Recherche Scientifique (INRS-Telecommunications), the Natural Sciences and Engineering Research Council of Canada (NSERC), and the University of Montreal.

The Program Committee reviewed, managed other reviewers, and helped in the establishment of the program. The Steering Committee, consisting of E.M. Clarke (Carnegie Mellon University), R.P. Kurshan (AT&T Bell Laboratories), A. Pnueli (Weizmann Institute), and J. Sifakis (LGI-IMAG), reviewed and offered council at appropriate moments. This year, the Program Committee members were: R. Alur (AT&T Bell Labs), R. Brayton (UC Berkeley), E. Brinksma (U. Twente), E. Cerny (U. Montreal), C. Courcoubetis (U. Crete), R. de Simone (INRIA), D. Dill (Stanford U.), A. Emerson (UT Austin), O. Grumberg (Technion), H. Hiraishi (Kyoto Sangyo U.), G. Holzmann (AT&T Bell Labs), W.A. Hunt Jr. (CLI), K. Larsen (Aalborg U.), P. Loewenstein (Sun), A. Mazurkiewicz (Polish Acad. Sci.), L. Paulson (Cambridge U.), D.K. Probst (Concordia U.), B. Steffen (TU Aachen), D. Taubner (sd&m GmbH) and P. Wolper (U. Liege). The names of additional reviewers are listed on the following page.

Gregor v. Bochmann was General and Program Chair. David K. Probst was Local Arrangements Chair and much more. Lucie Levesque was Registration Chair and resource person. Anindya Das was Treasurer. Stan Swiercz and Daniel Ouimet provided technical support for tool demonstrations. Most of the articles in this volume were typeset using the LaTeX document preparation system and Springer-Verlag's LNCS style file, slightly modified.

Gregor v. Bochmann
David K. Probst

Montreal, January 1993

Additional Reviewers

P. Attie (UT Austin), A. Aziz (UC Berkeley), W. Baker (UC Berkeley), F. Balarin (UC Berkeley), D. Barnard (TU Munich), H. Baumer (U Twente), R. Bayardo (UT Austin), O. Bernholtz (Technion), A. Borjesson (Aalborg U), B. Botma (U Twente), A. Bouajjani (LGI-IMAG), A. Bouali (INRIA), G. Boudol (INRIA), O. Burkart (RWTH Aachen), I. Castellani (INRIA), A. Claen (RWTH Aachen), H. Eertink (U Twente), P. Eijk (U Twente), U. Engberg (Aarhus U), T. Filkorn (Siemens), N. Francez (Technion), M. Fujita (Fujitsu), H. Garavel (Verilog), P. Godefroid (U Liege), C. Godskesen (Aalborg U), M. Gordon (Cambridge), S. Graf (LGI-IMAG), P. Gutwin (UC Berkeley), N. Halbwachs (LGI-IMAG), K. Hamaguchi (Kyoto U), T. Henzinger (Cornell U), R. Hojati (UC Berkeley), A. Hu (Stanford U), H. Huttel (Aalborg U), C. Jard (IRISA), T. Jeron (Alcatel), C. Jutla (IBM), M. Kaltenbach (UT Austin), T. Kam (UC Berkeley), P. Kars (U Twente), S. Katz (Technion), S. Kimura (Kobe U), A. Kindler (RWTH Aachen), M. Klein (RWTH Aachen), J. Knoop (Kiel), S. Krishnan (UC Berkeley), W. Lam (UC Berkeley), R. Langerak (U Twente), L. Lavagno (UC Berkeley), C. Loiseaux (LGI-IMAG), A. Mader (TU Munich), J. Makowsky (Technion), A. Mendelson (Technion), F. Mignard (INRIA), C. Moon (UC Berkeley), D. Ouimet (U Montreal), R. Rajaraman (UT Austin), C. Ratel (LGI-IMAG), D. Russinoff (CLI), S. Sagiv (Haifa), A. Scholz (Siemens), M. Sekine (UC Berkeley), N. Shankar (SRI), T. Shiple (UC Berkeley), M. Sinderen (U Twente), A. Skou (Aalborg U), P. Stephan (UC Berkeley), J. Tretmans (U Twente), F. Vaandrager (INRIA), J. Vaucher (U Montreal), T. Villa (UC Berkeley), H. Wang (UC Berkeley), C. Weise (RWTH Aachen), G. Whitcomb (UC Berkeley), H. Wong-Toi (Stanford U), W. Yi (Aalborg U), M. Yoeli (Technion), G. York (UC Berkeley), S. Yovine (LGI-IMAG).

Table of Contents

Computer-Hindered Verification
(Humans Can Do It Too)

Abstract

Leslie Lamport

Digital Equipment Corporation

Writing proofs is easy. It is so easy that mathematicians and computer scientists seem to have little difficulty writing proofs of incorrect theorems. We need to make it harder to prove things that aren't true. There is an inevitable conflict between the goals of making a proof easy to write and making it likely to be correct. Ordinary mathematical proofs are easy to write, but error prone. Mechanical proof checkers can make it almost impossible to prove an incorrect theorem, but they make it very difficult to prove a correct one. Little attention has been paid to proof methods that lie between these two extremes.

Hierarchically structured hand-checked proofs are more likely to be correct than conventional, unstructured proofs. A modest amount of extra effort in writing the proof yields an enormous increase in confidence compared with ordinary mathematical proofs. By increasing the depth of a hierarchically structured proof, one can increase the likelihood that it is correct. We do not know how reliable such proofs can be. It is possible that they can be made almost as error free as mechanically checked proofs.

Even if hand proofs can be made very rigorous, mechanical verification will still be appropriate for some applications. However, what is proved should depend on the application, not on the limitations of the verification system. The properties to be proved should be expressed in a formalism that is appropriate to the problem. It is then possible to decompose the proof so that different parts are proved by different methods–some mechanically, others by hand. The proof method can depend on the formal structure of the particular property and on how important that property is. For an avionics system, one might use three different methods to prove that (i) the load on a wing is never great enough to make it fail, (ii) a landing is never attempted before the landing gear has been lowered, and (iii) the coffee maker never overheats the coffee.

Modular Abstractions for Verifying Real-Time Distributed Systems

Hana De-Leon and Orna Grumberg
Computer Science Department
The Technion
Haifa 32000, Israel
orna@cs.technion.ac.il

1 Introduction

Temporal logics are widely used as languages for specifying system behaviors. Within temporal logics, qualitative reference to time (e.g., *"eventually"*, *"always"*) is possible. Real-time systems are systems in which the correct behavior depends not only on the actions performed, but also on the time duration of each action. In order to specify the behavior of such systems, quantitative reference to time is necessary. Real-time temporal logics include quantitative reference to time (e.g., *"within 5 time units"*) and therefore are suitable to express properties of real-time systems.

Considerable research has recently been done on the specification and verification of finite-state real-time systems ([ACD90], [AH89],[Alu91], [EMSS89], [Ha88], [HLP90], and others). A number of specification languages have been suggested, models to describe real-time systems have been presented and the problems of satisfiability and model checking have been investigated. A comprehensive survey of recent work appears in [AH91].

In this work, we address the verification of finite-state, real-time distributed systems. The number of states of a distributed system may grow exponentially with the number of its components, thus state explosion may occur. Following solutions that work well with untimed systems, our verification methodology is based on two main ideas, modularity and abstraction. We exploit the modular structure of the system to reduce each of the components by abstracting away from details that are irrelevant for the required specification. The abstract components are then composed to form an abstract system to which a model checking procedure is applied. The abstraction relation and the specification language are chosen to guarantee that if the abstract system satisfies a specification then the original system satisfies it as well.

Since each of the components is abstracted independently, our methodology enables easy and modular changes of a verified distributed system. When replacing a component in an already verified system, it is enough to show that the original component is an abstraction of the new one. This immediately implies that the new system satisfies the specification. Thus, an application of a model checking procedure to the new system is avoided. Moreover, by proving a system correct we actually prove correct a whole family of instantiations of the system.

Similar verification methodologies appear in [Ku90] for the linear-time case and in [SG90] and [GL91] for the branching-time case. However, none of them considers the real-time framework. Real-time models for processes and composed systems are suggested in [NS90] in the context of process algebra. However, they consider strong bisimulation while our abstraction is a preorder. Also, they do not consider any temporal specification language.

The logic RTL is a branching-time version of the linear-time, real-time logic $TPTL$, presented in [AH89]. A formula in the logic is:

$$E \,\Box\, x.(p \rightarrow A \Diamond y.(q \,\wedge\, y \leq x + 10))$$

It means that for *some* path, it is *always* true (at time x) that if p holds then along *every* path, *eventually* (at time y) q holds and $y \leq x + 10$. In other words, whenever p becomes true, then q becomes true within 10 time units. x and y are variables that *freeze* the value of the clock at certain events. The freezing variables range over the natural numbers. They can be compared by means of $\geq$ and modulo a time constant.

We developed a model checking procedure for RTL, which is exponential in the size of the formula and linear in the size of the model. The exponent arises from the time constants, represented in the formula by $log\ n$ symbols, but induce n computation steps. $TPTL$ is a powerful language ([AH90]) however, model checking for $TPTL$ although linear in the size of the model is double exponential in the size of the formula. Thus, we are motivated to choose the branching version of $TPTL$ as our specification language. Due to lack of space, we do not present our model checking here. Its details can be found in [DG92].

Other branching-time real-time logics are suggested in [EMSS89], [ACD90] and [Alu91], all solving the model checking problem for global systems. The first one suggests a simplified model of computation in which each transition takes exactly one time unit. The others discuss dense time and it is not clear how to introduce the notions of processes and composition into this framework.

In this work, real-time processes and real-time systems are modeled by state transition graphs in which states are labeled by atomic propositions and transitions are labeled by action names and time duration. We adopt the concept of *two alternating phases* of synchronous and asynchronous behaviors, suggested in [NS90]. All processes synchronize on time progress, while between two time progresses, processes cooperate asynchronously. Processes communicate via *handshaking* message passing.

Four types of actions are introduced: internal actions, message passing actions, interrupt actions and alternative actions. The first two types are self explanatory. Interrupts are communication actions with higher priority, i.e., a process that can receive an interrupt must do so, unless it is involved in another interrupt. Alternative actions are performed by a process only if the communication actions associated with them are not enabled. Their aim is to avoid deadlocks caused by waiting for communications to be enabled. By means of alternative actions a bounded delay may be modeled.

Two notions of abstraction are introduced, each defining a preorder on the model domain. One is an adaptation of the preorder presented in [SG90] to include reference to time duration of actions. The language preserved by this abstraction is a sublanguage of RTL, denoted RTL_A, in which only universal path quantifiers are allowed. The other is based on the stuttering equivalence for CTL_{-X} and CTL^*_{-X}, presented in [BCG88]. This abstraction allows further reduction, since a sequence of events can be abstracted to one event, provided that this sequence is 'unobservable' with respect to the specification. i.e., all states along the sequence are identically labeled, all actions are

4

internal and the sequence takes zero time. Note that, since our time is discrete, zero time means time duration that is smaller than the chosen time unit. The stuttering preorder preserves the language RTL_{A-next}, which is a sublanguage of RTL_A from which the *next* operator has been eliminated. Thus, stuttering preorder enables further reduction but preserves a smaller set of properties. We present an example in which stuttering preorder is used to verify a specification expressible in RTL_{A-next}.

The rest of the paper is organized as follows. The logic RTL is described in Section 2. In Section 3 the framework for verifying distributed systems is presented. Sections 3.1, 3.2 and 3.3 describe the structures used to model distributed systems. Section 3.4 describes the abstraction relation and the logic RTL_A. Section 3.5 presents the verification methodology and Section 3.6 includes the stuttering abstraction. In Section 4, an application of the methodology is exemplified on an alternating bit protocol. We conclude in Section 5 with a discussion of our results.

2 The logic RTL

Let AP be a set of atomic propositions and let V be a set of variables. $\forall c \in \mathbb{N}, \forall x \in V$, x, c and $(x + c)$ are *time expressions*.

Defenition : The set of atomic formulas consists of all $p \in AP$. Also, if π_1 and π_2 are time expressions then $\pi_1 \leq \pi_2$ and $\pi_1 \equiv_c \pi_2$ are atomic formulas.

We use the symbol $\sim$ to represent the relation $\equiv_c$ or $\leq$.

Defenition : The logic RTL is the set of formulas inductively defined as follows:

1. If f is an atomic formula then $f \in$ RTL.
2. If $f, g \in$ RTL then $\neg f$, $f \wedge g$, $A \circ x.f$, $E\,x.f\,U\,y.g$, $A\,x.f\,U\,y.g \in$ RTL.

We use the following abbreviations (where E/Af denotes the formulas Ef or Af):
$E \circ x.f = \neg A \circ x.\neg f$ $E/A \Diamond x.f = E/A\,true\,U\,x.f$ $E/A \Box x.f = \neg A/E \Diamond x.\neg f$

Defenition : A timed Kripke structure $M = (S, R, L)$ is a Kripke structure in which each transition is labeled with a value over the natural numbers, denoting the time duration of the transition. $(s_0, t_0), (s_1, t_1), (s_2, t_2) \ldots$ is a path in M from s_0 iff $\forall i \in \mathbb{N}\,(s_i, t_i, s_{i+1}) \in R$.

Defenition : Let T be a variable which represents the "current time" $(T \notin V)$. ε is an environment iff ε is a function from the time expressions over $V \cup \{T\}$ to $\mathbb{N}$ which satisfies the following: $\forall x \in V \cup \{T\}$, $\forall c \in \mathbb{N}$, $\varepsilon(c) = c$ and $\varepsilon(x+c) = \varepsilon(x) + \varepsilon(c)$.

Defenition : Let ε be an environment. $\varepsilon[x_1 := c_1, x_2 := c_2, \ldots, x_n := c_n]$ is an environment in which $\forall 1 \leq i \leq n$ the value of x_i is c_i. The values of all other variables are the same as in ε.

The semantics of RTL is defined with respect to a timed Kripke structure $M = (S, R, L)$, $s \in S$ and an environment ε. We use the notation $M, s, \varepsilon \models f$ to denote that f is true in state s, in the structure M, with respect to environment ε. M is omitted when no confusion may occur.

Defenition : The satisfaction relation $\models$ is inductively defined as follows:

1. if $a \in AP$ then $s, \varepsilon \models a$ iff $a \in L(s)$.
   $s, \varepsilon \models \neg f$ iff $s, \varepsilon \not\models f$ and $s, \varepsilon \models f \wedge g$ iff $s, \varepsilon \models f$ and $s, \varepsilon \models g$.

2. $s, \varepsilon \models \pi_1 \sim \pi_2$ iff $\varepsilon(\pi_1) \sim \varepsilon(\pi_2)$.

3. $s, \varepsilon \models A \circ x.f$ iff $\forall s' \in S, \forall t \in \mathbb{N}$ such that $s \xrightarrow{t} s'$,

$$s', \varepsilon[T := \varepsilon(T) + t , \ x := \varepsilon(T) + t] \models f.$$

4. $s, \varepsilon \models E \ x.f \ U \ y.g$ iff there exists a path $(s_0, t_0), (s_1, t_1) \ldots$ in M such that $s_0 = s$ and there exists $i \in \mathbb{N}$ such that

$$s_i, \varepsilon[T := \varepsilon(T) + \textstyle\sum_{l=0}^{i-1} t_l , \ y := \varepsilon(T) + \textstyle\sum_{l=0}^{i-1} t_l \ ] \models g$$

and for all $0 \leq j < i$

$$s_j, \varepsilon[T := \varepsilon(T) + \textstyle\sum_{l=0}^{j-1} t_l , \ x := \varepsilon(T) + \textstyle\sum_{l=0}^{j-1} t_l \ ] \models f.$$

$s, \varepsilon \models A \ x.f \ U \ y.g$ is defined similarly for *every* path starting from s.

theorem 1 *Let $\varphi \in RTL$, $M = (S, R, L)$, $s \in S$ and ε an environment. The time required to determine whether $s, \varepsilon \models \varphi$ is linear in the size of M and exponential in the size of φ.*

In [DG92], a model checking procedure MC for RTL is described, proved correct, and shown to have the above complexity.

3   The verification of distributed systems

In this section we present a methodology for the verification of real-time properties for synchronous, distributed systems, based on their decomposition into processes. For this purpose we introduce a composition operation that composes n processes into a system. Since the resulting system might be too large for a computer memory to hold, our aim is to find an abstraction for each of the system's components, that is smaller by the number of states than the original process. Composing the abstract components will result in a system which is, hopefully, much smaller than the original one. Our notion of abstraction and the chosen specification language are such that every property of the abstract system described by means of the language, is guaranteed to hold in the original system. Thus, the original system is never constructed and model checking is applied to the abstract system. Consequently, space and time are saved. We start the description by specifying how distributed systems are modeled.

3.1   The action set

Defenition : The set of process actions denoted by $ACTION_1$, consists of 4 disjoint sets:

1. A set of internal actions $\Lambda = \{(\lambda, 0), (\lambda, 1)\}$.
2. A set of message passing actions, $MES = SMES \cup RMES$, where $SMES$ and $RMES$ are disjoint and contain actions denoting sending of messages and receiving of messages, respectively. $(a, k) \in SMES$ iff $(\bar{a}, k) \in RMES$ where $k \in \{0, 1\}$.

3. A set of interrupt actions, $INT = SINT \cup RINT$, where $SINT$ and $RINT$ are disjoint and contain actions denoting sending of interrupts and receiving of interrupts, respectively. $(a, k) \in SINT$ iff $(\bar{a}, k) \in RINT$ where $k \in \{0, 1\}$.
4. A set of alternative actions, ξ. $(a, k) \in SMES \cup SINT$ iff $(\varepsilon a, k), (\varepsilon \bar{a}, k) \in \xi$.

The motivation for the above definition is as follows.

- A communication action is performed via handshaking between the sender and the receiver. Therefore, such an action may occur only when the two processes are ready to execute it. In many cases, we would like to have an alternative action which will be perform only when the communication action cannot be done. The alternative action of a communication action a $(\bar{a})$, is denoted by εa $(\varepsilon \bar{a})$.
- An interrupt is different from an ordinary message passing in the following way. In a composed system, a process that can receive an interrupt, must do so, unless it is involved in another interrupt action. A process that can receive a message, may choose to do another action.
- A process, willing to receive an interrupt, does not oblige the sending of the interrupt.
- By partitioning the communication actions into two groups, INT and MES, we establish two priority levels. This idea can be extended to construct several levels of priority.

3.2 The process model

Defenition : A process model is a 6-tuple $M = (AC, AP, S, s_0, R, L)$ where, $AC \subseteq ACTION_1$ is the subset of $ACTION_1$ used in R, AP is a set of atomic propositions, S is a finite set of states, s_0 is the initial state, and $R \subseteq S \times ACTION_1 \times S$ is a transition relation which is total in its first argument. The notation $s \xrightarrow{\alpha} t$ is used to indicate that $(s, \alpha, t) \in R$. $L : S \to P(AP)$ is a function that labels each state with a set of atomic propositions. We only consider processes that satisfy the following three requirements:

1. Along every path, time eventually advances, i.e., there are no zero time cycles.
2. The set of transitions originating from a state always includes at least one internal action or alternative action.
3. If the set of transitions originating from a state contains a transition labeled with εa $(\varepsilon \bar{a})$ then it contains also a transition labeled with a $(\bar{a})$.

The totality of R implies that processes contain no deadlock. The second requirement guarantees that deadlock does not occur when processes are composed into systems. The above requirements are not crucial for the verification methodology described below and could be released with some changes of definitions.

3.3 The system model

Given n processes $M_1, \ldots, M_n$ to be composed into a system, we consider two possible definitions. One possibility is to define a set of composition operators, one for each arity, such that a system composed of n processes will be obtained by applying the n-ary composition operator to the n processes, i.e., $\|_n (M_1, \ldots, M_n)$. Another possibility is to define one binary composition operator, that applied to two processes results in a new process. Additional operator will be needed to transform a process into a system. The main purpose of the additional operator is to omit transitions which are not enabled in the global system, e.g., transitions that correspond to communications on which only one participant is waiting (since we assume handshaking message passing, such transitions will never occur). Unreachable subgraphs should also be omitted.

The second definition, although more commonly used, has a severe drawback. Processes constructed in intermediate stages, might be much larger than the resulting system. Consequently, the first possibility is chosen. For conveniency, we use the notation $M_1 \| M_2 \| \ldots \| M_n$ instead of $\|_n (M_1, M_2, \ldots, M_n)$. Recall that we assume two alternating phases of synchronization and handshaking message passing. Also, each message is assumed to have a unique sender and an arbitrary number of receivers.

Defenition: For each $2 \leq n \in \mathbb{N}$ the set of actions $ACTION_n$ is defined as follows:
$(x_1, \ldots, x_n, 1) \in ACTION_n$ iff $\forall 1 \leq i \leq n, \ (x_i, 1) \in ACTION_1$
$(x_1, \ldots, x_n, 0) \in ACTION_n$ iff $\forall 1 \leq i \leq n \ [((x_i, 0) \in ACTION_1) \lor (x_i = \rho)]$
where, $x_i = \rho$ means that process i does not perform any action, and therefore, does not change its state. The tuple $(\rho, \ldots, \rho, 0) \notin ACTION_n$.

$$ACTION = \bigcup_{n=1}^{\infty} ACTION_n$$

Defenition: Let $M_1, \ldots M_n$ be process models where, $M_i = (AC_i, AP_i, S_i, s_0^i, R_i, L_i)$ then $\forall 1 \leq i \leq n, SEND_i = \{(a, k) | (a, k) \in (SMES \cup SINT) \cap AC_i\}$.

Defenition: $M_1, \ldots M_n$ are composable if $\forall j \neq i: AP_i \cap AP_j = \emptyset$ and $SEND_i \cap SEND_j = \emptyset$.

Defenition: Let $M_1, \ldots M_n$ be composable processes. The model $M = M_1 \| M_2 \| \ldots \| M_n$ of the composed system is defined as follows:

1. If $n = 1$ then $M = M_1$.
2. If $n > 1$ then $M = (AC, AP, S, s_0, R, L)$ where:
   - $s_0 = (s_0^1, s_0^2, \ldots, s_0^n)$.
   - $S \subseteq S_1 \times \ldots \times S_n$ is the maximal set of states, reachable from s_0 by transitions in R.
   - $AP = AP_1 \cup AP_2 \cup \ldots \cup AP_n$.
   - $L: S \to P(AP)$ is the labeling function such that,
     $\forall (s_1, \ldots s_n) \in S, \quad L((s_1, \ldots, s_n)) = L_1(s_1) \cup \ldots \cup L_n(s_n)$.
   - R is the set of all transitions of the form $(s_1, \ldots s_n) \xrightarrow{x_1, \ldots x_n, k} (t_1, \ldots t_n)$ that satisfy the following four conditions (where $I = \{1, 2, \ldots n\}$):
     (a) One of the two conditions bellow holds:
        i. $k = 1 \ \land \ \forall i \in I \ (s_i, (x_i, k), t_i) \in R_i$.
        ii. $k = 0$ and there exist $I' \subseteq I, I' \neq \emptyset$ such that $\forall i \in I', \ (s_i, (x_i, k), t_i) \in R_i$ and $\forall i \in I - I' \ (s_i = t_i \ \land \ x_i = \rho)$.
     (b) $\exists i \in I$ such that $x_i = a$ iff $\exists j \in I$ such that $x_j = \bar{a}$.
     (c) $\neg \exists i, j \in I$ such that $x_i = \varepsilon a \ \land \ x_j = \varepsilon \bar{a}$.
     (d) If there are $i \in I, (a, k) \in SINT$ such that $x_i = a$ or $x_i = \varepsilon a$, then
        $\forall j \in I, \forall t \in S_j \ [(s_j, (\bar{a}, k), t) \in R_j \Rightarrow (x_j, k) \in INT]$

8

- AC is the set of actions such that $\forall (s_1, \ldots s_n), (t_1, \ldots t_n) \in S, \forall \alpha \in ACTION_n$ if $((s_1, \ldots s_n), \alpha, (t_1, \ldots t_n)) \in R$ then $\alpha \in AC$.

Note that each process model is also a system model with $n = 1$.
Comments to the definition of R:
Condition (a)i: In a transition that takes 1 time unit, each one of the system's component performs a transition that takes 1 time unit. (This is similar to the time action χ, suggested in [NS90]).
Condition (a)ii: In a transition that takes 0 time units, at least one of the system's component performs a transition which takes 0 time units. All other components may be idle, i.e., may not take any action. Figure 1 demonstrates conditions $(a)i$ and $(a)ii$.

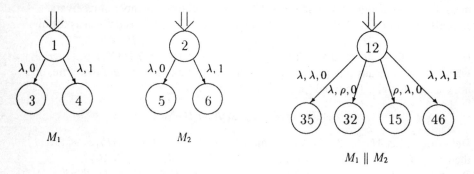

Fig. 1. Demonstration of condition (a)

Condition (b): The communication is done by handshaking.
Condition (c): An alternative action εa is performed by a process only if there is no suitable partner for the communication action a. Therefore, it is impossible for alternative actions of corresponding communication actions $(\varepsilon a, \varepsilon \bar{a})$, to occur in the same transition. (If both processes prefer to do the communication action $(a, \bar{a})$ then the communication action will be performed).
Condition (d): If there is a process M_i, that either sends interrupt a or is forced to perform εa, then every process M_j that could receive interrupt a is involved in some interrupt action (either a or another one). Example: when M_1, M_2 and M_3 of figure 2 are composed, then if $a \in SINT, b \in SMES$ then M_4 is obtained. If $a, b \in SINT$ then M_5 is obtained.

3.4 The abstraction relation $\geq$

Let $M = (AC, AP, S, s_0, R, L)$ and $M' = (AC', AP', S', s'_0, R', L')$ be system models. We define a sequence of relations $F_i \subseteq S' \times S$ as follows.
Definition: For every $s \in S, s' \in S'$:

1. $s' F_0 s$ iff $L(s) \cap AP' = L'(s')$.
2. $s' F_{n+1} s$ iff $s' F_n s$ and

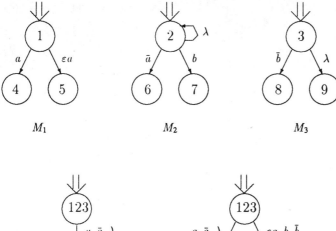

Fig. 2. Demonstration of condition (d)

(a) $\forall t \in S, \forall a \in ACTION \; (s \xrightarrow{\alpha} t \Rightarrow \exists t' \in S' \; (s' \xrightarrow{\alpha} t' \wedge t' F_n t))$

(b) $\forall t' \in S', \forall (\bar{a}, k) \in RINT \; (s' \xrightarrow{\bar{a},k} t' \Rightarrow \exists t \in S \; (s \xrightarrow{\bar{a},k} t \wedge t' F_n t))$

The relation $F \subseteq S' \times S$ is defined as follows: $\forall s \in S, \forall s' \in S'$, $s' F s$ iff $\forall i \geq 0$, $s' F_i s$.
Defenition : $M' \geq M$ iff $AP' \subseteq AP$ and $s_0' F s_0$.

Condition 2b of the definition of F_{n+1} is relevant only when M and M' are models of processes. Its aim is to guarantee the monotonicity of composition with respect to $\geq$. Consider Figure 3. Eliminating condition 2b from F, $M_1 \geq M_2$ holds. However, $M_1 \parallel M_3 \not\geq M_2 \parallel M_3$, thus, monotonicity is not accomplished.

RTL_A is a sublanguage of RTL that includes only universal path quantifiers. Formulas in the logic are assumed to be in negation normal form, so that existential path quantifiers do not arise via negation. The semantics of RTL_A is identical to that of RTL. In the sequel, we interpret RTL_A formulas with respect to a system model M. When this is done, the meaning of $\varphi \in RTL_A(AP)$ is determined with respect to the structure obtained from M by eliminating the action labels and the initial state. For $\varphi \notin RTL_A(AP)$, $M, s, \varepsilon \not\models \varphi$ for every s and every ε.

theorem 2 *Let $M' \geq M$. $\forall s \in S, \forall s' \in S'$, if $s' F s$ then for every $\varphi \in RTL_A$ and for every environment ε, $M', s', \varepsilon \models \varphi \Rightarrow M, s, \varepsilon \models \varphi$.*

Let $M_1, \ldots M_n, M_1', \ldots M_n'$ be models of processes such that $M_1, \ldots M_n$ are composable, and so are $M_1', \ldots M_n'$. The theorems below establish the validity of the verification methodology, presented in Section 3.5.

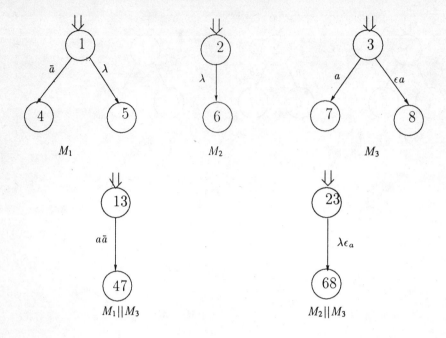

$$\bar{a}, a \in INT$$

Fig. 3. Motivating condition $2(b)$ of the relation F_{n+1}

theorem 3 *If* $\forall 1 \leq i \leq n$, $M_i' \geq M_i$ *then*

$$M_1' \parallel M_2' \parallel \ldots \parallel M_n' \geq M_1 \parallel M_2 \parallel \ldots \parallel M_n.$$

theorem 4 *If* $\forall 1 \leq i \leq n$, $M_i' \geq M_i$ *then,* $\forall \varphi \in RTL_A$ *and for every environment* ε

$$M_1' \parallel \ldots \parallel M_n', (s_0'^1, \ldots s_0'^n), \varepsilon \models \varphi \quad \Rightarrow \quad M_1 \parallel \ldots \parallel M_n, (s_0^1, \ldots s_0^n), \varepsilon \models \varphi$$

3.5 The verification methodology

Given a system composed of processes $M_1, \ldots M_n$ and a specification φ, the following steps are performed: (1) Construct reduced processes $M_1', \ldots, M_n'$. (2) Check that $\forall i \, [M_i' \geq M_i]$, and (3) Apply the procedure MC to the reduced system $M_1' \parallel \ldots \parallel M_n'$, to check whether it satisfies φ.

While the first step should be suggested by the user, the two other step are performed automatically. If the reduced system satisfies the specification, Theorem 4 implies that the original system satisfies it as well. If the reduced system does not satisfy the specification, there are two possibilities: either the original system does not satisfy the specification, or the reduction eliminates some information which is relevant for the specification. In the second case, another reduction should be tried, that includes the necessary information. This part is based on the user understanding of the verified system. The advantages of the proposed methodology:

1. Space is saved since the number of states of the reduced system is smaller.
2. The run time of MC depends on the number of states, therefore reducing the number of states, reduces also the run time.
3. Given that $M_1 \| \ldots \| M_n \models \varphi$, if M_i should be replaced by M_i^*, then $M_i \geq M_i^*$ will guarantee that $M_1 \| \ldots \| M_i^* \| \ldots \| M_n \models \varphi$. Thus, an application of MC to the complete system is replaced by checking "$\geq$" for one of the components. This enables easy modular changes of an existing system. Moreover, by proving $M_1 \| \ldots \| M_n \models \varphi$, a whole family of systems, composed of n components M_i^*, such that $M_i \geq M_i^*$, are shown to satisfy φ.

3.6 The stuttering abstraction $\geq^*$

Defenition : Let $M = (AC, AP, S, s_0, R, L)$ and $M' = (AC', AP', S', s_0', R', L')$ be system models, each composed of m processes. $F_i^* \subseteq S' \times S$ is a sequence of relations such that for every $s \in S, s' \in S'$:

$s' F_0^* s$ iff $L(s) \cap AP' = L'(s')$.

$s' F_{n+1}^* s$ iff $s' F_n^* s$ and one of the following holds:

$m = 1$ and

1. $\forall t \in S$, $\forall \alpha \in ACTION \; [s \xrightarrow{\alpha} t \Rightarrow [\exists t' \in S' \, (s' \xrightarrow{\alpha} t' \wedge t' F_n^* t) \vee (\alpha = (\lambda, 0) \wedge s' F_n^* t)]]$

2. $\forall t' \in S'$, $\forall (\bar{a}, k) \in RINT \; [s' \xrightarrow{\bar{a}, k} t' \Rightarrow \exists t \in S \, (s \xrightarrow{\bar{a}, k} t \wedge t' F_n^* t)]$

$m > 1$ and

$\forall t \in S$, $\forall \alpha \in ACTION \; [s \xrightarrow{\alpha} t \Rightarrow [\exists t' \in S' \, (s' \xrightarrow{\alpha} t' \wedge t' F_n^* t) \vee (\alpha = (x_1, \ldots x_m, 0) \wedge s' F_n^* t)]]$

F_i^* is defined similarly to F_i, except that it is possible for a sequence of states in S to be related to one state s' in S' (even when s' does not have a self loop). Since these states are all related to the same state, their labels with respect to AP' are identical. Also, they are all connected by zero time transitions. However, when the related systems consist of one process, only zero time λ actions are allowed, while for systems composed of $m > 1$ processes, any zero time action is allowed. Note that we assume that there are no zero time cycles, therefore along a path, only finitely many occurrences of states will be F^*-related to one state. F^* and $\geq^*$ are defined similarly to the non stuttering case.

The specification language in accord with the stuttering abstraction $\geq^*$ is the logic RTL_{A-next} obtained from RTL_A by eliminating the operator $A\circ$. As for the abstraction relation $\geq$ we get:

theorem 5 *Let $M_1, M_2, \ldots M_n, M_1', M_2' \ldots M_n'$ be models of processes such that $M_1, M_2 \ldots M_n$ are composable and so are $M_1', M_2' \ldots M_n'$.*
If $\forall 1 \leq i \leq n$, $M_i' \geq^* M_i$ then $\forall \varphi \in RTL_{A-next}$ and for every environment ε:

$$M_1' \| \ldots \| M_n', (s_0'^{\,1}, \ldots s_0'^{\,n}), \varepsilon \models \varphi \;\Rightarrow\; M_1 \| \ldots \| M_n, (s_0^1, \ldots s_0^n), \varepsilon \models \varphi$$

The consequence of this theorem is that the verification methodology described before is applicable in this context as well.

4 Examples

The example considered here is a version of the alternating bit protocol suggested in [SL87]. Two processes, P_1, P_2, and a data pool M are involved in this protocol. P_1 may choose nondeterministically among the following actions:[1] Rec_data - receiving data from the data pool, Send_data - sending data to P_2, and Rec_ack - receiving acknowledge from P_2. P_2 may choose nondeterministically among the following actions:[2] Send_ack - sending acknowledge to P_1, and Rec_data - receiving data from P_1.

P_1 and P_2 communicate via two channels. The process C_1 represents the channel from P_1 to P_2 and the process C_2 represents the channel from P_2 to P_1. The communication between the data pool M and P_1 is direct. The purpose of C_1 and C_2 is to model failures. Below, the algorithms run by P_1 and P_2 are described.

P_1: Rec_data :   if (acked=true) then {if rec_m(data) then {s:=1-s; acked:=false}}
Send_data :   if (acked=false) then $send_1$(data,1-s);
Rec_ack :   if (acked=false) then {if (rec_2(Ack,nr) $\wedge$ (s=nr)) then acked:=true}
P_2: Rec_data :   if (rec_1(data,ns) $\wedge$ (r=ns)) then {accept(data); r:=1-r}
Send_ack : $send_2$(ack,r);

Assumptions on the behavior of the algorithms:

1. s and r are initialized to 0. acked is initialized to true.
2. rec_i and $send_i$ for $i = 1, 2$, denote receiving a message from P_i and sending a message by P_i, respectively. rec_m denotes receiving a message from M. rec_i and $send_i$ are actions, returning true when they terminate successfully and false otherwise. We assume that sending of messages always terminates successfully since channels are always willing to accept a message. On the other hand, receiving of a message may fail, either because it has not been sent or because it has been lost (actually, a lose may occur only on rec_1 and rec_2).
3. Whenever a data from the data pool is successfully received by P_1 (rec_m returns true), P_1 must send it before receiving any other message.
4. Whenever a data is successfully received by P_2, it must send an acknowledge before being ready to receive another message.
5. The channels can lose messages.

In Figure 4, the models of P_1, P_2, C_1, C_2 and M are described. Following is an explanation to the transition labels in the figure:

- $\bar{m}$ - receiving of data by P_1 (from M).
- a, b - sending data by P_1 (to C_1). a and b are the alternating values of s in the algorithm.
- a_1, b_1 - passing data through C_1 (i.e., data received by C_1 is sent to P_2).
- $acka, ackb$ - sending acknowledge by P_2 (to C_2).
- $acka_2, ackb_2$ - passing acknowledge through C_2 (i.e., acknowledge received by C_2 is sent to P_1).

---

[1] with the exception imposed by assumption 3 below.
[2] with the exception imposed by assumption 4 below.

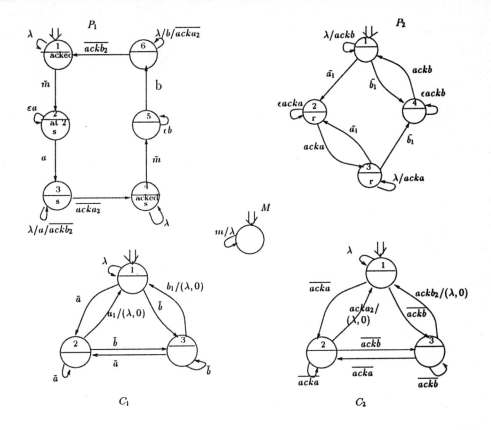

Fig. 4. Example - The Processes

$a, b, acka, ackb$ are interrupt actions. $m, a_1, b_1, acka_2, ackb_2$ are ordinary message sending actions. The time duration of the transitions is 1 time unit, unless mentioned otherwise. Note that, since messages sent by the channels to the processes are not interrupts, the processes might never choose to accept them.

Consider the following RTL_{A-next} formula:

$$\varphi = A\,\Box x.\,(at2 \rightarrow (A\,\Box y.\,y \le x+3 \rightarrow \neg acked)).$$

With respect to the system $M \parallel P_1 \parallel C_1 \parallel C_2 \parallel P_2$, the meaning of φ is that at least 3 time units pass from the time at which P_1 receives a message, until it gets the corresponding acknowledge.

The reduced processes P_1', P_2', C_1', C_2' are presented in figure 5. It can easily be shown that

$$P_1' \ge^* P_1\,,\quad P_2' \ge^* P_2\,,\quad C_1' \ge^* C_1\,,\quad C_2' \ge^* C_2.$$

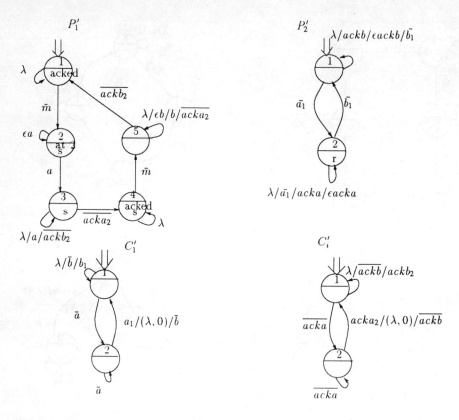

Fig. 5. Example - The Reduced Processes

(note that it is also true that $P_1' \geq P_1$ and $P_2' \geq P_2$). $M \parallel P_1' \parallel C_1' \parallel C_2' \parallel P_2'$ has 14 states, while $M \parallel P_1 \parallel C_1 \parallel C_2 \parallel P_2$ has 26 states. $M \parallel P_1' \parallel C_1' \parallel C_2' \parallel P_2' \models \varphi$ and therefore $M \parallel P_1 \parallel C_1 \parallel C_2 \parallel P_2 \models \varphi$.

5 Conclusions

This paper presents a framework for the verification of finite-state real-time distributed systems with real-time temporal specification. For specification we choose branching-time logics, since both the model checking algorithm and the algorithms to check the abstractions have a much better complexity than those for linear-time logics. Two notions of abstractions are introduced, presenting the tradeoff between the amount of reduction and the preserved language. If further reduction is enabled, a smaller set of properties is preserved.

The suggested model of computation is low level but rich. It is detailed enough to enable applying a model checking procedure directly to it, without the need to go through a transformation stage. It is rich enough to model high level constructs, useful for real-time systems, like bounded delays (including notions suggested in [NS90]) and interrupts. Unlike [NS90], we do not have a special action to denote time action and every action can be associated with time progress. However, we adopt the concept of two alternating phases of synchronous and asynchronous behaviors. This concept together with the convention that a communication has one sender and possibly many receivers, make this model adequate to describe hardware designs.

In [ACD90], a branching-time real-time logic over dense time has been introduced. It should be interesting to develop a methodology for modular verification in this framework. Checking more practical examples will indicate how useful the notions of abstraction are for real-time systems. This will require implementing the model checking algorithm and the algorithms for checking the preorders.

Acknowledgment: This research was partially supported by the U.S.-Israeli Binational Science Foundation.

References

[ACD90] R. Alur, C. Courcoubetis, D. Dill, Model-Checking for Real-time Systems, 5th LICS, 1990.

[AH89] R. Alur, T.A. Henzinger, A Really Temporal Logic, 30th FOCS, 1989

[AH90] R. Alur, T.A. Henzinger, Real Time Logics: complexity and expressiveness, 5th IEEE LICS, 1990.

[AH91] R. Alur, T.A. Henzinger, Logics and Models of Real Time: A Survey, REX 1991.

[Alu91] R. Alur, Techniques for Automatic Verification of Real-time Systems, PhD thesis, Stanford University, 1991.

[BCG88] M.C. Browne, E.M. Clarke, O. Grumberg, Characterizing Finite Kripke Structures in Propositional Temporal Logic, Theoretical Computer Science 59,pp.115-131,1988.

[DG92] H.De-leon, O. Grumberg, Modular Abstractions for Verifying Real-Time Distributed Systems, TR #713, July 1992, Computer Science Dept., Technion, Haifa. To appear in the journal on Formal Methods in System Design.

[EMSS89] E.A Emerson, A.K. Mok, A.P. Sistla, J. Srinivasan, Quantitative Temporal Reasoning, Workshop on Automatic Verification Methods for Finite-State Systems, Grenoble, France, 1989.

[GL91] O. Grumberg and D.E. Long, Model Checking and Modular Verification, CONCUR, Amsterdam, August 1991.

[Ha88] E. Harel, Temporal Analysis of Real-Time Systems, M.S Thesis, Weizmann Institute 1988.

[HLP90] E. Harel, O. Lichtenstein, A. Pnueli, Explicit Clock Temporal Logic, 5th LICS, 1990.

[Ku90] R.P. Kurshan, Analysis of Discrete Event Coordination, stepwise Refinement of Distributed Systems, LNCS 430, pp.414-453, 1990.

[NS90] X. Nicollin and J. Sifakis, The Algebra of Timed Processes ATP: Theory and Application, IMAG, RT-C26, December 1990.

[SG90] G. Shurek, O. Grumberg, The Modular Framework of Computer-Aided Verification, Workshop on Computer Aided Verification, Rutgers, NJ, June 1990.

[SL87] A.U Shankar, S.S Lam, Time-Dependent Distributed Systems: Proving Safety, Liveness and Real-Time Properties, Distributed Computing 2, pp.61-79, 1987.

Layering Techniques
for Development of Parallel Systems

An Algebraic Approach [*]

Mannes Poel & Job Zwiers,
University of Twente,
Dept. of Computer Science
P.O. Box 217,
7500 AE Enschede,
The Netherlands
E-mail:{mpoel,zwiers}@cs.utwente.nl

Abstract

A process language is presented which makes a clear distinction between temporal order and causal order. This allows for several algebraic laws that are particularly interesting for the *design* of concurrent systems. One of these is an algebraic formulation of the communication closed layers principle by [EF82]. These laws suffice to rewrite process terms that avoid specification of temporal ordering into a unique normal form. Other transformations allow for *gradually* imposing temporal ordering on an already functionally correct design. The combination of such laws enables a design strategy where architecture independent designs are transformed towards a form that matches a particular implementation architecture. We apply this style of design to various distributed algorithms, including an algorithm for the "point-in-polygon" problem transformed to a form suitable for pipelined execution on a tree network, and the Floyd-Warshall algorithm for the all-points shortest path transformed to a form suitable for execution on a SIMD architecture.

1 Introduction

In order to have a transformational algebraic approach that suits both specification and design of concurrent systems, a clear distinction should be made between temporal order and causal order between actions. In this paper we present a process language where a distinction is made between language constructs for specifying temporal order, such as the sequential composition operator, and causal order, using the *layer composition* operator, cf. [JPZ91]. Layer composition, denoted by $P \bullet Q$, gives rise to several important algebraic laws. For instance the communication closed layers principle from [EF82] can be formulated as the following algebraic law:

$$(P \bullet Q) \parallel (R \bullet S) = (P \parallel R) \bullet (Q \parallel S),$$

provided there is no "conflict" (communication) between P and S, and between Q and R. Another algebraic law, called the Left-Right Movers law states in its simplest form that

$$(P \bullet Q) \bullet (R \bullet S) = (P \bullet R) \bullet (Q \bullet S)$$

if there is no conflict between Q and R. The above laws would not be valid if we replaced layer composition by sequential composition.

Layer composition is a valuable tool in the *initial design stage* of a system. Such operations allow for an architecture independent design strategy. In this initial phase of design, the above laws together

---

[*] Part of this work has been supported by Esprit/BRA Project 6021 (REACT)

with an *expansion* theorem make it possible to rewrite a process term that avoids specification of temporal order into an unique normal form. This normal form is the maximal parallelization of that process term, and resembles the normal form for Mazurkiewicz traces. Other transformations and implementation relations, cf. section 2, then allow for a transformation of this normal form towards a process that can be implemented on a particular architecture.

This style of design is demonstrated on various distributed algorithms. First the "point-in-polygon" algorithm presented in the book of Akl, [Akl89] is considered. After removing all the irrelevant temporal order, but preserving the causal order induced by the temporal order (i.e. changing every sequential composition in a layer composition), this algorithm is rewritten into normal form. Afterwards this normal form is transformed to several distributed processes, all suitable for pipelining on a tree network.
Next the Floyd-Warshall algorithm for the "all-points shortest path" problem is discussed. Again after all the temporal order is deleted, but the induced causal order is preserved, this algorithm is transformed into normal form. Afterwards several optimal parallelizations are obtained, both for a CREW-PRAM and an EREW-PRAM.
Other applications to for instance protocols can be found in [JZ92b, JZ92a], and to parsing in [JPSZ91].

In section 2 we introduce the language together with informal discussion of the semantics. Also the algebraic laws and the theorem on normal forms are presented. In section 3 we apply the transformational algebraic approach to the point in polygon algorithm on a tree network. Section 4 gives several transformations of the Floyd-Warshall algorithm for the all-points shortest path problem. One transformation is suitable for a CREW-PRAM and another for an EREW-PRAM. Both are optimal parallelizations of the sequential Floyd-Warshall algorithm.

2   Language, Algebraic Laws, and Normal Forms

In this section we introduce a language which contains both layer composition and sequential composition. Assume that processes perform actions a that read and write shared variables $x, y, z, \ldots \in Var$, and perform (boolean valued) tests on shared variables. We employ the usual (simultaneous) assignment notation x := f where x and f are a list of variables and a list of expressions. Such assignments are guarded by means of a boolean expression b which must evaluate to true before executing the assignment. For such actions, that we denote by $b \& x := f$, the evaluation of the guard together with the assignment constitute a single *atomic* action. When the guard b is identically true, we omit it and employ the usual simultaneous assignment notation x := f. Similarly we regard boolean tests b as degenerate cases where the assignment part has been left out. Such guards can be used to model more conventional constructs. For instance we use

if b then P else Q fl   as an abbreviation for $(b \bullet P)$ or $(\neg b \bullet Q)$

For an action a of the form $b \& x := f$ the set of variables $\{x\}$ is called the write-set $W(a)$ of a. Similarly, we define the read-set $R(a)$ as the set of variables occurring (free) in b and the expression list f. Finally we define the *base* of a as $base(a) = R(a) \cup W(a)$. Two actions a_0 and a_1 *conflict* if one of them writes a variable x that is read or written by the other one. Formally we define a conflict relation on actions, denoted by $a_0 — a_1$ as follows:

$a_0 — a_1$ iff $W(a_1) \cap base(a_0) \neq \emptyset$ or $W(a_0) \cap base(a_1) \neq \emptyset$

Other models can be easily obtained by changing the conflict relation, for example by introducing also read-read conflicts, which is in correspondence with the EREW-PRAM.
The syntax for DL is as follows:

$P \in DL$,

$P ::= b \& x := f \mid P \parallel Q \mid P \bullet Q \mid P \, ; Q \mid P \text{ or } Q$

$\mid \quad \text{skip} \mid \quad \text{empty} \mid \quad P \backslash x \mid \quad \langle P \rangle \mid \quad io(P)$

We will now provide the intuition for the language operations of DL. A process P as a whole denotes the set $[\![P]\!]$ of all possible runs for that system. Execution of an action a results in a single

event. Therefore, actions are executed atomically. Our semantic domain is such that events, say e_0 and e_1, are in conflict, then they are ordered. Hence each run consists of a set of events, an a partial order $\longrightarrow$ on events, such that events which are in conflict are ordered with respect to $\longrightarrow$. Summarizing:
Each run $(E, \longrightarrow)$ of P satisfies:

- $(E, \longrightarrow)$ is a pomset of events, i.e. a partially ordered multiset.

- $\longrightarrow$ is a partial order on E such that if e and e' are in *conflict* then e and e' are ordered with respect to $\longrightarrow$.

Consequently we regard two processes P and Q as equal, denoted by $P = Q$ iff their sets of possible runs are equal, i.e. iff $[\![P]\!] = [\![Q]\!]$.

For *parallel composition*, the order that necessarily must exists between conflicting P and Q events is *nondeterministically* determined. The nondeterministic choices for different pairs of conflicting events are of course subject to the condition that the order must remain a partial order, so certain choices are excluded. Each choice corresponds to a (potential) different net effect of the whole run.

For *layer composition* $P \bullet Q$ the situation is the reverse: any P event e_0 precedes any Q event e_1 with which it conflicts. This resembles the sequential composition construct, but there is a substantial difference. For sequential composition P ; Q all P events precede *any* Q event . This is not so for layer composition. In the latter case any Q event e must wait only for its causal predecessors, implying that it need not wait for all P events.

Nondeterministic choice P or Q is a straightforward construct that either executes P or Q.

The process skip performs no action at all, and the empty process, cannot perform any computation at all, not even the computation executed by skip which contains no events. Both processes aid in formulating some algebraic properties of DL, where they act as a unit element and as a zero element respectively.

Atomic execution. Atomic brackets $\langle P \rangle$ serve to indicate that P should execute "atomically", i.e. without interference by other processes.

The *hiding* construct $P \backslash x$ hides the variable x in each run of P,i.e. it is removed from the write-set and read-set of each event. (Moreover events with empty read- and write-set are removed from the run.) The complement of the hiding operator is the projection operator; let S be a set of variables and let A be all the variables of a process P then

$$P_{|S} \stackrel{\text{def}}{=} P \backslash (A - S)$$

All the variables except those contained in S are hidden in each run of P.

$io(P)$ denotes execution of a single action that captures the net effect of executing P without admitting interference by other events. The $io(\cdot)$ operation is also called the *contraction* operation, since it contracts complete P runs into single events. Intuitively $io(P)$ represents the input-output behavior of a process P if we execute that process in isolation, i.e. without interference from outside. This operation induces an interesting process equivalence, called IO-equivalence, and an associated *implementation* relation, denoted by $P \stackrel{IO}{sat} Q$.

$$P \stackrel{IO}{=} Q \text{ iff } io(P) = io(Q), \text{ and } P \stackrel{IO}{sat} Q \text{ iff } io(P) \subseteq io(Q).$$

Such equivalences play an important role in the book by K.R. Apt and E.-R. Olderog [AO]. Specification of what is often called the *functional behavior* of a process P is really a specification of $io(P)$, i.e. of the IO-equivalence class of P. The $io(\cdot)$ operation does (obviously) not distribute through parallel composition. For the case of layer composition though, we have the following laws:

$$P \bullet Q \stackrel{IO}{=} io(P) \bullet io(Q) \text{ and } P \text{ ; } Q \stackrel{IO}{=} P \bullet Q$$

The intuition here is that although execution of "layer" P might overlap execution of "layer" Q *temporally*, one can pretend that all of P, here represented as an atomic action $io(P)$, precedes all of Q as far as IO behavior is concerned.

2.1 Algebraic Laws

In this section we provide some algebraic laws for model informally introduced here and extensively studied in [JPZ91]. The well-known laws for sequential composition, such as associativity, are not stated.

Lemma 2.1
Commutativity and Associativity:

$$
\begin{array}{rcll}
P \parallel Q & = & Q \parallel P & \text{(COM1)} \\
P \text{ or } Q & = & Q \text{ or } P & \text{(COM2)} \\
P \parallel (Q \parallel R) & = & (P \parallel Q) \parallel R & \text{(ASSOC1)} \\
P \bullet (Q \bullet R) & = & (P \bullet Q) \bullet R & \text{(ASSOC2)} \\
P \text{ or } (Q \text{ or } R) & = & (P \text{ or } Q) \text{ or } R & \text{(ASSOC3)}
\end{array}
$$

Distributivity:

$$
\begin{array}{rcll}
P \parallel (Q \text{ or } R) & = & (P \parallel Q) \text{ or } (P \parallel R) & \text{(DIST1)} \\
P \bullet (Q \text{ or } R) & = & (P \bullet Q) \text{ or } (P \bullet R) & \text{(DIST2)} \\
(P \text{ or } Q) \bullet R & = & (P \bullet R) \text{ or } (Q \bullet R) & \text{(DIST3)}
\end{array}
$$

Idempotency:

$$
P \text{ or } P \; = \; P
$$

Units and zeros:

$$
\begin{array}{rcllcll}
\text{skip} \parallel P & = & P \parallel \text{skip} & = & P & \text{(SKIP1)} \\
\text{skip} \bullet P & = & P \bullet \text{skip} & = & P & \text{(SKIP2)} \\
\text{empty or } P & = & P \text{ or empty} & = & P & \text{(EMPTY1)} \\
\text{empty} \parallel P & = & P \parallel \text{empty} & = & \text{empty} & \text{(EMPTY2)} \\
\text{empty} \bullet P & = & P \bullet \text{empty} & = & \text{empty} & \text{(EMPTY3)}
\end{array}
$$

□

More interesting is the relationship between parallel composition and layer composition. We can formulate here a (simple form of) the principle of communication closed layers in the form of an algebraic law. The communication closed layers law (CCL) deviates somewhat from the usual style of algebraic laws in that there is a (syntactic) side condition that should be checked concerning conflicts between processes. Let $act(P)$ denote the (finite) set of actions that (syntactically) occur in a DL process P. Let Act denote the set of actions, we extend the conflict relation on Act to sets of Act elements as follows: for $X, Y \subseteq Act$,

$$
X - Y \text{ iff there exist } a \in X,\ b \in Y \text{ such that } a - b.
$$

Conflicts between DL processes are then defined thus: $P - Q$ iff $act(P) - act(Q)$.

As usual, $P \nmid Q$ denotes that $P - Q$ is not the case, i.e. P actions do not conflict with Q actions.

The CCL laws can now be formulated as follows.

Lemma 2.2
Communication Closed Layers:

Provided that $P \nmid S$, and $Q \nmid R$:

$$
\begin{array}{rcll}
(P \bullet Q) \parallel (R \bullet S) & = & (P \parallel R) \bullet (Q \parallel S) & \text{(CCL)} \\
(P \bullet Q) \parallel S & = & P \bullet (Q \parallel S) & \text{(CCL-L)} \\
(P \bullet Q) \parallel R & = & (P \parallel R) \bullet Q & \text{(CCL-R)} \\
Q \parallel R & = & Q \bullet R & \text{(Independence)}
\end{array}
$$

□

In order to state a generalized version of the CCL and related laws, we introduce the abbreviations:

for $i \leftarrow [n \dots m]$ **dopar** $P(i)$ **rof** abbreviating: $P(n) \parallel \cdots \parallel P(m)$

for $i \leftarrow [n \dots m]$ **layer** $P(i)$ **rof** abbreviating: $P(n) \bullet \cdots \bullet P(m)$

for $i \leftarrow [n \dots m]$ **choice** $P(i)$ **rof** abbreviating: $P(n)$ or $\cdots$ or $P(m)$

for $i \leftarrow [n \dots m]$ **doseq** $P(i)$ **rof** abbreviating: $P(n) ; \cdots ; P(m)$

Lemma 2.3

- *Generalized Communication Closed Layers Law.*
  Assume that if there is a conflict between P_{ij} and P_{kl} then either $i = k$ or $j = l$ is satisfied, for $1 \le i, j, k, l \le n$. Then
  > for $i\leftarrow[1\ldots n]$ dopar
  >   for $j\leftarrow[1\ldots m]$ layer $P_{i,j}$ rof
  > rof

  $=$

  > for $j\leftarrow[1\ldots m]$ layer
  >   for $i\leftarrow[1\ldots n]$ dopar $P_{i,j}$ rof
  > rof

- *Left-Right Movers Law.*
  Assume that, for $1 \le i < k \le n$ and $1 \le l < j \le m$, $P_{i,j} \not\rightarrow P_{k,l}$. Then
  > for $i\leftarrow[1\ldots n]$ layer
  >   for $j\leftarrow[1\ldots m]$ layer $P_{i,j}$ rof
  > rof

  $=$

  > for $j\leftarrow[1\ldots m]$ layer
  >   for $i\leftarrow[1\ldots n]$ layer $P_{i,j}$ rof
  > rof

□

2.2 Normal Forms

Let DL' denote the language DL with the sequential composition operator omitted. If P is in DL' then for each P run $(E, \rightarrow)$ the order $\rightarrow$ is generated by conflicts only. That is, if $e \in E$ and e' is a direct successor of e with respect to $\rightarrow$, then e and e' are in conflict. (This is not the case if one adds the sequential composition to the language.)

Define layer $L(k)$ as

$L(k) = \{e \in E \mid$ the longest chain below e has length $k\}$

Since runs are assumed to be finite, $L(k) = \emptyset$ for sufficient large k. Enumerate the elements in each layer $L(k)$ such that

$L(k) = \{e_{k,j} \mid 1 \le j \le l(k)\}$

where $l(k)$ is the number of elements in $L(k)$.
Observe that there can be no conflict between events in the same layer, and for all events e in layer $L(k)$, $k > 1$, there exists an event e' in layer $L(k - 1)$ such that $e \rightarrow e'$. The run $(E, \rightarrow)$ is can be denoted syntactically by:

> for $k\leftarrow[0\ldots n]$ layer for $j\leftarrow[1\ldots l(k)]$ dopar $e_{k,j}$ rof rof

where n is such that

$(0 \le k \le n \Rightarrow L(k) \ne \emptyset) \wedge k > n \Rightarrow L(k) = \emptyset$

(Formally speaking $e_{k,j}$ is not an action but an event, and should replace $e_{k,j}$ by $\mu(e_{k,j})$, where $\mu(e_{k,j})$ is the action corresponding to the event $e_{k,j}$.) This can be done for every run of P, hence if we let r denote the number of runs of P then

$P = $ for $i\leftarrow[1\ldots r]$ choice
>   for $k\leftarrow[1\ldots n(r)]$ layer for $j\leftarrow[1\ldots k(n(r))]$ dopar $e_{i,k,j}$ rof rof
> rof

The above decomposition of P has the following properties:

- For each j and j', with $j \ne j'$, $e_{i,k,j} \not\rightarrow e_{i,k,j'}$.

- For each $k > 1$ and each $e_{i,k,j}$ there exists an event $e_{i,k-1,j'}$ such that $e_{i,k,j} - e_{i,k-1,j'}$.

Hence we have written P as a choice over layered maximal parallel processes. This above decomposition of P leads to following definition

Definition 2.4 *Normal Form*
A normal form is a process term of the form

> for $i \leftarrow [1 \ldots r]$ **choice**
>> for $k \leftarrow [1 \ldots n(r)]$ **layer**
>>> for $j \leftarrow [1 \ldots k(n(r))]$ **dopar** $e_{i,k,j}$ **rof**
>> **rof**
> **rof**

where each $e_{i,k,j}$ is an elementary process term. Moreover the process term should satisfy

1. For each j and j', with $j \neq j'$, $e_{i,k,j} \not{-} e_{i,k,j'}$.

2. For each $k > 1$ and each $e_{i,k,j}$ there exists an event $e_{i,k-1,j'}$ such that $e_{i,k,j} - e_{i,k-1,j'}$.

3. All mutually distinct branches of the **choice** construct are syntactically different.

□

This normal form resembles the normal form for Mazurkiewicz traces.

It follows from the observations above that each process term in DL' has a normal form. But there is more to it:

Theorem 2.5 *Expansion theorem*
Let $L_P \bullet P$ and $L_Q \bullet Q$ be process terms in DL' such that any two actions in L_P and any two actions in L_Q are non-conflicting. Furthermore assume that for every action $a'_P \in P$ ($a'_Q \in Q$) there exists an action $a_P \in L_P$ ($a_Q \in L_Q$) such that $a'_P \overset{*}{-} a_P$ ($a'_Q \overset{*}{-} a_Q$), where $\overset{*}{-}$ is the transitive closure of the conflict relation $-$. Then

$$(L_P \bullet P) \parallel (L_Q \bullet Q) =$$
> for $a_P \in L_P$ choice $a_P \bullet (((L_P - \{a_P\}) \bullet P) \parallel (L_Q \bullet Q))$ rof

> or

> for $a_Q \in L_Q$ choice $a_Q \bullet ((L_P \bullet P) \parallel ((L_Q - \{a_Q\}) \bullet Q))$ rof

□

The expansion theorem, together with the Left-Right Movers law, is crucial for transforming every process term P in DL' into normal form. The normal form is the maximal parallelization of P.

Theorem 2.6
Each process term $P \in DL'$ has an unique normal form (up to permutations of the indices). Moreover P can be algebraically transformed into this normal form in an algorithmic way using the algebraic laws of section 2.1 and the expansion theorem, theorem 2.5. □

A proof can be found in [PZ92].

3 The 'Point in polygon' algorithm: Pipelining on a tree network

The aim of this section is to show how to transform an *initial, algorithmic design* to a form that is suitable for implementation on a *pipelined architecture*. The (functional) correctness of the initial design is not our concern; we assume that it is the result from an initial design stage where it has been developed from a specification of the required *functional* behavior. We concentrate on the stage *following* the initial design phase, where not only functional correctness is of importance, but where also the architecture of the implementation must be taken into account.

The functional specification of the algorithm, that we do not formalize here, amounts to the following: Given a (fixed) polygon with edges $E_1, \cdots, E_N$ and a set $\{p_0, p_1, \cdots, p_m\}$ of points in a two dimensional Euclidean space, it is required to determine which of the points in $\{p_0, p_2, \ldots, p_m\}$ lay inside the polygon.

Our initial design has been essentially taken over from [Akl89]. It is based on the fact that a point p lies inside the polygon if and only if the vertical line through p intersects an odd number of edges above p. Thus the problem reduces to computing the number of intersections above p. The intuition for the algorithm in [Akl89] is as follows. Assuming that $N + 1$ is a power of 2, put $s = \log(N + 1)$. A tree-like arrangement of processes of depth s is used, containing one process for each edge. The coordinates of the points are stored in an array c, with $c[a]$ the coordinates of point p_a, $a = 0, \ldots, m$. The coordinates of the candidate points p are read by the top process and are broadcast during so called descend phases. A separate descend phase is executed for each 'level' in the tree, starting with the top node and ending with the level consisting of all leaf nodes. Each process receives the coordinates of the candidate point, determines locally whether the vertical line through p intersects the edge associated with that process, and broadcasts the results "downwards" to its children. After these descend phases, the total number of intersections is calculated during a number of ascend phases, where processes add together partial counts calculated by their children. If this count reaches the top process, then this top process assigns the appropriate boolean value to $inside[a]$, where $inside$ is a boolean array, such that $inside[a]$ holds if and only if the point p_a lies in the polygon. The algorithm in [Akl89] is presented in the form of a *sequential composition of "layers"* $D(l)$ and $A(l)$, each consisting of independent, parallel executed, actions. Communication between processes is by means of shared variables, where variables d_i and p_i are used during the descend phases and variables u_i during ascend phases. (Apart from these, there are *local* variables s_i, t_i, and q_i. q_i is used to store a local copy of coordinates of the point under consideration) Each descend layer $D(l)$ is itself divided into a reading phase $D^R(l)$ and a writing phase $D^W(l)$, and similarly, $A(l)$ is split into $A^R(l)$ and $A^W(l)$. The layer corresponding to the "leaf" nodes is an exception; there is no writing for the descend phase, and no reading for the ascend phase. The algorithm given in Akl [Akl89], adapted to our notation, is:

Program 0

> for $a \leftarrow [0 \ldots m]$ **doseq**
>
> $\quad d_1 := 0$; $p_1 := c[a]$;
>
> $\quad$ for $l \leftarrow [1 \ldots s-1]$ **doseq** $D^R(l)$; $D^W(l)$ **rof** ;
>
> $\quad D^R(s)$; $A^W(s)$;
>
> $\quad$ for $l \leftarrow [s-1 \ldots 1]$ **doseq** $A^R(l)$; $A^W(l)$ **rof** ;
>
> $\quad inside[a] := odd(u_1)$
>
> **rof**

This describes the "layered" structure of the algorithm. The layers $D^R(l)$, $D^W(l)$, $A^R(l)$ and $A^W(l)$ can each be described by means of parallel composition of independent actions. This implies that there is no interference among parallel processes, and consequently the (functional) correctness of the algorithm can be shown relying essentially on techniques for *sequential* programs, as explained for instance in [AO91]. The reason for this is that for independent processes P and Q, parallel composition $P \parallel Q$ is (semantically) identical to layer composition $P \bullet Q$; the latter in turn is, though not identical, IO-equivalent to sequential composition P ; Q.

The layers for the algorithm presented in [Akl89] can be specified as follows
The descending read phase for level l:

$D^R(l) = $ for $j \leftarrow [2^{l-1} \ldots 2^l - 1]$ **dopar**
$\quad\quad$ if $Intersects(e_j, p_j)$ then $s_j := d_j + 1$ else $s_j := d_j$ **fi** $\parallel$ $q_j := p_j$
$\quad$ **rof**

The descending write phase:

$D^W(l) =$

for $j \leftarrow [2^{l-1} \ldots 2^l - 1]$ dopar $p_{2j} := q_j \parallel p_{2j+1} := q_j \parallel d_{2j} := s_j \parallel d_{2j+1} := 0$ rof

The ascending read phase:

$A^R(l) =$ for $j \leftarrow [2^{l-1} \ldots 2^l - 1]$ dopar $t_j := u_{2j} + u_{2j+1}$ rof

Finally the ascending write phase is given by:

$A^W(l) =$ for $j \leftarrow [2^{l-1} \ldots 2^l - 1]$ dopar $u_j := t_j$ rof

except for $l = s$, in that case:

$A^W(s) =$ for $j \leftarrow [(N+1)/2 \ldots N]$ dopar $u_j := s_j$ rof

The presentation in [Akl89] is in terms of *sequential* composition of layers. From the point of view of functional correctness this is unnecessary; replacing all sequential composition by *layer composition* results in a process that is IO-equivalent. Moreover, this allows for algebraic manipulation that would be invalid for the version based on sequential composition. In particular, the layer composition version allows for *overlapping* execution of different layers, resulting in a *pipelined* execution where layers that have to be executed for different candidate points are executed in parallel. Thus, we will use, as starting point for a series of transformations, the following version:

Program 1

for $a \leftarrow [0 \ldots m]$ layer

$G(a) \bullet$

for $l \leftarrow [1 \ldots s-1]$ layer $D^R(l) \bullet D^W(l)$ rof $\bullet$

$D^R(s) \bullet A^W(s) \bullet$

for $l \leftarrow [s-1 \ldots 1]$ layer $A^R(l) \bullet A^W(l)$ rof $\bullet$

$P(a)$

rof

where

$G(a) = d_1 := 0 \parallel p_1 := c[a]$ and $P(a) = inside[a] := odd(u_1)$

First we will rename the processes $D^R(l)$, $D^W(l)$, $A^R(l)$ and $A^W(l)$, according to read or write actions. Put $t = 2s$ and define

$$R(l) = \begin{cases} D^R(l) & \text{if } 1 \leq l \leq s \\ A^R(t-l) & \text{if } s+1 \leq l \leq t-1 \end{cases}$$

$$W(l) = \begin{cases} D^W(l) & \text{if } 1 \leq l \leq s-1 \\ A^W(t-l) & \text{if } s \leq l \leq t-1 \end{cases}$$

Then Program 1 can be rewritten as

Program 1'

for $a \leftarrow [0 \ldots m]$ layer

$G(a) \bullet$

for $l \leftarrow [1 \ldots t-1]$ layer $R(l) \bullet W(l)$ rof $\bullet$

$P(a)$

rof

Conceptually we chanced the tree structure in a reflected tree structure, two identical trees with the leaves merged, such that all the data flows from top to bottom.

Observe that the above program is actually in pseudo normal form. It can be transformed into normal form, using the Left-Right Movers law and the Independence law, where one should check the side-conditions for these laws based on the following pattern of conflicts:

$$R(j) - R(j),\ W(j) - W(j),\ R(j) - W(j) \text{ and } R(j) - W(j-1)$$

Indeed, using that **skip** is a unit for layer composition, the above program is (semantically) equal to:

> for $a \leftarrow [0 \ldots m]$ layer for $l \leftarrow [0 \ldots m+t]$ layer $\tilde{R}(a,l) \bullet \tilde{W}(a,l)$ rof rof

where

$$\tilde{R}(a,l) = \begin{cases} P(a) & \text{if } l = a+t \\ R(l-a) & \text{if } a < l < a+t \\ \textbf{skip} & \text{otherwise} \end{cases}$$

$$\tilde{W}(a,l) = \begin{cases} G(a) & \text{if } l = a \\ W(l-a) & \text{if } a < l < a+t \\ \textbf{skip} & \text{otherwise} \end{cases}$$

The side-conditions for the Left-Right Movers Law are fulfilled, hence the program can be transformed into

> for $l \leftarrow [0 \ldots m+t]$ layer for $a \leftarrow [0 \ldots m]$ layer $\tilde{R}(a,l) \bullet \tilde{W}(a,l)$ rof rof

Again applying the Left-Right Movers and Independence Law to the inner layered loop gives that the program equals

Program 2

> for $l \leftarrow [0 \ldots m+t]$ layer
>
> for $a \leftarrow [0 \ldots m]$ dopar $\tilde{R}(a,l)$ rof $\bullet$
>
> for $a \leftarrow [0 \ldots m]$ dopar $\tilde{W}(a,l)$ rof
>
> rof

This last transformation results, for large enough m and again using that **skip** is unit for layer composition, in a program consisting of a phase where the tree is gradually filled, a phase where all the nodes of the tree execute simultaneously, and a final phase where the tree is emptied. For instance the layered loop

> for $a \leftarrow [0 \ldots m]$ dopar $\tilde{R}(a,l)$ rof

equals, by definition of $\tilde{R}(a,l)$

> if $(l-t) \geq 0$ then $P(l-t)$ fi $\ \|\ $ for $a \leftarrow [max(0, l-t+1) \ldots min(m, l-1)]$ dopar $R(l-a)$ rof

which on it's turn equals, by substituting $i = l - a$

> if $(l-t) \geq 0$ then $P(l-t)$ fi $\ \|\ $ for $i \leftarrow [max(1, l-m) \ldots min(t-1, l)]$ dopar $R(i)$ rof

If we apply similar substitutions to the layered loop with $\tilde{W}(a,l)$, the resulting program is

Program 3

> for $l \leftarrow [0 \ldots m+t]$ layer
>
> (if $(l-t) \geq 0$ then $P(l-t)$ fi $\ \|$
>
> for $i \leftarrow [max(1, l-m) \ldots min(t-1, l)]$ dopar $R(i)$ rof) $\bullet$
>
> (if $l \leq m$ then $G(l)$ fi $\ \|$
>
> for $i \leftarrow [max(1, l-m) \ldots min(t-1, l)]$ dopar $W(i)$ rof)
>
> rof

The variable boundaries at the inner parallel loops are due to "filling" of the tree, for $0 \leq l \leq t-1$, and "emptying" of the tree, for $m+1 \leq l \leq m+t$. The "filling" of the tree consists of two phases analogous to the descend and ascend phases in the original algorithm. First the information is broadcast "downwards", layer after layer, into the tree, until this downwards fill reaches the leaves. Then the results are broadcast "upwards", again layer after layer, towards the root of the tree, until it reaches layer 1. At that moment the tree is filled, this is the case for $l = t - 1$. Thereafter all cells compute in parallel for $t \leq l \leq m$ and afterwards the tree is emptied in the reverse order for $m < l \leq m + t$.

Although this program admits pipelined execution, it has the disadvantage that at each moment of time there is a different set of active processes. This is well known for pipelining in general: there is a phase where the pipeline is gradually 'filled', a phase where all processes in the pipeline are simultaneously executing, and a final phase where the pipeline is 'emptied'. This picture of "filling" and "emptying" is adequate on the abstraction level of *processes* only. On a low level where allocation of processes to *processors* is considered, there is no corresponding "starting" and "halting" of processors. Rather, during the filling and emptying phase there will be processors executing the same algorithm as others, but on non-relevant data so to say. We model this by adding 'dummy' actions to Program 3, in order to obtain a regular pattern.

Program 4

> for $l \leftarrow [0 \ldots m + t]$ **layer**
>
> > (**if** $(l - t) \geq 0$ **then** $P(l - t)$ **fi** $\parallel$
> >
> > **for** $j \leftarrow [1 \ldots t - 1]$ **dopar** $R(j)$ **rof**) •
> >
> > (**if** $l \leq m$ **then** $G(l)$ **fi** $\parallel$
> >
> > **for** $j \leftarrow [1 \ldots t - 1]$ **dopar** $W(j)$ **rof**)
>
> **rof**

Although this program doesn't semantically equal program 3, it has the property that it preserves functional correctness. More precisely program 4 projected onto the variables c and *inside* is semantically equal to program 3 projected onto the variables c and *inside*. Hence program 4 has the IO behavior with respect to c and *inside* as the original program 1. This can be seen by applying the inverse of the transformation steps above to program 4.

Next we take a step in the design that no longer preserves semantic equality, but only IO-equivalence, by imposing *extra* order by replacing the layer composition by a corresponding sequential composition in program 4. This cannot affect functional correctness, but it does allow for allocation of processes on (sequentially executing) processors.

Program 6

> for $l \leftarrow [0 \ldots m + t]$ **doseq**
>
> > (**if** $(l - t) \geq 0$ **then** $P(l - t)$ **fi** $\parallel$ **for** $j \leftarrow [1 \ldots t - 1]$ **dopar** $R(j)$ **rof**) ;
> >
> > (**if** $l \leq m$ **then** $G(l)$ **fi** $\parallel$ **for** $j \leftarrow [1 \ldots t - 1]$ **dopar** $W(j)$ **rof**)

Note that for each sequential phase, there are at most $(3N + 1)/2$ and at least $(3N - 1)/2$ processes active, which suggest a rather obvious allocation onto $(3N + 1)/2$ processors. In essence there are $(3N + 1)/2$ processes executing in parallel their contribution to some read phase and afterwards there are $(3N + 1)/2$ processes executing part of some ascend phase. Note that the *structure* of the program matches the class of SIMD machines, where a number of processors execute in lockstep the same (parameterized) program.

Applying the Independence law and commutativity of parallel composition to the program fragment

> (**if** $(l - t) \geq 0$ **then** $P(l - t)$ **fi** $\parallel$ **for** $j \leftarrow [1 \ldots t - 1]$ **dopar** $R(j)$ **rof**) •
>
> (**if** $l \leq m$ **then** $G(l)$ **fi** $\parallel$ **for** $j \leftarrow [1 \ldots t - 1]$ **dopar** $W(j)$ **rof**)

yields the following program fragment

for $j \leftarrow [1 \ldots s]$ dopar $R(j)$ rof •

(for $j \leftarrow [1 \ldots s - 1]$ dopar $W(j)$ rof $\parallel$ if $l \leq m$ then $G(l)$ fi) •

(for $j \leftarrow [s + 1 \ldots t - 1]$ dopar $R(j)$ rof $\parallel$ if $(l - t) \geq 0$ then $P(l - t)$ fi) •

for $j \leftarrow [s \ldots t - 1]$ dopar $W(j)$ rof

Invoking the definition of $R(j)$ and $W(j)$ and replacing layer composition by sequential composition results in $N + 1$ processes that alternate between four phases, corresponding to the read/write and the descend/ascend phase. As before, the algorithm matches an SIMD architecture. The final results is

Program 7

for $l \leftarrow [0 \ldots m + t]$ doseq

for $j \leftarrow [1 \ldots s]$ dopar $D^R(j)$ rof ;

(for $j \leftarrow [1 \ldots s - 1]$ dopar $D^W(j)$ rof $\parallel$ if $l \leq m$ then $G(l)$ fi);

(for $j \leftarrow [1 \ldots s - 1]$ dopar $A^R(j)$ rof $\parallel$ if $(l - t) \geq 0$ then $P(l - t)$ fi);

for $j \leftarrow [1 \ldots s]$ dopar $A^W(j)$ rof

rof

In this program each cell, $Cell(i)$, $1 \leq i \leq N$, executes the following program:

$Cell(i) =$

for $l \leftarrow [0 \ldots m + t]$ doseq

$q_i := p_i$;

if $Intersects(e_i, q_i)$ then $s_i := d_i + 1$ else $s_i := d_i$ fi ;

if $i < 2^{s-1}$ then $p_{2i} := q_i$; $p_{2i+1} := q_i$; $d_{2i} := s_i$; $d_{2i+1} := 0$ fi ;

if $i < 2^{s-1}$ then $t_i := u_{2i} + u_{2i+1}$ fi ;

if $i < 2^{s-1}$ then $u_i := t_i$ else $u_i := s_i$ fi

rof

It's clear that in this program for $Cell(i)$ we can take the local variables s_i and t_i equal.

4 The All-Points Shortest Path Problem

We have given some weighted directed graph of n nodes. The weights of the edge from node i to node j is given as w_{ij}, where $w_{ij} \geq 0$. If there is no edge from i to j in the graph, then we add one with weight $w_{ij} = \infty$.

The problem is to find the shortest distance d_{ij} from node i to j for all i and j. A *path* from node i to node j is a sequence of nodes $(i_0 i_1 \ldots i_k)$ where $i_j \in 1..n$ for $j \in 0..k$ and where $i_0 = i$ and $i_k = j$. The *length* of a path $(i_0 i_1 \ldots i_k)$ is the number of edges k, whereas the distance along it (its *weight*) is $w_{i_0 i_1} + w_{i_1 i_2} + \cdots + w_{i_{k-1} i_k}$. Note that since all weights are non-negative the shortest path from i to j is well defined, it will never cross itself, and so has length smaller than n. We denote the collection of paths from i to j with length smaller than m by $path(i, j, m)$. Then the distance d_{ij} along the *shortest path* from i to j is defined as:

$$i = j \rightarrow d_{ij} = 0, \text{ and } i \neq j \rightarrow d_{ij} = \min\{w_{i_0 i_1} + w_{i_1 i_2} + \cdots + w_{i_{k-1} i_k}\},$$

where the minimum is over all sequences in $path(i, j, n)$. A simple fact that follows directly from the definition: If node p is on the shortest path from i to j, then the subpaths from i to p and from p to j are the *shortest* paths from i to p and from p to j. Moreover, $d_{ij} = d_{ip} + d_{pj}$. (For instance, if the subpath from i to p would *not* be the shortest one, then we could improve the $i - j$ path, contrary to the assumption that it was the shortest $i - j$ path.)

A well-known sequential algorithm for computing the shortest path, based on the above observations, is the Floyd-Warshall, cf. [Akl89], Chapter 10.

Program *Floyd-Warshall*

    for $i\leftarrow[1\dots n]$ **doseq**

        for $j\leftarrow[1\dots n]$ **doseq** $m[0,i,j] := w[i,j]$ **rof**

    rof ;

    for $k\leftarrow[1\dots n]$ **doseq**

        for $i\leftarrow[1\dots n]$ **doseq**

            for $j\leftarrow[1\dots n]$ **doseq** $m[k,i,j] := min\{m[k-1,i,j], m[k-1,i,k] + m[k-1,k,j]\}$ **rof**

        rof

    rof

An invariant of the above program is; $m[k,i,j]$ is the shortest path from node i to node j with all the intermediate nodes taken from $\{1,\dots,k\}$. From which the correctness easily follows. Put

$$e_{i,k,j} = m[k,i,j] := min\{m[k-1,i,j], m[k-1,i,k] + m[k-1,k,j]\}$$

The Floyd-Warshall is a sequential algorithm where all actions are ordered in time. Again from point of functional correctness this is unnecessary; we can replace each sequential composition by a layer composition to get a process which is IO-equivalent to the initial process:

    for $i\leftarrow[1\dots n]$ **layer**

        for $j\leftarrow[1\dots n]$ **layer** $m[0,i,j] := w[i,j]$ **rof**

    rof •

    for $k\leftarrow[1\dots n]$ **layer**

        for $i\leftarrow[1\dots n]$ **layer**

            for $j\leftarrow[1\dots n]$ **layer** $\langle e_{i,k,j}\rangle$ **rof**

        rof

    rof

This process without sequential composition allows for algebraic transformations towards a specific architecture. Take for instance a CREW-PRAM, then there is only a conflict between $e_{i,k,j}$ and $e_{i,k',j}$. This yields, invoking the Left-Right Movers law, in that case the following normal form:

Program *Floyd-Warshall Normal Form I*

    for $i\leftarrow[1\dots n]$ **dopar**

        for $j\leftarrow[1\dots n]$ **dopar** $m[0,i,j] := w[i,j]$ **rof**

    rof •

    for $k\leftarrow[1\dots n]$ **layer**

        for $i\leftarrow[1\dots n]$ **dopar**

            for $j\leftarrow[1\dots n]$ **dopar** $\langle e_{i,k,j}\rangle$ **rof**

        rof

    rof

This leads to an implementation on a CREW-PRAM by changing every layer composition in a sequential composition, with complexity $O(n)$ time, on $O(n^2)$ processors. This is an optimal parallelization of the sequential Floyd-Warshall algorithm.

If we consider a EREW-PRAM then for fixed k $e_{i,k,j}$ is in conflict with $e_{i',k,j'}$ if and only if $i = i'$ or $j = j'$, because in that case they want to read both the same shared variable. The conflict order imposed by the sequential Floyd-Warshall algorithm is, again for fixed k

$$e_{i,k,j}\rightarrow e_{i',k,j} \text{ iff } i < i' \text{ and } e_{i,k,j}\rightarrow e_{i,k,j'} \text{ iff } j < j'$$

cf. figure 1, where one has to take the transitive closure in each row and column.

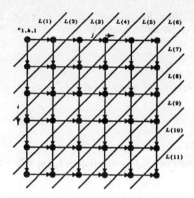

Figure 1: The causal ordering and layering for fixed k.

If we write this in pseudo normal form the computation becomes

Program *Floyd-Warshall Normal Form II*

> for $i \leftarrow [1 \ldots n]$ dopar
>
> > for $j \leftarrow [1 \ldots n]$ dopar $m[0, i, j] := w[i, j]$ rof
>
> rof •
>
> for $k \leftarrow [1 \ldots n]$ layer
>
> > for $l \leftarrow [1 \ldots 2 * n - 1]$ layer $L(k, l)$ rof
>
> rof

where for $l \leq n$

$$L(k, l) = \text{ for } j \leftarrow [1 \ldots l] \text{ dopar } \langle e_{j,k,l+1-j} \rangle \text{ rof}$$

and for $n < l \leq 2 * n - 1$

$$L(k, l) = \text{ for } j \leftarrow [1 \ldots 2 * n - l] \text{ dopar } \langle e_{l-n+j,k,n+1-j} \rangle \text{ rof}$$

which leads to an algorithm with time complexity $O(n^2)$ and processor complexity $O(n)$ on an EREW-PRAM, which is again optimal.

Observe that the causal ordering on the $e_{i,k,j}$ for fixed k is only induced by Read/Read conflicts, which means that the choice of the ordering doesn't influence the total result of the computation. Hence we can take another minimal conflict closed ordering, for instance the one given in figure 2. Writing this computation in a pseudo normal form gives:

Program *Floyd-Warshall Normal Form III*

> for $i \leftarrow [1 \ldots n]$ dopar
>
> > for $j \leftarrow [1 \ldots n]$ dopar $m[0, i, j] := w[i, j]$ rof
>
> rof •
>
> for $k \leftarrow [1 \ldots n]$ layer
>
> > for $l \leftarrow [1 \ldots n]$ layer $L'(k, l)$ rof
>
> rof

where

$$L'(k, l) = \text{ for } i \leftarrow [1 \ldots n] \text{ dopar } \langle e_{i,k,i \oplus l} \rangle \text{ rof}$$

with

$$i \oplus l = (n + l - i) \bmod n + 1$$

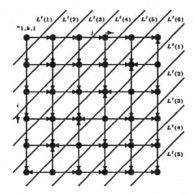

Figure 2: Another causal ordering for fixed k and the corresponding layering.

5 Conclusion

A language is presented which makes clear distinction between temporal order and causal order. This allows for a transformational approach, in an algebraic way, for the specification and verification of concurrent systems. Each process term without sequential composition can be transformed, in an algorithmic way, using the algebraic laws, into a normal form. This normal form is the maximal parallelization of the process under consideration. The techniques involved are exemplified by some examples from pipelining on a tree network, and the Floyd-Warshall algorithm for the all-points shortest path.

References

[Akl89]   S.G. Akl. *The Design and Analysis of Parallel Algorithms*. Prentice Hall, 1989.

[AO91]   K.R. Apt and E.-R. Olderog. *Verification of sequential and concurrent programs*. Springer-Verlag, 1991.

[EF82]   Elrad and N. Francez. Decomposition of distributed programs into communication closed layers. *Science of Computer Programming*, 2, 1982.

[JPSZ91] W. Janssen, M. Poel, K. Sikkel, and J. Zwiers. The primordial soup algorithm: A systematic approach to the specification and design of parallel parsers. In *Proc. of CSN'91*, 1991.

[JPZ91]   W. Janssen, M. Poel, and J. Zwiers. Action systems and action refinement in the development of parallel systems. In *Proc. of CONCUR '91*, pages 298–316. Springer-Verlag, LNCS 527, 1991.

[JZ92a]   W. Janssen and J. Zwiers. From sequential layers to distributed processes, deriving a distributed minimum weight spanning tree algorithm. In *Proc. 11th PODC Symposium*, pages 215–227. ACM, 1992.

[JZ92b]   W. Janssen and J. Zwiers. Protocol design by layered decomposition, a compositional approach. In *Proc. Formal Techniques in Real-Time and Fault-Tolerant Systems*. Springer-Verlag, LNCS 571, 1992.

[PZ92]   M. Poel and J. Zwiers. Layering techniques for development of parallel systems. Technical report, University of Twente, 1992. To appear.

Efficient Local Correctness Checking

Kim Guldstrand Larsen
Aalborg University, Denmark *

Motivation

This paper deals with the problem of verifying the correctness of a finite-state parallel system presented in terms of a finite labeled transition system. More precisely, we consider *logical* as well as *behavioural* specifications and the associated correctness checking problems (model–checking and equivalence/preorder–checking).

A number of theoretical techniques and tools have been developed. Here we mention the algorithms presented in [EL86, CS91b, PT87, PS90] and the tools [LMV88, RRSV87, EES86, CPS88]. However, traditionally the techniques applied are *global*, in the sense that they prerequire the generation (and storage) of the complete transition system before verification. As the size of the the global transition systems may grow exponentially in the number of parallel components, the main limitations of these traditional tools has been a space problem. In the last few years there have been a growing interest in techniques that avoid this global preconstruction. Here we mention the work of [FM91, CS91a, GW91b, GW91a, And92]. In particular the work in [CS91a] and [And92] are closely related to ours.

However, existing work in this direction has been developed mainly for specific correctness problems. In this paper we provide an abstract and uniform description of an efficient and local technique, which we show applicable to a variety of model–checking and equivalence/preorder–checking problems. In fact, the abstract technique we present is the very heart of all tools of the TAV–system [JGZ89].

Our general technique is based on a notion of consistency of Boolean Equation Systems (section 1), in terms of which a number of correctness problems may be represented (section 2). We show briefly how consistency may be checked using a well-known global technique (section 3). In the paper we provide two *proof systems* for determining consistency with respect to a Boolean Equation System. We provide suitable soundness and completeness theorems for the proof systems, and indicate how to extract *local* consistency checking algorithms. The first proof system (section 4) captures the essence of a number of recently developed (and implemented) model–checking techniques for the modal mu-calculus [Lar90, SW89, Cle90, Win89]. However, these techniques yield exponential time worst case complexity. The second proof system (section 5) remedies this deficiency and yields a polynomial–time local consistency checking algorithm. In the conclusion we discuss how the presented local technique — which is based on the behavioural semantics of processes — may be combined with algebraic properties of processes.

* Address: Dep. of Math. and Comp. Sc., Aalborg University, Fredrik Bajersvej 7, 9220 Aalborg, Denmark. Telephone: +45 98158522. Email: kgl@iesd.auc.dk. This work is done in the context of ESPRIT Basic Research Action 7166, CONCUR2. Also the work has been supported in part by the Danish Natural Science Research Council through the DART project.

1 Boolean Equation Systems

In this section we shall present the notion of *Boolean Equation Systems*. As we shall see in the next section, many correctness problems encountered in the area of parallel and reactive systems may by represented and solved through the use of Boolean Equation Systems.

The basis of Boolean Equation Systems is that of a negation–free, propositional formula. Let V be a set of (propositional) variables. The set $\mathcal{L}_V$ of negation–free, propositional formulae over V is given by the following abstract syntax:

$$\phi \ ::= \ x \mid \mathbf{tt} \mid \mathbf{ff} \mid \phi_1 \wedge \phi_2 \mid \phi_1 \vee \phi_2$$

where $x \in V$. We say that a formula ϕ is *simple* if it is in one of the forms $\mathbf{tt}$, $\mathbf{ff}$, $x_1 \wedge x_2$ or $x_1 \vee x_2$, where x_1 and x_2 are variables from V.

Semantically, we interpret formulae with respect to an *environment* $\rho : V \longrightarrow \text{Bool}$ mapping variables to booleans (Bool = $\{0, 1\}$). More precisely, for ρ an environment and ϕ a formula we define the boolean value $[\![\phi]\!]\rho$ inductively on ϕ as follows:

$$[\![x]\!]\rho = \rho(x)$$

$$[\![\mathbf{tt}]\!]\rho = 1$$

$$[\![\mathbf{ff}]\!]\rho = 0$$

$$[\![\phi_1 \wedge \phi_2]\!]\rho = \min\{[\![\phi]\!]\rho, [\![\phi_2]\!]\rho\}$$

$$[\![\phi_1 \vee \phi_2]\!]\rho = \max\{[\![\phi]\!]\rho, [\![\phi_2]\!]\rho\}$$

Syntactically the desired semantics of variables of V is specified recursively through the use of an *equation system*, $E : V \longrightarrow \mathcal{L}_V$ over V. That is, E is a function which for each variable x gives the (recursive) definition, $E(x) \in \mathcal{L}_V$, for x. We shall write $x =_E \phi$ to indicate that $E(x) = \phi$. We are now able to give a succinct definition of a *Boolean Equation System*:

Definition 1. *A Boolean Equation System is a pair*

$$\mathcal{E} = \langle V, E \rangle$$

where V is a finite set of variables and E is an equation system over V. The Boolean Equation System $\langle V, E \rangle$ is said to be simple in case $E(x)$ is a simple formula for any variable x.

An equation system E specifies a semantic requirement to an environment ρ. In particular, for any variable x, $[\![x]\!]\rho$ must equal $[\![E(x)]\!]\rho$. If ρ has this property, we call it a *model* with respect to E. We identify on this basis two sets of variables:

Definition 2. *Let $\mathcal{E} = \langle V, E \rangle$ be a Boolean Equation System. A variable x is said to be consistent with respect to $\mathcal{E}$ if $\rho(x) = 1$ for some model ρ of $\mathcal{E}$. We denote by $C_{\mathcal{E}}$ the set of all consistent variables. If a variable x is not consistent we call it inconsistent. A variable x is said to be factual with respect to $\mathcal{E}$ if $\rho(x) = 1$ whenever ρ is a model of $\mathcal{E}$. We denote by $S_{\mathcal{E}}$ the set of all factual variables.*

Given a Boolean Equation System $\mathcal{E} = \langle V, E \rangle$ we may define a functional $\mathcal{F}_{\mathcal{E}} : 2^V \longrightarrow 2^V$ by:

$$\mathcal{F}_{\mathcal{E}}(A) = \{x \in V \mid [\![E(x)]\!]\rho_A = 1\}$$

where $A \subseteq V$, and ρ_A is the characteristic function for A yielding 1 for any variable in A and 0 for variables outside A. As we only allow the use of negation–free formulae in an equation system it may be shown that $\mathcal{F}_{\mathcal{E}}$ is a monotonic function on the complete lattice of subsets of V ordered by set–inclusion. Using the standard fixed–point result due to Tarski [Tar55], this implies that $\mathcal{F}_{\mathcal{E}}$ has a maximal fixedpoint, $\nu\mathcal{F}_{\mathcal{E}}$, as well as a minimal fixedpoint, $\mu\mathcal{F}_{\mathcal{E}}$. It is routine to show that $\nu\mathcal{F}_{\mathcal{E}}$ coincides with the set of consistent variables $C_{\mathcal{E}}$ and that $\mu\mathcal{F}_{\mathcal{E}}$ coincides with the set of factual variables $S_{\mathcal{E}}$.

Example 1. Let $\mathcal{E} = \langle V, E \rangle$ be the Boolean Equation System, where $V = \{x_1, x_2, x_3, x_4\}$ and E is defined by the following four equations:

$$x_1 =_E x_1 \wedge x_2 \qquad x_3 =_E \mathtt{ff}$$

$$x_2 =_E x_3 \vee x_4 \qquad x_4 =_E \mathtt{tt}$$

It should then be obvious that $C_{\mathcal{E}} = \{x_1, x_2, x_4\}$ and $S_{\mathcal{E}} = \{x_2, x_4\}$. ☐

In logic a formula is called *consistent* provided one cannot infer contradictions from it. Our notion of consistency corresponds closely to this usage of the term: a variable x is consistent provided you cannot infer $0 = 1$ from the assumption that $x = 1$. Similarly, our use of the term *factuality* corresponds to the standard notion of theoremhood in logic. In the following sections we shall concentrate on methods for checking consistency. Methods for factuality checking may be obtained by straightforward dualisation.

In the analysis we shall state our complexity results in terms of the *size* of a Boolean Equation System $\mathcal{E} = \langle V, E \rangle$ defined as $|\mathcal{E}| = \sum_{x \in V} |E(x)|$, where the size of a formula ϕ is defined inductively as: $|\mathtt{tt}| = |\mathtt{ff}| = |x| = 1$ and $|\phi_1 \wedge \phi_2| = |\phi_1 \vee \phi_2| = |\phi_1| + |\phi_2|$. Also, we shall make some general assumptions about the representation of a Boolean Equation System. Firstly, we shall assume that variables are represented by natural numbers (which we in turn assume to be representable in constant amount of memory). Secondly, functions from finite subsets of natural numbers (e.g. E of a Boolean Equation System $\mathcal{E} = \langle V, E \rangle$) will be represented with efficient access to the value of one particular element in the domain (constant time as for "array" in many programming languages). Finally, note that any Boolean Equation System $\mathcal{E} = \langle V, E \rangle$ may be transformed into a Simple Boolean Equation System with only a linear blow–up: if $x =_E \phi_1 \vee \phi_2$ and ϕ_1 and ϕ_2 are compound formulae themselves simply add two new variables x_{ϕ_1} and x_{ϕ_2} and replace the above equation with the following three: $x =_E x_\phi \vee x_{\phi_2}$, $x_{\phi_1} =_E \phi_1$ and $x_{\phi_2} =_E \phi_2$. Repeating this procedure will eventually result in the desired Simple Boolean Equation System.

2 Representing Correctness Problems

We adopt the reactive view of parallel processes advocated in [Pnu85]; i.e. we model the behaviour of a process in terms of a *labelled transition system* describing its potential interaction with the environment. Having adopted this view, the *correctness* of a process may be formulated in a variety of ways: In the *process algebraic* framework [Mil80, Mil89, Hoa85, BK85, Bou85, BB87], a number of behavioural equivalences and preorders exists for comparing (concrete and abstract) processes. Alternatively, one may use formulae of Temporal and Modal Logic [BAPM83, Koz82] for specifying the desired behaviour of a process.

We claim that several of these notions of correctness may be represented as consistency (and factuality) problems of Boolean Equation Systems, thus allowing a single, uniform treatment. Due to lack of space we justify this claim by only a few illustrating examples. In particular, we show in this section how to represent bisimulation equivalence problems [Par81, Mil83] and simulation problems [Mil83, Lar87] between (finite–state) processes as Boolean Equation Systems. These two correctness problems are just a small sample of problems representable in terms of Boolean Equation Systems, and they have been selected because of their simplicity. Other problems which might have been presented include: $\frac{2}{3}$–bisimulation [LS91] (or ready bisimulation [Blo88]), m–nested simulation, refinement between modal transition systems [LT88], equation solving problems [Shi, Par89, LX90] and other synthesis problems. Also, model–checking problems as well as satisfiability problems with respect to the modal nu–calculus are representable as Boolean Equation Systems.

Definition 3. *A labelled transition system is a structure* $\mathcal{P} = (S, A, \longrightarrow)$ *where S is a set of states, A is a set of actions and* $\longrightarrow \subseteq S \times A \times S$ *is the transition relation. A labeled transition system $\mathcal{P}$ is said to be* finite *provided S and A (and hence $\longrightarrow$) are finite.*

The well–known notions of *simulation* and *bisimulation* [Par81, Mil83, Lar87] provide means of identifying processes based on their operational behaviour. Below we recall their formal definitions:

Definition 4. *Let* $\mathcal{P} = (S, A, \longrightarrow)$ *be a labelled transition system. Then a simulation R is a binary relation on S such that whenever $(P, Q) \in R$ and $a \in A$ then the following holds:*

– *Whenever* $P \xrightarrow{a} P'$, *then* $Q \xrightarrow{a} Q'$ *for some Q' with $(P', Q') \in R$,*

Q *is said to simulate P in case (P, Q) is contained in some simulation R. We write $P \preceq Q$ in this case. A binary relation R on S is a bisimulation in case both R and R^T are simulations* [2]. *P and Q are said to be bisimilar in case (P, Q) is contained in some bisimulation R. We write $P \sim Q$ in this case.*

We now provide the representation of simulation and bisimulation as Boolean Equation Systems:

Definition 5. *Let* $\mathcal{P} = (S, A, \longrightarrow)$ *be a finite labelled transition system. Then the Boolean Equation System* $\mathcal{E}_{\mathcal{P}}^{\preceq} = \langle V, E \rangle$ *is defined as $X_{P,Q} \in V$ whenever $P, Q \in S$, and*

$$ X_{P,Q} =_E \bigwedge_{P \xrightarrow{a} P'} \left(\bigvee_{Q \xrightarrow{a} Q'} X_{P',Q'} \right) $$

---

[2] For R a binary relation the transposed relation R^T is defined as $R^T = \{(Q, P) | (P, Q) \in R\}$.

The Boolean Equation System $\mathcal{E}_{\mathcal{P}}^{\simeq} = \langle V, E \rangle$ *is defined as* $Y_{P,Q} \in V$ *whenever* $P, Q \in S$, *with*

$$Y_{P,Q} =_E \bigwedge_{P \xrightarrow{a} P'} \left(\bigvee_{Q \xrightarrow{a} Q'} Y_{P',Q'} \right) \wedge \bigwedge_{Q \xrightarrow{a} Q'} \left(\bigvee_{P \xrightarrow{a} P'} Y_{P',Q'} \right)$$

The correctness of the above representations are stated in the following theorem:

Theorem 6. *Let* $\mathcal{P} = (S, A, \longrightarrow)$ *be a finite labelled transition system. Then* $X_{P,Q}$ *is consistent with respect to* $\mathcal{E}_{\mathcal{P}}^{\preceq}$ *if and only if* Q *simulates* P. *Also,* $Y_{P,Q}$ *is consistent with respect to* $\mathcal{E}_{\mathcal{P}}^{\simeq}$ *if and only if* P *and* Q *are bisimilar.*

3 Global Correctness Checking

For a Boolean Equation System $\mathcal{E} = \langle V, E \rangle$ the set of *consistent* variables may be computed in a straightforward and well–known manner, which is applied in several existing tools (e.g. [LMV88, CPS88]): simply compute the following decreasing sequence of variable–sets:

$$V \supsetneq \mathcal{F}_{\mathcal{E}}(V) \supsetneq \mathcal{F}_{\mathcal{E}}^2(V) \supsetneq \cdots \cdots \mathcal{F}_{\mathcal{E}}^n(V) = \mathcal{F}_{\mathcal{E}}^{n+1}(V) \tag{1}$$

That is, starting with the set of all variables V, we simply apply the functional $\mathcal{F}_{\mathcal{E}}$ repeatedly until convergence is reached (in (1) this happens after $n + 1$ iterations). As there are only finitely many variables, termination is guaranteed, and standard fixedpoint theory [Tar55] ensures that the set obtained at convergence is the maximal fixedpoint of $\mathcal{F}_{\mathcal{E}}$, i.e. the set of consistent variables.

As for complexity of this method, convergence is clearly obtained after at most $|V|$ iterations. In each iteration we must compute the semantic value of $E(x)$ for each variable x. Assuming that the access time for each variable is constant, this can be computed in time $\sum_{x \in V} |E(x)| = |\mathcal{E}|$. Hence, the complete worst case time complexity is $O(|V||\mathcal{E}|)$, which for Simple Boolean Equation Systems is the same as $O(|V|^2)$.

4 Local Correctness Checking

Using the global approach to consistency (or dually, factuality) checking, one is forced to consider all variables (in fact all variables are considered in each iteration). However, the initial problem might be concerned with the consistency (or factuality) of a *particular* variable, in which case the global technique seems to be an overkill. Instead we would want consistency of a given variable to be determined based on information of only a few (related) variables. For correctness problems in the world of parallel, reactive systems the global technique prerequires a total state–space construction with the familiar state–space explosion as a likely consequence. In contrast, we would prefer to settle the correctness problem of a parallel system in a manner that would minimize the construction and examination of its state–space.

In the following we shall present a *local* technique for consistency (and factuality) checking in a manner that exploits the Boolean Equation System in a minimal fashion.

Example 2. Consider the Simple Boolean Equation System given below:

$$x_1 = x_1 \wedge x_1 \qquad x_2 = x_1 \vee x_3 \qquad x_3 = \mathbf{tt}$$

Clearly, $C_{\mathcal{E}} = \{x_1, x_2\}$. However, as x_1 is completely independent of x_2 (and x_3) it should be possible to infer consistency of x_1 without any information of x_2 (and x_3). □

In Figure 1 we present the proof system $\mathcal{A}$ for inferring (relative) consistency of variables of a *simple* Boolean Equation System $\mathcal{E} = \langle V, E \rangle$. The statements of the proof system are of the form

$$\{x_1, \ldots, x_n\} \vdash_{\mathcal{E}} x \tag{2}$$

where $x_1, \ldots, x_n$ and x are variables of V. The statement in (2) may informally be interpreted as: the variable x is consistent under the assumption of consistency of $x_1, \ldots, x_n$. Most of the rules are obvious. However, note in rule $\mathbf{A_3}$ that the consistency of a variable x may be inferred from the consistency of its definition, under an assumption–set *augmented* with the variable itself. As consistency is defined using a *maximal* fixedpoint, this turns out to be a sound rule.

$$\mathbf{A_1} \ \frac{\overline{}}{\Gamma \vdash_{\mathcal{E}} x} \ x \in \Gamma \qquad \mathbf{A_2} \ \frac{\overline{}}{\Gamma \vdash_{\mathcal{E}} \mathbf{tt}}$$

$$\mathbf{A_3} \ \frac{\Gamma, x \vdash_{\mathcal{E}} \phi}{\Gamma \vdash_{\mathcal{E}} x} \ x =_{\mathcal{E}} \phi, \ x \notin \Gamma$$

$$\mathbf{A_4} \ \frac{\Gamma \vdash_{\mathcal{E}} x \quad \Gamma \vdash_{\mathcal{E}} y}{\Gamma \vdash_{\mathcal{E}} x \wedge y}$$

$$\mathbf{A_5} \ \frac{\Gamma \vdash_{\mathcal{E}} x}{\Gamma \vdash_{\mathcal{E}} x \vee y} \qquad \mathbf{A_6} \ \frac{\Gamma \vdash_{\mathcal{E}} y}{\Gamma \vdash_{\mathcal{E}} x \vee y}$$

Fig. 1. $\mathcal{A}$: Local Checking of Consistency

Formally, we may show the following soundness theorem:

Theorem 7. *Let* $\mathcal{E} = \langle V, E \rangle$ *be a Simple Boolean Equation System. Then*

$$\Gamma \vdash_{\mathcal{E}} x \ \Rightarrow \ \exists C. \begin{Bmatrix} C \backslash \Gamma \subseteq \mathcal{F}_{\mathcal{E}}(C) \ \wedge \\ x \in C \end{Bmatrix}$$

Proof By induction on the inference structure. Here we only consider the case when $\Gamma \vdash_{\mathcal{E}} x$ has been established using rule $\mathbf{A_3}$. That is, $\Gamma, x \vdash_{\mathcal{E}} \phi$ where $x =_{\mathcal{E}} \phi$. As $\mathcal{E}$ is simple, ϕ will be either a disjunction or a conjunction of variables. Assuming the latter — i.e. $\phi = x_1 \wedge x_2$ — then $\Gamma, x \vdash_{\mathcal{E}} \phi$ must have been inferred using $\mathbf{A_4}$ and thus $\Gamma, x \vdash_{\mathcal{E}} x_1$ and $\Gamma, x \vdash_{\mathcal{E}} x_2$. Appealing now to the Induction Hypothesis, we may conclude that $C_i \backslash (\Gamma \cup \{x\}) \subseteq \mathcal{F}_{\mathcal{E}}(C_i)$

and $x_i \in C_i$ for some C_i $(i = 1, 2)$. Now let $C = C_1 \cup C_2 \cup \{x\}$, then clearly $x \in C$. Also $C \backslash \Gamma \subseteq \mathcal{F}_{\mathcal{E}}(C)$ due to monotonicity and definition of $\mathcal{F}_{\mathcal{E}}$. □

As an easy corollary we may infer that the inference system is sound with respect to consistency:

Corollary 8. *Let* $\mathcal{E} = \langle V, E \rangle$ *be a Simple Boolean Equation System. Whenever* $\emptyset \vdash_{\mathcal{E}} x$ *then* $x \in C_{\mathcal{E}}$.

Example 3. Reconsider the Simple Boolean Equation System from Example 2. Using the proof system $\mathcal{A}$, consistency of x_1 may be inferred as follows:

$$
\mathbf{A}_3 \cfrac{\mathbf{A}_4 \cfrac{\mathbf{A}_1 \cfrac{\overline{}}{\{x_1\} \vdash_{\mathcal{E}} x_1} \qquad \cfrac{\overline{}}{\{x_1\} \vdash_{\mathcal{E}} x_1} \mathbf{A}_1}{\{x_1\} \vdash_{\mathcal{E}} x_1 \wedge x_1}}{\emptyset \vdash_{\mathcal{E}} x_1}
$$

Note, that the consistency of x_1 has been inferred in a local fashion without information about x_2 and x_3. □

The following theorem claims that Figure 1 constitutes a complete inference system for consistency.

Theorem 9. *Let* $\mathcal{E} = \langle V, E \rangle$ *be a Simple Boolean Equation System. Whenever* $x \in C_{\mathcal{E}}$ *then* $\emptyset \vdash_{\mathcal{E}} x$.

Proof Now let $\Gamma \prec \Omega$ whenever $\Omega \subset \Gamma$. Given that V only contains finitely many variables $\prec$ will be a well-founded ordering. Now, using well-founded induction on Γ we may show that $\Gamma \vdash_{\mathcal{E}} x$ whenever x is contained in some postfixed point relative to Γ. □

Using the inference rules of $\mathcal{A}$ in a goal–directed and backwards manner with possible backtracking (due to the choice between the or–rules $\mathbf{A}_5$ and $\mathbf{A}_6$) we clearly obtain a decision procedure for consistency checking (easily implemented in PROLOG). However, as we shall see the induced decision procedure has exponential worst–case time complexity and is thus — though clearly a local checking technique — inferior to the classical global technique of the previous section. We shall see in the next section how to remedy this deficiency.

5 Efficient Local Correctness Checking

The local checking technique of the previous section describes the essence of a number of recent techniques for modelchecking in the modal mu–calculus [Koz82], including the proof–system of [Lar90], the tableau system of [SW89, Cle90] (which has been incorporated into the Concurrency Workbench [CPS88]) and the rewrite system in [Win89]. However, in all cases the techniques have an exponential worst case time complexity as illustrated by the following Simple Boolean Equation System:

$$x_0 = x_1 \vee x_1, \quad x_1 = x_2 \vee x_2, \; \cdots\cdots x_{n-1} = x_n \vee x_n, \quad x_n = \mathbf{tt} \qquad (3)$$

Trying (and obviously failing) to demonstrate consistency of x_0 using the inference rules of figure 1 in a goal–directed manner with possible backtracking will lead to a computation with $2^{n+1} - 1$ recursive invocations as illustrated in figure 2 for the case $n = 2$. Here the superscripts indicate the order in which the invocations fails. The subscripts describe a sequence of rules that when applied to a node will yield the parent node.

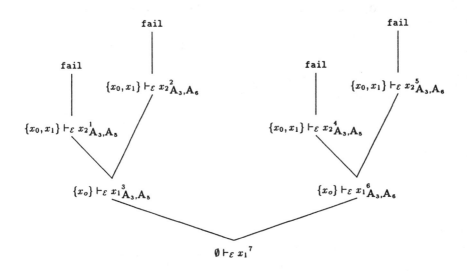

Fig. 2. Exponential Time Computation in $\mathcal{A}$.

Clearly, the source of the inefficiency is caused by the fact that *failing* attempts of establishing (relative) consistency are not remembered, and hence must necessarily result in recomputations when reencountered.

In figure 3 we present a proof system $\mathcal{B}$ for consistency checking in a manner which remembers and recalls previously discovered *in*consistency results. Given a Simple Boolean Equation System $\mathcal{E} = \langle V, E \rangle$ the proof system $\mathcal{B}$ permits the inference of statements of the form:

$$\langle x, B, N \rangle \rightsquigarrow_{\mathcal{E}} \langle b, C, M \rangle \tag{4}$$

where x is a variable of V; B, N, C and M are subsets of V, and b is a boolean value. In (4), $\langle x, B, N \rangle$ should be thought of as the problem given: is x consistent under the *assumption* that the variables in B are consistent and *knowing* that the variables in N are inconsistent? $\langle b, C, M \rangle$ then describes the answer to this question: the boolean b directly indicates the consistency of x with respect to B and N, whereas C and M are extensions of B and N containing results of consistency gathered during the process of answering the question $\langle x, B, N \rangle$ [3]. In particular, these extensions will be useful in "pruning" subsequent computations.

$$\mathbf{B_1} \langle x, B, N \rangle \leadsto_\varepsilon \langle 1, B \cup \{x\}, N \rangle \qquad \text{when } x \in B \text{ or } x =_\varepsilon \mathtt{tt}$$

$$\mathbf{B_2} \langle x, B, N \rangle \leadsto_\varepsilon \langle 0, B, N \cup \{x\} \rangle \qquad \text{when } x \in N \text{ or } x =_\varepsilon \mathtt{ff}$$

$$\mathbf{B_3} \frac{\langle \phi, B \cup \{x\}, N \rangle \leadsto_\varepsilon \langle 1, C, M \rangle}{\langle x, B, N \rangle \leadsto_\varepsilon \langle 1, C, M \rangle} \quad \text{when } x \notin B \cup N \text{ and } x =_\varepsilon \phi$$

$$\mathbf{B_4} \frac{\langle \phi, B \cup \{x\}, N \rangle \leadsto_\varepsilon \langle 0, C, M \rangle}{\langle x, B, N \rangle \leadsto_\varepsilon \langle 0, B, M \cup \{x\} \rangle} \quad \text{when } x \notin B \cup N \text{ and } x =_\varepsilon \phi$$

$$\mathbf{B_5} \frac{\langle x_1, B, N \rangle \leadsto_\varepsilon \langle 0, C, M \rangle}{\langle x_1 \wedge x_2, B, N \rangle \leadsto_\varepsilon \langle 0, C, M \rangle}$$

$$\mathbf{B_6} \frac{\langle x_1, B, N \rangle \leadsto_\varepsilon \langle 1, C, M \rangle \qquad \langle x_2, C, M \rangle \leadsto_\varepsilon \langle b, D, R \rangle}{\langle x_1 \wedge x_2, B, N \rangle \leadsto_\varepsilon \langle b, D, R \rangle}$$

$$\mathbf{B_7} \frac{\langle x_1, B, N \rangle \leadsto_\varepsilon \langle 1, C, M \rangle}{\langle x_1 \vee x_2, B, N \rangle \leadsto_\varepsilon \langle 1, C, M \rangle}$$

$$\mathbf{B_8} \frac{\langle x_1, B, N \rangle \leadsto_\varepsilon \langle 0, C, M \rangle \qquad \langle x_2, C, M \rangle \leadsto_\varepsilon \langle b, D, R \rangle}{\langle x_1 \vee x_2, B, N \rangle \leadsto_\varepsilon \langle b, D, R \rangle}$$

Fig. 3. $\mathcal{B}$: Efficient Local Checking of Consistency

For a given problem $\langle x, B, N \rangle$, the proof system $\mathcal{B}$ is using the set B as an assumption set similar to the use of assumptions in the previous proof system $\mathcal{A}$. In fact, the following formal relationship between the two proof systems may be shown:

Whenever $\langle x, B, N \rangle \leadsto_\varepsilon \langle 1, C, M \rangle$ in $\mathcal{B}$ then $B \vdash_\varepsilon x$ in $\mathcal{A}$.

We first give an informal description of the rules of $\mathcal{B}$:

$\mathbf{B_1, B_2}$: Axioms for inferring immediate (relative) consistency/inconsistency of a variable x. The rule $\mathbf{B_1}$ corresponds closely to the rule $\mathbf{A_1}$ of $\mathcal{A}$.

$\mathbf{B_3, B_4}$: In case the variable x is not included in any of the sets B and N the consistency of x is reduced to the consistency of its definition (ϕ). However, similar to the rule $\mathbf{A_3}$ of $\mathcal{A}$, we are allowed to use x itself as an assumption, during the consistency checking of ϕ. In case ϕ turns out consistent under the extended assumption set, we simply inherit

---

[3] Those familiar with the terminology of Structured Operational Semantics [Plo81] may view the inference system $\mathcal{B}$ as a *natural* semantics in the sense that it models *full* computations.

the complete result obtained from ϕ as the result of x. Otherwise — i.e. if ϕ is found inconsistent — also x is inconsistent, reflected in the augmentation of the result set M. In this case, we are not able to use any information gathered in the set C as it may be based on the (erroneous) assumption of x being consistent.

B_5, B_6, B_7, B_8: The obvious rules for (simple) conjunctive and disjunctive formulae with information gathered being passed from the first conjunct (disjunct) to the subsequent processing of the second conjunct (disjunct).

Now reconsider the Simple Boolean Equation System of (3) again for $n = 2$. In figure 4 we use the new proof system B to infer the inconsistency of x_o. Here $\Gamma_i = \{x_0, \ldots x_i\}$ and $\Omega_i = \{x_i, \ldots, x_2\}$ for $i = 0, 1, 2$. In contrast to a goal–directed use of the previous proof system A, we note that recomputation is totally avoided. In particular, we note that inconsistency of x_1 is only computed once; the second time x_1 is encountered $(*)$ the assumption-sets prevents a recomputation. As a consequence, as we shall state more precisely shortly, we avoid the exponential time complexity.

$$
\begin{array}{l}
B_8 \; \overline{} \\
B_4 \; \dfrac{(x_2 \vee x_2, \Gamma_1, \emptyset) \rightsquigarrow_\varepsilon (0, \Gamma_1, \Omega_2)}{(x_1, \Gamma_0, \emptyset) \rightsquigarrow_\varepsilon (0, \Gamma_0, \Omega_1)} \qquad \dfrac{ - }{(x_1, \Gamma_0, \Omega_1) \rightsquigarrow_\varepsilon (0, \Gamma_0, \Omega_1)} B_2{}^* \\
B_8 \; \overline{} \\
\qquad \dfrac{(x_1 \vee x_1, \Gamma_0, \emptyset) \rightsquigarrow_\varepsilon (0, \Gamma_0, \Omega_1)}{} \\
B_4 \; \overline{} \\
\qquad \langle x_0, \emptyset, \emptyset \rangle \rightsquigarrow_\varepsilon \langle 0, \emptyset, \Omega_0 \rangle
\end{array}
$$

Fig. 4. Inconsistency in B.

Formally, we have shown the following soundness result for B:

Theorem 10. *Let* $\mathcal{E} = \langle V, E \rangle$ *be a Simple Boolean Equation System. Then, whenever* $\langle x, B, N \rangle \rightsquigarrow_\varepsilon \langle b, C, M \rangle$ *the following holds:*

i) $C \backslash B \subseteq \mathcal{F}_\varepsilon(C)$

ii) $N \cap \nu \mathcal{F}_\varepsilon = \emptyset \Rightarrow M \cap \nu \mathcal{F}_\varepsilon = \emptyset$

iii) $B \subseteq C$

iv) $N \subseteq M$

v) $b = 1 \Rightarrow x \in C$

vi) $b = 0 \Rightarrow x \in M$

As an easy corollary we may infer that B is sound with respect to consistency.

Corollary 11. *Let* $\mathcal{E} = \langle V, E \rangle$ *be a Simple Boolean Equation System.*

1. *Whenever* $\langle x, \emptyset, \emptyset \rangle \rightsquigarrow_\varepsilon \langle 1, C, M \rangle$ *then* x *is consistent, i.e.* $x \in C_\varepsilon$.

2. *Whenever* $\langle x, \emptyset, \emptyset \rangle \rightsquigarrow_\varepsilon \langle 0, C, M \rangle$ *then* x *is inconsistent, i.e.* $x \notin C_\varepsilon$.

In contrast to the proof system A, where a statement may be inferred in a number of ways due to the open choice between A_5 and A_6 of A, the imposed left–to–right sequentiality in B makes proofs of statements unique. Formally, we have the following:

Theorem 12. Let $\mathcal{E} = \langle V, E \rangle$ be a Simple Boolean Equation System. Then the following holds:

$$\forall \langle x, B, N \rangle \exists! \langle b, C, M \rangle. \ \langle x, B, N \rangle \leadsto_{\mathcal{E}} \langle b, C, M \rangle$$

where $\exists!$ indicates unique existence.

Proof Now let $(B, N) \prec (B', N')$ if either $B \supsetneq B'$ and $N = N'$ or $N \supsetneq N'$ (i.e. $\prec$ is a lexicographical ordering on pairs with the first component being minor). As V is finite, $\prec$ will be a well–founded ordering. Now, the above theorem may be proved using well–founded induction on (B, N) and appealing to Theorem 10. □

In fact, not only does $\mathcal{B}$ provide a unique answer $\langle b, C, M \rangle$ for any given problem $\langle x, B, N \rangle$, the *proof* that $\mathcal{B}$ provides may also be shown to be unique.

From Theorem 10 and Theorem 12 it is clear that $\mathcal{B}$ is complete with respect to consistency in the following sense:

Corollary 13. Let $\mathcal{E} = \langle V, E \rangle$ be a Simple Boolean Equation System.

1. Whenever x is consistent, i.e. $x \in C_{\mathcal{E}}$, then $\langle x, \emptyset, \emptyset \rangle \leadsto_{\mathcal{E}} \langle 1, C, M \rangle$ for some sets C and M,

2. Whenever x is inconsistent, i.e. $x \notin C_{\mathcal{E}}$, then $\langle x, \emptyset, \emptyset \rangle \leadsto_{\mathcal{E}} \langle 0, C, M \rangle$ for some sets C and M.

For results of complexity, we need a minimum amount of terminology concerning *proof trees*. A proof tree T of $\mathcal{B}$ contains statements of $\mathcal{B}$ as nodes and is either an instance of one of the axioms $\mathbf{B_1}$ and $\mathbf{B_2}$ or is of the form:

$$T = \frac{T_1 \cdots \cdots T_n}{s} \tag{5}$$

where s is a statement of $\mathcal{B}$, and $T_1 \ldots T_n$ are themselves proof trees. s is the *conclusion* of T and should be obtainable from the conclusions of $T_1 \ldots T_n$ using one of the rules of $\mathcal{B}$. We now introduce a *total* ordering $\ll$ between the nodes of a proof tree (5) inductively as follows: s is the smallest node with respect to $\ll$; all nodes of T_i are smaller than the nodes of T_j whenever $i < j$. For the ordering among nodes of any T_i we appeal to the inductive construction. Clearly, $\ll$ is a total ordering with statements increasing in an 'up–or–right' direction.

The following lemma states the relation between $\prec$ and $\ll$:

Lemma 14. Let T be a proof tree of $\mathcal{B}$ and let $s_i = (\langle x_i, B_i, N_i \rangle \leadsto_{\mathcal{E}} \langle b_i, C_i, M_i \rangle)$ for $i = 1, 2$ be nodes in T. Then $(B_2, N_2) \prec (B_1, N_1)$ whenever $s_1 \ll s_2$.

As $\ll$ is total ordering among the nodes of a proof tree T, it follows that there can be no more nodes in T than the length of the longest decreasing $\prec$–sequence. Thus, for a given Simple Boolean Equation System $\mathcal{E} = \langle V, E \rangle$, any $\mathcal{B}$ proof tree will have no more than $|V|^2$ nodes. Under the assumption of constant access time for each variable of V, checking the side–condition of any of the rules of $\mathcal{B}$ may be done in constant time. Hence, using the rules in a goal–directed manner will yield an algorithm with $O(|V|^2)$ worst case running time.

Concluding Remarks

In this paper we have presented a proof system for efficient consistency–checking of variables of a (Simple) Boolean Equation System. We claim that several model–checking and equation/preorder–checking problems may be dealt with using the developed techniques. However, the techniques of this paper only leads to a model–checking method for pure *saftety* properties. Properties which can be expressed in the modal mu–calculus using only minimal fixedpoints may be dealt with by a simple dualization of the proof system $\mathcal{B}$. For properties requiring the used of both minimal and maximal fixedpoints our techniques may be extended to the modal mu–calculus of alternation depth one (i.e. any recursive subformula with alternating fixedpoint must be closed). To deal with mixed fixedpoints in this restricted sense, we simply consider lists of Boolean Equation Systems $[\mathcal{E}_1, \ldots, \mathcal{E}_n]$, where we alternate between consistency and factuality of variables and with variables of $\mathcal{E}_i$ only depending on variables of $\mathcal{E}_{i+1}, \ldots, \mathcal{E}_n$. Local model–checking for the *full* modal mu–calculus is contained in [Xin92], where an $O\left(m \times n \times \left(\frac{m \times n}{k}\right)^k\right)$ algorithm is presented. Here m is the size of the process P, n is the size of the formula F, and k is the alternation depth of F.

Applying the proof system $\mathcal{B}$ to $\mathcal{E}_P^{\sim}$ and $\mathcal{E}_P^{\preceq}$ we obtain local techniques for checking bisimulation equivalence and simulation preorder. The techniques will clearly be based entirely on the behavioural semantics of processes, and will in no way take account of their possible syntactic structure. However, it is possible to extend $\mathcal{B}$ so that certain algebraic properties of processes may be utilized. More precisely, for any consistency–preserving relation $\equiv$ [4] we may change the rule $\mathbf{B}_1$ as follows:

$$\mathbf{B}_1^{\equiv}\langle x, B, N \rangle \rightsquigarrow_{\mathcal{E}} \langle 1, B \cup \{x\}, N \rangle \qquad \text{when } \exists y \in B.x \equiv y, \text{ or } x =_{\mathcal{E}} \mathbf{tt}$$

while maintaining a sound proof system with respect to consistency. Thus, it is sufficient that x is $\equiv$–related to some member of B in order to invoke the axiom (and hence avoid further computation). Now, we may represent various algebraic laws between processes as a relation $\equiv$ between variables of $\mathcal{E}_P^{\sim}$ and $\mathcal{E}_P^{\preceq}$. The fact that the parallel operator of CCS [Mil80, Mil89] is commutative and has *nil* as unit with respect to bisimulation may be represented as:

$$Y_{P|Q,R} \equiv Y_{Q|P,R}$$
$$Y_{P|nil,R} \equiv Y_{P,R}$$

Taking in this way account of commutativity (and similarly associativity) of the parallel operator will clearly yield a much improved algorithm in verification of systems with many identical components, as we may identify system states with the same number of components in any particular state. Also, the fact that *nil* is the smallest process with respect to $\preceq$ may be reflected as $X_{nil,P} \equiv \mathbf{tt}$ thus avoiding computation completely. However, checking the side–condition of $\mathbf{B}_1^{\equiv}$ may no longer necessarily be done in constant time, and it will depend highly on the combination of the particular example and the choice of $\equiv$ as to whether $\mathbf{B}_1^{\equiv}$ yields an improvement.

---

[4] $\equiv$ is consistency-preserving if $y \in C_{\mathcal{E}}$ and $x \equiv y$ implies $x \in C_{\mathcal{E}}$.

Finally, it is clear that the global technique (with the required state–space precomputation) cannot be used for processes with infinite state space. We are currently investigating the relationship between our proof system $\mathcal{B}$ and the tableau–technique of [HS91] for contextfree processes.

Acknowledgement

The author would like to thank Liu Xinxin for many inspiring discussions on the subject of local correctness checking. Also, we would like to thank Hans Hüttel for reading and commenting on drafts of this paper.

References

[And92]   H.R. Andersen. Model checking and boolean graphs. *Lecture Notes In Computer Science, Springer Verlag*, 1992. In Proceedings of CAAP'92.

[BAPM83] M. Ben-Ari, A. Pnueli, and Z. Manna. The temporal logic of branching time. *Acta Informatica*, 20, 1983.

[BB87]   T. Bolognesi and E. Brinksma. Introduction to the ISO specification language LOTOS. *Computer Networks and ISDN Systems*, 14, 1987.

[BK85]   J.A. Bergstra and J.W. Klop. Algebra of communicating processes with abstraction. *Theoretical Computer Science*, 37:77–121, 1985.

[Blo88]   Meyer Bloom, Istrail. bisimulation can't be traced. *Proceedings of Principles of Programming Languages*, 1988.

[Bou85]   G. Boudol. Calcul de processus et verification. Technical Report 424, INRIA, 1985.

[Cle90]   R. Cleaveland. Tableau–based model checkin in the propositional mu–calculus. *Acta Informatica*, 1990.

[CPS88]   R. Cleaveland, J. Parrow, and B. Steffen. The concurrency workbench. University of Edinburgh, Scotland, 1988.

[CS91a]   R. Cleaveland and B. Steffen. Computing behavioural relations, logically. *Lecture Notes In Computer Science, Springer Verlag*, 510, 1991.

[CS91b]   R. Cleaveland and B. Steffen. A linear–time model–checking algorithm for ethe alternation–free modal mu–calculus. *Lecture Notes In Computer Science, Springer Verlag*, 1991. To appear in Proceedings of Third Workshop on Computer Aided Verification.

[EES86]   E.M.Clarke, E.A. Emerson, and A.P. Sistla. Automatic verification of finite–state concurrent systems using temporal logic specifications. *TOPLAS*, 8(2), 1986.

[EL86]   E.A. Emerson and C.L Lei. Efficient model checking in fragments of the propositional mu–calculus. *Proceedings of Logic in Computer Science*, 1986.

[FM91]   J.C. Fernandez and L. Mounier. A tool set for deciding beharioural equivalence. *Lecture Notes In Computer Science, Springer Verlag*, 527, 1991.

[GW91a]   P. Godefroid and P. Wolper. A partial approach to model–checking. *In Proceedings of Logic in Computer Science*, 1991.

[GW91b]   P. Godefroid and P. Wolper. Using partial orders for the efficient verification of deadlock freedom and safety properties. *Lecture Notes In Computer Science, Springer Verlag*, 1991. To appear in Proceedings of Third workshop on Computer Aided Verification.

[Hoa85]   C.A.R. Hoare. *Communicating Sequential Processes*. Prentice-Hall, 1985.

[HS91]   H. Hüttel and C. Stirling. Actions speak louder than words: proving bisimilarity for context-free processes. *Proceedings of Logic in Computer Science*, 1991.

[JGZ89]   K.G. Larsen J.C. Godskesen and M. Zeeberg. Tav — tools for automatic verification — users manual. Technical Report R 89-19, Department of Mathematics and Computer Science, Aalborg University, 1989. Presented at workshop on Automatic Methods for Finite State Systems, Grenoble, France, Juni 1989.

[Koz82]   D. Kozen. Results on the propositional mu–calculus. *Lecture Notes In Computer Science, Springer Verlag*, 140, 1982. in Proc. of International Colloquium on Algorithms, Languages and Programming 1982.

[Lar87]   K.G. Larsen. A context dependent bisimulation between processes. *Theoretical Computer Science*, 49, 1987.

[Lar90]   K.G. Larsen. Proof systems for satisfiability in Hennessy–Milner logic with recursion. *Theoretical Computer Science*, 72, 1990.

[LMV88]   V. Lecompte, E. Madelaine, and D. Vergamini. Auto: A verfication system for parallel and communicating processes. INRIA, Sophia–Antipolis, 1988.

[LS91]   K.G. Larsen and A. Skou. Bisimulation through probabilistic testing. *Information and Computation*, 94(1), 1991.

[LT88]   Kim G. Larsen and Bent Thomsen. A modal process logic. In *Proceeding on Logic in Computer Science*, 1988.

[LX90]   K.G. Larsen and L. Xinxin. Equation solving using modal transition systems. In *Proceedings on Logic in Computer Science*, 1990.

[Mil80]   R. Milner. *Calculus of Communicating Systems*, volume 92 of *Lecture Notes In Computer Science, Springer Verlag*. Springer Verlag, 1980.

[Mil83]   R. Milner. Calculi for synchrony and asynchrony. *Theoretical Computer Science*, 25:267–310, 1983.

[Mil89]   R. Milner. *Communication and Concurrency*. Prentice–Hall, 1989.

[Par81]   D. Park. Concurrency and automata on infinite sequences. *Lecture Notes In Computer Science, Springer Verlag*, 104, 1981. Proceedings of 5th GI Conference.

[Par89]   J. Parrow. Submodule construction as equation solving in CCS. *Theoretical Computer Science*, 68, 1989.

[Plo81]   G. Plotkin. A structural approach to operational semantics. FN 19, DAIMI, Aarhus University, Denmark, 1981.

[Pnu85]   A. Pnueli. Linear and branching structures in the semantics and logics of reactive systems. *Lecture Notes In Computer Science, Springer Verlag*, 194, 1985. Proceedings of 12th International Colloquium on Automata, Languages and Programming.

[PS90]   P.C.Kanellakis and S.A.Smolka. Ccs expressions, finite state processes, and three problems of equivalence. *Information and Control*, 86, 1990.

[PT87]   Paige and Tarjan. Three partition refinement algorithms. *SIAM Journal of Computing*, 16(6), 1987.

[RRSV87] J.L. Rixchier, C. Rodriguez, J. Sifakis, and J. Voiron. Xesar: a tool for protocol validation. users' guide. Technical report, LGI–IMAG, 1987.

[Shi]   M.W. Shields. A note on the simple interface equation. Technical report, University of Kent at Canterbury.

[SW89]   C. Stirling and D. Walker. Local model checking in the modal mu–calculus. *Lecture Notes In Computer Science, Springer Verlag*, 352, 1989. In Proc. of Tapsoft'89.

[Tar55]   A. Tarski. A lattice–theoretical fixpoint theorem and its applications. *Pacific Journal of Math.*, 5, 1955.

[Win89]   G. Winskel. Model checking the modal nu–calculus. *Lecture Notes In Computer Science, Springer Verlag*, 372, 1989. In Proceedings of International Colloquium on Algorithms, Languages and Programming 19'89.

[Xin92]   Liu Xinxin. *Specification and Decomposition in Concurrency*. PhD thesis, Aalborg University, 1992. R 92–2005.

Mechanical Verification of Concurrent Systems with TLA

Urban Engberg[1], Peter Grønning[2], and Leslie Lamport[3]

[1] Aarhus University
[2] Technical University of Denmark
[3] Digital Equipment Corporation
Systems Research Center

Abstract. We describe an initial version of a system for mechanically checking the correctness proof of a concurrent system. Input to the system consists of the correctness properties, expressed in TLA (the temporal logic of actions), and their proofs, written in a humanly readable, hierarchically structured form. The system uses a mechanical verifier to check each step of the proof, translating the step's assertion into a theorem in the verifier's logic and its proof into instructions for the verifier. Checking is now done by LP (the Larch Prover), using two different translations—one for action reasoning and one for temporal reasoning. The use of additional mechanical verifiers is planned. Our immediate goal is a practical system for mechanically checking proofs of behavioral properties of a concurrent system; we assume ordinary properties of the data structures used by the system.

1 Introduction

TLA, the Temporal Logic of Actions, is a logic for specifying and reasoning about concurrent systems. Systems and their properties are described by logical formulas; the TLA formula $\Pi \Rightarrow \Phi$ asserts that the system represented by Π satisfies the property, or implements the system, represented by Φ. TLA is a linear-time temporal logic [4] that can express liveness (eventuality) as well as safety (invariance) properties. Although TLA is a formal logic, the TLA specification of a concurrent system is no more difficult to write than the system's description in a conventional programming language.

Since TLA is a formal logic, it allows completely rigorous reasoning. It is clear that TLA proofs can, in principle, be checked mechanically. In 1991, we began a one-year effort to determine if mechanical verification with TLA is practical. We decided to use the LP verification system [1, 2], initially planning to write proofs directly in LP. However, we found the LP encoding to be distracting, making large proofs difficult. We therefore decided to write a TLA to LP translator, so specifications, theorems, and proof steps could be written in TLA. Writing specifications and theorems directly in TLA avoids the errors that can be introduced when hand translating what one wants to prove into the language of a verifier. The translator also allows mechanically checked proofs to have the same structure as hand proofs, making them easier to write and understand.

Working on the translator has thus far allowed us time to verify only a few simple examples, including an algorithm to compute a spanning tree on an arbitrary graph. Experience with more realistic examples is needed to determine if mechanical verification of TLA formulas can be a practical tool for concurrent-system design. It will never be easy to write rigorous proofs. However, we find it very encouraging that mechanically checkable proofs written in the translator seem to be only two to three times longer than careful hand proofs.

TLA, its LP encoding, and the translator are described in the following three sections, using the spanning-tree algorithm as an example. In this example, we prove that a system satisfies a property. An important feature of TLA is the ability to prove that one system implements (is a refinement of) another. However, space does not permit an example of such a proof.

2   TLA

For the purposes of this paper, we can consider TLA to be ordinary predicate logic, except with two classes of variables called *rigid variables* and *flexible variables*, extended with the two operators ′ (prime) and □. Quantification is over rigid variables only. (Full TLA also includes quantification over flexible variables, which serves as a hiding operator.) We often refer to flexible variables simply as variables.

The semantics of TLA is based on the concept of a *state*, which is an assignment of values to (flexible) variables. The meaning of a TLA formula is a set of *behaviors*, where a behavior is a sequence of states. The operator □ is the standard temporal-logic "always" operator [7]; the prime is a "next-state" operator. The complete semantics of TLA can be found elsewhere [6]; here we explain TLA informally through simple examples.

As a first example, we write a TLA formula specifying a program that starts with the variable x equal to any natural number, and keeps incrementing x by 1 forever. Letting Nat denote the set of natural numbers, the obvious way to express this with the prime and □ operators is

$$(x \in Nat) \;\wedge\; \Box(x' = x + 1) \tag{1}$$

The predicate $x \in Nat$ asserts that the value of x in the initial state is an element of Nat; the action $x' = x + 1$ asserts that the value of x in the next state is always 1 greater than its value in the current state, and the temporal formula $\Box(x' = x + 1)$ asserts that this is true for all steps—that is, for all pairs of successive states.

Formula (1) asserts that the value of x is incremented in each step of a behavior. For reasons explained in [5], we want also to allow steps that leave x unchanged. Letting $[\mathcal{A}]_f$ denote $\mathcal{A} \vee (f' = f)$, this is expressed by the TLA formula

$$(x \in Nat) \;\wedge\; \Box[x' = x + 1]_x \;\wedge\; \mathrm{WF}_x(x' = x + 1) \tag{2}$$

The conjunct $\Box[x' = x + 1]_x$ asserts that every step of the program either increments x by 1 or leaves it unchanged. It allows behaviors in which x remains unchanged forever. The conjunct $\mathrm{WF}_x(x' = x+1)$ expresses the liveness property that infinitely many $x' = x+1$ steps (ones that do increment x) occur. The reader is referred to [6] for an explanation of the WF operator and its definition in terms of $'$ and $\Box$.

In general, the canonical form of a TLA formula describing an algorithm is

$$Init \;\wedge\; \Box[\mathcal{N}]_v \;\wedge\; F \tag{3}$$

where $Init$ is a predicate describing the initial state, $\mathcal{N}$ is an action describing how the variables may change, v is the tuple of all program variables, and F is a liveness condition. The conjunct $\Box[\mathcal{N}]_v$ asserts that every step is either an $\mathcal{N}$ step or else leaves all variables unchanged (since a tuple is unchanged iff every component is unchanged).

Our major example is a simple algorithm that, given a finite connected graph and a root, constructs a spanning tree. For each node n, the algorithm computes the distance $d[n]$ from n to the root and, if n is not the root, its father $f[n]$ in the spanning tree.

When the algorithm is expressed formally, d and f are variables whose values are functions with domain equal to the set of nodes. Before describing the algorithm, we introduce some notation for expressing functions. The expression $\lambda x \in S : e(x)$ denotes a function f whose domain is S, such that $f[x]$ equals $e(x)$ for all x in S. If f is a function, then $f[s := v]$ is the function that is the same as f except with $f[s] = v$. This is defined formally as follows, where $dom\,f$ denotes the domain of f, and $\stackrel{\Delta}{=}$ means *equals by definition*.

$$f[s := v] \;\stackrel{\Delta}{=}\; \lambda x \in dom\,f : \text{if } x = s \text{ then } v \text{ else } f[x]$$

(Thus, $s \notin dom\,f$ implies $f[s := v] = f$.) If f is a function and T a set, then $f[s :\in T]$ is the set of all functions $f[s := v]$ with $v \in T$. Finally, $[S \to T]$ denotes the set of all functions f with domain S such that $f[x] \in T$ for all $x \in S$.

We now describe the spanning-tree algorithm. Initially, $d[n]$ equals 0 for the root and equals ∞ for all other nodes. For each node n, there is a process that repeatedly executes *improvement steps* that choose a neighbor m with $d[m] + 1 < d[n]$, decrease $d[n]$, and set $f[n]$ to m. The improvement step could simply decrease $d[n]$ to $d[m]+1$, but for reasons that are irrelevant to this discussion, we consider a more general algorithm in which $d[n]$ is set to a nondeterministically chosen number between its old value and $d[m]$. The algorithm terminates when no more improvement steps are possible.

The TLA formula Π describing this algorithm is defined in Figure 1, where *Node* is the set of nodes, *Root* is the root, $Nbrs(n)$ is the set of neighbors of node n in the graph, and $[a, b)$ is the set of natural numbers c such that $a \le c < b$. We adopt the convention that a list bulleted with $\wedge$'s denotes the conjunction of the items, and we use indentation to eliminate parentheses. We have found this convention extremely helpful in making large formulas easier to read.

The initial condition is described by the predicate *Init*. It asserts that $d[n]$ has the appropriate value (0 or ∞) and that $f[n]$ is a node, for each $n \in Node$.

Action $\mathcal{N}_2(n, m)$ describes an improvement step, in which $d[n]$ is decreased and $f[n]$ set equal to m. However, it does not assert that m is a neighbor of n. The action is enabled only if $d[m] + 1 < d[n]$. (In this formula, d and f are flexible variables, while m and n are rigid variables.)

Action $\mathcal{N}$ is the disjunction of the actions $\mathcal{N}_2(n, m)$ for every node n and neighbor m of n. It is the next-state relation of the algorithm, describing how the variables d and f may change. We define v to be the pair (d, f) of variables, and Π to be the canonical formula describing the algorithm. The weak fairness condition $\mathrm{WF}_v(\mathcal{N})$ asserts that $\mathcal{N}$ steps are eventually taken as long as they remain possible—that is, as long as the action $\mathcal{N}$ remains enabled. Concurrency is represented by the nondeterministic interleaving of the different processes' (atomic) improvement steps.

$$
\begin{aligned}
Init \;&\triangleq\; \wedge\; d = \lambda n \in Node : \text{if } n = Root \text{ then } 0 \text{ else } \infty \\
&\quad\; \wedge\; f \in [Node \rightarrow Node] \\[4pt]
\mathcal{N}_2(n, m) \;&\triangleq\; \wedge\; d[m] \neq \infty \\
&\quad\; \wedge\; d' \in d[n :\in [d[m] + 1, \, d[n])] \\
&\quad\; \wedge\; f' = f[n := m] \\[4pt]
\mathcal{N} \;&\triangleq\; \exists n \in Node : \exists m \in Nbrs(n) : \mathcal{N}_2(n, m) \\[4pt]
v \;&\triangleq\; (d, f) \\[4pt]
\Pi \;&\triangleq\; Init \wedge \Box[\mathcal{N}]_v \wedge \mathrm{WF}_v(\mathcal{N})
\end{aligned}
$$

Fig. 1. The spanning-tree algorithm.

The correctness property to be proved is that, for every node n, the values of $d[n]$ and $f[n]$ eventually become and remain correct. Letting $Dist(n, m)$ denote the distance in the graph between nodes n and m, the correctness of these values is expressed by the predicate *Done*, defined to equal

$$
\forall n \in Node : \wedge\; d[n] = Dist(Root, n) \\
\qquad\qquad\;\; \wedge\; 0 < d[n] < \infty \;\Rightarrow\; \wedge\; f[n] \in Nbrs(n) \\
\qquad\qquad\qquad\qquad\qquad\qquad\qquad \wedge\; Dist(Root, f[n]) = Dist(Root, n) - 1
$$

(If the graph is not connected, then for every node n not in the root's connected component, *Done* asserts only that $d[n] = \infty$.) The assertion that *Done* eventually becomes and remains true is expressed by the TLA formula $\Diamond\Box \, Done$, where $\Diamond F$, read *eventually F*, is defined to equal $\neg\Box\neg F$. Correctness of the algorithm is expressed by the formula $\Pi \;\Rightarrow\; \Diamond\Box \, Done$, which asserts that $\Diamond\Box \, Done$ holds for every behavior satisfying Π.

The usual first step in reasoning about a concurrent algorithm is to prove an invariant. The appropriate invariant *Inv* for our algorithm is the following, where \ denotes set difference.

$$\land\ d \in [Node \rightarrow Nat \cup \{\infty\}]$$
$$\land\ f \in [Node \rightarrow Node]$$
$$\land\ d[Root] = 0$$
$$\land\ \forall n \in Node \setminus \{Root\} : d[n] < \infty \Rightarrow \land\ Dist(Root, n) \leq d[n]$$
$$\land\ f[n] \in Nbrs(n)$$
$$\land\ d[f[n]] < d[n]$$

The invariance of *Inv* is asserted by the formula $\Pi \Rightarrow \Box Inv$. For brevity, we prove the invariance only of the first two conjuncts of *Inv*, which we call *TC*. A careful hand proof of the TLA formula $\Pi \Rightarrow \Box TC$ expressing the invariance of *TC* appears in Figure 2 and is discussed below. A similar proof for the complete invariant *Inv* takes about two pages, but has the same basic structure.

The proof in Figure 2 uses a structured format that we find quite helpful for managing the complexity of proofs. Step 1 proves that *TC* holds in the initial state. Step 2 proves that any single step starting in a state with *TC* true leaves it true. Step 3 applies the following standard TLA proof rule [6], where I' denotes the formula obtained from I by replacing x with x', for each flexible variable x.

$$INV1: \quad \frac{I \land [\mathcal{N}]_v \Rightarrow I'}{I \land \Box[\mathcal{N}]_v \Rightarrow \Box I}$$

The theorem follows trivially from steps 1 and 3. Step 2, the "induction step", is the major part of an invariance proof. For this simple invariant, its proof is easy.

The proof that $\Pi \Rightarrow \Box Inv$ is like the invariance proof for *TC*, except step 2 is more difficult. The proof of the correctness property $\Pi \Rightarrow \Diamond \Box Done$ then uses ordinary temporal-logic reasoning and the TLA proof rule WF1 [6]; space does not permit its description.

3 Encoding TLA in LP

LP is based on a fragment of multisorted first-order logic. To reason about TLA with LP, one must encode TLA formulas in LP's logic. Our initial plan was to have a single encoding. However, as Figure 2 shows, two different kinds of reasoning are used in TLA proofs: steps 1 and 2 illustrate *action reasoning*, not involving temporal operators; step 3 illustrates *temporal reasoning*. Since it is formally a special case, action reasoning is possible in any encoding that allows temporal reasoning. However, such reasoning can be made easier with a special encoding for formulas not containing the temporal operator $\Box$. Action reasoning is almost always the longest and most difficult part of a proof, so we decided to use separate encodings for the action and temporal reasoning. We have found

Theorem $\Pi \Rightarrow \Box TC$

1. $Init \Rightarrow TC$
   Proof We assume $Init$ and prove TC.
   1.1. $d \in [Node \rightarrow Nat \cup \{\infty\}]$
      Proof By definition of $Init$, considering separately the cases $n = Root$
      and $n \neq Root$.
   1.2. $f \in [Node \rightarrow Node]$
      Proof By definition of $Init$.
   qed Step 1 follows from 1.1, 1.2, and the definition of TC.

2. $TC \wedge [\mathcal{N}]_v \Rightarrow TC'$
   Proof We assume TC and $[\mathcal{N}]_v$ and prove TC'.
   2.1. $\mathcal{N} \Rightarrow TC'$
      Proof Since $\mathcal{N} = \exists n \in Node, m \in Nbrs(n) : \mathcal{N}_2(n, m)$, it suffices to
      assume $n \in Node$, $m \in Nbrs(n)$, and $\mathcal{N}_2(n, m)$, and to prove TC'.
      2.1.1. $d' \in [Node \rightarrow Nat \cup \{\infty\}]$
         Proof By definition of TC and $\mathcal{N}_2$, since $[d[m] + 1, d[n]) \subseteq Nat \cup$
         $\{\infty\}$.
      2.1.2. $f' \in [Node \rightarrow Node]$
         Proof By definition of TC and $\mathcal{N}_2$, since $Nbrs(n) \subseteq Node$, for all
         nodes n.
      qed Step 2.1 follows from 2.1.1, 2.1.2, and the definition of TC.
   2.2. $(v' = v) \Rightarrow TC'$
      Proof Follows trivially from the definitions.
   qed Step 2 follows from 2.1 and 2.2, since $[\mathcal{N}]_v = \mathcal{N} \vee (v' = v)$.

3. $TC \wedge \Box[\mathcal{N}]_v \Rightarrow \Box TC$
   Proof By step 2 and rule INV1.
qed The theorem follows from 1, 3, and the definition of Π.

Fig. 2. The proof of invariance of TC.

the resulting simplification of action reasoning to be worth the inconvenience of
having two different encodings.

The encoding of action reasoning in LP is straightforward. TLA's rigid variables become LP variables. For each TLA flexible variable x, we encode x and
x' as two distinct LP constants..Thus, the TLA action $(x' = x + 1) \wedge (y' = y)$ is
encoded in LP as `(x'=x+1)&(y'=y)`.

The encoding of temporal reasoning is more subtle. In TLA, a formula is
an assertion that is true or false for a behavior. Let $\sigma \models F$ denote that the
behavior σ satisfies the TLA formula F. Formula F is valid iff $\sigma \models F$ is true for
all behaviors σ. The validity of F is represented in LP's logic by $\forall \sigma : \sigma \models F$.
Neglecting details of the precise ASCII syntax, this formula is written in LP
as $\sigma \models F$, universal quantification over the free variable σ being implicit. The
semantic operator $\models$, which cannot appear in a TLA formula, becomes part of
the formula's LP translation.

TLA's (temporal) proof rules have straightforward translations into LP. For example, the proof rule INV1 asserts

$$\frac{\forall \sigma : \sigma \models (I \wedge [N]_f \Rightarrow I')}{\forall \sigma : \sigma \models (I \wedge \Box[N]_f \Rightarrow \Box I)}$$

In this rule, $\wedge$, $\Rightarrow$, and $'$ are operators declared in LP to represent the corresponding TLA cperators. In particular, $\wedge$ and $\Rightarrow$ are different from LP's built-in conjunction (&) and implication (=>) operators. Propositional reasoning about temporal formulas is done in LP using such axioms as

$$\sigma \models (F \wedge G) \quad = \quad (\sigma \models F) \,\&\, (\sigma \models G)$$

4 The Translator

The TLA translator is a program written in Standard ML [3] that translates "humanly readable" TLA specifications and proofs into LP proof scripts. Their readability makes proofs easier to maintain when the specifications change than they would be if written directly in LP. The different encodings for action reasoning and temporal reasoning are translated into two separate LP input files. Formulas proved in the action encoding are asserted in the temporal encoding. The proof succeeds if LP successfully processes both files.

4.1 Specifications

Figure 3 is the input to the TLA translator corresponding to the spanning-tree algorithm of Figure 1. (All translator input is shown exactly as typed by the user, except that multiple fonts have been used for clarity.) It begins with a declaration of *Span* as the name of the specification, followed by a directive to read the file *frame*, which contains declarations of all constants such as 0, +, *Nbrs*, and *Node*. The next two lines declare d and f to be (flexible) variables. (In TLA's typeless logic, the only sorts are Boolean and Any.) The rest of the specification is a direct transliteration of Figure 3, except for two differences: the action $N1(n)$ is defined for use in the proofs, and $*$ is used instead of comma to denote ordered pairs. The translation of these definitions into LP rewrite rules is straightforward, except for quantified expressions and the lambda-construct. LP does not now support full first-order quantification, so we have defined LP operators and associated proof rules for quantification and lambda abstraction. Each occurrence of a quantifier or "lambda" requires the definition of an auxiliary function, which is named for reference in proofs by a term in brackets [* ... *].

In TLA, prime ($'$) is an operator that can be applied to predicates like *Init* and to state functions like v, where priming an expression replaces all variables by their primed versions. In the LP action encoding, primed and unprimed variables become distinct constants, so the prime operator cannot be expressed. The "bar operator" used in refinement [6, Section 9.3.2] and TLA's *Enabled* operator [6, Section 3.7] are similarly inexpressible. The translator must therefore add to the LP encoding rewrite rules explicitly defining such expressions as $Init'$, $\overline{v}$,

Name *Span*
Use *frame*
Variables
    d, f : **Any**
Predicates
    Init   == $/\ d =$ **Lambda** n in *Node* :
                    If $n = Root$ **Then** 0 **Else** *infty* [* dist : **Any** *]
            $/\ f$ in [*Node* -> *Node*]
Actions
    $N2(n, m)$ == $/\ d[m]$ $\tilde{}=$ *infty*
                $/\ d'$ in $d[n$:in *openInter*$(d[m] + 1, d[n])]$
                $/\ f' = f[n := m]$
    $N1(n)$ == **Exists** m in *Nbrs*(n) : $N2(n, m)$ [* n1(n) *]
    N == **Exists** n in *Node* : $N1(n)$ [* n *]
Statefunctions
    v == $(d * f)$
Formulas
    Pi   == *Init* $/\$ [][N]_v $/\$ **WF**(v, N)

Fig. 3. The spanning-tree algorithm, in the translator's input language.

and *Enabled* $\mathcal{N}$. Definitions for the primed and barred expressions are generated automatically by the translator. Definitions for the *Enabled* predicates must now be provided by the user; future versions of the translator will generate them as well.

4.2 Proofs

The invariant *TC* of our spanning-tree algorithm is specified in the translator's language as

    TC == d in [*Node* -> *NatInf*] $/\ f$ in [*Node* -> *Node*]

where *NatInf* denotes $Nat \cup \{\infty\}$. The hand proof of invariance of *TC* was based on certain tacit assumptions about *Root*, *Node*, and *Nbrs*. The formal statement of these assumptions is the assertion *Assump*, defined in the translator input to be the conjunction of the following two assertions. (Since the set construct has a bound variable, it requires the same kind of auxiliary function used for quantifiers and "lambda".)

    Assump1 == *Root* in *Node*
    Assump2 == **Forall** n in *Node* :
                  Nbrs$(n) = \{m$ in *Node* :
                          NbrRel(n, m) [* a22(n) *]$\}$ [* a21 *]

where *NbrRel* denotes the neighbor relation on the graph. Further assumptions about *NbrRel* are needed for the complete correctness proof of the algorithm.

Figure 4 contains the translator version of the invariance proof of Figure 2. It has the same structure as the hand proof in Figure 2. Steps are numbered in the more compact fashion $\langle level\rangle step$, with **Step**$\langle 2\rangle 3$ denoting the third substep of level two and **Hyp**$\langle 1\rangle.2$ denoting the second hypothesis of level one of the current proof.

The proof is written in a natural deduction style, the translator input **Assume** A **Prove** B denoting that $A \Rightarrow B$ is to be proved by assuming A and proving B. The goal B can be omitted if it is the same as the current goal. (In the temporal encoding, assuming A and proving B means assuming $\sigma \models A$ and proving $\sigma \models B$, for an arbitrary constant σ.) The construct **Reduce by** A **To** B expresses an argument of the form "By A it suffices to prove B." It is converted into LP's style of direct reasoning by rearranging the proof steps. **Normalize**, **Apply**, and **Crit** are LP commands. The applied rules, such as BoxElim1, are defined in LP for reasoning about the translator output. In step $\langle 1\rangle 3$, INV1 applies the INV1-rule and **Crit**'s the current hypotheses with the resulting fact.

Figure 5 shows the LP input in the action-reasoning file generated from step $\langle 3\rangle 1$ in the proof of step $\langle 1\rangle 2$. Additional translator constructs allow arbitrary LP input to be inserted into the output, making the full power of LP available through the translator. (Soundness is maintained if no LP `assert` commands are inserted.) Such direct use of LP was not needed in this proof; our ultimate goal is to make it unnecessary in general.

The predicate TC is just one part of the entire invariant Inv. About three more pages of translator input completes the proof of invariance of Inv. The rest of the correctness proof takes about six more pages. These proofs required additional properties of numbers (elements of $NatInf$), functions, and the distance function $Dist$—including the well-foundedness of the ordering on $[Node \rightarrow Nat \cup \{\infty\}]$ defined by $f \leq g$ iff $f[n] \leq g[n]$ for all $n \in Node$. Properties of the natural numbers (associativity of addition etc.) were expressed directly in LP. Properties of the distance function needed for the proof were asserted in the translator input. Although these properties can be proved from more primitive definitions, we have ignored such conventional verification in order to concentrate on the novel aspects of TLA.

5 Future Directions

It is obviously easier to write a TLA proof in TLA than in an LP encoding of TLA. It was not obvious to us how much easier it would be. Our initial experience indicates that writing a proof with the translator can be an order of magnitude faster than doing the proof directly in LP. Such a speed-up is possible only if the proof can be written in the translator with no direct use of LP. We are planning to enhance the translator to eliminate all direct LP reasoning.

Translating the steps of a proof rather than just the property to be proved permits the use of multiple verification methods. The translator now generates separate LP input for action and temporal reasoning. We plan to generate input to other verification systems as well. Steps that are provable by simple temporal

Theorem TC
  Assume [] *Assump* Prove *Pi* => [] *TC*

Proof
  ⟨1⟩1 Assume *Assump, Init* Prove *TC*

    ⟨2⟩1 *d* in [*Node -> NatInf*]
    Reduce by Normalize Hyp⟨1⟩.2 with *Init*,
              Apply ProveFuncSpaceLambda to Red
    To Assume *n* in *Node* Prove *d*[*n*]in *NatInf*

      ⟨3⟩1 Case *n* = *Root*
      Qed by Normalize Hyp⟨1⟩.2 with *Init*

      ⟨3⟩2 Case *n* ~= *Root*
      Qed by Normalize Hyp⟨1⟩.2 with *Init*

    Qed by Cases

    ⟨2⟩2 *f* in [*Node -> Node*]
    Qed by Normalize Hyp⟨1⟩.2 with *Init*

  Qed by Normalize Goal with *TC*

  ⟨1⟩2 Assume *Assump, TC,* [*N*]_*v* Prove *TC'*

    ⟨2⟩1 Case *N*
    Reduce by Normalize Hyp with *N*
    To Assume *n* in *Node* /\ *N*1(*n*)
    Reduce by Normalize Hyp with *N*1
    To Assume *m* in *Nbrs*(*n*) /\ *N*2(*n, m*)

      ⟨3⟩1 *d'* in [*Node -> NatInf*]

        ⟨4⟩1 Assume *k* in *openInter*(*d*[*m*] + 1, *d*[*n*]) Prove *k* in *NatInf*
        Qed by Normalize Hyp with UseOpenInterval

      Qed by Normalize Hyp⟨1⟩.2 with *TC*,
                Normalize Hyp⟨2⟩ with *N*2,
                Apply ProveFuncSpaceUpdateIn to Hyp⟨1⟩.2 Hyp⟨2⟩ Step⟨4⟩1

      ⟨3⟩2 *f'* in [*Node -> Node*]

        ⟨4⟩1 *m* in *Node*
        Qed by Normalize Hyp⟨1⟩.1 with *Assump Assump2*

      Qed by Normalize Hyp⟨1⟩.2 with *TC*,
                Normalize Hyp⟨2⟩ with *N*2,
                Apply ProveFuncSpaceUpdateEq to Hyp⟨1⟩.2 Hyp⟨2⟩ Step⟨4⟩1

    Qed by Normalize Goal with *TC*

    ⟨2⟩2 Case Unchanged(*v*)
    Qed by Normalize Hyp with *v*,
              Normalize Hyp⟨1⟩.2 with *TC*,
              Normalize Goal with *TC*

  Qed by Cases

  ⟨1⟩3 Assume [] *Assump, TC,* [][*N*]_*v* Prove [] *TC*
  Qed by INV1 on Step⟨1⟩2

Qed by Normalize Hyp with Pi,
          Apply BoxElim1 to Hyp,
          Crit Hyp with Step1 Step3

Fig. 4. Proof of invariance of *TC*, in the translator's input language.

```
set name Theorem_Tc1_2_1_1
prove in(d', funcSpace(Node, NatInf))
  set name Theorem_TC_2_1_1_1
  prove (in(v_k_, openInter(((d@v_m_c)+1), (d@v_n_c))) => in(v_k_,NatInf))
    resume by =>
    <> 1 subgoal for proof of =>
      normalize Theorem_TC_2_1_1_1ImpliesHyp with UseOpenInterval
      [] => subgoal
    [] conjecture
  set name Theorem_TC_2_1_1
  normalize Theorem_TC_2ImpliesHyp.2 with TC
  normalize Theorem_TC_2_1ImpliesHyp with N12
  apply ProveFuncSpaceUpdateIn to Theorem_TC_2ImpliesHyp.2 Theorem...
  [] conjecture
```

Fig. 5. Translator output for step ⟨3⟩1 in the proof of step ⟨1⟩2 of Figure 4.

reasoning will be verified automatically by a decision procedure for propositional temporal logic. Some steps might be proved with a model checker by enumerating all possibilities. We may also investigate the use of theorem provers other than LP as "back ends" for the translator.

References

1. Stephen J. Garland and John V. Guttag. An overview of LP, the Larch Prover. In N. Dershowitz, editor, *Proceedings of the Third International Conference on Rewriting Techniques and Applications*, volume 355 of *Lecture Notes on Computer Science*, pages 137–151. Springer-Verlag, April 1989.
2. Stephen J. Garland and John V. Guttag. A guide to LP, the Larch Prover. Technical Report 82, Digital Equipment Corporation Systems Research Center, December 1991.
3. Robert Harper, David MacQueen, and Christopher Wadsworth. Standard ML. Internal Report ECS–LFCS–86–2, Edingburgh University, March 1986.
4. Leslie Lamport. 'Sometime' is sometimes 'not never': A tutorial on the temporal logic of programs. In *Proceedings of the Seventh Annual Symposium on Principles of Programming Languages*, pages 174–185. ACM SIGACT-SIGPLAN, January 1980.
5. Leslie Lamport. What good is temporal logic? In R. E. A. Mason, editor, *Information Processing 83: Proceedings of the IFIP 9th World Congress*, pages 657–668, Paris, September 1983. IFIP, North-Holland.
6. Leslie Lamport. The temporal logic of actions. Technical Report 79, Digital Equipment Corporation, Systems Research Center, December 1991.
7. Amir Pnueli. The temporal logic of programs. In *Proceedings of the 18th Annual Symposium on the Foundations of Computer Science*, pages 46–57. IEEE, November 1977.

Using a Theorem Prover for Reasoning about Concurrent Algorithms

Joakim von Wright and Thomas Långbacka

Department of Computer Science, Åbo Akademi University
Lemminkäinengatan 14, SF-20520 Turku, Finland

Abstract. An attempt to mechanise reasoning about concurrent algorithms is described. The HOL theorem prover is used to formalise the semantics of the Temporal Logic of Actions (TLA). Using this formalisation, the proof rules of TLA are proved as theorems in the HOL system. The use of HOL in reasoning about algorithms in TLA is illustrated by two examples: a proof of a program property and an implementation proof.

1 Introduction

The Temporal Logic of Actions (TLA) is a logic for reasoning about concurrent algorithms, developed recently by Leslie Lamport [5, 6]. Algorithms are expressed directly as formulas in TLA, rather than in terms of a separate programming language. In this paper we describe an attempt to mechanise TLA reasoning using the theorem prover HOL [4]. Since reasoning about algorithms using TLA involves a lot of tedious proof details, much would be gained if the reasoning could be verified and partly automated using a proof assistant.

The HOL system has mainly been used for hardware verification. However, the higher order features of HOL also makes it useful for formalising logics and programming semantics [1, 2]. The fact that TLA expresses algorithms directly in the logic is an advantage, since this means that there is only one formalism that has to be implemented.

The HOL system is an interactive proof assistant, based on higher order logic (a polymorphic version of the simple theory of types [3]). Other logics can be embedded in HOL, using the HOL logic as a meta-logic. In this paper, which extends the previous work in [8], we formalise TLA in HOL by defining the semantics of TLA in HOL. The proof rules of TLA are then proved as HOL theorems. After this, these rules can be used for reasoning about programs. This means that we can show that a program has a certain property, or that one program implements another one, by proving a corresponding HOL theorem. We restrict ourselves to *Simple TLA*. This means that we do not consider hiding of variables and refinement mappings.

We assume that the reader is familiar with the HOL system and its version of higher order logic, as described in the documentation of the HOL system [4]. When referring to HOL-terms and interaction with the HOL system we use the syntax of HOL. In particular, we note that the scope of binders and quantifiers extends as far to the right as possible. To make formulas more readable, w e often omit type information which can be inferred from the context. Also, we use the ordinary logical symbols (the boolean truth values are denoted **F** and **T**).

2   Basic Concepts of TLA in HOL

In this section, we first give an overview of TLA and then describe how TLA is semantically embedded in HOL.

2.1   The Temporal Logic of Actions

One of the main ideas of TLA is that algorithms are expressed directly in the logic, rather than in a separate programming notation. TLA is based on a simple temporal logic, with □ ("always") as the only primitive temporal operator.

An *action* is a boolean expression that states how initial and final states are related. As an example,

$$(x' = x + 1) \wedge (y' = y) \tag{1}$$

is an action that increments x by 1 and leaves y unchanged (thus primed variables always stand for final states).

Predicates can always be interpreted as actions (as actions, they put no restrictions on the final states). Similarly, both predicates and actions can be interpreted as temporal formulas. A predicate asserts something about the state at time 0 while an action relates the states at time 0 and time 1.

If $\mathcal{A}$ is an action and f is a state function, then $[\mathcal{A}]_f$ is the action

$$[\mathcal{A}]_f \stackrel{\text{def}}{=} \mathcal{A} \vee (f = f')$$

where f' is the same as f but with all occurrences of program variables primed.

As an example, if $\mathcal{A}$ is the action $(x' = x + 1) \wedge (y' = y)$ then the action $[\mathcal{A}]_{(x,y)}$ permits arbitrary changes of all other variables than x and y. In this way stuttering can be modelled.

Variables and Types. TLA assumes that there is an infinite supply of program variables, though a given algorithm always mentions only a finite number of them. The values that variables can take are not organised in types. Instead, TLA assumes that there exists only one single set of values, and a variable can take any value from this set.

Expressing Algorithms in TLA. An algorithm is described by a formula

$$\Pi = \textit{Init} \wedge \Box[\mathcal{N}]_f \wedge F \tag{2}$$

where *Init* is a predicate that characterises the permitted initial states, $\mathcal{N}$ is the disjunction of all the actions of the algorithm and F is a formula that describes a fairness condition (thus safety and liveness are treated within a single framework). Note that the predicate *Init* is used as such in the TLA-formula (2). This shows how TLA permits predicates, actions and temporal formulas to be combined.

The safety part of (2) is $\Box[\mathcal{N}]_f$ which states that every step of the program must be permitted by $\mathcal{N}$ or it must leave f unchanged. Typically, f is a tuple containing all variables that the algorithm works on. Then $\Box[\mathcal{N}]_f$ states that every step is an $\mathcal{N}$-step or a stuttering step.

The liveness part F is typically a conjunction of fairness conditions on actions of the algorithm. Fairness requirements are easily expressed in TLA. Weak and strong fairness with respect to an action $\mathcal{A}$ is expressed as

$$WF_f(\mathcal{A}) \stackrel{\text{def}}{=} (\Box\Diamond\langle\mathcal{A}\rangle_f) \vee (\Box\Diamond\neg Enabled\langle\mathcal{A}\rangle_f)$$
$$SF_f(\mathcal{A}) \stackrel{\text{def}}{=} (\Box\Diamond\langle\mathcal{A}\rangle_f) \vee (\Diamond\Box\neg Enabled\langle\mathcal{A}\rangle_f)$$

where $\langle\mathcal{A}\rangle_f = \neg[\neg\mathcal{A}]_f$ and $Enabled(\mathcal{A})$ is true of those states in which it is possible to perform $\mathcal{A}$.

As a proof system, TLA has only a small set of basic proof rules. In addition to this, simple temporal reasoning is used, as well as ordinary mathematical reasoning about actions. In TLA, proving that program Π has property $\Box\Phi$ means proving that the TLA formula

$$\Pi \Rightarrow \Box\Phi$$

is valid. Similarly, proving that Π is implemented by another program Π' means proving that the formula $\Pi' \Rightarrow \Pi$ is valid.

An Example Algorithm. As an example we consider a simple algorithm, which increments variables x and y indefinitely. The initial state is characterised by the predicate

$$Init_1 \stackrel{\text{def}}{=} (x = 0) \wedge (y = 0)$$

The incrementation is defined by the following two actions:

$$\mathcal{M}_1 \stackrel{\text{def}}{=} x' = x + 1 \wedge y' = y$$
$$\mathcal{M}_2 \stackrel{\text{def}}{=} y' = y + 1 \wedge x' = x$$

The fairness requirement is weak fairness with respect to both actions, so the algorithm is described by the following formula:

$$\Pi_1 = Init_1 \wedge \Box[\mathcal{M}_1 \vee \mathcal{M}_2]_{(x,y)} \wedge WF_{(x,y)}(\mathcal{M}_1) \wedge WF_{(x,y)}(\mathcal{M}_2) \tag{3}$$

2.2   States, Predicates and Actions in HOL

In our formalisation, we assume that every variable has a well-defined type. Much can be said about advantages and disadvantages of typing. Our choice is dictated by the typing rules of HOL, and in Sect. 4.2 we will se how the typing supports implementation proofs.

We formalise states as tuples where every component corresponds to one variable of the state (the type of the component indicates what type its values must have). The state is made potentially infinite by adding a final component with polymorphic type. This final component ("the rest of the universe") can be instantiated to any tuple.

As an example, we consider the state space containing the variables x and y which range over natural numbers. The corresponding state space in HOL has type `:num#num#*` (type variables have names beginning with an asterisk).

Predicates and actions are formalised as boolean expressions with lambda-bound program variables. For example, in the above mentioned state space, the action (1) is formalised as

```
λ(x,y,z)(x',y',z'). (x'=x+1) ∧ (y'=y)
```

and the state predicate $x > 0$ is formalised as

```
λ(x,y,z). x>0
```

With this way of treating predicates and actions, substitutions can be formalised neatly as a combination of an application and an abstraction. For example, the predicate $x + y > 0$, with y substituted for x, is formalised as

```
λ(x,y,z). (λ(x,y,z). x+y>0)(y,y,z)
```

which beta-reduces to

```
λ(x,y,z).y+y>0
```

as it should. Note that the variables are anonymous, in the sense that the action (1) is equivalently expressed by

```
λ(a,z,x)(c,t',z'). (c=a+1) ∧ (t'=z)
```

However, we avoid confusion if we use the TLA rules for priming as a convention when writing actions in HOL. In passing, we note that the variables of ordinary programs are also anonymous, in the sense that we can usually change the name of a variable throughout the program without changing the effect of executing the program.

Constants (called *rigid variables* in TLA) are formalised as variables that are not bound by λ-abstraction.

Connectives for Predicates and Actions. The boolean connectives are lifted to predicates and actions in a straightforward way. The connectives for predicates are called pnot, pand, por, pimp etc. Similarly, the connectives for actions are called anot, aand, etc. As examples, we show the theorems that define the lifted conjunctions:

$\vdash_{def}$ p pand q = λs. p s $\land$ q s
$\vdash_{def}$ a aand b = λs s'. a s s' $\land$ b s s'

where s and s' are states.

We also define functions that represent validity:

$\vdash_{def}$ pvalid p = $\forall$s. p s
$\vdash_{def}$ avalid a = $\forall$s s'. a s s'

2.3 Temporal Logic in HOL

We have formalised the TLA logic by semantically embedding in HOL in a straighforward way. Time is represented by natural numbers and *behaviors* have type :num$\rightarrow$state where :state is the type of the state (in the generic case, :state is just a polymorphic type). Temporal formulas are represented as *temporal properties*, i.e., as boolean functions on behaviors. The following theorem defines the □-operator:

$\vdash_{def}$ box f t = $\forall$i. f(λn. t(i+n))

for temporal formula f and behavior t.

We also lift the boolean connectives to temporal formulas, giving them the names tnot, tand, etc. For example, the following theorems define lifted conjunction and lifted validity:

$\vdash_{def}$ f tand g = λt. f t $\land$ g t
$\vdash_{def}$ tvalid f = $\forall$t. f t

where t is a behavior.

2.4 TLA Formulas in HOL

We have formalised TLA in HOL by directly defining the semantics of TLA. The HOL system also permits another approach, where one defines a new type corresponding to TLA formulas and then define the semantics separately. However, the syntax of TLA is such that it would be quite involved to define TLA formulas as a new type.

One consequence of our approach is that TLA formulas are a subset of the of type : (num$\rightarrow$state)$\rightarrow$bool which represents temporal properties. Thus we do not formalise the notion of "well-formed TLA formula" at all. This is justified by a pragmatic viewpoint: our aim is to mechanise TLA-reasoning about algorithms, not to reason about the properties of the TLA logic itself.

TLA Formulas as Temporal Properties. In TLA, every predicate can also be interpreted as an action or as a temporal formula. I n our formalisation this is not true. Instead, predicates, actions and temporal formulas have distinct types. We define functions that do the "lifting" from predicates to the action and temporal levels (see Fig. 1).

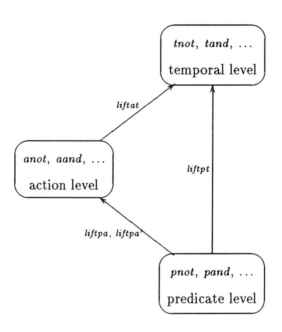

Fig. 1. Levels of the TLA logic

The functions `liftpa` and `liftpa'` that lift predicates to actions are defined as follows:

$$\vdash_{def} \texttt{liftpa p} = \lambda\texttt{s s'. p s}$$
$$\vdash_{def} \texttt{liftpa' p} = \lambda\texttt{s s'. p s'}$$

Similarly, the functions `liftpt` and `liftat` that lift predicates and actions to the temporal level are defined as follows:

$$\vdash_{def} \texttt{liftpt p t} = \texttt{p (t 0)}$$
$$\vdash_{def} \texttt{liftpa a t} = \texttt{a (t 0) (t 1)}$$

The square function $[\mathcal{A}]_f$ and the *Enabled* predicate are formalised by the following defining theorem:

$$\vdash_{def} \texttt{square a f} = \texttt{a aor } (\lambda\texttt{s s'. f s} = \texttt{f s'})$$
$$\vdash_{def} \texttt{enabled a} = \lambda\texttt{s. }\exists\texttt{s'. a s s'}$$

where f is a function from states to an arbitrary type.

Finally, we consider how an algorithm is represented. We assume that we are given a predicate (the initialisation init), an action (action) and a temporal formula (the liveness part live). The algorithm is then described by the formula

(liftpt init) tand (box (liftat (square action w))) tand live

where w represents the function $\lambda(x_1, ..., x_n, z).(x_1, ..., x_n)$ which takes the global state as argument and returns the part of the state that the algorithm works on (i.e., the state with the last component removed).

An Example Algorithm. As an example we consider the algorithm described in (3). The following defining theorems show how this algorithm is formalised:

$\vdash_{def}$ Init1 = λ(x,y,z). (x=0) $\wedge$ (y=0)
$\vdash_{def}$ M1   = λ(x,y,z)(x',y',z'). (x'=x+1) $\wedge$ (y'=y)
$\vdash_{def}$ M2   = λ(x,y,z)(x',y',z'). (y'=y+1) $\wedge$ (x'=x)
$\vdash_{def}$ w   = λ(x,y,z). (x,y)
$\vdash_{def}$ F   = (WF M1 w) tand (WF M2 w)
$\vdash_{def}$ Prog1 = (liftpt Init1) tand
                (box (liftat (square (M1 aor M2) w))) tand F

3   The TLA Logic in HOL

We will not state all the proof rules of Simple TLA. Instead, we consider two typical rules in some detail. The first rule is called $INV1$ and is used to prove invariance properties:

$$\frac{I \wedge [\mathcal{N}]_f \Rightarrow I'}{I \wedge \Box[\mathcal{N}]_f \Rightarrow \Box I}$$

This rule expresses the fact that if all program actions preserve I, then $\Box I$ holds provided I holds initially.

In HOL, the rule $INV1$ becomes

$\vdash$ avalid (((liftpa I) aand (square N f)) aimp (liftpa' I))
    $\Rightarrow$
    tvalid (((liftpt I) tand (box (square N f))) timp (box (liftpt I)))

Note how the HOL implication corresponds to the meta-implication in the rule.

The TLA rules that are used for reasoning about liveness are generally more complicated than the above rule. An example is the rule $SF1$ which permits the deduction of liveness properties from strong fairness assumptions:

$$P \wedge [\mathcal{N}]_f \Rightarrow (P' \vee Q')$$
$$P \wedge \langle \mathcal{N} \rangle_f \Rightarrow Q'$$
$$\frac{\Box P \wedge \Box[\mathcal{N}]_f \wedge \Box F \Rightarrow \Diamond Enabled\langle \mathcal{A} \rangle_f}{\Box[\mathcal{N}]_f \wedge SF_f(\mathcal{A}) \wedge \Box F \Rightarrow (P \rightsquigarrow Q)}$$

The formalisation of this rule in HOL is quite a big expression. When the rule is applied, however, one never has to work with the rule as a whole. Instead, the present goal is matched against the conclusion of the rule, and three subgoals are produced, one for each assumption of the rule.

Rules of TLA, such as the above two, are represented as theorems in HOL which are proved using the definition of the semantics. At first sight the rules in HOL may look ugly, since we cannot mix predicates, actions and temporal formulas as neatly as TLA does; we have to use the lifting functions. However, this is sometimes an advantage, since we avoid the confusion which can arise when the same term is sometimes a predicate and sometimes a temporal formula. The proofs (in HOL) of the above rules are quite straighforward, using rewriting and (in the case of the liveness rules) induction.

From the basic proof rules, further rules can easily be derived. The proofs of such rules in HOL mirror the paper-and-pen proofs almost exactly.

Use of Well-founded Sets. An important rule in liveness proofs is the Lattice rule, which encodes the principle of well-founded ranking. This rule presupposes the existence of a well-founded order on some set involved in the reasoning. To support the use of this rule in HOL reasoning, we have created a separate theory of well-founded sets where the notion of well-foundedness is defined and basic properties of well-founded sets are proved.

4 Reasoning about Algorithms

Once we have proved the proof rules of Simple TLA, we can use them to reason about algorithms in HOL. We shall now give examples of two kinds of reasoning: proving that a program has a certain property and proving that one program implements another one. Formally, these amount to the same thing in TLA, since programs are formulas in the logic.

4.1 Verifying Properties of Programs

As an example, we shall show how mutual exclusion is proved for a simple algorithm. The example is taken from [6]. It is a refinement of the simple example considered earlier which incremented variables x and y indefinitely. This algorithms works on the variables x, y, pc_1, pc_2 and sem. The variables pc_1 and pc_2 are program counters, taking values $"A"$, $"B"$ and $"G"$, and sem is a semaphore.

The initial state is characterised by the predicate

$$Init_2 \overset{\text{def}}{=} pc_1 = "A" \wedge pc_2 = "A" \wedge x = 0 \wedge y = 0 \wedge sem = 1$$

64

There are six actions; two for the actual incrementing of x and y and four for handling the semaphore:

$$\alpha_1 \stackrel{\text{def}}{=} pc_1 = "A" \land sem > 0 \land pc_1' = "B" \land sem' = sem - 1 \land Unch(x, y, pc_2)$$

$$\alpha_2 \stackrel{\text{def}}{=} pc_2 = "A" \land sem > 0 \land pc_2' = "B" \land sem' = sem - 1 \land Unch(x, y, pc_1)$$

$$\beta_1 \stackrel{\text{def}}{=} pc_1 = "B" \land pc_1' = "G" \land x' = x + 1 \land Unch(y, pc_2, sem)$$

$$\beta_2 \stackrel{\text{def}}{=} pc_2 = "B" \land pc_2' = "G" \land y' = y + 1 \land Unch(x, pc_1, sem)$$

$$\gamma_1 \stackrel{\text{def}}{=} pc_1 = "G" \land pc_1' = "A" \land sem' = sem + 1 \land Unch(x, y, pc_2)$$

$$\gamma_1 \stackrel{\text{def}}{=} pc_2 = "G" \land pc_2' = "A" \land sem' = sem + 1 \land Unch(x, y, pc_1)$$

where $Unch\ f$ is defined to mean $f' = f$. An intuitive picture of this algorithm is given in Fig. 2).

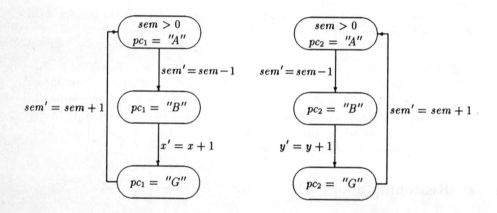

Fig. 2. Intuitive description of the algorithm Π_2

The algorithm is described formally by the formula

$$\Pi_2 \stackrel{\text{def}}{=} Init_2 \land \Box[\mathcal{N}_1 \lor \mathcal{N}_2]_w \land SF_w(\mathcal{N}_1) \land SF_w(\mathcal{N}_2)$$

where $\mathcal{N}_1 = \alpha_1 \lor \beta_1 \lor \gamma_1$ and $\mathcal{N}_2 = \alpha_2 \lor \beta_2 \lor \gamma_2$ and $w = (x, y, pc_1, pc_2, sem)$. In the fairness condition strong fairness is used in order to guarantee that the refined program implements the program Π_1 (cf. Sect. 4.2).

We are interested in the mutual exclusion property of this algorithm, i.e., the property that the algorithm never reaches a situation where $pc_1 = pc_2 = "B"$ holds. This is shown by proving the formula:

$$\Pi_2 \Rightarrow \Box(pc_1 = "A" \lor pc_2 = "A")$$

The translation of this algorithm into our HOL-formalisation is straightforward. The state is represented by the tuple (x,y,pc1,pc2,sem) which has the type :num#num#tri#tri#num#**. Here :tri is a flat type with the three elements A, B and G, defined by the means of the built-in type definition package of the HOL system. The possibility to define types in this way turns out to be very handy in program verification. If the program counters were defined to be, e.g., of the type :num, we would have needed additional arithmetic reasoning, which is tedious in HOL.

The initialisation is defined by the defining theorem

$\vdash_{def}$ Init2 =
      λ(x,y,pc1,pc2,sem,z).
        (pc1=A) $\wedge$ (pc2=A) $\wedge$ (x=0) $\wedge$ (y=0) $\wedge$ (sem=1)

As an example of the actions, we show the theorem which defines the action β_1:

$\vdash_{def}$ Beta1 =
      λ(x,y,pc1,pc2,sem,z)(x',y',pc1',pc2',sem',z').
        (pc1=B) $\wedge$ (pc1'=G) $\wedge$ (x'=x+1) $\wedge$ (y'=y) $\wedge$ (sem'=sem) $\wedge$ (pc2'=pc2)

The other five actions are defined accordingly. We also define

$\vdash_{def}$ N1   = Alpha1 aor Beta1 aor Gamma1
$\vdash_{def}$ N2   = Alpha2 aor Beta2 aor Gamma2
$\vdash_{def}$ w   = λ(x,y,pc1,pc2,sem,z).(x,y,pc1,pc2,sem)
$\vdash_{def}$ F2   = (SF N1 w) tand (SF N2 w)
$\vdash_{def}$ Prog2 = (liftpt Init2) tand
            (box (liftat (square (N1 aor N2) w))) tand F2

Now the mutual exclusion property of this algorithm can be proved in the theorem

$\vdash$ tvalid
      (Prog2 timp (box (liftpt(λ(x,y,pc1,pc2,sem,z).(pc1=A) $\vee$ (pc2=A)))

This theorem is proved by means of a rule for proving invariance properties using invariants. The invariant is in this case the following:

$$sem + (pc_1 = \ ''A'' \mapsto 0|1) + (pc_2 = \ ''A'' \mapsto 0|1) \ = \ 1$$

where we use the notation $b \mapsto e|f$ for conditional expressions.

Using this invariant, the proof of the mutual exclusion property is quite straighforward. However, it involves some arithmetic which means that it is not trivial in HOL.

4.2 Proving Correctness of Implementations

The two algorithms we have considered were chosen so that Π_2 is an implementation of Π_1. To prove this, we have to prove the validity of the formula $\Pi_2 \Rightarrow \Pi_1$. This can be reduced to proving the following:

$$Init_2 \Rightarrow Init_1 \tag{4}$$
$$\Box[\mathcal{N}_1 \vee \mathcal{N}_2]_w \Rightarrow \Box[\mathcal{M}_1 \vee \mathcal{M}_2]_{(x,y)} \tag{5}$$
$$\Pi_2 \Rightarrow WF_{(x,y)}(\mathcal{M}_1) \wedge WF_{(x,y)}(\mathcal{M}_2) \tag{6}$$

where w is the state tuple of Π_2.

Note that the types of the state spaces of the two programs are as follows:

$$\texttt{Prog1} : \texttt{num\#num\#*}$$
$$\texttt{Prog2} : \texttt{num\#num\#tri\#tri\#num\# * *}$$

These types match, since the type variable : * ("the rest of the world" for `Prog1`) can be instantiated to `:tri#tri#num#**`. In fact, this instantiation is done automatically by the HOL system.

Formulas (4–6) can be translated directly into HOL goals. The proofs of (4) and (5) are straightforward, though time-consuming, as HOL is quite slow in working with tuples.

The proof of (6) is more complicated and rather lengthy. The complication arises partly from the use of TLA's Lattice-rule. Informally this kind of proof is easy to handle, as one can refer to pictures when reasoning about simple well-founded sets, but in HOL it quickly becomes complicated. Furthermore, the formulas used for proving liveness properties are the most complex ones in the TLA proof system.

A general source of complication is the fact that the goals often must be transformed before they can be matched to the proof rules of the TLA logic. These transformations can generally be justified by appealing to some simple tautology. This means that a lot of effort goes into proving tautologies on both the predicate, action and temporal levels, and into doing transformations on the goals.

5 Conclusion

Our work shows that TLA can be represented in HOL in such a way that reasoning about algorithms can be mechanically checked. We have defined the semantics of the basic concepts of TLA and proved part of the basic proof rules of TLA as HOL theorems. Once this was done, reasoning about algorithms could be done in HOL in a way which corresponds closely to the way reasoning is carried out on paper. Thus HOL works as a proof checker for TLA reasoning.

Since we embed TLA semantically in HOL, our formalisation does not permit meta-level reasoning about the TLA logic. It is possible to formalise TLA in HOL in a way which would permit such reasoning, but such a formalisation would be much more difficult to use in practice. Melham discusses this problem in his formalisation of the pi-calculus in HOL [7].

TLA reasoning involves proofs on two levels: the temporal level and the level of actions. Proofs on the temporal level involve using the proof rules of TLA and simple temporal reasoning. Proofs on the action level involve reasoning over the datatypes that the program handles (integers, lists, etc.). We have built a theory for the first kind of reasoning; action reasoning in HOL is supported by the numerous libraries that are part of the HOL system.

Reasoning using HOL can be slow and tedious, for many reasons. A lot of effort goes into the transformation of goals into a form which matches the conclusion of some proof rule of TLA. Reasoning using well-founded sets involves a lot of straighforward but tedious proof details. Furthermore, reasoning on the action level is often arithmetic reasoning, at which HOL is notoriously inefficient. Many of these problems could be avoided if HOL could be made to support automatic proofs. In particular, we think that much of TLA reasoning could be automated if the user could supply the system with hints (e.g., invariants and definitions of well-founded orders) and if good libraries (e.g., for semi-automatic arithmetic) were added to the HOL system, for use in action level proof.

In the near future we will investigate to what extent the proofs reported in this paper can be re-used in other similar examples. This will give an indication of the degree of automation that is possible. Certainly such automation will require a substantial amount of programming in ML, the meta-language of HOL.

The definition of algorithms in HOL notation is unnecessarily difficult. This problem could be solved by designing some kind of interface which allows the user to describe algorithms in a TLA-like notation which would then be automatically translated into HOL. Such interfaces are not supported by the HOL system at present.

One important aspect of TLA is the treatment of simulation relations between programs. Simulation is proved using *refinement mappings*. In TLA this is based on existential quantification of program variables. Expressing this in HOL is left for future work.

Acknowledgements

We wish to thank the anonymous referees for their comments and helpful suggestions.

References

1. R.J.R. Back and J. von Wright. Refinement concepts formalised in higher-order logic. *Formal Aspects of Computing*, 2:247–272, 1990.
2. A.J. Camilleri. Mechanizing CSP trace theory in higher order logic. *IEEE Transactions of Software Engineering*, 16(9):993–1004, 1990.
3. A. Church. A formulation of the simple theory of types. *Journal of Symbolic Logic*, 5:56 –68, 1940.

68

4. The HOL System Documentation. Cambridge, 1989.
5. L. Lamport. A temporal logic of actions. Techn. Rep. 57, DEC Systems Research Center, April 1990.
6. L. Lamport. The temporal logic of actions. Manuscript, January 1991.
7. T.F. Melham. A mechanized theory of the π-calculus in HOL. Techn. Rep. 244, University of Cambridge Computer Laboratory, January 1992.
8. J. von Wright. Mechanising the temporal logic of actions in HOL. In *Proceedings of the 1991 HOL Tutorial and Workshop*. ACM, August 1991.

Verifying a Logic Synthesis Tool in Nuprl: A Case Study in Software Verification

Mark Aagaard, Miriam Leeser*

School of Electrical Engineering, Cornell University, Ithaca NY 14853, USA

Abstract. We have proved a logic synthesis tool with the Nuprl proof development system. The logic synthesis tool, *Pbs*, implements the weak division algorithm, and is part of the *Bedroc* hardware synthesis system. Our goal was to develop a proven and usable implementation of a hardware synthesis tool. *Pbs* consists of approximately 1000 lines of code implemented in a functional subset of Standard ML. The program was verified by embedding this subset of SML in Nuprl and then verifying the correctness of the implementation of *Pbs* in Nuprl. In the process of doing the proof we learned many lessons which can be applied to efforts in verifying functional software. In particular, we were able to safely perform several optimizations to the program. In addition, we have invested effort into verifying software which will be used many times, rather than verifying the output of that software each time the program is used. The work required to verify hardware design tools and other similar software is worthwhile because the results of the proofs will be used many times.

1 Introduction

This paper describes our experiences in using the Nuprl proof development system to verify the correctness of a logic synthesis tool. The lessons that we have learned are applicable to researchers using theorem proving based methods to verify functional programs.

We have implemented and proved *Pbs*: Proven Boolean Simplification. *Pbs* is based on Brayton and McMullen's weak division algorithm for logic synthesis [BM82]. The implementation of *Pbs* required approximately 1000 lines of Standard ML code. The proof of *Pbs* consists of a formal description of the properties to be proved, a formal semantics for the implementation language (a functional subset of Standard ML), and a mechanized formal proof showing that the implementation satisfies the properties claimed by the weak division algorithm. The proof was done in the Nuprl proof development system [C+86], and involved emulating a subset of SML in Nuprl, verifying the implementation of *Pbs* in Nuprl and showing that the semantics for the subset of SML that we

---

* Mark Aagaard is supported by a fellowship from Digital Equipment Corporation. This research was supported in part by the National Science Foundation under Award No. MIP-9100516.

emulated in Nuprl are equivalent to those defined for SML. Although the development of the proof required a significant amount of time, the results are used over and over again. Thus, the expenditure was well worth the effort.

The weak division algorithm was first described in a paper by Brayton and McMullen in 1982 [BM82]. It is currently used in several CAD tools, including *Mis*, which is part of the Berkeley Synthesis System [BR⁺87]. Our work is based upon the definitions, algorithms, and proof outlines presented in these articles. In some cases we have clarified previous definitions and algorithms, and in many instances we have developed formal proofs from the informal outlines presented earlier. The aim of this work is to prove an *implementation* of the weak division algorithm. Because of this, we reason about the algorithm at a much more specific and lower level than that of earlier efforts.

Theorem proving based formal methods have used mathematics to model and reason about a wide variety of different subjects. Originally, most theorem proving based work in digital hardware was done by proving the correctness of an implementation after it was designed [CGM86, Hun86]. This methodology suffers from the fact that such a *post hoc* verification process is invariably time-consuming and labor intensive. Many researchers are proving hardware design tools correct and investigating synthesis by proven transformations. For example, Martin [Mar90] uses proved correct transformations to synthesize delay insensitive circuits, Chin [Chi90] uses verified design procedures to synthesize array multipliers. More recently, McFarland [McF91] found several errors in the System Architect's Workbench [TDW⁺88] while proving their transformations correct. *Pbs* is the only work being done in applying formal methods to logic synthesis.

Our implementation of *Pbs* is described in Sect. 2. We outline our proof techniques in Sect. 3. Sect. 4 analyzes the results of the verification of *Pbs*. More detailed descriptions of the algorithms used in *Pbs* can be found elsewhere [AL91, Aag92].

2 Implementation of PBS

Pbs implements the weak division algorithm, which is a global approach to Boolean simplification. This means that the algorithm works with an entire system of Boolean equations at once. In contrast, local optimization techniques examine and optimize individual or small sets of equations independently.

The weak division algorithm seeks to decrease circuit area by removing redundant combinational logic. A sub-circuit contains redundant logic if it implements precisely the same function as another. Weak division removes redundant logic by finding common subexpressions among the *divisors* of different functions. The common subexpressions are replaced by new intermediate variables. This results in the duplicated logic being implemented only once, thereby reducing the area of the circuit.

For example, (1) contains two functions, one defining the variable p and one defining the variable q.

$$p = (a \wedge b \wedge c) \vee (a \wedge b \wedge d) \vee (a \wedge b \wedge e)$$
$$q = (g \wedge c) \vee (g \wedge d) \vee h \tag{1}$$

There is one common subexpression, $(c \vee d)$, among the divisors of p and q. We can substitute a new variable z into the equations in place of $(c \vee d)$. Next, we can substitute a new variable (x) for the term $(a \wedge b)$, which appears twice in the expression for p. This results in the set of equations shown below.

$$p = x \wedge z \vee x \wedge e$$
$$q = (g \wedge z) \vee h$$
$$z = c \vee d$$
$$x = a \wedge b \tag{2}$$

These substitutions have reduced the size of the circuit from twelve two input gate equivalents to seven, because the factors $(c \vee d)$ and $(a \wedge b)$ are now only implemented once. The substitutions increased the delay through the circuit from two gate delays to three, because the signals z and x added an additional layer of logic to the circuit. We have found that as the size of circuits increase the reduction in area increases significantly, but the additional delay converges rapidly: we are able to achieve reductions in area of 88% for circuits with more than three thousand gates, but yet add only nine additional layers of logic.

Our goals were for *Pbs* to be a proven *and* usable implementation of the weak division algorithm. In order to meet these two goals, we decided to embed a functional subset of the Standard ML (SML) programming language in the Nuprl proof development system. This allows the code for *Pbs* to be reasoned about in Nuprl and compiled and run using an SML compiler. Thus there is a very high degree of confidence that the SML implementation has the same behavior as the Nuprl implementation.

Standard ML is a very high level programming language and is based upon a formal definition which prescribes the precise semantics of the language [RM90]. SML is primarily a higher order functional language, but it does support some non-functional features, such as sequential operations, references, and exception handling. SML is strongly typed and polymorphic, thus it closely parallels much of the Nuprl type system.

Nuprl [C+86] is a mechanical proof development system based upon Martin-Löf's constructive type theory. In Nuprl, the user begins by entering a theorem to be proved. The theorem represents the *goal* of a proof. The user applies *tactics* which manipulate the goal, usually by breaking it down into a set of subgoals. This process of using tactics to break goals down into subgoals creates a structure known as a proof tree. In order to successfully complete a proof, the subgoals should become increasingly simple. Eventually an individual sub-goal will be simple enough that it matches one of the primitive rules in the Nuprl logic. When all of the leaves of the proof tree have been shown to be true, the proof is completed and the original theorem is proved.

Nuprl contains a set of primitive operations which are the basis for its computation system. Many SML instructions are very similar to these primitive operations. By limiting *Pbs* to use only these instructions, we were able to emulate a subset of SML in Nuprl. The primitive operations upon which we based our subset include integer arithmetic, list recursion, integer equality, string equality, and pairing. The principal features which we did not include in our subset (because of the difficulty of implementing them in terms of the Nuprl primitives) are: references, exceptions, sequentiality, explicit recursion, pattern matching, real numbers, modules, streams, and records.

We now demonstrate this method by showing the definition of our primitive list recursion function in Nuprl and SML. Nuprl provides a primitive list recursion operation *(list_ind)*, while SML does explicit recursion (the name of the function appears within the body of the function). Equation (3) shows the semantics for *list_ind* in Nuprl by describing its behavior on an empty list and on a non-empty list.

$$list\_ind(nil;\ nil\_val;\ h,t,rest.\ f(h)(t)(rest)) \qquad = nil\_val$$
$$list\_ind(hd::tl;\ nil\_val;\ h,t,rest.\ f(h)(t)(rest)) \qquad =$$
$$f(hd)(tl)(list\_ind(tl;nil\_val;\ h,t,rest.\ f(h)(t)(rest))) \tag{3}$$

Following the approach outlined above, we wrote a function *(recurse)* in SML (Equation (4)) which has the same behavior as the list recursion primitive in Nuprl.

$$fun\ recurse\ f\ nil\_val\ nil \qquad = nil\_val$$
$$|\quad recurse\ f\ nil\_val\ (hd::tl) \quad = f(hd)\ (tl)\ (recurse\ f\ nil\_val\ tl) \tag{4}$$

Equation (5) shows the definition of *recurse* in Nuprl. All other recursive functions in *Pbs* are written in terms of *recurse*. By using this methodology we have isolated the functions that are dependent upon primitives in Nuprl down to a very small number of low level functions.

$$recurse\ f\ nil\_val\ a\_list =$$
$$list\_ind(a\_list;\ nil\_val;\ h,t,rest.\ f(h)(t)(rest)) \tag{5}$$

To complete the process, we proved Thms 1 and 2, which show that the Nuprl definition of *recurse* has the same behavior as the SML function. Using this methodology we defined and verified each of the constructs in the subset of SML that we emulated. Having defined the function *recurse*, we can now use it in our implementation of other functions and can use Thms 1 and 2 to prove theorems describing the behavior of functions built upon *recurse*. Using this methodology, the SML code for a function is identical to the Nuprl object representing the function.

The only informal link in the connection between Nuprl and SML arises because Nuprl uses lazy evaluation and SML uses eager evaluation. In reality, this does not pose a problem for us, because the subset of SML that we are using is purely functional and all of the functions are guaranteed to terminate. (We are able to prove termination because the only recursion done in *Pbs* is list recursion using Nuprl's list induction primitive, which always terminates.) Purely functional programs with guaranteed termination will exhibit identical

Thm 1 *Recurse – base case*

⊢∀*f, nil_val.*
   recurse f nil_val nil = nil_val

Thm 2 *Recurse – inductive case*

⊢∀*f, hd, tl, nil_val.*
   recurse f nil_val (hd::tl) = f(hd)(tl)(recurse f nil_val tl)

---

behavior in eager and lazy evaluation environments. Thus, for the subset that we are using, programs will have identical behavior in Nuprl and in an SML compiler. Ongoing research at Cornell includes work aimed at creating a type theoretic semantics for SML within Nuprl. Once this has been done, programs will be able to be verified without relying on informal arguments to show the correspondence between the Nuprl and SML semantics.

3 Verification of PBS

The proof of *Pbs* shows two things. First, the output circuits generated by *Pbs* are functionally equivalent to the input circuits. Second, all output circuits satisfy the minimality property claimed by the weak division algorithm. Informally, a circuit with this property is completely irredundant – that is, there is no duplicated logic in the circuit. Others have shown that circuits which satisfy this minimality property are completely single stuck-at fault testable [HJKM89].

In doing the proof of *Pbs* we began with a specification of the overall algorithm and our implementation in Standard ML, which we had tested on a number of sample circuits. Our approach was to write several theorems describing the behavior of each function in *Pbs* and then to prove that the code used to implement the function satisfied the theorems that we had written. In general we worked in a bottom up fashion. We began with very simple functions, such as adding an element to a list, and testing if an element is a member of a list. After proving that these function had their intended behavior, we were able to move up a level in the hierarchy, and prove theorems describing the behaviors of more complicated functions.

There are two basic categories of theorems in the proof of *Pbs*. The first is theorems which describe abstract properties of functions. The second, and more common, category is theorems which describe the behavior of functions at a level which is very close to the actual implementation. The first category of theorems includes the theorem that the output of *Pbs* satisfies the correctness criteria for the weak division algorithm. Theorems in the second category usually describe how a function behaves for certain inputs. For example, the function for dividing Boolean expressions is partially characterized by a theorem which states that dividing an empty expression by any expression produces an empty expression.

For the first category of theorems, we did not find any specific methodology which was applicable to all proofs. For the second category of theorems, we found a technique which was used for these theorems throughout the proof of *Pbs*. This technique consists of four steps: list induction, unfolding definitions, rewriting and application of previously proven lemmas. As an example of these techniques, we describe the proof of a theorem describing membership in a list (Theorem 3). This is a trivial example; it is included here because it illustrates the techniques which we used throughout the verification of *Pbs*.

Thm 3 *Membership in a non-empty list*

$\vdash \forall A$, *eq_fn*, *tl*, *hd*, *a*.
    mem eq_fn a (hd::tl) $\iff$
    (eq_fn a hd) $\lor$ *(mem eq_fn a tl)*

As an alternative to the approach taken here, we could have defined the membership function in such a way that Nuprl could have completed the proof of this function automatically. This approach would have been similar to that of proof systems which are capable of automatically verifying many inductively defined functions [BM88]. We could have done this by writing the function directly in terms of Nuprl's primitive list induction operator, which was described in Sect. 2. In Nuprl, there are several disadvantages to choosing this alternative. Most importantly, it would prevent our implementation of *Pbs* in Nuprl from being the same as our implementation in SML. Secondly, verifying more complicated functions in this alternative style would be more difficult than in the style which we used. By using the function *recurse* as the only primitive function for recursion, we were able to hide the implementation details of recursion and thereby prevent our proofs from becoming cluttered with low level details.

The complete proof of the theorem describing the membership function is shown in Figure 1 and is discussed in the following paragraphs. In the proof, only the conclusion and the rule for each step are shown. The hypotheses contain variable declarations and are not modified in the proof. The rules, which appear after "**BY**", are the only text other than the initial goal that the user types in.

Because lists are so pervasive in *Pbs*, most of the functions in *Pbs* are defined in terms of list recursion. This also means that most proofs rely on list induction. Thm 3 shows the inductive case for membership in a list, which says that an element is a member of a list if and only if it is equal to the head of the list or it is a member of the tail of the list. Another theorem (which is not shown), describes the base case for this function. The theorem for the base case says that an empty list does not have any members.

One of the first steps of each proof is to unfold the definition of the function

$\vdash$ (mem eq_fn a (hd::tl))

$\Longleftrightarrow$

(eq_fn a hd) ∨ (mem eq_fn a tl)

BY   (RewriteConcl (NthC 1 (UnfoldC 'mem')))...)

$\vdash$ (reduce (fn hd => fn result =>

(eq_fn a hd) orelse result) false (hd::tl))

$\Longleftrightarrow$

(eq_fn a hd) ∨ (mem eq_fn a tl)

BY   (RewriteConcl reduce_ht_convn...)

$\vdash$ (eq_fn a hd) orelse

reduce (fn hd => fn result =>

(eq_fn(a))(hd) orelse result) false tl)

$\Longleftrightarrow$

(eq_fn a hd) ∨ (mem eq_fn a tl)

BY   (RewriteConcl mem_fold_convn...)

$\vdash$ (eq_fn a hd) orelse (mem eq_fn a tl)

$\Longleftrightarrow$

(eq_fn a hd) ∨ (mem eq_fn a tl)

BY   (RewriteConcl orelse_x_x_convn...)

Fig. 1. Proof of Theorem 3

being described. In Nuprl "unfolding" means to replace an instantiation of a function with the code used to implement the function. It is analogous to the compiler optimization of in-line expansion. The purpose of unfolding definitions is to reveal the implementation of functions. When this has been done, rewrite rules or lemmas describing lower level functions can be used in the proof. In the first step of the proof the definition of the function *mem* is unfolded to reveal that it is implemented in terms of *reduce*. The function *reduce* (Equation (6)) is a higher order recursive function which is defined using the function *recurse* (Equation (4)).

fun reduce f nil_val a_list =
    let
        fun f2 hd tl result = f hd result
    in
        recurse f2 nil_val a_list
    end   (6)

As illustrated here, unfolding is really just one type of rewriting that can be performed. Nuprl has a very powerful rewriting package, which is used to replace one term with another term, where the two terms are related by some property. This property does not have to be equality, it may be any relation which the user has proved to be reflexive and transitive. The rewrite package supports rewriting terms in hypotheses as well as in the conclusion. Rewrite rules may be constructed from previously proven lemmas, hypotheses in the current proof, or direct computation. Lemmas may be used to construct *conditional* rewrite rules, that is, a rule which only holds under certain conditions. We made extensive use of these features throughout the proof of *Pbs*.

In the proof of Thm 3, four different rewrite rules are used. In the first and third steps, direct computation rules are used to fold and unfold the instantiation of *mem*. The rewrite rules used in steps two and four are derived from lemmas that were proved about the functions *reduce* and *orelse*.

Although not a proof technique, Autotactic is a very important tactic which was used throughout the proof of *Pbs*. Autotactic is comprised of a collection of tactics which can be used to handle many of the minor details involved in using mechanical proof systems. These proof systems offer a high degree of confidence in the correctness of the theorems proved with their use, but the tradeoff is that the user is exposed to a great many details that are usually ignored in paper proofs. Common uses of Autotactic include automatically introducing universally quantified variables that appear in conclusions and proving type checking goals. In each step of the proof, Autotactic was used after applying the rewrite rule. Using Nuprl's display forms, Autotactic is represented by the (...) in the proof steps.

By adopting the proof style described here, we are able to write concise theorems describing complex functions. An example of this appears in Thm 4, which describes the behavior of the quotient function for dividing an expression by a cube (2). Theorem 4 says that a cube (*co*) is a member of the quotient of an expression (*ei1*) and another cube (*ci2*) if and only if there is a cube (*ci1*) in *ei1* such that *ci2* is a subset of *ci1* and *co* is equal to *ci2* deleted from *ci1*. This theorem was proved in a total of fourteen steps, which included seven rewrites and three lemma applications (Lemma application is one of the four primary techniques used throughout *Pbs*, but was not demonstrated in the proof of the membership function).

4   Discussion

This section describes reasons for verifying software, lessons that we learned about theorem proving techniques for software verification, an analysis of the amount of time required to verify *Pbs* with Nuprl, and some directions for future research.

The verification of *Pbs* was valuable because we found several errors while formalizing the proof, we were able to safely perform several optimizations to the code, and we gained a much deeper understanding of the algorithm. In the process of verifying *Pbs*, several obscure errors in the implementation and

---

Thm 4 *Membership in a quotient*

⊢∀*ei1:Expr_t.*
  ∀*ci2,co:Cube_t.*
    is_valid_expr e1 ⇒
        tr(*MEM_ce*(*co*)(*QUOT_ec*(*ei1*)(*ci2*))) ⟺
        ∃ *ci1:Cube_t.*
            tr(*MEM_ce*(*ci1*)(*ei1*)) &
            tr(*IN_cc ci2 ci1*) &
            tr(*EQc co* (*DEL_cc*(*ci1*)(*ci2*)))

```
fun QUOT_ec ei1 ci2 =
    let
        fun f c_hd result =
            if IN_cc ci2 c_hd
            then (DEL_cc c_hd ci2)::result
            else result
    in
        Cs2E(reduce f NIL_e (E2Cs ei1))
    end
```

Fig. 2. Function for quotient of an expression and a cube

---

formal description of *Pbs* were found. The nature of the errors was such that they would most likely manifest themselves only in rare occurrences in large systems of equations, exactly the times when they would be least likely to be detected. These errors are described elsewhere [Aag92].

If a program or optimization is not completely understood, performing the optimization on the code may introduce bugs into the program. For most of the operations in the weak division algorithm there is both a Boolean and an algebraic function which may be used. The algebraic functions are much faster, but return the correct result only under certain conditions. In the original implementation of *Pbs*, only Boolean operations were used. This sacrificed speed for increased assurance that the code was correct. In doing the proof in Nuprl, several instances were discovered where the correctness conditions for the algebraic operations could be guaranteed. When these occurrences were found, Boolean operations were replaced by algebraic operations. This increased the speed of the code and also simplified the proof, because the lemmas describing the algebraic operations were simpler than those describing the Boolean ones.

In the process of verifying *Pbs*, we discovered several guidelines which are useful when writing code which will be verified or when reasoning about a program. Beginning with a mathematically defined, very high level language greatly eases the process of proving a program. In addition there are certain programming techniques and styles which can significantly increase the ability to reason about a program.

- All functions should be very short
- Code should be written in an extremely modular style
- Higher order functions should be used wherever possible

These guidelines may seem to be very obvious, but their importance can not be over emphasized. Ideally, each function performs only a single operation and the behavior can be summarized in one or two lemmas. By writing code in a very modular style, a single function and its corresponding lemmas may be used many times. When just writing code, it may seem easier to simply duplicate a piece of code if it is extremely short and is only used a few times. But, when proving code correct, not only must the code be duplicated, but the proofs describing the code must also be duplicated. Along these same lines, the use of higher order functions to handle such tasks as recursion is a much better approach than to try to do explicit recursion.

When we began the verification effort, we quickly learned that each lemma should only bridge two adjacent levels of abstraction. That is, only one function should be unfolded in each proof. This means that each proof is only dependent upon the implementation of a single function. Following this guideline helps ensure that lemmas are as general as possible, which makes them more useful, and requires that fewer total lemmas be written.

Although we learned most of these guidelines while in the process of working on the proof of *Pbs*, a few were not recognized until we had completed the proof and were able to analyze our work as a whole. A technique which did not occur to us was to try to generalize the reasoning to general mathematical principles. The operations in *Pbs* can be described as an algebra. There is a large body of existing knowledge about algebras, which we could have used. Instead, we proved special theorems for each function. Had we shown that the operators in *Pbs* were an algebra, we could have used general theorems about algebras to do the more complicated and abstract reasoning in *Pbs*.

An important tool which we could have made use of, but did not, was the ability to execute our code as we were verifying it. When we developed *Pbs* we did substantial amounts of debugging using informal techniques before beginning to formally verify the code. But we made a number of changes to the implementation as we developed the proof (some were minor bug fixes, others were done to make the proof easier or optimize the code). We did not try running the code with any of these modifications, instead we relied solely upon our proof for debugging these changes.

Looking back on this decision, it is now apparent that it would have been more efficient to do some informal debugging of the modified code, before we spent the time to do the formal verification. The primary reason for this is that testing code on a few test cases can be an extremely fast method to gain some measure of confidence that the code behaves as desired. Also, with complicated specifications, there may be some doubt as to whether the specification actually describes the intended behavior of the program. For these reasons, such techniques as executable specifications can be very useful.

The implementation of weak-division consists of approximately one thousand lines of code. In the process of implementing *Pbs* and doing the proof in Nuprl there was a large learning curve and several new tools were written to make the proof easier. We estimate that if we were to do it over again, it would take approximately one month to implement the code and an additional two months to complete a formal proof on paper. We believe that using the knowledge gained and tools written, it would take a total of four months to do the proof in Nuprl all over again. Thus, doing the proof in Nuprl would take approximately twice as long as doing the proof on paper.

One of the lessons learned in the process of doing the proof is that there is a potential for automating several aspects of the proof process for software verification. This area has not yet been fully explored, so it is difficult to say exactly how much of the proof could be automated, but we estimate that it is feasible to reduce the time to do the proof in Nuprl from four months to three months. (Compared with two months for doing the formal proof on paper.) We are currently investigating some of these ideas. Ideally, doing the proof in a mechanical theorem prover would not take any longer than doing the formal proof on paper, but that time has not yet arrived.

5   Conclusion

A piece of software is verified in order to have higher confidence that it does what it is meant to do. It is very unlikely that the day will come when all software is formally verified, so it is important to decide how much verification should be done for a given piece of software. Often, there are informal proofs that describe an algorithm at an abstract level, but there may be a great disparity between the level of detail of the proof and the implementation. It is in this process of going from an abstract description of an algorithm to the concrete implementation that many errors are introduced. An informal proof that the algorithm is correct is a good first step toward a correct implementation, but unless formal verification is done at the level of implementation, there can not be a high level of assurance that the final implementation is correct. The tradeoff for this increased assurance is that there are a great many details that the proof must take into account. One of the most important advantages of mechanical proof systems is their ability to manage proof efforts and potentially automate a significant portion of this process.

Such was the case with *Pbs*. Brayton and McMullen had provided informal arguments that the weak division algorithm was correct, but by using Nuprl we were able to formally prove *Pbs* at the implementation level. The extra effort of performing a formal proof definitely *was* worthwhile. The proof provided us with greater understanding of the algorithm and allowed us to take advantage of optimizations to the program. The code will be used many, many times, thus amortizing the initial work. Finally, people without any knowledge of formal methods can easily use *Pbs* and there is no need for *post hoc* verification of the circuits generated by *Pbs*.

6 Acknowledgements

We would like to thank Robert Constable and Jim Caldwell for reading an earlier draft of this paper and Paul Jackson, who implemented the rewrite package, for his advice and assistance in using Nuprl. In addition we would like to thank Chet Murthy and Doug Howe, who were always willing to help and gave us a number of useful suggestions.

References

[Aag92]   Mark Aagaard. A verified system for logic synthesis. Master's thesis, Department of Electrical Engineering, Cornell University, January 1992.

[AL91]   Mark Aagaard and Miriam Leeser. The implementation and proof of a boolean simplification system. In Geraint Jones and Mary Sheeran, editors, *Designing Correct Circuits, Oxford 1990*. Springer-Verlag, 1991.

[BM82]   R. K. Brayton and C. McMullen. Decomposition and factorization of boolean expressions. In *International Symposium on Circuits and Systems*, 1982.

[BM88]   R. S. Boyer and J. S. Moore. *A Computational Logic Handbook*. Academic Press, 1988. Volume 23 of Perspectives in Computing.

[BR+87]   R. K. Brayton, R. Rudell, et al. MIS: A multiple-level logic optimization system. *IEEE Transactions on Computer-Aided Design*, CAD-6(6), 1987.

[C+86]   R. L. Constable et al. *Implementing Mathematics with the Nuprl Proof Development System*. Prentice Hall, 1986.

[CGM86]   A. J. Camillieri, M. J. C. Gordon, and T. F. Melham. Hardware verification using higher-order logic. In D. Borrione, editor, *From HDL Descriptions to Guaranteed Correct Circuit Designs*. North Holland, September 1986.

[Chi90]   Shiu-Kai Chin. Combining engineering vigor with mathematical rigor. In *Proceedings of the MSI Workshop on Hardware Specification, Verification, and Synthesis: Mathematical Aspects*. Springer Verlag, 1990. LNCS 408.

[HJKM89]   G. Hachtel, R. Jacoby, K. Keutzer, and C. Morrison. On the relationship between area optimization and multifault testability of multilevel logic. In *International Conference on Computer Aided Design*, pages 316–319. ACM/IEEE, 1989.

[Hun86]   W. A. Hunt, Jr. *FM8501: A Verified Microprocessor*. PhD thesis, Institute for Computing Science, The University of Texas at Austin, 1986.

[Mar90]   A. J. Martin. The design of a delay-insensitive microprocessor: An example of circuit synthesis by program transformation. In *Proceedings of the MSI Workshop on Hardware Specification, Verification, and Synthesis: Mathematical Aspects*. Springer Verlag, 1990. LNCS 408.

[McF91]   Michael C. McFarland. A practical application of verification to high-level synthesis. In *International Workshop on Formal Methods in VLSI Design*. ACM, 1991.

[RM90]   R. Harper R. Milner, M. Tofte. *The Definition of Standard ML*. The MIT Press, 1990.

[TDW⁺88] D. E. Thomas, E. M. Dirkes, R. A. Walker, J. V. Rajan, J. A. Nestor, and R. L. Blackburn. The system architect's workbench. In 25th *Design Automation Conference*, pages 337–343. ACM/IEEE, 1988.

This article was processed using the LaTeX macro package with LLNCS style

Higher-Level Specification and Verification With BDDs *

Alan J. Hu, David L. Dill, Andreas J. Drexler, and C. Han Yang

Department of Computer Science, Stanford University

Abstract. Currently, many are investigating promising verification methods based on Boolean decision diagrams (BDDs). Using BDDs, however, requires modeling the system under verification in terms of Boolean formulas. This modeling can be difficult and error-prone, especially when dealing with constructs like arithmetic, sequential control flow, and complex data structures. We present new techniques for automatically translating these constructs into BDDs. Furthermore, these techniques generate Boolean next-state relations in a form that allows efficient image computation without building the full BDD for the next-state relation, thereby side-stepping the commonly-encountered BDD-size blowup of next-state relations.

1 Introduction

With the high complexity of hardware designs and protocols, improved debugging tools and methodologies are critical to avoiding the expenses and delays resulting from discovering bugs late in the design phase [9, 4]. Simulation catches some problems, but bugs frequently slip through. The increasing concurrency and complexity of hardware designs exacerbates this problem: detecting by simulation every bug resulting from the complex interaction of concurrent events becomes highly improbable (or prohibitively time-consuming). This situation has prompted interest in verification techniques.

Verification by state enumeration is particularly attractive because it is highly automatic: Given a specification, the verification system performs the verification with no further user intervention [4]. The main disadvantage of this technique is the potentially huge number of possible states. To address this state-explosion problem, many recent results have used symbolic expressions to specify sets of states (e.g. [2, 5, 4, 9]). In fact, all of the above cited works use a particularly promising data structure for the symbolic expressions: Boolean decision diagrams (BDDs) [7].

One drawback of BDDs is the requirement to describe the system being verified using Boolean formulas. This modeling is difficult, time-consuming, and

---

* This research was supported by the National Science Foundation (grant number MIP-8858807), the Defense Advanced Research Projects Agency (contract number N00014-87-K-0828) and by gifts from the Powell Foundation and Mitsubishi Electronics. The first author was supported by an ONR Graduate Fellowship. Most of this work was done using equipment generously donated by Sun Microsystems.

error-prone [17]. Worse, revising the description to, for example, scale the number processes, enlarge buffers, or increase word sizes, entails a laborious rewriting of the entire description. Working with common programming language constructs like scalar-valued variables [18], arrays, records, and sequential assignment would be much more natural.

Another problem confronting verification with BDDs is that the next-state relation of the system being verified frequently results in a BDD that is too large to build [10, 19, 3]. For verifying deterministic finite-state machines (*e.g.* a digital synchronous circuit), Boolean Functional Vectors [10] have proven quite successful. Unfortunately, higher-level specifications tend to be non-deterministic, necessitating other approaches to avoiding this problem.

We are working on two languages to address these problems. One, called Murφ, is a high-level language much like common structured programming languages. We can compile Murφ both into C++ (for simulation and non-symbolic verification) and also into our second language. We discuss Murφ in another paper [11]. The second language, called Ever, is a BDD-based verifier. In addition to the usual Boolean and verification operators common to other BDD-based verifiers, however, Ever provides direct support for many higher-level features, including scalars, arrays, records, and sequentiality. These higher-level features, besides providing expressive power, allow us to avoid building the full BDD for the next-state relation. Supporting these features involves some novel techniques that we discuss here.

2   Design Objectives

We started with some abstract design objectives. As Ever is intended to be an intermediate language, it must be easily machine-generated. Furthermore, the language must allow compact expression of the semantics of the higher-level language. On the other hand, the language should be human-readable and human-writable to allow writing Ever code directly, facilitate modifying automatically-generated code, and ease debugging the automatic generators.

Like other BDD-based verifiers, Ever must support the usual Boolean and temporal logic operators, as well as standard verification operations like reachability and trace generation. Our experience also indicated that parameterized predicates would be convenient.

Complex data structures are imperative. For example, while verifying a real, industrial link-level protocol, we needed to specify queues that were arrays of packets. Each packet, in turn, was a record including fields for packet type, sequence number, and other data. The fields were integers, enumerated types, or records. Clearly, then, we must provide scalar values and variables, with the concomitant arithmetic and relational operators, as well as array and record constructors, to allow arbitrarily complex data structures. Beyond expressive convenience, these higher-level data structures provide an additional pay-off: scalability. By simply changing a few constants and array bounds, we can easily take a large and detailed description of a system and scale it to a smaller version that can be fully verified.

One particularly difficult aspect of modeling with Boolean formulas is an instance of the famous Frame Problem in artificial intelligence [16]. We refer to our instance as the problem of *stability:* for a given operation, how does one determine which variables retain their current values, which variables change, and which variables are non-deterministic. In a normal programming language, a variable that is not explicitly modified keeps its current value. In the Boolean context, however, any variable that is not constrained can take on any value. This semantic difference gives Boolean formulas much of their expressive power, but is also the source of many subtle specification bugs. For example, it is easy to see that an imperative statement like:

```
x := 17;
```

corresponds to the Boolean next-state relation:

```
(next(x)=17) AND (everything except x doesn't change).
```

It is not obvious how to correctly translate a code fragment (taken from an industrial directory-based cache-coherence protocol modeled in our imperative specification language Murϕ) like:

```
If (i < Homes[h].Dir[a].Shared_Count) & (Homes[h].Dir[a].Entries[i] = n)
Then
  -- overwrite this entry with last entry.
  Homes[h].Dir[a].Entries[i] :=
    Homes[h].Dir[a].Entries[Homes[h].Dir[a].Shared_Count-1];
  -- clear last entry
  Homes[h].Dir[a].Entries[Homes[h].Dir[a].Shared_Count-1] := 0;
  Homes[h].Dir[a].Shared_Count := Homes[h].Dir[a].Shared_Count-1;
Endif;
```

To handle such expressions, then, we felt it necessary to support deterministic assignment, which handles stability exactly as the user would expect, *directly* in Ever, along with facilities to build correct next-state formulas for complex statements from the formulas for simpler ones.

3 A Simple Example

An example is perhaps the easiest way to acquaint oneself with the Ever language. We will look at a simple link-level protocol. (See Figure 1.) There are four processes: a source, a transmitter, a receiver, and a destination. These four operate asynchronously, handshaking via ports.[2] The source has a string of data, which it sends a character at a time to the transmitter. The transmitter packs the characters into packets, appends a checksum, and sends the packet to the receiver. The receiver unpacks the characters, and sends them one at a time to the destination. The destination receives characters and stores them in a buffer.

---

2 The computational model underlying Ever is a non-deterministic finite-state machine. We can easily model the asynchronous, interleaved concurrency in this example using non-deterministic choice. Synchronous parallelism currently requires some contortions.

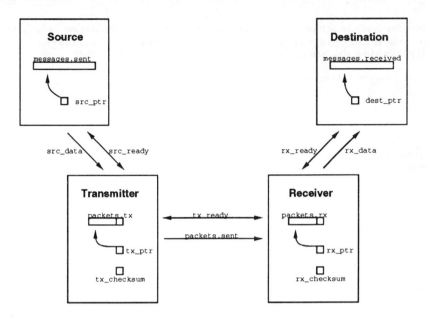

Fig. 1. In this simple example, a message travels from source to destination. The transmitter and receiver handle packets and checksums.

The syntax is simple in order to simplify automatically generating Ever code. A program consists of a sequential list of declarations and commands. Within a declaration or command, expressions are in LISP-like prefix notation. Array and record accesses are denoted by square brackets and periods, as in Pascal or C.

The first few lines:

```
deftype signal (bits 1 "low" "high");
deftype char (bits 1 "a" "b");
deftype integer (bits 4);
deftype packet (record data (array 0 3 char) check char);
```

declare some types. In Ever, we declare scalar types by the number of bits needed. (The strings following the bit width are used for output.) Thus, types signal and char are both 1 bit, type integer is 4 bits, and type packet is a record with two fields: data, a four-element array, and check, of type char. The next few lines declare variables for the source and destination:

```
defvar src_ready signal;   -- Variable src_ready is of type signal,
defvar src_ptr integer;    -- and so forth.
defvar src_data char;

defvar dest_ptr integer;

defvar messages (interleaved record
                        sent (array 0 7 char)
                        received (array 0 7 char)
            );
```

The source sends the contents of `messages.sent` to the destination, which writes the data into `messages.received`. We will discuss the `interleaved` keyword later. We then declare variables for the transmitter and receiver.

```
defvar packets (interleaved record
                        tx packet
                        sent packet
                        rx packet
              );

defvar tx_ptr integer;
defvar tx_checksum char;
defvar tx_ready signal;

defvar rx_ptr integer;
defvar rx_data char;
defvar rx_checksum char;
defvar rx_ready signal;
```

The next lines define the set of possible start states:

```
defprop StartState (and
                    (eq src_ptr^c 0)    -- src_ptr must be 0
                    (eq src_ready^c 0) -- src_ready must be 0
                    (eq tx_ptr^c 0)     -- etc.
                    (eq tx_ready^c 0)
                    (eq rx_ptr^c 4)
                    (eq rx_ready^c 0)
                    (eq dest_ptr^c 0)
                );
```

The suffix `^c` specifies the current value of the variable, whereas the suffix `^n` specifies the next value. The formula initializes the control variables, but leaves the data unspecified, allowing them to assume any value.

Next, we define the next-state relation. The definition is in parts. First, we define the source:

```
defprop Source (if (and (le src_ptr^c 7)
                   (eq src_ready^c 0)) -- If we can send another char
               (compose        --then send it to Tx
               (becomes src_data^n messages.sent[src_ptr^c]^c)
               (becomes src_ptr^n (add src_ptr^c 1))
               (becomes src_ready^n 1)
               )
               FALSE         --else block
            );
```

which simply writes the next character to a port if the port is ready. Note that scalar arithmetic makes it easy to maintain counters. The `becomes` operator provides deterministic assignment: it generates the BDD next-state relation that assigns an expression to a variable, while keeping all other variables constant. Combining the `becomes` operator with the `compose` operator, which provides next-state relation composition, produces code resembling sequential execution, but which actually defines a next-state relation for *all* legal executions. Next, we define the transmitter:

```
defprop Tx (if (and (le tx_ptr^c 3)
               (eq src_ready^c 1)) -- If incoming char
```

```
(compose         --then add it to packet and update checksum
    (becomes packets.tx.check^n (add packets.tx.check^c
                                     src_data^c))
    (becomes packets.tx.data[tx_ptr^c]^n src_data^c)
    (becomes tx_ptr^n (add tx_ptr^c 1))
    (becomes src_ready^n 0)
)
(if (and (gt tx_ptr^c 3)
         (eq tx_ready^c 0)) --else if ready to send packet
    (compose      --then send it to Rx
        (becomes packets.sent^n packets.tx^c)
        (becomes packets.tx^n 0)
        (becomes tx_ptr^n 0)
        (becomes tx_ready^n 1)
    )
    FALSE        --else block
)
);
```

The transmitter reads characters from the source, appends them to a packet, and computes a checksum. Whenever it has a complete packet and the channel to the receiver is clear, it sends the packet. The receiver unpacks characters from the packets:

```
defprop Rx (if (and (gt rx_ptr^c 3) (eq tx_ready^c 1)) --If we can receive packet
        (compose          --then get the packet
            (becomes packets.rx^n packets.sent^c)
            (becomes packets.sent^n 0)
            -- Error detection and recovery code would go here.
            (becomes rx_ptr^n 0)
            (becomes tx_ready^n 0)
        )
        (if (and (le rx_ptr^c 3)
                (eq rx_ready^c 0)) --else if we have data for Dest
            (compose    --then send it
                (becomes rx_data^n packets.rx.data[rx_ptr^c]^c)
                (becomes rx_ptr^n (add rx_ptr^c 1))
                (becomes rx_ready^n 1)
            )
            FALSE        --else block
        )
);
```

In a real link-level protocol, we would insert code to check the checksum and handle errors at the indicated point. The destination is easy:

```
defprop Destination (if (eq rx_ready^c 1) --If Rx has data for us
            (compose              --then get it
                (becomes messages.received[dest_ptr^c]^n rx_data^c)
                (becomes dest_ptr^n (add dest_ptr^c 1))
                (becomes rx_ready^n 0)
            )
            FALSE                 --else block
        );
```

We define the next-state relation for the entire system

```
defprop NextState (or (Source) (Tx) (Rx) (Destination));
```

as the non-deterministic choice of the preceding next-state relations.

The remaining lines of the program:

```
defprop Ok (if (gt dest_ptr^c 7) (eq messages.sent^c messages.received^c));

printtrace (StartState) (NextState) (not (Ok));
```

define a simple verification condition and invoke the reachability verifier. We use verification conditions to check safety properties. The state-reachability computation starts from all states that satisfy the start-state formula and, using the specified next-state relation, outputs a trace that reaches the end condition (or is as long as possible).

This program takes thirteen and a half minutes on a SUN 4/75, using less than 6.4MB of memory, to compute all reachable states and to find and print a longest acyclic trace (37 states long). Interestingly, even this short example has 84 billion reachable states (out of a state space of 1.8×10^{16} states) putting it well-beyond the reach of non-symbolic state-enumeration verifiers.

4 Translation into Logic

Much of the Ever language is similar to other BDD-based verifiers. We will only briefly mention these aspects here. Logical operations are directly supported by BDDs [7]. Our implementation uses Brace *et al.*'s BDD implementation [6]. Symbolic verification algorithms (reachability, trace generation, etc.) are standard and can be found in several sources [9, 2, 4, 5]. Very recently, Clarke *et al.* [8], as part of a larger work on building approximate abstract models of programs, have proposed a solution to the problems of stability and sequentiality that is essentially a special case (no complex data structures) of the deterministic assignment rules in Section 4.3 combined with the sequentiality rule in Section 4.4.

4.1 Scalars

We represent a scalar variable as a vector of Boolean functions. We map scalars to Booleans using the binary representation of the ordinal value of the scalar. A variable a would be represented by (a_3, a_2, a_1, a_0), where the a_i are the Boolean variables corresponding to a. The scalar quantity $a+4$ would be $(a_3 \oplus a_2, \overline{a_2}, a_1, a_0)$. This mapping permits, for instance, using a simple ripple-carry adder to compute the sum $z = x + y$ of two scalar variables:

$$z_i = x_i \oplus y_i \oplus c_{i-1}$$
$$c_i = x_i y_i + c_{i-1}(x_i + y_i).$$

Similar expressions correspond to other operators. We have implemented a larger set of arithmetic and relational operators than Srinivasan *et al.* [18], including comparison, addition, and subtraction between arbitrary scalar-valued expressions. Note that these expressions are computed logically on the Boolean characteristic functions, so that, for example, if $P(x)$ and $Q(y)$ specify the subsets of possible values for x and y, we can express that z can be *all possible values of the sum* by writing $\exists x, y[P(x) \wedge Q(y) \wedge (z = x + y)]$.

4.2 Data Structures

As illustrated in the example in Section 3, Ever permits Pascal-like records and arrays. Implementing the variable declarations is much like compiling the variable declarations of a structured programming language, except that instead of allocating bits of memory for storage, we allocate entries in an array of BDD variables. Let us call this array V. We can easily compute the size of V using a standard recursive computation: the size of a scalar is the number of bits used to represent it, the size of a record is the sum of the sizes of its fields, and the size of an array is the product of the number of elements in the array and the size of an array element.

A more interesting problem is to generate the correct vector of Boolean formulas to correspond to a variable reference. For a simple variable reference, we look up the offset to the correct BDD variables much as a compiler would generate the offset to the start of the correct block of memory. The BDD variables starting at that offset form the correct vector of Boolean formulas. For a record access, we start with the base variable as before, add the field offset, and proceed as in the case of the simple variable reference. Array indexing is the most complex. If the index were a constant, we could proceed as for records. The index, however, can be an arbitrary scalar-valued expression, which is a vector of Boolean functions denoting a *set* of possible values. For example, an expression like $x[a+4]$ denotes a vector of Boolean formulas that, when restricted to having $a = 0$, are equivalent to the Boolean formulas for $x[4]$; when restricted to having $a = 1$, are equivalent to $x[5]$; and so forth. If $f(a)$ is the proposition $1 < a < 5$, then the proposition $(z = x[a + 4]) \wedge f(a)$ says that z can be equal to any of $x[5]$ through $x[9]$. Therefore, the formulas we generate for an array access must perform a case analysis for each possible value of the array index.

In more formal terms, define a *modifier* as either a field name or an array-indexing expression. We will consider a variable name to be a field name in a global record. In this notation, a variable reference is simply a string of modifiers. For any field name or constant array index, define OFFSET(*modifier*) to be the offset from the beginning of the record or array to the start of the referenced field or array entry. OFFSET is a common computation in compilers: the offset for a record field is the sum of the sizes of the fields that precede it, and the offset for the ith array entry is the product of i (minus the array lower bound) and the size of an array element. Denote by $V(n, s)$ the s BDD variables in the storage array V going from $V[n]$ to $V[n + s - 1]$. Since this quantity is a vector of Boolean formulas, we can consider it to be an Ever scalar. For notational convenience, a Boolean operator applied to a vector of Boolean formulas is assumed to apply in parallel to each element. Given an arbitrary variable reference ρ, define s_ρ to be the number of bits that ρ describes, or equivalently, the size of the referenced variable. The vector of Boolean formulas for the variable reference ρ is given by

$BDD(0, \rho)$, where the function BDD is defined by:

$$BDD(n, \epsilon) = V(n, s_\rho)$$
$$BDD(n, field\_name\, \sigma) = BDD(n + OFFSET(field\_name), \sigma)$$
$$BDD(n, index\_expr\, \sigma) = \bigwedge_{i=l}^{u} [(index\_expr = i) \Rightarrow BDD(n + OFFSET(i), \sigma)]$$

where σ is a (possibly empty) string of modifiers, ϵ is the empty string, and l and u are the lower and upper bounds of the array. Note that these expressions generate a vector of complex Boolean formulas, rather than a set of particular BDD variables. Intuitively, the generated formulas are multiplexors whose select lines are driven by the array-indexing expressions and whose inputs are the BDD variables. (The formula for array indexing can be considered a scalar-valued generalization of work by Beatty et al. [1].)

4.3 Deterministic Assignment

To implement deterministic assignment, we use a computation similar to the variable reference computation described above, except that we must specify that every BDD variable that isn't referenced must keep its current value. Also, for variable referencing, we are generating a vector of Boolean formulas; in the case of deterministic assignment, we want to generate a single Boolean relation between the current state of the system and the next state of the system that is true iff the current and next states correspond to the deterministic assignment.

For records, generating this relation is straightforward. For each field not being accessed, we AND into the Boolean relation being generated the further requirement that the field not change. For the field that we do access, we equate a variable reference expression like that generated in the previous section with the right-hand side of the assignment. For arrays, we must again perform a case analysis.

Formally, the next-state relation for deterministic assignment of an expression new_value to a variable reference ρ is given by $BECOMES(0, \rho, new\_value)$, where the function BECOMES is defined by:

$$BECOMES(n, \epsilon, v) = (V(n, s_\rho) = v)$$

$$BECOMES(n, field\_name\, \sigma, v) = \bigwedge_{f \in record\_fields} \left[\begin{array}{l} \text{if } (f = field\_name) \\ \text{then} \\ \qquad BECOMES(n + OFFSET(f), \sigma, v) \\ \text{else } V(n + OFFSET(f), s_f) \\ \text{remains constant.} \end{array} \right]$$

$$BECOMES(n, index\_expr\, \sigma, v) = \bigwedge_{i=l}^{u} \left[\begin{array}{l} \text{if } (i = index\_expr) \\ \text{then } BECOMES(n + OFFSET(i), \sigma, v) \\ \text{else } V(n + OFFSET(i), s_a) \text{ remains constant.} \end{array} \right]$$

where s_f is the size of record field f, s_a is the size of an array element, and the other variables are defined as before.

4.4 Stability

Once we have deterministic assignment, the problem of stability becomes easy. Here are the rules we need to build larger next-state relations from smaller ones with correct stability. (Correctness follows trivially by a structural induction.) If p is some code fragment in a higher-level language, define $EVER(p)$ to be the corresponding Ever next-state relation.

Assignment: If p is an assignment statement "variable := expression", then $EVER(p)$ is "(becomes variable expression)."

Sequentiality: If p is a sequence of statements "$s_1; s_2; \ldots; s_n$", then $EVER(p)$ is "(compose $EVER(s_1)$ $EVER(s_2)$ ... $EVER(s_n)$)." (The compose operator is simply Boolean relation composition. For example, if $N_1(x, y)$ and $N_2(x, y)$ are two Boolean relations, we can compute $N_2 \circ N_1(x, y) = \exists z[N_1(x, z) \wedge N_2(z, y)]$.)

Conditional: If p is the conditional statement "if c then s_1 else s_2 endif", then $EVER(p)$ is "(if c $EVER(s_1)$ $EVER(s_2)$)."

Non-Determinism: If p is the non-deterministic choice between s_1 and s_2, then $EVER(p)$ is simply "(or $EVER(s_1)$ $EVER(s_2)$)."

Note that these rules essentially provide a denotational semantics for a higher-level, sequential specification language in terms of Ever. We are currently using a structured protocol description language Murφ that, by applying these rules, compiles efficiently into Ever for symbolic verification. For example, the complex statement presented in Section 2 is a Murφ statement that compiles by a trivial rewriting into the following Ever code:[3]

```
(if
  (and
    (lt i^c Homes[h^c].Dir[a^c].Shared_Count^c)
    (eq Homes[h^c].Dir[a^c].Entries[i^c]^c n^c)
  )
  (compose                          -- if body
    (becomes
      Homes[h^c].Dir[a^c].Entries[i^c]^n
      Homes[h^c].Dir[a^c].Entries[(sub Homes[h^c].Dir[a^c].Shared_Count^c 1)]^c
    )
    (becomes
      Homes[h^c].Dir[a^c].Entries[(sub Homes[h^c].Dir[a^c].Shared_Count^c 1)]^n
      0
    )
    (becomes
      Homes[h^c].Dir[a^c].Shared_Count^n
      (sub Homes[h^c].Dir[a^c].Shared_Count^c 1)
    )
  )
  CurNextEq                         -- else body
)
```

---

[3] The code fragment given in Section 2 is actually from a procedure, which Murφ inlines. Therefore, in the translation of the real protocol, the parameters i,h,a, and n are replaced by the complex expressions in the procedure call. This situation presents no problem to Ever, but would needlessly complicate our illustrative example.

(CurNextEq is a next-state relation that requires the state not to change.) Translation from other protocol description languages into Ever should also be straightforward.

4.5 Image Computation

The preceding techniques are sufficient to convert a high-level specification into a Boolean next-state relation expressed as a BDD. Given a next-state relation $N(x, x')$, computing foward and backward images of characteristic functions $\chi(x)$ and $\chi'(x')$ is easy and efficient: the forward image is simply $\exists x[\chi(x) \wedge N(x, x')]$, and the backward image is simply $\exists x'[\chi'(x') \wedge N(x, x')]$. Efficiently computing these operations is important because they are the basis for most verification algorithms. For large problems, however, the BDD for $N(x, x')$ is frequently too large to compute [10, 19, 3]. Because of this problem, many researchers have turned to Boolean Functional Vectors [10, 14, 13] or closely related methods [19] to successfully verify large gate-level digital circuits.

Unfortunately, these methods, in addition to complicating image computation, do not support non-deterministic next-state relations. In the domain of gate-level digital circuits, this limitation does not matter; a gate-level circuit is typically considered deterministic. To model and verify higher-level protocols, however, non-determinism is essential, both to model unpredictable events (e.g. noise corrupting a data transmission) and to allow abstraction (e.g. modeling a cache without full details of the line-replacement policy).

Fortunately, the translation of higher-level language constructs into Ever automatically gives us the next-state relation in a form that allows efficient computation of both forward and backward images without building the BDD for the full next-state relation. Let $\mathrm{Image}(\chi, N)$ be the forward image of the characteristic function χ under next-state relation N. Recall from Section 4.4 that we generate Ever code from a higher-level language using a set of recursive rules. Therefore, an Ever next-state relation always has one of the following forms:

- $N(x, x')$ is a deterministic assignment. This case is the basis. We must build the BDD for N and compute $\mathrm{Image}(\chi, N) = \exists x[\chi(x) \wedge N(x, x')]$.
- $N(x, x') = (N_n \circ \cdots \circ N_1)(x, x')$, where the operator $\circ$ denotes composition: $(N_2 \circ N_1)(x, x') = \exists x''[N_1(x, x'') \wedge N_2(x'', x')]$. In this case, $\mathrm{Image}(\chi, N)$ is just the forward image of $\mathrm{Image}(\chi, N_1)$ under $(N_n \circ \cdots \circ N_2)(x, x')$.
- $N(x, x') = $ if $C(x)$ then $N_1(x, x')$ else $N_2(x, x')$. In this case, $\mathrm{Image}(\chi, N)$ equals $\mathrm{Image}(\chi \wedge C, N_1) \vee \mathrm{Image}(\chi \wedge \overline{C}, N_2)$.
- $N(x, x') = N_1(x, x') \vee \cdots \vee N_n(x, x')$. This case is Burch *et al.*'s [3] disjunctive partitioned transition relation. We compute $\mathrm{Image}(\chi, N)$ as simply $\mathrm{Image}(\chi, N_1) \vee \cdots \vee \mathrm{Image}(\chi, N_n)$.

The computation of backward images is almost identical. These rules require building the BDD only for the next-state relations corresponding to each individual assignment, thereby eliminating the problem of building an enormous BDD for the entire next-state relation.

This technique represents an instance of the classic space-time trade-off. The number of nodes in the BDD for the full next-state relation is, in the worst case, the product of the number of nodes in the component next-state relations (yielding exponential behavior). Using the above technique, the number of BDD nodes is the *sum* of the number of nodes in the component next-state relations (yielding linear growth). On the other hand, one image computation on the full next-state relation becomes one image computation for *each* of the component next-state relations, yielding slower execution. Finally, in some instances, the BDD for the full next-state relation is substantially smaller than the worst-case behavior. Ever provides an evaluate operator to force the construction of the BDD for a given expression. Using this operator gives flexibility in trading space for time. For the small example described in Section 3, forcing complete evaluation of the next-state relation only increased memory usage to 6.8MB while cutting runtime to four and a half minutes. In contrast, on a large model of a real directory-based cache-coherence protocol (approximately 1000 lines of Murφ code and 10^{34}-state state space), both the fully-evaluated next-state relation and the disjunctive partitioned next-state relation were unable to build the required BDDs (with a 60MB memory limit), whereas the technique described above enabled reachability computation and verification using less than 24MB memory and one hour of CPU time. (All figures are for a SUN 4/75.)

5   Future Work and Conclusion

One issue that definitely needs further research is the problem of variable ordering. The size of the BDD representation of a Boolean function depends critically on the ordering of the variables [7]. One heuristic that has proven useful for scalars is to interleave the corresponding bits (most significant bits first, followed by the next most significant bits, etc.) [18]. In many cases, this ordering produces a substantially smaller BDD. For example, to check the equality of two scalars $x = y$, this ordering $(x_n, y_n, \ldots, x_1, y_1)$ produces the optimum $3n$-node BDD, whereas a naïve ordering $(x_n, \ldots, x_1, y_n, \ldots, y_1)$ produces an exponential-sized BDD. Jeong *et al.*'s Non-Interleaving Lemma [14] provides theoretical justification for this heuristic.[4] The `interleaved` keyword mentioned in Section 3 implements this ordering on each subtype to which it is attached. We plan to introduce additional variable-ordering heuristics to permit verification of larger examples.

Another issue is the question of relating specifications at different levels of abstraction. For example, we may wish to check that a synthesized circuit corresponds to a higher-level specification. We have developed an efficient technique to find *simulation preorders*, which check that one specification implements an-

---

4 In an unfortunate clash of terminology, what we and Srinivasan *et al.* call an interleaved variable order, because the bits comprising the scalars are interleaved, creates what Jeong *et al.* call a non-interleaved order, because the Boolean relations for the individual bit-slices have disjoint supports and are grouped together.

other [15, 12]. We are currently investigating the integration of this technique into Ever.

We have demonstrated the efficient implementation of higher-level language features in a BDD-based verifier and expect that these techniques will be applicable to other verifiers as well. These features have greatly simplified writing specifications for verification, as they provide a much more natural means of expression. Furthermore, they can also increase the efficiency of the verification by obviating the expensive computation of the full BDD for the next-state relation. In addition, the translation from a higher-level specification language like Murφ is straightforward. As we have already been using Murφ for several real, industrial problems, we are excited by progress in this direction.

References

1. Derek L. Beatty, Randal E. Bryant, and Carl-Johann H. Seger, "Synchronous Circuit Verification by Symbolic Simulation: An Illustration," *Advanced Research in VLSI: Proceedings of the Sixth MIT Conference*, William J. Dally, ed., MIT Press, 1990.

2. S. Bose and A. Fisher, "Automatic Verification of Synchronous Circuits Using Symbolic Logic Simulation and Temporal Logic," *IMEC-IFIP International Workshop on Applied Formal Methods For Correct VLSI Design*, Luc J.M. Claesen, ed., North Holland, 1989.

3. J.R. Burch, E.M. Clarke, and D.E. Long, "Symbolic Model Checking with Partitioned Transition Relations," *VLSI '91: Proceedings of the IFIP TC 10/WG 10.5 International Conference on Very Large Scale Integration*, Edinburgh, Great Britain, 1991.

4. J.R. Burch, E.M. Clarke, K.L. McMillan, and David L. Dill, "Sequential Circuit Verification Using Symbolic Model Checking," *27th ACM/IEEE Design Automation Conference*, 1990, pp. 46-51.

5. J.R. Burch, E.M. Clarke, K.L. McMillan, D.L. Dill, and L.J. Hwang, "Symbolic Model Checking: 10^{20} States and Beyond," *Proceedings of the Conference on Logic in Computer Science*, 1990, pp. 428–439.

6. Karl S. Brace, Richard L. Rudell, and Randal E. Bryant, "Efficient Implementation of a BDD Package," *27th ACM/IEEE Design Automation Conference*, 1990, pp. 40–45.

7. Randal E. Bryant, "Graph-Based Algorithms for Boolean Function Manipulation," *IEEE Transactions on Computers*, Vol. C-35, No. 8 (August 1986), pp. 677–691.

8. Edmund M. Clarke, Orna Grumberg, and David E. Long, "Model Checking and Abstraction," *Proceedings of the ACM Symposium on Principles of Programming Languages*, 1992, pp. 343–354.

9. Olivier Coudert, Christian Berthet, and Jean Christophe Madre, "Verification of Synchronous Sequential Machines Based on Symbolic Execution," *Automatic Verification Methods for Finite State Systems*, J. Sifakis, ed., Lecture Notes in Computer Science Vol. 407, Springer-Verlag, 1989.

10. Olivier Coudert, Christian Berthet, and Jean Christophe Madre, "Verification of Sequential Machines Using Boolean Functional Vectors," *IMEC-IFIP International Workshop on Applied Formal Methods For Correct VLSI Design*, Luc J.M. Claesen, ed., North Holland, 1989.

11. David L. Dill, Andreas J. Drexler, Alan J. Hu, and C. Han Yang, "Protocol Verification as a Hardware Design Aid," to appear in *IEEE International Conference on Computer Design*, 1992.

12. David L. Dill, Alan J. Hu, and Howard Wong-Toi, "Checking for Language Inclusion Using Simulation Preorders," *Computer-Aided Verification: Third International Workshop*, July 1–4, 1991, K.G. Larsen and A. Skou, eds., Lecture Notes in Computer Science Vol. 575, Springer-Verlag, published 1992.

13. Thomas Filkorn, "Functional Extension of Symbolic Model Checking," *Computer-Aided Verification: Third International Workshop*, July 1–4, 1991, K.G. Larsen and A. Skou, eds., Lecture Notes in Computer Science Vol. 575, Springer-Verlag, published 1992.

14. S.-W. Jeong, B. Plessier, G.D. Hachtel, and F. Somenzi, "Variable Ordering for FSM Traversal," *Proceedings of the International Workshop on Logic Synthesis*, MCNC, Research Triangle Park, NC, May 1991.

15. Paul Loewenstein and David Dill, "Formal Verification of Cache Systems using Refinement Relations," *IEEE International Conference on Computer Design*, 1990, pp. 228-233.

16. J. McCarthy and P.J. Hayes, "Some Philosophical Problems from the Standpoint of Artificial Intelligence," in *Machine Intelligence 4*, B. Meltzer and D. Michie, eds., Edinburgh University Press, 1969.

17. K. L. McMillan and J. Schwalbe, "Formal Verification of the Gigamax Cache-Consistency Protocol," *Proceedings of the International Symposium on Shared Memory Multiprocessing*, Information Processing Society of Japan, 1991, pp. 242–251.

18. Arvind Srinivasan, Timothy Kam, Sharad Malik, and Robert K. Brayton, "Algorithms for Discrete Function Manipulation," *IEEE International Conference on Computer-Aided Design*, 1990, pp. 92–95.

19. Herve J. Touati, Hamid Savoj, Bill Lin, Robert K. Brayton, and Alberto Sangiovanni-Vincentelli, "Implicit State Enumeration of Finite State Machines using BDD's" *IEEE International Conference on Computer-Aided Design*, 1990, pp. 130–133.

Symbolic Bisimulation Minimisation

Amar Bouali[1] and Robert de Simone[2]

[1] ENSMP Centre de Mathématiques Appliquées
B.P. 207 F-06904 Sophia-Antipolis
FRANCE
amar@cma.cma.fr
[2] I.N.R.I.A.
2004 route des Lucioles
F-06904 Sophia-Antipolis
FRANCE
rs@cma.cma.fr

Abstract. We describe a set of algorithmic methods, based on symbolic representation of state space, for minimisation of networks of parallel processes according to bisimulation equivalence. We compute this with the Coarsest Partition Refinement algorithm, using the Binary Decision Diagram structures. The method applies to labelled synchronised vectors of finite automata as the description of systems. We report performances on a couple of examples of a tool being implemented.

1 Introduction

Bisimulation is a central notion in the domain of verification for parallel communicating systems [17]. It was defined as an equivalence in the abstract formal setting of process algebras [17,2], through interpretation by labelled transition systems.

Bisimulation's algorithmic properties in the finite automata case have been widely studied [15,19,10], leading to a large body of automata-theoretic methods, complexity theory results and experimental comparisons based on verification tools [24,6,10,11]. Studies were also pursued with the additional concern of *observational* bisimulations, with a particular hidden action. Various treatments of this action were considered (*weak, branching ...*) [17,23].

The usual drawback of bisimulation is that, being defined on underlying automata, its computation requires all the informations (on states and transitions) collected in this global structure. Building the full automaton can lead to combinatorial explosion, while recomputing information dynamically is a time penalty. Several methods have nevertheless be proposed in the latter direction, either in the general case or in specific subcases (bisimulation comparaison with a determinate process for instance), with some success [12,3,20,18]. Anyhow most of these methods require to keep track at least of the reachable state space –if not of the transitions–, even though the problem of efficient representation or approximation of this state space has also been tackled [13,14].

In this paper we study one such efficient representation of the state space, using the symbolic Binary Decision Diagrams [4]. These data structures have been now widely recognised for their ability to concisely represent sets and relations in practice, and applied to generate state spaces in several frameworks [7,22,16]. They have also been already applied to the problem of bisimulation, but inside a quite general setting, through formulation of the bisimulation property in general logical terms, based on the μ-calculus [5,9]. The solution here is more closely algorithmic in a sense directly related to the early methods in bisimulation checking. We first introduce a "concrete" formalism to represent Networks of Process Automata and shortly discuss its relation to process algebraic constructions in the finitary case. Then we recall the computational definition of bisimulation and rephrase it in a way that anticipates on the functions and techniques available with the particular BDD data structures. We then describe some of these functions on BDD, that will be used in our approach. In the two following sections we actually describe the algorithms for (symbolic) state space construction and bisimulation refinement; we do this on the model of Process Automata Networks, and in terms of the BDD functions just introduced. We end with a discussion on efficiency and implementation, and experimental results.

2 The Model and the Verification Method

We now introduce our description model formally. Then we sketch its relations with process algebraic static networks and its way of compilation into global automata. Last in this section we introduce bisimulation and characterize it in set-theoretic fashion.

We recall briefly the celebrated definition of automata:

Notation 2.1 *A* finite labelled transition system (lts) $A = < S, Sort(A), s^0, T >$ *-or* automaton- *is a 4-uple with S and $Sort(A)$ finite sets of respectively* states *and* labels, $s^0 \in S$ *an* initial *state and $T \in (S \times Sort(A) \times S)$ a set of (labelled)* transitions.

T *can be sorted by labels into relations $T_a \subset S \times S, a \in Sort(A)$. As usual we note $s \xrightarrow{a} s'$ for $(s, a, s') \in T$ (or $(s, s') \in T_a$). We shall assume w.l.o.g. all T_a to be nonempty.*

Also $T_a^{-1} = \{(s', s) \in S \times S \mid (s, s') \in T_a\}$. For $C \subseteq S$, we note $s \xrightarrow{a} C$ if $\exists s' \in C$ such that $s \xrightarrow{a} s'$.

2.1 Networks of Processes

A *Labelled Synchronised Automata Vector* consists in a finite vector of automata components (individual processes), together with a set of *Labelled Synchronisation Vectors* to constrain their relative behaviors. This model has been introduced by Arnold and Nivat [1]. The only difference here is that our synchronisation vectors are themselves labelled, introducing compositionality: a network could itself be expanded into an automaton, and act as component to a larger system. Another way to go is by flattening a structured description, with subnetworks used as components of larger networks, into a single vector, with only "leaf" individual processes remaining.

Still in this paper we shall concentrate on flat networks, so that each rational process component is a finite labelled transition system.

Definition 1. A *Labelled Synchronised Automata Vector (LSAV)* N (of size n) is a 4-uple $< \mathbf{A}, V, Sort(N), label >$ consisting of:

- a n-ary Automata Vector $\mathbf{A}$ of $A_i = < S_i, Sort(A_i), s_i^0, T_i >$ as automata components,
- a finite set V of n-ary Labelled Synchronisation Vectors, so that, for each $sv \in V$, $sv_i \in Sort(A_i)$ or $sv_i = \star$. The particular symbol $\star$ indicates inaction: the corresponding component does not engage in this global behavior.
- a finite set of labels $Sort(N)$.
- a labelling surjective function $label : V \rightarrow Sort(N)$

Notation 2.2 *We note $n]$ the integer interval $[1..n]$. For sv a given synchronisation vector we note $support(sv)$ the set $\{i \in n], sv_i \neq \star\}$.*

Definition 2. Let N be a LSAV. The *global automaton* A_N *associated to* N is given by:

- $Sort(A_N) = Sort(N)$ as (global) label space,
- $S = S_1 \times S_2 \times \ldots \times S_n$, as (global) state space,
- $s^0 = (s_1^0, s_2^0, \ldots, s_n^0)$ as initial state,
- $T = \{((s_1, s_2, \ldots, s_n), a, (s_1', s_2', \ldots, s_n')), \exists sv \in V, label(sv) = a \wedge$
  $((s_i, sv_i, s_i') \in T_i \vee (s_i = s_i' \wedge sv_i = \star))\}$ as transition relation.

Later we shall of course only be interested in the global states that are reachable from s^0. This subset will be computed symbolically, using BDDs.

We end this section with informal motivations of our description formalism in the light of process algebraic constructors.

Because of closure by composition the LSAV model allows to represent a large body of process calculi expressions, namely the non-recursive ones built only from so-called static operators in [17]. Recursion is then only used for the creation of individual automata components with dynamic operators. This was shown in [8]. Shortly, such operators have SOS semantic rules such that the residual expression keeps unchanged the shape of the term (parallel rewrites into parallel, etc...). In this sense the various *parallel / scoping / relabelling* operators describing the network can be thought of as an elegant syntax for shaping the description of the network.

Note that, in addition to the static operators, production of actual synchronisation vectors also require the *Sorts* of (uninstanciated) components.

While simplifying the construction of global state spaces and automata, since a number of successive static constructions may here be combined at once, our concrete formalism of *LSAVs* do not favour compositional reduction (minimisation applied on subsystems). This latter method is dramatically used in AUTO for example. This is not a penalty in the symbolic approach, where intermediate automata are not built anyway. Of course the two approaches could be juxtaposed independantly, wherever more beneficial.

2.2 Bisimulation Equivalence

The present section recalls the notion of bisimulation, a "behavioral" equivalence defined on transition systems. We derive from this definition a set-theoretic formulation to compute it as a fix-point on finite transition systems.

We shall not motivate the philosophy behind bisimulation equivalence, see [17]. Its main characteristic is that equivalent states all have the same behavior ability, so that there exists a canonical minimal form, based on classes as states, even for nondeterministic transition systems.

Bisimulation equivalence is used in the setting of verification both to reduce an underlying automaton and to compare two distinct automata. We are here interested in the former role, and we want to extract the equivalence classes, from the LSAV description and a representation of the reachable state space. Actually constructing the minimal automaton is then straightforward (and possibly useless).

Notation 2.3 *Given an equivalence relation $\mathcal{R}$ on a set E we note $[e]_\mathcal{R}$ the equivalence class of $e \in E$.*

Definition 3. Let $A =< S, Sort(A), s^0, T >$ be a lts. A binary symmetric relation $\mathcal{R} \in S \times S$ is a bisimulation if:

$$\forall s, s' \in S, (s\mathcal{R}s') \Rightarrow \left(\forall a \in Sort(A), \forall t \in S, (s \xrightarrow{a} t \Rightarrow \exists t', (s' \xrightarrow{a} t') \wedge (tRt')) \right)$$

We note $\sim$ the largest bisimulation relation $\mathcal{R}$ verifying the previous definition.

The bisimulation property above is defined recursively. Now consider the following chain of equivalence relations:

$$\mathcal{R}_0 = S \times S$$
$$\mathcal{R}_{n+1} = \{(s, s') \in \mathcal{R}_n \mid \forall a \in Sort(A),$$
$$((s \xrightarrow{a} s_1) \Rightarrow (\exists s_1', s' \xrightarrow{a} s_1' \wedge (s1, s_1') \in \mathcal{R}_n)) \wedge$$
$$((s' \xrightarrow{a} s_1') \Rightarrow (\exists s_1, s \xrightarrow{a} s1 \wedge (s_1, s_1') \in \mathcal{R}_n))\}$$

It is folklore that for finite automata $\mathcal{R}_\infty = \bigcap \mathcal{R}_n$ corresponds to $\sim$, and is obtained through finite iteration: it exists n_0 such that $\mathcal{R}_{n_0} = \mathcal{R}_\infty$. Each $\mathcal{R}_j$ belonging to the sequence of relations can be seen as a union of n_j equivalence classes, that is

$$\mathcal{R}_j = \bigcup_{i=1}^{n_j} C_{i,j} \times C_{i,j}$$

with the $C_{i,j}$ ranging over the equivalence classes of R_j. To each $\mathcal{R}_j$, we associate the related partition $P_j = \{C_{i,j} | i \in n_j]\}$

For convenience we introduce the auxiliary values:

$$E_{j,a} = \bigcup_{i=1}^{n_j} C_{i,j} \times T_a^{-1}(C_{i,j})$$

Now we can rewrite the definition of $\mathcal{R}_{j+1}$ from $\mathcal{R}_j$ as

$$\mathcal{R}_{j+1} = \mathcal{R}_j \cap \left(\bigcap_{a \in Sort(A)} \{(s_1, s_2) \mid \forall s, (((s, s_1) \in E_{j,a} \iff (s, s_2) \in E_{j,a})\} \right)$$

$$= \mathcal{R}_j \cap \left(\bigcap_{a \in Sort(A)} \{(s_1, s_2) \mid \neg \exists s, (((s, s_1) \in E_{j,a} \iff (s, s_2) \notin E_{j,a})\} \right)$$

This set-theoretic identity will base an algorithm to compute $\sim$ by refinement in the second part of the paper. Note already that each iteration requires **a single application** of T_a^{-1}, in the computation of $E_{j,a}$.

3 Symbolic Representation of LSAV and Bisimulation

We now shortly discuss the symbolic encoding of state spaces into Binary Decision Diagrams. We describe the simple computation of their reachable parts, and then the symbolic computation of bisimulation on (the encoding of) LSAVs.

3.1 Sets and BDD Encodings

A BDD is an acyclic graph representation of (the truth table of) a Boolean propositional formula, on a finite predefined support of predicate variables. It is based on decision trees, where branching splits according to the alternative values of the variables, encountered in some fixed order. BDDs are then obtained by sharing subtrees as much as possible. BDDs are canonical, relative to a given ordering of the variables, in the sense that different syntaxic formulas with the same truth values have identical (minimal) representations. See [4] for full details.

As usual in the BDD litterature we shall identify *finite* sets and relations with their characteristic functions, and further with an encoding using boolean variables of this characteristic functions. We shall now be more specific on our notion of encoding.

Definition 4. Let E be a finite set. An *encoding* for E consists of: a finite, totally ordered *encoding array* of size m (say $x = [x_1 < x_2 < \ldots < x_m]$) of boolean variables together with a surjective partial function $\xi : Bool^m \longrightarrow E$.

Notation 3.1 *We note $\underline{x}_m$ the ordered (encoding) array $[x_1 < x_2 < \ldots < x_m]$ of propositional variables. x is then called the* basename, *and m the* size. *We omit the size subscript and the underline when clear from context.*

With our definition an element of E needs not be represented by a *unique* boolean valuation, nor does *any* boolean valuation represent an element of E. Just a boolean valuation may not be associated with two elements of E ambiguously. As previously mentioned we will abusively call E for its encoding syntactic BDD also (this makes an implicit reference to a specific encoding). We extend this and note $\overline{E}$ for the BDD representing $Bool^m \setminus \xi^{-1}(E)$ on the proper encoding array.

The value m in the previous definition is not fixed *a priori*. Encodings of sets usually range from those minimal variables numbers $(m = \lceil log(\#E) \rceil$ to *One-hot* encodings where a variable is assigned to each element $(m = \#E)$. Since a key issue in BDDs lies not so much in the symbolic representation of states as in this of transition relations, our choice of encoding should try and make the encoding of transitions as small as possible. This was one reason why we gave such a broad definition of encodings.

Encoding arrays are needed in the definition since boolean variables in BDDs are syntactic elements. Later on we will need at places to introduce disjoint samples of encoding sets for the same E and the same *coding* function, so they will differ only by their explicit range of variables.

Coming down to our precise needs for symbolic modelisation, we shall have to represent: local states, global states (as vectors of local states), T_a transition relations and $\mathcal{R}_i$ equivalence relations (as couples of global states). So local states will require basic encoding, from which we deduce the other encodings by taking product encodings, on disjoint unions of encoding arrays.

The "good encoding" issue now splits into: first, find appropriate local encodings; second, find interesting order extensions when putting different (disjoint) encodings together in disjoint union.

We now introduce two natural ordering extensions of encodings in case of cartesian products E^k.

Definition 5. Let $\{\underline{x}^1, \ldots, \underline{x}^k\}$, compose k pairwise disjoint encoding arrays of size m for a common set E (with the same encoding function), such that $\forall i \in k]$, $\underline{x}^i = [x^i_1, \ldots, x^i_m]$. We introduce two extensions $\ll$ and $\lhd$ of the total orders on the $\underline{x}_i$'s by

$$\ll: \forall i \in (k-1)] x^i_m \ll x^{i+1}_1$$
$$\lhd : \ \forall i \in (k-1)], \forall j \in m] \ \ x^i_j \lhd x^{i+1}_j$$
$$\forall j \in (k-1)] x^m_j \lhd x^1_{j+1}$$

We call $\ll$ the concatenated extension, for it will not mix (variables from) different coding sets. On the contrary $\lhd$ the shuffled extension will put as close as possible corresponding variables from various coding sets.

The ordering extension to (vector) global states here should also be discussed. A brute force solution consists in concatenating these orders without mixing. A more insighful solution should bring as close as possible those variables which are correlated, no matter which local component they encode. This corresponds to an attempt at bringing together (when feasible) the different local aspects of a same global event. Still, it will be the case that, in the encoding of a global state, each variable helps in encoding exactly one local component. We note $\underline{x}_i$ the subarray obtained by collecting in increasing order all boolean variables that deal with automata component A_i, and $\underline{x}_{sv}$ for the concatenation (still in increasing order) of the $\underline{x}_i, i \in support(sv)$.

We end this section by recalling some less familiar boolean operators to be used later in algorithms.

Definition 6. Let f be a boolean function. The smoothing of f by boolean variables $X = (x_{i_1}, \ldots, x_{i_p})$ is defined as

$$S(x_{i_1}, \ldots, x_{i_p})(f) = S_{x_{i_1}} \circ \ldots \circ S_{x_{i_p}}(f)$$
$$S_{x_{i_j}}(f) = f_{x_{i_p}} + f_{\overline{x_{i_p}}} \text{ where}$$
$$f_{x_i}(x_1, \ldots, x_{i-1}, x_i, x_{i+1}, \ldots, x_r) = (x_1, \ldots, x_{i-1}, 1, x_{i+1}, \ldots, x_r) \text{ and}$$
$$f_{\overline{x_i}}(x_1, \ldots, x_{i-1}, x_i, x_{i+1}, \ldots, x_r) = (x_1, \ldots, x_{i-1}, 0, x_{i+1}, \ldots, x_r)$$

Logically, the smoothing operator performs existential quantification on the smoothed variables: $S_{(x_{i_1}, \ldots, x_{i_p})}(f) = \exists x_{i_1} \ldots \exists x_{i_p} f$.

Definition 7. Let f be a boolean function. Substitution of array of boolean variables $X = [x_1, x_2, \ldots, x_p]$ by array $Y = [y_1, y_2, \ldots, y_p]$ in f, noted $[Y \leftarrow X]f$, consists of the simultaneous replacement of (boolean variables) array items x_i by corresponding y_i. Formally

$$[Y \leftarrow X]f \equiv_{def} S_X \left(\bigwedge_{i \in p]} (y_i \iff x_i) \wedge f \right)$$

The resulting BDD may be very different from f due to different respective ordering of x's and y's and other variables.

A third boolean operator we shall use on BDD is the *cofactor* operation. For lack of room we shall not describe it here. Intuitively $cofactor(B, C)$ represents *"B provided C"*, or what is strictly needed to recover B under the assumption of C being true.

3.2 The Reachable States Algorithm

The space of all reachable states in a *LSAV* will be attained in a breadth-first search iterative manner, where at each iteration all states directly following the ones just obtained are reached. To do this, one should just apply the transition relation once. The main problem here is that encoding the full transition relation proves in practice to be much more space consuming than the state space itself. We solve this problem by splitting the application of the transition relation according to the synchronisation vectors. We now discuss this issue in relation with our model.

When building a global (unlabelled) transition relation $T(x, y)$ from the synchronisation vectors and the local transitions of individual automata, one needs to encode the identity where $\star$ (inaction) is indicated (leading to *stable*$_i$ BDDs in [9]). This completion does not seem too dramatic when considering a single synchronisation vector, but when building the union of all transitions it does not behave friendly according to sharing of subtrees. The resulting BDD is thus frequently very large.

On the other hand, if one considers building T_{sv} the part of the transition relation corresponding to an only synchronisation vector sv, nice features show up.

Then the full transition is then applied in steps by iteration on synchronisation vectors. The algorithm is shown in figure 1.

Nice features just mentioned are:

- first, the synchronisation vector allows a priori any combination of local transitions properly labelled. Thus the union of equaly labelled transitions can be formed locally, and this indicates natural sharing,
- second, T_{sv} can be defined and applied on $support(sv)$ only, disregarding the other components, which will therefore be left unchanged. This drops the need for the stable completion.

Definition 8. $T_{sv}(\underline{x}_{sv}, \underline{y}_{sv}) \equiv_{def} \bigwedge_{i \in support(sv)} \left(\bigvee_{t_i \in T_{i_{label}(sv_i)}} T_{t_i}(\underline{x}_{\{i\}}, \underline{y}_{\{i\}}) \right)$

where $T_t(\underline{x}, \underline{y})$ encodes transition t's local source/target states with respective encoding arrays $\underline{x}$ and $\underline{y}$.

Application of transitions corresponding to sv to a state space St is expressed as:

$$Apply(T_{sv}(\underline{x}_{sv}, \underline{y}_{sv}), St(\underline{x})) = [\underline{x}_{sv} \leftarrow \underline{y}_{sv}] S_{\underline{x}_{sv}}(St(\underline{x}) \wedge T_{sv}(\underline{x}_{sv}, \underline{y}_{sv}))$$

```
(1)    States(x) = S⁰(x)
(2)    New(x) = States(x)
(3)    while New ≠ 0
(4)    begin
(5)        Temp(x) = States(x)
(6)        for each sv ∈ V do
(7)        begin
(8)            States(x) = States(x) ∨ Apply(Tₛᵥ(x, y), States(x))
(9)        end
(10)       New(x) = States(x) ∧ Temp(x)
(11)   end
```

Fig. 1. Reachable states with vector transition relation

3.3 The Real Transition Relation

No matter whether it is fully constructed or applied by chunks along the synchronisation vectors, the transition relation above is actually syntactically derived as a superset of the real one: not everything needs to be applicable. Certain conjunctions of local transitions, while legible from the synchronisation point of view, may leave from non-reachable states and therefore not be fireable. More generally, the transition relation may pay attention to behaviors outside the state space.

We define below the (very simple) way to restrict this relation to its useful part. We shall need this in the bisimulation partitioning algorithm.

Definition 9.

$$\tilde{T}_{sv}(\underline{x}, \underline{y}) \equiv_{def} T_{sv}(\underline{x}_{sv}, \underline{y}_{sv}) \wedge States(\underline{x}) \wedge \left(\bigwedge_{i \notin support(sv)} Stable_i \right)$$

$$\tilde{T}_a(\underline{x}, \underline{y}) \equiv_{def} \bigvee_{label(sv)=a} \tilde{T}_{sv}(\underline{x}, \underline{y})$$

3.4 BDD Bisimulation

With explicit reference to variables encoding, the relation between R_j and R_{j+1} can now be expressed as:

$$E_{j,a}(x, z) = S_y(R_j(x, y) \wedge \tilde{T}_a(y, z))$$

$$Bad_j(x, y) = [x \leftarrow z] \left(\bigvee_{a \in sort(N)} S_x \left([y \leftarrow z] E_{j,a}(x, z) \Leftrightarrow \overline{E_{j,a}(x, z)} \right) \right)$$

$$R_{j+1}(x, y) = R_j(x, y) \wedge \overline{Bad_j(x, y)}$$

One starts with $R_0 = S_N \times S_N$, or taking coding sets into account: $R_0(x, y) = S_N(x) \wedge S_N(y)$. The algorithm of figure 2 implements this: lines (8-9) compute $E_{j,a}$, while lines (10-14) compute bad couples on a label, not with a XOR operation but as a two-fold union, this due to the fact that our implementation package allowed to perform simultaneously the conjunction and smoothing in lines 13 or 14, which is an interesting save-up in complexity. The loop at lines (5-17) accumulates bad couples for all actions. Lines 18 computes the termination test.

Figure 2 refines the computation at lines 1 and 8, where the cofactor function is introduced, so that all sets are given "provided" $S_N \times S_N$, into which they are all included.

4 Observational Bisimulation Equivalences

Two main variations on bisimulation have been proposed in order to deal with a specific actions (τ) as invisible: *weak* bisimulation and *branching* bisimulation. We shall not detail them here. We briefly indicate how to modify our previous algorithms to cope with these two extensions.

Weak bisimulation equivalence simply uses a new transition relation, deduced straightforwardly from the original one.

Definition 10. The weak transition relation $\Rightarrow$ of a lts A is:

$$s \xRightarrow{\tau} s' \text{ iff } \exists s_0, s_1, \ldots, s_n, n \geq 0, s = s_0 \xrightarrow{\tau} s_1 \xrightarrow{\tau} \ldots \xrightarrow{\tau} s_n = s'$$
$$s \xRightarrow{a} s' \text{ iff } \exists s_1, s_2, s \xRightarrow{\tau} s_1 \xrightarrow{a} s_2 \xRightarrow{\tau} s'$$

```
(1)    NewR(x, y) = cofactor(R₀(x, y), R₀(x, y))
(2)    i = 0
(3)    while NewR(x, y) ≠ 0
(4)    begin
(5)        Badⱼ(x, y) = ∅
(6)        For all a ∈ Sort(N)
(7)        begin
(8)            trans(z, y) = [z ← x]cofactor(Tₐ(x, y), R₀(x, ))
(9)            E¹ⱼ,ₐ(x, z) = Sᵧ(Rᵢ(x, y) ∧ trans(z, y))
(10)           E²ⱼ,ₐ(x, y) = [y ← z]E¹ⱼ,ₐ(x, z)
(11)           T₁(x, z) = ‾E¹ⱼ,ₐ(x, z)‾
(12)           T₂(x, y) = ‾E²ⱼ,ₐ(x, y)‾
(13)           B₁(z, y) = Sₓ(E¹ⱼ,ₐ(x, z) ∧ T₂(x, y))
(14)           B₂(z, y) = Sₓ(T₁(x, z) ∧ E²ⱼ,ₐ(x, y))
(15)           Badⱼ(x, y) = Badⱼ(x, y) ∨ [x ← z](B₁(z, y) ∨ B₂(z, y))
(17)       end
(16)       Rᵢ₊₁(x, y) = Rᵢ(x, y) ∧ ‾Badⱼ(x, y)‾
(18)       NewR(x, y) = Rᵢ(x, y) ∧ Rᵢ₊₁(x, y)
(19)       i = i + 1
(20)   end
```

Fig. 2. Bisimulation with BDD

One may either computes these relations symbolically, or composes dynamically the application of three relations ($T_{\tau^*}^{-1}$, then T_a^{-1} and $T_{\tau^*}^{-1}$ again). We use the iterative squaring method (see [22]) to compute $\xrightarrow{\tau}$ as the fixpoint of

$$F(x, y) = (x \xrightarrow{\tau} y) \vee \exists z(F(x, z) \wedge F(z, y))$$

Branching bisimulation instead restricts the above application of surrounding τ^* to state inverse images that preserve equivalence (so far). It can be proven in this case that τ^* need only be applied once (either before or after the "real action"), without affecting the resulting equivalence. Also, when τ is used as the discriminating action, only τ transitions joining (already) non-equivalent states need be applied. Thus, we define a set of transition relations Tb^j at each step in the equivalence partitioning. Noticeably these sets are very easy to recompute dynamically, as all they do is gather two informations already present: $\mathcal{R}_j$ equivalence, and the fixed global τ^* transition relation.

$$Inert_{\tau^*}^j = T_{\tau^*} \cap \mathcal{R}_j$$
$$Tb_a^j = Inert_{\tau^*}^j \circ T_a$$
$$Tb_\tau^j = Inert_{\tau^*}^j \circ (T_\tau \cap \overline{\mathcal{R}_j})$$

5 Applications

5.1 Encoding and Variable Ordering

It is shown in [9] that the interleaved order extension was theoretically best for the representation of transitions and states, during the Reachable State Space construction. Now the question is: would the same considerations apply for the representation of equivalent state couples during the Partition Refinement step?

As a rule of thumb it seems that, while the interleaved order gets better as the final relation is more discriminating and states are less identified, the concatenated order takes advantage of coarser cases where classes are fewer and more state identifications take place. This is understandable: in this order, the description of either instance of the class is factorised independantly (as first or second component of couples). In the former case use of BDDs may be questioned, for its interest is based on gain of sharing for sets representation. As more elements are isolated, they each tend to consume space individually in the BDD. Of course this is rough estimation. Weak bisimulation often allows more identifications to take place, specially when not all actions are kept visible. This case is certainly the most beneficial for the symbolic approach to bisimulation minimisation.

Sensibility to the alternative ($\ll$ /$\lhd$) variable orderings is illustrated and contrasted below on two examples with opposite teachings.

5.2 Test Examples

Two examples are exposed in this section. The first one is the LSAV specification of the scheduler with different number of cyclers. The second one is the Dekker Mutual Exclusion algorithm. For a precise presentation of these examples, the reader should refer to [17] for the former example, and [21] for the latter.

Table displayed in figure 3 shows the results obtained on the different instanciations of the scheduler specification problem, namely $4, 8, 16, 18$, and 20 cyclers for which a specific row is attributed in the table, and for the Dekker algorithm whose results row begins with a "D". All results have been obtained on a SPARC Station 2 with 24 MBytes of memory. Each row contains from letf to right: the concerned example, the number of reachable states followed by the size of the corresponding BDD and the time taken by the tool to compute it; for each type of variable order in ($\lhd$, $\ll$), the related time taken to compute the bisimulation equivalence on the reachable state space and the size of the corresponding BDD; finally, the number of equivalent pairs under bisimulation. The symbol "-" means that the tool was aborted during execution, due to lack of memory. In the case of the scheduler example, the $\lhd$ order is better than $\ll$,unlike in the other examples.

Conclusion

We have described an implementation of Bisimulation Minimisation based on symbolic representation using Binary Decision Diagrams. This implementation

	States	BDD	Time	Var	~ Time	~ BDD	Pairs
4	128	16	0.29	◁	4.88	59	256
				≪	24.83	859	
8	4096	16	0.29	◁	4.88	59	256
				≪	24.83	859	
16	2097152	64	11.99	◁	131.11	251	4194304
				≪	-	-	
18	9437184	72	16.26	◁	165.42	283	18874368
				≪	-	-	
20	41943040	80	22.47	◁	213.90	315	83886080
				≪	-	-	
D	126	74	1.36	◁	104.20	962	450
				≪	20.50	686	450

Fig. 3. Performances of the tool

tried to optimize computations and BDD sizes wherever possible, and in particular:

- works on LSAV as a compound version of process algebraic networks, so that several operators may be applied at once, and impossible behaviors detected as soon as possible,
- applies transitions as events individually, eliminating the need for storing the full transitions, with its out-of-support intricacies. Event-parted transitions allow well BDD sharing,
- applies backward behavior image only once for the coarsest partition fixpoint algo- rithm (instead of on both components of equivalent couples),
- performs simultaneous splitting of all classes by all classes.

References

1. A. Arnold and M. Nivat. Comportements de processus. In *Les Mathématiques de l'Informatique*, pages 35–68. Colloque AFCET, 1982.
2. D. Austry and G. Boudol. Algèbre de processus et synchronisation. *Theorical Computer Sciences*, 1(30), 1984.
3. A. Bouali. Weak and branching bisimulation in fctool. Technical Report 1575, INRIA, 1991.
4. Randal E. Bryant. Graph-based algorithms for boolean function manipulaiton. *Transactions on Computers*, C-35(8):677–691, August 1986.
5. J.R. Burch, E.M. Clarke, L. McMillan, D̃.L. Dill, and J. Hwang. Symbolic model checking: 10^{20} and beyond. In *5th IEEE Symposium on Logic in Computer Science*, pages 428–439, Philadelphia, 1990.
6. R. Cleaveland, J. Parrow, and B. Steffen. The concurrency workbench. In *Automatic Verification Methods for Finite State Systems*, pages 24–37. LNCS, 1989.

7. O. Coudert, C.. Berthet, and J.C. Madre. Verification of sequential machines using boolean vectors. In *IFIP Internationnal Workshop, Applied Formal Methods for Correct VLSI design*, Leuven, November 1990.

8. R. de Simone and A. Bouali. Causal models for rationnal algebraic processes. In J.C.M. Baeten and J.F. Groote, editors, *2nd internationnal Conference on Concurrency Theory*, Amsterdam, August 1991. CONCUR'91, Springer-Verlag.

9. R. Enders, T. Filkorn, and D. Taubner. Generating bdds for symbolic model checking. In *Third Workshop on Computer Aided Verification*, volume 1, pages 263–278. University of Aalborg, July 1991.

10. J.C. Fernandez. *Aldébaran: un système de vérificatoin par réduction de processus communiquants*. PhD thesis, Grenoble, 1989.

11. J.C. Godskesen, K.G. Larsen, and M. Zeeberg. Tav, tools for automatic verification. In *Automatic Verification Methods For Finite State Systems*, pages 232–246, Grenoble, France, 1989. LNCS, Springer-Verlag.

12. J.F. Groote and F. Vaandrager. An efficient algorithm for branching bisimulation and stuttering equivalence. *ICALP '90*, 1990.

13. G.J. Holzmann. Algorithms for automated protocol validation. In *International Workshop on Automatic Verification Methods for Finite State Systems*, Grenoble, France, June 1989.

14. C. Jard and T. Jéron. Bounded-memory algorithm for verification on-the-fly. In Larsen.K.G. and A. Skou, editors, *Third Workshop on Computer Aided Verification*, volume 1, pages 251–262, July 1991.

15. P.C. Kanellakis and S.A. Smolka. Ccs expressions, finite state processes, and three problems of equivalence. In *ACM Symposium on Principles of Distributed Computing*, pages 228–240, 1983.

16. B. Lin and A.R. Newton. Efficient manipulation of equivalence relations and classes. In *ACM International Workshop on Formal Methods in VLSI design*, Miami, January 1991.

17. Robin Milner. *Communication and Concurrency*. International Series in Computer Science. Prentice Hall, 1989.

18. Laurent Mounier. *Méthodes de vérification de spécifications comportementales: étude et mise en oeuvre*. PhD thesis, LGI Grenoble, 1991.

19. R. Paige and R. Tarjan. Three partition refinement algorithms. *SIAM*, 16(6), 1987.

20. Huajun Qin. Efficient verification of determinate processes. Technical report, Dep. of Comp. Sc., SUNY, Stony Brook, 1991.

21. M. Raynal. *Algorithmes du Parallélisme: le Problème de l'Exclusion Mutuelle*. Dunod Informatique, 1984.

22. H.J. Touati, H. Savoj, B. Lin, and Sangiovanni-Vincentelli. Implicit state enumeration of finite state machines using bdd's. In *Internationnal Conference on Computer Aided Design*, 1990.

23. R.J. Van Glabbeek and W.P. Weijland. Branching time and abstraction in bisimulation semantics (extended abstract). *Information processing '89 (G.X. Ritter, ed.) Elsevier Science*, pages 613–618, 1984.

24. D. Vergamini. *Vérification de réseau d'automates finis par equivalence observationnelle: le système AUTO*. PhD thesis, Université de Nice, 1987.

Towards A Verification Technique for Large Synchronous Circuits

Prabhat Jain,   Prabhakar Kudva,   and Ganesh Gopalakrishnan

Department of Computer Science,
University of Utah,
Salt Lake City, UT 84112

Abstract. We present a symbolic simulation based verification approach which can be applied to large synchronous circuits. A new technique to encode the state and input constraints as *parametric Boolean expressions* over the state and input variables is used to make our symbolic simulation based verification approach efficient. The constraints which are encoded through parametric Boolean expressions can involve the Boolean connectives $(\cdot, +, \neg)$, the relational operators $(<, \leq, >, \geq, \neq, =)$, and logical connectives $(\wedge, \vee)$. This technique of using parametric Boolean expressions vastly reduces the number of symbolic simulation vectors and the time for verification. Our verification approach can also be applied for efficient modular verification of large designs; the technique used is to verify each constituent sub-module separately, however in the context of the overall design. Since regular arrays are part of many large designs, we have developed an approach for the verification of regular arrays which combines formal verification at the high level and symbolic simulation at the low level(e.g., switch-level). We show the verification of a circuit called *Minmax*, a pipelined cache memory system, and an LRU array implementation of the least recently used block replacement policy, to illustrate our verification approach. The experimental results are obtained using the COSMOS symbolic simulator.

1 Introduction

Most digital VLSI circuits are checked for correct operation through *scalar valued simulation*. In this approach, *scalar* bit vectors—vectors over 0 and 1—are used as inputs to the circuit being simulated. As most real-world circuits require an impracticably large number of scalar vectors to check for all possible execution paths, scalar simulation alone is insufficient to verify a digital VLSI circuit.

Several formal verification approaches have been suggested for the verification of digital VLSI circuits. But, current formal hardware verification approaches cannot accurately model low-level circuit details (e.g., charge sharing). On the other hand, formal verification at the high level can provide useful information (e.g., circuit state invariants) for efficient symbolic simulation at the low level, in addition to its other advantages. Since the simulators (e.g., switch-level) can model low-level circuit details accurately, an approach combining the capabilities of formal verification at the high level and symbolic simulation at the low-level can derive the advantages of both the approaches.

Bryant has proposed *symbolic* switch-level simulation for formal hardware verification [4]. In [4, 1], it is shown that a symbolic simulator can be used to *verify* (check for all possible execution paths) many non-trivial circuits. His verification approach has been applied to verify a static RAM, data paths, and pipelined circuits [5, 6, 7]. Our verification approach for datapath and control circuits is based on a simple hardware specification formalism called HOP [9], a parallel composition algorithm called PARCOMP, and a switch-level simulator(COSMOS). In the past, we have studied the problem of generating minimally instantiated symbolic simulation vectors for non-regular designs, and also developed techniques to integrate the formal verification phase with the symbolic simulation phase. The combination of formal verification at the high-level and symbolic simulation based verification at the low-level has been proposed in [11, 14]. We have obtained encouraging results in this regard [11, 13, 12].

In order to reduce the symbolic simulation effort, a new technique to encode the state and input constraints as parametric Boolean expressions on the state and input variables is incorporated in our verification approach. This technique of using parametric Boolean expressions vastly reduces the number of symbolic simulation vectors and the time for verification, and thus makes our verification approach applicable to large synchronous circuits. Parametric forms have also been used in [2, 8] for the verification of finite state machines.

Our verification approach can be applied for efficient modular verification of large designs. Parametric Boolean expressions can be used to encode the input and state constraints of the sub-modules of the design. Each sub-module is individually verified. When verifying a sub-module, it is assumed that its context operates correctly, and so the inputs expected by the sub-module are derived directly from the input constraints of the sub-module. (The input constraints of each sub-module are typically known to the designer (*e.g.* a certain internal bus carries only unary values), and can be proved to be a consequence of the design, during high level verification.) The outputs of the sub-module being verified are not isolated from its context, and so the sub-module being verified is subject to the true electrical loadings.

Since regular arrays are part of many large designs, we have developed an approach for the verification of regular arrays which combines formal verification at the high level and symbolic simulation at the low level(e.g., switch-level). The verification approach is based on a simple hardware specification formalism called HOP, a parallel composition algorithm for regular arrays called PCA, and a switch-level symbolic simulator(COSMOS). We illustrate our verification approach on the Least Recently Used(LRU) page replacement policy implemented as a two-dimensional array of LRU cells in VLSI.

1.1 Outline of the Paper

In the following section, we present the basic idea of parametric Boolean expressions and the encoding of the state and input constraints as parametric Boolean expressions. In Section 3, 4, and 5 we present our symbolic simulation based verification approach and the use of parametric Boolean expressions through examples. In Section 3, we show the verification of a circuit called *Minmax*. In Section 4, we show the verification of a pipelined cache memory system. In Section 5, we present our verification approach for regular arrays using an LRU array as an example. In Section 6, we summarize the results, report the ongoing effort, and outline the future work.

2 Parametric Boolean Expressions

We explain the idea of parametric Boolean expressions with the help of an example. Suppose a circuit with four inputs $in1$, $in2$, $in3$, and $in4$ has to obey the constraint that exactly one of these inputs be a 1. This constraint is captured by the sum of products formula:

$$(in1 \wedge \neg in2 \wedge \neg in3 \wedge \neg in4) \vee (\neg in1 \wedge in2 \wedge \neg in3 \wedge \neg in4) \vee$$
$$(\neg in1 \wedge \neg in2 \wedge in3 \wedge \neg in4) \vee (\neg in1 \wedge \neg in2 \wedge \neg in3 \wedge in4) \tag{1}$$

Alternatively, this constraint is also captured by the formula:

$$= \exists b1\, b2\, .\, ((in1 = b1 \wedge b2) \wedge (in2 = b1 \wedge \neg b2) \wedge$$
$$(in3 = \neg b1 \wedge b2) \wedge (in4 = \neg b1 \wedge \neg b2)) \tag{2}$$

Formula 2 is logically equivalent to formula 1. However, formula 2 has the following advantage: the inputs $in1$ through $in4$ are expressed directly in terms of *parametric expressions* over *parametric variables* $b1$ and $b2$. These parametric expressions cover all possible values of $in1$ through $in4$ which satisfy the required constraint. Each permissible combination of $in1$ through $in4$ is obtained by every value assignment to the parametric variables. By applying the parametric expressions directly through input ports $in1$ through $in4$ during symbolic simulation, one symbolic simulation vector is tantamount to simulating the desired combinations of $in1$ through $in4$ separately. Thus, the parametric form of input constraints can be seen to effect a trade-off between the number of symbolic simulation vectors (which goes down exponentially) and the number of extra variables in symbolic input vectors (which goes up only by a logarithmic value, at worst). We find that this trade-off can reduce the symbolic simulation time significantly.

Many automatic ways to obtain the parametric form are well known, e.g., Boole's and Löewenheim's procedures [3]. We have improved these standard procedures in a number of ways. Some details are provided in section 6. In the rest of the paper, we focus on the applications of the parametric form, and not on procedures for obtaining them *per se*.

Constraints on the State and Input Vectors

In many situations, it is convenient to express the constraints of a circuit as a Boolean expression on the state and/or input bit-vectors. For example, a set-associative cache would require all the tags (bit-vectors) in a set to be different

($\neq$) for its correct operation. Here we consider the constraints which may involve relational operators ($<, \leq, >, \geq, \neq, =$) and logical connectives ($\wedge, \vee$). These constraints on the bit-vectors can also be expressed as Boolean expressions containing individual bit-variables of the bit-vectors, and parametric Boolean expressions can be obtained for these individual bit-variables. However, the direct generation of parametric Boolean expressions for bit-vectors, taking advantage of the recursive nature of the relations on the bit-vectors (*e.g.* $\neq$ on an N bit vector can be expressed using the *xor* function and $\neq$ on an $N - 1$ bit vector) would be computationally more efficient. Moreover, symbolic simulation is more efficient using the vectors generated by taking advantage of the recursive nature of the relations on the bit-vectors.

$$a_3 = x_{ab} \cdot y_{ab} + p_3 \qquad b_3 = (\overline{x_{ab}} + \overline{y_{ab}}) \cdot p_3$$
$$a_2 = x_{ab} \cdot \overline{y_{ab}} + p_2 \qquad b_2 = x_{ab} \cdot y_{ab} \cdot q_2 + \overline{x_{ab}} \cdot p_2$$
$$a_1 = \overline{x_{ab}} \cdot y_{ab} + p_1 \qquad b_1 = x_{ab} \cdot q_1 + \overline{x_{ab}} \cdot \overline{y_{ab}} \cdot p_1$$
$$a_0 = \overline{x_{ab}} \cdot \overline{y_{ab}} + p_0 \qquad b_0 = (x_{ab} + y_{ab}) \cdot q_0$$

Fig. 1. Parametric Boolean Expressions for $A : [a_3, a_2, a_1, a_0] > B : [b_3, b_2, b_1, b_0]$

To illustrate the generation of parametric Boolean expressions for the constraints involving bit-vectors, consider two 4-bit vectors $A : [a_3, a_2, a_1, a_0]$ and $B : [b_3, b_2, b_1, b_0]$ and the constraint $A > B$. The parametric Boolean expressions for the bit-variables of these two vectors are shown in Figure 1. The instantiations of these variables result in minimally instantiated symbolic A and B vectors which satisfy the constraint $A > B$. For example, with $x_{ab} = 0$ and $y_{ab} = 1$, we obtain $A : [p_3, p_2, 1, p_0]$ and $B : [p_3, p_2, 0, q_0]$. We call x_{ab} and y_{ab} *control parametric variables* and $p_i (0 \leq i \leq 3)$ and $q_j (0 \leq j \leq 2)$ parametric Boolean variables.

Boolean expressions on bit-vectors containing the logical connectives $\wedge$ and $\vee$ can be first simplified into a disjunction of conjunctive-forms (or "cubes"). Then, the parametric Boolean expressions for each conjunctive-form can be obtained and combined to get the parametric Boolean expression for the given Boolean expression. The parametric Boolean expressions can be obtained using a Boolean equation solving procedure [3, 8], but we are working on automating the generation of the parametric Boolean expressions for bit-vectors, taking advantage of the recursive nature of the relations on the bit-vectors.

3 Verification of *Minmax*

In this section, we take a simple example that was also studied in [11]. *Minmax* (Figure 2) [15] has three registers, MAXI, MINI, and LASTIN. It implements five operations, Iclr_en, Iclr_dis, Idis, Ireset, and Ien. Here, we consider Ien

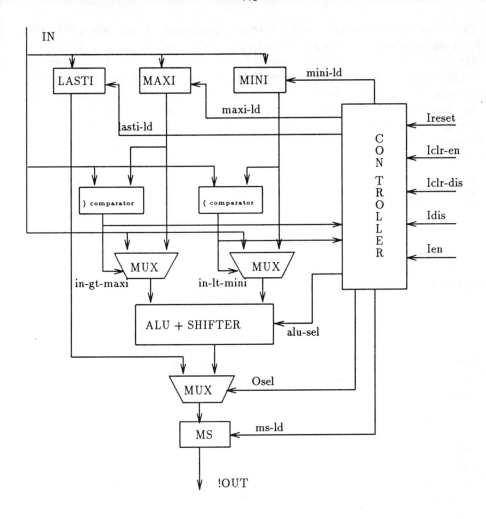

Fig. 2. Schematic of *Minmax*

operation which reads the current input, updates **MAXI** and **MINI**, with the (running) maximum value so far and the minimum value so far respectively. It also causes an output equal to the average of the max-so-far and min-so-far to be produced on the output port !**OUT**. A formal verification of *Minmax* was carried out using algebraic/equational reasoning techniques [10].

3.1 Verification with Minimally Instantiated Symbolic Vectors

Since every circuit requires some state and/or input constraints to be obeyed for its correct operation, one needs to instantiate the symbolic state and input vectors to the right degree so that the state and/or input constraints of the circuit are satisfied in the symbolic simulation based verification of that circuit. We refer to these vectors as *minimally instantiated symbolic simulation vectors*. In [11], we approached the verification of *Minmax* by enumerating minimally instantiated symbolic simulation vectors; we used Prolog to generate the minimally instantiated symbolic vectors for *Minmax*. We generated symbolic simulation vectors for each condition of a data dependent conditional branch, augmented with the circuit invariant MINI $\leq$ MAXI. Some of the sixteen vectors generated, for the case IN > MAXI (also taking the circuit invariant MINI $\leq$ MAXI into account) are now listed:

```
MINI`0  = [0,0,MINI1,MINI0],  IN`0  = [1,IN2,IN1,IN0],  MAXI`0  = [0,1,MAXI1,MAXI0]
MINI`1  = [0,MINI2,0,MINI0],  IN`1  = [1,IN2,IN1,IN0],  MAXI`1  = [0,MINI2,1,MAXI0]
MINI`2  = [0,MINI2,MINI1,0],  IN`2  = [1,IN2,IN1,IN0],  MAXI`2  = [0,MINI2,MINI1,1]
...
MINI`15 = [IN3,IN2,IN1,0],     IN`15 = [IN3,IN2,IN1,1],  MAXI`15 = [IN3,IN2,IN1,0]
```

Here, MINI_i represents the ith vector to be loaded into the register MINI, and so on for the other vectors. Verification time using this approach, for the cases (IN > MAXI) and (MINI $\leq$ IN $\leq$ MAXI), are listed in Figure 5 under the circuit name **Minmax4** and the column "minimal instantiation"(this does not include the time required to generate the minimally instantiated symbolic vectors).

3.2 Verification with Parametric Boolean Expressions

Verification of the *Minmax* circuit for the **Ien** operation required the verification of three transitions whose state and input constraints were: IN < MINI $\leq$ MAXI, MINI $\leq$ IN $\leq$ MAXI, and MINI $\leq$ MAXI < IN. We generated parametric Boolean expressions for the state and input vectors satisfying these three constraints to verify the three transitions for **Ien** operation of the *Minmax* circuit, using the technique outlined in Section 2. The use of parametric Boolean expressions for the verification of *Minmax* reduced the number of symbolic simulation vectors to 1 for each of the three constraints mentioned above and it also reduced the verification time significantly. The verification time for *Minmax* using this approach is listed in Figure 5 under the column "Parametric Expressions"(this does not include the time required to generate the parametric Boolean expressions).

4 Verification of A Pipelined Cache Memory System

In this section we consider the verification of a pipelined cache memory system to illustrate our technique to verify large designs.

4.1 A Pipelined Cache Memory System

The pipelined cache memory considered here has a 2-way set-associative cache with 4 sets in the cache. The size of a block in each set is one byte and the tag associated with each block is 3 bits. A set is selected by the two higher-order bits of the Read/Write address.

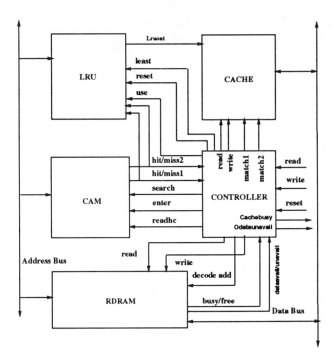

Fig. 3. The Pipelined Cache Memory System

The least recently used(LRU) block replacement policy is used for the cache miss on a Read or Write operation. Since each set has only two blocks, the LRU policy is implemented by one flip-flop for each set; output of the flip-flop indicates the least recently used block in the corresponding set. For higher set sizes, an LRU array would be used to implement the LRU block replacement policy. Verification of regular arrays, with LRU array as an example, is discussed in Section 5.1.

The main memory is updated using the write-through policy (i.e., for a Write operation, the data is written into the main memory and the cache at the same time). Since it takes more time to write the data into the main memory than into the cache for a Write operation, pipelining can be achieved by allowing more operations on the cache, while the data is being written into the main memory. In our pipelined cache system design, pipelining is achieved by allowing one or two Read operations (two Read operations, if the first Read operation following the Write operation results in a hit in the cache), while the data is being written into the main memory for a Write operation.

The block diagram of the pipelined cache memory system is shown in Figure 3. The pipelined cache system design consists of four main modules, as shown in Figure 3. The CACHE module stores the data part of all the blocks in the cache. The LRU module contains the data storage and the logic necessary to implement the LRU block replacement policy. The CAM module stores the tag part of the addresses currently in the cache. It also contains the logic necessary to implement set selection and parallel search for the tag part of the address of a Read/Write operation. The CONTROLLER module controls the operation of the pipelined cache memory system. This pipelined cache memory system was implemented on a Tiny Chip (about 5,700 transistors) and the simulation files necessary for switch-level symbolic simulation in COSMOS were derived from the NET description of the design.

4.2 Verification Using Parametric Boolean Expressions

Symbolic simulation cannot be naively applied to verify the entire cache memory system. For example, if symbolic vectors are applied as the address inputs and the memory is asked to Read, all the locations covered by the symbolic address are "simultaneously read"; this can cause conflicting drives of values on the data output. Therefore, we resort to the technique of separately verifying the sub-modules of the cache memory. Specifically, the following sub-modules have to be separately verified: (a) the CACHE; (b) the DRAM; and (c) all remaining units treated as the third submodule. Notice that the DRAM and the CACHE modules of the pipelined cache memory system can be separately verified using the switch-level verification techniques outlined in [5].

To verify the pipelined cache memory system, we wrote the behavioral and structural description for the design in HOP. The inferred behavior of the design from the structural description by PARCOMP was used to determine the Read/Write operation sequences necessary to verify the pipelined cache memory system. Since our example cache memory system is pipelined, it is necessary to verify its operation over the sequences of Reads and Writes listed in the middle of Figure 5. Verification is separately carried out for each of these Read/Write sequences. For a particular sequence, the tags in the CAM are initialized to symbolic expressions that satisfy the CAM *invariant* (i.e., no two tags in a set have the same value). The Read/Write addresses are then set to symbolic expressions that cause the particular scenario (*e.g.* "Write Miss → Read Hit → Read Miss") to manifest.

In our first attempt, we used Prolog to encode the constraint among the tags of the CAM (captured by the CAM invariant) and the constraints on Read/Write addresses required to make each scenario manifest, and ran the Prolog description to generate minimally instantiated symbolic values that satisfied the constraints. An impracticably large number of symbolic vectors were obtained (e.g., the operation sequence Write Miss → Read Hit → Read Hit resulted in 191232 symbolic vectors).

We then explored the idea of using parametric Boolean expressions by generating the tags in the CAM and the Read/Write addresses satisfying the constraints as described above. The constraints involved the $\neq$ relation and the logical connective $\wedge$. The use of parametric Boolean expressions reduced the number of symbolic vectors required for verification to *one* for all the Read/Write operation sequences beginning with a Write Hit operation and to *eight* for rest of the Read/Write operation sequences beginning with a Write Miss operation. The reason why eight symbolic vectors were required for each Read/Write operation sequence beginning with a Write Miss operation is the following: since a Write Miss operation would write the address tag in the CAM and the data in the CACHE, the set part of the Write address and the LRU value for the corresponding set were required to be instantiated to scalar values; there are four possible sets, and for each set, there are two possible LRU values. The symbolic simulation and verification times required for all the Read/Write operation sequences are shown in Figure 5.

We verified the pipelined cache memory system by supplying (using the `freeze` command in COSMOS symbolic simulator) the expected inputs from the DRAM and the CACHE module during the symbolic simulation of the Read/Write operation sequences, assuming that the DRAM and CACHE operate correctly.

4.3 Verification of Large Cache Sizes

We believe that the technique of using parametric Boolean expressions can be applied for the verification of large cache sizes. If the number of symbolic variables which can be used in the COSMOS symbolic simulator is a limitation for the verification of large cache sizes, the technique of using parametric Boolean expressions can be applied in the following way. The set part of the Write operation's address in an operation sequence can be instantiated to the scalar value and the tags of CAM for the sets in which addresses of the Read/Write operation sequence map to can be initialized to contain the parametric Boolean expressions satisfying the required constraints; the tags in all the other sets can be kept to the unknown value X. This would reduce the number of symbolic variables required in the verification of an operation sequence, but would increase the number of symbolic vectors required in the verification of the operation sequence. The number of symbolic vectors required would be proportional to the number of sets in the cache.

5 Verification of Regular Arrays

Regular arrays form an important class of VLSI circuit designs, and with regular array designs being employed in numerous applications, the verification of regular arrays becomes an important step in their design and implementation as VLSI circuits. Also, it is important to develop efficient ways to handle state and input constraints for the verification of regular arrays, because many regular arrays are designed to operate under input constraints (*e.g.*, "inputs must be unary"). In this section, we show our verification approach for regular arrays and show the application of parametric Boolean expressions in the verification of regular arrays. The hardware implementation of LRU page replacement policy

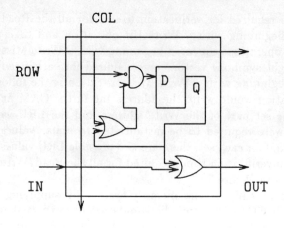

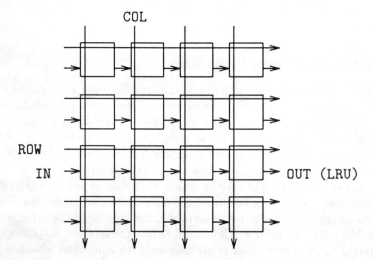

Algorithm: Set row; reset col; find row with all zeros

Fig. 4. LRU Cell and its HOP state diagram; LRU Array

which we consider here maintains an array of $n \times n$ bits, initially all zeros, for a machine with n page frames. Whenever page k is referenced, the hardware sets all the bits of the row k to 1 and sets all the bits of the column k to 0. At any instant, the row with all bits set to 0 indicates the least recently used row, hence the least recently used page frame.

5.1 The LRU Array

The LRU array is realized as a two-dimensional regular array of LRU cells. Each LRU cell of the regular array consists of a state bit which can be set to 1 by keeping the ROW input to 1 and COL input to 0; the state bit can be set to 0 by keeping the COL input to 1. On rising edge of the clock, the state bit of the LRU cell is set to 0 or 1 depending upon ROW and COL inputs. On falling edge of the clock, the output OUT is computed as logical OR of IN input of the cell (which is OUT output of the previous cell) and the state bit of the LRU cell. The output of each row is logical OR of the state bits of the LRU cells in the row.

The functionality of an LRU cell is shown in Figure 4(a). A 4×4 LRU array is shown in Figure 4(c). The operation of the LRU array relies on the input constraint that only the ith $(0 \leq i \leq 3)$ ROW bit and the ith COL bit are 1, when page i is referenced.

The LRU array implementation of the LRU policy is verified at two levels. At the first level, the LRU regular array behavior determined by PCA (a parallel composition algorithm for regular arrays) is verified against the abstract specification of the LRU array algorithm. The formal verification at this level is based on the homomorphism relation between states of the inferred behavior and the states of the abstract specification. We are skipping the details of this proof in this paper.

At the second level, the transistor level implementation of the LRU array corresponding to the structural description in HOP is verified against the behavior inferred by PCA. However, the PCA-inferred behavior cannot directly be used as the reference specification because PCA does not take into account the input constraints. Therefore, we first obtain the PCA-inferred behavior and then substitute into it the input and initial state values applied during the transistor level symbolic simulation; *this* forms the reference specification.

5.2   Verification with Parametric Boolean Expressions at the Inputs

The LRU array was verified for all combinations of row and column input values, which satisfied the input constraint for the LRU array. Each cell in the LRU array was initialized to a distinct symbolic variable, to verify the LRU array for all possible state values. (this is possible as the LRU array does not have any non-trivial circuit invariants.) We illustrate our technique to handle the input constraint on the 4×4 LRU array, and report the results for higher sizes. We first used *scalar values* on the row and column inputs, satisfying the input constraint, and verified the resulting new state and output values against the expected values. It required four symbolic simulation vectors to verify the 4×4 LRU array.

Then, we encoded the input constraint as parametric Boolean expressions on the row and column inputs, with two parameter Boolean variables $b1$ and $b2$ as described in in Section 2. With the use of this technique, the number of symbolic simulation vectors reduced from *four* to *one*. In general, $\log_2 n$ parametric Boolean variables are required to encode the input constraint of an $n \times n$ LRU array. In the LRU array verification, this technique reduces the number of symbolic simulation vectors to *one*, independent of the size n of the LRU array. Symbolic simulation and verification times for various sizes of the LRU array are shown in Figure 5 under "parametric expressions as inputs".

Circuit Name	No. of Transistors	IN > MAXI				MINI ≤ IN ≤ MAXI			
		Minimal Instantiation		Parametric Expressions		Minimal Instantiation		Parametric Expressions	
		No. of Vectors	Total time	No. of Vectors	Total time	No. of Vectors	Total time	No. of Vectors	Total time
Minmax4	1232	16	4.83	1	2.42	21	6.13	1	3.07

Operation Sequence	No. of Vectors	Total time
Write Hit → Read Miss	1	12.40
Write Hit → Read Hit	1	9.58
Write Hit → Read Hit → Read Hit	1	15.0
Write Hit → Read Hit → Read Miss	1	17.90
Write Miss → Read Miss	8	70.65
Write Miss → Read Hit	8	70.0
Write Miss → Read Hit → Read Hit	8	185.75
Write Miss → Read Hit → Read Miss	8	222.03

Circuit Name	No. of Transistors	Scalar Input Values		Parametric Expressions as Inputs	
		No. of Vectors	Total time	No. of Vectors	Total time
LRU 4 × 4	448	4	0.63	1	0.27
LRU 8 × 8	1792	8	6.93	1	2.29
LRU 16 × 16	7168	16	134.63	1	34.68

Fig. 5. Experimental Results[1] for Minmax, LRU array, and Pipelined Cache Memory System

The improvement in the symbolic simulation and verification time, with the use of parametric Boolean expressions, is significant for the large LRU array sizes. We find that the use of parametric Boolean expressions can lead to significant reduction in the number of symbolic vectors and the verification time in the symbolic simulation based verification of regular arrays.

6 Conclusions and Future Work

Symbolic simulation based verification is a powerful approach for the verification of hardware designs, which can complement formal verification using theorem provers. There is considerable incentive to make symbolic simulation based verification scale up to large circuits, as this would provide digital system designers with a familiar tool (a simulator) to verify the designs almost automatically. Results reported in this paper indicate that the symbolic simulation based verification approach can scale up to large circuit sizes in many cases. The main

---

[1] Total user time is shown in seconds.

motivation of our work has been to discover techniques that would help expand the class of circuits, and the circuit sizes that can be verified by the symbolic simulation based verification approach. One of the main observations is that the parametric Boolean expressions can be used in variety of ways for efficient symbolic simulation based verification of large synchronous circuits. Even though the generation of the parametric Boolean expressions can involve some computational effort, the parametric Boolean expressions, once generated, can be re-used during the debugging of the circuit being verified. In all the circuits we have verified, the use of parametric Boolean expressions enhanced the speed of the symbolic simulation process, mainly through a favorable tradeoff between the the number of simulation vectors (which is very much reduced) and the average number of symbolic variables per vector (which goes up only by a small amount).

We have automated our method for the generation of parametric Boolean expressions for the state and input constraints. We have also implemented two known methods, namely, Boole's and Löwenheim's method, to generate parametric Boolean expressions for comparison with our method. The comparison of our method with these methods shows that our method generates smaller parametric Boolean expressions which result in more efficient symbolic simulation. By studying more examples, we hope to get further insight into the technique(s) that would work best for a given example.

References

1. Derek L. Beatty, Randal E. Bryant, and Carl-Johan H.Seger. Synchronous circuit verification by symbolic simulation: An illustration. In *Sixth MIT Conference on Advanced Research in VLSI, 1990*. MIT Press, 1990.
2. Christian Berthet, Olivier Coudert, and Jean-Christophe Madre. New ideas on symbolic manipulations of finite state machines. In *Proceedings of the ICCD, 1990*, pages 224–227, 1990.
3. F. M. Brown. *Boolean Reasoning*. Kluwer Academic Publishers, 1990.
4. Randal E. Bryant. A methodology for hardware verification based on logic simulation. Technical Report CMU-CS-90-122, Computer Science, Carnegie Mellon University, March 1990. *Accepted for publication in the JACM*.
5. Randal E. Bryant. Formal verification of memory circuits by switch-level simulation. *IEEE Transactions on Computer-Aided Design*, 10(1):94–102, January 1991.
6. Randal E. Bryant, Derek L. Beatty, and Carl-Johan H. Seger. Formal hardware verification by symbolic ternary trajectory evaluation. In *Proc. ACM/IEEE 28th Design Automation Conference*, pages 397–402, June 1991.
7. Randal E. Bryant and Carl-Johan H. Seger. Formal verification of digital circuits using ternary system models. Technical Report CMU-CS-90-131, School of Computer Science, Carnegie Mellon University, May 1990. *Also in the Proceedings of the Workshop on Computer-Aided Verification*, Rutgers University, June, 1990.
8. Olivier Coudert, Christian Berthet, and Jean-Christophe Madre. Verification of sequential machines using boolean functional vectors. In *Proceedings of the IMEC-IFIP Workshop on Applied Formal Methods for Correct VLSI Design, Leuven, Belgium*, pages 179–196, November 1989.

122

9. Ganesh Gopalakrishnan. Hop: A formal model for synchronous circuits using communicating fundamental mode symbolic automata. Technical Report UUCS-TR-92-006, Dept. of Computer Science, University of Utah, Salt Lake City, UT 84112, 1992. Submitted to "Formal Methods in System Design".

10. Ganesh Gopalakrishnan and Prabhat Jain. A practical approach to synchronous hardware verification. In *Proc. VLSI Design '91: The Fourth CSI/IEEE International Symposium on VLSI Design, New Delhi, India,* January 1991.

11. Ganesh Gopalakrishnan, Prabhat Jain, Venkatesh Akella, Luli Josephson, and Wen-Yan Kuo. Combining verification and simulation. In Carlo Sequin, editor, *Advanced Research in VLSI : Proceedings of the 1991 University of California Santa Cruz Conference.* The MIT Press, 1991. *ISBN 0-262-19308-6.*

12. Prabhat Jain and Ganesh Gopalakrishnan. Some techniques for efficient symbolic simulation based verification. Technical Report UUCS-TR-91-023, University of Utah, Department of Computer Science, October 1991.

13. Prabhat Jain, Ganesh Gopalakrishnan, and Prabhakar Kudva. Verification of regular arrays by symbolic simulation. Technical Report UUCS-TR-91-022, University of Utah, Department of Computer Science, October 1991.

14. Carl-Johan H. Seger and Jeffrey Joyce. A two-level formal verification methodology using HOL and COSMOS. Technical Report 91-10, Dept. of Computer Science, University of British Columbia, Vancouver, B.C., June 1991.

15. D. Verkest and L. Claesen. The minmax system benchmark, November 1989.

Verifying Timed Behavior Automata with Nonbinary Delay Constraints*

David K. Probst and Hon F. Li
Department of Computer Science
Concordia University
1455 de Maisonneuve Blvd. West
Montreal, Quebec H3G 1M8

Abstract. Timed behavior automata allow surprisingly efficient model checking of delay-constrained reactive systems when partial-order methods for delay-insensitive systems are adapted for real time. The complexity of timing verification is a sensitive function of the precise abstraction of real time used in the model. Untimed behavior automata [14] are modified in two ways: (i) process output actions are performed inside a timing window relative to the holding of their presets, and (ii) acknowledgment of process input actions is replaced by observing minimum delays between old and new inputs. We prove timing-window bounds on system responses, and show that system inputs do not arrive too fast. Since non-singleton presets are common, we develop a semantics to reason about nonbinary delay constraints. Model checking starts by coupling specification mirror to implementation network; in timed systems, questions of graph connectivity become questions of constraint graph satisfaction that are computed by optimized linear-time shortest-path algorithms. In the generalized TBA model, nondeterministic input choice is process-scheduled testing of an environment-controlled state predicate; the generalized model, which focuses on mixed-type critical races, is deferred.

1 Introduction

There is widespread interest in real-time reactive systems, such as control and communication systems and embedded real-time systems. Formal methods for modelling, specifying and reasoning about real-time systems have been proposed [1–5,7–9]. These models and reasoning systems for real time have thrown light on problem complexity (including decidability), verification efficiency and modelling expressiveness in many instances. Given the perceived complexity of real-time model checking, we show how restrictions on powerful models permit tractable (polynomial-time) automatic verification of finite-state real-time systems. We adapt partial-order methods [12–14] for verifying asynchronous reactive systems with acknowledgment protocols to real-time reactive systems. We alter the model

* This research was supported in part by the Natural Sciences and Engineering Research Council of Canada under grants A3363, A0921 and MEF0040121. E-mail: probst@crim.ca and probst@vlsi.concordia.ca.

of untimed behavior automata by introducing minimum and maximum delays in the scheduling of enabled actions, and using special "concentrators" to allow nonbinary maximum-delay constraints, such as the bounded-response property $c \leq \max\{a, b\} + 4$, to be verified efficiently by simple shortest-path algorithms in graphs.

One way to find an efficient model-checking algorithm for real-time systems is to find a factorization of the real-time enabling relation into: (i) one part that is the causality relation of an untimed system, and (ii) another part in which delay bounds are additional (scheduling) constraints. Actions can then be generated without the need to advance clocks. Factorization is simplest when delay bounds simulate rather than replace acknowledgment protocols. Precedence constraints in timed systems are enforced by bounded invariance (which quantifies "push-away" causality) and bounded response (which quantifies "pull-back" weak fairness). A given timing constraint is enforced by: (i) pure bounded invariance, (ii) pure bounded response, or (iii) both. These concepts will be made precise after we have defined push-away and pull-back arrows—for both process *and* environment—and their semantics. In powerful models, even the reachability problem of deciding whether a given configuration appears on one of the real-time trajectories of a timed system is PSPACE-complete [4]. We choose formal models that are only as powerful as the properties that need to be proved.

The branching structure in timed behavior automata can model how delay bounds affect the resolution of nondeterministic choice. A model that cannot capture the interplay between delay bounds and nondeterminism is unsatisfactory. In generalized TBA, the interesting differences between the timed and untimed enabling relations (essentially, timeout and exception handling) are put into the conflict-resolution part of the timed behavior automaton, which then models both same-type nondeterministic choice and mixed-type critical races. While process-controlled delay constraints are natural extensions of a causality relation with weak fairness, nondeterministic properties of real-time systems such as timeout and exception handling should be modelled as branching (nondeterministic choice) whose outcome is determined by critical races between tests and conditions. These races are affected by changes to delay bounds on scheduling. In this paper, we take the branching and recurrence structure of behavior automata for granted, and focus on efficient model checking of nonbinary pull-back constraints, for which we propose a new, "disjunctive-path" semantics.

Previous work on delay insensitivity has been extended to delay-constrained reactive systems [15]. Here, we build a more general reasoning system for delays, assuming some familiarity with [14]. The following features of untimed behavior automata are retained in timed versions: (i) a finite partial-order representation that explicitly distinguishes concurrency, choice and recurrence, and (ii) a state encoding that is causality comprehensive (includes all causality) and state minimal (has fewest states). *Pace* Lamport [1], time does not appear in TBA state encodings of timed systems, avoiding additional state explosion.

2 Abstract Specification of Delay-Constrained Reactive Systems

Abstract specifications refer to externally-visible computational behaviors. An untimed behavior automaton specifies a set of (zero-valued) minimum-delay precedence constraints with implicit weak fairness [12–14]. Here, (i) no event may occur until its preset holds, and (ii) once enabled, an output event must occur eventually. A timed behavior automaton specifies two disjoint sets of minimum-delay and maximum-delay precedence constraints, called **push-away** and **pull-back** constraints. Here, (i) no event may occur until its preset has held continuously for a minimum delay, and (ii) once enabled, an output event must occur before its preset has held continuously for a maximum delay. Untimed behaviors are obtained from timed behaviors by relaxing all timing windows of the form $\langle \min, \max \rangle$ to $\langle 0, \infty \rangle$. In real-time systems, we say that an action is **enabled** as soon as its preset holds, but may not occur unless it is **scheduled**.

In the simple TBA model, an output action remains scheduled during a timing window relative to its enabling, while an input action remains scheduled until it occurs; in the generalized model, input actions also have timing windows and output actions may be (briefly) disrupted inside their timing window. We distinguish safety and liveness properties in the untimed system, and view delay bounds as additional (scheduling) constraints. If each precedence constraint in the timed system is enforced by pure bounded invariance or pure bounded response, then correctness of the untimed system is a precondition for correctness of the timed system. For a timed system to be correct, the timing constraint graph produced by coupling specification mirror mP to implementation network *Net* must be feasible. Feasibility verifies precedence constraints with either "pure" or "mixed" support.

A process P has disjoint sets of input and output ports. In the generalized model, ports are the loci of generalized control elements such as tests and conditions. An unrolled timed behavior automaton is an infinite delay-constrained pomtree, which is like a computation tree except that arcs are finite weighted directed graphs, and vertices are branch points that correspond to nondeterministic choice. Process behaviors result from use of process P by P's environment. In the simple TBA model, P's input actions are under the control of P's environment, while P's output actions are under the control of P. In the generalized model, an input action is process-scheduled testing of an environment-controlled state predicate. Critical races occur when P tests a condition whose value is determined by P's environment.

Safety properties constrain both the process and its environment. A safety violation is the performance of an action that is either not enabled or not yet scheduled. A process receiving unsafe input logically fails. In simple TBA, **liveness properties** only constrain the process. A liveness (progress) violation is the non-performance of an enabled output action before the expiration of its scheduling window or — a fortiori — indefinitely. By simple convention, we view push-away (resp., pull-back) constraints as safety (resp., liveness) properties.

2.1 Untimed Behavior Automata

Untimed behavior automata are constructed in three phases; these machines are succinct encodings of infinite sets of infinite pomsets [11,12]. First, there is a "small" deterministic finite-state machine D that expresses the branching and recurrence structure of the process. Second, there is an expansion of each transition of dfsm D into an (unlabelled) finite poset, with (leading) sockets to define nonsequential concatenation. Third, there is a nonnumeric labelling of all successor arrows in posets to define the process state encoding.

We sketch the formal definition of behavior automaton. Given disjoint alphabets Act (process actions), Arr (successor arrow labels), Com (dfsm D transitions) and Soc (sockets), define Pos as the set of finite labelled posets over Act $\cup$ Soc. Each member of Pos is a labelled poset (B,Γ,ν), where (i) Γ is a partial order over $B \subseteq$ Act $\cup$ Soc, and (ii) $\nu : \Omega \to$ Arr assigns a label to each element in the successor relation Ω (the transitive reduction of Γ). A behavior automaton is a 3-tuple (D,ξ,ψ), where (i) D is a dfsm over Com, (ii) ξ: Com $\to$ Pos maps dfsm transitions to labelled posets, and (iii) ψ: Soc $\to$ powerset(Act) maps sockets to sets of process actions. ψ defines which process actions may fill a socket when a command is concatenated to a sequence of earlier commands. There is an imaginary reset action •. In timed behavior automata, unlabelled posets are replaced by weighted directed graphs whose push-away and pull-back projections are acyclic. Pull-back assertions are interpreted disjunctively when they pull back to nonsingleton presets.

3 Timed Behavior Automata

Figure 1 shows an untimed behavior automaton for a C-element, where the state encoding is provided by nonnumeric labels on successor arrows. Each solid or dashed arrow in Figure 1 is a causality constraint implicitly labelled with a lower bound of 0 time units on the delay; $a \to b$ means that action b may not be performed until at least 0 units after action a. When the state contains $n1$, the environment may perform action a^+, removing $n1$ and adding $n3$. When the state contains $n3$ and $n4$, the process may (in fact must, because of the bracket) perform action $\underline{c}^+$, removing $n3$ and $n4$ and adding $n5$ and $n6$. In both timed and untimed cases, asymmetry of control between process and environment is fundamental. A bracket signifies that incoming arrows are implicitly labelled with an upper bound of ∞ time units on the delay (solid arrows incident to bracketed actions are both zero-valued push-away and "maximally-loose" pull-back constraints). In the untimed case, the lower bounds of zero are strict, and ∞ denotes "finite but unbounded". The solid push-away arrows model input/output causality, while the *implicit* solid pull-back arrows model input/output weak fairness. The dashed push-away arrows model the (output/input) acknowledgment protocol. We propose conservative real-time extensions to the interprocess assumption protocol (given by the dashed arrows) and the intraprocess guarantee protocol (given by the solid arrows). We achieve modelling expressiveness without sacrificing verification efficiency; by analogy to the untimed case, we define real-time correctness as a simple relation on the infinite weighted directed graph produced by coupling mirror mP to implementation *Net*.

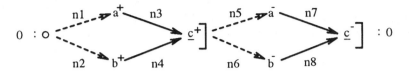

Fig. 1. Untimed behaviour automaton for a C-element

Figure 2 shows an unlabelled half-timed behavior automaton for a wire, with a real-time extension to the intraprocess protocol. Figure 2 specifies that the wire must remain unstable (after being excited by an *a* action) for at least 2 units, but not longer than 5 units, before responding with a *b* action. We say that: *a* enables *b*, and *b* remains scheduled during the timing window $\langle 2, 5 \rangle$ relative to *a*. To encode this, we could label each $a \rightarrow b$ with the interval $\langle 2, 5 \rangle$ specifying a minimum and maximum delay, or we could use a pair of "matched" arrows: a push-away (bounded-invariance) arrow $a \rightarrow b$ labelled with $+2$, and a pull-back (bounded-response) arrow $a \leftarrow b$ labelled with -5 (upper bounds are expressed as negative lower bounds in the opposite direction) [3]. Formally, both push-away and pull-back arrows in constraint graphs are minimum-delay constraints. Each minimum-delay arrow is explicitly labelled as a push-away or a pull-back; these labels are used by the model-checking algorithm to achieve greater verification efficiency. The triangle inequality (transitivity rule) in constraint graphs is now as follows: to derive a timing label *t* on an arbitrary $a \rightarrow b$, find all directed paths from *a* to *b*, and compute the sum of minimum delays along each path; if there are distinct sums, then take the maximum.

$$0 \; : \; \circ \dashrightarrow^{+0} a^+ \underset{-5}{\overset{+2}{\rightleftarrows}} b^+ \Big] \dashrightarrow^{+0} a^- \underset{-5}{\overset{+2}{\rightleftarrows}} b^- \Big] \; : \; 0$$

Fig. 2. Half-timed behavior automaton for a wire

As illustrated in Figure 3, we use a different semantics for pull-back arrows. This is physically reasonable and leads to superior verification algorithms. In Figure 3(a), the push-away arrows from *d* and *e* to *f* indicate that $\{d, e\}$ is the preset of *f*. Although *d* and *e* are asynchronous, we assume that these minimum delays can be enforced by the process. The semantics of the pull-back arrows is different. If *d* occurs later than *e*, then the lower bound of -5 on the delay from *f* to *e* does not hold. The bound holds only when *e* occurs last. For this reason, we adopt a "disjunctive-path" semantics, as shown in Figure 3(b). Every pull-back constraint is specified relative to the holding of a preset (pseudoaction ξ is the last of *d* and *e*). Let pre(c) be the preset of c. A pull-back of $-u$ to pre(c) means that $\underline{c}$ is performed by the process no later than u units after the last action in pre($\underline{c}$). Let β be the last of a and b. Then β is a or b, and a pull-back to β is a pull-back to a or b. With this semantics, there is no minimum delay from $\underline{f}$ to d or e. Rather, pull-backs to these actions are specified disjunctively: either $d - \underline{f} \geq -6$ or $e - \underline{f} \geq -6$. We say that pull-back arrows $d \leftarrow \underline{f}$ and $e \leftarrow \underline{f}$ form a complete disjunctive set in the sense that at least one of their assertions must be true.

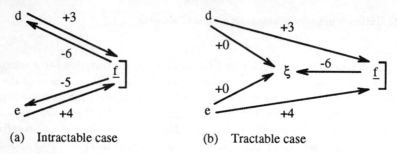

(a) Intractable case   (b) Tractable case

Fig. 3. Two temporal structures of unequal verification complexity

Figure 4 shows a timed behavior automaton for a "real-time" C-element. It illustrates conservative real-time extensions to both interprocess and intraprocess protocols, and includes nonbinary delay constraints. Let $\beta = \max\{a, b\}$ and $\alpha = \min\{a, b\}$, where actions are identified with the real times at which they occur. The pseudoaction β (resp., α) occurs when the last of (resp., first of) a and b occurs. Action $\underline{c}$ remains scheduled during a timing window relative to β, while α remains scheduled until it occurs. In Figure 4, $\psi(\circ) = \{\bullet, \alpha\}$, so α may fill $\circ$. We draw special push-away arrows with timing label $+0$ between presets and their maxima and minima; these constraints are enforced, not by process or environment, but by arithmetic (i.e., the definitions of minimum and maximum). For the purposes of applying the triangle inequality, special push-away arrows in the appropriate context may be read as zero-valued pull-back or push-away arrows in the opposite direction provided their assertions are interpreted disjunctively. In Figure 4, by following directed paths from $\underline{c}$ to a and b, we obtain: either "$a \leftarrow \underline{c}$ with label -4" or "$b \leftarrow \underline{c}$ with label -4". Similarly, there would be a disjunctive push-away $x \rightarrow \circ$ if there were push-aways $x \rightarrow a$ and $x \rightarrow b$. The asymmetry between conjunction and disjunction introduces an asymmetry in the use of the triangle inequality. To derive a timing label t on a pull-back arrow $a \leftarrow b$, find all complete disjunctive sets of directed paths from b to a, and compute the sum of minimum delays along each path; if there are distinct sums in a given disjunctive set, then take the minimum. Repeat this process recursively until only a single conjunctive path (assertion) remains.

Consider the intraprocess guarantee protocol. Figure 4 specifies that process action $\underline{c}$ is performed no earlier than 2 units, and no later than 4 units, after $\beta = \max\{a, b\}$. The use of matched pairs makes it easier to spot inconsistencies.

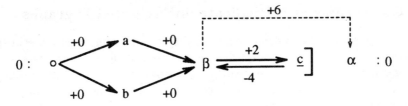

Fig. 4. Timed behavior automaton for a "real-time" C-element

Sockets and pseudoactions are removed by transitive closure. By transitivity, there are push-away arrows from a and b to $\underline{c}$ with timing label $+2$ that hold conjunctively. By definition of β, there are pull-back arrows from $\underline{c}$ to a and b with timing label -4 that hold disjunctively. The intraprocess protocol contains a nonbinary delay constraint; it asserts: $\underline{c} \geq \max\{a, b\} + 2$ and $\underline{c} \leq \max\{a, b\} + 4$.

Consider the interprocess assumption protocol. The environment is required to wait at least 6 units after β (the last of a and b) before performing α (the first of the next a and b). By transitivity, there are push-away arrows from each of the first a and b to each of the next a and b, with timing label $+6$, that hold conjunctively. The interprocess protocol contains a nonbinary delay constraint; it asserts: $\min\{a', b'\} \geq \max\{a, b\} + 6$, where a' and b' are the next a and b. Since socket $\circ$ can be filled by pseudoaction α, we could sum along the chain $\underline{c} \to \beta \to \alpha \to a'$ ($-4+6+0 = 2$) to derive timing label $+2$ on push-away arrow $\underline{c} \to a'$. We intend no use of this logical acknowledgment protocol simulated by delay bounds; we prefer the generality of timed systems that may not even *have* (possibly simulated) acknowledgment protocols.

3.1 Restrictions on Processes

Which delay-constrained reactive systems can be model checked efficiently? We will propose a set of well-behavedness conditions—in another paper—after we have worked out the details of the generalized TBA model, with its mixed-type critical races. Clearly, delay constraints should not obscure the causality relation. For example, a delay constraint between two input actions (if any) should not obscure the fact that they are both members of the same preset. We are comfortable with connectivity analysis in posets, and shortest-path analysis in weighted directed graphs. The significance of the work lies in the efficient checkability of timed behavior automata with rich modelling expressiveness, where automaton branching captures all same-type nondeterministic choice and all mixed-type critical races (that is, all nondeterministic choice) without the state explosion of unfactored powerful real-time models. The clean separation of concurrency and nondeterministic choice may prove to be a precondition of tractable (polynomial-time) model checking of general real-time systems.

4 Correctness as a Predicate on Weighted Digraphs

We define correctness of a delay-constrained system by using mirror mP of specification P as a conceptual implementation tester [6,9]. We form closed real-time system S by linking mirror mP to implementation *Net*. This produces a delay-constrained pomtree of system events containing weighted arrows from all assumption and guarantee protocols; system correctness is defined as a simple relation on this infinite weighted directed graph.

Mirror mP is formed by inverting the type of P's actions and the assumption/guarantee interpretation of P's arrows, turning P's dashed arrows into solid arrows and vice versa. Brackets on mP actions and special arrows are preserved unchanged. Every action that can be performed in S is either a linked (output action, input action) pair or a pseudoaction; some system actions inherit brackets from mP. As a result, we can check whether intraprocess guarantee protocols support interprocess assumption protocols in closed real-time system S. The essence of our model-checking strategy is: (i) whenever a set of solid weighted directed paths from a to b holds conjunctively, we use the triangle inequality; (ii) whenever a set of solid weighted directed paths from a to b holds disjunctively, we use the concentrator lemma. We then check whether these guaranteed solid-path weights support the assumed dashed-path weights.

4.1 Concentrator Lemma

(i) Let $\beta = \max\{A\}$. If $\forall a \in A : \exists\, x \leftarrow a$ with timing label t_a, then $\exists\, x \leftarrow \beta$ with timing label $t = \min\{t_a : a \in A\}$. Proof: Since β is the maximum of A, only the weakest pull-back in $\{x \leftarrow a : a \in A\}$ can be guaranteed to hold for $x \leftarrow \beta$.

(ii) Let $\alpha = \min\{A\}$. If $\forall a \in A : \exists\, x \rightarrow a$ with timing label t_a, then $\exists\, x \rightarrow \alpha$ with timing label $t = \min\{t_a : a \in A\}$. Proof: Since α is the minimum of A, only the weakest push-away in $\{x \rightarrow a : a \in A\}$ can be guaranteed to hold for $x \rightarrow \alpha$.

4.2 Safety Correctness

For each dashed push-away arrow $a \rightarrow b$ with timing label t, there must be a solid directed path from a to b whose weight is at least t. Whenever delay bounds enforce a precedence constraint without simulating an acknowledgment protocol, portions of the solid path will consist of chains of solid pull-back arrows. This correctness condition subsumes safety correctness of the untimed system [14], viz., if there is a dashed push-away arrow $a \rightarrow b$, then there must be a chain of solid push-away arrows from a to b. By allowing pull-backs in the supporting solid chain, we have generalized our notion of underlying untimed system to account for both bounded invariance (causality) and bounded response (weak fairness) as support for precedence constraints in timed systems. One solid path from a to b with enough minimum-delay weight is sufficient to verify a push-away constraint. In general TBA, mixed support may be necessary for dashed push-away and pull-back arrows in interprocess assumption protocols.

4.3 Liveness Correctness

For each dashed pull-back arrow $\beta \leftarrow c$ with timing label t — where c is a bracketed system action and β is $\max\{\text{pre}(c)\}$ — the minimum path weight in the complete disjunctive set of solid directed pull-back paths from c to β must be at least t. This condition presupposes the liveness correctness of the untimed system, viz., the causal preset of c as determined by solid push-away chains must not be a proper superset of the noncausal preset of c as determined by dashed push-away arrows; this implies there is no solid directed path to c from some concurrent mP-attributed system action that is not a member of the noncausal preset. All the solid directed paths in a complete disjunctive set are necessary to verify a pull-back constraint.

We restate this condition without concentrators. Consider the complete disjunctive set of dashed pull-back arrows from a bracketed system action c to each of the members of its noncausal preset $A = \text{pre}(c)$. Each dashed pull-back arrow $a \leftarrow c$, $a \in A$, must be supported by the weakest solid pull-back chain $a \leftarrow c$ in the complete disjunctive set of solid directed pull-back paths from c to a. By well-behavedness, there is only one such disjunctive set for each preset action $a \in A$.

There is an asymmetry between safety and liveness of intraprocess guarantee protocols coming from conjunction and disjunction. The interesting case is interprocess assumption protocols that both (i) have mixed supporting chains of push-away and pull-back arrows, and (ii) determine branching structure in timed behavior automata. In this case, every critical race is between process output actions and process input actions.

5 Model Checking of Real-Time Systems

We enumerate system actions in computations of the untimed system. Consider a nonbracketed system action σ. We step back along single dashed push-away arrows to find each noncausal predecessor τ. We must find a solid directed path $\tau \to \sigma$ whose weight is at least the label t on dashed push-away arrow $\tau \to \sigma$. We repeatedly step back along directed paths of solid push-away arrows until encountering an mP action, recording separate push-away and pull-back weights for each path. The required solid path starts with a pull-back chain leaving τ, continues with an mP push-away arrow, and ends with a push-away chain entering σ. Consider a bracketed system action σ. We step back along single dashed push-away arrows to compute the noncausal preset $\text{pre}(\sigma)$ [14]. We repeatedly step back along directed paths of solid push-away arrows, until encountering an mP action, to compute the causal preset. There is no safety or liveness violation of the untimed system iff the two presets are equal. (For the branching case, see [14]). In this case, consider $\tau \in \text{pre}(\sigma)$. We must find a solid directed push-away path $\tau \to \sigma$ and a complete disjunctive set of solid directed pull-back paths $\tau \leftarrow \sigma$ whose weights are at least the labels t on dashed push-away arrow $\tau \to \sigma$ and dashed pull-back arrow $\tau \leftarrow \sigma$, respectively. To verify a dashed push-away arrow, we step back to mP actions along chains of solid push-away arrows. To verify a dashed pull-back arrow, we step "forward" to mP actions, branching recursively, along disjunctive directed paths of solid pull-back arrows. We explore all solid paths between σ and τ, $\forall \tau \in \text{pre}(\sigma)$, and compute their path weights. The comparison of path weights after traversal is a direct translation of Section 4 [15].

During verification, we perform actions that are enabled in the closed system. We update the state of both processes to which the action is attributed. Until branching and/or recurrence points are encountered, we perform these actions in an arbitrary order. This is different from "verification" algorithms patterned on distributed event simulation, where an elaborate calculation precedes each performance [10]. Checkpointing of system states follows the rules for untimed model checking [13,14].

Figure 5 shows a simple delay-constrained system verification example. Implementation *Net* is a network containing the real-time C-element of Figure 4, plus three timed wires attached to the ports of the C-element. The two input wires assume input separation 3 (resp., 4), and guarantee response within $\langle 1, 2 \rangle$ (resp., $\langle 2, 3 \rangle$; the output wire is like the first input wire. Not all delay constraints are shown in Figure 5. Specification P is a real-time C-element that assumes an input separation of 10 between β and α, and guarantees $\underline{c}$ response within $\langle 4, 9 \rangle$ (relative to β). No mirror dashed arrows are shown in Figure 5; there is only the solid arrow showing that an input separation of 10 between β and α is guaranteed by mirror mP.

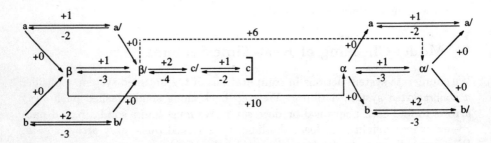

Fig. 5. Delay-constrained system verification example

Internal system actions are distinguished by slashes. When mP is coupled to *Net*, no delay constraints appear between $\beta = \max\{a, b\}$ and $\beta/ = \max\{a/, b/\}$; these must be obtained by application of the concentrator lemma. Intuitively, when a occurs last, $\beta/$ may be separated from β by as little as 1 unit. Similarly, when b occurs last, $\beta/$ may be separated from β by as much as 3 units. To derive a timing label on $\beta \rightarrow \beta/$, we take the weakest constraint among the two disjunctive paths from β to $\beta/$. We fill in the pairs of matched arrows between β and $\beta/$, and between α and $\alpha/$. Is the input separation of 6 units assumed by the implementation-component C-element guaranteed when implementation *Net* is driven by specification mirror mP? We derive a timing label on $\beta/ \rightarrow \alpha/$;

we sum along the chain $\beta/ \to \beta \to \alpha \to \alpha/$ $(-3 + 10 + 1 = 8)$; since $8 \geq 6$, the component C-element does not fail (receive unsafe input). Verifying the assumption protocol of an internal component depends primarily on the internal subnetwork that provides its input; for this reason, we have $\Theta(V+E)$ search on small graphs.

The suppressed detail in Figure 5 includes a pair of matched dashed arrows coming from mirror mP. Specifically, there is a dashed push-away arrow $\beta \to c$ with label $+4$ and a dashed pull-back arrow $\beta \leftarrow c$ with label -9. Using the pair of matched solid arrows between β and $\beta/$, we derive solid $\beta \to c$ with label $+4$ and solid $\beta \leftarrow c$ with label -9, guaranteeing both dashed-arrow assumptions with zero slack.

Figure 6 shows a second verification example for an intraprocess guarantee protocol. In this example, a timed fork and a timed C-element implement a timed wire. The disjunctive solid directed pull-back paths show clearly. We verify the intraprocess guarantee protocol. There are two solid directed paths from a to d that hold conjunctively; either solid path supports the dashed push-away arrow. There are two solid directed paths from d to a that hold disjunctively; this complete disjunctive set of solid paths supports the dashed pull-back arrow, with a slack of 1 time unit.

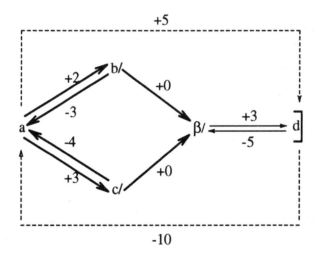

Fig. 6. Second delay-constrained system verification example

6 Sketch of the Generalized Model

Consider the following closed real-time system with two processes originally proposed by Pnueli and sometimes called the increment/decrement system [8]. The system contains a critical race. Condition stop is originally false. One process (the player) repeatedly tests stop and increments a local counter until stop is true; it then decrements the counter to zero and halts. The other process (the referee) sets stop to true. We view the test as a player-scheduled input action in which a nonblocking receive periodically tests whether a stop message has arrived (message delivery is instantaneous). Actions are also assumed to be instantaneous. Question: How long may/must the player run before halting? Suppose the first test occurs at system reset and subsequent tests remain scheduled during the timing window $\langle 3, 4 \rangle$ relative to the previous test. We assume some timing window for the decrement loop, which has no race. The referee's stop action remains scheduled during the timing window $\langle 1, 10 \rangle$ relative to system reset. Let n be the number of subsequent tests. We unroll the player's loop and derive timing windows of $\langle 3n, 4n \rangle$ and $\langle 3(n-1), 4(n-1) \rangle$ for the last and previous test, respectively. Since the stop action must occur between the two tests, two feasibility checks establish that $1 \leq n \leq 4$, which answers both questions. Answer: A speedy player with a slow referee can squeeze in four increments, while a slow player with a speedy referee can only manage one.

Unfortunately, this system is too sequential to show the power of generalized TBA; it contains nondeterminism but no concurrency. The automaton for the player contains a branch point to model the critical race, but it is a **sequential** nondeterministic automaton. Insofar as many real-time problems in the real world tend to resemble some variant of the timed dining philosophers problem, where there are both nonbinary delay constraints (i.e., concurrency) and nondeterminism, we may find that only generalized TBA retains both its modelling expressiveness and its verification efficiency. For example, if the interprocess assumption protocol of the real-time C-element were specified with a timing window, then the new α would be pushed away, and the new β would be pulled back, from the current β. No delay bounds would be specifiable to states or control locations "between" the new α and the new β. This may cause subtle problems for sequential nondeterministic automata in modelling and verifying timeout and exception handling. We suggest that "concentrators" reduce the semantic distance between sequential nondeterministic and timed behavior automata.

We need concurrency for modelling expressiveness and verification efficiency. Generalized TBA explicitly distinguishes concurrency and choice because its critical races are between process output actions and "concentrators" of process input actions.

7 Conclusion

At the level of processes, our timed partial-order model puts upper and lower delay bounds on "adjacent" process actions only. Process-controlled push-away and pull-back constraints are annotations of a causality/weak fairness relation. A process action is enabled as soon as its preset holds, but may not occur unless delay bounds relative to its enabling are satisfied. Pull-back constraints are expressed relative to "concentrators" of presets. The advantages during model checking are two-fold: (i) the causality relation allows the next action to be generated without reference to the passage of time (a precedence constraint can be checked without reference to any number of temporally-intermediate actions), and (ii) when concentrators are used, nonbinary delay constraints still allow the use of shortest-path techniques for checking feasibility of timing constraint graphs (the concentrator lemma allows all nonbinary precedence information to be encoded using binary constraints). Moreover, these shortest-path algorithms take advantage of the explicit push-away and pull-back labels on minimum-delay arrows; in this way, the linear-time shortest-path algorithms run on small graphs. In the absence of nondeterminism, verifying timing-window constraints in intraprocess guarantee protocols is scarcely more expensive than verifying precedence constraints in untimed systems [13,14]. Interprocess assumption protocols that specify minimum delays between old and new inputs are also easily verified. In the worst case (ignoring any special structure in the graph), for each dashed arrow, we can always use a single-source shortest-path algorithm in a finite weighted directed acyclic graph made up of solid arrows (we compute only simple paths by ignoring inappropriate members of matched pairs of solid arrows); the cost of each such use is $\Theta(V+E)$.

Nevertheless, all real real-time systems contain timeouts (just as all real computers contain interrupts). This is one place where we cannot select the next action without reference to the passage of time. When time and nondeterminism interact (that is, when processes refer to physical clocks and time out), the outcomes of nondeterministic choice are determined by critical races that are affected by delay bounds. These bounds are not annotations of a conflict relation; they are an integral part of the branching structure of the timed behavior automaton. We continue to study the generalized TBA model. We see a special role for "concentrators" in allowing the efficient verification of timed nonsequential nondeterministic automata. Lin Jensen continues to make changes to the POM verification system to accommodate real time; several toy examples have been run, including Figure 5 with checkpointing of system states for termination, rings of up to 8 timed DME-elements and Fischer's real-time protocol for mutual exclusion [1]. The cost for latter two is $\Theta(n^2)$. We are now designing a timed dining philosophers benchmark. An intriguing question is, what will be the size of the system timed behavior automaton constructed while verifying a nondeterministic real-time system? How many finite constraint graphs of what size will there be? If both these quantities are polynomial in the number of components, then the real-time state explosion problem goes away. We conjecture that efficient model checking of general real-time systems will depend on seeing precisely to what extent time should be abstracted out of state encodings of timed systems.

References

1. M. Abadi and L. Lamport, *An Old-Fashioned Recipe for Real Time*, in W.-P. de Roever (Ed.), Real-Time: Theory in Practice, REX Workshop on Real-Time, Proceedings, Lecture Notes in Computer Science 600, Springer–Verlag, 1992.

2. R. Alur, *Techniques for automatic verification of real-time systems*, Ph.D. Thesis, Department of Computer Science, Stanford University, Report STAN-CS-91-1378, August 1991.

3. R. Casley, R.F. Crew, J. Meseguer and V.R. Pratt, *Temporal Structures*, Math. Structures in Computer Science, **1:2**, July 1991, pp. 179–213.

4. C. Courcoubetis and M. Yannakakis, *Minimum and maximum delay problems in real-time systems*, in K.G. Larsen and A. Skou, (Eds.), Third Workshop on Computer-Aided Verification, Proceedings, Department of Mathematics and Computer Science, Aalborg University, Report IR-91-5, July 1991, pp. 467–477. Also Lecture Notes in Computer Science 575, Springer–Verlag, 1992.

5. W.-P. de Roever (Ed.), Real-Time: Theory in Practice, REX Workshop on Real-Time, Proceedings, Lecture Notes in Computer Science 600, Springer–Verlag, 1992.

6. D.L. Dill, *Trace theory for automatic hierarchical verification of speed-independent circuits*, Ph.D. Thesis, Department of Computer Science, Carnegie Mellon University, Report CMU-CS-88-119, February 1988. Also MIT Press, 1989.

7. D.L. Dill, *Timing assumptions and verification of finite-state concurrent systems*, in J. Sifakis, (Ed.), Automatic Verification Methods for Finite State Systems, Proceedings, First Workshop on Computer-Aided Verification, Lecture Notes in Computer Science 407, Springer–Verlag, 1990, pp. 197–212.

8. T.A. Henzinger, *The temporal specification and verification of real-time systems*, Ph.D. Thesis, Department of Computer Science, Stanford University, Report STAN-CS-91-1380, August 1991.

9. F. Jahanian and A.K.-L. Mok, *A graph-theoretic approach for timing analysis and its implementation*, IEEE Trans. on Computers, **C-36:8**, August 1987, pp. 961–975.

10. P.K. Khordoc et al., *A stimulus/response system based on hierarchical timing diagrams*, Proceedings of ICCAD '91, Santa Clara, CA, November 1991.

11. V.R. Pratt, *Modelling concurrency with partial orders*, Int. Journal of Parallel Prog., **15:1**, February 1986, pp. 33–71.

12. D.K. Probst and H.F. Li, *Abstract specification, composition and proof of correctness of delay-insensitive circuits and systems*, Technical Report, Department of Computer Science, Concordia University, CS-VLSI-88-2, April 1988 (Revised March 1989).

13. D.K. Probst and H.F. Li, *Using partial-order semantics to avoid the state explosion problem in asynchronous systems*, in E.M. Clarke and R.P. Kurshan, (Eds.), Second Workshop on Computer-Aided Verification, June 1990, DIMACS Series, Vol. 3, 1991, pp. 15–24. Also Lecture Notes in Computer Science 531, Springer–Verlag, 1991.

14. D.K. Probst and H.F. Li, *Partial-order model checking: A guide for the perplexed*, in K.G. Larsen and A. Skou, (Eds.), Third Workshop on Computer-Aided Verification, Proceedings, Department of Mathematics and Computer Science, Aalborg University, Report IR-91-5, July 1991, pp. 405–416. Also Lecture Notes in Computer Science 575, Springer–Verlag, 1992, pp. 322–331.

15. D.K. Probst and L.C. Jensen, *Controlling state explosion during automatic verification of delay-insensitive and delay-constrained VLSI systems using the POM verifier*, in S. Whitaker, (Ed.), Proceedings of the 3rd NASA Symposium on VLSI Design, Moscow, ID, October 1991, pp. 8.2.1–8.2.8.

Timing Verification by Successive Approximation

R. Alur   A. Itai   R. Kurshan   M. Yannakakis

AT&T Bell Laboratories
Murray Hill, NJ 07974

Abstract. We present an algorithm for verifying that a model M with timing constraints satisfies a given temporal property T. The model M is given as a composition of ω-automata P_i, where each automaton P_i is constrained by the bounds on delays. The property T is given as an ω-automaton as well, and the verification problem is posed as a language inclusion question $\mathcal{L}(M) \subseteq \mathcal{L}(T)$. In constructing the composition M of the constrained automata P_i, one needs to rule out the behaviors that are inconsistent with the delay bounds, and this step is (provably) computationally expensive. We propose an iterative solution which involves generating successive approximations M_j to M, with containment $\mathcal{L}(M) \subseteq \mathcal{L}(M_j)$ and monotone convergence $\mathcal{L}(M_j) \rightarrow \mathcal{L}(M)$ within a bounded number of steps. As the succession progresses, the M_j become more complex, but at any step of the iteration one may get a proof or a counter-example to the original language inclusion question.

We first construct M_0, the composition of the P_i ignoring the delay constraints, and try to prove the language inclusion $\mathcal{L}(M_0) \subseteq \mathcal{L}(T)$. If this succeeds, then $\mathcal{L}(M) \subseteq \mathcal{L}(M_0) \subseteq \mathcal{L}(T)$. If this fails, we can find $\mathbf{x} \in \mathcal{L}(M_0) \backslash \mathcal{L}(T)$ of the form $\mathbf{x} = \sigma' \sigma^\omega$. We give an algorithm to check for consistency of $\mathbf{x}$ with respect to the delay bounds of M: the time complexity of this check is linear in the length of $\sigma' \sigma$ and cubic in the number of automata. If $\mathbf{x}$ is consistent with all the delay constraints of M, then $\mathbf{x}$ provides a counter-example to $\mathcal{L}(M) \subseteq \mathcal{L}(T)$. Otherwise, we identify an "optimal" set of delay constraints D inconsistent with $\mathbf{x}$. We generate an automaton P_D which accepts only those behaviors that are consistent with the delay constraints in the set D. Then we add P_D as a restriction to M_0, forming M_1, and iterate the algorithm.

In the worst case, the number of iterations needed is exponential in the number of delay constraints. Experience suggests that in typical cases, however, only a few delay constraints are material to the verification of any specific property T. Thus, resolution of the question $\mathcal{L}(M) \subseteq \mathcal{L}(T)$ may be possible after only a few iterations of the algorithm, resulting in feasible language inclusion tests. This algorithm is being implemented into the verifier COSPAN at AT&T Bell Laboratories.

1   Overview

We address the problem of automata-theoretic verification of coordinating processes, in the case that the coordinating processes have certain associated events understood as "delays", and these delays are constrained by lower and upper bounds on their allowed duration in time.

Given a "system" modeled by an ω-automaton M, and a temporal property modeled by an ω-automaton T, we want to verify that M has the property T, or more precisely, that the language inclusion $\mathcal{L}(M) \subseteq \mathcal{L}(T)$ holds. The language $\mathcal{L}(M)$ can be understood as the set of "behaviors" possible in the system M, while $\mathcal{L}(T)$ can be interpreted as the set of all behaviors consistent with the property T.

While our development here is fairly general, we make one basic requirement on the semantic nature of the automata used to model the system (M above). We require that the automata (over a common alphabet) are closed under a composition operator, denoted by $\otimes$, supporting the language intersection property:

$$\mathcal{L}(M \otimes N) = \mathcal{L}(M) \cap \mathcal{L}(N). \tag{1}$$

We will refer to any such class of automata as *processes*. Examples of process classes are *L-processes* [Kur87, Kur90] with composition defined by the tensor product, *deterministic Muller automata* [Cho74] and *deterministic Rabin-Scott acceptors* (conventional automata accepting strings) with composition defined by the Cartesian product (more precisely, the $\wedge$ operator defined in [Kur87]). Such processes support models of both synchronous and asynchronous coordination, including interleaving semantics [Kur90].

A "system" M is commonly defined in terms of coordinating components, each component restricting the behavior of the other components with which it coordinates. Therefore, processes provide a natural class of automata for modeling such coordination. We make further use of this property when we consider processes subject to timing constraints: the timing constraints not only constrain the process itself, but also the other processes with which it coordinates.

While we impose no requirements of associativity on $\otimes$, in the following development, for simplicity, we will write successive compositions without parentheses. Furthermore, we assume that if Σ is the underlying alphabet, then there exists a process $\mathbf{1}$ with $\mathcal{L}(\mathbf{1}) = \Sigma^+$ or $\mathcal{L}(\mathbf{1}) = \Sigma^\omega$. [1]

In this paper we address the issue of verification subject to timing constraints imposed upon the component processes. We begin with a system model P expressed as a composition of processes: $P = \otimes_{i=1}^{K} P_i$, with no reference yet to timing constraints. Next, suppose that certain events $x \in \Sigma$ correspond to the beginning or the end of a "delay event" relative to various P_i. Specifically, for each P_i we are given a finite set Δ_i of *delays*; let Δ_P be $\cup_i \Delta_i$. The association between the events in Σ and the delays is given, for each P_i, by two partial functions b_i ("begin") and e_i ("end"), mapping some of the events in Σ to the delays in Δ_i. For an event $x \in \Sigma$, if $b_i(x) = \delta$, then this means that process P_i begins delay $\delta \in \Delta_i$ at event x, and if $e_i(x') = \delta$ then P_i ends this delay at x'. For example, x may correspond to the receipt of a signal by P_i, marking the onset of an internal delay $\delta \in \Delta_i$: $b_i(x) = \delta$; or, x may correspond to the subsequent emission of a signal from P_i marking the end of that delay: $e_i(x) = \delta$. If process P_i did not begin a delay at event x, then $b_i(x)$ is undefined; likewise for $e_i(x)$. If processes P_i and P_j both begin a delay at event x, then $b_i(x) \in \Delta_i$ and $b_j(x) \in \Delta_j$ are defined. For example, x may correspond to the simultaneous receipt of a signal by P_i and emission of a (perhaps unrelated) signal from P_j. For more examples of how this arises naturally in modeling systems of concurrent processes, see [Kur87, Kur90].

Now, recall that the verification problem is to prove $\mathcal{L}(P) \subseteq \mathcal{L}(T)$ for some process T. However, it may be the case that while $\mathcal{L}(P) \not\subseteq \mathcal{L}(T)$, it nonetheless holds that $\mathcal{L} \subseteq \mathcal{L}(T)$ for the subset $\mathcal{L} \subset \mathcal{L}(P)$ which is consistent with timing constraints we impose on the delays. Specifically, suppose that each delay $\delta \in \Delta_P$ has associated with it two nonnegative numbers: $0 \leq \alpha(\delta) \leq \beta(\delta)$ where $\alpha(\delta)$ is rational and $\beta(\delta)$ is rational or is ∞. The intended interpretation is that the delay δ has duration at least $\alpha(\delta)$ and at most $\beta(\delta)$. A *delay constraint* is a 3-tuple $D = (\Delta, \alpha, \beta)$ where $\Delta \subseteq \Delta_P$. Now we define the notion of timing consistency:

A sequence $\mathbf{x} \in \mathcal{L}(P)$ is *timing-consistent* with respect to a delay constraint $D = (\Delta, \alpha, \beta)$, provided there exist real numbers $t_1 < t_2 < \cdots$ such that for all processes P_i, and any $\delta \in \Delta \cap \Delta_i$, if $b_i(x_j) = \delta$, $e_i(x_k) = \delta$ for $k > j$ and both $b_i(x_l)$ and $e_i(x_l)$ are undefined for $j < l < k$, then $\alpha(\delta) \leq t_k - t_j \leq \beta(\delta)$.

In other words, $\mathbf{x}$ is timing-consistent if it is possible to assign an increasing succession of real times to the events of P modeled by $\mathbf{x}$, in such a way that the durations of delays of the respective component processes P_i as given by these time assignments are within the allowed bounds. For any delay constraint D, let

$$\mathcal{L}_D(P) = \{\mathbf{x} \in \mathcal{L}(P) \mid \mathbf{x} \text{ is timing-consistent with } D\}.$$

For convenience, we define any string $\sigma = (x_1, \ldots, x_n)$ to be *timing-consistent* (with D) provided there are real numbers $t_1 < \cdots < t_n$ satisfying these same conditions.

We seek an algorithm to answer the language inclusion question

$$\mathcal{L}_D(P) \subseteq \mathcal{L}(T) \tag{2}$$

for $D = (\Delta_P, \alpha, \beta)$. Such an algorithm is already known, because using the method of [AD90], we can construct an automaton P_D which rules out timing-inconsistent sequences; that is, $\mathcal{L}(P \otimes P_D) = \mathcal{L}_D(P)$.

---

[1] In this paper we refer both to strings: finite words over Σ, and sequences: infinite words over Σ.

Unfortunately, the size of P_D is exponential in the number of processes comprising P and is proportional to the magnitudes of the bounds given by α and β. Furthermore, it was shown there that this problem is PSPACE-complete. The purpose of this paper is to develop a heuristic for circumventing this computational complexity. Our heuristic works like this. We first try to prove the language inclusion

$$\mathcal{L}(P) \subseteq \mathcal{L}(T) . \tag{3}$$

If this succeeds, then surely (2) holds, as $\mathcal{L}_D(P) \subseteq \mathcal{L}(P)$. If (3) fails, then for some $\mathbf{x} \in \mathcal{L}(P)$, $\mathbf{x} \notin \mathcal{L}(T)$.

Let us first consider the case that the counter-example $\mathbf{x}$ has a finite prefix σ such that every extension of σ does not belong to $\mathcal{L}(T)$. This is the case, for instance, when the temporal property defined by T is a "safety" property. The problem of testing consistency of σ can be reduced to the problem of finding negative cost cycles in a weighted graph as described in the next section. In this case, the timing-consistency of $\mathbf{x}$ can be checked in time $O(|\sigma| \cdot K^2)$, where K is the number of processes. For the general case with $\mathbf{x}$ infinite (*e.g.*, T specifies a "liveness" property) we can find a counter-example $\mathbf{x}$ of the form $\mathbf{x} = \sigma' \sigma^\omega$ for strings σ and σ'. The algorithm for testing consistency of $\mathbf{x}$ in this case is of time complexity $O((|\sigma'| + |\sigma|) \cdot K^2 + K^3 \cdot \lceil \log K \rceil)$.

If $\mathbf{x}$ is timing-consistent, then (2). Otherwise, we identify first a minimal set of processes, and for those, a minimal set of delays Δ_1, giving a delay constraint $D' = (\Delta_1, \alpha, \beta)$ with respect to which $\mathbf{x}$ is not timing-consistent. Next, we relax the delay bound maps α and β by decreasing respective $\alpha(\delta)$'s and increasing $\beta(\delta)$'s, in a fashion which preserves the non-timing-consistency of $\mathbf{x}$ but which, after dividing each bound by their collective greatest common divisor, results in bounds which are as small as possible. The result of these operations gives an "optimized" delay constraint D_1 with respect to which $\mathbf{x}$ is timing inconsistent. Using an algorithm from [AD90], we generate a process P_{D_1} such that $\mathcal{L}(P_{D_1}) = \mathcal{L}_{D_1}(\mathbf{1})$, where $\mathbf{1}$ is a process satisfying $\mathcal{L}(\mathbf{1}) = \Sigma^\omega$. We apply state minimization to P_{D_1}, getting E_1 with $\mathcal{L}(E_1) = \mathcal{L}_{D_1}(\mathbf{1})$. If D_1 involves only a few processes, then the size of E_1 is small. In fact, experience suggests that in typical cases, only a few delay bounds are material to the verification of any specific property T, especially in case T is a "local" property (derived, perhaps, through decomposition [Kur90] of a global property).

We test the language inclusion

$$\mathcal{L}(P \otimes E_1) \subseteq \mathcal{L}(T) \tag{4}$$

and proceed as before, either verifying (4) and thus (2), or finding a counter-example $\mathbf{x}$ to (4). In the latter case, either $\mathbf{x}$ is a counter-example to (2), or it is not timing-consistent. In this last case, we find a set of delays D_2 as before, with respect to which $\mathbf{x}$ is not timing-consistent, and generate an E_2' with $\mathcal{L}(E_2') = \mathcal{L}_{D_2}(\mathbf{1})$. We minimize $E_1 \otimes E_2'$ giving E_2, and test $\mathcal{L}(P \otimes E_2) \subseteq \mathcal{L}(T)$.

The outline of the algorithm is shown in Figure 1. Note that as $\Delta_P = \cup \Delta_i$ is finite, there are only finitely many choices for $\Delta(\mathbf{x})$ at step 4. The optimization heuristic used at step 5 can construct only a finitely many choices of the bounding functions α' and β' for a given set $\Delta(\mathbf{x})$ of delays. This guarantees termination. To ensure faster convergence, α and β are optimized only once for a specific choice of $\Delta(\mathbf{x})$. With this restriction, this algorithm terminates in at most $n = 2^{|\Delta_P|}$ steps, in the worst case generating $E_1, \ldots, E_n$ with

$$\mathcal{L}(P) \supset \mathcal{L}(P \otimes E_1) \supset \mathcal{L}(P \otimes E_2) \supset \cdots \supset \mathcal{L}(P \otimes E_n) = \mathcal{L}_D(P). \tag{5}$$

2   Checking Timing Consistency

In this section, we address the problem of checking timing consistency of $\mathbf{x}$ with respect to a delay constraint $D = (\Delta, \alpha, \beta)$.

2.1   A graph-theoretic formulation of the problem

Consider a sequence $\sigma = x_1 x_2 \ldots$. Recall that σ is timing consistent with respect to D if and only if we can assign "time" values t_i to the respective events x_i such that

Input: Processes $P_1, \ldots P_k, T$, and a delay constraint $D = (\Delta_P, \alpha, \beta)$.
Output: Decides whether the inclusion $\mathcal{L}_D(\otimes_i P_i) \subseteq \mathcal{L}(T)$ holds.
Algorithm:
Initially: $P = \otimes_i P_i$ and $E = 1$.
Loop forever
    1. If $\mathcal{L}(P \otimes E) \subseteq \mathcal{L}(T)$ then stop (the desired inclusion holds).
    2. Choose $x = \sigma' \sigma^\omega$ in $\mathcal{L}(P \otimes E) - \mathcal{L}(T)$.
    3. If x is timing consistent with the delay constraint D
       then stop (the desired inclusion does not hold).
    4. Find a minimal set of delays $\Delta(x) \subseteq \Delta_P$ such that
       x is timing inconsistent with $(\Delta(x), \alpha, \beta)$.
    5. Find an optimal delay constraint $D(x) = (\Delta(x), \alpha', \beta')$ such that
       x is timing inconsistent with $D(x)$.
    6. Construct the region automaton $P_{D(x)}$.
    7. Set E to the minimized version of the product $E \otimes P_{D(x)}$.

Figure 1: Algorithm for timing verification

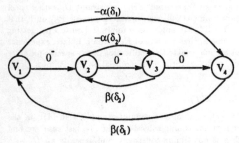

Figure 2: The weighted graph for $\sigma = b_1 b_2 e_2 e_1$

1. $t_1 < t_2 < \ldots$, and

2. if process P_i begins a delay $\delta \in \Delta$ at x_j (i.e., $b_i(x_j) = \delta$), and the matching end is at x_k (i.e., $e_i(x_k) = \delta$ and both $b_i(x_l)$ and $e_i(x_l)$ are undefined for $j < l < k$), then

$$\alpha(\delta) \leq t_k - t_j \leq \beta(\delta).$$

Checking feasibility of this system of inequalities can be reduced to detecting negative cost cycles in a weighted graph. Let us first consider an example.

Example 1 Consider two processes P_1 and P_2. The process P_1 has a delay δ_1, and the process P_2 has a delay δ_2. Let b_i and e_i denote the beginning and ending of the respective delays of P_i. Consider the string $\sigma = (b_1, b_2, e_2, e_1)$. Checking consistency of σ corresponds to testing consistency of the following set of inequalities:

$$t_1 < t_2 < t_3 < t_4, \quad \alpha(\delta_1) \leq (t_4 - t_1) \leq \beta(\delta_1), \quad \alpha(\delta_2) \leq (t_3 - t_2) \leq \beta(\delta_2).$$

The graph associated with these inequalities is shown in Figure 2. The graph has a node v_i for each t_i, and each inequality gives rise to an edge. Thus, the constraint $\alpha(\delta_1) \leq (t_4 - t_1) \leq \beta(\delta_1)$ gives rise to two edges: a forward edge from v_1 to v_4 with weight $-\alpha(\delta_1)$ and a backward edge from v_4 to v_1 with weight $+\beta(\delta_1)$. Similarly the constraint $\alpha(\delta_2) \leq (t_3 - t_2) \leq \beta(\delta_2)$ gives rise to two edges. For every constraint $t_i < t_{i+1}$, i.e. $t_i - t_{i+1} < 0$, there is an edge from v_i to v_{i+1} with weight 0^-. The superscript "$-$" indicates that, on account of the strict inequality, nonzero time must have elapsed.

The cost of a cycle is the sum of the costs of its edges. While adding the costs we need to account for the superscripts also: the sum of two costs has the superscript "$-$" iff one of the costs has the superscript "$-$". It is easy to see that the string σ is timing inconsistent iff the graph has a negative cost cycle (the cost 0^- is considered to be negative). Assuming $\alpha(\delta_1) \leq \beta(\delta_1)$ and $\alpha(\delta_2) \leq \beta(\delta_2)$, the graph has a negative cost cycle iff $\alpha(\delta_2) \geq \beta(\delta_1)$. Note that if $\alpha(\delta_2) = \beta(\delta_1)$, then there is a negative cost cycle with cost 0^-. ∎

The domain of bounds

The above example illustrates that the cost of an edge reflects whether the corresponding constraint is a strict or a nonstrict inequality. In order to deal with different types of bounds uniformly, we define the domain of bounds, similar to [Dil89], to be the set

$$\mathcal{B} = \{\ldots - 2, -1, 0, 1, 2, \ldots\} \cup \{\ldots - 2^-, -1^-, 0^-, 1^-, 2^-, \ldots\} \cup \{-\infty, \infty\}.$$

The costs of the edges of the graph will be from the domain $\mathcal{B}$. To compute shortest paths, we need to add costs and compare costs. The ordering $<$ over the integers is extended to $\mathcal{B}$ by the following law: for any integer a, $-\infty < a^- < a < (a+1)^- < \infty$. The addition operation $+$ over integers is extended to $\mathcal{B}$ by: (i) for all $b \in \mathcal{B}$, $b + \infty = \infty$, (ii) for all $b \in \mathcal{B}$ with $b \neq \infty$, $b + (-\infty) = -\infty$, and (iii) for integers a and b, $a + b^- = a^- + b = a^- + b^- = (a+b)^-$.

Now the constraints corresponding to a sequence σ can be rewritten as follows. A constraint of the form $t_i < t_{i+1}$ is written as $t_i - t_{i+1} \leq 0^-$. A constraint of the form $a_1 \leq t_k - t_j \leq b_1$ gives rise to two constraints: $t_k - t_j \leq b_1$ and $t_j - t_k \leq -a_1$.

The weighted graph $G(\mathbf{x})$

For a sequence $\mathbf{x}$, now we define an infinite weighted graph $G(\mathbf{x})$, where the costs of the edges are from the set $\mathcal{B}$, as follows. The graph $G(\mathbf{x})$ has a node v_i for every variable t_i; for each constraint $t_j - t_k \leq b$, $b \in \mathcal{B}$, there is an edge from v_j to v_k with cost b. Thus if a process begins its delay at x_i with a matching end at x_j, then the graph has a forward edge from v_i to v_j with negative cost showing the lower bound and a backward edge from v_j to v_i with positive cost showing the upper bound. The problem of checking consistency reduces to finding negative cost cycles in this graph:

Lemma 1 *The sequence $\mathbf{x}$ is timing inconsistent iff the graph $G(\mathbf{x})$ has a negative cost cycle.*

For a string σ of length N, a weighted graph $G(\sigma)$ with N vertices is defined similarly, and the corresponding lemma holds as well.

2.2 Testing consistency of strings

For a string σ of length N, the graph $G(\sigma)$ is finite with N vertices and $O(N \cdot K)$ edges, where K is the number of processes. There exist standard polynomial-time algorithms to detect negative cost cycles. However, the best known time complexity is $O(N^2 \cdot K)$. Since N is much larger than K, we prefer an alternative solution with time complexity $O(K^2 \cdot N)$.

Input: A string $\sigma = x_1, \ldots x_N$.
Output: Decides if σ is timing consistent, and if so, outputs the reduced graph $G^*(\sigma)$.
Algorithm:

    Initially: Let G be the graph with a single vertex v_1.
    For $j := 2$ to N do
      { Comment: G equals $G^*(x_1, \ldots x_{j-1})$.}
      1. To G, add the vertex v_j and all edges of $G(\sigma)$
         that connect v_j with the vertices of G.
      2. Compute new shortest distances within G;
         if a negative cost cycle is detected, stop (σ is timing inconsistent).
      3. Remove all the vertices not in $V^*(x_1, \ldots x_j)$.

Figure 3: Algorithm for testing consistency of finite strings

The reduced graph $G^*(\sigma)$

Consider a string $\sigma = x_1 x_2 \ldots x_N$. The graph $G(\sigma)$ has N vertices $v_1, v_2, \ldots v_N$. Let $V_b^*(\sigma)$ consist of vertices v_j such that some process P_i finishes a delay δ at x_j with no prior matching beginning of the delay (i.e., $e_i(x_j) = \delta$ and for all $1 \leq k < j$, both $b_i(x_k)$ and $e_i(x_k)$ are undefined). Similarly, let $V_e^*(\sigma)$ consist of vertices v_j such that some process P_i begins a delay δ at x_j and there is no matching end of the delay (i.e., $b_i(x_j) = \delta$ and for all $j < k \leq N$, both $b_i(x_k)$ and $e_i(x_k)$ are undefined). Let $V^*(\sigma)$ be the union of $V_b^*(\sigma)$ and $V_e^*(\sigma)$. Observe that the size of $V^*(\sigma)$ is at most $2K$. Now consider a superstring σ'. Clearly, the graph $G(\sigma)$ is a subgraph of $G(\sigma')$. A vertex in the subgraph $G(\sigma)$ has an edge going out of this subgraph only if this vertex is in $V^*(\sigma)$. Thus the vertices not in $V^*(\sigma)$ are "internal" to the subgraph $G(\sigma)$.

From the graph $G(\sigma)$ let us define another weighted graph $G^*(\sigma)$, called the *reduced graph* of σ, as follows: the vertex set is $V^*(\sigma)$, and for every pair of vertices v_j and v_k in $V^*(\sigma)$ there is an edge from v_j to v_k with cost equal to the cost of the shortest path from v_j to v_k in the graph $G(\sigma)$ (note that this cost can be ∞ if there is no path from v_j to v_k, and can be $-\infty$ if there is no "shortest" path because of a negative cost cycle). Thus, the graph $G^*(\sigma)$ is obtained from $G(\sigma)$ by first computing the shortest paths and then discarding the internal vertices. Thus, if we replace the subgraph $G(\sigma)$ by $G^*(\sigma)$ in $G(\sigma')$, the resulting graph has a negative cost cycle iff $G(\sigma')$ does.

Constructing the reduced graph

Using these ideas, the consistency of strings can be checked efficiently using a dynamic programming approach. The outline of the algorithm is shown in Figure 3. Given a string σ, it checks if the graph $G(\sigma)$ has a negative cost cycle, and if not, computes the reduced graph $G^*(\sigma)$. While implementing the algorithm, a graph will be represented by a matrix that gives, for every pair of vertices, the cost of the edge connecting them (the entries in the matrix are from the domain $\mathcal{B}$).

Consider a matrix A representing the reduced graph $G^*(x_1, \ldots x_{j-1})$. Step 1 corresponds to adding an extra row and column to A. At step 2, we need to check if the updated matrix has a negative cost cycle, and if not, compute the new shortest distances. Observe that, for any pair of vertices v and v', the new shortest distance between v and v' is different from the old one, only if the new shortest path visits the new vertex v_j. This fact can be used to compute the new shortest distances efficiently: in time $O(m^2)$, where m is the number of vertices in the current graph. Step 3 ensures that the updated matrix A stores only the vertices that are external to $x_1, \ldots x_j$, and hence at most $2K$ vertices. Thus, the overall time complexity of the algorithm is $O(N \cdot K^2)$.

Theorem 1 *The problem of deciding whether a string σ is timing consistent can be solved in time $O(|\sigma| \cdot K^2)$.*

2.3 Testing consistency of sequences

If the language inclusion $\mathcal{L}(P) \subseteq \mathcal{L}(T)$ fails, since P and T have finite state spaces, we can find a sequence $\mathbf{x} \in \mathcal{L}(P)\backslash\mathcal{L}(T)$ of the form $\mathbf{x} = \sigma'\sigma^{\omega}$ (for strings $\sigma', \sigma \in \Sigma^{+}$).

First observe that it is possible that $\sigma'\sigma$ is consistent, while for some i, $\sigma'\sigma^i$ is not.

Example 2 Consider two processes P_1 and P_2. The process P_1 has a delay δ_1, and the process P_2 has a delay δ_2. We use b_i and e_i to denote the beginning and ending of the delays of the processes P_i, as in Example 1. Let

$$\sigma' = (b_1)$$
$$\sigma = (b_2, \{e_1, b_1\}, e_2).$$

If $\alpha(\delta_1) = \beta(\delta_1) = n$ and $\alpha(\delta_2) = \beta(\delta_2) = n+1$, it is easy to see that $\sigma'\sigma^i$ is consistent iff $i \leq n$. ∎

Now we proceed to develop an algorithm for checking consistency of $\mathbf{x}$. We start by showing how to reduce the problem of checking consistency of a sequence to checking consistency of its subsequences.

Combining two reduced graphs

Consider a string σ_1 that is the concatenation of two strings σ_2 and σ_3. If either σ_2 or σ_3 is timing inconsistent then so is σ_1. Consider the reduced graphs $G^*(\sigma_2)$ and $G^*(\sigma_3)$. We can put these two graphs together by connecting the vertices in $V_e^*(\sigma_2)$ to the vertices in $V_b^*(\sigma_3)$ by the appropriate edges (i.e., by connecting the begin-delay events in σ_2 with their matching end-delay events in σ_3). If the resulting graph has a negative cycle, then σ_1 is timing inconsistent. Otherwise, we can compute the shortest distances in this new graph, and then delete the vertices not in $V^*(\sigma_1)$ to obtain $G^*(\sigma_1)$. This step takes only time $O(K^3)$.

Lemma 2 *For a string σ, the reduced graph $G^*(\sigma^m)$ can be computed in time $O(|\sigma| \cdot K^2 + K^3 \cdot \lceil \log m \rceil)$.*

The lemma follows from the facts that $G^*(\sigma)$ can be computed in time $O(|\sigma| \cdot K^2)$, and the reduced graph $G^*(\sigma^m)$ can be computed from $G^*(\sigma^{m/2})$ in time $O(K^3)$.

Now consider a sequence $\mathbf{x}$ that is the concatenation of a string σ' and a sequence $\mathbf{x}'$. In the previous section, we defined reduced graphs for strings, we can define reduced graphs for sequences similarly (note that for a sequence $\mathbf{x}'$, $V^*(\mathbf{x}') = V_b^*(\mathbf{x}')$). Now we can test consistency of $\mathbf{x}$ by putting together the reduced graphs $G^*(\sigma')$ and $G^*(\mathbf{x}')$. From this, it follows that

> If there is an algorithm which tests whether σ^{ω} is timing consistent, and if so, computes the reduced graph $G^*(\sigma^{\omega})$, then it is possible to check timing consistency of $\sigma'\sigma^{\omega}$ with additional time complexity $O(|\sigma'| \cdot K^2 + K^3)$.

Computing the shortest distances within the periodic graph $G(\sigma^{\omega})$

The periodic graph $G(\sigma^{\omega})$ can be considered as the concatenation of infinitely many copies of the graphs $G^*(\sigma)$. Suppose $G^*(\sigma)$ has m vertices, $m \leq 2K$, and let us denote the vertices in the j-th copy of $G^*(\sigma)$ by $v_1^j, \ldots v_m^j$. We will use G_l^k, $1 \leq k \leq l$, to denote the subgraph of $G(\sigma^{\omega})$ consisting of l copies of $G^*(\sigma)$ starting from k-th copy, and G^k to denote the subgraph consisting of infinite number of copies starting from k-th copy. It should be clear that for every k, k', l, the graphs G_l^k and $G_l^{k'}$ are isomorphic, and the graphs G^k and $G^{k'}$ are also isomorphic.

Now the problem of computing $G^*(\sigma^{\omega})$ can be rephrased as computing the shortest distances between every pair of vertices v_i^1 and v_j^1 in the first copy. Let $d^k(i,j)$ denote the shortest distance between v_i^1 and v_j^1 in the subgraph G_k^1 (i.e., the graph with only first k copies), and let $d(i,j)$ be the shortest distance between v_i^1 and v_j^1 in the entire graph $G(\sigma^{\omega})$. Equivalently, $d^k(i,j)$ is the shortest distance between v_i^1 and v_j^1 in the subgraph G_k^l, and $d(i,j)$ the shortest distance between v_i^l and v_j^l in the subgraph G^l, for any $l > 0$.

144

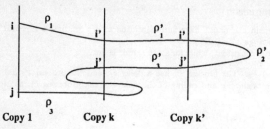

Copy 1   Copy k   Copy k'

Figure 4: The splitting of the path ρ

The question is whether $d(i,j)$ can be determined by computing the values of $d^k(i,j)$ up to a small k. The following lemma gives the answer in the case where there is a shortest path between v_i^1 and v_j^1 (i.e., the case where $d(i,j) \neq -\infty$). It shows that if the shortest distance between v_i^1 and v_j^1 can be reduced by considering additional copies of $G(\sigma)$ beyond m^2 copies, then, in fact, it can be reduced repeatedly by "pumping" appropriate paths, and hence, is unbounded.

Lemma 3 *For every pair of vertices v_i^1 and v_j^1, either $d(i,j)$ is $-\infty$ or equals $d^{m^2}(i,j)$.*

Proof. Consider a pair of vertices v_i^1 and v_j^1 such that $d(i,j) < d^{m^2}(i,j)$. We will show that, in such a case, $d(i,j)$ is $-\infty$. Let ρ be the smallest, in terms of the number of edges, path between v_i^1 and v_j^1 such that the cost of ρ is less than $d^{m^2}(i,j)$. Let us denote the cost by $c(\rho)$.

Let us say that a pair (i',j') *belongs* to the path ρ, iff for some k, ρ can be written as

$$v_i^1 \xrightarrow{\rho_1} v_{i'}^k \xrightarrow{\rho_2} v_{j'}^k \xrightarrow{\rho_3} v_j^1$$

such that the path ρ_2 lies entirely in the subgraph G^k. Since there are only m^2 such pairs, and the path ρ does not lie entirely within $G_{m^2}^1$, it follows that there exists a pair (i',j') that belongs to ρ and also to ρ_2. That is, the path ρ can be split as:

$$v_i^1 \xrightarrow{\rho_1} v_{i'}^k \xrightarrow{\rho_1'} v_{i'}^{k'} \xrightarrow{\rho_2'} v_{j'}^{k'} \xrightarrow{\rho_3'} v_{j'}^k \xrightarrow{\rho_3} v_j^1$$

such that the path ρ_2' lies entirely within the subgraph $G^{k'}$ and the path $\rho_2 = \rho_1'\rho_2'\rho_3'$ lies entirely within G^k (see Figure 4).

Recall that the subgraphs G^k and $G^{k'}$ are isomorphic, and hence ρ_2' can be considered to be a path between $v_{i'}^k$ and $v_{j'}^k$, (to be precise, the superscripts of the vertices appearing on ρ_2' need to be shifted by $(k'-k)$, but we will slightly abuse the notation). In fact, for every $n \geq 0$, we have the path $(\rho_1')^n \rho_2'(\rho_3')^n$ between $v_{i'}^k$ and $v_{j'}^k$.

Now consider the path $\rho_1\rho_2'\rho_3$ between v_i^1 and v_j^1. If $c(\rho_1\rho_2'\rho_3) \leq c(\rho)$ then we have a path from v_i^1 and v_j^1 with cost less than $d^{m^2}(i,j)$ and with less edges than ρ. Hence, by the choice of ρ, $c(\rho_1\rho_2'\rho_3) > c(\rho)$. This implies that $c(\rho_1') + c(\rho_3') < 0$. This means that the segments ρ_1' and ρ_3' can be "pumped" to reduce the cost further and further: $c((\rho_1')^n \rho_2'(\rho_3')^n)$ forms a strictly decreasing sequence with increasing values of n. This implies that there is no "shortest" path between the vertices $v_{i'}^k$ and $v_{j'}^k$, and hence, $d(i,j) = -\infty$. ∎

The next question is to determine the pairs of vertices v_i^1 and v_j^1 for which there is no "shortest" path and $d(i,j)$ is $-\infty$. Clearly, if $d^{2m^2}(i,j) < d^{m^2}(i,j)$ then $d(i,j)$ is $-\infty$ by the above lemma. But the converse of this statement does not hold.

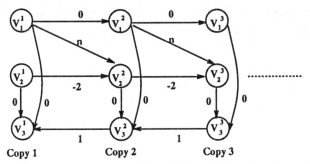

Figure 5: The periodic graph of Example 3

Example 3 Consider the graph shown in Figure 5. A single copy consists of 3 vertices. Note that the distance between the vertices v_2^1 and v_3^1 decreases at every step: $d^k(2,3) = -k+1$. Thus $d^{18}(2,3) < d^9(2,3)$, and this allows us to correctly conclude that $d(2,3) = -\infty$. The situation is quite different for the distance between v_1^1 and v_3^1: $d^k(1,3) = 0$ for $k \leq n+4$ and $d^k(1,3) = n+4-k$ for $k > n+4$. Thus the shortest distance does not change in the beginning. If the cost n exceeds 14, then $d^{18}(1,3) = d^9(1,3)$, and yet, $d(1,3) = -\infty$. Thus a different criterion is required to conclude $d(1,3) = -\infty$; it should follow from the facts that $d(2,3) = -\infty$ and there exists a finite cost edge from v_1^1 to v_2^1 and from v_3^2 to v_3^1. ∎

The next lemma characterizes pairs (i,j) such that $d(i,j) = -\infty$.

Lemma 4 *Let v_i^1 and v_j^1 be a pair of vertices such that $d(i,j) = -\infty$ and $d^{m^2}(i,j) \neq -\infty$. Then there exists some pair (i',j') such that $d^{2m^2}(i',j') < d^{m^2}(i',j')$ and in the graph G^1 there exist paths from v_i^1 to $v_{i'}^k$ and from $v_{j'}^k$ to v_j^1, for some $k > 0$.*

Proof. Consider a pair of vertices v_i^1 and v_j^1 such that $d(i,j) < d^{m^2}(i,j)$. The proof is very similar to the proof of Lemma 3. Let ρ be the smallest, in terms of the number of edges, path between v_i^1 and v_j^1 such that the cost of ρ is less than $d^{m^2}(i,j)$. Let (i',j') be a pair such that the path ρ can be split as

$$v_i^1 \xrightarrow{\rho_1} v_{i'}^k \xrightarrow{\rho_1'} v_{i'}^{k'} \xrightarrow{\rho_2'} v_{j'}^{k'} \xrightarrow{\rho_3'} v_{j'}^k \xrightarrow{\rho_3} v_j^1$$

such that the path $\rho_2 = \rho_1'\rho_2'\rho_3'$ visits least number of different copies. This added restriction on the choice of (i',j') implies that the path ρ_2 lies within the subgraph $G_{m^2}^k$. Let ρ_2'' be the shortest path between $v_{i'}$ and $v_{j'}$ that lies within m^2 copies, that is, $c(\rho_2'') = d^{m^2}(i',j')$. Now the path $\rho_1'\rho_2''\rho_3'$ lies within $2m^2$ copies, and, since $c(\rho_1') + c(\rho_3') < 0$ (as in the proof of Lemma 3), has cost less than $c(\rho_2'')$. This means that $d^{2m^2}(i',j') < d^{m^2}(i',j')$, and this proves the lemma. ∎

To find all pairs (i,j) with $d(i,j) = -\infty$ using the above lemma, we construct an edge-labeled graph G_{inf} over the vertex set $\{v_1, \ldots v_m\}$ with the labels $\{a,b,c,d\}$ as follows:

1. If $G^*(\sigma)$ has an edge from v_i to v_j then G_{inf} has a-labeled edge from v_i to v_j.

2. If $d^{2m^2}(i,j) < d^{m^2}(i,j)$ then G_{inf} has b-labeled edge from v_i to v_j.

3. If G_2^1 has an edge from v_i^1 to v_j^2 then G_{inf} has c-labeled edge from v_i to v_j.

4. If G_2^1 has an edge from v_i^2 to v_j^1 then G_{inf} has d-labeled edge from v_i to v_j.

Next we define a language L_{inf} over the alphabet $\{a,b,c,d\}$ to consist of all the words w such that

1. the number of c's is equal to the number of d's;

2. in every prefix of w, the number of c's is at least as large as the number of d's;

3. there is at least one b.

From the graph G_{inf} we build the desired set S_{inf}:

$(i,j) \in S_{inf}$ iff there exists a path ρ from v_i to v_j in G_{inf} such that ρ spells a word in L_{inf}.

The next lemma follows from the previous lemmas and the definitions:

Lemma 5 *For every pair of vertices v_i^1 and v_j^1, if $(i,j) \in S_{inf}$ then $d(i,j) = -\infty$, otherwise $d(i,j) = d^{m^2}(i,j)$.*

Computing the set S_{inf}

Given an edge-labeled graph and a language L, the L-transitive closure problem is to compute all pairs of nodes (v_i, v_j) for which there exists a path from v_i to v_j that spells a word in L. Thus computing the set S_{inf} corresponds to computing the L_{inf}-transitive closure of the graph G_{inf}.

It is easy to see that the language L_{inf} can be recognized by a deterministic 1-counter machine A (a special case of a pushdown automaton). Let A be a machine which reads the symbols of the input word one by one and does the following: on symbol a it does nothing, on b it moves to a state that signifies that A has seen at least one b, on symbol c it increments the counter (staying in the same state), and on d it decrements the counter if it was positive and rejects the whole input if the counter was 0. The machine accepts if after processing the input word it has seen some b and the counter is 0. Thus, the language L_{inf} is context-free. The L-transitive closure problem for a context-free language can be solved in cubic time $O(m^3)$ in the number m of nodes [Yan90] giving the following lemma:

Lemma 6 *The set of pairs S_{inf} can be computed in time $O(m^3)$.*

The algorithm is derived from a context-free grammar for L_{inf} in Chomsky normal form. We will describe now in more concrete terms the algorithm for our case. It uses the following grammar:

$$
\begin{aligned}
A &\rightarrow a \mid b \mid AA \mid A'd \\
A' &\rightarrow c \mid cA \\
B &\rightarrow b \mid BA \mid AB \mid B'd \\
B' &\rightarrow cB
\end{aligned}
$$

We will compute iteratively four sets A, A', B, B' of pairs of nodes. A pair (v_i, v_j) will be in A at the end of the algorithm iff there is a path from v_i to v_j which spells a word that satisfies conditions 1 and 2 in the definition of L_{inf} (but possibly not 3); it will be in A' iff the word satisfies the following modified conditions: 1'. the number of c's is one more than the number of d's; and 2'. in every prefix the number of c's is strictly larger than the number of d's. The sets B and B' are defined analogously except that, in addition, the word must also contain one b (i.e., satisfy condition 3 in the definition of L_{inf}). Thus, the desired set S_{inf} is given by the final value of B. These sets are represented by Boolean matrices whose rows and columns are indexed by the nodes of the graph. In addition, for each of the four sets we have a list of "unprocessed" pairs, $S_A, S_{A'}$ etc.

The data structures are initialized as follows: For every a-labeled edge, insert the corresponding pair of nodes to A (i.e., set the corresponding entry of matrix A to 1) and to the list S_A. For every b-labeled edge, insert the corresponding pair to A, B, S_A, S_B. For every c-labeled edge, insert the pair to A' and $S_{A'}$; we do nothing for the d-labeled edges.

In the iterative step, we remove a pair from one of the lists and "process" it; the algorithm terminates when the lists are empty. A pair (v_i, v_j) is processed as follows depending on the list it is taken from.

Input: Two strings σ' and σ.
Output: Decides if $\sigma'\sigma^\omega$ is timing consistent.
Algorithm:
1. If σ' is timing inconsistent then stop
   else compute $G^*(\sigma')$.
2. If σ is timing inconsistent then stop
   else compute $G^*(\sigma)$ (with vertex set $\{v_1, \cdots v_m\}$).
3. Compute $G^*(\sigma^{m^2})$ and $G^*(\sigma^{2m^2})$.
4. Compute the set of pairs S_{inf}.
5. Construct $G^*(\sigma^\omega)$ using the rule:
   If $(i,j) \in S_{inf}$ then $d(i,j) = -\infty$ else $d(i,j) = d^{m^2}(i,j)$.
6. Check if $G^*(\sigma')$ connected with $G^*(\sigma^\omega)$ has a negative cost cycle.

Figure 6: Algorithm for testing consistency of infinite sequences

---

- Case 1: List S_A. For every member (v_j, v_k) of A (respectively B), if (v_i, v_k) is not in A (resp. B), then add it to A and to S_A (resp. B and S_B). For every member (v_k, v_i) of A (respectively B), if (v_k, v_j) is not in A (resp. B), then add it to A and to S_A (resp. B and S_B). For every edge (v_k, v_i) labeled c, if (v_k, v_j) is not in A', then add it to A' and to $S_{A'}$.

- Case 2: List S_B. For every member (v_j, v_k) of A, if (v_i, v_k) is not in B, then add it to B and to S_B. For every member (v_k, v_i) of A, if (v_k, v_j) is not in B, then add it to B and to S_B. For every edge (v_k, v_i) labeled c, if (v_k, v_j) is not in B', then add it to B' and to $S_{B'}$.

- Case 3: List $S_{A'}$. For every edge (v_j, v_k) labeled d, if (v_i, v_k) is not in A, then add it to A and to S_A.

- Case 4: List $S_{B'}$. For every edge (v_j, v_k) labeled d, if (v_i, v_k) is not in B, then add it to B and to S_B.

Removing a pair from a list and processing it takes time $O(m)$. Since every pair is inserted (and therefore also removed) at most once in each list, it follows that the time complexity is $O(m^3)$.

Algorithm for testing consistency of x

Now we can put together all the pieces to obtain the algorithm of Figure 6. Algorithm of Figure 3 is used to test the consistency of σ' and σ, and to compute the reduced graphs $G^*(\sigma')$ and $G^*(\sigma)$. Step 3 takes time $O(m^3 \cdot \lceil \log m \rceil)$. Computing the set S_{inf} at step 4 can be performed in time $O(m^3)$ as outlined earlier. Combining the two graphs $G^*(\sigma')$ and $G^*(\sigma^\omega)$, and testing for negative cost cycles is easy. This gives the following theorem:

Theorem 2 *The problem of deciding whether a sequence $\sigma'\sigma^\omega$ is timing consistent is solvable in time* $O((|\sigma'| + |\sigma|) \cdot K^2 + K^3 \cdot \lceil \log K \rceil)$.

3 Finding the optimal delay constraint

Given a delay constraint $D = (\Delta, \alpha, \beta)$ it is possible to construct an automaton P_D that accepts precisely those sequences that are timing-consistent with respect to D. This is done by using the algorithm for constructing the *region automaton* of [AD90]. The size of the region automaton grows exponentially with the size of the delay constraints as follows. Let I be the set $\{i \mid \Delta \cap \Delta_i \neq \emptyset\}$, and for a delay δ, let $\gamma(\delta)$ be

$\beta(\delta)$ when it is not ∞, and $\alpha(\delta)$ otherwise. Then the number of states of the region automaton is bounded by

$$|I|! \cdot \prod_{i \in I} |\Delta_i \cap \Delta| \cdot max_{\delta \in \Delta_i \cap \Delta} \{\gamma(\delta) + 1\}.$$

On finding that $\mathbf{x}$ is timing inconsistent with the delay constraint $D = (\Delta_P, \alpha, \beta)$, the next step is to find an "optimal" delay constraint, namely a delay constraint $D(\mathbf{x})$ with $P_{D(\mathbf{x})}$ as small as possible, subject to:

1. $\mathbf{x}$ is timing inconsistent with $D(\mathbf{x})$, and

2. $\mathcal{L}(P_D) \subseteq \mathcal{L}(P_{D(\mathbf{x})})$.

Notice that the condition 2 ensures that to prove that the implementation augmented with P_D satisfies the specification, it suffices to prove that the implementation augmented with $P_{D(\mathbf{x})}$ satisfies the specification.

We find the desired delay constraint in two steps: in the first step we find a small set $\Delta(\mathbf{x})$ of delays such that $\mathbf{x}$ is timing inconsistent with the delay constraint $(\Delta(\mathbf{x}), \alpha, \beta)$; and in the second step we try to modify the bounds α and β to obtain $D(\mathbf{x}) = (\Delta(\mathbf{x}), \alpha', \beta')$. Our approach does not guarantee the minimality of the size of $P_{D(\mathbf{x})}$; it is only a heuristic to reduce the size.

3.1 Finding a minimum set of inconsistent delays

First observe that, if $D = (\Delta, \alpha, \beta)$ and $D' = (\Delta', \alpha, \beta)$ with $\Delta' \subseteq \Delta$, then $\mathcal{L}_D(1) \subseteq \mathcal{L}_{D'}(1)$. Thus we can discard delays that do not contribute to the inconsistency of $\mathbf{x}$. Consequently, we try to find a minimal set of delays that is necessary for the timing inconsistency of $\mathbf{x}$. This is done in two steps.

First we find a set Δ of delays such that $\mathbf{x}$ is timing inconsistent with (Δ, α, β), and Δ involves the least number of processes, that is, $|\{i \mid \Delta \cap \Delta_i \neq \emptyset\}|$ is minimum. We, therefore, look for a minimum size subset $I \subseteq \{1, ..., K\}$, such that $\mathbf{x}$ is inconsistent also with the delay constraint $D_I = (\cup_{i \in I}\Delta_i, \alpha, \beta)$. That is to say, if we run the algorithm of the previous section ignoring the delay events of the processes not in I, we should still end up with timing inconsistency.

We can show that

The problem of finding a subset $I \subseteq \{1, ... K\}$ of minimum size such that a string σ is timing inconsistent with respect to $(\cup_{i \in I}\Delta_i, \alpha, \beta)$ is NP-complete.

Therefore, we exhaustively consider subsets of $\{1, ..., K\}$ in order of increasing size, starting with subsets of size 2. If the smallest I has size n, then the time complexity increases by a factor of $min\{2^K, K^n\}$. Hopefully, n will indeed be small. When n is much larger, then the region automaton is far too large to implement in general, and thus, this exhaustive search is not a bottleneck of the algorithm.

Having identified the minimal set I of processes, the second step is to find a minimal subset $\Delta(\mathbf{x})$ of $\cup_{i \in I}\Delta_i$ preserving the timing-inconsistency of $\mathbf{x}$. This is again done by an exhaustive search over all the subsets of $\cup_{i \in I}\Delta_i$. Clearly, the set $\Delta(\mathbf{x})$ consists of only the delays corresponding to the edges involved in the negative cost cycle.

3.2 Relaxing the bounds

Having identified the optimal set $\Delta(\mathbf{x})$ of delays, we want to adjust the bounding functions α and β so as to reduce the sizes of the constants.

We start with a simple observation that dividing all bounds by a common factor does not affect timing consistency. Let D be a delay constraint (Δ, α, β), and k be the greatest common divisor of all the constants bounding the delays in Δ. Define new lower and upper bounds for the delays by: $\alpha'(\delta) = \alpha(\delta)/k$ and $\beta'(\delta) = \beta(\delta)/k$. It is easy to prove that $\mathcal{L}_D(1) = \mathcal{L}_{D'}(1)$. This property can be used to reduce the size of the region automaton. Instead of using the delay constraint $D = (\Delta(\mathbf{x}), \alpha, \beta)$ we use scaled down versions of α and β, and construct the region automaton $P_{D'}$. If the greatest common divisor k is large, this leads to a big saving: the size of $P_{D'}$ is smaller than that of P_D by a factor of $k^{|I|}$.

It is unlikely that we can apply the optimization of dividing by the greatest common divisor, by itself. However, the situation may improve dramatically if we "preprocess" the bounding functions by relaxing the lower and upper bounds. Again let $D = (\Delta, \alpha, \beta)$ be a delay constraint. Consider a delay $\delta \in \Delta$ with lower bound a and upper bound b. Suppose we replace these bounds by $a' \leq a$ and $b' \geq b$, respectively; that is, we relax the delay bounds by decreasing the lower bound and increasing the upper bound. Let D' be the new delay constraint. It is obvious that any sequence that is timing-consistent with D is also consistent with D' (bu not vice versa). Hence, $\mathcal{L}_D(1) \subseteq \mathcal{L}_{D'}(1)$. However, if we use D' obtained by this transformation as it is, there is no computational benefit; in fact, since we are increasing the upper bounds the size of the region automaton increases. But note that the scaling transformation may be applicable to the new delay bounds in a more effective way than it was to the original bounds. Thus the objective of changing the bounds is to make them all integral multiples of some large common factor. However we should not relax the bounds too much: in particular, we require that the counter-example x is timing inconsistent with respect to D' also. This can be easily understood by an example:

Example 4 Consider two delays: delay δ_1 of P_1 with lower bound 0 and upper bound 2, and delay δ_2 of P_2 with lower bound 5 and upper bound ∞. Suppose in the counter-example x both P_1 and P_2 begin their delays at the first step, and end their delays at the second step: $b_1(x_1) = e_1(x_2) = \delta_1$, and $b_2(x_1) = e_2(x_2) = \delta_2$. Clearly this scenario is timing inconsistent. If we construct a region automaton, the number of states is $2 \cdot 5 \cdot l$ (for some l). To reduce the size, we first replace the lower bound $\alpha(\delta_2)$ by 4 which imposes a weaker bound. Now we can divide all bounds by their common factor, 2. Then δ_1 has lower bound 0 and upper bound 1, whereas δ_2 had lower bound 2 and upper bound ∞. The number of states in the new region automaton is $1 \cdot 2 \cdot l$, a saving by a factor of 5. Note that had we replaced the original lower bound for δ_2 by 2, we could have eventually reduced all bounds to 1 after scaling. But this would not have been helpful because x would have been timing-consistent with the new constraints. ∎

Thus the problem is to construct new lower and upper bound maps α' and β' from the delay constraint $(\Delta(x), \alpha, \beta)$ by replacing, for each delay $\delta \in \Delta(x)$, its lower bound $\alpha(\delta)$ by $\alpha'(\delta) \leq \alpha(\delta)$, and its upper bound $\beta(\delta)$ by $\beta'(\delta) \geq \beta(\delta)$, such that x is timing inconsistent with $(\Delta(x), \alpha', \beta')$, so as to minimize the magnitudes of constants after scaling (dividing by the greatest common divisor of all the bounds). Recall that the algorithm to test consistency of x reports that x is inconsistent when it finds a negative cost cycle in the associated weighted graph $G(x)$. We adjust the delay bounds so that the negativeness of the cost of this cycle is preserved. Recall that in the weighted graph all upper bounds appear as positive costs and all lower bounds appear as negative costs. Now the optimization problem can be stated precisely as follows.

> Given a set of nonnegative integers $C = \{a_1, \ldots a_m, b_1, \ldots b_n\}$ such that $\Sigma_j b_j < \Sigma_i a_i$ find another set of nonnegative integers $C' = \{a'_1, \ldots a'_m, b'_1, \ldots b'_n\}$ such that
>
> 1. $a'_i \leq a_i$ for $1 \leq i \leq m$,
> 2. $b'_j \geq b_j$ for $1 \leq j \leq n$,
> 3. $\Sigma_j b'_j < \Sigma_i a'_i$
>
> so as to minimize the maximum of the set $\{n / gcd(C') \mid n \in C'\}$.

We solve the problem using the following facts:

1. The greatest common divisor of the optimal solution set C' cannot exceed the maximum of $a_1, \ldots a_m$.

2. If the greatest common divisor of the optimal solution set is k then it is easy to find the optimal solution. First, choose $a'_i = \lfloor a_i/k \rfloor$ and $b'_j = \lceil b_j/k \rceil$, and then keep subtracting k from the largest a'_i as long as condition 3 holds (this does not involve much computation assuming that a_i's are sorted initially).

Putting these two pieces together, we get a pseudo-polynomial algorithm which runs in time $O[(m+n)\cdot max\{a_i\}]$.

Now the delay constraint $D(\mathbf{x}) = (\Delta(\mathbf{x}), \alpha', \beta')$ is chosen as follows. For a delay $\delta \in \Delta(\mathbf{x})$, if $\alpha(\delta)$ equals some $a_i \in C$ then we set $\alpha'(\delta)$ to be a_i' of the optimal solution; if $\alpha(\delta)$ is not in C (that is, the lower bound edge is not in the negative cost cycle) then we set $\alpha'(\delta) = 0$. Similarly, if $\beta(\delta) = b_j$ then we set $\alpha'(\delta) = b_j'$; if $\beta(\delta)$ is not in C then we set $\beta'(\delta) = \infty$.

Acknowledgements

We thank Edith Cohen, David Johnson, and Jeff Lagarias for helpful discussions.

References

[AD90] R. Alur and D.L. Dill. Automata for modeling real-time systems. In *Automata, Languages and Programming: Proceedings of the 17th ICALP*, Lecture Notes in Computer Science 443, pages 322–335. Springer-Verlag, 1990.

[Cho74] Y. Choueka. Theories of automata on ω-tapes: a simplified approach. *Journal of Computer and System Sciences*, 8:117–141, 1974.

[Dil89] D.L. Dill. Timing assumptions and verification of finite-state concurrent systems. In J. Sifakis, editor, *Automatic Verification Methods for Finite State Systems*, Lecture Notes in Computer Science 407. Springer-Verlag, 1989.

[Kur87] R. P. Kurshan. Reducibility in analysis of coordination. In *Lecture Notes in Computer Science*, volume 103, pages 19–39. Springer-Verlag, 1987.

[Kur90] R. P. Kurshan. Analysis of discrete event coordination. In *Lecture Notes in Computer Science*, volume 430, pages 414–453. Springer-Verlag, 1990.

[Yan90] M. Yannakakis. Graph-theoretic methods in database theory. In *Proceedings of the 9th ACM Symposium on Principles of Database Systems*, pages 230–242, 1990.

A Verification Strategy for Timing Constrained Systems

Felice Balarin   Alberto L. Sangiovanni-Vincentelli

Department of Electrical Engineering and Computer Science
University of California, Berkeley, CA 94720

Abstract. Verification of many properties can be done without regard to the speed of the components of a finite-state system. However, some of the properties can be verified only under certain timing constraints. We propose a new verification strategy for timing constrained finite-state systems. The strategy can avoid the state space explosion problem for a class of systems. A model of such systems, called *timed L-process*, compatible with the strategy, is also developed.

1 Introduction

Recently, Dill [Dil89] and Alur and Dill [AD90] proposed a method for incorporating timing restriction into a model of communicating finite-state systems by introducing the notion of a timed automaton, containing fictitious time-measuring elements called clocks [AD90] or timers [Dil89]. The verification problem is shown to be equivalent to the speed-independent verification problem on an appropriate automaton. The fundamental problem with both approaches is state space explosion, i.e. state space growing exponentially in the number of timers (clocks).

Kurshan [Kur91] suggested to carry out the verification process on timed systems with COSPAN [HK88], a verification system for untimed processes, by relaxing the time constraints, verifying the relaxed system and if the verification is unsuccessful check whether the run that violates the property to be verified is infeasible under the timing constraints. If this is so, Kurshan removes the run and repeats the process. This strategy is appealing but heuristic in nature. There was no proof that the process would eventually converge to provably the correct answer.

In this paper, we introduce the notion of *pauses*, and construct an equivalent (non-pausing) automaton. In contrast to previous approaches, we build an equivalent automaton as a composition of the speed-independent (or unrestricted) automaton and many small automata. This decomposition of timing constraints enable us to perform the verification on a smaller, abstracted automaton which includes only some aspects of timing constraints. This leads to an iterative verification strategy similar to the heuristic proposed by Kurshan, where a verification process is started with the unrestricted automaton, which is then composed with simple automata imposing timing constraints, but only after the verification has failed, and imposing only those constraints which are violated in the failure report.

The rest of this paper is organized as follows. In section 2, we introduce the notion of timed L-process, and then we construct the equivalent (not timed) L-process in section 3. In section 4 two main steps of the proposed verification strategy are described: extracting timing violations from the failure report, and imposing that subset of timing constraints to the model of the system. Final remarks are provided in section 5.

2 Timed L-Processes

An L-process [Kur90] is an automaton over infinite sequences, distinguished from others by its alphabet and its acceptance conditions.

An alphabet of L-processes is a set of atoms of Boolean algebra L. It is convenient to think of atoms of L as distinct assignments to several variables taking values in finite domains. A boolean algebra L can be than thought of as a power set of a set of atoms, which is obviously closed under intersection (or product) $*$, union (or sum) $+$ and complement $\sim$. A partial order $\leq$ can be thought of as a set inclusion, multiplicative identity 1, as a set of all atoms, and additive identity 0 as an empty set.

Although ideas presented here are applicable to other automata, we have chosen to develop them in the framework of L-processes, because algebraic structure on the alphabet enables us to describe easily manipulations we use, like adding additional variables, or changing the transition structure

Acceptance conditions of L-processes (called cycle sets and recur edges) are particular because of their negative nature, i.e. a run is accepted unless it is excepted by cycle sets or recur edges. Hence, if no acceptance conditions are given a language of the L-process contains all sequences that have a run from some of the initial states. A product $\otimes$ (or "composition") of L-processes satisfying: $\mathcal{L}(P_1 \otimes P_2) = \mathcal{L}(P_1) \cap \mathcal{L}(P_2)$, has been defined in [Kur90].

It can be verified automatically whether the language of an L-process is contained in the language describing some properties (e.g. [HK88]). If this is not the case, there exists at least one loop of states reachable from the initial states, that is an accepting run of some sequence not in the language of the task. Usually, one such a loop is included in the failure report produced by automatic tools.

We extend L-processes by allowing them to remain in designated "pause" states a limited amount of time. This extension is called a *simple timed L-process*. Intuitively, we describe one pause by a pair of states $\{v_i^@, v_i^d\}$, as shown in Figure 1. When a system enters a state $v_i^@$, a pause begins. A symbol p_i, uniquely associated with that state indicates that a pause is in progress. A pause finishes when a system exits a state v_i^d. The time spent in these two states must satisfy the lower bound l_i and the upper bound u_i. To be able to treat uniformly both constraints of type $x < c$ and of type $x \leq c$ we adopt the concept of *bounds* introduced in [AIKY92]. The set of bounds is an extension of the set of integers with expression of the form n^- which can be thought of as a number infinitesimally smaller than the integer n. Addition and comparison are then naturally extended.

Formally, a simple timed L-process T is a pair (P,d), where P is an L-process (called *unrestricted process of T*) and d is a set of pauses. A *pause* $i \in d$ is a 5-tuple $(v_i^@, v_i^d, p_i, l_i, u_i)$ satisfying the following:

- l_i and u_i are bounds satisfying $-\infty < l_i < 0,$[1] $0 < u_i \le \infty$ and of course $-l_i \le u_i$,
- $v_i^@$ and v_i^d are states of P and $p_i \in L$ is such that $M_P(v_i^@, v_i^@) = M_P(v_i^@, v_i^d) = p_i$, no other transitions depend on p_i, $v_i^@$ has no other fanouts and v_i^d has no other fanins,
- $V^@$ (a set of all $v_i^@$), V^d (a set of all v_i^d) and the set of initial states of P are mutually disjoint.

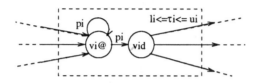

Fig. 1. A pair of states representing one pause

Figure 2a shows three examples of simple timed L-processes. Each process contains one pause, with associated bounds $-2^-, \infty; -1, 2^-$ and $-1, 3$, respectively.

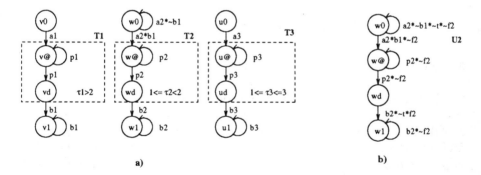

a)   b)

Fig. 2. Examples of simple timed L-processes (a) and corresponding unrestricted $\widehat{L}$-process (b)

A *timed sequence* (a,t) consists of a sequence a and a timing function t assigning a real positive time t_k to every a_k in a. A timing is naturally extended

---

[1] It is convenient to represent lower bound constraint of type $x \ge n$ as $-x \le -n$, and of type $x > n$ as $-x \le n^-$.

to some run v of a by: $t(v_k) = t(a_k) = t_k$. If pause i is active, the *elapsed time* of pause i at v_k, $(\tau_i)_k$ is defined to be the difference between $t(v_k)$ and the time the pause i has last started. It is convenient to extend this definition to the whole v by setting $(\tau_i)_k = 0$, if v_k is not an element of pause i.

We say that a t is a *proper timing* of v if all of the following consistency conditions hold:

1. $t_1 = 0$, $t_{k+1} \geq t_k$, for all $k \geq 1$ (time is non-decreasing),
2. if $v_k \notin V^d$ and $v_k \neq v_{k-1}$, then $t_k = t_{k-1}$ (all state changes outside a pause are instantaneous, the time can advance only inside a pause, or in a self-loop),
3. if $v_k = v_i^d \in V^d$ then $-(\tau_i)_k \leq l_i$ (pause-finishing times satisfy lower bounds),
4. $(\tau_i)_k \leq u_i$ (elapsed times satisfy upper bounds).

We do not make an usual requirement that time progresses without bounds, or equivalently we do allow that infinitely many events happen in a bounded amount of time. Hence, a failure to complete a pause can be acceptable. The time progress requirement can be easily added by making $\{v_i^@\}$ a cycle set. Since this has no implications to results presented here, we leave it out of the definition, as the users choice.

We say that a timed sequence (a, t) is in the *language* of a simple timed L-process $T = (P, d)$, and write $(a, t) \in \mathcal{L}(T)$, if and only if there exists v such that v is an accepting run of a in P, and t is a proper timing of v.

Pauses are tied with states, so in a simple timed L-process only one pause can be active at one time. To overcome this limitation we define a *timed L-process* as a N-tuple of simple timed processes $(T_1, \ldots, T_N)$. We say that T_n, $1 \leq n \leq N$ are the components of T. A language of the timed process T is defined to be an intersection of languages of T_n's. An *untimed language* of T is defined by: $Untime(\mathcal{L}(T)) = \{a | \exists t, (a, t) \in \mathcal{L}(T)\}$.

3 Equivalent Non-Pausing Process

In this section we will sketch the construction of the equivalent untimed process $\widehat{P}$ for some timed L-process T. We will define such a process in some extension $\widehat{L}$ of Boolean algebra L. $\widehat{P}$ and T are equivalent in a sense that the projection on L of the language of $\widehat{P}$ is exactly equal to the untimed language of T. Therefore, to prove $Untime(\mathcal{L}(T)) \subseteq \mathcal{L}(A)$, where A is some L-automaton (hence also $\widehat{L}$-automaton), it is enough to prove: $\mathcal{L}(\widehat{P}) \subseteq \mathcal{L}(A)$. Full details of the construction, as well as the proof of equivalence are given in [BSV92].

Given a timed L-process $T = (T_1, \ldots, T_N)$ defined by its components' unrestricted L-processes $P_1, \ldots, P_N$, and its components' sets of pauses $d_1, \ldots, d_N$, we construct $\widehat{P}$ as a product of the *unrestricted $\widehat{L}$-process* U the *region $\widehat{L}$-process* R.

The unrestricted $\widehat{L}$-process U is a composition of $\widehat{L}$-processes $U_1, \ldots, U_N$, each U_n being basically the same as P_n, except that we add some additional information to its output. This information is needed to coordinate U with R.

The first piece of information we add is whether or not a transition in P_n can take some time, as required by consistency condition 2. We will extend the Boolean algebra L by a new variable t and use it to label all transition that must take some time. If we also label by $\sim t$ all transition that must not take any time, we will ensure that transition from these two classes will not happen simultaneously. Specifically, we multiply with $\sim t$ all entries in the transition matrix of P_n, except the diagonal (i.e. self-loops), and the entries corresponding to transitions inside a pause. Similarly, we will add a new "flag variable" f_i for each pause i in d_n. We use f_i as a signal that pause i is finishing. Consequently, we multiply with f_i all entries of the transition matrix corresponding to the fanouts of v_i^d, and multiply by $\sim f_i$ all other entries. The process U_2 for the example in Figure 2a is shown in Figure 2b.

It is easy to see that the projection of the language of U on algebra L contains exactly those sequences that are accepted by all P_n's, including those sequences that can not be properly timed, hence are not in $Untime(\mathcal{L}(T))$. It is the purpose of the process R to eliminate such sequences from the language. Basically, R keeps record of possible elapsed times in all pauses, and does not allow a finish of some pause if the elapsed can not satisfy given bounds. Alur and Dill [AD90] have shown that it is not necessary to remember exact values of the elapsed time, but only the integer part and the ordering of fractional parts. They have also shown that if no upper bound is given all values larger than the lower bound can be considered equivalent.

To keep track of the values of elapsed times we extend the Boolean algebra with one "multi valued variable" $\widehat{\tau}_i$ for each pause i. A variable $\widehat{\tau}_i$ is a finite abstraction of τ_i, more precisely if $u_i < \infty$ it takes a distinct value for each integer and open interval between integers in $[0, u_i]$. If $u_i = \infty$, all values of τ_i larger then the lower bound correspond to single value of $\widehat{\tau}_i$. In slight abuse of notation we use bounds to represent a domain of $\widehat{\tau}_i$. More precisely, we use integers to represent themselves and bounds of the form n^- to represent intervals $(n-1, n)$, or $(n-1, \infty)$ if $u_i = \infty$ and $l_i = (n-1)$ or $l_i = (n-1)^-$.

We construct the region process as a product of *difference tracking* automata $R_{\tau_i - \tau_j \leq c}$ and *zero tracking* automata $R_{\tau_i = 0}$. We build one automaton $R_{\tau_i = 0}$ for each pause i and one automaton $R_{\tau_i - \tau_j \leq c}$ for each pair of pauses i and j and every bound c necessary to uniquely determine the value of $\widehat{\tau}_i$ (or $\widehat{\tau}_j$) given that $\tau_i = 0$ ($\tau_j = 0$, respectively), and that truth values of $\tau_i - \tau_j \leq c$ for all c's are known. For example, variables $\widehat{\tau}_2$ and $\widehat{\tau}_3$ take values in $\{0, 1^-, 1, 2^-\}$ and $\{0, 1^-, 1, 2^-, 2, 3^-, 3\}$ respectively, so we need $R_{\tau_3 - \tau_2 \leq c}$ for each c in

$$\{-1^-, -1, 0^-0, 1^-, 1, 2^-, 2, 3^-\}$$

The purpose of the $R_{\tau_i - \tau_j \leq c}$ is to establish whether $\tau_i - \tau_j \leq c$ is satisfied or not. Its state space is an abstraction of a (possibly infinite) rectangle containing all possible pairs of values of τ_i and τ_j. All points satisfying $\tau_i - \tau_j \leq c$ are contained in a "good" state and all others make a "bad" state. A unique initial state is the one containing point $(0, 0)$. It has no cycle sets nor recur edges, and its transition matrix reflects possible *trajectories* in the rectangle containing feasible values of τ_i and τ_j. The trajectory can be constructed for any sequence $a \in \mathcal{L}(U)$ and any timing t of a. The trajectory is constructed incrementally, adding a segment from $((\tau_i)_k, (\tau_j)_k)$ to $((\tau_i)_{k+1}, (\tau_j)_{k+1})$ according to a_k and t_k. The construction rules are as follows:

Rule 1 : we begin at point $(0,0)$ and stay there as long as neither pause i nor j are active, i.e. $a_k \leq \sim p_i* \sim p_j$,

Rule 2(3) : if pause i (j) is active and pause j (i) is not, i.e. if $a_k \leq p_i* \sim p_j$ $(a_k \leq \sim p_i * p_j)$, we move forward, along the τ_i (τ_j) axis,

Rule 4 : if both pauses i and j are active, i.e. if $a_k \leq p_i * p_j$, we move forward, along a 45° line,

Rule 5(6) : if pause j (i) is finishing pausing and pause i (j) is not, i.e. if $a_k \leq f_j* \sim f_i$ $(a_k \leq \sim f_j * f_i)$ we move to the point $((\tau_i)_k, 0)$ $((0, (\tau_j)_k)$ respectively),

Rule 7 : if both pauses i and j are finishing, i.e. if $a_k \leq f_j * f_i$, we move to the point $(0,0)$.

The length of all forward movements is determined by $t_{k+1} - t_k$. A transition between states of $R_{\tau_i - \tau_j \leq c}$ exists if a segment of some properly timed trajectory connects two points in those states. The transition is enabled if the conditions stated in the rule that generated the segment are met. More precisely, for any pair $v, w \in \{good, bad\}$ the corresponding transition matrix entry is of the form:

$$M(v, w) = \sum (enabling\_condition * \sum ((\hat{\tau}_i = \hat{x}) * (\hat{\tau}_j = \hat{y})))$$

where the outer sum goes over all eight enabling conditions in the left column of Table 1, and the inner sum goes over all abstracted values $(\hat{x}, \hat{y})$ of some pair of positive real numbers[2] $(x, y) \in w$ satisfying the corresponding constraint in the right column of Table 1.

Table 1. Rules for building a transition matrix of difference tracking L-processes

enabling condition	applied rule(s)	constraints on $(x,y) \in w$
$t* \sim p_i* \sim p_j$	1	$x = y = 0, (x, y) \in v$
$t * p_i* \sim p_j$	2	$y = 0, \exists \delta > 0 : (x - \delta, y) \in v$
$t* \sim p_i * p_j$	3	$x = 0, \exists \delta > 0 : (x, y - \delta) \in v$
$t * p_i * p_j$	4	$\exists \delta > 0 : (x - \delta, y - \delta) \in v$
$\sim t* \sim f_i * f_j$	5	$y = 0, \exists z \leq u_j : -z \leq l_j, (x, z) \in v$
$\sim t * f_i* \sim f_j$	6	$x = 0, \exists z \leq u_i : -z \leq l_i, (z, y) \in v$
$\sim t * f_i * f_j$	7	$\exists (q, z) \in v : q \leq u_i, -q \leq l_i, z \leq u_j, -z \leq l_j$
$\sim t* \sim f_i* \sim f_j$	1-7	$(x, y) \in v$

[2] If w is a good state $(x, y) \in w$ stands for $x - y \leq c$, and if w is a bad state it stands for $x - y > c$.

One possible trajectory for pauses 3 and 2 in Figure 2a is shown in Figure 3a. Each segment of the trajectory is labeled with the number of the rule that generated it. An $\widehat{L}$-process $R_{\tau_3 - \tau_2 \leq 2}$ is shown in 3b. The only transition which has a small enough expression to fit in the figure is $bad \to good$. The rest of the transitions are given in Table 2. Each transition expression is formed as a sum over all rows of products of the expression in the first column and the expression in the column corresponding to that transition.

Table 2. An example of the transition matrix of a difference tracking L-process

enabling condition	transition expression		
	$good \to good$	$good \to bad$	$bad \to bad$
$t* \sim p_3 * \sim p_2$	$\widehat{\tau}_3 = 0 * \widehat{\tau}_2 = 0$	0	0
$t * p_3 * \sim p_2$	$0 < \widehat{\tau}_3 \leq 2 * \widehat{\tau}_2 = 0$	$\widehat{\tau}_3 > 2 * \widehat{\tau}_2 = 0$	$\widehat{\tau}_3 > 2 * \widehat{\tau}_2 = 0$
$t* \sim p_3 * p_2$	$\widehat{\tau}_3 = 0 * \widehat{\tau}_2 > 0$	0	0
$t * p_3 * p_2$	$\widehat{\tau}_3 > 0 * \widehat{\tau}_2 > 0*$ $(\widehat{\tau}_3 < 3 + \widehat{\tau}_2 \geq 1)$	0	$\widehat{\tau}_3 > 2 * 0 < \widehat{\tau}_2 < 1$
$\sim t* \sim f_3 * f_2$	$0 < \widehat{\tau}_3 \leq 2 * \widehat{\tau}_2 = 0$	$\widehat{\tau}_3 > 2 * \widehat{\tau}_2 = 0$	0
$\sim t * f_3* \sim f_2$	$\widehat{\tau}_3 = 0$	0	0
$\sim t * f_3 * f_2$	$\widehat{\tau}_3 = 0 * \widehat{\tau}_2 = 0$	0	0
$\sim t* \sim f_3* \sim f_2$	$\widehat{\tau}_3 \leq 2 + \widehat{\tau}_2 \geq 1+$ $\widehat{\tau}_3 < 3 * \widehat{\tau}_2 > 0$	0	$\widehat{\tau}_3 > 2 * \widehat{\tau}_2 < 1$

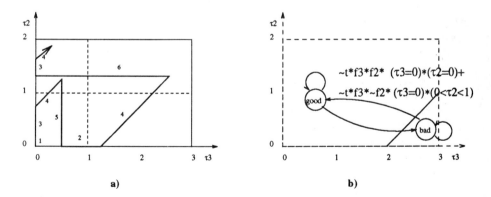

Fig. 3. A trajectory (a) and one difference tracking L-process (b)

Next, we define processes $R_{\tau_i = 0}$ which track whether the elapsed time in pause i can be zero or not. For each pause i we define an $\widehat{L}$-process $R_{\tau_i = 0}$ with two states v_i^0 and v_i^1, the first one being a unique initial state, no recur edges nor cycle sets and transition matrix:

$$M_{Q_i}(v_i^0, v_i^0) = (t* \sim p_i + \sim t* \sim f_i) * (\hat{\tau}_i = 0) \quad M_{Q_i}(v_i^0, v_i^1) = t * p_i * (\hat{\tau}_i > 0)$$
$$M_{Q_i}(v_i^1, v_i^1) = \quad \sim f_i * (\hat{\tau}_i > 0) \quad M_{Q_i}(v_i^1, v_i^0) = f_i * (\hat{\tau}_i = 0)$$

Intuitively, $R_{\tau_i=0}$ is in v_i^0 if $\tau_i = 0$ and in v_i^1 if $\tau_i > 0$. A transition from v_i^0 to v_i^1 must absolutely take some time. A transition from v_i^1 to v_i^0 occurs if the pause i has finished. Note that f_i is not accepted in v_i^0.

4   Verification Strategy

Verifying a task on $\hat{P}$ can run into difficulties, due to the large size of the state space that has to be searched. We propose a verification strategy to avoid this problem. We start a verification process with the unrestricted L-process U. If the verification succeeds, we have verified the task. If the verification fails, there is at least one sequence which is in the language of the current abstraction of $\hat{P}$, but not in the language of the task. We analyze one run of such a sequence. If that run violates no timing constraints, we have proved that the task is not satisfied. However, if the run does violate some timing constraints, we compose the current abstraction of $\hat{P}$ with some simple abstraction of the process R, which is guaranteed to eliminate that run. We repeat this process until the verification is terminated, either successfully or unsuccessfully. This strategy can lead to significant savings in time and space, provided that the behavior of the system is not heavily dependent on the timing constraints. The verification strategy is outlined in Algorithm 1.

Algorithm 1: verification strategy
```
procedure verify_task()
   initialize P_c = U
   while not stop
       try to verify a task on P_c
       if success then stop, the task is verified
       find a timing violating loop G
       if such a loop does not exist then stop, the task is not verified
       P_c =eliminate_loop(G, P_c)
   end while
end procedure
```

4.1   Identifying Timing Violation

Assume that the error report from the verifier contains a loop and a path to that loop from the initial state. We can unfold the loop, thus forming an infinite sequence of states. We form a graph with nodes being states in the sequence and the edges representing constraints on elapsed time between states. There are four kinds of edges corresponding to four consistency constraints:

backward non-pause edges: (induced by consistency condition 1) for all $k >$ 1 we add an edge $(k, k-1)$ and label it with "≥ 0",

forward non-pause edges: (induced by consistency condition 2) if $t(v_k) = t(v_{k+1})$ must be satisfied by consistency condition 2, we add an edge from $(k, k+1)$ and label it with "≤ 0",

backward pause edges: (induced by consistency condition 3) if some pause i starts at node k and is finishing at node k', we add an edge (k', k) and label it with "$-\tau_i \leq l_i$",

forward pause edges: (induced by consistency condition 4) if some pause i starts at node k and is still active at node k' and $u_i < \infty$, we add an edge (k, k') and label it with "$\tau_i \leq u_i$".

The sequence can not be consistently timed only if there exists a loop in the graph such that every sum of numbers satisfying upper-bound constraints in forward edges is smaller than any sum of number satisfying lower-bound constraints in backward edges. We call such a loop an overconstrained loop. If we set a weight of an edge to be the right hand side of its label, then overconstrained loops are exactly those with weights smaller than zero. Finding a negative weighted loop is well studied problem running in a low polynomial time in the size of the graph (e.g. [Tar83]). However, in our case the graph is infinite. Therefore we have have modified the existing algorithm to process nodes in natural order (determined by the sequence) and to stop as soon as a solution to constraints which can be repeated infinitely often is found. It can be shown that if such a solution exists it will be found in finite number of steps.

Without loss of generality, we assume that the loop is minimal, in the sense that removing any edge enables proper timing of nodes. Once a loop has been identified, we collapse all non-pause edges, by merging their incident nodes. However, we mark nodes obtained by collapsing forward non-pause edges. Such a loop is an input to the algorithm which eliminates a timing constraint, described in the next subsection.

For example, for the timed L-process in Figure 2a, a sequence of states:

$$v_1 = \begin{pmatrix} v_0 \\ w_0 \\ u_0 \end{pmatrix}, v_2 = \begin{pmatrix} v^@ \\ w_0 \\ u^@ \end{pmatrix}, v_3 = \begin{pmatrix} v^d \\ w_0 \\ u^@ \end{pmatrix}, v_4 = \begin{pmatrix} v_1 \\ w^@ \\ u^@ \end{pmatrix}, v_5 = \begin{pmatrix} v_1 \\ w^d \\ u^@ \end{pmatrix}, \ldots \quad (1)$$

is not possible under the timing restrictions, because no timing can satisfy conflicting constraints in the following table:

constraint	edge	edge label
$t(v_5) - t(v_2) \leq 3$	$v_2 \rightarrow v_5$	$\tau_3 \leq 3$
$t(v_5) - t(v_4) \geq 1$	$v_5 \rightarrow v_4$	$-\tau_2 \leq -1$
$t(v_4) - t(v_3) \leq 0$	$v_4 \rightarrow v_3$	≤ 0
$t(v_3) - t(v_2) > 2$	$v_3 \rightarrow v_2$	$-\tau_1 \leq -2^-$

The overconstrained loop corresponding to the edges in the table is shown in Figure 4a with non-pause edges collapsed.

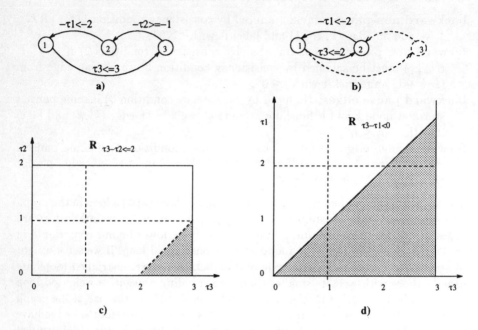

Fig. 4. An overconstrained loop and processes to eliminate it

4.2 Eliminating Timing Violations

Given an overconstrained loop G, we want to build some abstraction of R which eliminates that run. The procedure is outlined in Algorithm 2. We will follow the execution of the algorithm for the overconstrained loop in Figure 4a.

Since no nodes are marked we skip the first two steps of the algorithm. We start with any "peak" node, i.e. a node with one in-coming forward edge and one outgoing backward edge. In our example, node 3 is the only peak node. Labels $\tau_3 \leq 3$ and $-\tau_2 \leq -1$ indicate that pause 2 finishes while pause 3 is still active or just finishing. This is possible only if those two conditions can be simultaneously satisfied, or in other words, if $R_{\tau_3-\tau_2\leq 2}$ is in the good state. If $R_{\tau_3-\tau_2\leq 2}$ is in the bad state at that time, a finish of pause 2 will not be accepted and the sequence will be eliminated from the language. Therefore, in step 3 of the Algorithm 2 we compose a current abstraction of $\widehat{P}$ with the process $R_{\tau_3-\tau_2\leq 2}$. We do not need to consider edges $(1,3)$ and $(3,2)$ any more, so in step 4 we remove them from the graph. However, we do need to consider under which conditions will the process $R_{\tau_3-\tau_2\leq 2}$ be in a good or bad state. It is clear from Figure 4c that it will be in the good state at node 3, only if $\tau_3 \leq 2$ when pause 2 starts at node 2. Therefore, in step 5 we add an edge $(1,2)$ and label it with $\tau_3 \leq 2$, as shown in Figure 4b. A dual case, when the start of the pause associated with the backward edge precedes the start of the pause associated with the forward edge, is considered in step 6.

We repeat steps 3–6 while there are peak nodes. In our example only one additional iteration is necessary, generating an abstracted pair region process $R_{\tau_3-\tau_1\leq 0-}$, shown in Figure 4d. These two processes are enough to eliminate the sequence (1), because the process $R_{\tau_3-\tau_1\leq 0-}$ will initially be in the bad state and remain there until pause 1 finishes, so it will accept the finish of pause 1 only if $\hat{\tau}_2 > 2$, which in turn will force $R_{\tau_3-\tau_2\leq 2}$ to move to the bad state, where it will not accept the finish of pause 2.

This new abstraction is also enough to verify the task: " b_3 *always appear before* b_2 ", which is not satisfied if timing constraints are ignored. Using our strategy, we have verified the property using the abstraction of R that has only 4 states, in contrast to the full process R that has 960 states.

Algorithm 2: eliminating a timing violation
   procedure eliminate_loop(G, P_c)
    /* G - an overconstrained loop, P_c - a current abstraction of $\widehat{P}$ */
step 1: **for each** (k, m), labeled $-\tau_i \leq b$, m marked **do** $P_c = P_c \otimes R_{\tau_i = 0}$
step 2: **for each** pair (k, m), (m, n) labeled $\tau_i \leq b$, $-\tau_j \leq c$, m marked **do**
    $P_c = P_c \otimes R_{\tau_i = 0} \otimes R_{\tau_i - \tau_j \leq c}$
    while there exist a pair of edges (k, m), (m, n) labeled $\tau_i \leq b$, $-\tau_j \leq c$
step 3: $P_c = P_c \otimes R_{\tau_i - \tau_j \leq b+c}$
step 4: remove from G edges (k, m) and (m, n)
step 5: **if** $k < n$ **then** add to G edge (k, n) and label it $\tau_i \leq b + c$
step 6: **if** $k > n$ **then** add to G edge (k, n) and label it $-\tau_j \leq b + c$
    end while
    return P_c
   end procedure

Step 1 is executed only if there is a backward edge coming into a marked node. For example, had the node 2 in Figure 4a been marked, the processes in Figure 4c and d would not eliminate the sequence (1). The marking of the node 2 would indicate that pause 2 starts before pause 1 finishes, but no time can elapse between these two events. The process in Figure 4d would still force $\hat{\tau}_3 > 2$ when pause 1 finishes, but this would not be enough to force the process in Figure 4c to the bad state, because pause 2 would be active, making for example $\hat{\tau}_3 = 3^-, \hat{\tau}_2 = 1$ a possible choice to remain in the good state. This could be easily fixed by composing P_c with $R_{\tau_2=0}$ which would ensure $\hat{\tau}_2 = 0$ until some transition that can take time occurs.

Step 2 is executed only if there is a marked node with in-coming forward edge and out-going backward, indicating that the pause associated with the forward edge finishes before the pause associated with the backward edge, but no time

162

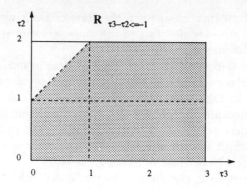

Fig. 5. Additional process needed when the peak node is marked

can elapse between these two events. Assume, for example, that the node 3 in Figure 4a is marked. Even if the process shown in Figure 4c is in a bad state, when pause 3 finishes it will move to the good state, where the finish of pause 2 is acceptable. We fix this in step 2 by composing P_c with $R_{\tau_3=0}$ and $R_{\tau_3-\tau_2\leq-1}$ (Figure 5). Now, when pause 3 finishes and the process Figure 4c is in the bad state it must be that $\widehat{\tau}_3 = 0$ and $\widehat{\tau}_2 = 1^-$, so the process in Figure 5 must be in the bad state. Since no time can elapse, it will remain there until pause 2 finishes. But $R_{\tau_3=0}$ will force $\widehat{\tau}_3 = 0$ (as long as no time elapses) and the process in Figure 5 accepts the finish of pause 2 only if $\widehat{\tau}_3 > 0$. Therefore, the sequence (1) is eliminated.

In general case, Algorithm 2 ensures, that the original sequence no longer has a run in the updated abstraction of $\widehat{P}$, because at least one of the difference tracking processes will be in the bad state at the corresponding peak node, hence it will not accept the finish of the "x-axis pause".

By Algorithm 2, it is possible to eliminate any timing inconsistent sequence, by composing the current abstraction of the system with some difference tracking and zero tracking processes. Since there are only finitely many of those, the iteration will converge in a finite number of steps.

5 Conclusions

To model timing behavior of finite-state systems, we have proposed timed L-processes. We believe that timed L-processes offer two major advantages over previous approaches. First, an equivalent L-process is defined as a composition of an unrestricted L-process and many smaller processes. We provide a transition matrix for each of these processes. In this way, the automatic generation of the equivalent process is simpler than in [Dil89] where there is one big region automaton and the computation of the next state function includes non-trivial matrix manipulation, and in [AD90] where the equivalent automaton is defined as a single automaton with a very large state space.

More importantly, we propose a verification strategy to deal with the state space explosion problem. Basically, we propose a "trial and error" strategy, starting with the unrestricted process, and using at each step only the minimum subset of timing constraints necessary to eliminate the reported error. Although in the worst case the construction of the full region process is necessary, in our experience that is rarely the case. In fact none of the examples we tried required it. However, even if the region process is only partially constructed, the verification of timing constrained systems remains a complex and time-consuming task, requiring further research and development of more efficient techniques.

Besides time and space saving, the proposed strategy could also have a positive impact on the design. Indeed, to perform the required task, a design does not have to meet all timing constraints, but only those used in the verification. Relaxing of constraints could be used to optimize the design.

Acknowledgment

The authors would like to thank Prof. R. Brayton, R. Murgai and T. Villa for many useful discussions. We also acknowledge R. Kurshan for his presentations at UCBerkeley that sparked our interest in the subject. This work has been supported by DARPA under contract JFBI90-073.

References

[AD90]   Rajeev Alur and David L. Dill. Automata for modelling real-time systems. In M.S. Paterson, editor, *ICALP 90 Automata, languages, and programming: 17th international colloquium*. Springer-Verlag, 1990. LNCS vol. 443.

[AIKY92] Rajeev Alur, Alon Itai, R. P. Kurshan, and M. Yannakakis. Timing verification by successive approximation. In *Proceeding of the Forth Workshop on Computer-Aided Verification (CAV '92)*, June 1992.

[BSV92]   Felice Balarin and Alberto L. Sangiovanni-Vincentelli. Formal verification of timing constrained finite-state systems. Technical report, University of California Berkeley, 1992. UCB ERL M92/8.

[Dil89]   David L. Dill. Timing assumptions and verifications of finite-state concurrent systems. In Joseph Sifakis, editor, *Automatic Verification Methods for Finite-State Systems*. Springer-Verlag, 1989. LNCS vol. 407.

[HK88]   Z. Har'El and R. P. Kurshan. Software for analysis of coordination. In *Proceedings of the International Conference on System Science*, pages 382–385, 1988.

[Kur90]   R. P. Kurshan. Analysis of discrete event coordination. In J.W. de Bakker, W.P. de Roever, and G. Rozenberg, editors, *Stepwise Refinement of Distributed Systems : Models, Formalisms, Correctness*, pages 414–453. Springer-Verlag, 1990. LNCS vol. 430.

[Kur91]   R. P. Kurshan, 1991. private communications.

[Tar83]   Robert Endre Tarjan. *Data Structures and Network Algorithms*. Society for Industrial and Applied Mathematics, Philadelphia, PA, 1983.

Using unfoldings to avoid the state explosion problem in the verification of asynchronous circuits

K. L. McMillan

School of Computer Science
Carnegie Mellon University

1 Introduction

A number of researchers have observed that the arbitrary interleaving of concurrent actions is a major contributor to the state explosion problem, and that substantial efficiencies could be obtained if the enumeration of all possible interleavings could be avoided. As a result, several have proposed verification algorithms based on partial orders [Val89, Val90, God90, GW91, PL89, PL90, PL91, YTK91]. The method presented in this paper is based on unfolding a Petri net into an acyclic structure called an *occurrence net*. The notion of unfolding was introduced by Nielsen, Plotkin and Winskel as a means for giving a concurrent semantics to nets, but in this case the goal is to avoid the state explosion problem. An algorithm is introduced for constructing the unfolding of a net, which terminates when the unfolded net represents all of the reachable states of the original net. The unfolding is adequate for testing reachability (to be more precise, *coverability*) and deadlock properties. Reachability testing can be used to prove safety properties of finite state systems, for example in Dill's trace theory for asynchronous circuits [Dil88]. It is shown using an asynchronous circuit example that the unfolding can be polynomial in the circuit size while the state space is exponential. In contrast, the stubborn sets method of Valmari [Val89, Val90] and trace automaton method of Godefroid [God90, GW91] are ineffective in reducing the state explosion problem for asynchronous circuit models, because of the ubiquity of confusion in such models. In addition, because the unfolding method is fully automatic, it has a certain advantage over behavior machines method of Probst [PL89, PL90, PL91], which requires a pomset grammar describing the circuit's behavior to be constructed by hand.

2 The unfolding operation

Briefly, an occurrence net is a Petri net without backward conflict (two transitions outputting to the same place), and without cycles. Such a net can be obtained from an ordinary place/transition net by an unfolding process. Figure 1 shows an example of a net and part of its unfolding. Since the occurrence net it is acyclic and rooted, there is a natural well founded (partial) order on the transitions and places of the net. This order is called the dependency order. It is impossible for a transition of the occurrence net to fire unless all of its predecessors in the dependency order have fired.

The most important theoretical notion regarding occurrence nets is that of a *configuration*. A configuration represents a possible partial run of the net – it is any set of transitions that satisfies the following conditions:

1. If any transition is in the configuration, then so are all of its predecessors in the dependency order (a configuration is *downward closed*).

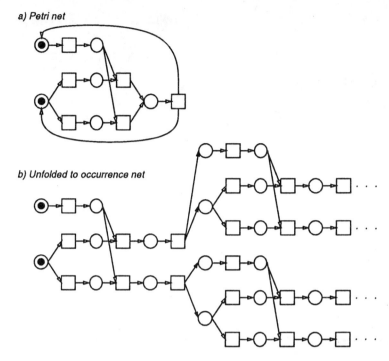

Fig. 1. Unfolding example.

2. A configuration cannot contain two transitions in *conflict*, meaning that both input from the same place.

An example of a configuration is shown in figure 2, with elements of the configuration filled in black. Two transitions in the figure are hatched in. Either of these transitions can be added to the black set to form a new configuration. Adding any other transition would be illegal, however, since it would either violate downward closure or conflict-freeness.

In an unfolding, each transition corresponds to a transition of the original net, and each place corresponds to a place of the original net. We can associate each configuration of the unfolding with a state (marking) of the original net by simply identifying those places whose tokens are produced but not consumed by the transitions in the configuration. This set is marked with black dots in figure 2. Mapping this set back onto the original net, we obtain the *final state* of the configuration.

The final theoretical notion we need regarding unfoldings is that of a *local configuration*. The local configuration associated with any transition consists of that transition and all of its predecessors in

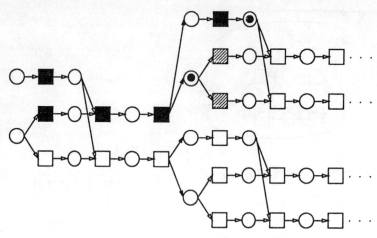

Fig. 2. Configuration

the dependency order (that is, the downward closure of the transition as a singleton). This is the set of transitions which necessarily are contained in any configuration containing the given transition. Note that a local configuration may not exist if this set contains two transitions in conflict.

We are now ready to consider the problem of building a fragment of the unfolding which is large enough to represent all of the reachable markings of the original net. Building the unfolding itself is straightforward. The process starts with a set of places corresponding to the initial marking of the original net. The unfolding is grown by finding a set of places in the unfolding which correspond to the inputs (preset) of a transition in the original net, then adding a new instance of that transition to the unfolding, as well as a new set of places corresponding to its outputs (postset). If the new transition has no conflicts in its local configuration (more precisely, if it *has* a local configuration) it is kept, otherwise it is discarded. This is because the existence of a conflict means that the new transition can occur in no configurations of the unfolding.

The key to termination of the unfolding is to identify a set of transitions of the unfolding to act as *cutoff points*. This set must have the following property: any configuration containing a cutoff point must be equivalent (in terms of final state) to some configuration containing no cutoff points. From this definition, it follows that any successor of a cutoff point can be safely omitted from the unfolding, without sacrificing any reachable markings of the original net. To see this, suppose we have built the unfolding only up to the cutoff points, in the sense that any new transition we can add must have a cutoff point as a predecessor. From this point on, any transition we add must be descended from some cutoff point. Thus, any configuration we might add to the unfolding must have the same final state as some configuration already present.

A sufficient condition for a transition to be a cutoff point is the following: the final state of its local configuration is the same as that of some other transition whose local configuration is smaller. The proof of this statement is as follows: suppose there are two transitions t_1 and t_2, whose local configurations have the same final state, with that of t_2 being smaller. Now imagine a configuration C_1 (local or otherwise) containing t_1. We can obtain C_1 from the local configuration of t_1 by adding the transitions in the difference one at a time, in an order consistent with the dependency relation. According to our construction, at each step of this process, there is a corresponding transition we can add to the local configuration of t_2 leading to the same final state. Hence, we can build a configuration C_2 containing t_2 which has the same final state, *but is at least one transition smaller than C_1*, since we started from a smaller set. Thus if any configuration contains a cutoff point, it is equivalent to a smaller configuration. Configurations cannot be made arbitrarily small, however, so any configuration containing a cutoff point must be equivalent to a configuration not containing a cutoff point. Since all the reachable states are represented by configurations containing no cutoff points, it is unnecessary to build the unfolding beyond any cutoff point.

We can find the cutoff points by simply keeping a hash table of all transitions, indexed by the final state of the local configuration. If when generating a transition, we find in the table a transition with equivalent but smaller local configuration, we discard the new transition. We can show, as follows, that this process is guaranteed to terminate if the original net is bounded and finite. First, the depth of the unfolding must be bounded by the number of number of reachable markings. The depth of a given transition in the unfolding is the longest chain of predecessors of that transition. Each transition in this chain has a local configuration, and these local configurations form a chain of increasing size. If the depth of the given transition is greater than the number of reachable markings of the original net, then by the pidgeon-hole principle, two of these local configurations must have the same final state. This cannot be, however, since in this case one of the transitions in the chain would have been determined to be a cutoff point. If the original net is bounded, it has a finite number of reachable markings, hence the depth of the unfolding is bounded. If the original net is finite, we can show by induction that the number of transitions at any given depth in the unfolding is finite. Hence the total number of transitions generated by the unfolding process is finite.

As an example of termination, consider the net of figure 3, which represents the dining philosophers paradigm. In this scenario, there are n concurrent processes (philosophers), each of which must acquire the use of two shared resources (forks) in order to execute its critical section (eating spaghetti). The processes are organized in a ring, with each neighboring pair sharing one resource. Figure 4 shows the completed unfolding for the case of three philosophers ($n = 3$). The cutoff points are marked with an X. The local configuration of each of these transitions is equivalent to the empty configuration. We observe that the size of the unfolding is not only bounded, but is linear in the number of philosophers, while the number of states is exponential as shown in table 1.

n	unfolding size (transitions)	reachable states
2	9	22
3	13	100
4	17	466
5	21	2164

Table 1. Unfolding size and number of states for Dining Philosophers

[t]

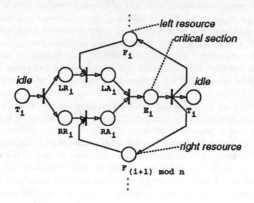

Fig. 3. Dining philosophers net.

Recall that in growing the unfolding, it is necessary to enumerate all of the subsets of places which correspond to the inputs of transitions. The complexity of this is $O\binom{n}{i}$, where n is the size of the unfolding, and i is the largest number of inputs of any transition. This is, of course, bounded by n^i, which is polynomial given a fixed value of i. In practice, however, the number of subsets which are considered can be reduced quite effectively, using the following two techniques. First, suppose we are enumerating the subsets: we need not add any place to the set if the result would not be contained in the set of inputs of any transition. Second whenever a place is added to the set, we can immediately eliminate from consideration all of the places which have a predecessor in conflict with a predecessor of the new element, since any transition with both places as inputs would be discarded. We add transitions to the net in order increasing size of the local configuration, so that we can use a hash table to determine whether or not each transition is a cutoff point. Thus, whenever a candidate for a transition in the unfolding is generated, it is placed in a queue ordered by increasing local configuration size. The places of the net are enumerated by pulling the first element t' from this queue, testing whether it is a cutoff point, and if not, generating places for its outputs. The procedure terminates when the queue of candidate transitions becomes empty. Figures 5 and 6 show a pseudo-code implementation of this procedure. The pseudo-code is written somewhat inefficiently in places for simplicity.

In function Unfold, the arguments P, T and M_0 are the places, transitions and initial marking of the original net. Each place in the unfolding is represented by a pair $(place, preds)$, where $place$ is the corresponding place in the original net, and $preds$ is the set of immediate predecessor transitions in the unfolding (note that since there is no backward conflict, the size of this set is at most one). Each transition in the unfolding is represented by a pair $(trans, preds)$, where $trans$ is the corresponding transition in the original net, and $preds$ is the set of immediate predecessor places in the unfolding. The function returns P' and T', the set of places and transitions, respectively, of the unfolding. There is also a queue Q' of transitions to be expanded, and a hash table (HashTable) used for identifying

[t]

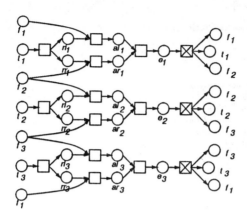

Fig. 4. Unfolding of the dining philosophers net.

cutoff points.

Coverability problems can be solved using the unfolding in the following way. Imagine we have a set of places in the original net, and we wish to determined whether this set can every be simultaneously marked. We simply add a new transition to the net, whose inputs are the given set, and then construct the unfolding. If the unfolding contains any instance of this new transition, the set is coverable, and otherwise not.

3 Application example

We now consider a more realistic example than the dining philosophers – a speed-independent [Sei80] circuit designed to implement a distributed mutual exclusion (DME) protocol. The circuit was designed by Alain Martin [Mar85] and has been analyzed using an abstracted trace theoretic model by Dill [Dil88].

Networks of logic gates in speed-independent circuits are readily modeled by Petri nets. A network of n gates can be modeled by a Petri net of $O(n)$ places. When we model a network of gates as a Petri net, we introduce two places for each input of each gate. One represents the the input in a logic low state, while the other represents the input in a logic high state. Transitions in the Petri net correspond to rising or falling transitions of gate outputs. A rising transition of a gate output removes all the logic low tokens from the inputs to which it is connected, and places tokens on the corresponding logic high places.

As an example, figure 7 shows the net fragment representing an AND gate. When both inputs of the gate are at the logic high state, we can move a token from the place representing logic low at the output to the place representing logic high. Similarly, if either input is at the logic low state, we can move a token from the place representing logic high at the output to the place representing logic low.

```
global P',T',Q',HashTable[]
function Unfold(P,T,M₀)
    P' = T' = Q' = ∅; clear HashTable
    for each p ∈ M₀ do
        add p' = (p,∅) to P'
        GenTrans({p'},T)
    end for
    while the queue Q' is not empty do
        pull the first t' off of Q'
        if not IsCutoffPoint?(t') do
            for each p in outputs of trans(t') do
                add p' = (p,{t'}) to P'
                GenTrans({p'},T)
            end for
        end if
    end while
    return(P',T')
end function

procedure GenTrans(S',T)
    if not exists t ∈ T such that place(S') ⊆ inputs of t then return
    if Predecessors(S') has forward conflict then return
    forall t ∈ T do if place(S') = inputs of t then
        add t' = (t,S') to set T'
        insert t' in Q' in order of |LocalConfig(t')|
    end for
    for all p' ∈ P where p' older than any member of S' do
        GenTrans(S' ∪ p',T)
end procedure
```

Fig. 5. Pseudo-code implementation of unfolding procedure

A dynamic hazard occurs, for example, if the AND gate's output is enabled to rise while one of the inputs is enabled to fall. The problem of whether or not a dynamic hazard can occur can thus be posed as a coverability problem. Alternatively, since dynamic hazards correspond to dynamic conflicts in the unfolding, the problem can be solved by constructing the unfolding and examining it for dynamic conflicts, *i.e.*, two transitions which are in conflict, and which may be simultaneously enabled. The DME circuit also uses special two-way mutual exclusion elements as components, which are immune to certain hazards. In checking the DME ring for hazards, we ignore conflicts between rising transitions of a mutual exclusion element's acknowledge outputs.

Figure 9 shows the results of the occurrence net unfolding procedure for the Petri net model of the DME circuit, for rings with one to nine cells. The depth of the occurrence net unfolding for the case of 5 cells was 141 transitions. The number of transitions in the unfolding, shown in part (a) of the figure, increases quadratically in the number of cells. This is because as the number of cells in the ring increases, a request must be relayed through a greater number of stages in order to obtain the

```
function IsCutoffPoint?(t'₁)
    C'₁ = LocalConfig(t'₁)
    S'₁ = FinalState(C'₁)
    L' = HashTable[HashFun(S'₁)]
    forall t'₂ in L' do
        C'₂ = LocalConfig(t'₂)
        if S'₁ = FinalState(C'₂) and Size(C'₂) < Size(C'₁) then return(1)
    end for
    add t'₁ to HashTable[HashFun(S'₁)]
    return(0)
end function

function LocalConfig(t')
    return(Predecessors({t'}) ∩ T')
end

function Predecessors(S')
    do
        S' = S' ∪ preds(S')
    until S' unchanged
end function

function FinalState(C')
    let S' be the set of all p' ∈ P' such that preds(p') ⊆ C'
    return(place(S' − preds(C')))
end function
```

Fig. 6. Pseudo-code, continued.

token, in the worst case. At the same time, the number of cells which are requesting also increases. The occurrence net therefore grows in both width and depth in proportion to the number of cells. The time to construct the unfolding (running a LISP implementation on a Sun3 workstatation) appears to increase quartically, as shown in part (b) of the figure. Finally, as we increase the number of cells in the ring, the number of reachable global markings increases exponentially, as shown in part (c) of the figure (on a logarithmic scale).[1] The number of states increases asymptotically by slightly less than a factor ten for each added cell.

How do these results compare to other methods for avoiding the state explosion problem? The trace theory approach of Dill [Dil88] required an abstract model of the arbiter cell to be created by hand. This reduces the state explosion problem, but does not entirely solve it, since even with the reduced model, the number of states still increases exponentially with the number of components. Probst [PL91] reports a method which requires quadratic space and time in the number of cells, but also is not fully automatic. The methods of Valmari [Val89, Val90] and Godefroid [God90, GW91]

---

[1] The number of reachable states was established using the symbolic model checking technique [BCM+90]

[t]

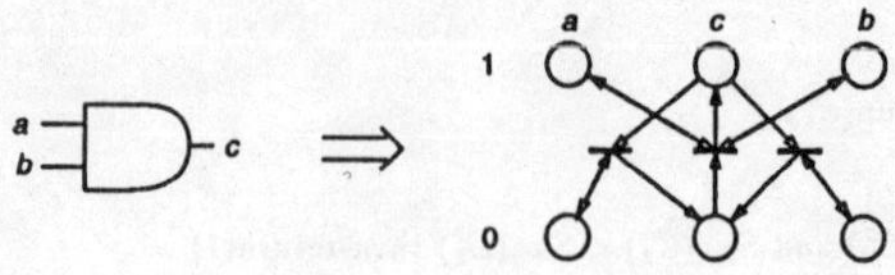

Fig. 7. Translation from circuit to net

and Yoneda [YTK91] cannot be effectively applied to this example or to other speed independent circuits, because in all states, all enabled transitions are in conflict with some disabled transition. Thus no transition can be statically guaranteed to be persistent. Experiments by Holger Schlingloff[2] have confirmed this to be the case. It is possible, perhaps, that some more clever static analysis technique could be used to show that some transitions are persistent, in which case these methods could be applied to some effect.

Finally, we consider the symbolic model checking technique [BCM+90]. For DME circuit, the basic symbolic model checking algorithm requires cubic time and linear space (in the number of cells). Burch and Long[3] have obtained $O(n^{2.5})$ time for the DME using symbolic model checking with a modified search order [BCL]. This method requires some hand optimization, however. In any event, it appears that the symbolic model checking method yields somewhat better asymptotic performance for the DME circuit, though both methods effectively solve the state explosion problem. The unfolding method has an advantage over the symbolic model checking method in that no variable ordering or other heuristic information is required. It is not difficult to construct a variation on the dining philosophers for which there is no good variable ordering for symbolic model checking, but for which the unfolding is still linear space (in the number of philosophers). However, the author is presently unaware of any practical circuits for which this is the case.

4 Deadlock and occurrence nets

Besides coverability, another interesting problem for Petri nets is the question of deadlock. A *terminal marking* of a Petri net is one in which no transitions are enabled. Reachability of a terminal (or deadlocked) state cannot be framed in terms of the coverability problem. However, since the unfolding represents all reachable markings, a net has a reachable terminal marking if and only if its unfolding has a reachable terminal marking. The problem of existence of a reachable terminal marking of an occurrence net is NP-complete. This is easily shown by reduction from 3-SAT.[4] To see this consider the formula $(x_1+y_1+z_1)(x_2+y_2+z_2)\cdots(x_n+y_n+z_n)$ where each x_i, y_i and z_i is a positive or negative literal. Assume the formula has m variables. Let the positive literals be $l_1,\ldots,l_m$, and the negative literals be $\bar{l}_1,\ldots,\bar{l}_m$. In polynomial time, we can construct a net which has a terminal marking if and only if the formula is satisfiable. The initial marking of the net is a set of places $\{v_1,\ldots,v_m\}$. There is a place representing each positive literal $l_1,\ldots,l_m$ and each negative literal $\bar{l}_1,\ldots,\bar{l}_m$. For

---

[2] Personal communication
[3] Personal communication
[4] Satisfiability of a Boolean formula in conjunctive normal form, with three literals in each conjunct.

[t]

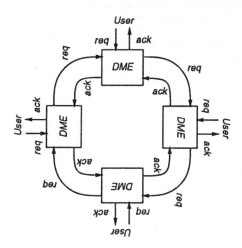

Fig. 8. Distributed mutual exclusion circuit

each variable v_i, there is a transition from v_i to l_i and from v_i to $\bar{l}_i$. For each conjunct $(x_i + y_i + z_i)$, there is a transition c_i, whose preset is $\{\bar{x}_i, \bar{y}_i, \bar{z}_i\}$. In other words, the transition c_i is enabled to fire if and only if $(x_i + y_i + z_i)$ is false. Thus, some transition c_i is enabled to fire if and only if the whole formula is false. The postset of each transition c_i is the single place $\{q\}$, and there is a transition from $\{q\}$ to $\{q\}$. Thus, if any c_i fires, the net may never reach a terminal marking. As a result, there is a terminal marking of the net if and only if the formula is satisfiable. For example, figure 10 shows the net constructed for the formula $(a + b + \bar{c})(b + c + \bar{d})$.

The reader may easily verify that the size of the unfolding of such a net (up to the cutoff points) is linear in the size of the original net. In fact, it is essentially the same net, except the the place q occurs n times in the unfolding. Since all reachable markings of the original net occur as configurations of the unfolding, the unfolding has a terminal marking if and only if the formula is satisfiable. Hence 3-SAT is P-time reducible to reachability of a terminal marking of an unfolding. Since the configuration representing the terminal marking can be guessed in P-time in the size of the unfolding, and also tested in P-time, it follows that the problem is in NP, and hence NP-complete.

Interestingly, however, the problem is readily solved in practice even for very large unfoldings, using an algorithm based on techniques of constraint satisfaction search. The key observation which leads to this algorithm is that there is no terminal marking exactly when all configurations the unfolding can reach some configuration containing a cutoff point. This is simply because if there is no terminal marking, then all configurations can reach a configuration which is arbitrarily large. A configuration C' can reach a configuration containing transition t' if and only if the union of C' and the local configuration of t' is a configuration. If it is not, then no set containing C' and t' is a configuration. If the union is not a configuration, we will say that C' and t' are in conflict. Hence, there is a terminal marking if and only if there is a configuration which is in conflict with every cutoff point. The search for such a configuration can be carried out using branch and bound techniques. For example, if a configuration C' is in conflict with a cutoff point t', there must be a transition $t'_1 \in C'$ which is in conflict with some transition in the local configuration of t'. Such a transition t'_1 will be called a *spoiler* of t'.

There exists a configuration in conflict with all of the all of the cutoff points (equivalently, there exists a terminal marking) if and only if there exists a configuration containing a spoiler for every cutoff point. The set of spoilers contained in this configuration will be called T_s. The algorithm of figure 11 uses branch and bound techniques to find such a set T_s if one exists.

Note that in line 3 of the procedure, the cutoff point with the smallest number of spoilers is chosen so that the number of choices in line 5 is minimized. Whenever a spoiler for a given cutoff point is chosen to belong to T_s in line 5, everything in conflict with T_s is eliminated from future consideration in line 7. Note that the cutoff points in conflict with T_s are also eliminated, which cuts down on the amount of future branching. Whenever there is a cutoff point with no remaining spoilers, the procedure backtracks, from line 4 to the most recent occurrence of line 5 where there are remaining choices. If there are no remaining choices, the procedure fails. Of course, when backtracking occurs, the the net is also returned to the state it was in at the point where execution is being resumed. This backtracking is easily implemented by keeping a stack of the remaining choices for t' in each iteration of the loop, and marking each transition in the net with the level of the stack at the time it was "removed". Interestingly, if the procedure terminates successfully, the remaining net has the property that every path leads to a terminal marking of the original net N. This makes it straightforward to extract a path leading to a terminal marking.

Obviously, because of the backtracking, this procedure is exponential (as it must be, if $\mathcal{P} \neq \mathcal{NP}$). However, this is only the worst case. The dining philosophers serve as an example of a case in which the exponential complexity is avoided. In fact, the procedure finds the terminal marking in time which is *linear* in the number of philosophers. This is easily seen by examining the unfolding of the Dining Philosophers net in figure 4. There is one cutoff point in this net for each process. Initially, each of these transitions has two spoilers, which correspond to the two resources required to enter the critical region being granted to the two neighboring processes. Regardless of which cutoff point is used first, the symmetry is then broken as the part of the net in conflict with one of the two spoilers is removed. This removes, in particular, the transition which granted one of the resources to the first philosopher, hence one of its neighbors now has only one spoiler, so there is only one choice available the next time line 5 is reached. After this spoiler is added to T_s, the remaining neighbor of the second philosopher now has only one spoiler. This process continues without backtracking until it has come full circle and the terminal marking is found. Note that if the cutoff point with the fewest spoilers were not chosen in line 3, the procedure might have examined an exponential number of candidates for T_s before a valid one was found.

For the DME circuit example, we find that the run time of the deadlock algorithm is 218 seconds for a ring of five cells, and 6600 seconds for a ring of 9 cells. Hence, even though the the algorithm is exponential in the worst case, in this case it runs in reasonable time for an unfolding of over 5000 transitions. It is clear that the branch and bound technique quickly narrows down the number of choices for this example.

5 Evaluation

When is unfolding a suitable strategy for problems in automatic verification? The most promising application is hazard checking for asynchronous control circuits. In these circuits, the state explosion seems to derive almost entirely from arbitrary interleavings of concurrent transitions. In such cases, the unfolding method can have a considerable advantage over methods that search the entire state space. Note, however, that other methods based on partial orders are not necessarily effective in reducing the state explosion for these circuits, because of the aforementioned problem of determining when transitions of the net are persistent.

In general, any problem which can be posed in terms of coverability or deadlock in a Petri net model is a possible application of the unfolding method. In addition, it is possible that heuristically efficient procedures can be found for deciding the existence of an infinite firing path in some ω-regular set, given an unfolding. In this case, specifications framed as linear time temporal logic formulas, or ω-automata could be evaluated.

References

[BCL]   J. R. Burch, E. M. Clarke, and D. E. Long. Symbolic model checking with partitioned transition relations. To appear in the Proceedings of VLSI'91.

[BCM+90] J. R. Burch, E. M. Clarke, K. L. McMillan, D. L. Dill, and J. Hwang. Symbolic model checking: 10^{20} states and beyond. In *Proceedings of the Fifth Annual Symposium on Logic in Computer Science*, June 1990.

[Dil88]   D. Dill. Trace theory for automatic hierarchical verification of speed-independent circuits. Technical Report 88-119, Carnegie Mellon University, Computer Science Dept, 1988.

[God90]   P. Godefroid. Using partial orders to improve automatic verification methods. In *Workshop on Computer Aided Verification*, 1990.

[GW91]   P. Godefroid and P. Wolper. A partial approach to model checking. In *LICS*, 1991.

[Mar85]   A. J. Martin. The design of a self-timed circuit for distributed mutual exclusion. In Henry Fuchs, editor, *1985 Chapel Hill Conference on VLSI*, pages 245–260. Computer Science Press, 1985.

[PL89]   D. K. Probst and H. F. Li. Abstract specification, composition, and proof of correctness of delay-insensitive circuits and systems. Technical report, Concordia University, Dept. of Computer Science, 1989.

[PL90]   D. K. Probst and H. F. Li. Using partial order semantics to avoid the state explosion problem in asynchronous systems. In *Workshop on Computer Aided Verification*, 1990.

[PL91]   D. K. Probst and H. F. Li. Partial-order model checking: A guide for the perplexed. In *Third Workshop on Computer-aided Verification*, pages 405–416, July 1991.

[Sei80]   C. L. Seitz. System timing. In Carver Mead and Lynn Conway, editors, *Introduction to VLSI Systems*, pages 218–262. Addison-Wesley, 1980.

[Val89]   A. Valmari. Stubborn sets for reduced state space generation. In *10th Int. Conf. on Application and Theory of Petri Nets*, 1989.

[Val90]   A. Valmari. A stubborn attack on the state explosion problem. In *Workshop on Computer Aided Verification*, 1990.

[YTK91]   Tomohiro Yoneda, Yoshihiro Tohma, and Yutaka Kondo. Acceleration of timing verification method based on time Petri nets. *Systems and Computers in Japan*, 22(12):37–52, 1991.

[1]

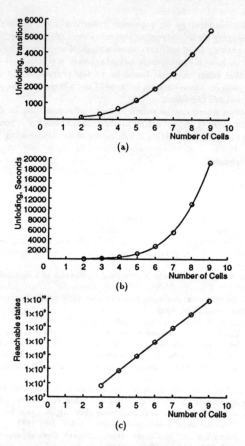

(a)

(b)

(c)

Fig. 9. Performance of unfolding method on hazard-detection problem for the distributed mutual exclusion circuit

[t]

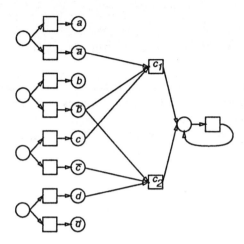

Fig. 10. Reduction from 3-SAT problem to a terminal marking problem.

1 let B be the set of the cutoff points, $T_s = \emptyset$
2 while B is not empty do
3   let t the the element of B with the fewest spoilers
4   if t has no spoilers, then <u>backtrack</u>
5   <u>choose</u> an element t' from the spoilers of t
6   add t' to T_s
7   delete all transitions in conflict with T_s
8 end do

Fig. 11. Procedure to detect terminal marking.

State Space Caching Revisited

Patrice Godefroid*
Université de Liège
Institut Montefiore B28
4000 Liège Sart-Tilman
Belgium

Gerard J. Holzmann
AT&T Bell Laboratories
600 Mountain Avenue
Murray Hill, NJ 07974
U.S.A.

Didier Pirottin*
Université de Liège
Institut Montefiore B28
4000 Liège Sart-Tilman
Belgium

Abstract

State space caching is a state space exploration method that stores all states of just one execution sequence plus as many previously visited states as available memory allows. So far, this technique has been of little practical significance. With a conventional reachability analysis, it allows one to reduce memory usage by only two to three times, before an unacceptable exponential increase of the run-time overhead sets in. The explosion of the run-time requirements is caused by redundant multiple explorations of unstored parts of the state space. Indeed, almost all states in the state space of concurrent systems are typically reached several times during the search. There are two causes for this: firstly, several different partial orderings of statement executions can lead to the same state; secondly, all interleavings of a same partial ordering of statement executions lead to the same state.

In this paper, we describe a method to completely avoid the effects of the second cause given above. We show that with this method, most reachable states are visited only once during the state space exploration. This makes for the first time state space caching a very efficient verification method. We were able, for instance, to completely explore a state space of 250,000 states while storing simultaneously no more than 500 states and with only a three-fold increase of the run-time requirements.

1   Introduction

Memory is the main limiting factor of most conventional reachability analysis algorithms. These verification algorithms perform an exhaustive exploration of the state space of the system being checked. This exploration amounts to simulating all possible behaviors the system can have from its initial state and storing all reachable states. To avoid significant run-time penalties for disk-access, reachable states can only be stored in a randomly accessed memory, i.e. in the main memory available in the computer where the algorithm is executed. Therefore the applicability of these verification algorithms is limited by the amount of main memory available. Typically, it only takes a few minutes of run-time to fill up the whole main memory of a classical computer.

*The work of these authors is partially supported by the European Community ESPRIT BRA project SPEC (3096) and by the Belgian Incentive Program "Information Technology" – Computer Science of the future, initiated by Belgian State – Prime Minister's Service – Science Policy Office. The scientific responsibility is assumed by its authors.

During the search, once states have been visited they are stored. Storing states avoids redundant explorations of parts of the state space. If a stored state is encountered again later in the search, it is not necessary to revisit all its successors. It is worth noticing that states that are reached only once during the search do not need to be stored. Storing them or not would not change anything about the time requirements of the method. Of course, it would be preferable not to store them in order to decrease the memory requirements, but with a conventional algorithm it is virtually impossible to predict if a given state will be visited once or more than once.

Typically, almost all states in the state space of concurrent systems are reached several times during the search. There are two causes for this:

- From the initial state, the exploration of different partial orderings of statement executions of the system can lead to the same state.

- From the starting state, the exploration of all interleavings of a same partial ordering of statement executions lead to the same state.

In this paper, we give a way to completely get rid of the second cause given above. Then we study the impact of this new technique on real-protocol state spaces. In many cases, when using this method, most of the states are now reached *only once* during the search.

Sadly, it is not possible to determine which states are visited only once before the search is completed. However, the risk of double work when not storing an already visited state becomes very small since the probability that this state will be visited again later during the search becomes very small. This enables us not to store most of the states that have already been visited without incurring too much redundant exploration of parts of the state space. The memory requirements can thus strongly decrease (more than 100 times) without seriously increasing the time requirements (only 3 or 4 times). This makes possible the complete exploration of very large state spaces (several tens of million states) that can not be explored exhaustively by any other known method. With this technique, time becomes the main limiting factor.

In the next Section, we recall the principles of state space caching and present some results obtained with this method for the verification of four real-protocols. Then we show how this verification method can be substantially improved by the use of *"sleep sets"*. Sleep sets were introduced in [God90, GW91b]. In Section 3, we recall the basic idea behind sleep sets. Then, we give a new simple and efficient implementation of the sleep set scheme. We study properties of sleep sets and prove two new theorems. Section 4 presents and compares the results obtained with the state space caching method with and without the use of sleep sets. In Section 5, some suggestions to further improve the effectiveness of the method are investigated.

2   State Space Caching

State space exploration can be performed by a classical depth-first search algorithm, as shown in Figure 1, starting from the initial state s_0 of the system. The main data structures used are a *Stack* to hold the states of the current explored path, and a hash table

```
Initialize: Stack is empty; H is empty;
Search() {
    enter s₀ in H;
    push (s₀) onto Stack;
    DFS();
}
DFS() {
    s = top(Stack);
    for all t enabled in s do {
        s' = succ(s) after t; /* execution of t */
        if s' is NOT already in H then {
            enter s' in H;
            push (s') onto Stack;
            DFS();
        }
        /* backtracking of t */
    }
    pop s from Stack
}
```

Figure 1: Algorithm 1 — classical depth-first search

H to store all the states that have already been visited during the search. Algorithm 1 simulates all possible transitions sequences the system is able to perform. The exploration can be performed "on-the-fly", i.e. without storing the transitions that are taken during the search. This reduces substantially the memory requirements. Unfortunately, the number of reachable states can be very large and it is then impossible to store all these states in H.

However, it is well-known that a completely exhaustive state space exploration can be performed without the storage of any other part of the full state space than a single sequence of states leading from the initial state to the currently explored state, i.e. the $Stack$ used in Algorithm 1. Such a search, termed "Type-3" or stack-search algorithm in [Hol90], reduces the memory requirements while still guaranteeing a complete exploration of any finite state space. This strategy was used in, for instance, the first Pan system [Hol81], and in the Pandora system [Hol84]. The problem is that, if an execution path joins a previously analyzed sequence in a state that is no more onto the stack, this search strategy will do redundant work. Hence the run-time requirements of this type of search go up dramatically. The result is that even state spaces that could otherwise comfortably be stored exhaustively become unsearchable with even the fastest implementations of a stack-search discipline.

A trade-off between these two strategies consists of storing all the states of the current path and storing as many other states as possible given the remaining amount of available memory. This strategy is called *state space caching* [Hol85]. It creates a restricted *cache* of selected system states that have already been visited. Initially, all system states encountered are stored into the cache. When the cache fills up, old states are deleted to accommodate new ones. This method never tries to store more states than possible in the cache. Thus, if the size of the cache is greater than the maximal size of the stack during the exploration, the whole state space can be explored without any problems.

We have implemented such a caching discipline in an efficient automated protocol validation system called SPIN[1] [Hol91], which includes an implementation of a classical search as described in Figure 1. The details of PROMELA, the validation language that SPIN accepts, can be found in [Hol91]. PROMELA defines systems of asynchronously executing concurrent processes that can interact via shared global variables or message channels. Interaction via message channel can be either synchronous (i.e. by rendez-vous) or asynchronous (buffered), depending on what type of channel is declared.

Experiments with our implementation were made on four sample real protocols:

1. PFTP is a file transfer protocol presented in Chapter 14 of [Hol91], modeled in 206 lines of PROMELA.

2. URP is the AT&T's Universal Receiver Protocol, modeled in 405 lines of PROMELA.

3. MULOG3 is a protocol implementing a mutual exclusion algorithm presented in [TN87], for 3 participants, modeled in 97 lines of PROMELA.

4. DTP is a data transfer protocol, modeled in 406 lines of PROMELA.

The results of our experiments with Algorithm 1 and different cache sizes are presented in Figure 4. All measurements were run on a SPARC2 workstation (64 Megabytes of RAM). Time is user time plus system time as reported by the UNIX system time command. The experiments were performed using a random replacement strategy (see Section 5).

The results show clearly that the number of stored states can be reduced by approximately two to three times without seriously affecting the run time. If the cache is further reduced, the run time increases dramatically.

These results confirm the ones presented in [Hol85, Hol87]. As first pointed out in [Hol87], whether a large reduction of the memory requirements without a significant blow-up of the time complexity can be achieved depends largely on the structure of the state space, which is protocol dependent and highly unpredictable. The conclusion from these early studies was that the effect of the state space caching discipline are too unpredictable to be useful in a general verification tool. Indeed, it is necessary to know how many states the full state space contains to find the optimal caching setup since the blow-up of execution time starts too soon, and is too steep. The results of these experiments were more recently confirmed in a series of independent experiments [JJ89, JJ91].

The critical point for a caching algorithm is the risk of double work incurred by joining a previously visited state that has been deleted from memory. This risk depends on the state space: if the states are reached several times during the search, the risk is greater than if they are reached only once. For the state spaces of the examples above, one can see in Table 1 that the number of transitions is about 3 times the number of states. This means that each state is, on average, reached 3 times during the search. The risk is too high. This is why this technique is not very efficient.

---

[1]The original version of SPIN can be obtained free of charge via email, for educational purposes. To get instructions, send an arbitrary one-line message to "netlib@research.att.com". The response is automated.

In the next section, we show how it is possible to strongly reduce the number of transitions that have to be explored during the search, which reduces the risk and makes state space caching manageable.

3 Sleep Sets

The classical depth-first search presented in Figure 1 explores all enabled transitions from each state encountered during the search. However, in case of concurrent systems, it is possible to explore all the reachable states of the state space *without* exploring systematically all enabled transitions in each state. This can be done by using *sleep sets*.

Sleep sets were introduced in [God90, GW91b] where it was shown that most of the state explosion due to the modeling of concurrency by interleaving can be avoided. The basic idea of this verification method was to describe the behavior of the system by means of partial orders rather than by sequences. More precisely, Mazurkiewicz's traces [Maz86] were used as a semantic model.

Traces are defined as equivalence classes of sequences. Given an alphabet Σ and a dependency relation $D \subseteq \Sigma \times \Sigma$, two sequences over Σ belong to the same trace with respect to D (are in the same equivalence class) if they can be obtained from each other by successively exchanging adjacent symbols which are independent according to D. For instance, if a and b are two symbols of Σ which are independent according to D, the sequences ab and ba belong to the same trace. A trace is usually represented by one of its elements enclosed within brackets and, when necessary, subscripted by the alphabet and the dependency relation. Thus the trace containing both ab and ba could be represented by $[ab]_{(\Sigma,D)}$. A trace corresponds to a partial ordering of symbol occurrences and represents all linearizations of this partial order. If two independent symbols occur next to each other in a sequence of a trace, the order of their occurrence is irrelevant since they occur concurrently in the partial order corresponding to that trace.

In a PROMELA program, dependency can arise between statements that refer to the same global objects, i.e. same global variables or same message channels. For instance, two write operations on a same shared global variable in two concurrent processes are dependent, while two concurrent read operations on the same object are independent since they can be shuffled in any order without changing the possible outcome of the read. Tracking dependencies between PROMELA statements is by no means a trivial point. We refer the reader to [HGP92] for a detailed presentation of that topic.

In the context of [God90, GW91b], sleep sets were one of the means used by an algorithm devoted to the exploration of at least one (sequence) interleaving for each possible trace (partial ordering of transitions) the concurrent system was able to perform. More precisely, the specific aim of sleep sets was to avoid the wasteful exploration of all possible shufflings of independent transitions.

Let us consider an example to illustrate the basic idea behind sleep sets. Consider a classical depth-first search and assume there are two independent transitions t_1 and t_1' from the current state s (see the top of the right part of Figure 2). Assume that transition t_1 is explored before transition t_1' and that t_1 leads to a successor state s'. When all immediate successor states of s' have been explored, the transition t_1 is backtracked and the depth-first

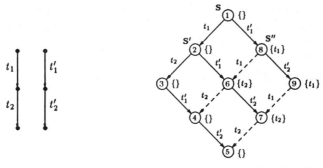

Figure 2: A concurrent system (left) and the exploration performed by Algorithm 2 (right)

Same as Algorithm 1 except:

- A variable *Sleep* is added. Its initial value is {}.
- Instead of executing systematically all enabled transitions from each state, execute only all enabled transitions that *are not in Sleep*.
- Each time a transition *t* is executed from a state *s*, delete all transitions from *Sleep* that are dependent with *t* (the result gives the value of *Sleep* that has to be associated to the successor state *s'* of *s*).
- Each time a transition *t* that has led to a state *s'* is backtracked, restore the value of *Sleep* before the execution of *t*. If *s'* is not in *Stack*, then add *t* to *Sleep*.

Figure 3: Algorithm 2 — depth-first search with sleep sets

---

search backs up to state s. Then t_1' is executed from s, leads to a successor node s'' and the search goes on from s''. Since t_1 and t_1' are *independent*, t_1 is still enabled in s''. But it is not necessary to explore transition t_1 from state s'' since the result of another shuffling of these independent transitions, namely the sequence $t_1 t_1'$, has already been explored from s. In order to prevent the execution of t_1 in s'', we use sleep sets: we put t_1 in the sleep set associated to s''.

A sleep set is defined as a set of transitions. One sleep set is associated with each state s reached during the search. The sleep set associated with s is a set of transitions that are *enabled* in s but *will not be executed* from s. The sleep set associated with the initial state s_0 is the empty set.

Note that, in the previous example, if t_1 and t_1' would have been dependent, then it would have been mandatory to explore both shufflings of t_1 and t_1'. (For example, the two shufflings of two write statements on a same global variable performed by two concurrent processes are dependent and leaves the system in two different states.)

Figure 3 shows how to introduce the sleep set scheme in the classical depth-first search algorithm. A single variable *Sleep* is added. The two last rules describe how to set and reset the value of *Sleep* properly during the state-graph traversal. The appropriate rule is applied each time a transition is executed or backtracked during the search.

A simple example of a state-graph traversal performed by Algorithm 2 is given in Figure 2. The system on the left is composed of two completely independent concurrent processes. For each state, the value of *Sleep* when that state has been added to the stack is given between braces beside the state. Dotted transitions are not explored by Algorithm 2.

Note that Algorithm 2 as presented above can be viewed as an efficient version of the procedure that was given in [GW91b] to compute sleep sets. Indeed, with this new version, it is no more necessary to store explicitly sleep sets on the stack as it was suggested in [GW91b]. It is sufficient to store only some information about sleep sets updates in order to restore the value of the sleep set before the execution of a transition when the transition is backtracked. (From our experience in designing several different versions of the sleep set scheme, implementing it as described above can imply a substantial speed-up in the sleep set computations.)

The following theorem ensures that all reachable states of the concurrent system are still visited by Algorithm 2.

Theorem 3.1 *All reachable states are visited by Algorithm 2.*

Proof:

Let s be a state reachable from the initial state s_0. Imagine that we fix the order in which transitions selected in a given state are explored and that we first run Algorithm 1 (depth-first search without sleep sets). Then, we run Algorithm 2 (depth-first search with sleep sets) while still exploring transitions in the same order. The important point is that the order used in both runs is the same, the exact order used is irrelevant. Let then S denote the spanning tree explored by Algorithm 1 and let S_s denote the part of S that contains all states from which the state s is reachable. Since s is reachable, S_s is nonempty and contains s (we do not prove here that a classical depth-first search visits all reachable states). Moreover, the leftmost path of S_s leads to s. We now prove that in the second run, i.e. when using Algorithm 2, the leftmost path of S_s is still explored.

Let $p = s_0 \xrightarrow{t_0} s_1 \xrightarrow{t_1} s_2 \ldots s_{n-1} \xrightarrow{t_{n-1}} s$ be this path. Since the order used in both runs is the same, p is the very first path of S_s that will be examined during both runs. The only reason for which it might not be fully explored (i.e. until s is reached) by the algorithm using sleep sets is that some transition t_i of p is not taken because it is in the sleep set associated to s_i. There are two possible causes for this. The first cause is that p might contain a state that has already been visited with a sleep set which contained t_i. This is not possible because if such a state existed, the path p would not be the leftmost path in S_s. The second possible cause is that t_i has been added to the sleep set at some point on the path p and then passed along p until s_i. Let us prove that this is also impossible.

Assume that t_i is in the sleep set associated to state s_i and that it has been added to *Sleep* at some previous point on the path p. Precisely, there are states s_j and s_{j+1}, $j < i$, in p such that $t_i \notin Sleep$ at s_j and $t_i \in Sleep$ at s_{j+1}. This implies that t_i has been explored *before* t_j from s_j since a transition is introduced in *Sleep* once it is backtracked (fourth rule in Figure 3). This also implies that, from s_j, t_i has not led to a state s_l, $l \leq j$ already visited in the path p. Moreover, all transitions that occur between t_j and t_i in p, i.e. all t_k such that $j \leq k < i$, are independent with respect to t_i. Indeed, if this were not the case, t_i would not be in the sleep set of s_i since transitions that are dependent with the transition taken are removed from the sleep set (third rule in Figure 3).

Consequently, $t_i t_j \ldots t_{i-1} \in [t_j \ldots t_{i-1} t_i]$, i.e. $t_i t_j \ldots t_{i-1}$ and $t_j \ldots t_{i-1} t_i$ are two interleavings of a single concurrent execution (i.e. a single trace) and hence $s_j \xrightarrow{t_i t_j \ldots t_{i-1}} s_{i+1}$. Given that s is reachable from s_{i+1}, it is reachable by a path that in state s_j takes the transition t_i. Since t_i has been explored before t_j in s_j and has not led to a state s_l, $l \leq j$ already visited in p, the path p is not the leftmost path in S_s. A contradiction.

■

Protocol	Algorithm	states	matched	transitions	depth	time (sec)
PFTP	1	409,257	771,265	1,180,522	5,044	219.4
	2	409,257	179,304	588,561	4,550	394.6
URP	1	15,378	27,709	43,087	202	6.9
	2	15,378	1,884	17,262	202	10.7
MULOG3	1	100,195	254,183	354,378	119	35.2
	2	100,195	3,736	103,931	119	53.6
DTP	1	251,409	397,058	648,467	545	97.8
	2	251,409	11,152	262,561	545	160.8

Table 1: Comparison of the performances of Algorithm 1 and 2

In practice, the previous theorem enables us to use Algorithm 2 to verify all properties that can be reduced to a state accessibility problem, like, for instance, deadlock detection, unreachable code detection, assertion violations, safety properties. Moreover, other problems like the verification of liveness properties and model checking for linear-time temporal logic formulae are reducible to a set of reachability problems (see for instance [CVWY90, Hol91, VW86]), for which the method developed in this paper is applicable. By construction, the state-graph G' explored by Algorithm 2 is a "sub-graph" of the state-graph G explored by Algorithm 1. Both state-graphs G and G' contain the same number of states, the only difference is that G' contains always less transitions than G. Of course, if no simultaneous enabled independent transitions are encountered during the search, G' is then exactly equivalent to G.

Since only states, not transitions, are stored during an on-the-fly verification and since the number of states is the same in G and G', Algorithm 1 and Algorithm 2 have exactly the same memory requirements. (As a matter of fact, Algorithm 2 requires a few hundred bytes more for the manipulation of $Sleep$; this overhead can be made insignificant with respect to the global memory requirements [HGP92].)

Table 1 compares the performances of and the state-graphs explored by Algorithm 1 and Algorithm 2 for the protocols presented in Section 2. The advantage of Algorithm 2 is that it explores much fewer transitions than Algorithm 1. The number of state matchings strongly decreases. If the reduction in the number of transitions is sufficient to make up the additional run-time overhead due to the manipulation of sleep sets, an improvement in the general run-time requirements can result. This is not the case for the protocols considered here. (In [HGP92], it is shown that the sleep set scheme can produce a significant reduction in the overall run-time requirements when it is combined with a state compression method.) "Depth" is the maximum size of the stack during the search.

One clearly sees in Table 1 that the number of matched states strongly decreases when using Algorithm 2. This phenomenon can be explained with the following theorem.

Theorem 3.2 *For every reachable state s, Algorithm 2 never completely explores more than one interleaving of a single trace (partial ordering of transitions) that leads to s, and thus never visits s twice because of the exploration of two interleavings of a same trace.*

Proof:

By definition, all $w' \in [w]$, i.e. all interleavings w' of a single concurrent execution $[w]$, can be obtained from w by successively permuting pairs of *adjacent independent* transitions. Let w and w' denote two interleavings of the single trace $[w]$. We now prove that Algorithm 2 does not completely explore both of them.

Let $Pref(w)$ denote the common prefix of w and w' that ends when w and w' differ. Assume the next transition of w after $Pref(w)$ is t and that the next transition of w' after $Pref(w)$ is t'. In state s such that $s_0 \overset{Pref(w)}{\Rightarrow} s$, both transitions t and t' are enabled. Moreover, t and t' are independent since w and w' differ only by the order of independent transitions. Assume that t and t' are not in the current *Sleep* and that the search explores t first. Later, when t is backtracked and the search backs up in s, t is introduced in *Sleep*. Then t' is explored and leads to a state s''. Since t and t' are independent, t is not removed from *Sleep* at state s''.

During the remainder of the exploration of w' starting from s'', t remains in *Sleep* and is never executed. Indeed, t could only be removed from *Sleep* after the execution of some transition t'' that is dependent with it. This is impossible because if t'' occurs before t in w' (since t has to occur eventually in w'), w' would differ from w by the order of two dependent transitions t and t'' and thus, w and w' would not be two interleavings of a same trace. Since t is never executed and has to occur in w', w' is not completely explored.

Note that, if an already visited state is reached during the exploration of w' from s'', the exploration of w' stops. It might then be the case that the remainder of w' has already been explored, but it was during the exploration of an interleaving of another trace that has the same suffix than w'.

∎

In other words, if a state is reachable by only several interleavings of a single trace, Algorithm 2 never completely explores more than one of these interleavings and visits that state only once. In the example of Figure 2, all states are visited only once by Algorithm 2. Of course, if one could know it in advance before starting the search, it would not be necessary to store *any* states! Unfortunately, it is impossible to determine which are the states that are encountered only once before the search being completed.

Let us now study the impact of sleep sets on state space caching.

4 State Space Caching and Sleep Sets

Figure 4 compares the performances of Algorithm 1 (classical depth-first search) and Algorithm 2 (depth-first search with sleep sets) for various cache sizes.

As already pointed out in Section 2, the number of transitions that are explored during the search performed by Algorithm 1 blows up when the cache size is approximately the half/third of the total number of states. This causes a run-time explosion, which makes state space caching inefficient under a certain threshold.

With Algorithm 2, for PFTP, this threshold can be reduced to the fourth of the total number of states. The improvement is not very spectacular because the number of matched states, even when using sleep sets, is still too important (see Table 1). The risk of double work when reaching an already visited state that has been deleted from memory is not reduced enough.

For the other three protocols, URP, MULOG3 and DTP, the situation is different: there is no run-time explosion with Algorithm 2. Indeed, the number of matched states is reduced so much (see Table 1) that the risk of double work becomes very small. When the cache size is reduced up to the maximal depth of the search (this maximal depth is the lower bound for the cache size since all states of the stack have to be stored to ensure the termination of the search), the number of explored transitions is still between only two and four times the total number of transitions in the state space. *These protocols, which have between 15,000 and 250,000 reachable states, can be analyzed with no more than 500 stored states. The memory requirements are reduced to 3% up to 0.2%. The only drawback is an increase of the run time by two to four times compared to the search where all states are stored (which may be impossible for larger state spaces).*

The efficiency of the method can be dynamically estimated during the search: if the maximum stack size remains acceptable with respect to the cache size and if the proportion of matched states remains small enough, the run-time explosion will likely be avoided. Else one cannot predict if the cache size is large enough to avoid the run-time explosion.

5   Further Investigations

An important factor when using the state space caching method is the selection criterion for determining which states are deleted when the cache is full.

Holzmann has studied several replacement strategies in [Hol85]. These strategies were based on the number of times that a state has been previously visited. These strategies were: replace the most frequently visited state; replace the least frequently visited state; replace a state from the largest class of states in the current state space (where a class contains states that have been visited equally often); replace randomly a state (blind round-robin replacement); replace the state corresponding to the lowest point in the search tree (smallest subtree). The conclusion of that study was that the best strategy seems to be a random selection. In [Hol87], the probability of recurrence of states (i.e. the probability that once a state has been visited n times it will be visited an $n + 1$st time as well) was investigated and turns out not to be strongly correlated with the number of previous visits.

We have experimented some different replacement strategies. Our motivation was to study the influence of the type of transitions that can lead to a state on the probability that the state is visited again later during the search. For instance, a "labeled" state, e.g. the target of a goto jump, is intuitively more susceptible to be matched than an "unlabeled" state.

First, let us classify transitions into different types:

1. control branches (goto jump, start of do loops, ...);

2. receives on message channels;

3. sends on message channels;

4. assignments to variables;

5. other transitions.

Each state encountered during the search is tagged with the type of the transition that has led to it. We have studied the impact of the following replacement strategy on the run-time requirements of the state space caching method, for each of the four first types of transitions:

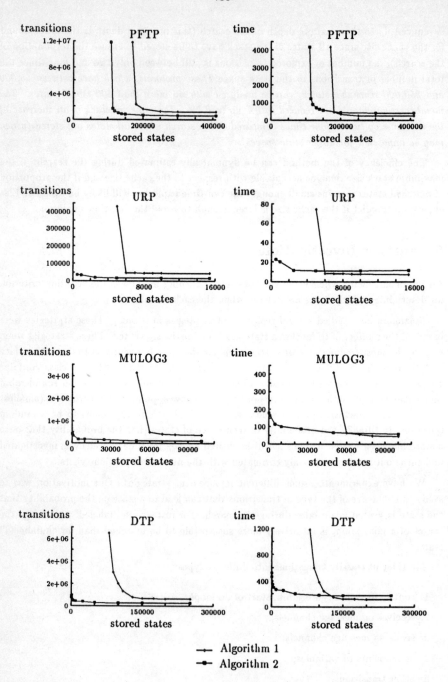

Figure 4: Performances of state space caching with Algorithm 1 and 2

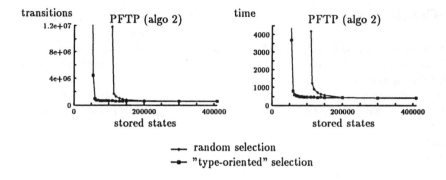

Figure 5: Random vs "type-oriented" replacement strategy

Each time a state has to be deleted, scan an arbitrarily given number of stored states (scanning too many states incurs an unacceptable overhead; this is why an arbitrary limit is given). If possible, select a state that *is not* tagged with the type considered. Otherwise, select randomly one of them.

The results are the following: for type 1, the procedure described above gives always better results than a simple random selection; for types 2, 3 and 4, the results are unpredictable. In other words, it is preferable not to remove states pointed by type 1 transitions, as far as possible.

Since protocols do not necessarily have transitions of each type, a good heuristic cannot be based only on the selection of states that follow transitions of a single type. Grouping all the four first types together and trying to delete only states that follow transitions of type 5 is not a good solution as well because it degenerates to a random selection since transitions of type 5 are usually not numerous enough. A possible trade-off is to use the following replacement strategy:

Each time a state has to be deleted, scan an arbitrarily given number of stored states and select one state that is tagged with the highest type (i.e. closest to 5).

The order of the types given above was chosen according to the results of the experiments we made with the different types taken separately. If a state is visited by several transitions, its tag is set to the smallest type of transitions that led to it.

Figure 5 shows the results obtained with this strategy (denoted "type-oriented" strategy) compared to a random replacement discipline for the PFTP protocol. One can see that this strategy does not involve a significant run-time overhead. Moreover, it yields a 50% reduction for the run-time blow-up threshold.

For the other three protocols, there is no significant difference with respect to a random selection strategy. As a matter of fact, in these examples, the random selection strategy is sufficient to reduce the cache size so close to the maximal stack size that no significant further reduction is possible.

6 Conclusions

We have presented a new technique which can substantially improve the state space caching discipline by getting rid of the main cause of its previous inefficiency, namely prohibitive state matching due to the exploration of all possible interleavings of concurrent statement executions all leading to the same state. We have shown with experiments on real protocol models that, thanks to sleep sets, the memory requirements needed to validate large protocol models can be strongly decreased (sometimes more than 100 times) without seriously increasing the time requirements (a factor of 3 or 4). This makes possible the complete exploration of very large state spaces, that could not be explored so far. However, exploring state spaces of several tens of million states takes time, since all these states are visited at least once during the search. Thus time becomes the main limiting factor.

Note that no attempts were made in this paper to reduce the number of states that need to be visited in order to validate properties of a system. However, sleep sets were originally introduced as part of a method intended to master the "state explosion" phenomenon [God90, GW91a, GW91b, HGP92]. Using the full method preserves the beneficial properties of sleep sets that were investigated in Section 3 while enabling a substantial reduction of the number of states that have to be visited for verification purposes.

Acknowledgements

We wish to thank Pierre Wolper for helpful comments on this paper.

References

[CVWY90] C. Courcoubetis, M. Vardi, P. Wolper, and M. Yannakakis. Memory efficient algorithms for the verification of temporal properties. In *Proc. 2nd Workshop on Computer Aided Verification*, volume 531 of *Lecture Notes in Computer Science*, pages 233–242, Rutgers, June 1990.

[God90] P. Godefroid. Using partial orders to improve automatic verification methods. In *Proc. 2nd Workshop on Computer Aided Verification*, volume 531 of *Lecture Notes in Computer Science*, pages 176–185, Rutgers, June 1990.

[GW91a] P. Godefroid and P. Wolper. A partial approach to model checking. In *Proceedings of the 6th IEEE Symposium on Logic in Computer Science*, pages 406–415, Amsterdam, July 1991.

[GW91b] P. Godefroid and P. Wolper. Using partial orders for the efficient verification of deadlock freedom and safety properties. In *Proc. 3rd Workshop on Computer Aided Verification*, volume 575 of *Lecture Notes in Computer Science*, pages 332–342, Aalborg, July 1991.

[HGP92] G. J. Holzmann, P. Godefroid, and D. Pirottin. Coverage preserving reduction strategies for reachability analysis. In *Proc. 12th International Symposium on Protocol Specification, Testing, and Verification*, Lake Buena Vista, Florida, June 1992. North-Holland.

[Hol81] G. J. Holzmann. Pan — a protocol specification analyzer. Technical report, Technical Memorandum 81-11271-5, Bell Laboratories, 1981.

[Hol84] G. J. Holzmann. The pandora system — an interactive system for the design of data communication protocols. *Computer Networks*, 8(2):71–81, 1984.

[Hol85]   G. J. Holzmann. Tracing protocols. *AT&T Technical Journal*, 64(12):2413–2434, 1985.

[Hol87]   G. J. Holzmann. Automated protocol validation in argos — assertion proving and scatter searching. *IEEE Trans. on Software Engineering*, 13(6):683–696, 1987.

[Hol90]   G. J. Holzmann. Algorithms for automated protocol validation. *AT&T Technical Journal*, 69(1):32–44, 1990. Special issue on Protocol Testing and Verification.

[Hol91]   G. J. Holzmann. *Design and Validation of Computer Protocols*. Prentice Hall, 1991.

[JJ89]   C. Jard and T. Jeron. On-line model-checking for finite linear temporal logic specifications. In *Workshop on automatic verification methods for finite state systems*, volume 407 of *Lecture Notes in Computer Science*, pages 189–196, Grenoble, June 1989.

[JJ91]   C. Jard and Th. Jeron. Bounded-memory algorithms for verification on-the-fly. In *Proc. 3rd Workshop on Computer Aided Verification*, volume 575 of *Lecture Notes in Computer Science*, Aalborg, July 1991.

[Maz86]   A. Mazurkiewicz. Trace theory. In *Petri Nets: Applications and Relationships to Other Models of Concurrency, Advances in Petri Nets 1986, Part II; Proceedings of an Advanced Course*, volume 255 of *Lecture Notes in Computer Science*, pages 279–324, 1986.

[TN87]   M. Trehel and M. Naimi. Un algorithme distribué d'exclusion mutuelle en log(n). *Technique et Science Informatiques*, pages 141–150, 1987.

[VW86]   M.Y. Vardi and P. Wolper. Automata-theoretic techniques for modal logics of programs. *Journal of Computer and System Science*, 32(2):182–21, April 1986.

Verification in process algebra of the distributed control of track vehicles—A case study*

Siegfried Fischer, Andreas Scholz, Dirk Taubner[†]

Siemens AG[‡], Germany

Abstract A real-life example of parallel processes, namely the distributed control of track vehicles, is modelled and analyzed on design level using process algebra techniques.

We report on the stepwise development, the verification performed, and the errors found. We show how the complexity of verification is handled and argue that the verification was only possible due to computer assistance which was available as the tool PVE (Process Verification Environment). This non-trivial, industrially motivated example may also serve as a benchmark for other methods and tools.

1 Introduction

Parallel processes more and more often occur in the design of applications such as telecommunication systems, operating systems, and embedded control systems. They are extremely hard to test and debug. Opposed to testing, verification aims at proving correctness. A number of approaches such as Petri nets [18], process algebras [14, 1], and parallel program verification techniques [16, 5] have been developed in order to verify correctness of parallel processes. Examples of applications found in textbooks are typically rather small such as mutual exclusion, dining philosophers, and the alternating bit protocol.

This paper is a case study in applying the techniques of process algebra to a real-life problem. We study the problem of safely controlling track vehicles in a distributed manner. Every track section and every vehicle has its own control processor. These processors have to communicate to ensure safe (e.g. collision-free) movement of vehicles.

This problem is industrially motivated. Such controls are developed in our company and some actual design draft served as the starting point for our study. However due to abstractions, further developments, and for reasons motivated by clarity of presentation the material given in this paper diverges from any actual design.

The aim is to show that the verification techniques supplied by process algebra can be used for practical applications. We want to present a useful approach to designing and verifying a system of parallel processes. We investigate the feasibility and limitations. This case study may also serve as a benchmark for other methods and tools.

It is important to emphasize that we apply verification to the design phase. The reason is twofold. Firstly this cuts short the traditional development cycle where certain errors are found in the test phase only (see Fig. 1). Secondly we believe that only on the design level the system to be verified has a complexity which can be handled with verification. This is true even if state-of-the-art tool support is used. Nevertheless, due to abstractions some errors will still be detected not earlier than in the test phase.

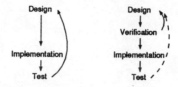

Figure 1: Traditional and refined development cycle

*This work has been partially supported by a BMFT grant under contract number TV8743.
[†]New address: D. Taubner, sd&m GmbH, Thomas-Dehler-Str. 27, W-8000 München 83, Germany
  Email: taubner@informatik.tu-muenchen.de
[‡]Address for correspondence: A. Scholz, Siemens AG, ZFE BT SE 1, Otto-Hahn-Ring 6, W-8000 München 83, Germany
  Email: scholz@newton.zfe.siemens.de

2 Process algebra techniques and the tool PVE

Research on process algebras was initiated by Milner's *Calculus of Communicating Systems* (CCS) [13], it progressed rapidly, cf. e.g. [3, 8, 2, 1]. As we use it, process algebra allows to reason about a system of concurrent finite state machines which communicate synchronously. Two techniques for verification are provided, equivalence checking and model checking. In both cases the external behaviour of the system which is to be verified is relevant.

For *equivalence checking* one needs a specification (i.e. a second description of this behaviour). The equality of both is then checked with respect to an adequate notion of equivalence. To this end we choose *weak bisimulation equivalence*, denoted $\approx$ [14].

For *model checking* one formulates certain desirable properties (such as deadlock freedom, ability to perform certain sequences of actions) in a logic called *propositional modal μ-calculus* [9]. Each property is checked for validity against the system. As such properties may cover separate small aspects this approach is feasible even if it is impossible to supply a specification for the whole system.

Let us recall how transition systems are combined to a system of communicating components by operators for parallel composition, restriction, and renaming. Assume a set $Act = \{\tau, a?, b?, c?, \ldots, a!, b!, c!, \ldots\}$ of actions. It contains the internal action τ which is not visible externally, and as many visible actions as needed. An input action a? will match the output action a! in communications. The basic building block of parallel systems is a transition system $T = \langle S, \longrightarrow, z \rangle$ which consists of a finite set S of states, a finite ternary transition relation $\longrightarrow \subseteq S \times Act \times S$, and a starting state $z \in S$. A transition $\langle r, \alpha, s \rangle \in \longrightarrow$ is also denoted as $r -\alpha\rightarrow s$.

The *parallel composition* $T_1 \mid T_2$ of two transition systems $T_1 = \langle S_1, \longrightarrow_1, z_1 \rangle$ and $T_2 = \langle S_2, \longrightarrow_2, z_2 \rangle$ is defined as $\langle S_1 \times S_2, \longrightarrow, \langle z_1, z_2 \rangle \rangle$ where

$$\longrightarrow := \{(\langle r_1, s_2 \rangle, \alpha, \langle s_1, s_2 \rangle) \mid r_1 -\alpha\rightarrow_1 s_1\} \cup \{(\langle s_1, r_2 \rangle, \alpha, \langle s_1, s_2 \rangle) \mid r_2 -\alpha\rightarrow_2 s_2\}$$
$$\cup \ \{(\langle r_1, r_2 \rangle, \tau, \langle s_1, s_2 \rangle) \mid r_1 -x?\rightarrow_1 s_1 \wedge r_2 -x!\rightarrow_2 s_2 \vee r_1 -x!\rightarrow_1 s_1 \wedge r_2 -x?\rightarrow_2 s_2\}.$$

The first two cases allow components to proceed independently asynchronously while the third case constitutes a synchronous communication via matching input and output actions. The joint action resulting from the communication is invisible. This is the parallel composition of CCS [14], for others see [20]. Note that it allows only binary synchronization, i.e. the result of a synchronization is invisible and hence cannot serve for an additional synchronization.

To enforce communication one has to disallow the asynchronous moves with the following *restriction* operator. Given $T = \langle S, \longrightarrow, z \rangle$ and a set A of visible actions, the restriction $T\backslash A$ is defined as $\langle S, \{\langle r, \alpha, s \rangle \mid r -\alpha\rightarrow s \wedge \alpha \notin A\}, z \rangle$. The restriction disallows all transitions labelled by actions in A. We often use the complementary restriction operator $T \ allowonly \ A := T\backslash(Act - (A \cup \{\tau\}))$.

The *renaming* operator is convenient to instantiate a copy of a transition system with modified actions. Let $f : Act \rightarrow Act$ be a function which does not change the invisible action, then $T \ map \ f$ is defined as $\langle S, \{\langle r, f(\alpha), s \rangle \mid r -\alpha\rightarrow s\}, z \rangle$.

The tool PVE (Process Verification Environment) We have built the software tool PVE [11] which automates process algebra techniques. See [11, 12] for overviews over similar tools. In essence PVE provides the basic functionality of the Concurrency Workbench [6] but is much more efficient in space and time. PVE supports the following points.

Parsing A machine-readable syntax for basic transition systems (adapted from [14]), for the process algebra operators, for formulas of the used modal logic, and for several commands has been defined. It is analyzed in a command line interpreter which initiates the appropriate functions.

Transition system generation For process algebra source code the transition systems are built internally as an appropriate linked data structure. The τ-closure, i.e. the $\Longrightarrow$ transition relation [11] is computed.

Equivalence checking and Minimization The partition refinement algorithm of Paige and Tarjan [17] has been generalized for the case that there is more than one action. We perform some equivalence-preserving reduction of transition systems before equivalence checking. In addition, the generalized Paige/Tarjan-algorithm is used for minimization of transition systems.

Model checking The model checker of Emerson and Lei [9] has been implemented. On an experimental basis we also implemented symbolic model checking [10, 4] and local model checking [19]. We plan to integrate the improvements of [7].

PVE has been implemented in C++ and runs on UNIX workstations (HP/Apollo, Sun SPARCstation 2). Currently the system is able to handle up to 10^6 states and transitions.

3 Distributed control technique for track vehicles

Problem description As is usual for the control of track vehicles, such as railway trains, the track is divided into sections. One such section is called a *block*. The point which is new here is that the track system is not controlled centrally (either by hand or machine), but in a decentralized manner. Each block has its own control computer which runs some software. Taking hardware and software together, we speak of a *block control*. In addition, each vehicle has its own control computer. The problem of our case study is to design and verify a *distributed block control*.

The most important safety requirement is that each block must not contain more than one vehicle (i.e. mutual exclusion is guaranteed). As a vehicle has spatial extension a vehicle may be in two blocks at the same time, cf. Fig. 2. However, we assume a *reference point* for each vehicle. The transition of this point from one block to the next is assumed to be atomic. A second important property of the control mechanism which we want to verify is the absence of deadlocks. Although a deadlock would not imply a safety risk such as a collision, we do not want to see passengers starving on the track.

All block controls and vehicles have to communicate in order to ensure the correct function of the system. To this end the block controls are linked according to the topologic structure of the track system. In this paper we consider only cyclic topologies. Communication between a vehicle and a block control is possible if and only if the reference point of the vehicle is within the block. In this case we say that the vehicle is controlled by the block control. Fig. 2 summarizes the communication structure.

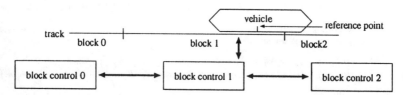

Figure 2: Communication between block controls and a vehicle

The aim of this paper is to present the development process of the design of the block control. We proceed in two steps, first the unidirectional case is considered, later changes of direction are supported additionally. The control system will allow changes of direction at any moment, i.e. the vehicles may attempt to change direction at any position in or "between" blocks.

Modelling of vehicles Developing the block control we will need some assumptions on the vehicles and their ability to communicate. In particular we assume that a vehicle which is controlled by a block control informs the control about all important changes of state. We will use the following actions.

Enter	The reference point of the vehicle enters the block.
EnterComp	The vehicle has completely entered the block, no other block is occupied anymore. We assume that blocks are much longer than vehicles.
ResReq	The vehicle requests the reservation of the successor block as it approaches the block boundary.
OccSucc	The vehicle has (partially) occupied the successor block. The distributed block control has to be designed in such a way that this action can be performed only if the successor block is not occupied by another vehicle. Of course automatic braking should start if this action cannot be performed in time. However, this mechanism is not modelled here.
ChDir	The vehicle changes its direction of movement.
ChDirOk	The vehicle receives a message that the change of direction has been processed by the control.
Exit	The reference point of the vehicle exits the block.

In essence these actions are an abstract model of a track vehicle and its physical movement.

Naming Conventions For the rest of this paper we use a structure for actions which shows the participants in a communication. Every action is prefixed by two characters which indicate the sender and the receiver respectively. For example the action *VIEnterComp* means that vehicle *V* sends an *EnterComp*-message to block control *I*. We will use the following letters in prefixes.

V   Vehicle
I   the currently considered block control; may be read as I=myself
P   Predecessor of the current block control with respect to the current direction of movement of the vehicle (if there is any in the block)
S   Successor of the current block, note that there are only cyclic topologies, so there is exactly one successor
L   Left neighbour of the current block with respect to the physical topology
R   Right neighbour
X   any

Note that these abbreviations are understood with respect to a specific block control. Consider, for example, the complete unidirectional system with movement from lower to higher block numbers. It is built from several instantiations of the block control such that an action *ISxxx* of block control 2 matches action *PIxxx* of block control 3. In process algebra we map both to *23xxx* replacing *I*, *P* and *S* by the corresponding block numbers. In diagrams of transition systems we use the additional convention to omit the '?' and '!' marks if they are clear from the two-character prefix. For example in the transition system of the block control *I* all actions *IXxxx* (*XIxxx*) implicitly have an '!' ('?') at the end.

4   Designing the distributed block control

This section describes the design process for the block control associated with each block of the track. In a first step we develop a version which is able to handle vehicles that never change their direction of movement. In 4.2 we refine the layout developed in 4.1 and the vehicles are allowed to change their direction of movement at any time.

4.1   Unidirectional vehicles

The unidirectional case of our block control will only be able to control vehicles passing from left to right (or in the opposite direction) through a block, but never allows a change of direction. Consequently we speak of predecessor blocks and of successor blocks with respect to a fixed direction of movement for the rest of 4.1. We chose the direction from lower to higher numbers (modulo cycle length).

Specification   One possibility for the specification would be to describe the behaviour of a single-block control. However, this is not realistic if nothing is known about the vehicle. Therefore, we start to assume that a vehicle performs the following sequence of actions when moving from block *I* to block *S*.

$$VIResReq!.VIOccSucc!.VEinBS!.VIExit!.VSEnter!.VSEnterComp!$$

The action *VEinBS* is to indicate externally (for verification purposes) that vehicle *V* is starting to move to block *S*. We start with a system of three blocks connected in a cycle. The transition system $VehicleUD_i$ given in Fig. 3 shows a vehicle which starts in block number *i* and which tries to move circularly in one direction through this ring.

The design of the block control has to be such that if we take one copy for each block and link the communication appropriately the vehicle is controlled in such a way that it actually can move in circles. In other words if we enforce communication with respect to all actions between block controls and the vehicle we expect the behaviour of the complete system to allow forever the sequence

$$VEinB1!\ VEinB2!\ VEinB0!\ \ldots$$

To put it formally, if *BC0wV*, *BC1*, and *BC2* are block controls such that *BC0wV* controls the vehicle initially we expect

$$(BC0wV \mid BC1 \mid BC2 \mid VehicleUD_0)\ allowonly\ \{VEinB0!, VEinB1!, VEinB2!\}$$

to be bisimulation equivalent to the transition system of Fig. 4(a). We call this transition system *SpecUD1*. It is the specification for a unidirectional ring of three blocks with one vehicle.

The specification for a ring which has two vehicles is more interesting. In principle each vehicle can be in one of the three blocks. This would result in 9 possible states. However, those combinations where both vehicles are in the same block have to be excluded. The transition system *SpecUD2* for the specification of a ring with two vehicles which both move in only one and the same direction is given in Fig. 4(b).

We are now ready for the design.

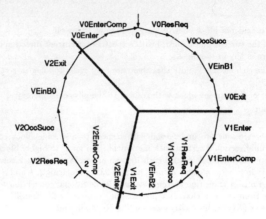

Figure 3: A unidirectional vehicle for a ring of three blocks

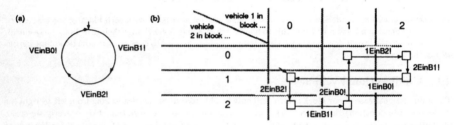

Figure 4: Specification for a unidirectional ring of three blocks with one (a) or two (b) vehicle(s)

Internal control As mutual exclusion on occupation of blocks is the main safety property which is to be ensured by the block control a semaphore is naturally chosen for the beginning of the design process. However, the control of a block is not informed directly by the vehicle about its entering. This is due to the assumption that vehicles communicate only with that block control whose block contains its reference point (see Fig. 2). Therefore, the semaphore has to be enhanced by a reservation phase which allows a vehicle to occupy the block without direct notification of the corresponding block control. In a symmetric way we add a release state for exiting vehicles. Fig. 5 shows the resulting 4-state process. We will refer to this process as *internal control process* (IC-process) and to its states as ICx where x is a state number.

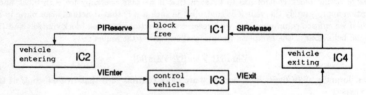

Figure 5: A semaphore enhanced by reservation

Predecessor and successor control As there is a reservation required before occupation there must be someone to make it. For the reasons mentioned above the vehicle cannot do that itself. We decided to add a second process for this task which is called *successor control process* (SC-process). It has to perform two subtasks. Firstly it has to perform the reservation procedure upon the receipt of a *V1ResReq*-message. Secondly the process has to ensure that a *V1OccSucc*-action cannot occur before the reservation is finished successfully. Fig. 6(a) shows the transition diagram for the SC-process.

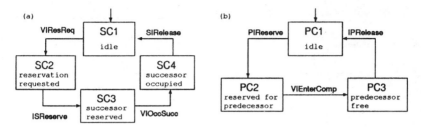

Figure 6: The successor (a) and predecessor (b) control processes

Note that an occupation of the successor block can occur only after a successful reservation. If the successor block cannot be reserved (i.e. the process is blocked in state SC2), the vehicle will be unable to perform a *VIOccSucc*-action and will be forced to stop by some sort of timeout mechanism within the vehicle which is not modelled in Fig. 3.

A further task which has to be carried out by the block control is to release the predecessor block if the vehicle has completely entered the block. Therefore we add a third process named *predecessor control process* (PC-process). It has roughly the layout of a boolean variable which indicates whether the predecessor block is occupied by (a part of) a vehicle. Fig. 6(b) shows the transition system of the process. State PC3 can be interpreted as a one-message buffer for the message coming from the vehicle.

Multiple synchronizations Note that the action *IPRelease* of the PC-process has to match the actions named *SIRelease* of the internal and the successor control processes of the predecessor's block control. This is an example for a synchronization of more than two processes which is called a *multiple synchronization*. Another example is the *XXReserve*-action.

The CCS-parallel composition presented in Section 2 allows to express binary synchronizations only. One possibility to overcome this restriction would be to use more powerful synchronizing constructs as proposed e.g. in MEIJE [8]. However the use of multiple synchronizations as a primitive raises the question of adequacy for the description of distributed designs and of implementability. We suggest to allow the use of multiple synchronizations only between processes which are located on the same computer. Otherwise we suggest to use only binary synchronizations.

In order not to limit the actual implementation we do not use multiple synchronizations as primitive construct in this paper. This also yields a deeper insight into the necessary synchronizations which is valuable for a later implementation.

For modelling of multi-synchronizations by binary synchronizations we introduce a communication pattern which we will often use below. We explain it with the example of *XXReserve*. Fig. 7(a) shows a block control A which requests reservation of its successor block B. Therefore it has to synchronize its own successor control process with the internal and predecessor control processes of its successor. We split the action *ISReserve* into two new actions called *ISResReq* and *SIResOk* which indicate a reservation request and a positive acknowledgement respectively. Careful design ensures that no deadlocking can occur in the new intermediate states shown in Fig. 7(b). This is of course verified using PVE. For internal synchronization another new action called *IIReserve* is introduced. A similar construction is applied to the action *XXRelease*, the new actions are called *XXRelReq*, *XXRelOk* and *IIRelease*.

The complete model and its verification Fig. 8 shows the complete three-process structure of one block control. Naming the component processes with their initial states we have the following definition.

$$BlockControlUD := (PC1 \mid IC1 \mid SC1) \setminus A_{II}$$

Where the set A_{II} contains all actions which start with II. A block control which controls a vehicle initially is defined as

$$BlockControlUDWithVeh := (PC1 \mid IC3 \mid SC1) \setminus A_{II}.$$

Three copies of the block control for the track are instantiated as follows.

$$
\begin{array}{llll}
BC0wV & := & BlockControlUDWithVeh & map \quad fPIS201 \\
BC1 & := & BlockControlUD & map \quad fPIS012 \\
BC2 & := & BlockControlUD & map \quad fPIS120
\end{array}
$$

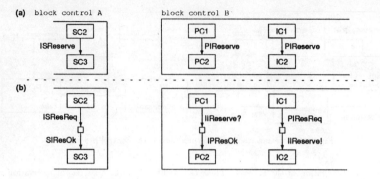

Figure 7: Modelling a multi-synchronization with binary synchronizations

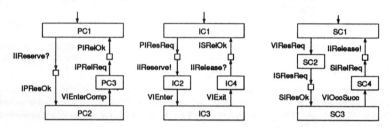

Figure 8: The complete block control for unidirectional vehicles

Here *fPIS201* maps every *P*, *I*, and *S* in the first two characters of actions to 2, 0, and 1 respectively. The functions *fPIS012* and *fPIS120* are analogous. The complete design of a unidirectional ring of three blocks with one vehicle is defined as

$$RingUD1 := (BC0wV \mid BC1 \mid BC2 \mid VehicleUD_0) \text{ allowonly } A_{XE}$$

where A_{XE} contains all actions whose second character is an *E*.

This complete design can now be verified against the specification *SpecUD1* of Fig. 4(a). We have performed not only this check with PVE, but also checked several intermediate drafts of the design. We found a number of errors, below in 4.2 we point to a particular error. For the above presented design we have $RingUD1 \approx SpecUD1$.

Similarly for a ring with two vehicles we instantiate block control 1 as *BlockControlUDWithVeh* and two vehicles which are located in block 0 and 1 respectively. Formally we get

$$
\begin{aligned}
BC1wV &:= & BlockControlUDWithVeh & \text{ map } & fPIS012 \\
V1 &:= & VehicleUD_0 & \text{ map } & fVE1E \\
V2 &:= & VehicleUD_1 & \text{ map } & fVE2E
\end{aligned}
$$

where *fVE1E* changes in every action which starts with *VE* the *V* to 1. The function *fVE2E* is analogous. The unidirectional ring with two vehicles is defined as

$$RingUD2 := (BC0wV \mid BC1wV \mid BC2 \mid V1 \mid V2) \text{ allowonly } A_{XE}.$$

Again we have $RingUD2 \approx SpecUD2$. We report on statistics and on our experience using PVE for verification in detail in Section 5.

4.2 Refinement for allowing changes of direction

We are now turning towards a design which allows vehicles to change their direction of movement. Opposed to the unidirectional case the notions predecessor and successor are no longer static. For an unambiguous reference to the neighbours of a block we use the notions *left* and *right* below. We assume the blocks of the track to be numbered in a linear order. We call the neighbour with a lower (higher) block number the *left* (*right*) neighbour. This definition can be extended easily for cyclic tracks (with at least 2 blocks). We will call the direction from left to right *positive* and the opposite direction *negative*.

Specification The specification of a ring with three blocks and one or two vehicles does not get much more complicated for the bidirectional case, see Fig. 9(a) for the transition system *SpecBD1* and Fig. 9(b) for the transition system *SpecBD2*.

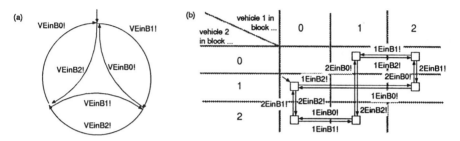

Figure 9: Specification of a bidirectional ring with three blocks and one (a) or two (b) vehicle(s)

The assumptions on the vehicle however are more involved as we allow the vehicle to change its direction of movement at any time. The transition system $VehicleBD_i$ for a vehicle which moves through a ring of three blocks starting in block i is illustrated in Fig. 10. Observe that the outer (inner) circle corresponds to positive (negative) direction of movement and that the vehicle is allowed to perform a change of direction at any time. Only when the vehicle's reference point crosses a block boundary (which is assumed to be an atomic transition) a change of direction is not allowed between the notifications of the corresponding block controls and of the external observer.

Duplication of states In process algebra the labels of transitions are static, consequently it is impossible to modify the previously used action patterns dynamically depending on the current direction. As a remedy we duplicate each process in the block control. One copy is modified for positive direction (predecessor=left, successor=right), the other copy is rewritten for negative direction.

Of course at each moment only one direction is valid in a block and consequently only one copy of a control process is allowed to be active (i.e. to perform actions). For the internal control process of a block control this is achieved by joining the initial states of the copies (cf. Fig. 12). We could do the same with the predecessor and successor control processes. However, if a vehicle changes its direction a reservation *of* a neighbour block will turn into a reservation *for* this neighbour. Therefore, we prefer to join the initial states of the predecessor control for positive direction and of the successor control for negative direction to form a new process which is called *left neighbour control process* (NCL-process). Symmetrically a *right neighbour control process* (NCR-process) is formed. The shaded parts in Fig. 12 indicate those parts of the NCL- and NCR-process which result from this join.

Additional transitions As may be seen from Fig. 12 there are a number of additional transitions within the three processes of a complete block control. Their need is best explained with Fig. 11. The figure shows ten significant *positions* of a vehicle, they are named by circled numbers. As in the unidirectional case for each position there is a corresponding state of the block control which is in turn a triple of the states of its components (cf. Fig. 12 for state names). However, as the vehicle may move in both directions for each position there are two triples. The pos-triple and the neg-triple correspond to positive and negative direction respectively.

The change from one position to the next usually involves several transitions of the block controls which are occupied by the vehicle. In Fig. 11 we only show one significant action. However, a few changes of position involve no transition of the block controls, the corresponding arrows are unlabeled. Solid (dashed) arrows correspond to positive (negative) direction of the vehicle.

Note that a vehicle is in position 1 with respect to a specific block if and only if it is in position 6 with respect to its left neighbour block. Similar facts hold for positions 2/7, 3/8, 4/9 and 5/0.

200

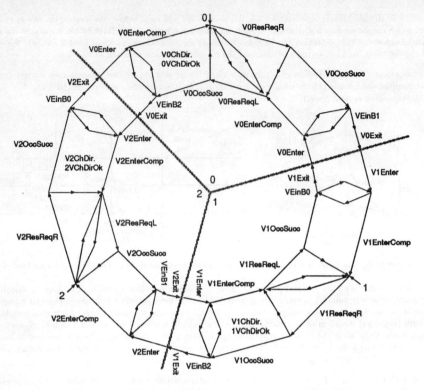

Figure 10: A bidirectional vehicle moving in a ring of three blocks

Fig. 11 shows which state changes within a block control are expected when a vehicle changes its position. The block control shown in Fig. 12 is enhanced by additional transitions in order to ensure these changes of state.

To explain these transitions let us look at a vehicle moving in positive direction which is in position 5 with respect to its controlling block A. This means that the vehicle is in position 0 with respect to A's right neighbour block B. A change in this situation is very simple, it just means that the IC-process of A has to change from IC3P to IC3N. Confer Fig. 12 to see how this is handled.

If the vehicle runs out of space as it approaches a block boundary it changes to position 6 and to position 1 respectively. Comparing the pos-triples shows that block control A has to change its NCR-process from NCR1 to NCR3 and block control B has to change its IC-process from IC1 to IC2P and its NCL-process from NCL1 to NCL2. It becomes clear that these three transitions are exactly what the construction in Fig. 7 does using the actions $ABResReq$, $BBReserveL$ and $BAResOk$.

Let us now turn to a change of direction. Assume a vehicle which has reached position 6 and position 1 respectively decides to change its direction of movement. A change of direction in this situation implies a change of position from 6 to 5 and from 1 to 0. Checking the differences between the pos-triple for position 6 and the neg-triple for position 5 as well as those between the corresponding triples for positions 1 and 0 one gets all state changes which have to be performed. In A the IC-process has to perform the transition from IC3P to IC3N, thus turning the direction, and the NCR-process has to change from NCR3 to NCR1, thus cancelling the reservation of block B. During this change from NCR3 to NCR1 the NCR-process issues the $IRRelReq$-signal to the block control B. To prevent a new reservation process to start before the release operation is completed, the NCR-process waits for an acknowledgement called $RIRelOk$. The state NCL2 of B's NCL-process indicates that the left neighbour (which is A in this case) has a reservation for block B. If a release request comes in, the process notifies its internal control process via $IIRelease$. The IC-process of B completes the cancellation with $ILRelOk$ which the NCR-process of block A is waiting for.

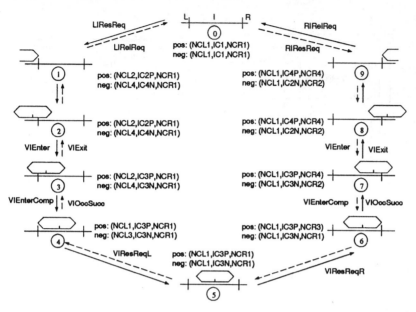

Figure 11: A vehicle passes through a block

Note that it is essential for absence of deadlocks in our design that the IC-process of B comes back to its inital state *after* the NCL-process did. In fact we have made the error to program the synchronizations in the wrong order. This may cause a deadlock if a new reservation starts before the release operation is completed.

In a similar way the change of direction of a vehicle which is in position 7 with respect to its controlling block A and in position 2 with respect to its right neighbour B is handled. In this case no change of position is implied. An exiting vehicle becomes an entering one and vice versa. Consequently a reservation of a neighbour block turns into a reservation for that block. Here it becomes clear why we decided to join an SC-process with a PC-process. We use the new action *IRDirExit* to notify B that the vehicle has switched its direction and hence is now exiting B. In a symmetrical manner we use the action *IRDirEnter* for a change from negative to positive direction in the same positions.

The full model and its verification So far our design has become quite complicated and again we wish to ensure the correct function. The block control which is shown in Fig. 12 is defined by the following process algebra term.

$$BlockControlBD := (NCL1 \mid IC1 \mid NCR1) \setminus A_{II}$$

Again A_{II} denotes the set of actions starting with II. Similarly a block control which already controls a vehicle with positive direction of movement is written as

$$BlockControlBDWithVeh := (NCL1 \mid IC3P \mid NCR1) \setminus A_{II}.$$

Processing this in PVE results in two transition systems each with 6867 states. This seems surprising since during our construction we had very few combinations of triples of states in mind (cf. Fig. 11). The reason for the large state space is that we have not made full use of the fact that communication between a block control and a vehicle occurs only if the vehicle is controlled by the block control. For example each NC-process is able to accept a *VIResReqX*-signal from a vehicle even if there is no vehicle in the block, i.e. even if the internal control is not in state IC3X.

The full system with one vehicle consists of three copies of the block control and the vehicle process shown in Fig. 10. It is given by the following definitions.

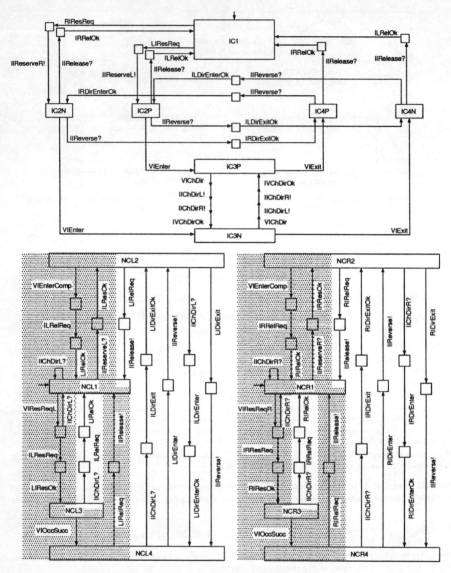

Figure 12: The block control for bidirectional vehicles

$$
\begin{aligned}
BC0wV \quad &:= \quad BlockControlBDWithVeh \quad map \quad fLIR201 \\
BC1 \quad &:= \quad BlockControlBD \quad\quad\quad\quad map \quad fLIR012 \\
BC2 \quad &:= \quad BlockControlBD \quad\quad\quad\quad map \quad fLIR120
\end{aligned}
$$

$$RingBD1 := (BC0wV \mid BC1 \mid BC2 \mid VehicleBD_0) \; allowonly \; A_{VE}$$

Here the function $fLIR201$ maps the letters L, I and R in the first and second position of action names to 2, 0 and 1 respectively. The set A_{VE} contains all actions which start with VE. A quick PVE-proof shows that $RingBD1 \approx SpecBD1$.

The same track carrying two vehicles is defined as follows.

$$RingBD2 := (BC0wV \mid BC1wV \mid BC2 \mid V1 \mid V2) \; allowonly \; A_{XE}$$

The processes $BC1wV$, $V1$, and $V2$ are understood in a similar way as in the previous section. Again we have $RingBD2 \approx SpecBD2$. Detailed statistics of the verification are reported in the following section.

Having reached the final solution it may be observed that the coupling of the three components within the block control is rather tight. Indeed it is possible to give a solution for the block control with just one component which has less than twenty states. However, the splitting into three components is motivated by a natural functional decomposition, furthermore in practice the components serve for additional tasks which should be separated correspondingly.

5   Verification in PVE

The main results of the verification were already described above. This section shows how PVE was used as a development tool along the whole process of refining the design. In addition, we give verification results on the mutual exclusion requirement which were skipped above. Some statistics on the performance of PVE prove that we are able to handle real life systems without hampering the design process.

Using PVE for supporting the design process   Developing the unidirectional version of the block control turned out to be straightforward from an earlier draft design and was easy to be proved correct.

A first, naive attempt to add changes of direction showed us that further development requires some method of "small development steps". We decided to make the development along a series of increasingly more complex vehicles. While the easiest vehicle does not perform changes of direction if any neighbour block is involved, the most complex vehicle (cf. Fig.10) performs changes of direction arbitrarily. After each step of improvement the system $RingBD1$ was checked against $SpecBD1$ for equivalence. The time for generating the system never exceeded a minute while equivalence checking for systems containing still some errors was very likely to take up to 30 minutes. Consequently it is very important to have a fast tool even for relatively small systems. During this case study almost every incorrect intermediate development of the block control had some deadlocking behaviour. On the other hand the mutual exclusion requirement turned out to be very stable with respect to modifications. Hence we concentrated our raid for errors on deadlocks. For practical use it is essential to get quick answers on questions like "Is there any τ-cycle which cannot be left by a visible action?" Our model checker takes no more than a few seconds for that (see the statistics below).

In the course of the refinement process the complexity of the errors found was increasing. One of them took a minimum of three changes of direction and a full run through the ring to get block controls confused. Later, when a second vehicle was added the length of pathes to erroneous behaviour grew even further. We believe that there is no possibility for detection of errors like these without a tool like PVE.

Additional verification results   To check the main safety property, i.e. the mutual exclusion of vehicles in blocks, we send a pair of special test vehicles along the track. In every state they indicate the number(s) of the occupied blocks. Fig. 13 shows a fragment of a vehicle which corresponds to a run through a block in positive direction. The complete transition system (like Fig. 10) consists of six copies of this fragment. Fig. 13 shows only one transition for a change of direction, the others are to be added canonically. Using the action $VEoccBI$ vehicle V indicates to an external observer that it is currently occupying block number I. The property "two vehicles never occupy the same block" is formalized in the following formula Γ of the μ-calculus:

$$
\begin{aligned}
\nu X.(\quad &\neg(\langle 0EoccB0\rangle \mathbf{true} \wedge \langle 1EoccB0\rangle \mathbf{true}) \quad \wedge \\
&\neg(\langle 0EoccB1\rangle \mathbf{true} \wedge \langle 1EoccB1\rangle \mathbf{true}) \quad \wedge \\
&\neg(\langle 0EoccB2\rangle \mathbf{true} \wedge \langle 1EoccB2\rangle \mathbf{true}) \quad \wedge [.]X \;)
\end{aligned}
$$

The last column of Table 2 shows how long it takes to check this property for the three-block ring.

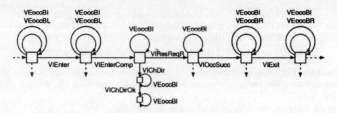

Figure 13: Verifying mutual exclusion of occupation of blocks

Statistics Below we present some statistics on the performance of PVE. They show that the tool's performance is feasible for the use in a stepwise refinement process. Since most time and space consuming problems occur when analyzing systems which contain errors (which are not listed here), performance must still be improved. All results were obtained on a Sun SPARCstation 2.

Table 1 summarizes results for the unidirectional version.

	generating transition system			checking $\cdots \approx SpecUD_i$
	#states	#trans	time	
BlockControlUD	180	425	$\ll 1$ s	
RingUD1	180	425	$\ll 1$ s	8 s
RingUD2	180	306	$\ll 1$ s	5 s

Table 1: Statistics for unidirectional version

The results for the bidirectional version are more interesting. The line for *minBlockControlBD* shows the size of the minimized version of the block control. It takes 80 s to compute it from *BlockControlBD*. The line for *RingBD2** refers to the system which contains two test vehicles as described above for checking the formula Γ.

	generating transition system			checking $\cdots \approx SpecBD_i$	checking formula Γ
	#states	#trans	time		
BlockControlBD	6867	19138	17 s		
minBlockControlBD	4266	17528			
RingBD1	5004	12342	26 s	38 s	
RingBD2	17280	48624	143 s	13 s	
RingBD2*	16320	56880	140 s		29 s

Table 2: Statistics for bidirectional version

6 Conclusion and future work

In this case study we have investigated the use of process algebra techniques for the design and verification of the distributed control of track vehicles. We have made a stepwise refinement and at each step the design has been verified using the automatic tool support PVE. We found several errors during our design. We claim that we have been able to locate these errors only due to the support given by PVE. This case study is industrially motivated. It concerns a certain aspect of a control problem only. However this aspect is treated in full depth on the design level. We see this case study as evidence that a formal verification of parallel processes with process algebra techniques is feasible if state-of-the-art tool support is available.

However using process algebra and PVE also indicated where further developments are needed. Firstly process algebra should be enhanced by a more user-friendly facility to express communication links. Several errors resulted from typos concerning actions. In addition, the limitation to a static use of actions made the bidirectional solution more complex. It would be interesting to see if e.g. the π-calculus [15] would ease the formulation of the solution. Secondly the debugging aid of PVE has to be made more powerful.

It should be noted that the verification approach in this paper verifies the correctness of particular topologies of the track with particular numbers of vehicles. It would be desirable to prove for the design of the block control that it behaves correctly in arbitrary topologies (e.g. in rings of arbitrary length). Future work will investigate suitable verification approaches.

Acknowledgement We thank our collegue Knigge for his cooperation. We also acknowledge joint work with Hans-Albert Schneider, Thomas Filkorn, and Reinhard Enders. Two anonymous referees have supplied helpful comments.

References

[1] J. Baeten and W. Weijland. *Process Algebra*, volume 18 of *Cambridge Tracts in Theoretical Computer Science*. Cambridge University Press, 1990.

[2] J. A. Bergstra and J. W. Klop. Algebra of communicating processes with abstraction. *Theoretical Computer Science*, 37:77–121, 1985.

[3] S. Brookes, C. Hoare, and A. Roscoe. A theory of communicating sequential processes. *Journal of the ACM*, 31:560–599, 1984.

[4] J. R. Burch, E. M. Clarke, K. L. McMillan, D. L. Dill, and L. J. Hwang. Symbolic model checking: 10^{20} states and beyond. In *Proceedings of the 5th IEEE Symposium on Logic in Computer Science, Philadelphia*, pages 428–439, 1990.

[5] K. M. Chandy and J. Misra. *Parallel Program Design: A Foundation*. Addison-Wesley Publishing Company, 1988.

[6] R. Cleaveland, J. Parrow, and B. Steffen. The concurrency workbench. In J. Sifakis, editor, *Automatic Verification Methods for Finite State Systems. Proceedings, Grenoble, 1989*, volume 407 of *Lecture Notes in Computer Science*, pages 24–37, Berlin et al., 1990. Springer.

[7] R. Cleaveland and B. Steffen. A linear-time model-checking algorithm for the alternation-free modal mu-calculus. In *Computer Aided Verification. Proceedings, Aalborg 1991*, pages 79–92, 1991.

[8] R. de Simone. Higher-level synchronizing devices in MEIJE-SCCS. *Theoretical Computer Science*, 37:245–267, 1985.

[9] E. A. Emerson and C.-L. Lei. Efficient model checking in fragments of the propositional mu-calculus. In *Proc. of the First Annual Symp. on Logic in Computer Science*, pages 267–278. Computer Society Press, 1986.

[10] R. Enders, T. Filkorn, and D. Taubner. Generating BDDs for symbolic model checking in CCS. In K. G. Larsen and A. Skou, editors, *Computer Aided Verification. Proceedings, Aalborg 1991*, pages 263–278, 1991.

[11] K. Estenfeld, H.-A. Schneider, D. Taubner, and E. Tidén. Computer aided verification of parallel processes. In A. Pfitzmann and E. Raubold, editors, *VIS '91 Verläßliche Informationssysteme. Proceedings, Darmstadt 1991*, volume 271 of *Informatik Fachberichte*, pages 208–226, Berlin, 1991. Springer.

[12] P. Inverardi and C. Priami. Evaluation of tools for the analysis of communicating systems. *EATCS Bulletin*, 45:158–185, 1991.

[13] R. Milner. *A Calculus of Communicating Systems*, volume 92 of *Lecture Notes in Computer Science*. Springer, Berlin, 1980.

[14] R. Milner. *Communication and Concurrency*. Prentice Hall, New York, 1989.

[15] R. Milner, J. Parrow, and D. Walker. A calculus of mobile processes, Parts I and II. LFCS Report Series ECS-LFCS-89-85 and 86, LFCS University of Edinburgh, June 1989.

[16] S. Owicki and D. Gries. An axiomatic proof technique for parallel programs I. *Acta Informatica*, 6(1):319–340, 1976.

[17] R. Paige and R. E. Tarjan. Three partition refinement algorithms. *SIAM J. Comput.*, 16(6):973–989, 1987.

[18] W. Reisig. *Petri Nets*, volume 4 of *EATCS Monographs on Theoretical Computer Science*. Springer-Verlag, Berlin, 1985.

[19] C. Stirling and D. Walker. Local model checking in the modal mu-calculus. In J. Díaz and F. Orejas, editors, *TAPSOFT '89. Volume 1., Proceedings, Barcelona 1989*, volume 351 of *Lecture Notes in Computer Science*, pages 369–383, Berlin, 1989. Springer.

[20] D. Taubner. *Finite Representations of CCS and TCSP Programs by Automata and Petri Nets*, volume 369 of *Lecture Notes in Computer Science*. Springer, Berlin, 1989.

Design Verification of a Microprocessor Using Branching Time Regular Temporal Logic[*]

Kiyoharu HAMAGUCHI[†], Hiromi HIRAISHI[‡] and Shuzo YAJIMA[†]

† Department of Information Science, Faculty of Engineering,
Kyoto University, Kyoto, 606, JAPAN.
(E-mail: hama@kuis.kyoto-u.ac.jp)
‡ Department of Information & Communication Sciences,
Kyoto Sangyo University, Kita-ku, Kyoto, 603, JAPAN.

Abstract. This paper reports about design verification of a real microprocessor using a symbolic model checking algorithm for a variant of branching time temporal logics, i.e. branching time regular temporal logic (BRTL).

The 8-bit microprocessor which was verified is KUE-CHIP2, which is an LSI chip developed for educational purpose. The KUE-CHIP2 contains approximately 1,600 gates and 68 flip-flops and supports 19 kinds of instructions, many of which can specify absolute/index addressing. The language for specification is BRTL, which is an enhancement of computation tree logic (CTL). BRTL has automaton connectives as temporal operators. Some examples of the specification in BRTL are shown.

The adopted verification technique is symbolic model checking using binary decision diagram (BDD). Some of the properties such as conditions for buses or behaviors for the instructions were chekced. The verifier succeeded in finding a bug. The total verification time for all the instruction was approximately 10 hours.

1 Introduction

In order to verify correctness of finite state machines automatically, various methods have been widely studied. Among them, the model checking approach based on computation tree logic (CTL) has been shown to be one of the most practical and effective methods. The model checking method, however, suffered from combinatorial explosion which can be observed in construction of state transition graphs or Kripke structures from sequential circuits.

On the other hand, as a new data structure to represent and handle logic functions, binary decision diagram (BDD) was formulated by R.E. Bryant[1]. Through the development of efficient BDD manipulators[2, 3], it has been known that BDD can relax effectively the exponential blowups which occur in manipulation of logic functions

The key idea of symbolic model checking proposed by Burch et al. [4] is to express sequential circuits by logic functions and to perform model checking

---

[*] This research was partially supported by Japan-USA Cooperative Research sponsored by JSPS and NSF. The first author was partially supported by Grant-in-Aid for Scientific Research (B)(1) under project number 04555079.

through logic function manipulation. Using BDD for manipulating logic functions, the symbolic model checker for CTL succeeded in verifying a pipelined ALU, which has 10^{20} states in the form of state transition diagrams[4]. The circuit size which can be handled has increased by several works [5, 6]. Recently, by introducing abstraction through homomorphism to reduce a register file composed of 64 registers to 3 registers, the pipelined ALU with 10^{1300} states was successfully verified[7].

The aim of this paper is to report about design verification of a real microprocessor based on the symbolic model checking method.

An 8-bit microprocessor which was verified is KUE-CHIP2 (Kyoto University Educational Chip 2), which is an LSI chip developed for educational purpose. The KUE-CHIP2 which is composed of approximately 1,600 gates and 68 flipflops is more complex in some points than the above pipelined ALU. For example, the processor supports 19 kinds of instructions, many of which specify absolute/index addressing modes and the phase length of the instructions varies in the range from 3 to 5.

The specification is described by using branching time regular temporal logic (BRTL)[8], which is an improvement of CTL in terms of expressive power. BRTL uses a restricted ω automaton of Büchi type to express temporal properties. Although the expressive power is smaller than extended CTL (ECTL)[9], the restriction to ω automata gives less computation cost in the symbolic model checking. For example, complex nested fixed point operations can be avoided.

The reason BRTL instead of CTL or μ calculus([10] etc.) was used, is that ω automaton is straightforward to express temporal properties especially when we handle the structure corresponding to *while*. Furthermore it is easier to understand intuitively than greatest or least fixed point operators of μ calculus. In a later section, we show some examples of how to describe specifications for the microprocessor in BRTL.

Using a symbolic model checking algorithm for BRTL, spme of the properties such as conditions for buses or behaviors for the instructions were checked and bugs were found. (In the verification, the abstraction method was not utilized.) The experimental results suggest that the verification of the whole chip (excluding the internal memory) can be performed in reasonable time.

This paper is organized as follows: Section 2 overviews design verification using BRTL. Section 3 explains the algorithm of symbolic model checking through an example. Section 4 describes some examples of specification for the KUE-CHIP2 and reports experimental results. Section 5 concludes this paper. The accurate definition of BRTL and the detail of the algorithm are shown in Appendix.

2 Overview of Design Verification

This section overviews how a given sequential machine is verified for a specification described in BRTL.

When we consider a tuple of input values and output values, i.e. an input/output tuple, the behavior of a sequential machine corresponds to a set of sequences composed of the input/output tuples. The model checking algorithm

208

checks whether the property which a given BRTL formula specifies is satisfied by the set of the sequences of the input/output tuples.

In the following, the values allowed to use as inputs and outputs are restricted to 1 or 0, without loss of generality. Boolean operators ∨, ¬, ∧, ≡ and ⇒ mean disjunction, negation, conjunction, equivalence and implication as usual. *true* and *false* represent tautology and inconsistency respectively. +, ⁻, · are sometimes used instead of ∨ ,¬, ∧ respectively.

(1) Transformation to Kripke structure

We assume designs are given as sequential machines. Since the semantics of BRTL formulas is determined over Kripke structures, A Kripke structure has to be obtained so that the structure reflects all the behaviors of the sequential machine.

The sequential machine of Moore type shown in Figure 1(a) is transformed to the Kripke structure shown in Figure 1(b). The part in the dashed line in (a) is transformed to the vertex s_1 in (b). The initial vertices corresponding to the initial state of the machine is pointed by ⇐

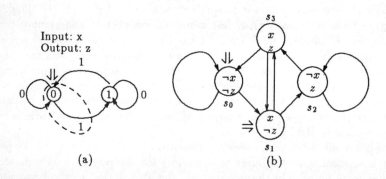

Fig. 1. Transformation to Kripke structure

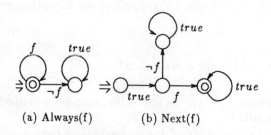

(a) Always(f)   (b) Next(f)

Fig. 2. Automata Connectives

(2) Description of specification

We see how the following specification is described in BRTL.

"It always holds that, when the input x becomes 1, then the output changes its value at the next time"

The property is expressed as follows:

$$\forall Always(x \Rightarrow ((z \Rightarrow \forall Next(\neg z)) \wedge (\neg z \Rightarrow \forall Next(z))))$$

Here $\forall$ means "over all paths on the Kripke structure". Always(f) and Next(f) mean "f always holds" and "f holds at the next time" respectively. The temporal properties such as Always and Next are described by finite automata shown in Figure 2.

The automata have propositional logic formulas (more generally, BRTL formulas) as their transition conditions. The finite automata in BRTL accept or reject infinite sequences of vectors composed of 0 or 1. The acceptance condition is Büchi type, that is, an automata accepts an infinite sequence if and only if it hits some accepting state infinitely often. Th automata satisfying the following conditions are allowed to use in BRTL.

- It has a unique initial state.
- The transition is deterministic and completely specified.
- There exists no path from an arbitrary rejecting state q_r to q_r via some accepting state.

For automata A, A_1 and A_2, $\forall A$, $\exists A$, $\forall(A_1 \vee A_2)$, $\forall \neg A$ and so on can be described in BRTL.

(3) Verification

Whether a BRTL formula holds or not is determined at each vertex on a Kripke structure. A formula $\forall A$ ($\exists A$) holds at a vertex if and only if all (some) paths on the Kripke structure starting from the vertex are accepted.

For example, in Figure 1(b), $\forall$ Next(z) holds at s_2 and $g \stackrel{\text{def}}{=} x \Rightarrow ((z \Rightarrow \forall$ Next($\neg z$))$\wedge$ ($\neg z \Rightarrow \forall$ Next(z))) holds at s_0, s_1, s_2 and s_3.

The given specification is satisfied if and only if the BRTL formula holds at every initial vertex of the Kripke structure.

3 Outline of Symbolic Model Checking

The detail of the algorithm of symbolic model checking is shown in Appendix.

The following notations are used. f is a logic function. $\exists x.f(x, y) \stackrel{\text{def}}{=} f(0, y) \vee f(1, y)$. For $\mathbf{x} = x_1, x_2, \cdots, x_n$, $\exists \mathbf{x}.f(\mathbf{x}, \mathbf{y}) \stackrel{\text{def}}{=} \exists x_1.(\exists x_2. \cdots (\exists x_n.f(\mathbf{x}, \mathbf{y})) \cdots)$

Furthermore, for $B = \{0, 1\}$, a subset $X \subseteq B^n$ is represented by a logic function with n variables f_X such that f_X satisfies the following condition:

$$x \in X \Leftrightarrow f_X(x) = 1$$

When a sequential machine is given as a design, a unique code word is assigned to each state of the machine and transition functions and output functions of the machine are used as inputs to the model checking algorithm.

Let $x_i(1 \leq i \leq l)$ and $y_j(1 \leq j \leq m)$ be input variables and state variables over B respectively. Vectors of variables are represented like $\mathbf{x} = x_1, x_2, \cdots, x_l$.

- Transition functions: $f_j : B^l \times B^m \to B$ $(1 \leq j \leq m)$
- Output functions: $z_k : B^m \to B$ $(1 \leq k \leq n)$ (Moore type)
  $z_k : B^l \times B^m \to B$ $(1 \leq k \leq n)$ (Mealy type)

Let $g_{init}(\mathbf{y})$ be a logic function representing the set of initial states of the machine.

At first, a logic function representing the set of edges of the Kripke structure obtained from the transition functions.

(1) Transformation to Kripke structure

The set of vertices of the Kripke structure comes to be the product space $B^l \times B^m$ composed from the domain of inputs and the domain of state variables. Let $\mathbf{s} \stackrel{\text{def}}{=} \mathbf{x}\#\mathbf{y}$. $\#$ expresses the concatenation of $\mathbf{x}$ and $\mathbf{y}$. For $\mathbf{x}$, new variables $\mathbf{x}' = x_1', x_2', \cdots, x_k'$ are introduced. Similarly, $\mathbf{y}'$ are introduced. Let $\mathbf{s}' = \mathbf{x}'\#\mathbf{y}'$. $\mathbf{s}$ and $\mathbf{s}'$ are used to represent starting points and ending points of edges. The logic function f_S representing the set of edges of the Kripke structure S can be constructed as follows:

$$f_S(\mathbf{s}, \mathbf{s}') = \bigwedge_{0 \leq j \leq m} (y_j' \equiv f_j(\mathbf{x}, \mathbf{y}))$$

The logic function f_{init} representing the initial vertices of the Kripke structure is defined by $f_{init}(\mathbf{s}) = g_{init}(\mathbf{y})$. The logic functions representing the set of vertices where the value of x_i or z_k is 1, come to be $f_{x_i}(\mathbf{s}) = x_i$, $f_{z_k}(\mathbf{s}) = z_k(\mathbf{y})$ (or $z_k(\mathbf{x}, \mathbf{y})$), respectively.

(2) Algorithm

Firstly, for each subformula ψ_i contained in the given BRTL formula ψ, the logic function satisfying the following conditions are calculated in bottom up manner.

$$f_{\psi_i}(\mathbf{s}) = 1 \Leftrightarrow \psi_i \text{ holds at s}$$

Secondly, $f_{init}(\mathbf{s}) \Rightarrow f_\psi(\mathbf{s})$ is obtained. The algorithm outputs 'yes' if and only if this logic function is $true$. The calculation of $f_\psi(\mathbf{s})$ is done by the algorithm shown in Appendix.

It is necessary to perform manipulation of logic functions efficiently, when we implement the above algorithm. Shared binary decision diagram (SBDD)[2] is an improvement of the original BDD[1], which shares all possible subgraphs among multiple functions. By using BDD, logical operations, substitution to logical variables and equivalence checking of two functions can be performed efficiently and many functions are represented compactly. The implemented system uses SBDD.

For the purpose of efficient model checking, the whole transition relation functions f_S are not generated. Each of transition functions is handled separately using the method shown in [5, 6].

4 Verification Results

4.1 Specification

In this section, examples of specification description are shown. The verified microprocessor is KUE-CHIP2. The KUE-CHIP2 is an 8-bit microprocessor based on CMOS technology and the second version of KUE-CHIP[11] which was developed for educational purpose. The microprocessor contains approximately 1,600 gates (exclusive of the internal memory) and 68 flipflops and supports 19 kinds of instructions, many of which can specify absolute/index addressing modes. The microprocessor does not contain a pipeline structure nor a multiplier. The architecture is shown in Figure 3.

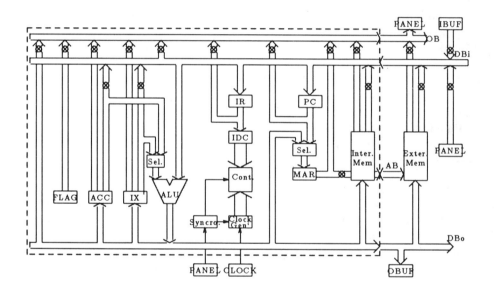

Fig. 3. The Architecture of KUE-CHIP2

The microprocessor has three kinds of operation modes: normal mode, single instruction mode and single phase mode. Under the single instruction (or phase) mode, only an instruction (or a phase) is performed by a start pulse.

The KUE-CHIP2 has an external memory and an internal memory. Since direct manipulation of 8 bit by 512 word memory is impossible even with BDD, inputs (or outputs) of the memory are modeled as outputs (or inputs) of the microprocessor. Specifications have to be described so that the contents of the memory are not accessed.

Phase signals

The following formula means that "if 'op' is always 1, then the phase number of each instruction is 3, 4 or 5, and the phase signals become 1 correctly". 'op' is a signal which indicates that the microprocessor is in operation. 'ph0' is an abbreviation of $ph0 \cdot \overline{ph1} \cdot \overline{ph2} \cdot \overline{ph3} \cdot \overline{ph4}$ and so on. $ph\,i$ is the signal representing the phase i at which the processor is operating.

$$\forall Always(\forall(Always(op) \Rightarrow A))$$

A is shown in Figure 4. The edges to the dead state are abbreviated.

Conditions for Buses

The condition for the bus shown in Figure 7 can be described as follows:

$$\forall Always(a\overline{b}\overline{c} + \overline{a}b\overline{c} + \overline{a}\overline{b}c)$$

The formula claims that one and only one control signal among the signals of the tristate buffers is 1. $Always$ is shown in Figure 2.

Behaviors for Instructions

The behavior for each instruction is verified by checking the behavior for each bit and for each phase. For example, the behavior of the instruction IN is informally described by Figure 5. The following formula specifies the behavior for (ibuf) $\rightarrow$ acc.

$$\forall Always(\forall(Always(op) \Rightarrow IN))$$

IN is shown in Figure 6. Instruction In fetches data from the input buffer and put it to the accumulator. 'ibuf0' and 'acc0' represents the 0th bit of input data and the 0th bit of the accumulator (ACC) respectively. Similar description for every bit is used as specification. 'op' is the signal representing that the processor is operating. ph_0 means phase 0 as shown in the above. 'opin' means the code for IN. 'opin' is a logic formula $\overline{mem7} \cdot \overline{mem6} \cdot mem5 \cdot mem4 \cdot mem3$, where $mem\,i$ represents the i-th bit of the outputs of the memory.

When the processor was verified, different descriptions were given for efficiency. Since the first two edges from the initial state of IN are the same for each bit, they can be shared. The automaton IN was split and the same property was expressed by nesting two automata.

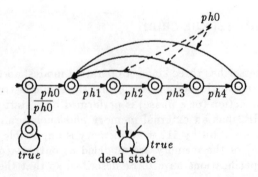

Fig. 4. Automaton connective A

213

Phase 0	Phase 1	Phase 2	Phase 3
(pc) → mar pc++	(mem) → ir	(ibuf) → acc 0 → ibuf_re	0 → ifc

Fig. 5. Behavior of IN (phase 2 and 3)

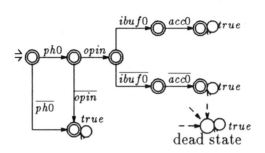

Fig. 6. Automaton connective *IN*

4.2 Experimental Results

A symbolic model checker for BRTL was implemented. The verifier was written in language C and runs on a SPARCstation 2. This program utilizes the Boolean function manipulator developed by Minato et.al. [2].

The transition functions and the output functions were obtained directly from the design data made on SOLO, a CAD tool developed by ES2 (European Silicon Structure).

Each flip-flop was expanded to a transition function using a next state variable. The internal memory (8 bit × 512 words) included in KUE-CHIP2 was detached in the translation, that is, it was treated as an external memory. The bus shown in Figure 7 was translated to the following formula.

$$bus = (a \Rightarrow d_a) \land (b \Rightarrow d_b) \land (c \Rightarrow d_c)$$

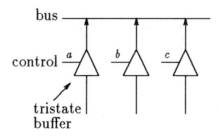

Fig. 7. Bus

In order to describe the ω finite automata, we implemented a simple language which has structures of 'while' or 'if' and can use macro definitions.

The number of nodes of SBDD was limited to 500,000 (11 M byte).

The conditions for all the control signals for the buses were checked. The verifier found that a bus floats under some condition, and the error was debugged.

Table 1 shows the experimental result of verifying some of the properties of the microprocessor. 'bus' shows the result for the conditions for the buses. 'phloop' shows the result for $\forall Always(\forall(Always(op) \Rightarrow A))$. Since the behaviors at phase 0 and 1 are common among all the instructions, they were checked separately without specifying any instruction. The results for the phases 0 and 1 are shown in 'ph0' and 'ph1' respectively. The result for each instruction does not consider the behaviors for phase 0 and 1. The given specifications include the conditions where the registers that should hold the values, for example, the index register in Figure 5, do not change their values.

In order to simplify the verification, some of the inputs to the processor were fixed to 0 or 1.

'ADC' in Table 1 is the instruction with the address modification by the index register. The behavior for the instruction is most complex.

The KUE-CHIP2 has about 170 instructions, if addressing modes and destination registers are distinguished. The behavior of all the instructions under the normal mode of the KUE-CHIP2 was verified. The total verification time was approximately 10 hours. The size of the files containing the specifications was approximately 2 Mbyte.

Table 1. Experimental Results for KUE-CHIP2

	time	# PH	
bus	12.8	–	Bus conditions
phloop	16.2	–	Phase signals
ph0	21.3	–	Behavior for phase 0
ph1	48.6	–	Behavior for phase 1
RCF	81.8	3	Reset Carry Flag
IN	114.8	4	INput to ACC
OUT	136.8	4	OUTput from ACC
LD†	234.7	5	LoaD from memory to ACC
ST†	242.3	5	STore from ACC to memory
ADC†	309.8	5	ADDition with Carry

time: CPU time (sec)

 # PH: the number of phases for each instruction

†: modified by the index register

5   Conclusion

In this paper, for an 8-bit microprocessor KUE-CHIP2, how to describe specification in a variant of branching time temporal logics, i.e. BRTL, was shown. The specifications were checked by using a symbolic model checking method. The experimental results show that the symbolic model checking method is suitable to the microprocessor design and that the verification of the whole chip (excluding the internal memory) can be done in reasonable time.

Although the KUE-CHIP2 has only 8-bit arithmetic operations excluding multiplication, the 16 or 32-bit multiplier increases the difficulties of verification drastically. In order to verify larger microprocessors, incorporation of the technique shown in [12] and so on has to be investigated.

The descriptions of specification in Section 3 and 4 are given for each phase. It would be better to describe the specification as a relation between the condition at the first phase and that at the last phase for each instruction as shown in [4]. In order to verify such descriptions, the part of the internal memory has to be handled as a sequential circuit. Abstraction mechanism seems powerful to handle large memories. We would like to introduce the technique and estimate its effectiveness in the near future.

Acknowledgment

The authors would like to express sincere appreciation to Prof. Hiroto Yasuura and Mr. Hiroyuki Kanbara who provided the design data of KUE-CHIP2. They would also like to thank Mr. Shin-ichi Minato who offered the Boolean function manipulation subroutines using SBDD representation, and Mr. Fuminobu Yatsuboshi who performed the verification of all the KUE-CHIP2 instructions.

References

1. R. E. Bryant. Graph-Based Algorithms for Boolean Function Manipulation. *IEEE Transactions on Computers*, C-35(8):677–691, August 1986.
2. Shinichi Minato, Nagisa Ishiura, and Shuzo Yajima. Shared Binary Decision Diagram with Attributed Edges for Efficient Boolean Function Manipulation. In *Proceedings of 27th Design Automation Conference*, pages 52–57, 1990.
3. K. S. Brace, R. L. Rudell, and R. E. Bryant. Efficient Implementation of a BDD Package. In *Proceedings of 27th Design Automation Conference*, pages 40–45, 1990.
4. J. R. Burch, E. M. Clarke, K. L. McMillan, and D. L. Dill. Sequential Circuit Verification Using Symbolic Model Checking. In *Proceedings of 27th Design Automation Conference*, pages 46–51, 1990.
5. J. R. Burch, E. M. Clarke, and D. E. Long. Representing Circuits More Efficiently in Symbolic Model Checking. In *Proceedings of 28th Design Automation Conference*, pages 403–407, June 1991.
6. H. Hiraishi, K. Hamaguchi, H. Ochi, and S. Yajima. Vectorized Symbolic Model Checking of Computation Tree Logic. In *Workshop on Computer-Aided Verification*, pages 279–290, July 1991.
7. E. M. Clarke and O. Grümberg and D. E. Long. Model Checking and Abstraction. Technical report, Carnegie Mellon University, 1991. manuscript.

8. K. Hamaguchi, H. Hiraishi, and S. Yajima. Branching Time Regular Temporal Logic for Model Checking with Linear Time Complexity. In *Workshop on Computer-Aided Verification*, June 1990.

9. E. M. Clarke, O. Grümberg, and R. P. Kurshan. A synthesis of two approaches for verifying finite state concurrent systems. In *Logic at Botik '89, Symposium on Logical Foundations of Computer Science*, volume 363 of *Lecture Notes in Computer Science*. Springer Verlag, July 1989.

10. J. R. Burch, E. M. Clarke, K. L. McMillan, D. L. Dill, and J. Hwang. Symbolic Model Checking: 10^{20} States and Beyond. In *Proceedings of 5th IEEE Symposium on Logic in Computer Science*, June 1990.

11. H. Kanbara. KUE-CHIP:A Microprocessor for education of Computer Architecture and LSI design. In *Proc. of IEEE ASIC Seminar & Exhibit*, 1990.

12. J. R. Burch. Using BDDs to verify multipliers. In *Proceedings of 28th Design Automation Conference*, pages 408–412, jun 1991.

13. A. V. Aho, J. E. Hopcroft, and J. D. Ullman. *The Design and Analysis of Computer Algorithms*. Addison-Wesley, 1974.

Appendix

Syntax and Semantics of BRTL

BRTL uses the following dfa-1 as temporal operators.

Definition 1. A *deterministic ω finite automaton type 1* (dfa-1) $A = (Q, P, Br, q_0, F)$ is defined as follows:

Q is a set of finite states, $P = \{p_1, \cdots, p_n\}$ is a set of propositional variables. $Br : Q \times Q \to BF$ (BF is a set of propositional formulas composed from P) is a partial function which assigns a propositional formula to a pair of two states. Let $Br(q, Q)$ be $\{f \mid \exists q'. Br(q, q') = f, q' \in Q\}$, for $q \in Q$.

Br satisfies the following conditions: "For all $f_1, f_2 \in Br(q, Q)$ such that $f_1 \neq f_2$, $f_1 \wedge f_2 = false$" and "$\bigvee_{f \in Br(q,Q)} f = true$." q_0 is an initial state and F is a set of accepting states. The elements of $Q - F$ are called rejecting states. Furthermore A satisfies the following condition.

"There exists no path from an arbitrary rejecting state q_r to q_r via some accepting state"

A accepts or rejects infinite sequences composed of the elements of $\Delta = 2^P$. The transition function $\delta : Q \times \Delta \to Q$ is defined as $\delta(q, v) = q' \Leftrightarrow Br(q, q')(v) = T$ for $q, q' \in Q$, $v \in \Delta$. $Inf(\sigma)$ represents of the set of states which A goes through infinitely often when σ composed of the elements of Δ is given to A as an input. The language which A accepts is $\{\sigma \mid Inf(\sigma) \cap F$ is not empty$\}$. □

Proposition 2. *[8]* For a dfa-1 $A = (Q, P, Br, \delta, q_0, F)$, the dfa-1 $\overline{A}$ which accepts the complementary set of A can be obtained by exchanging the accepting states with the rejecting states. Furthermore, the dfa-1 $(A_1|A_2)$ which accepts the union of the sets accepted by A_1 and A_2 can be constructed. In other words, dfa-1's are closed under Boolean operations. □

Definition 3. Syntax

BRTL formula : BRF represents the set of BRTL formulas.

$p \in AP$, $\psi, \phi \in BRF$. If A is an automaton connective, then $p, (\neg\psi), (\psi \vee \phi), (\exists A) \in BRF$.

Automaton connective

Let AP be a set of propositional variables and A_i $(i = 1, \cdots, m)$ be dfa-1's. We assume that $\{\psi_1, \psi_2, \cdots, \psi_n\} \subseteq BRF$. $A(\psi_1, \psi_2, \cdots, \psi_n)$ is obtained by replacing each propositional variable $p_1, p_2, \cdots, p_n \in AP$ in A with $\psi_1, \psi_2, \cdots, \psi_n$ simultaneously. The value of $Br(q, q')$ changes accordingly. Any description which is obtained by finite number of applications of $\neg$ (unary operator) and $\vee$ (binary operator) to $A_i(\psi_1, \psi_2, \cdots, \psi_n)$, is called an automaton connective. □

Proposition 2 shows that $\exists\neg A$ and $\exists(A_1 \vee A_2)$ can be expressed by $\exists\overline{A}$ and $\exists(A_1|A_2)$ respectively.

The semantics of BRTL formulas is defined for Kripke structures. Let AP be the set of atomic propositions $p_1, p_2, \cdots, p_n$.

Definition 4. $S = \langle \Sigma, I, R, \Sigma_0 \rangle$ is called Kripke structure. Σ is a set of vertices. $I : \Sigma \to 2^{AP}$ assigns the truth value of each atomic proposition to each vertex. $R \subseteq \Sigma \times \Sigma$ is a set of directed edges over Σ and Σ_0 is a set of initial states. □

Definition 5. Semantics

$S, s \models \psi$ means that a BRTL formula ψ holds at the vertex $s \in \Sigma$ (or ψ is true at s). We assume $p \in AP$, and $\psi, \phi, \psi_1, \psi_2, \cdots, \psi_n$ are BRTL formulas. A is a dfa-1.

- $S, s \models p \Leftrightarrow p \in I(s)$
- $S, s \models (\psi \vee \phi) \Leftrightarrow S, s \models \psi$ or $S, s \models \phi$
- $S, s \models (\neg\psi) \Leftrightarrow S, s \not\models \psi$
- $S, s \models (\exists A(\psi_1, \psi_2, \cdots, \psi_n)) \Leftrightarrow$ There exist an infinite sequence $s_0 s_1 s_2 \cdots$ starting from s on the Kripke structure S and an infinite sequence of states of A such that $S, s_i \models Br(q_i, q_{i+1})$ $(i = 0, 1, 2, \cdots)$ and at least one state which appears infinitely often along $q_0, q_1, \cdots$ is an accepting state of A.
- $S, s \models (\exists\neg A) \Leftrightarrow S, s \models (\exists\overline{A})$

- $S, s \models (\exists(A_1 \vee A_2)) \Leftrightarrow S, s \models (\exists(A_1 \mid A_2))$

When $S, s \models \psi$ holds for all $s \in \Sigma_0$, then we describe $S \models \psi$. □

$\forall$ is defined as follows: $\forall A \stackrel{\text{def}}{=} \neg\exists\neg A$.

Symbolic model checking

Algorithm 1 Symbolic model checking algorithm

- Input: f_S, f_{init}, f_{x_i} and f_{z_k}, for a BRTL formula ψ and a Kripke structure S.
- Output: If $S \models \psi$ then yes. Otherwise no.

– Method:

1. By Proposition 2, '¬' and '∨' are removed from each automaton connective A_j.
2. For each subformula ϕ_i in ψ, $f_{\phi_i}(s)$ which represents the set of vertices such that $S, s \models \phi_i$ is obtained in bottom up manner.

   Let f_{h_1}, f_{h_2}, f_h represent the set of vertices s such that $S, s \models h_1$, $S, s \models h_2$, $S, s \models h$ respectively.

   (a) Case: ϕ_i is an atomic proposition.

   f_{x_i} and f_{z_i} are given.

   (b) Case: $\phi_i = h_1 \vee h_2$ or $\neg h$.

   $f_{h_1 \vee h_2} = f_{h_1} \vee f_{h_2}$, $f_{\neg h} = \neg f_h$.

   (c) Case: $\phi_i = \exists A_j$

   Regarding A_j as a directed graph (V, E), strongly connected components (SCC's) are calculated. See the definition and the algorithm for SCC's in [13, Chap. 5.5]. (The definition claims that an SCC may consists of only one vertex without a selfloop. Let q_0 be the initial state of A_j. Then $f_{\phi_i} =$ fixpoint(q_0).

   The procedure fixpoint and label_accept and label_all are shown in Figure 8, Figure 9 and Figure 10. label_function(q, f) labels f to the state q of the automaton A_j. labeled_function(q) returns the logic function labeled to q. $\bigvee_{i \in S} f_i$ (f_i is a logic function) is assumed to be $false$, if S is an empty set. BF is shown in Section 3.
3. If $(f_{init}(s) \Rightarrow f_\eta(s)) = true$, yes. Otherwise no. □

procedure fixpoint(q)
/* (V_q, E_q) is an SCC containing q. */
  begin

1 .   **for all** $q' \in V_q$ **do** label_function($q', false$);
2 .   **if** q is an accepting state **then** label_accept(q);
3 .   **for all** $q' \in V_q$ **do**
        begin
4 . $f =$ labeled_function(q') $\vee$
$$\bigvee_{(q', q'') \in E, q'' \notin V_q} (\, BF(\text{fixpoint}(q'')) \wedge f_{Br(q', q'')}\,);$$
5 .   labeled_function(q', f);
        end
6 .   label_all(q);
7 .   **return** (labeled_function(q));
  end

Fig. 8. Procedure fixpoint

procedure label_accept(q)
/* (V_q, E_q) is an SCC containing q. */
   begin
1 .   **for** all $q' \in V_q$ **do** label_function(q',$true$); **end**
2 .   **repeat**
3 .   **for** all $q' \in V_q$ **do**
4 .   **begin**
5 . $f = $ labeled_function(q') $\wedge$

$$\bigvee_{(q',q'') \in E_q} (\ \mathrm{BF}(\text{labeled\_function}(q'')) \wedge f_{Br(q',q'')});$$

6 .   labeled_function(q', f);
       end
7 .   **until** (For every state $q' \in V_q$, labeled_function(q') does not change)
   end

Fig. 9. Procedure label_accept

procedure label_all(q)
/* (V_q, E_q) is an SCC containing q. */
   begin
1 .   **repeat**
2 .   **for** all $q' \in V_q$ **do**
3 .   **begin**
4 . $f = $ labeled_function(q') $\vee$

$$\bigvee_{(q',q'') \in E_q} (\ \mathrm{BF}(\text{labeled\_function}(q'')) \wedge f_{Br(q',q'')});$$

5 .   labeled_function(q', f);
       end
6 .   **until** (For every state $q' \in V_q$, labeled_function(q') does not change)
   end

Fig. 10. Procedure label_all

A Case Study in Safety-Critical Design

Glenn Bruns

Department of Computer Science, University of Edinburgh
Edinburgh EH9 3JZ, UK

Abstract. We have modelled the design of a safety-critical railway system in the process calculus CCS, described important properties of the design in temporal logic, and verified with the Concurrency Workbench that some of the properties hold of the model. Verifying properties of a design, rather than an implementation, presented special problems, particularly in capturing in the formal model the kinds of abstraction found in the design, and in showing that the verified properties would also hold in all implementations of the design.

1 Introduction

Many case studies demonstrating the verification of distributed systems involve communication protocols, low-level algorithms, or hardware. A less-studied topic is the verification of system designs. A design describes structure, such as the top-level components of a system and their interconnection, as well as behaviour, such as the responses of components to inputs. Verifying properties of a design allows design decisions to be checked before spending much, possibly wasted, implementation effort. Since the design contains less detail than a full implementation, the verification task may also be more tractable.

We describe here our experience in attempting to verify properties of the design of a safety-critical system. We had three specific goals. First, to formalize the key parts of the system design as a CCS process, leaving more detailed design issues open. Second, to formalize safety-critical properties of the system as temporal logic formulas and show, using an automatic verification tool, that these properties hold of the model. Finally, to prove that any "acceptable implementation" would also possess the properties shown to hold of the design model. By "acceptable implementation" we are intentionally vague. Such an implementation could be one reached from the design systematically according to a set of refinement rules, or simply one satisfying certain ad-hoc, application-specific constraints.

2 Background

The function of British Rail's Solid State Interlocking (SSI) [7] is to adjust, at the request of the signal operator, the settings of signals and points in the railway to permit the safe passage of trains. "Safe", in this context, means that the system will protect the signal operator from inadvertently sending trains along routes that could lead to a collision or derailment. The entire BR network is controlled by many SSI's, each responsible for one sub-network.

Figure 1 depicts an SSI and the devices it controls. Safe commands issued from the control panel are allowed to effect signals and points via messages sent over a high-speed communication link to trackside functional modules (TFM's). Each message is received by all TFM's connected to the link, but only acted on by the TFM with the address specified in the message.

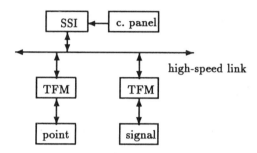

Fig. 1. The SSI and its environment

A safety-related features of the SSI is its pattern of communication with the TFM's. Instead of sending signal or point commands only as needed, the SSI sends a message of the form $\langle TFM\ address, state\rangle$ to each attached TFM about once every second, giving the intended current setting. These messages are sent in a predefined cyclic pattern, called a *major cycle*, one TFM after another. After sending a message, the SSI waits at most a few milliseconds for the addressed TFM to respond with the current state of the device. This scheme allows failures of the TFM's and communication link to be detected quickly, and forces devices that have autonomously changed state to return to their proper state.

In some sections of the BR network, many miles of track lie between TFM's, making the high-speed link very expensive. A cheaper low-speed link could not be directly adopted as it would not provide the bandwidth needed for the TFM command cycling scheme. On the other hand, dropping the scheme would compromise safety and force changes to the SSI and TFM's. A solution is to employ a *slow-scan* system, built of a low-speed link (also called a *low-grade link*, or *LGL*) with *protocol converters* at each end (see Figure 2). The SSI-side protocol converter (SPC) accepts TFM commands once every second, and responds immediately with trackside device status, but only sends the TFM command along the low-grade link occasionally. The TFM-side protocol converter (TPC) sends a command to each attached TFM once every second. Responses from the TFM's are occasionally sent by the TPC to the SPC, in order to update the SPC's device status information. Because the SPC mimics a TFM, and the TPC mimics an SSI, the slow-scan system can replace a section of high-speed link, although the safety and performance properties will be altered.

The slow-scan system must also mimic the high-speed link in its failure be-

222

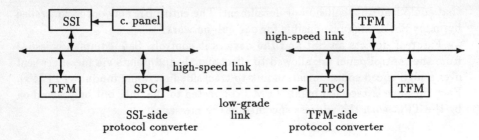

Fig. 2. The slow-scan system

haviour. For example, if the high-speed link fails so that the attached TFM's stop receiving messages, then the TFM's will detect the problem and put their outputs to a safe state: signals to red; points locked in their current setting. Therefore, if the low-grade link of the slow-scan system fails, the TPC should stop sending commands to the attached TFM's.

3 Safety Considerations

The development of any formal model is guided by the purposes to which that model will be put. Here we are interested in showing safety-critical properties of our model, so before building the model we should consider the kinds of properties that we will try to show.

Taken on its own, the slow-scan system cannot be considered safety-critical, since it does not directly control physical devices. However, by first looking at the safety-critical properties of the train routing system as a whole, and then working through the levels of the system, it is possible to obtain derived safety requirements of the slow-scan system. There is not room here to present such a hierarchical safety analysis. We will simply observe that the safe routing of trains depends on the *timely and error-free delivery of commands* and *timely detection of failures.*

The SSI can satisfy these requirements if a high-speed link is used. The bandwidth of the link and the error coding of messages ensures that the first requirement is met. The TFM-command cycling scheme ensures the second is met. Both requirements are threatened by slow-scan, however. Its low-grade link slows the delivery of messages and lacks the bandwidth needed to send many redundant messages. In this study, we focus on failures of the low-grade link and their detection by the slow-scan system.

4 A Simple Model of Slow-Scan

We first present a simple model of the slow-scan system and then show how the model can be extended to include the occurrence and handling of LGL failures.

Our goal is to capture the aspects of the design relevant to the safety-critical properties of interest, and to leave detailed design issue open. For example, we would like our model to be independent of a policy that determines when TFM commands should be passed along the low-grade link. Furthermore, we want to keep the model simple enough to enable mechanical verification with the Concurrency Workbench.

We will model the slow-scan system as CCS processes. Only a brief and informal overview of CCS will be given here.

Processes are described in CCS by terms for which the only possible behaviour is to perform *actions*, which are either names $(a,b,c,...)$, co-names $(\bar{a},\bar{b},\bar{c},...)$, or the special action τ.

Process terms have the following syntax, where L ranges over sets of actions and f ranges over functions from actions to actions:

$$ P ::= 0 \mid a.P \mid P_1 + P_2 \mid P_1 \mid P_2 \mid P\backslash L \mid P[f] $$

The term 0 denotes the nil process, which can perform no actions. The operator . expresses sequential action. The process $a.P$ can perform the action a and thereby become process P. The operator $+$ expresses choice. If P_1 can perform a and become P_1', then so can $P_1 + P_2$, and similarly for P_2. The operator $\mid$ expresses parallel execution. If process P_1 can perform a and become P_1', then $P_1 \mid P_2$ can perform a and become $P_1' \mid P_2$, and similarly for P_2. Furthermore, if P_1 can perform a and become P_1', and P_2 can perform $\bar{a}$ and become P_2', then $P_1 \mid P_2$ can perform τ and become $P_1' \mid P_2'$. The operator $\backslash$ expresses the restriction of actions. If P can perform a and become P', then $P\backslash L$ can only perform a to become $P'\backslash L$ if $a, \bar{a} \notin L$. Finally, $P[f]$ expresses the relabelling of actions. if P can perform a and become P', then $P[f]$ can perform $f(a)$ and become $P'[f]$. A relabelling function f has the property that $f(\tau) = \tau$, and $f(\bar{a}) = \overline{f(a)}$.

The idea of repetition is captured by allowing recursive process definitions of the form $P \stackrel{\text{def}}{=} E$, where P is a process constant and E is a process term possibly containing P. For example, the process defined by $P \stackrel{\text{def}}{=} a.P + b.0$ has the possibility of performing either a or b, and continues to have this possibility as long as action a is performed. Once action b is performed, the process terminates.

The set of actions that can be eventually performed by a process is called its *sort*. For example, the sort of $P \stackrel{\text{def}}{=} a.P + b.0$ is $\{a, b\}$.

We are ready to present the first, simple model of the slow-scan system. The flow diagram for our first model (see Figure 3) shows that the SSI and TFM's are considered outside the boundary of the slow-scan system. Because we are using CCS to model the system, we will admittedly be able to say little about real-time and probabilistic aspects of the system's behaviour.

The LGL component of the model will be formalized first. Few details about the LGL interface are given in the high-level design, so the model is based on what one might expect in a typical communication link. For example, messages can be written to the input port or read from the output port at any time. This feature ensures that the protocol converters need never wait on the LGL ports. We would like our model to say as little as possible about the content of messages

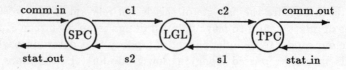

Fig. 3. Flow diagram for a simple slow-scan model

and the message buffering capacity of the LGL, although we naturally expect it to have only finite buffering capacity. Our CCS model of the LGL is as follows:

$$LGL \stackrel{\text{def}}{=} Comm[c1/in, c2/out, c2_u/out_u] \mid Comm[s1/in, s2/out, s2_u/out_u]$$

$$Comm \stackrel{\text{def}}{=} in.Comm' + \overline{out_u}.Comm$$

$$Comm' \stackrel{\text{def}}{=} in.Comm' + \overline{out}.Comm$$

The model contains two concurrent processes, one for each direction of message flow. Messages are modelled simply as content-less "pulses". Each link process can buffer a single message, because it is not possible in CCS to describe a buffer with finite but arbitrary capacity. If a message arrives at the input port of a link already buffering a message, the buffer is overwritten. If the output port of a link is read while the link is empty, the special action $\overline{out_u}$ occurs.

The slow-scan design requires of the SPC that SSI commands are responded to immediately with TFM status information. This requirement ensures that the slow-scan system properly mimics the behaviour of a high-speed link. The design also states that the SPC must pass commands along the LGL to the TFM, but the policy for determining which commands should be passed, and when they should be passed, is left open. Similarly, the policy for updating TFM status information with messages sent from the TFM is left open in the design. The CCS process that models the SPC is as follows:

$$SPC \stackrel{\text{def}}{=} comm\_in.\overline{stat\_out}.SPC +$$
$$\overline{c1}.SPC + s2.SPC + s2_u.SPC$$

We have attempted to leave a policy for passing command and status messages open by allowing actions $\overline{c1}$ and $s2$ to occur at any time (except just after the receipt of an SSI command). This SPC model says too little about a message-passing policy in one sense – since our model need never pass command messages along – and too much in another sense – since a message-passing policy need not be capable of sending a command at every instant. Unfortunately, it does not seem possible to express the model we would like with a process algebra such as CCS.

The TPC is modelled much like the SPC. Here we would like the model to say nothing about passing status information along the TFM and reading command information from the LGL. Our CCS model of the TPC is as follows:

$$TPC \stackrel{\text{def}}{=} \overline{comm\_out}.stat\_in.TPC +$$
$$\overline{s1}.TPC + c2.TPC + c2_u.TPC$$

By composing processes TPC, LGL, and SPC, we get the complete model SS, with sort $\{comm\_in, \overline{comm\_out}, stat\_in, \overline{stat\_out}\}$.

$$SS \stackrel{\text{def}}{=} (SPC \mid LGL \mid TPC) \backslash \{c1, c2, c2_u, s1, s2, s2_u\}$$

5 Modelling Low-grade Link Failures

Our simple model captures the basic operation of the slow-scan system: the SPC immediately responds to SSI commands with TFM state information; the SPC and TPC occasionally write command or status messages to the LGL input ports; and the SPC and TPC occasionally read the LGL output ports. The slow-scan design additionally discusses failure detection, but does not describe any specific failure detection mechanisms. Since we are most interested in the safety-critical aspects of the system, we will add some failure modes to our model, and a mechanism for failure detection and handling.

We will consider two LGL failure modes. The LGL can fail if its buffering capacity is exceeded, and it can fail spontaneously because of a break in the communication medium. We assume that once a failure occurs the LGL will continue to accept messages, but will never deliver messages. The revised model of the LGL incorporating these failure modes is as follows:

$$LGL \stackrel{\text{def}}{=} Comm[c1/in, c2/out, c2_u/out_u] \mid Comm[s1/in, s2/out, s2_u/out_u]$$
$$Comm \stackrel{\text{def}}{=} in.Comm' + \overline{out_u}.Comm + \overline{fail}.Comm''$$
$$Comm' \stackrel{\text{def}}{=} in.\overline{fail}.Comm'' + \overline{out}.Comm + \overline{fail}.Comm''$$
$$Comm'' \stackrel{\text{def}}{=} in.Comm'' + \overline{out_u}.Comm''$$

The new action $\overline{fail}$ occurs when a failure occurs on either of the links comprising the LGL.

Because the slow-scan system is intended to simulate a high-speed link, an LGL failure should cause the slow-scan system to simulate a high-speed link failure. The SSI detects such a failure when the TFM fails to respond to a command. Conversely, the TFM detects a high-speed link error when the SSI fails to send a command. Therefore, once an LGL failure is detected, the slow-scan system should stop responding to SSI commands and stop sending TFM commands.

The problem in detecting an LGL failure in the basic slow-scan model is that the LGL may be inactive for long periods in the normal course of events. An LGL failure detection strategy cannot report that a failure has occurred simply because no message has been received over the LGL after some period of time. Thus, to detect failures, additional messages have to be introduced along the LGL.

Consider the more general problem of having two distributed processes detect failures in a communication medium connecting them. Assume that both processes receive pulses from a clock. If one process sends a message once every clock pulse, and the other process increments a local counter once every clock pulse (clearing the counter if a message is received), then a failure must have occurred in the medium if the counter exceeds a certain bound. The following process Mon illustrates this idea, with S as the sending process and $R(i)$ as the receiving process having local counter value i:

$$Clock \stackrel{\text{def}}{=} \overline{tick}.\overline{ts}.\overline{tr}.Clock$$
$$S \stackrel{\text{def}}{=} ts.\overline{out}.S$$
$$R(i) \stackrel{\text{def}}{=} tr.(\text{ if } i > n \text{ then } \overline{det}.R(0)$$
$$\text{else } R(i+1))$$
$$+in.R(0)$$
$$Mon \stackrel{\text{def}}{=} (Clock \mid S \mid R(0))\backslash\{tr, ts\}$$

Some new notational features have been introduced here: parameterized actions and conditional statements. The process term $R(i)$ can be regarded as shorthand for the indexed process constant R_i. The term **if** b **then** P_1 **else** P_2 behaves as process P_1 if the boolean expression b evaluates to true, or as the process P_2 if b evaluates to false.

Two such distributed channel monitors can be combined, with a single clock, to check both directions of a bidirectional channel. Each process sends a message each clock pulse and expects to receive a message at least every n clock pulses. Note that although the synchronizing process is named 'Clock', there is no notion of real time in the model.

Incorporating this channel monitoring strategy into our simple model of the slow-scan system, we get the following SSI-side protocol converter process:

$$SPC(i) \stackrel{\text{def}}{=} comm\_in.\overline{stat\_out}.SPC(i)$$
$$+\overline{c1}.SPC(i) + s2.SPC(0) + s2_u.SPC(i)$$
$$+mcs.\overline{c1}.(\text{ if } i > n \text{ then } \overline{det}.SP \text{ else } SPC(i+1))$$
$$SPCF \stackrel{\text{def}}{=} comm\_in.SPCF + s2.SPCF + s2_u.SPCF + mcs.SPCF$$

As before, the SPC accepts commands from the SSI, responds to the SSI with TFM status information, and sometimes sends a command over the LGL. In this new model, the SPC is guaranteed to send at least one message over the LGL each clock tick. Also, if n clock ticks pass without the receipt of a message from the TPC, then the SPC enters failure mode, in which it never again sends messages to the SSI or LGL. Of course, a more detailed model would contain a mechanism by which the SPC could exit failure mode.

Similarly, the TFM-side protocol converter process is as follows:

$$TPC(i) \stackrel{\text{def}}{=} \overline{comm\_out}.stat\_in.TPC(i)$$
$$+\overline{s1}.TPC(i) + c2.TPC(0) + c2_u.TPC(i)$$
$$+mct.\overline{s1}.(\text{ if } i > n \text{ then } \overline{det}.TPCF \text{ else } TPC(i+1))$$
$$TPCF \stackrel{\text{def}}{=} stat\_in.TPCF + c2.TPCF + c2_u.TPCF + mct.TPCF$$

The clock process is as follows:

$$Clock \stackrel{\text{def}}{=} \overline{tick}.\overline{mcs}.\overline{mct}.Clock$$

The complete model of the slow-scan with LGL failure detection:

$$SS \stackrel{\text{def}}{=} (SPC(0) \mid LGL \mid TPC(0) \mid Clock) \backslash \{c1, c2, c2_u, s1, s2, s2_u, mcs, mct\}$$

6 Analysis of the Model

6.1 Formalizing the Safety Properties

We will try to show that two safety-critical properties hold of our slow-scan model:

- After a low-grade link fails, the slow-scan system will eventually detect the failure and stop responding to the SSI and TFM.
- A failure is detected only if a failure has actually occurred.

We use the modal mu-calculus [10] in a slightly extended form [15] as a temporal logic to formalize behavioural properties. The syntax of the mu-calculus is as follows, where L ranges over sets of actions and Z ranges over variables:

$$\phi ::= \neg\phi \mid \phi_1 \wedge \phi_2 \mid [L]\phi \mid Z \mid \nu Z.\phi$$

Informally, the formula $\neg\phi$ holds of a process P if ϕ does not hold of P. The formula $\phi_1 \wedge \phi_2$ holds of P if both ϕ_1 and ϕ_2 hold of P. The formula $[L]\phi$ holds of P if ϕ holds for all processes P' that can be reached from P through the performance of action $\alpha \in L$. The formula $\nu Z.\phi$ is the greatest fixed point of the recursive modal equation $Z = \phi$, where Z appears in ϕ. Some intuition about fixed point formulas can be gained by keeping in mind that $\nu Z.\phi$ can be replaced by its "unfolding": the formula ϕ with Z replaced by $\nu Z.\phi$ itself. Thus, $\nu Z.\psi \wedge [\{a\}]Z = \psi \wedge [\{a\}](\nu Z.\psi \wedge [\{a\}]Z) = \psi \wedge [\{a\}](\psi \wedge [\{a\}](\nu Z.\psi \wedge [\{a\}]Z)) = $ ... holds of any process for which ψ holds along any execution path of a actions.

The operators $\vee$, $\langle \alpha \rangle$, and μ can be defined as duals to existing operators (where $\phi[\psi/Z]$ is the property obtained by substituting ψ for free occurrences of Z in ϕ):

$$\phi_1 \vee \phi_2 \stackrel{\text{def}}{=} \neg(\neg\phi_1 \wedge \neg\phi_2)$$

$$\langle L \rangle \phi \stackrel{\text{def}}{=} \neg[L]\neg\phi$$

$$\mu Z.\phi \stackrel{\text{def}}{=} \neg\nu Z.\neg\phi[\neg Z/Z]$$

Informally $\langle L \rangle \phi$ holds of a process that can perform an action in L and thereby evolve to a process satisfying ϕ. As with $\nu Z.\phi$, the formula $\mu Z.\phi$ can be understood through unfolding, except here only finitely many unfoldings can be made. Thus, $\mu Z.\psi \vee \langle \{a\} \rangle Z$ holds of a process that can evolve to a process satisfying ψ after finitely many occurrences of action a.

These additional abbreviations are also convenient (where L ranges over sets of actions, and Act is the set of CCS actions):

$$[\alpha_1, \ldots, \alpha_n]\phi \stackrel{\text{def}}{=} [\{\alpha_1, \ldots, \alpha_n\}]\phi$$
$$[-]\phi \stackrel{\text{def}}{=} [Act]\phi$$
$$[-L]\phi \stackrel{\text{def}}{=} [Act - L]\phi$$

The booleans are defined as abbreviations: $\text{tt} \stackrel{\text{def}}{=} \nu Z.Z$, $\text{ff} \stackrel{\text{def}}{=} \neg\text{tt}$. An example using these abbreviations is $\langle a, b\rangle\text{tt}$, which holds of processes that can perform either an a or a b action. As another example, the formula $\nu Z.\langle-\rangle\text{tt} \wedge [-]Z$ holds of deadlock-free processes.

The mu-calculus along with the abbreviations presented so far constitutes an expressive but still low-level temporal logic for describing properties of processes. In practice it is usually convenient to define additional abbreviations that capture important concepts of the application. Before considering specific properties of the slow-scan system we present two more abbreviations that often make it possible to avoid the fixed-point operators:

$$[L]^\infty\phi \stackrel{\text{def}}{=} \nu Z.\phi \wedge [L]Z$$
$$\langle L\rangle^*\phi \stackrel{\text{def}}{=} \mu Z.\phi \vee \langle L\rangle Z$$

Informally, $[L]^\infty\phi$ holds if ϕ always holds along all paths composed of actions in the set L. For example, the absence of deadlock can be written $[-]^\infty\langle-\rangle\text{tt}$ — in every state some action is possible. The dual operator $\langle L\rangle^*\phi$ holds of processes having a finite execution path composed of actions from L leading to a state in which ϕ holds.

We are ready now to formalize the two important slow-scan properties. Recall the first property:

> After either of the low-grade links fail, the slow-scan system will eventually detect the failure and stop responding to the SSI and TFM.

There are two distinct parts to this property: a) failures are eventually detected, and b) after detection eventually no responses are made to the TFM's or SSI. On the way to formalizing the first part, we have the idea "after a $\overline{fail}$ action occurs then eventually a $\overline{det}$ action occurs". Care needs to be taken here with the notion of eventuality, however, because we want to consider only executions in which the clock continues to tick. Our CCS model contains execution paths in which the clock does not continue to tick, and we do not expect $\overline{det}$ to eventually occur in all these paths. The next step is therefore to define an abbreviation for the property "if the clock continues to tick then eventually action α will occur":

$$even(\alpha) \stackrel{\text{def}}{=} \mu Z.[-\overline{tick}, \alpha]^\infty[\overline{tick}]Z$$

A reasonable translation of this formula to English is "no execution path exists containing infinitely many $\overline{tick}$ actions and no α actions". A useful and closely-related abbreviation captures the property "if the clock continues to tick then eventually property ϕ holds":

$$even(\phi) \stackrel{\text{def}}{=} \mu Z.(\nu Y.\phi \vee ([\overline{tick}]Z \wedge [-\overline{tick}]Y))$$

Now we can formalize "after a $\overline{fail}$ action occurs then eventually a $\overline{det}$ action occurs":

$$failures\text{-}detected \stackrel{\text{def}}{=} [-\overline{fail}]^{\infty}[\overline{fail}]even(\overline{det})$$

The formula begins with $[-\overline{fail}]^{\infty}$ rather than $[-]^{\infty}$ because we are concerned only with the first failure that occurs.

A potential pitfall is that *failures-detected* is vacuously true if a failure never occurs. So, for example, the nil process 0 satisfies the formula. The formula is also vacuously true of processes in which the clock cannot continue to tick, such as $\overline{fail}.\overline{tick}.0$. To ensure that the slow-scan model does not satisfy failures-detected in one of these ways, we can write two more formulas:

$$failures\text{-}possible \stackrel{\text{def}}{=} \langle-\rangle^{*}\langle\overline{fail}\rangle\texttt{tt}$$

$$can\text{-}tick \stackrel{\text{def}}{=} [-]^{\infty}\langle-\rangle^{*}\langle\overline{tick}\rangle\texttt{tt}$$

The formula *failures-possible* says that there is some execution path containing the action $\overline{fail}$. The formula *can-tick* says that, from any state, there is some execution path containing the action $\overline{tick}$. Note that *can-tick* is stronger than the property we need: "$\overline{tick}$ can occur infinitely often after a $\overline{fail}$ action".

To complete the formalization of the first property, we need to also express the second part: "after detection eventually no responses are made to the TFM's or SSI". Using the auxiliary formula *silent*, the property can be expressed as follows:

$$silent \stackrel{\text{def}}{=} [-]^{\infty}[\overline{comm\_out}, \overline{stat\_out}]\texttt{ff}$$

$$eventually\text{-}silent \stackrel{\text{def}}{=} [-]^{\infty}[\overline{det}]even(silent)$$

The property *silent* expresses that no occurrence of actions $\overline{comm\_out}$ or $\overline{stat\_out}$ is ever possible. The first property of interest is thus fully captured by the conjunction of *failures-detected*, *eventually-silent*, *failures-possible*, and *can-tick*.

The second property, "a failure is detected only if a failure has actually occurred", is much simpler to express:

$$no\text{-}false\text{-}alarms \stackrel{\text{def}}{=} [-\overline{fail}]^{\infty}[\overline{det}]\texttt{ff}$$

Other properties could be formalized besides the two important safety-critical ones. For example, we have already seen that the absence of deadlock can be expressed as $[-]^{\infty}\langle-\rangle\texttt{tt}$. However, this property is weaker than the property *can-tick*, which states that not only is some action possible in every state, but that actions leading to a $\overline{tick}$ action are possible in every state.

6.2 Checking the Safety Properties

By formalizing the behaviour of the slow-scan design, we enable precise and even automated reasoning about it. Since the slow-scan model has a finite and reasonably small state space (of 3842 states), the Concurrency Workbench [6] can check whether the properties formulated in the last section hold of the model.

The complexity of some of the properties means that they cannot be checked by the Workbench in 24 hours on a powerful workstation. For each of these properties, checking was made of a smaller model derived from the slow-scan model by hiding actions not relevant to the particular property. Then, by using a technique [3] that cannot be described here because of space, the properties were shown by hand to hold of the full model if and only if they held in the smaller model. In what follows, we will write that a property was checked *indirectly* if this technique was used, and checked *directly* if the Workbench alone was sufficient.

Recall that the first property of interest involved detection of LGL failures. The property *failures-detected* was checked indirectly and shown to hold. The properties *failures-possible* and *can-tick* were also shown to hold, the first directly and the second indirectly.

The property *eventually-silent*, which holds if the slow-scan system eventually stops performing output actions after a failure is detected, could not practically be checked even indirectly. The property is expensive to check because after any $\overline{det}$ action a complicated eventuality property must be shown to hold.

The second property, *no-false-alarms*, expresses that failures cannot be detected before they occur. This property could be checked directly, but was found not to hold. It fails to hold because the action $\overline{fail}$ occurs after a failure, not simultaneously with it. A failure can be detected, and the corresponding action $\overline{det}$ can occur, between the moment of failure and the moment action $\overline{fail}$ occurs. Using the simulation facility of the Workbench, we were able to guide the slow-scan model through such a course of events. The state reached immediately after the $\overline{det}$ action occurred was as follows:

$$(SPCF \mid \overline{fail}.Comm''[f] \mid \overline{fail}.Comm''[f] \mid \overline{s1}.TPC(1) \mid \overline{mct}.Clock)\backslash L$$

Knowing that *no-false-alarms* fails to hold, other questions become interesting, such as "can both protocol converters signal detection of failure before $\overline{fail}$ occurs?", and "if a failure is detected before $\overline{fail}$ occurs, must $\overline{fail}$ eventually occur?". The formula *detects-before-failure* expresses the property that two $\overline{det}$ actions can occur before a $\overline{fail}$ action:

$$detects\text{-}before\text{-}failure \stackrel{\text{def}}{=} \langle -\overline{fail}\rangle^*\langle\overline{det}\rangle\langle -\overline{fail}\rangle^*\langle\overline{det}\rangle\mathrm{tt}$$

This property was checking indirectly (by hiding all actions except $\overline{fail}$ and $\overline{det}$) and shown not to hold. However, it was shown in a similar way that two $\overline{fail}$ actions *can* occur before any $\overline{det}$ actions occur.

The two following formulas express the idea that $\overline{det}$ and $\overline{fail}$ are related by property "if a $\overline{fail}$ occurs before a $\overline{det}$, then eventually a $\overline{det}$ will occur, and conversely":

$$even\text{-}detect \stackrel{\text{def}}{=} [-\overline{fail}, \overline{det}]^{\infty}[\overline{fail}]even(\overline{det})$$
$$even\text{-}fail \stackrel{\text{def}}{=} [-\overline{fail}, \overline{det}]^{\infty}[\overline{det}]even(\overline{fail})$$

Note that the property *failures-detected* is slightly stronger than *even-detect*; the former property requires that $\overline{det}$ occurs after $\overline{fail}$ even if $\overline{det}$ occurred before $\overline{fail}$. These properties were checked indirectly and shown to hold. To perform the indirect checking, the actions $comm\_in, stat\_in, \overline{comm\_out}$, and $\overline{stat\_out}$ were hidden, yielding a model of 641 states.

In summary, we have verified that LGL failures are detected in our model. To ensure that this property is meaningful we have also shown that in all states the clock can continue to tick, and that it is possible for such failures can occur. However, we have not verified that output actions will eventually cease after an LGL failure is detected.

7   Showing Properties of Implementations

An important goal of this study was to avoid putting features in the model that are not present in the design, so that properties shown of the model would hold of the actual system, regardless of specific choices made during detailed design and implementation. For example, the model of the SPC does not specify when messages are passed along the LGL, only that they can be passed. Less success was achieved in leaving the LGL buffering capacity unspecified; we settled for an LGL model with a capacity of one message.

Unfortunately, we cannot claim that properties shown of our CCS model will hold for all slow-scan implementations, in part because we have given no precise rules governing how a CCS model can be refined.

The observation equivalence relation of CCS is sometimes used to show that a specification and implementation (both described as CCS processes) have the same behaviour. Generally, however, we do not want a refinement relation to be symmetrical. Instead, we expect refinement to be modelled as a pre-order relation in which detail can be added in a refinement step according to some rules.

Bisimulation preorders [16] use the idea that a refinement must be "at least as defined" as a specification. For example, a CCS process that evolves to an error-handling state after an *error* action occurs is a refinement of a process that evolves to an undefined state after such an action. This preorder relation can be characterized logically [14]: process P is a refinement of process Q exactly when P possesses more properties than Q. However, the properties here are those expressible in an intuitionistically-interpreted sub-language of the mu-calculus. Liveness properties, such as *eventually-silent*, cannot be expressed in this logic.

Another refinement preorder comes from the modal process logic of Larsen and Thomsen [11]. Specifications in this logic resemble CCS processes except that both *necessary* and *admissible* actions are possible. A specification R is a refinement of another specification S if R must perform every action S must perform, and if S may perform every action R may perform. This preorder also has a logical characterization [12], but here the logical language is an intuitionistically-interpreted form of Hennesy-Milner logic, which cannot express the safety and liveness properties of interest to us.

Holmstrom's refinement calculus [9] allows CCS processes to be refined from specifications given in Hennessy-Milner logic with recursion. An implementation is guaranteed to have the property expressed by its specification, but the meaning of a recursive specification is taken to be its greatest fixed point, and so again this approach does not allow liveness properties to be expressed.

8 Conclusions

Our aim was to model the slow-scan design as a CCS process, to prove that the model possessed safety-critical properties expressed in the modal mu-calculus, and to show that these properties would be possessed by implementations based on the design model.

We were able to model most of the slow-scan design directly in CCS. Timing and probabilistic aspects of the design could obviously not be captured. As has been described elsewhere [11], CCS agents are not ideal for specifying systems, since only a single process can be described (up to equivalence), while one often would like to describe a broad class of processes. A notion of priority [4] or of interrupt [2] would have been useful in modelling the *tick* action of the clock process. It would have also been convenient to ascribe simple process fairness [8] to the model, allowing simpler expression of the eventuality properties. In adding a failure detection mechanism to the basic slow-scan model, a notion of superposition [5] would have been helpful. However, a notation with all of these features would lack the appealing simplicity of CCS.

The slow-scan model lacked some features described in the design, such as system initialization. The modelling of failures and failure detection was also overly simple. In particular, many more failure modes of the system could be modelled, and the failure modes could be made more realistic. For example, it may not be valid to assume that the LGL is quiet after failure.

In specifying the safety-critical properties of the system, the modal mu-calculus was expressive enough to capture all the properties of interest. Abbreviations were necessary to keep the formulas small and understandable. As just mentioned, the eventuality properties were complicated by the lack of priority and fairness in the design model. The inability of the Concurrency Workbench to check certain properties in a reasonable period of time reflects both the complexity of the properties and the relative lack of concern with efficiency issues in the development of the Workbench.

Probably the biggest shortcoming of the study was our failure to show that properties of our design model also hold for for slow-scan implementations. This problem is the subject of current study. Also to be studied is the applicability of timed process calculi [1, 13] to this system.

233

Acknowledgements

We thank Ian Mitchell, Chris Gurney, and others at British Rail Research, Derby, for their help, and Stuart Anderson, Terry Stroup, Colin Stirling and Matthew Morley of Edinburgh, for their comments. The comments of the anonymous referees were also helpful. This work was supported by SERC grant "Mathematically-Proven Safety Systems", IED SE/1224.

References

1. J.C.M. Baeten and J.A. Bergstra. Real time process algebra. *Formal Aspects of Computing*, 3, 1991.
2. J.C.M. Baeten, J.A. Bergstra, and J.W. Klop. Syntax and defining equations for an interrupt mechanism in process algebra. Technical Report CS-R8503, CWI, Amsterdam, 1985.
3. Glenn Bruns. Verifying properties of large systems by abstraction. To be submitted for publication, 1991.
4. Juanito Camilleri. A conditional operator for CCS. In *Proceedings of CONCUR '91*. Springer Verlag, 1991.
5. K. Mani Chandy and Jayadev Misra. *Parallel Program Design*. Addison Wesley, 1988.
6. Rance Cleaveland, Joachim Parrow, and Bernhard Steffen. The concurrency workbench: A semantics based tool for the verification of concurrent systems. Technical Report ECS-LFCS-89-83, Laboratory for Foundations of Computer Science, University of Edinburgh, 1989.
7. A.H. Cribbens. Solid-state interlocking (SSI): an integrated electronic signalling system for mainline railways. *IEE Proceedings*, 134(3), May 1987.
8. Nissim Francez. *Fairness*. Springer-Verlag, 1986.
9. Sören Hölmstrom. A refinement calculus for specifications in hennessy-milner logic with recursion. *Formal Aspects of Computing*, 1:242–272, 1989.
10. D. Kozen. Results on the propositional mu-calculus. *Theoretical Computer Science*, 27:333–354, 1983.
11. Kim G. Larsen and Bent Thomsen. A modal process logic. In *Proceedings of the Third Annual Symposium on Logic in Computer Science*, 1988.
12. Kim Guldstrand Larsen. Modal specifications. Technical Report 89-9, Institute for Electronic Systems, Department of Mathematics and Computer Science, Denmark, 1989.
13. F. Moller and C. Tofts. A temporal calculus of communicating systems. In *Proceedings of CONCUR '90*. Springer-Verlag, 1990.
14. Bernhard Steffen. Characteristic formulae for CCS with divergence. Technical Report ECS-LFCS-89-76, Laboratory for Foundations of Computer Science, University of Edinburgh, 1989.
15. Colin Stirling. An introduction to modal and temporal logics for CCS. In A. Yonezawa and T. Ito, editors, *Concurrency: Theory, Language, and Architecture*. Springer Verlag, 1989. Lecture Notes in Computer Science, volume 391.
16. D. J. Walker. Bisimulations and divergence. In *Proceedings of the Third Annual Symposium on Logic in Computer Science*, 1988.

Automatic Reduction in CTL Compositional Model Checking

Thomas R. Shiple*   Massimiliano Chiodo†
Alberto L. Sangiovanni-Vincentelli*   Robert K. Brayton*

*Department of EECS, University of California, Berkeley, CA 94720
†Magneti Marelli, Pavia, Italy

Abstract. We describe a method for reducing the complexity of temporal logic model checking of a system of interacting finite state machines, and prove that it yields correct results. The method consists essentially of reducing each component machine with respect to the property we want to verify, and then verifying the property on the composition of the reduced components. We demonstrate the method on a simple example. We assess the potential of our approach on real-world examples.

1   Introduction

Temporal logic model checking procedures are potentially powerful verification tools for finite state systems. However, when the system under examination consists of several communicating parallel machines, the potential arises for an explosion in the size of the representation of the composition. Traditionally, the size of a system is identified with the number of states, and hence the issue is referred to as the *state-explosion* problem. The introduction of symbolic representations, based on binary decision diagrams (BDDs) [1], and symbolic verification procedures [8, 15, 2], made it possible to verify complex systems that could not be handled by techniques based on explicit representations [5]. However, just as with explicit representations, the size of the parallel composition may still be too large to handle.

Methods proposed to avoid the construction of the complete state graph, and therefore to avoid the representation explosion, can be split into two categories, *compositional verification* and *compositional minimization* [9]. In the first category, one tries to deduce properties of a composition of processes by reasoning on the individual components and their interactions, without ever building the composed system. In the second category, one tries to reduce or minimize the components in such a way that their composition yields a smaller yet semantically equivalent model of the total system.

As an example of the first, Wolper [16] inductively verifies complex systems by looking for *network invariants*, that is properties that, if satisfied by a network of n identical processes, will be satisfied by a network of $n + 1$ processes. Kurshan and McMillan have attempted a similar approach [12].

As for compositional minimization, Kurshan [13] uses homomorphic reductions, which "relax" the behavior of the component machines, to produce component machines that have fewer states than the original ones. The ω-regular properties he wants to verify are preserved under such user-provided reductions. Similarly, Clarke et al. [10, 7] define subsets of the logics CTL* and CTL, namely ∀CTL* and ∀CTL, where only universal path quantification is allowed. For these logics, satisfaction is preserved under composition and homomorphic reduction. However, these logics are strictly less expressive than CTL* and CTL, respectively.

As additional examples of compositional minimization, the compositional model checking algorithm based on the *interface rule*, proposed by Clarke *et al.* [6], is a technique that allows verification of a CTL property [5] on a single (main) machine within a system of interacting machines. Here, the other (side) machines are reduced by hiding those output variables of the side machines which the main machine cannot observe. This reduction is property *independent* in that the reduction is valid for any property on the main machine. The main limitation of this approach is that it cannot handle CTL formulas which specify properties of multiple interacting machines. Burch describes a technique for efficiently computing the existential quantification of variables from a product of component transition relations, a central computation in symbolic model checking [3]. By quantifying out variables from such a product as early as possible, one can avoid forming explicitly the complete product machine, and hence, potentially avoid an explosion in the BDDs. However, the applicability of this technique, and the amount of reduction achieved, depend heavily on the structure of the system and on the user-supplied order in which the component transition relations are processed.

It is our opinion that to make formal verification a usable tool in design, fully automatic techniques whose details are transparent to the user must be developed to attack large, complex problems typical of electronic system design. Our goal is to verify CTL properties on a system of interacting finite state machines.

The approach we take is to extract from the component machines the information relevant to the verification of a given property, and use only this to build the representation of a reduced system that preserves all of the behavior needed to verify the property. In this regard, our approach falls into the compositional minimization category. Our approach is fully automated and returns an exact result; that is the reduced system is verified if and only if the complete system is verified. Our finite state machine model allows non-deterministic transitions and incomplete specification, and thus can be used to represent reduced machines.

In Section 2 we present an overview of our approach, with references to the sections where the topics are addressed in detail. Section 3 gives definitions that will be used in the paper. In Section 4 we fully describe the details of our technique. In Section 5, we apply our technique to a simple example and discuss the results. Finally, in Section 6 we present conclusions and future developments. Detailed proofs of the theorems presented in the body of the paper are given in [4].

2 Overview

Techniques for CTL model checking on a *single* finite state machine are well known: given the transition relation for a single machine, and a CTL property on the machine, a *single machine model checker* will return the set of states of the machine which satisfy the property. The model checker operates on the BDD of the characteristic function of the transition relation.

Our goal is to perform CTL model checking on a *system* of interacting FSMs, where the CTL formulas express properties of the entire system, and not just of a component of the system. This is known as *compositional model checking*. In this setting, we are given the transition relation for each component machine. Since the interaction between the components affects the behavior of each component, we cannot directly apply the *single* machine model checker to each component. Nonetheless, by forming the complete product of all the component transition relations, we can produce a single transition relation which can be used as input to the model checker. However, this is a naive approach, because there is a distinct possibility that the size of the representation for the product machine will explode. In other words, the size of the representation for each component may be reasonable, but the size of the product may be intractable.

In our approach to compositional model checking, we use the single machine model checker, but not applied to the complete product of the component machines. Instead, we first extract the "interesting" part of each component to yield a "reduced" transition relation for each component. We then take the product of the reduced components, and finally, apply the model checker to the reduced product. In this manner, we hope to avoid an explosion in the size of the product machine.

We have reformulated the single machine model checker computations to better suit our needs for compositional model checking (Section 4.1). Specifically, the output it produces is a transition relation rather than a set of states. To produce the set of states which satisfy a formula, we simply project the transition relation onto the state space. Thus, our model checker takes a CTL formula F and a transition relation T as input, and produces a transition relation T^* as output. The proof of correctness of our compositional model checker relies on two important properties of our single machine model checker. The first is that T contains T^*. The second is that we can delete transitions from T *before* passing it to the model checker, and still get the same final result, as long as we do not delete any transitions that would be in T^*.

A novel aspect of our approach is how we determine the interesting part of each component machine. For a state in the product machine to satisfy a given formula, each state component of the global state must satisfy the formula projected onto the state component's associated machine. Thus, for each component, we project the CTL formula of interest onto the component (Section 4.2), and then apply the model checker to the component machine with the projected formula. The output of the model checker will have the same or fewer transitions than the input transition relation. Hence, by first eliminating some transitions from each component, the hope is that the size of the reduced product machine will be smaller than the complete product machine. Since the reduction of each component depends on the property of interest, we say that the reduction is *property dependent*.

To see why this technique gives the correct result, that is, computes the set of states of the product machine satisfying the input CTL formula, consider Figure 1. We are given a system M composed of interacting machines A and B, and a CTL formula F. The state space of M is the entire box, and the state space of A is the projection of the box onto any horizontal line. Likewise, the state space of B is any vertical line. Let Q_M be the set of states of M satisfying F. Consider the formula F_A produced by projecting the formula F onto machine A. By applying the model checker to machine A with formula F_A, we find the set of states Q_A of A which satisfy the projected formula, *disregarding the interaction of A and B*. Similarly, we produce Q_B by applying the model checker to B with F_B. By this procedure, $Q_A \times Q_B \supseteq Q_M$. Finally, we apply the model checker to the product of the subset of A containing Q_A, and the subset of B containing Q_B, to yield Q_M (Section 4.2).

In addition to the property-dependent reduction of each component machine described above, we apply several other techniques to reduce the size of each component before forming the product machine (Sections 4.2 and 4.2). If we were using an explicit representation (e.g. state transition graph) for the transition relations, then just by removing transitions, we would be decreasing the size of the representation. However, we are using an implicit representation, namely BDDs. Therefore, our actual goal is to find the smallest possible subset, containing the interesting behavior, of the original transition relations. This gives us a large don't care set within which to choose a transition relation with a small BDD representation.

It is important to note that in our work, "reduction" of a machine means reducing the size of the representation of the machine by removing "uninteresting" behavior. This differs, for example, from the usage of the term reduction in COSPAN [13], where reduction means making a machine smaller by adding behavior.

By avoiding the possible explosion in the size of the product machine, we hope to verify complex systems that cannot be verified with present techniques. There are two important features of our method to bear in mind. First, our reduction is fully automatic - it requires no guidance from the user. Second, our approach gives an exact result: it produces exactly the set of states satisfying a given CTL formula.

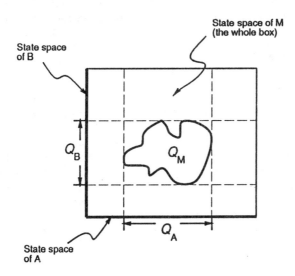

Fig. 1. State spaces in a system of interacting FSMs

3 Background

In the sequel, we use the following notation: The symbol "$\cdot$" is used for Boolean AND, the symbol "$+$" for Boolean OR, and the symbols "$\neg$" and overbar for Boolean NOT. $[T]_{x \to y}$ denotes the substitution of each occurrence of the variable x in the function T, by the variable y.

$S_x T$ denotes the *smoothing* of the relation T by x, computed as $S_x T = T_{\overline{x}} + T_x$, where T_x is the cofactor of T with respect to x [15]. This is interpreted as the projection of T onto the subspace orthogonal to x, or equivalently as the existential quantification of the variable x on the relation T. We will make use of the following properties of the smoothing operator: (a) $S_x f$ is the smallest function independent of x that contains f, and (b) $S_{x,y} f = S_x(S_y f) = S_y(S_x f)$.

Our model of finite state machines is based on the Moore model. A *synchronous finite state machine* with states X and inputs I is specified by a *transition relation* $T \subseteq X \times I \times X$. Each $(x, i, x') \in T$ is a *transition* from *present state* $x \in X$ to *next state* $x' \in X$ enabled by input i. We require each state to have a next state. Otherwise, we allow non-deterministic and incompletely specified machines. Lastly, in place of the Moore model's explicit outputs, which are functions of the state variables, our model simply allows the environment to directly observe the state variables.

In a *system* of interacting FSMs, the input to each component machine consists of the present states of the other components, plus external inputs. The definition of the parallel composition of two interacting machines follows.

Definition 1. Let $A(x, i, x')$ and $B(y, j, y')$ be transition relations describing two interacting FSMs. Furthermore, let $x, x' \in X$, $i \in Y \times I$, $y, y' \in Y$, and $j \in X \times I$. The transition relation M defining the behavior of the parallel composition of the two synchronous machines A and B is given by a subset of $(X \times Y) \times I \times (X \times Y)$ where

$$((x, y), k, (x', y')) \in M \text{ iff } (x, (y, k), x') \in A$$
$$\text{and } (y, (x, k), y') \in B. \quad \blacksquare$$

This definition is easily extended to a system of n interacting machines $A_1, A_2, \ldots, A_n$. Each machine A_i has present state variable $x_i \in X_i$ and next state variable $x_i' \in X_i$, and takes as input $\underline{x}_{\neq i} = [x_1, \cdots, x_{i-1}, x_{i+1}, \cdots, x_n]$, the present state variables of the other machines. The global state of the system is $\underline{x} = [x_1, \ldots, x_n] \in \underline{X} = X_1 \times X_2 \times \ldots \times X_n$. We restrict our attention to *closed* systems, that is systems that do not take inputs from the external environment. Interaction with the external environment is modeled by other state machines that produce (possibly non-deterministically) the inputs to which the system is sensitive. Thus we can represent each A_i by the transition relation $A_i(x_i, \underline{x}_{\neq i}, x_i') = A_i(\underline{x}, x_i')$ (see Figure 2).

In Section 4, we use the notion of path to define the output of the model checker computations.

Definition 2. A *path* on the transition relation T, from state x_0 to state x_k and of length k, is a finite sequence of transitions $< (x_0, i_0, x_1), (x_1, i_1, x_2), \ldots, (x_{k-1}, i_{k-1}, x_k) >$. (A path may have cycles.) If x_k belongs to a cycle, the path is said to be *infinite*. $\blacksquare$

Note that every set of transitions, be it a transition relation or a path, is denoted by its characteristic function implemented as a BDD.

3.1 Computation Tree Logic

In this work we use Computation Tree Logic, or CTL [5], to specify properties of FSMs. The set of all CTL formulas can be defined inductively in terms of a subset of

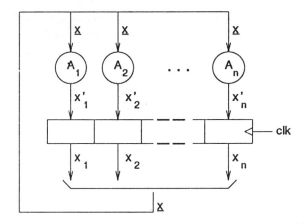

Fig. 2. Interacting Finite State Machines

base CTL formulas. The choice of the subset is not unique. In the following definition, an *atomic proposition* f is a function of the state variables of a FSM. That is, f is true in a state $x \in X$ if $f(x) = 1$.

Definition 3. The set of CTL formulas $\mathcal{F}$ is defined inductively as follows:

1. Every atomic proposition f is a CTL formula.
2. If f and g are CTL formulas, then $\neg f$, $f \cdot g$, $\exists X f$, $\exists G f$, and $\exists [f R g]$ are CTL formulas. ∎

The formula $\exists X f$ is true in a state s if f is true in some successor of s. The formula $\exists G f$ is true in a state s if f is true in every state of some infinite path beginning with s. The formula $\exists [f R\ g]$ is true in a state s if f is true in s and there is some path beginning with a successor of s along which f is true in every state until g is true.

The basis we have chosen is the same as the one presented by other researchers [5, 2] except that the *until* operator $\exists [f U g]$ is replaced by the *repeat* operator $\exists [f R g]$ (see Figure 3). The semantics of $\exists [f R g]$ is similar to that of $\exists [f U g]$, but the paths must have length at least one. More formally, $\exists [f U g] \equiv \exists [f R g] + g$.

Syntactic abbreviations, such as $\forall F f$, which is equivalent to $\neg \exists G \neg f$, are often used for notational convenience. We assume the semantics of CTL formulas is known to the reader. For example, the formula $\forall G \forall F$**enabled** specifies that the signal **enabled** holds infinitely often along every computation path.

A non-nested CTL formula, that is one whose arguments f and g are atomic propositions (where g may be NIL, as in the case of $\exists G f$), will be referred to as a *simple* formula.

4 Model Checking

4.1 Single Machine Model Checker

The input to our single machine model checker is a transition relation T and a base CTL formula F. The output is a set of transitions T^* such that F holds at the present state of each transition.

240

Definition 4. The *model checker* implements a function $mc : 2^{(X \times I \times X)} \times \mathcal{F} \to 2^{(X \times I \times X)}$. We denote the output of the model checker as T^*, that is, $T^* = mc(T, F)$. ∎

Since the output is a set of transitions, we have chosen for Definition 3 a set of base formulas that expresses all of CTL logic and can be given semantics in terms of sets of transitions. In this way we can easily define which paths, and consequently, which transitions, are relevant to each property.

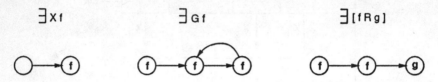

Fig. 3. Base CTL Formulas

Definition 5. $(\exists X f)$: $T^* = mc(T, \exists X f)$ contains all transitions $(x, i, x') \in T$ such that $f(x') = 1$. T^* is computed as $T^* = f(x') \cdot T$ ∎

Definition 6. $(\exists G f)$: $T^* = mc(T, \exists G f)$ contains all transitions $(x, i, x') \in T$ that belong to some infinite path on which f is true at each state. T^* is computed by the following *greatest* fixed point computation.

$$T_0 = T \cdot f(x) \cdot f(x')$$
$$T_{n+1} = T_n \cdot [S_{i,x'}(T_n)]_{x \to x'}$$
$$T^* = T_n, \text{ s.t. } T_{n+1} = T_n \quad \blacksquare$$

Definition 7. $(\exists [f R \; g])$: $T^* = mc(T, \exists [f R g])$ contains all transitions $(x, i, x') \in T$ that have present state in f and belong to some path where f is true until g is true. T^* is computed by the following *least* fixed point computation.

$$\tilde{T} = T \cdot f(x) \cdot f(x')$$
$$T_0 = T \cdot f(x) \cdot g(x')$$
$$T_{n+1} = \tilde{T} \cdot [S_{i,x'}(T_n)]_{x \to x'} + T_n$$
$$T^* = T_n, \text{ s.t. } T_n = T_{n+1} \quad \blacksquare$$

Since the set T is finite, the fixed point computations are guaranteed to terminate.

We prove two properties on the relation between the input and output of the model checker.

Proposition 8. Let $T^* = mc(T, F)$. Then $T^* \subseteq T$, for any base CTL formula F.

This result follows since the model checker only removes transitions from T; it never adds transitions. As a consequence, the transition relation returned by the model checker generally describes an incompletely specified machine.

Proposition 9. Let $T^* = mc(T, F)$. If M is another transition relation such that $T^* \subseteq M \subseteq T$, then $mc(M, F) = T^*$.

Think of T as the full transition relation for a machine. As usual, T^* is the output of the model checker when T is the input. Proposition 9 tells us that we can use as input to the model checker any transition relation M that is contained in T and contains T^*, and still get T^* as output. This result will be used in the compositional model checker to justify the removal of "uninteresting" transitions from the component machines.

4.2 Compositional Model Checker

The input to the compositional model checker is an array of transition relations specifying a system of n interacting machines $A_1, A_2, \ldots, A_n$ and a base CTL formula F. The output is the set of states of the global system that satisfy F.

Definition 10. The *compositional model checker* implements a function $cmc : 2^{\underline{X} \times \underline{X}} \times \mathcal{F} \rightarrow 2^{\underline{X}}$. We denote the output of the compositional model checker as $Q(\underline{x}) = cmc(A_1, \cdots, A_n, F)$. ∎

```
    function cmc(array[A_i], F) {
1       for i = 1 to n {      /* project F on A_i and run mc on A_i */
            A_i* = mc(A_i, F_A_i);
        }
2       R = ∏(S_x'_i A_i*);      /* compute reducing term */
        for i = 1 to n {      /* find minimum onset of A_i */
            A_i*' = A_i* · R;
        }
3       for i = 1 to n {      /* use don't cares to minimize BDD for A_i */
            Â_i = min_bdd(A_i, A_i*');
        }
4       M̂ = mc(∏_i Â_i, F);   /* run mc on reduced product */
        Q = S_x' M̂;           /* states that satisfy F */
        return Q;
    }
```

Fig. 4. Compositional Model Checker

The compositional model checker procedure cmc consists of four phases (Figure 4).

Phase 1 The first phase is to check the components independently. For each machine A_i we compute the reduced component A_i^* by applying the model checker to A_i and the projection of F onto A_i.

Definition 11. Let $A_i(x_i, \underline{x}_{\neq i}, x_i')$ be a transition relation in a system $A_1, A_2, \ldots, A_n$. Let F be a base CTL formula with atomic propositions $f(\underline{x})$ and $g(\underline{x})$. The *projection* F_{A_i} of F onto A_i is obtained by replacing $f(\underline{x})$ with $f(x_i) = S_{\underline{x}_{\neq i}} f(\underline{x})$ and $g(\underline{x})$ with $g(x_i) = S_{\underline{x}_{\neq i}} g(\underline{x})$ in F.

Phase 2 The second phase is to reduce statically each component with respect to the interaction of the other components.

Proposition 12. Consider a system of interacting machines $A_1, A_2, \ldots, A_n$. Let

$$R(\underline{x}) = \prod_{j=1}^{n}(S_{x'_j} A_j)$$

Then $A'_i = A_i \cdot R$ is the smallest subset of A_i which contains $\prod A_j$ and is independent of $\underline{x}'_{\neq i}$.

We apply this proposition in this phase by intersecting each A^*_i with $R(\underline{x}) = \prod(S_{x'_j} A^*_j)$ to obtain $A^{*'}_i$. The transition relations of these machines contain the smallest possible sets of transitions (the minimum onsets) that are needed to verify the given property F.

Phase 3 In the worst case, the size of the AND of two BDDs is the product of the number of nodes of each BDD. Hence, in the third phase, we want to minimize the size of the component BDDs by applying heuristics such as the *restrict operator* [8]. Given an incompletely specified function with onset $f \cdot c$ and don't care set $\bar{c}$, the restrict operator $P_c f$ is a function $f \cdot c \subseteq P_c f \subseteq f + \bar{c}$ that in most cases has a smaller BDD than f. Here, the don't care set derived from phases 1 and 2 is $\bar{c} = A_i - A^{*'}_i$. Thus, we apply the restrict operator to each transition relation with $f = A^{*'}_i$ and $c = \overline{A}_i + A^{*'}_i$, to yield $\hat{A}_i$. Unfortunately, minimizing the sizes of the BDDs for the A_i's does not guarantee that we are minimizing the size of the BDD for the product. Only thorough experimentation will indicate the effectiveness of this heuristic.

Phase 4 The fourth and final phase of the procedure *cmc* is to apply the single machine model checker to the original formula F and the product $\prod \hat{A}_i$ of the minimized components, to determine the states of the product machine that satisfy F. In fact, we can form the product of the minimized components incrementally, applying the model checker after taking the composition with each component. The following theorem states that applying the model checker to the reduced product, gives the same result as if we had taken the naive approach and applied the model checker to the complete product machine.

Theorem 13. Consider a system of interacting machines $A_1, A_2, \ldots, A_n$. Let F be any base CTL formula. Then

$$mc(\prod_{i=1}^{n} \hat{A}_i, F) = mc(\prod_{i=1}^{n} A_i, F).$$

The correctness of our technique relies on our choice of the base formulas for CTL. By allowing only existential path quantifiers in our base formulas, we can guarantee that each reduced component A^*_i contains every transition that would be present in the output of the model checker when applied to the complete product machine. The intuition behind this is that a component "loses behavior" when composed with the rest of the system, relative to its behavior when viewed independently of the system.

On the other hand, our technique fails if we choose as our base formulas those with universal path quantifiers (e.g. $\forall Xp$). To illustrate this, in the example of Figure 5 we have communicating machines $A(x, y, x')$ and $B(y, x, y')$ and propositions $p(x)$ and $q(y)$. State $(0,0)$ in the product machine $A \cdot B$ satisfies the formula $\forall G(p \cdot q)$, even though no state of A satisfies the projected formula $\forall Gp$. In the notation of Section 2, $Q_A = \emptyset$, and thus, $Q_M \not\subseteq Q_A \times Q_B \subseteq X \times Y$.

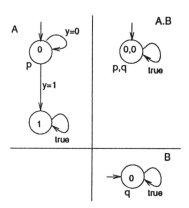

Fig. 5. Interacting FSMs (state $(1,0)$ is not reachable)

4.3 Nested Formulas

A general CTL formula can be nested, that is the propositions can either be explicit sets of states or formulas to be computed. For example, the CTL formula $F = \forall G(\text{req} \rightarrow \forall F\text{ack})$ is a nested formula. For this reason, a general CTL formula is represented as a binary tree. Each node of the tree is a structure composed of a type (e.g. $\exists G$), and two pointers (f and g) to sub-formulas which can either be atomic propositions or other CTL formulas. As in [5], we verify a nested CTL formula by traversing the formula from the leaves to the root. At each level of nesting, we verify one or more simple CTL formulas whose propositions are either given or computed from the previous level. In the example above, the atomic propositions req, ack, and reset are given as BDDs. The formula is then verified as follows. Let $M = array[A_i]$. The formula $F = \forall G(\text{req} \rightarrow \forall F\text{ack})$ can be rewritten as $\neg(\exists[1 R \neg(\text{req} \rightarrow \neg\exists G\neg\text{ack})] + \neg(\text{req} \rightarrow \neg\exists G\neg\text{ack}))$, and is satisfied by the set Q of states of M given by:

$$Q_0 = cmc(M, F = \neg\text{ack})$$
$$Q_1 = cmc(M, F = \exists GQ_0)$$
$$Q_2 = cmc(M, F = \neg Q_1)$$
$$Q_3 = cmc(M, F = \text{req} \rightarrow Q_2)$$
$$Q_4 = cmc(M, F = \neg Q_3)$$
$$Q_5 = cmc(M, F = \exists[1 R Q_4)$$

$$Q_6 = cmc(M, F = Q_4 + Q_5)$$
$$Q = cmc(M, F = \neg Q_6)$$

To verify a nested formula F, we embed the cmc function, which verifies a simple CTL formula, in a recursive procedure $rcmc$ (Recursive Compositional Model Checker) that traverses the tree of the formula F from the leaves to the root (see Figure 6).

```
function rcmc(array[A_i], F) {
    if (NESTED(F.f)) {      /* if f is nested, apply rcmc to f */
        F.f = rcmc(array[A_i], F.f);
    }
    if (NESTED(F.g)) {      /* if g is nested, apply rcmc to g */
        F.g = rcmc(array[A_i], F.g);
    }
    Q = cmc(array[A_i], F);   /* run cmc on root formula */
    return Q;
}
```

Fig. 6. Recursive Compositional Model Checker

5   Example

In this section, we assess the potential of our compositional technique by verifying a simple system of four interacting machines.

The structure of the system is shown in Figure 7. A resource *server* is shared by two *user* processes. Each user can request the server at any time. If both require it at the same time, the server non-deterministically decides which user to serve. Once acknowledged, a user can release the server at any time, but after a time t_{max} the server is automatically released. The fourth component is an 8-bit *counter* that is started whenever *server* acknowledges a user, and is reset to t_0 when the *server* is released. When the counter reaches the state t_{max} the server is forcefully released. The sizes of the components in BDD nodes are 29 for the server, 14 for each user, and 769 for the counter. The size of the complete product transition relation is 27796. Note that the counter is the component that most contributes to the size of the system.

We first want to check which states satisfy the following property: *if* req_1 *is present and* req_2 *is not present, then* ack_1 *must be present sometime in the future.* In CTL notation this is

$$F = \text{req}_1 \cdot \neg\text{req}_2 \rightarrow \forall F \text{ack}_1.$$

This formula is rewritten in base formulas as

$$F = \text{req}_1 \cdot \neg\text{req}_2 \rightarrow \neg\exists G \neg\text{ack}_1.$$

The largest BDD computed in this verification has a size of 15405 nodes, which is about 55% of the complete product machine. This BDD is computed in verifying the sub-formula $\exists G\neg\text{ack}_1$, which is the only significant sub-formula in this case. Analyzing the component reductions, we find that only *server* is actually reduced (from 29 to 16 nodes). In fact, the paths in *server* that visit ack_1 are removed. The other components, including the counter, remain unchanged. This is because the variable ack_1 depends on *server* only. The projection of the sub-formula $\exists G\neg\text{ack}_1$ onto the other components is $\exists G1$, which means: *there exists some infinite path.* Consequently, since all components are completely specified, all transitions belong to some infinite path, and therefore no reduction is achieved. In general, a formula with propositions that depend on only a few machines will yield less reduction than one with propositions on many machines.

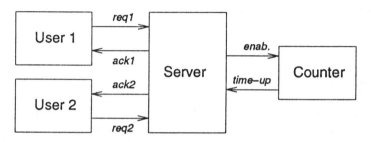

Fig. 7. Four machine system

This result seems promising. However, it is not hard to come up with a case where there is no reduction. For example, let us check for which states the property above is globally true. That is: *for all states of all paths, if* req_1 *is present and* req_2 *is not present, then* ack1 *must be present sometime in the future.* In CTL notation we have

$$H = \forall G(\text{req}_1 \cdot \neg\text{req}_2 \rightarrow \forall F\text{ack}_1)$$

rewritten as

$$H = \neg(\exists[1\ R\ \neg F] + \neg F),$$

where F is defined as above. This property is not satisfied by any state of the system. In fact, from every state of the product machine, there is at least one path to a state where the implication above does not hold. In this case, the complete product machine must be computed. This happens because the sub-formula $\exists[1\ R\ \neg F] + \neg F$, which reads *there exists some path to* $\neg F$, is trivially true for every state of a strongly connected system where $\neg F$ is true in at least one state. Thus, no paths are removed and no reduction is achieved in verifying this sub-formula.

This example shows how the amount of reduction depends on the structure of the machine being checked and on the formula being verified. If the machine is strongly connected, little reduction is expected because the paths tend to span the machine. On the other hand, if the machine is not strongly connected, then more reduction may be possible because the paths may be bound to some regions of the graph. Formulas that have the tautology as a proposition (notably $\forall Gp$ rewritten as $\exists[1\ R\ \neg p] + \neg p$) are most sensitive to the structure of the machine.

In this example, if we could compute $\forall GF$ directly, without reexpressing it in terms of a formula with an existential path quantifier, then we would achieve some reduction. However, this does not fit in our method because Theorem 13 does not hold

under the universal path quantifier. Nonetheless, in many cases it may be useful to
trade off the exact (i.e. necessary and sufficient) result for a sufficient but computable
result.

6 Conclusions

We have described a method for verifying a CTL property on a system of interacting
FSMs. It turns out that for some properties, by first applying property-dependent
reductions to the component machines before building the product machine, we will be
able to verify larger systems than is currently possible. Our method is fully automatic,
and produces the exact set of states which satisfy a given CTL property.

The core of the compositional model checker has been implemented. It remains to
provide an interface to the verification system being developed at UC Berkeley, a system that will be tightly linked with the Sequential Interactive Synthesis system [14].
Once this interface is completed, we plan to test thoroughly the effectiveness of our
method on large examples.

Several ideas to increase the power of our approach deserve investigation. Clarke's
interface rule could be added as a preprocessor to our approach for those properties
on a single machine, and Burch's method for computing relational products could be
used to handle the product of the reduced components. Another idea is to *add* transitions to each component to reduce the size of the BDDs. Of course, these transitions
must be chosen judiciously so that the final result is not altered. We would like to
further investigate the general problem of finding a cover, with a minimal BDD representation, of an incompletely specified function. Also, using a formula as a criterion
for repartitioning the original system into a new set of FSMs, may lead to smaller
BDDs for each component.

We could relax the exact nature of our approach by never taking the product of
the reduced components. In this case, we would be limited to stating conclusively
that a certain state does *not* satisfy a given property. Conversely, as suggested by
the example, we could compute the universally quantified properties directly, as in
COSPAN, and be content with knowing that a certain state *does* satisfy a given property, although others may also. Similarly, another interesting development would be
to combine automatic reduction with homomorphic abstraction. Finally, we may consider extending our approach to other logics, such as ECTL and ω-regular languages.

7 Acknowledgements

We wish to thank Kolar L. Kodandapani for his contribution in the early stages of
this work, and Bob Kurshan for stimulating discussions which sparked our interest in
automatic reduction.

References

1. R. E. Bryant, "Graph-Based Algorithms for Boolean Function Manipulation," *IEEE Trans. on Computers*, C-35(8), pp. 677-691, Aug. 1986.
2. J. R. Burch, E. M. Clarke, K. L. McMillan, and D. L. Dill, "Sequential Circuit Verifica-
tion Using Symbolic Model Checking," in *Proc. of 27th Design Automation Conference*,
pp. 46-51, June 1990.

3. J. R. Burch, E. M. Clarke, and D. E. Long, "Representing Circuits More Efficiently in Symbolic Model Checking," in *Proc. of 28th Design Automation Conference,* pp. 403-407, June 1991.

4. M. Chiodo, T. R. Shiple, A. Sangiovanni-Vincentelli, and R. K. Brayton, "Automatic Reduction in CTL Compositional Model Checking," Memorandum No. UCB/ERL M92/55, Electronics Research Laboratory, College of Engineering, University of California, Berkeley, Jan. 1992.

5. E. M. Clarke, E. A. Emerson, and P. Sistla, "Automatic Verification of Finite-State Concurrent Systems Using Temporal Logic Specifications," *ACM Trans. Prog. Lang. Syst.,* 8(2), pp. 244-263, 1986.

6. E. M. Clarke, D. E. Long, and K. L. McMillan, "Compositional Model Checking," in *Proc. of the 4th Annual Symposium on Logic in Computer Science,* Asilomar, CA, June 1989.

7. E. M. Clarke, O. Grumberg and D. E. Long, "Model Checking and Abstraction," in *Proc. of Principles of Programming Languages,* Jan. 1992.

8. O. Coudert, C. Berthet, and J. C. Madre, "Verification of Synchronous Sequential Machines Based on Symbolic Execution," in *Lecture Notes in Computer Science: Automatic Verification Methods for Finite State Systems,* vol. 407, editor J. Sifakis, Springer-Verlag, pp. 365-373, June 1989.

9. S. Graf and B. Steffen, "Compositional Minimization of Finite State Systems," in *Lecture Notes in Computer Science: Proc. of the 1990 Workshop on Computer-Aided Verification,* vol. 531, editors R. P. Kurshan and E. M. Clarke, Springer-Verlag, pp. 186-196, June 1990.

10. O. Grumberg and D. E. Long, "Model Checking and Modular Verification," in *Lecture Notes in Computer Science: Proc. CONCUR '91: 2nd Inter. Conf. on Concurrency Theory,* vol. 527, editors J. C. M. Baeten and J. F. Groote, Springer-Verlag, Aug. 1991.

11. J. E. Hopcroft, "An $n \log n$ Algorithm for Minimizing the States in a Finite Automaton," in *The Theory of Machines and Computation,* New York: Academic Press, pp. 189-196, 1971.

12. R. P. Kurshan and K. L. McMillan, "A Structural Induction Theorem for Processes," in *Proc. of 8th ACM Symp. on Principles of Distributed Computing,* Aug. 1989.

13. R. P. Kurshan, "Analysis of Discrete Event Coordination," in *Lecture Notes in Computer Science: Proc. REX Workshop on Stepwise Refinement of Distributed Systems, Models, Formalisms, Correctness,* vol. 430, editors J. W. de Bakker, W. -P. de Roever, and G. Rozenberg, Springer-Verlag, May 1989.

14. E. M. Sentovich, K. J. Singh, C. Moon, H. Savoj, R. K. Brayton, and A. Sangiovanni-Vincentelli, "Sequential Circuit Design Using Synthesis and Optimization," in *Proc. of International Conference on Computer Design,* Oct. 1992.

15. H. J. Touati, H. Savoj, B. Lin, R. K. Brayton, and A. Sangiovanni-Vincentelli, "Implicit State Enumeration of Finite State Machines using BDDs," in *Proc. of IEEE International Conference on Computer-Aided Design,* pp. 130-133, Nov. 1990.

16. P. Wolper and V. Lovinfosse, "Verifying Properties of Large Sets of Processes with Network Invariants," in *Lecture Notes in Computer Science: Automatic Verification Methods for Finite State Systems,* vol. 407, editor J. Sifakis, Springer-Verlag, pp. 68-80, June 1989.

Compositional Model Checking for Linear-Time Temporal Logic

Roope Kaivola

University of Helsinki, Department of Computer Science
Teollisuuskatu 23, SF-00510 Helsinki, Finland
tel. +358-0-708 4163, fax. +358-0-708 4441
email rkaivola@cc.helsinki.fi

Abstract. *Temporal logic model checking is a useful method for verifying properties of finite-state concurrent systems. However, due to the state explosion problem modular methods are essential in making the verification task manageable. One such method is to verify that certain properties ϕ_i are true of the submodules M_i of the system in all environments, and that the required property ϕ is a logical implication of these. This paper presents an algorithm deciding whether a nexttime-less linear temporal logic formula ϕ is true of a distributed variable module M in all environments. There are two versions of the algorithm: one allowing no fairness requirements and one for strongly fair concurrency. Both versions run in time $O(|M| \cdot 2^{c \cdot |\phi|})$. In addition to presenting the algorithms it is shown that given some reasonable assumptions the method is complete in the sense that all formulas ϕ true of $M_1 \parallel M_2$ can be verified by it.*

1 Introduction

One of the most important approaches to practical verification of propositional temporal logic properties of finite-state programs is automated model-checking: the execution of a program is modelled by a finite graph which can be directly interpreted as a temporal logic model, and a model-checking algorithm for the appropriate temporal logic can be run on the model. For many propositional temporal logics the model checking algorithms are of relatively low time-complexity, e.g. linear in size of the model and singly exponential in the size of the formula for the standard linear temporal logic [LP85].

However, despite the low time-complexity of model checking, the size of the execution graph is still often a prohibitive factor. An essential reason for this state-explosion problem is the modelling of concurrency by arbitrary interleavings of the atomic actions of the concurrent processes. In the general case the size of the complete model is exponential in the number of concurrent processes.

One way to avoid this problem is verifying the system directly on the basis of the individual processes without constructing a global execution graph. Here we follow the approach advocated by [MP91]. In this method a system M consists of several concurrent modules $M_1 \parallel \ldots \parallel M_n$. Verifying that ϕ is true of M is done by finding lemmas $\phi_1, \ldots, \phi_n$ such that each ϕ_i holds of M_i in every possible environment and $\phi_1 \wedge \ldots \wedge \phi_n \Rightarrow \phi$ is a theorem.

In this paper we describe an algorithm deciding whether a nexttime-less temporal logic formula ϕ is true of a module M in every possible environment. There are two versions of the algorithm: the basic case in which the concurrency is modelled by potentially unfair interleavings, and the enhanced case with fair concurrency. Both versions run in a time $O(|M| \cdot 2^{c \cdot |\phi|})$. In other words, using this algorithm it costs no more to decide whether ϕ_i is true of M_i in all (fair) environments than it costs in the standard linear temporal logic model checking [LP85] to decide whether ϕ_i is true of M_i without any environment. The method of communication between processes is by distributed variables. These are shared variables with the restriction that only the process owning a variable may change its value.

We do not discuss the issue of how the lemmas ϕ_i are to be found, and leave it to the responsibility of the human verifier of a system. However, in Section 5 we prove that given certain reasonable assumptions the lemmas always exist. This means that the method is complete in the sense that every formula ϕ true of $M_1 \parallel M_2$ is, at least in theory, verifiable by it.

The modularity issues discussed here have been addressed by several researchers. [BKP84], [Pnu85] and [Bar86] describe compositional linear temporal logic semantics for distributed-variable systems similar to ours. However, their point of interest lies more in the axiomatic semantics and compositional proof rules than in presenting an explicit algorithm for modular verification. A method for compositional model-checking using $MCTL$, an extension of CTL allowing restricted linear temporal logic formulas and fairness requirements as assumptions, is discussed in [Jos89]. A modular model checking algorithm for a logic tailored for Petri-nets is presented in [BE91]. It is unclear whether either of these methods can be applied to the model and the linear temporal logic used here. An approach to CTL^* model checking in which the environment of a module is modelled by an additional interface module is presented in [CLM89]. This differs from our approach in the use of interface processes and in the underlying communication method. The problem of modular verification of communicating Moore-machines is addressed by [GL91]. However, it does not seem possible to transfer their results directly into an asynchronous distributed-variable model.

The paper proceeds as follows: we first recall some standard definitions and properties of nexttime-less linear temporal logic and present the concepts of a module and parallel composition of modules. Then we define the core concept of a *satisfiability graph* and show that in a sense it encodes all the necessary information about the behaviour of a module in any environment. To illustrate the approach in practice, a mutual exclusion protocol is verified as an example. In Section 5 the results are extended to deal with fair concurrency.

2   Linear temporal logic

In this section we recall the definitions of standard nexttime-less linear temporal logic.

Definition 2.1 The *alphabet of propositional linear temporal logic LTL'* consists of the set AP of atomic propositions and of the symbols $(,), \neg, \vee, \mathcal{U}$. The *well-formed formulas* (wffs) of LTL' are as follows:

- if $\phi \in AP$, then ϕ is a wff,
- if ϕ_1 and ϕ_2 are wffs, then $(\neg\phi_1)$, $(\phi_1 \vee \phi_2)$ and $(\phi_1 \mathcal{U} \phi_2)$ are wffs, and
- there are no other wffs.

We use the abbreviations $\top \equiv_{df} (p \vee (\neg p))$ for some fixed $p \in AP$, $(\phi_1 \wedge \phi_2) \equiv_{df} (\neg((\neg\phi_1) \vee (\neg\phi_2)))$, $(\phi_1 \Rightarrow \phi_2) \equiv_{df} ((\neg\phi_1) \vee \phi_2)$, $(\Diamond\phi) \equiv_{df} (\top \mathcal{U} \phi)$, $(\Box\phi) \equiv_{df}$

250

$(\neg(\Diamond(\neg\phi)))$, $(\phi_1 \mathcal{U}_w \phi_2) \equiv_{df} ((\phi_1 \mathcal{U} \phi_2) \vee (\Box\phi_1))$, and the ordinary precedence rules to reduce the number of parentheses. ☐

Definition 2.2 A *truth set* v is a set of atomic propositions, $v \subseteq AP$. A *truth set sequence* σ is a finite or infinite sequence of truth sets, $\sigma = (v_1, v_2, \ldots)$. If σ is a truth set sequence, σ_n is the n:th element of σ, $\sigma^{(n)}$ is the truth set sequence obtained by leaving the first n elements out of σ, and $\sigma \cap A$ is the truth set sequence $(v_1 \cap A, v_2 \cap A, \ldots)$. ☐

Definition 2.3 A *Kripke-model* K is an ordered 4-tuple $K = (S, I, R, V)$, where S is the set of *states*, $I \subseteq S$ is the set of *initial states*, $R \subseteq S \times S$ is the *transition relation*, and $V : S \to P(AP)$ is a *valuation* expressing the atomic formulas true in a state. ($P(X)$ denotes the powerset of X.)

A *path* p in a Kripke-model K is a finite or infinite sequence $p = (s_1, s_2, \ldots)$ such that $s_1 \in I$, and each $(s_i, s_{i+1}) \in R$. A path p is a *fullpath* iff either p is infinite or there is no further state reachable from the last state of p, i.e. if s_n is the last state of p then for all s, $(s_n, s) \notin R$. The truth set sequence corresponding to a fullpath $p = (s_1, s_2, \ldots)$, denoted $V(p)$, is $(V(s_1), V(s_2), \ldots)$. ☐

Next we augment Kripke-models with fairness constraints expressed in terms of transition sets [LP85]. The notion of fairness used is the so-called strong fairness, meaning that if an event is possible infinitely often it has to be realised infinitely often, too.

Definition 2.4 A *fair Kripke-model* K_f is an ordered 5-tuple $K_f = (S, I, R, V, F)$, where (S, I, R, V) is a Kripke-model and F is a finite set of fairness sets $F = \{f_1, \ldots f_n\}$ such that $\bigcup_{f_i \in F} f_i = R$.

The paths and fullpaths of K_f are those of the Kripke-model (S, I, R, V). A fairness set $f_i \in F$ is *enabled* in a state $s \in S$ iff there is an s' such that $(s, s') \in f_i$. A fairness set f_i is *active* in a transition (s, s') iff $(s, s') \in f_i$. A fullpath p is *fair* iff every fairness set f_i that is enabled in infinitely many states of p is active in infinitely many transitions of p, too. ☐

Definition 2.5 An *LTL'-formula* ϕ is true in a truth set sequence $\sigma = (v_1, v_2, \ldots)$ i.e. $\sigma \models \phi$, according to the following rules:

- If $\phi \in AP$, then $\sigma \models \phi$ iff $\phi \in v_1$.
- $\sigma \models \neg\phi$ iff not $\sigma \models \phi$.
- $\sigma \models \phi_1 \vee \phi_2$ iff $\sigma \models \phi_1$ or $\sigma \models \phi_2$.
- $\sigma \models \phi_1 \mathcal{U} \phi_2$ iff $\exists : 0 \leq i < |\sigma|$, such that $\sigma^{(i)} \models \phi_2$ and for all $0 \leq j < i$, $\sigma^{(j)} \models \phi_1$.

If ϕ is true in every truth set sequence σ we say that ϕ is a theorem and write $\models \phi$. An *LTL'-formula* ϕ is true in a (fair) Kripke-model K, denoted $K \models \phi$, iff $V(p) \models \phi$ for every (fair) fullpath p of K. ☐

The operators have their conventional meanings. The reflexivity of $\mathcal{U}$ and the lack of a nexttime-operator allow us to overlook truth sets in a truth set sequence if they do not differ from their predecessor.

Definition 2.6 Let $\sigma = (v_1, v_2, \ldots)$ be a truth set sequence. The *reduced form of* σ, denoted by $red(\sigma)$ is constructed by removing from σ all v_i such that $v_i = v_{i-1}$. If $A \subseteq AP$ and $red(\sigma \cap A) = red(\sigma' \cap A)$ we say that σ and σ' are *stuttering equivalent modulo A* and write $\sigma \approx \sigma'$ (mod A). ☐

Proposition 2.7 Let $A \subseteq AP$ and σ, σ' be truth set sequences such that $\sigma \overset{u}{\approx} \sigma'$ (mod A) and ϕ a formula containing only atomic propositions in A. Then $\sigma \models \phi$ iff $\sigma' \models \phi$.

Proof: Induction on the structure of ϕ [Lam83]. □

Corollary 2.8 Let $A \subseteq AP$ and ϕ be a formula containing only atomic propositions in A. Let K and K' be (fair) Kripke-models such that for every (fair) fullpath p in K there is a (fair) fullpath p' in K' such that $V(p) \overset{u}{\approx} V(p')$ (mod A) and vice versa for all (fair) fullpaths p' in K'. Then $K \models \phi$ iff $K' \models \phi$. □

3 Modules

In this section we give the formal definitions of modules and the parallel composition operator. Each module M has a set of its own variables that cannot be modified by the environment of M. In addition to its own variables a module may refer to a set of external variables and base decisions about its behaviour on their values. As in [MP81] a module is modelled by a directed graph, the states of which correspond to the execution states and the transitions to atomic actions. Here this model is simplified by allowing only boolean variables, by labelling the states of the model with the values of module's own variables, by dropping the assignment labels and by allowing only transition conditions consisting of a single proposition or its negation.

Definition 3.1 Let $A \subseteq AP$. By $\neg A$ we denote the set $\{\neg a \mid a \in A\}$, and by $L(A)$ the set $L(A) = A \cup \neg A \cup \{\top\}$, where $\top$ is an element not in A or $\neg A$. If $a \in L(A)$ and $A' \subseteq A$, we write $A' \models a$ iff either $a = \top$ or $a \in A'$ or $a = \neg a'$ where $a' \in A$ and $a' \notin A'$. □

Definition 3.2 A *module* M is an ordered 6-tuple (A_o, A_e, S, I, R, V), where
- $A_o \subseteq AP$ is the set of atomic propositions owned by module M,
- $A_e \subseteq AP \setminus A_o$ is the set of external atomic propositions visible to M,
- S is the set of states,
- $I \subseteq S$ is the set of initial states,
- $V : S \rightarrow P(A_o)$ is the truth valuation of module's own propositions, and
- $R \subseteq S \times L(A_e) \times S$ is the set of transitions. Each transition is labelled by a transition label which can be either trivially true $\top$, an external atomic proposition or a negation of such. If $(s_1, l, s_2) \in R$, we write $s_1 \overset{l}{\rightarrow} s_2 \in R$. □

Definition 3.3 A *fair module* M_f is an ordered 7-tuple $M_f = (A_o, A_e, S, I, R, V, F)$, where (A_o, A_e, S, I, R, V) is a module and F is a finite set of fairness sets $F = \{f_1, \ldots f_n\}$ such that $\bigcup_{f_i \in F} f_i = R$. A *basic fair module* M_f is a fair module such that $F = \{R\}$. □

Modules may be combined using binary parallel composition $\parallel$ which can be generalised to deal with n modules in the standard fashion. Concurrency is represented by interleaving the atomic actions of the submodules. If a transition in one of the submodules is labelled by an atomic proposition owned by the other submodule, a corresponding transition in the combined module can be taken only if the proposition evaluates to true in the initial state of the transition.

Definition 3.4 Let $M_1 = (A_{o1}, A_{e1}, S_1, I_1, R_1, V_1)$ and $M_2 = (A_{o2}, \ldots, V_2)$ be modules such that $A_{o1} \cap A_{o2} = \emptyset$. The *parallel composition* of them, $M_1 \parallel M_2$, is the module (A_o, A_e, S, I, R, V) defined as follows:

- $A_o = A_{o1} \cup A_{o2}$
- $A_e = (A_{e1} \cup A_{e2}) \setminus A_o$
- $S = S_1 \times S_2$
- $I = I_1 \times I_2$
- $R = \{(s_1, t) \xrightarrow{l} (s_2, t) \mid s_1 \xrightarrow{l} s_2 \in R_1 \text{ and } l \in L(A_e)\} \cup$
  $\{(s_1, t) \xrightarrow{\tau} (s_2, t) \mid \exists l : s_1 \xrightarrow{l} s_2 \in R_1 \text{ and } l \in L(A_{o2}) \text{ and } V_2(t) \models l\} \cup$
  $\{(s, t_1) \xrightarrow{l} (s, t_2) \mid t_1 \xrightarrow{l} t_2 \in R_2 \text{ and } l \in L(A_e)\} \cup$
  $\{(s, t_1) \xrightarrow{\tau} (s, t_2) \mid \exists l : t_1 \xrightarrow{l} t_2 \in R_2 \text{ and } l \in L(A_{o1}) \text{ and } V_1(s) \models l\}$
- $V(s_1, s_2) = V_1(s_1) \cup V_2(s_2)$ $\qquad\square$

In the parallel composition of fair modules the fairness sets of the submodules are propagated to the resulting module. If a system is modelled by a parallel composition of basic fair modules, the definition guarantees that the fair fullpaths of the complete system are exactly those that are strongly fair with respect to each module.

Definition 3.5 Let $M_{f1} = (A_{o1}, A_{e1}, S_1, I_1, R_1, V_1, \{f_{11}, \ldots, f_{1n_1}\})$ and $M_{f2} = (A_{o2}, \ldots, V_2, \{f_{21}, \ldots, f_{2n_2}\})$ be fair modules. Then $M_{f1} \parallel M_{f2}$, is the fair module $(A_o, \ldots, V, \{f_1, \ldots, f_{n_1+n_2}\})$ where $(A_o, \ldots, V) = (A_{o1}, \ldots, V_1) \parallel (A_{o2}, \ldots, V_2)$ and for $i = 1, \ldots, n_1$
$f_i = \{(s_1, t) \xrightarrow{l} (s_2, t) \in R \mid s_1 \xrightarrow{l} s_2 \in f_{1i} \text{ and } l \in L(A_e)\} \cup$
$\quad \{(s_1, t) \xrightarrow{\tau} (s_2, t) \in R \mid \exists l : s_1 \xrightarrow{l} s_2 \in f_{1i} \text{ and } l \in L(A_{o2}) \text{ and } V_2(t) \models l\}$
and for $i = 1, \ldots, n_2$
$f_{i+n_1} = \{(s, t_1) \xrightarrow{l} (s, t_2) \in R \mid t_1 \xrightarrow{l} t_2 \in f_{2i} \text{ and } l \in L(A_e)\} \cup$
$\quad \{(s, t_1) \xrightarrow{\tau} (s, t_2) \in R \mid \exists l : t_1 \xrightarrow{l} t_2 \in f_{2i} \text{ and } l \in L(A_{o1}) \text{ and } V_1(s) \models l\}$ $\quad\square$

The availability of a transition in a module that does not have any nontrivial transition conditions cannot be influenced by its environment. Therefore, we treat such a module as corresponding to a complete system, and interpret formulas in the naturally induced Kripke-model.

Definition 3.6 Let $M = (A_o, A_e, S, I, R, V)$ be a module. M is *closed* iff $A_e = \emptyset$ and the *Kripke-model* $K(M)$ *corresponding to the closed module* M is defined as $K(M) = (S, I, R_K, V)$, where $(s_1, s_2) \in R_K$ iff $s_1 \xrightarrow{\tau} s_2 \in R$.

Let $M_f = (A_o, \ldots, V, \{f_1, \ldots, f_n\})$ be a fair module. M_f is closed iff $A_e = \emptyset$ and the fair Kripke-model $K(M_f)$ corresponding to M_f is defined as $K(M_f) = (S, I, R_K, V, \{f_{K1}, \ldots, f_{Kn}\})$, where R_K is as above and for all $1 \leq i \leq n$: $(s_1, s_2) \in f_{Ki}$ iff $s_1 \xrightarrow{\tau} s_2 \in f_i$.

A formula ϕ is true of a closed (fair) module M, $M \models \phi$, iff $K(M) \models \phi$. $\quad\square$

4 Compositional model checking

The basic method of compositional verification applied in this paper is that of [MP91]: when verifying that ϕ holds of $M_1 \parallel M_2$, find ϕ_1 and ϕ_2 such that ϕ_i holds of M_i in any environment and $\models \phi_1 \wedge \phi_2 \Rightarrow \phi$.

Definition 4.1 A formula ϕ is *modularly true* of M iff $M \parallel M' \models \phi$ for all modules M' such that $M \parallel M'$ is closed. If this is the case we write $M \stackrel{m}{\models} \phi$. $\quad\square$

The correctness of the verification method is asserted by the following result, which can be generalised to n processes.

Proposition 4.2 If $M_1 \models^m \phi_1$ and $M_2 \models^m \phi_2$, then $M_1 \| M_2 \models^m \phi_1 \wedge \phi_2$. $\qquad \square$

The aim now is to find a method for verifying that $M \models^m \phi$. This can be done by constructing a Kripke-model K on the basis of M so that $M \models^m \phi$ iff $K \models \phi$ and by applying the standard linear temporal logic model checking algorithm [LP85] to check whether $K \models \phi$ holds. A straighforward approach is to construct a single environment of M so that it exhibits all the possible behaviours that any environment of M can produce and to combine this environment with M.

Definition 4.3 Let $M = (A_o, \ldots, V)$ be a module. The *chaotic environment* of M, $ce(M)$ is the module $(A_e, \emptyset, P(A_e), P(A_e), P(A_e) \times P(A_e), V')$, where $V'(s) = s$. $\qquad \square$

Proposition 4.4 Let $M = (A_o, \ldots, V)$ be a module and ϕ a formula such that every atomic proposition occurring in ϕ is in $A_o \cup A_e$. Then $M \models^m \phi$ iff $M \| ce(M) \models \phi$.
Proof: If $M \models^m \phi$, then $M \| ce(M) \models \phi$ by the definition of $\models^m$. If $M \not\models^m \phi$, then there is an M' and a path p_1 in $K_1 = K(M \| M')$ such that $V_1(p_1) \not\models \phi$ holds. If $p_1 = ((s_1, t_1), (s_2, t_2), \ldots)$, then $p_2 = ((s_1, V_1(t_1) \cap A_e), (s_2, V_1(t_2) \cap A_e), \ldots)$ is a path in $K_2 = K(M \| ce(M))$. What is more, $V_1(p_1) \stackrel{\approx}{\approx} V_2(p_2)$ (mod $A_o \cup A_e$). By 2.7, $V_2(p_2) \not\models \phi$ which implies $M \| ce(M) \not\models \phi$. $\qquad \square$

Please note that the set A_e can always be extended so that every atomic proposition occurring in ϕ is in $A_o \cup A_e$. Therefore, without loss of generality we suppose that this is the case in the following.

Checking whether $M \models^m \phi$ can be done by checking that $M \| ce(M) \models \phi$. This is exactly the method proposed in [MP91], where a transition system equivalent to $K(M \| ce(M))$ is denoted by S_M. As $|M \| ce(M)| = |M| \cdot 2^{|A_e|}$, the model checking will take $O(|M| \cdot 2^{|A_e|} \cdot 2^{c \cdot |\phi|})$ time. This is sensible only if $|A_e| < log(|M'|)$, where M' is the actual environment in which M is to work.

In this naive approach we are, in fact, doing a lot of unnecessary work. What we are actually interested in is the validity of ϕ in all the fullpaths of all the systems consisting of M and an environment M'. The only influence of the external atomic propositions not occurring in ϕ is the availability of some transitions in some states and, consequently, the existence or nonexistence of some fullpaths. However, if a certain transition is labelled by an external atomic proposition, there is always both an environment in which the transition is disabled and an environment in which the transition is enabled. The first possibility is always present, anyway, since an infinite execution of the environment unfair to M might prevent M from taking a transition even if it were enabled. Therefore, we do not need to pay any attention to whether transition conditions not occurring in ϕ are true or false, and we may simply drop them.

Definition 4.5 Let $M = (A_o, \ldots, V)$ be a module and $A \subseteq A_o \cup A_e$. The *satisfiability graph* corresponding to M and A, $sg(M, A)$, is the Kripke-model (S_g, I_g, R_g, V_g) where
- $S_g = S \times P(A \setminus A_o)$
- $I_g = I \times P(A \setminus A_o)$
- $R_g = \{((s, A_1), (s, A_2)) \in S_g \times S_g\} \cup$
  $\{((s_1, A_1), (s_2, A_1)) \in S_g \times S_g \mid \exists l : s_1 \stackrel{l}{\to} s_2 \in R$ and $l \notin L(A)$ or $A_1 \models l\}$

- $V_g(s, A_1) = V(s) \cup A_1$ □

Proposition 4.6 Let $M = (A_o, \ldots, V)$ be a module, $A \subseteq A_o \cup A_e$ and ϕ a formula containing only atomic propositions from A. Then $M \overset{m}{\models} \phi$ iff $sg(M, A) \models \phi$.

Proof: By 4.4, $M \overset{m}{\models} \phi$ iff $M \parallel ce(M) \models \phi$. Here it is shown that $M \parallel ce(M) \models \phi$ iff $sg(M, A) \models \phi$.

Let us denote $M \parallel ce(M)$ by $M_c = (A_{co}, A_{ce}, S_c, I_c, R_c, V_c)$ and $sg(M, A)$ by $K_g = (S_g, I_g, R_g, V_g)$. The result is obtained by showing that given any fullpath p in $K(M_c)$ there is a fullpath p' in K_g such that $V_c(p) \overset{\approx}{\approx} V_g(p')$ (mod A) and vice versa, and by applying 2.8.

Assume that $K(M_c)$ has a fullpath p. From the definitions of $K()$ and M_c it is known that p is of the form $p = ((s_1, A_1), (s_1, A_2), \ldots)$, where each $s_i \in S$, $A_i \in P(A_e)$, and either $s_i = s_{i+1}$ or $A_i = A_{i+1}$ and there is an l such that $s_i \overset{l}{\to} s_{i+1} \in R$ and $A_i \models l$. If $s_i = s_{i+1}$, it is clear that $((s_i, A_i \cap A), (s_{i+1}, A_{i+1} \cap A)) \in R_g$. If $s_i \neq s_{i+1}$, then $A_i = A_{i+1}$ and either $l \notin L(A)$ or $l \in L(A)$ and $A_i \cap A \models l$. In both cases $((s_i, A_i \cap A), (s_{i+1}, A_{i+1} \cap A)) \in R_g$ follows. As $(s_1, A_1 \cap A) \in I_g$, $p' = ((s_1, A_1 \cap A), (s_2, A_2 \cap A), \ldots)$ is a fullpath in K_g. What is more, $V_c(p) \overset{\approx}{\approx} V_g(p')$ (mod A) since $V_c((s_i, A_i)) \cap A = (V(s_i) \cup A_i) \cap A = V_g((s_i, A_i \cap A)) \cap A$.

Assume now that K_g has a fullpath p. From the definition of K_g it is known that $p = ((s_1, A_1), (s_2, A_2), \ldots)$ where for each $((s_i, A_i), (s_{i+1}, A_{i+1}))$ either $s_i = s_{i+1}$ or $A_i = A_{i+1}$ and there is an l such that $s_i \overset{l}{\to} s_{i+1} \in R$ and either $A_i \models l$ or $l \notin L(A)$. If $s_i = s_{i+1}$, it is clear that $(s_i, A_i) \overset{\top}{\to} (s_{i+1}, A_{i+1}) \in R_c$. If $A_i = A_{i+1}$ and $A_i \models l$, $(s_i, A_i) \overset{\top}{\to} (s_{i+1}, A_{i+1}) \in R_c$, again. If $A_i = A_{i+1}$ and $l \notin L(A)$ and l is of the form $\neg l_1$, $l_1 \notin A_i$ which implies that $A_i \models l$. Consequently, $(s_i, A_i) \overset{\top}{\to} (s_{i+1}, A_{i+1}) \in R_c$. Finally, if $A_i = A_{i+1}$ and $l \notin L(A)$ and l is not of the form $\neg l_1$, R_c has the transitions $(s_i, A_i) \overset{\top}{\to} (s_i, A_i \cup \{l\}) \overset{\top}{\to} (s_{i+1}, A_{i+1} \cup \{l\}) \overset{\top}{\to} (s_{i+1}, A_{i+1})$. Therefore, for each transition of p in K_g we can construct a sequence of transitions in R_c so that they contain the same initial and final states. The required path p' in $K(M_c)$ is constructed by joining these sequences together. By the structure of p', $V_g(p) \overset{\approx}{\approx} V_c(p')$ (mod A) as well. □

By proposition 4.6 we can check whether $M \overset{m}{\models} \phi$ by taking A as the set containing only the atomic propositions in ϕ and by checking whether $sg(M, A) \models \phi$. Noticing that $|sg(M, A)| = |M| \cdot 2^{|A \setminus A_o|}$ and that $|A \setminus A_o|$ is limited by $|\phi|$, we acquire an upper limit $|M| \cdot 2^{|\phi|}$ to the size of the satisfiability graph. Since the satisfiability graph can be constructed in a time linear to its size, the model checking takes $O(|M| \cdot 2^{|\phi|} \cdot 2^{c \cdot |\phi|})$, i.e. $O(|M| \cdot 2^{c \cdot |\phi|})$ time. The total time requirement of the method consists of three parts: verifying that $M_1 \overset{m}{\models} \phi_1$, which takes $O(|M_1| \cdot 2^{c \cdot |\phi_1|})$ time, verifying that $M_2 \overset{m}{\models} \phi_2$, which takes $O(|M_2| \cdot 2^{c \cdot |\phi_2|})$ time, and verifying that $\models \phi_1 \wedge \phi_2 \Rightarrow \phi$, which takes $O(2^{c \cdot (|\phi_1| + |\phi_2| + |\phi|)})$ time [LPZ85]. Assuming $|\phi_1| \approx |\phi_2|$, the total time needed is thus $O((|M_1| + |M_2| + 2^{c \cdot |\phi|}) \cdot 2^{c \cdot |\phi_1|})$. Furthermore, if $|\phi| \approx |\phi_1|$, this is $O((|M_1| + |M_2|) \cdot 2^{c \cdot |\phi|})$.

This should be contrasted with the time requirement $O(|M_1| \cdot |M_2| \cdot 2^{c \cdot |\phi|})$ of the simple approach of just constructing the whole state space of the system and then running the model checker on it. If M_1 and M_2 are large and the required lemmas ϕ_1 and ϕ_2 relatively short, the compositional method presented here can therefore yield substantial savings. As an additional note, the restriction that transitions are labelled by single propositions or their negations can be dropped in favour of arbitrary formulas in the disjunctive normal form without affecting the time requirement.

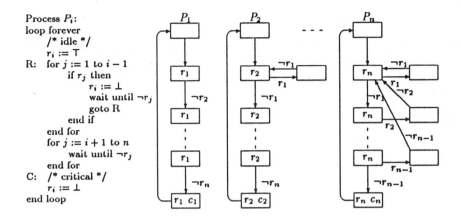

```
Process P_i:
loop forever
    /* idle */
    r_i := T
R:  for j := 1 to i − 1
        if r_j then
            r_i := ⊥
            wait until ¬r_j
            goto R
        end if
    end for
    for j := i + 1 to n
        wait until ¬r_j
    end for
C:  /* critical */
    r_i := ⊥
end loop
```

Figure 1: Mutual exclusion protocol

Although no systematic way of finding suitable lemmas is developed in this paper, the issue is naturally very important for real-world applications. Ideally, when creating a concurrent system the designer sets some requirements to each module so that the requirements to the complete system are met if the requirements to the individual modules are met. These requirements naturally form a good basis for the required lemmas. The applications of the method are best illustrated by an example.

Example 4.7 Figure 1 contains a textual description of a mutual exclusion protocol and the corresponding module graphs. Each state in the picture is labelled by the atomic propositions true in that state. The only propositions shown are r_i, which has the meaning *process i requests access to the critical section*, and c_i meaning *process i is in the critical section*. For each module P_i, $A_{oi} = \{r_i, c_i\}$ and $A_{ei} = \{r_j \mid 1 \leq j \leq n, j \neq i\}$. An obvious requirement to the system is that two processes are never together in the critical section, i.e. that $\bigwedge_{i \neq j} \Box(\neg c_j \vee \neg c_i)$.

If we analyse a system consisting of n such processes, the number of global states is $O(n^n)$. This means that e.g. for $n = 32$ the number of global states would be in the range 2^{160}, which rules out straightforward model checking.

Let us denote by ϕ the formula $\Box(\neg c_j \vee \neg c_i)$ for some fixed i and j. If we can show that ϕ holds for all $i \neq j$, the required result follows. As lemma ϕ_1 we may take the formula $\neg r_i \wedge \Box(c_i \Rightarrow r_i) \wedge \Box(\neg r_i \Rightarrow (\neg c_i)\mathcal{U}_w(r_i \wedge \neg r_j))$ and as lemma ϕ_2 the same formula with i:s and j:s reversed. It is easy to check that $\models \phi_1 \wedge \phi_2 \Rightarrow \phi$.

If we tried to verify that $P_i \models^m \phi_1$ using the naive method of 4.4, the size of the resulting Kripke-model would have a minimum of 2^{36} states. Even this would very likely be infeasible.

When verifying that $P_i \models^m \phi_1$ using the satisfiability graph construction, the only external proposition that we need to keep track of is r_j, and consequently the satisfiability graph has a maximum of 128 states. The same applies to verifying that $P_j \models^m \phi_2$. The advantages of the method are clear in this case. □

5 Fair concurrency

Despite the advantages of the verification method presented in the previous section, it still suffers from an important drawback: when two modules are combined in parallel, the resulting system in not required to be fair with respect to both modules. One counter-intuitive result of this is that even if M is a closed module, $M \models \phi$ does not necessarily imply $M\overset{m}{\models}\phi$. In this section we present a remedy to these problems in the form of a variant of the satisfiability graph construction which can takes fairness requirements into consideration.

Definition 5.1 A formula ϕ is *modularly true* of a fair module M_f, i.e. $M_f\overset{fm}{\models}\phi$, iff $M_f \parallel M_f' \models \phi$ for all fair modules M_f' such that $M_f \parallel M_f'$ is closed. □

The following result states that for a closed fair module it does not matter whether M is considered in or without an environment, i.e. that the fairness requirements remove the problem stated above.

Proposition 5.2 If M_f is a closed fair module, then $M_f\overset{fm}{\models}\phi$ iff $M_f \models \phi$. □

Definition 5.3 Let $M_f = (A_o, \ldots, F)$ be a fair module. The *fair chaotic environment* of M_f, $ce(M_f)$ is the fair module $(A_o', \ldots, V', \{P(A_e) \times P(A_e)\})$, where $A_o', \ldots, V'$ are as in 4.3. □

Proposition 5.4 Let $M_f = (A_o, \ldots, F)$ be a fair module and ϕ a formula such that every atomic proposition occurring in ϕ is in $A_o \cup A_e$. Then $M_f\overset{fm}{\models}\phi$ iff $M_f \parallel ce(M_f) \models \phi$.

Proof: If $M_f\overset{fm}{\models}\phi$, then $M_f \parallel ce(M_f) \models \phi$ by the definition of $\overset{fm}{\models}$. If $M_f\overset{fm}{\not\models}\phi$, then there is an M_f' and a fair path p_1 in $K_1 = K(M_f \parallel M_f')$ such that $V_1(p_1) \not\models \phi$ holds. As in 4.4 there is a path p_2 in $K_2 = K(M_f \parallel ce(M_f))$ such that $V_1(p_1)\overset{\cdot\cdot}{\approx}V_2(p_2)$ (mod $A_o \cup A_e$). As p_1 is fair with respect to every fairness set $f \in F$, p_2 is, by its structure, also fair with respect to all the corresponding fairness sets of K_2. However, p_2 is not necessarily fair with respect to the one fairness set of K_2 corresponding to the single fairness set of $ce(M_f)$. This can be rectified by interleaving an infinite number of non-state-changing transitions of $ce(M_f)$ into p_2 without affecting $V_1(p_1)\overset{\cdot\cdot}{\approx}V_2(p_2)$ (mod $A_o \cup A_e$). □

In the construction of the satisfiability graph we have now the additional concern of discerning fair paths from unfair ones. What essentially happens when we move from the naive approach with the chaotic environment to the satisfiability graph is grouping together states (s, A') where the A':s differ only with respect to propositions not in A. This grouping, however, may introduce new dependencies between the enabled fairness sets, and may therefore have unwanted effects on which paths are regarded fair. The way to do away with these dependencies in order to reflect the original structure faithfully is to make as many copies of a state (s, A') as there are possible combinations of enabled fairness sets in the module, i.e. 2 copies in the case of a basic fair module, and $2^{|F|}$ copies in the general case. Each copy (s, A', F'), where $F' \subseteq F$, represents the possibility that in the chaotic environment it is possible to reach a state (s, A'') such that $A'' \cap A = A'$ and all the enabled fairness sets are in F'.

Definition 5.5 Let $M_f = (A_o, \ldots, F)$ be a fair module, $A \subseteq A_o \cup A_e$, $A_1 \subseteq A_e \cap A$, $A_1' \subseteq A_e$, $s \in S$ and $F_1 \subseteq F$. We say that (s, A_1') is an F_1-*enabled A-extension of* (s, A_1) iff $A_1' \cap A = A_1$ and for every $f \in F$ the following holds: if there are l and s' such that $s \xrightarrow{} s' \in f$ and $A_1' \models l$, then $f \in F_1$. □

Definition 5.6 Let $M_f = (A_o, \ldots, F)$ be a fair module, where $F = \{f_1, \ldots, f_n\}$, and $A \subseteq A_o \cup A_e$. The *fair satisfiability graph* corresponding to M_f and A, $sg(M_f, A)$ is the fair Kripke-model $(S_g, I_g, R_g, V_g, F_g)$ defined as follows:

- $S_g = \{(s, A_1, F_1) \in S \times P(A \setminus A_o) \times P(F) \mid$
  $\exists A_1' : (s, A_1')$ is an F_1-enabled A-extension of $(s, A_1)\}$
- $I_g = (I \times P(A \setminus A_o) \times P(F)) \cap S_g$
- $R_g = \bigcup_{i=1}^{n+1} f_{gi}$, where for all $1 \le i \le n$
  $f_{gi} = \{((s_1, A_1, F_1), (s_2, A_2, F_2)) \in S_g \times S_g \mid f_i \in F_1$ and $A_1 = A_2$ and
  $\exists A_1' : \exists l : A_1' \models l$ and $s_1 \xrightarrow{} s_2 \in f_i$ and
  (s_1, A_1') is an F_1-enabled A-extension of (s_1, A_1) and
  (s_2, A_1') is an F_2-enabled A-extension of $(s_2, A_2)\}$
  $f_{g\,n+1} = \{((s, A_1, F_1), (s, A_2, F_2)) \in S_g \times S_g\}$
- $V_g(s, A_1, F_1) = V(s) \cup A_1$
- $F_g = \{f_{g1}, \ldots, f_{gn}, f_{g\,n+1}\}$ □

Proposition 5.7 Let $M_f = (A_o, \ldots, F)$ be a fair module, where $F = \{f_1, \ldots, f_n\}$, and $A \subseteq A_o \cup A_e$. If ϕ is a formula containing only atomic propositions from A, then $M_f \overset{\underset{lm}{}}{\models} \phi$ iff $sg(M_f, A) \models \phi$.

Proof: In the proof we use following notation: $M_f \parallel ce(M_f)$ is denoted by $M_c = (A_{co}, A_{ce}, S_c, I_c, R_c, V_c, F_c)$, where $F_c = \{f_{c1}, \ldots, f_{cn+1}\}$, and $sg(M_f, A)$ by $K_g = (S_g, I_g, R_g, V_g, F_g)$, where $F_g = \{f_{g1}, \ldots, f_{g\,n+1}\}$. The indexing of the fairness sets F_c and F_g is supposed to correspond to the indexing of the original fairness set F. If $(s_i, A_i) \in S_c$, then $en(s_i, A_i) = \{f_j \in F \mid f_{cj}$ is enabled in $(s_i, A_i)\}$.

The following facts are direct consequences of the definitions:

1. If $((s_i, A_i), (s_{i+1}, A_{i+1})) \in f_{cj}$, then
   $((s_i, A_i \cap A, en(s_i, A_i)), (s_{i+1}, A_{i+1} \cap A, en(s_{i+1}, A_{i+1}))) \in f_{gj}$.

2. If $1 \le j \le n$, then f_{gj} is enabled in $(s_i, A_i, F_i) \in S_g$ only if $f_j \in F_i$. Consequently, if f_{gj} is enabled in $(s_i, A_i \cap A, en(s_i, A_i))$ then f_{cj} is enabled in (s_i, A_i).

3. If $((s_i, A_i, F_i), (s_{i+1}, A_{i+1}, F_{i+1})) \in f_{gj}$, then there exist A_i'' and A_{i+1}' such that $((s_i, A_i''), (s_{i+1}, A_{i+1}')) \in f_{cj}$, $A_i'' \cap A = A_i$, $A_{i+1}' \cap A = A_{i+1}$, and for all $1 \le k \le n+1$: if $f_k \in en(s_i, A_i'')$ then f_{ck} is enabled in (s_i, A_i, F_i), and if $f_k \in en(s_{i+1}, A_{i+1}')$ then f_{ck} is enabled in $(s_{i+1}, A_{i+1}, F_{i+1})$.

As in 4.6, the proof proceeds by showing that if $K(M_c)$ has a fair fullpath p then K_g has a fair fullpath p' such that $V_c(p) \overset{\approx}{} V_g(p')$ (mod A) and vice versa.

Assume that $p = ((s_1, A_1), (s_2, A_2), \ldots)$ is a fair fullpath of $K(M_c)$. The required p' can be obtained as $p' = ((s_1, A_1 \cap A, en(s_1, A_1)), (s_2, A_2 \cap A, en(s_2, A_2)), \ldots)$. By 1 above and by the definition of R_g, p' is a fullpath. As p is fair, 1 and 2 imply that p' is fair as well. $V_c(p) \overset{\approx}{} V_g(p')$ (mod A) is established as in 4.6.

Assume that $p = ((s_1, A_1, F_1), (s_2, A_2, F_2), \ldots)$ is a fair fullpath of K_g. The required p' can be obtained as $p' = ((s_1, A_1''), (s_2, A_2'), (s_2, A_2''), (s_3, A_3'), \ldots)$, where A_i' and A_i'' are as in 3 above. Note that for every transition in p there are two transitions in p'. By 3 above, p' is a fullpath. As p is fair, 3 implies that p' is fair as well. Finally, the definitions of A_i' and A_i'' used in constructing p' guarantee that $V_g(p) \overset{\approx}{} V_c(p')$ (mod A). □

The size of the satisfiability graph is $|M| \cdot 2^{|F|} \cdot 2^{|A \setminus A_o|}$. In constructing the satisfiability graph the essential step is deciding whether $s_1 \overset{!}{\rightarrow} s_2 \in f_i$ implies $((s_1, A_1, F_1), (S_2, A_2, F_2)) \in f_{gi}$. This can be done by checking whether formula

$$ l \wedge \bigwedge_{f \in F \setminus F_1 \ (s_1, a, s_1') \in f} \bigwedge \neg a \wedge \bigwedge_{f \in F \setminus F_2 \ (s_2, a, s_2') \in f} \bigwedge \neg a $$

is satisfiable, which can be done in linear time. Therefore, the satisfiability graph can be constructed in a time linear to its size. As checking the truth of ϕ over $sg(M_f, A)$ takes $O(|F| \cdot |sg(M_f, A)| \cdot 2^{c \cdot |\phi|})$ time, checking modular truth of ϕ in a fair module M_f requires $O(|F| \cdot |M_f| \cdot 2^{|F|} \cdot 2^{|\phi|} \cdot 2^{c \cdot |\phi|})$, i.e. $O(|M_f| \cdot 2^{c \cdot |F|} \cdot 2^{c \cdot |\phi|})$ time. This is less than that of the naive approach as long as $|F| < |AP_e \setminus A|$. Although the time requirement is exponential in $|F|$, this is unlikely to cause problems in practice as $|F|$ is typically very low.

Fairness between concurrent processes in a system is a special case of the more general fairness notion treated above. In order to model it only basic fair modules are needed. These have the property that all the transitions of a module form a single fairness set, i.e. that $|F| = 1$. In this case the time requirement reduces to $O(|M_f| \cdot 2^{c \cdot |\phi|})$, which means that we can answer the question about the truth of ϕ over module M in all strongly fair environments in the same time as over M in all environments.

As the last issue we discuss briefly the existence of the lemmas ϕ_1 and ϕ_2, and draw attention to a particular case in which we can be sure of their existence. Intuitively the following result shows that if every state of a module can be uniquely characterised by the atomic propositions true in that state, the lemmas always exist. This should come as no suprise, as the characterisability means that the structure of the modules can be axiomatised.

Proposition 5.8 Let M_1, M_2 be (fair) modules such that both V_1 and V_2 are injective, i.e. that for all $s, s' \in S_1$: $V_1(s) = V_1(s')$ implies $s = s'$ and alike for V_2.

If $M_1 \| M_2 \models \phi$, there exist formulas ϕ_1 and ϕ_2 such that $M_1 \overset{fm}{\models} \phi_1$, $M_2 \overset{fm}{\models} \phi_2$ and $\models \phi_1 \wedge \phi_2 \Rightarrow \phi$.

Proof: Thanks to the characterisability of M_i we can construct formulas $ch(M_i)$ so that they completely describe the behaviour of M_i.

$$ ch(s) = \bigwedge_{a \in V(s)} a \wedge \bigwedge_{a \in A_o \setminus V(s)} \neg a \qquad\qquad tr(s) = ch(s) \mathcal{U}_w(\bigvee_{(s,l,s') \in R} (ch(s') \wedge l)) $$

$$ ch(R) = \Box \bigwedge_{s \in S} (ch(s) \Rightarrow tr(s)) $$

$$ ch(f_i) = (\Box \Diamond \bigvee_{(s,l,s') \in f_i} (ch(s) \wedge l)) \Rightarrow (\Box \Diamond \bigvee_{(s,l,s') \in f_i} (ch(s) \mathcal{U} ch(s'))) \qquad ch(F) = \bigwedge_{f_i \in F} ch(f_i) $$

$$ ch(M) = \Box \bigvee_{s \in S} ch(s) \wedge \bigvee_{s \in I} ch(s) \wedge ch(R) \wedge ch(F) $$

$$ int(M, M') = \bigwedge_{a \in L(A_o)} \bigwedge_{a' \in L(A_o')} a \wedge a' \Rightarrow ((a \wedge a') \mathcal{U}_w((\neg a \wedge a') \vee (a \wedge \neg a'))) $$

(The formula $int(M, M')$ decrees that two propositions owned by different modules cannot change their truth-value at the same time.) Now $M_1 \overset{fm}{\models} ch(M_1) \wedge int(M_1, M_2)$ and alike for M_2. It remains to show that if $M_1 \| M_2 \overset{fm}{\models} \phi$ then $\models ch(M_1) \wedge int(M_1, M_2) \wedge ch(M_2) \Rightarrow \phi$. This can be done by supposing that, on the contrary, there were a Kripke-model K and a path p falsifying the implication, and by constructing a path p' in $(M_1 \parallel M_2) \parallel ce(M_1 \parallel M_2)$ falsifying ϕ as well, and thus creating a contradiction. □

It is clear that the lemmas constructed in the proof are of purely theoretical value due to their length. However, knowing that the method is complete in the sense that any property can be verified by it naturally adds confidence to it.

6 Discussion

In this paper we have presented algorithms deciding the truth of a nexttime-less linear temporal logic formula ϕ over a distributed-variable module M in all environments and in all fair environments. An interesting result obtained is that the time-complexity of checking whether a property holds of a module in all environments is essentially no higher than that of checking whether it holds without any environment. The method of modular verification suggested here seems to be very promising. However, what is still needed for a fully-fledged system is a methodology for creating the required lemmas.

References

[Bar86] Barringer, H.: Using Temporal Logic in the Compositional Specification of Concurrent Systems, in Galton, A. (ed.): *Temporal Logics and Their Applications*, Academic Press, 1987, pp. 59-90

[BKP84] Barringer, H. & Kuiper, R. & Pnueli, A.: Now You May Compose Temporal Logic Specification, in *Conference Record of the Sixteenth Annual ACM Symposium on Theory of Computing*, 1984, pp. 51-63

[BE91] Best, E. & Esparza, J.: *Model Checking of Persistent Petri Nets*, Hildesheimer Informatikberichte 11/91, Universität Hildesheim, Institut für Informatik, 1991, also presented in Computer Science Logic '91

[CLM89] Clarke, E. M. & Long, D. E. & McMillan, K. L.: Compositional Model Checking, in *Proceedings of the Fourth IEEE Symposium on Logic in Computer Science*, 1989, pp. 353-362

[GL91] Grümberg, O. & Long, D. E.: Model Checking and Modular Verification, in Baeten, J. C. M. & Groote, J. F. (eds.): *Proceedings of CONCUR'91, the 2nd International Conference on Concurrency Theory*, LNCS, vol. 527, Springer-Verlag, 1991, pp. 250-265

[Jos89] Josko, B.: Verifying the Correctness of AADL-modules Using Model Checking, in de Bakker, J.W. & de Roever, W.-P. & Rozenberg, G. (eds.): *Proceedings of the REX Workshop on Stepwise Refinement of Distributed Systems, Models, Formalisms, Correctness*, LNCS, vol. 430, Springer-Verlag, 1989, pp. 386-400

[Lam83] Lamport, L.: What Good is Temporal Logic?, in *Proceedings of the IFIP 9th World Computer Congress*, 1983, pp. 657-668

[LP85] Lichtenstein. O, & Pnueli, A.: Checking That Finite State Concurrent Programs Satisfy Their Linear Specification, in *Conference Record of the Twelfth Annual ACM Symposium on Principles of Programming Languages*, 1985, pp. 97-107

[LPZ85] Lichtenstein. O, & Pnueli, A. & Zuck, L.: The Glory of The Past, in Parikh, R. (ed.): *Logics of Programs, Proceedings*, LNCS, vol. 193, Springer-Verlag, 1985, pp. 196-218

[MP81] Manna, Z. & Pnueli. A.: Verification of Concurrent Programs: The Temporal Framework, in Boyer, R. S. & Moore, J. S. (eds.): *The Correctness Problem in Computer Science*, Academic Press, 1981, pp. 215-273

[MP91] Manna, Z. & Pnueli. A.: *The Temporal Logic of Reactive and Concurrent Systems, vol. 1, Specification*, Springer-Verlag, 1991

[Pnu85] Pnueli, A.: In Transition from Global to Modular Temporal Reasoning About Programs, in Apt, K. R. (ed.): *Logics and Models of Concurrent Systems*, NATO ASI Series, vol. F13, Springer-Verlag, 1985, pp. 123-146

Property preserving simulations*

S. Bensalem A. Bouajjani C. Loiseaux J. Sifakis

IMAG-LGI, BP 53X, F-38041 Grenoble
e-mail: {bensalem,bouajjan,loiseaux,sifakis}@imag.imag.fr

Abstract. We study property preserving transformations for reactive systems. A key idea is the use of $<\varphi, \psi>$-simulations which are simulations parameterized by a Galois connection (φ, ψ), relating the lattices of properties of two systems.

We propose and study a notion of preservation of properties expressed by formulas of a logic, by a function φ mapping sets of states of a system S into sets of states of a system S'. Roughly speaking, φ preserves f if the satisfaction of f at some state of S implies that f is satisfied by any state in the image of this state by φ.

The main results concern the preservation of properties expressed in sublanguages of the branching time μ-calculus when two systems S and S' are related via $<\varphi, \psi>$-simulations. They can be used in particular to verify a property for a system by proving this property on a simpler system which is an abstraction of it.

1 Introduction

A central idea in a rigorous program development methodology is that a designer starting from a formal requirements specification obtains an implementation by performing successive semantics preserving transformations. In this process, semantics can be expressed by a set of properties specified as formulas of an appropriate program logic; the transformations applied should preserve these properties.

The investigation of property preserving implementations or abstractions of reactive systems has been the object of intensive research during the last years. However, the existing theoretical results are too fragmented. They strongly depend on the choice of the specification formalism and the underlying semantics.

Some results [Kur89,AL88,LT88] adopt a linear time semantics framework where specifications are the conjunction of a safety and a liveness property. The safety part is usually expressed as a transition relation (automaton) while the liveness constraint is characterized either by an acceptance condition on the states or by a formula. The notions of implementation proposed are based on the use of structure or language homomorphisms preserving correctness.

For process algebras the problem of the adequacy of a logic used to express process properties, has been studied [HM85,GS86b,GS86a,NV90]. Adequacy means compatibility of the behavioral equivalence of the process algebra with the semantics of the logic. That is, equivalent processes satisfy the same formulas and consequently cannot be distinguished in the logic. Clearly, adequacy corresponds to a particular case of property preservation; in general, the

* This work was partially supported by ESPRIT Basic Research Action "SPEC"

property preserving relations need not to be equivalences.

This paper is based on ideas originally presented in [Sif82a,Sif83]. We propose a notion of preservation of a property f by an arbitrary function φ from the powerset of the states of a program S_1 to the powerset of the states of a program S_2. The function φ is said to preserve f if for any state of S_1 which satisfies f, all the states of S_2 in its image satisfy f too. If the converse is also true, then we say that φ strongly preserves f. Some general results are provided allowing to prove that a given function preserves (or strongly preserves) the meaning of the formulas of a language by induction on its structure.

These results are applied to show both preservation and strong preservation of sublanguages of the branching time μ-calculus for functions that represent some general form of homomorphism between the transition structures of the considered programs. Homomorphisms or simulation relations between transition structures are at the base of the definitions of most of the relations used to compare behaviors [Bra78,KM79,Mil71]. Their use allows the application of algebraic techniques and reduces the study of a relation on programs to the study of relations on elements of their structure.

The simulation relations used are parameterized by a pair of functions (φ, ψ) which defines a Galois connection between powersets of the state sets of the programs considered. The results presented concern preservation of properties expressed in fragments of the μ-calculus when programs are related via $<\varphi, \psi>$-simulations. The functions φ and ψ determine precisely state correspondences that preserve the satisfaction of formulas.

These results generalize some results in [CGL92] where this problem is studied in the particular case where the restriction of the property preserving function φ on the states is an abstraction. The idea of using simulations parameterized by Galois connections is quite natural as connections have been proven to be very useful for studying correspondences between partially ordered structures [Ore44], in our case the lattices of state properties of two programs. In the domain of verification and abstract interpretation of programs they have been extensively used by Patrick and Rhadia Cousot (see for example [CC79,CC90]). Our results specialize their approach as far as $<\varphi, \psi>$-simulations induce a particular case of abstract interpretations. These interpretations under some additional conditions preserve the validity of properties on abstractions.

The paper is organized as follows. Section 2 presents the notion of property preservation and general results allowing to prove that a function preserves the validity of formulas of a given language. In section 3, the definition and properties of $<\varphi, \psi>$-simulations are given. Section 4 gives results about the preservation of sublanguages of the μ-calculus. Section 5 shows how the results can be applied to obtain abstractions or implementations of a given program.

2 General results on property preservation

A program is considered to be a transition system defined as follows:

Definition 1. A *transition system* is a tuple $S = (Q, R)$, where Q is a set of states and R is a transition relation on Q ($R \subseteq Q \times Q$).

We adopt the following conventions and notations:

- We identify a unary predicate on Q with its characteristic set as the lattice of unary predicates is isomorphic to 2^Q. Thus, for a unary predicate P and a state $q \in Q$, the notations $P(q) = true$, $P(q)$ and $q \in P$ are equivalent.

- Given two sets Q_1 and Q_2, we represent by $[Q_1 \rightarrow Q_2]$ (resp. $[Q_1 \xrightarrow{m} Q_2]$) the set of (resp. monotonic) functions from Q_1 to Q_2.
- We denote by Id the *identity* function on 2^Q. For a set $\Pi \subseteq Q$, we denote by Id_Π the restriction of Id to 2^Π.

We suppose that program properties are expressed by formulas of a logical language $\mathcal{F}(\mathcal{P})$ where $\mathcal{P} = \{P_1, P_2, ...\}$ is a set of propositional variables. For a given system $S = (Q, R)$ and an *interpretation function* $\mathcal{I} \in [\mathcal{P} \rightarrow 2^Q]$, the semantics of $\mathcal{F}(\mathcal{P})$ is given by means of a function $|\ |_{s,\mathcal{I}} \in [\mathcal{F}(\mathcal{P}) \rightarrow 2^Q]$. This function is such that $\forall P \in \mathcal{P}$, $|P|_{s,\mathcal{I}} = \mathcal{I}(P)$. Furthermore, it associates with a formula its characteristic set i.e., the set of states satisfying it.

To simplify notations, either one or both of the subscripts S and $\mathcal{I}$ in $|f|_{s,\mathcal{I}}$ will be omitted whenever their values can be determined by the context.

Definition 2. Let $f \in \mathcal{F}(\mathcal{P})$ be a formula, $S_1 = (Q_1, R_1)$ and $S_2 = (Q_2, R_2)$ be two transition systems, Π be a subset of Q_1 $\mathcal{I} \in [\mathcal{P} \rightarrow 2^{Q_1}]$ an interpretation function and $\varphi \in [2^{Q_1} \rightarrow 2^{Q_2}]$. We say that φ *preserves* (resp. *strongly preserves*) f for $\mathcal{I}$ on Π if and only if for any $q \in \Pi$,

$$q \in |f|_{S_1, \mathcal{I}} \text{ implies (resp. iff) } \varphi(\{q\}) \subseteq |f|_{S_2, \varphi \circ \mathcal{I}}.$$

If $\Pi = Q_1$, we omit to precize that the preservation is on Π.

Definition 3. Let $f \in \mathcal{F}(\mathcal{P})$ be a formula, $S_1 = (Q_1, R_1)$ and $S_2 = (Q_2, R_2)$ be two transition systems, $\mathcal{I} \in [\mathcal{P} \rightarrow 2^{Q_1}]$ be an interpretation function and $\varphi \in [2^{Q_1} \rightarrow 2^{Q_2}]$.

We say that φ *semi-commutes* (resp. *commutes*) with f for $\mathcal{I}$ if and only if $\varphi(|f|_{S_1, \mathcal{I}}) \subseteq |f|_{S_2, \varphi \circ \mathcal{I}}$ (resp. $\varphi(|f|_{S_1, \mathcal{I}}) = |f|_{S_2, \varphi \circ \mathcal{I}}$).

In these definitions, the function φ establishes a correspondence between properties of S_1 and properties of S_2. Preservation means that the function φ is compatible with the satisfaction relation. The notion of semi-commutativity is used in the sequel to prove preservation. The following lemma relates preservation and commutativity.

Lemma 4. *Let f be a formula of $\mathcal{F}(\mathcal{P})$, $\varphi \in [2^{Q_1} \xrightarrow{m} 2^{Q_2}]$ a monotonic function and $\mathcal{I} \in [\mathcal{P} \rightarrow 2^{Q_1}]$.*

1. *If φ semi-commutes with f for $\mathcal{I}$ then φ preserves f for $\mathcal{I}$.*
2. *If φ commutes with f for $\mathcal{I}$, φ is one-to-one and φ^{-1} is monotonic then φ strongly preserves f for $\mathcal{I}$.*

Proof. The first point is immediate, from $q \in |f|_{\mathcal{I}}$, we obtain by monotonicity of φ and its semi-commutativity with f, $\varphi(\{q\}) \subseteq \varphi(|f|_{\mathcal{I}}) \subseteq |f|_{\varphi \circ \mathcal{I}}$.

For the second point it remains to prove that for any $q \in Q_1$, $\varphi(\{q\}) \subseteq |f|_{\varphi \circ \mathcal{I}}$ implies $q \in |f|_{\mathcal{I}}$. $\varphi(\{q\}) \subseteq |f|_{\varphi \circ \mathcal{I}} = \varphi(|f|_{\mathcal{I}})$ by commutativity of φ with f. From $\varphi(\{q\}) \subseteq \varphi(|f|_{\mathcal{I}})$ we deduce that $q \in |f|_{\mathcal{I}}$ as φ^{-1} is monotonic and φ is one-to-one.

Theorem 5. *Let $S_1 = (Q_1, R_1)$ and $S_2 = (Q_2, R_2)$ be two transition systems. For any set $\Pi \subseteq Q_1$ and for any monotonic functions $\varphi \in [2^{Q_1} \xrightarrow{m} 2^{Q_2}]$ and $\psi \in [2^{Q_2} \xrightarrow{m} 2^{Q_1}]$ such that $\psi \circ \varphi \circ \psi = \psi$ and $Id_\Pi \subseteq \psi \circ \varphi$, if φ semi-commutes with f for $\mathcal{I} \in [\mathcal{P} \rightarrow Im(\psi)]$ and ψ semi-commutes with f for $\varphi \circ \mathcal{I}$ then φ strongly preserves f for $\mathcal{I}$ on Π.*

Proof. The preservation is obtained by lemma 4 since φ semi-commutes with f for $\mathcal{I}$.

In order to show strong preservation, suppose that, for $q \in \Pi$, $\varphi(\{q\}) \subseteq |f|_{\varphi \circ \mathcal{I}}$. We have,

$\psi \circ \varphi(\{q\}) \subseteq \psi(|f|_{\varphi \circ \mathcal{I}})$ (monotonicity of ψ),
$q \in \psi(|f|_{\varphi \circ \mathcal{I}})$ $(Id_{\Pi} \subseteq \psi \circ \varphi)$,
$q \in |f|_{\psi \circ \varphi \circ \mathcal{I}}$ (semi-commutativity of ψ for $\varphi \circ \mathcal{I}$).

Since $\mathcal{I} \in [\mathcal{P} \rightarrow Im(\psi)]$, there exists an interpretation function $\mathcal{I}' \in [\mathcal{P} \rightarrow 2^{Q_2}]$ such that $\mathcal{I} = \psi \circ \mathcal{I}'$. Thus $\psi \circ \varphi \circ \mathcal{I} = \psi \circ \varphi \circ \psi \circ \mathcal{I}' = \psi \circ \mathcal{I}' = \mathcal{I}$ which implies $q \in |f|_{\mathcal{I}}$.

3 Simulations based on connections ($<\varphi, \psi>$-simulations)

The notion of $<\varphi, \psi>$-simulation plays a central role for the preservation of properties of two transition systems $S_1 = (Q_1, R_1)$ and $S_2 = (Q_2, R_2)$. To introduce it, the following definitions and well-known results are needed.

Definition 6. Given a relation R from a set Q_1 to a set Q_2 $(R \subseteq Q_1 \times Q_2)$ we define two predicate transformers $pre[R] \in [2^{Q_2} \rightarrow 2^{Q_1}]$ and $post[R] \in [2^{Q_1} \rightarrow 2^{Q_2}]$:

$$pre[R] \overset{def}{=} \lambda X. \{q_1 \in Q_1 \; : \; \exists q_2 \in X \wedge q_1 \, R \, q_2\}$$
$$post[R] \overset{def}{=} \lambda X. \{q_2 \in Q_2 \; : \; \exists q_1 \in X \wedge q_1 \, R \, q_2\}$$

In the sequel, we denote by $\widetilde{\varphi}$ the dual of a function $\varphi \in [Q_1 \rightarrow Q_2]$ that is
$$\widetilde{\varphi} \overset{def}{=} \lambda X. \neg \varphi(\neg X).$$
Notice that for $Q_2' \subseteq Q_2$, $pre[R](Q_2')$ represents the set of "predecessors" of the states of Q_2' via the relation R and for $Q_1' \subseteq Q_1$, $post[R](Q_1')$ represents the set of "successors" of the states of Q_1' via R. The following proposition states that the operator *pre* is strict and distributive over union.

Proposition 7. *For any relation R from a set Q_1 to a set Q_2 $(R \subseteq Q_1 \times Q_2)$, we have:*

1. $pre[R](\emptyset) = \emptyset$,
2. *For any X_1, X_2 subsets of Q_2, $pre[R](X_1 \cup X_2) = pre[R](X_1) \cup pre[R](X_2)$,*

Definition 8. A connection from 2^{Q_1} and 2^{Q_2} is a pair of monotonic functions (φ, ψ), $\varphi \in [2^{Q_1} \overset{m}{\rightarrow} 2^{Q_2}]$ and $\psi \in [2^{Q_2} \overset{m}{\rightarrow} 2^{Q_1}]$, such that $Id_{Q_1} \subseteq \psi \circ \varphi$ and $\varphi \circ \psi \subseteq Id_{Q_2}$.

Proposition 9. *[San77] Let φ and ψ be two monotonic functions $\varphi \in [2^{Q_1} \overset{m}{\rightarrow} 2^{Q_2}]$, $\psi \in [2^{Q_2} \overset{m}{\rightarrow} 2^{Q_1}]$. If (φ, ψ) is a connection between 2^{Q_1} and 2^{Q_2} then φ is distributive w.r.t. union and ψ is distributive w.r.t. intersection.*

Proposition 10. *Let ρ be a relation from a set Q_1 to a set Q_2 $(R \subseteq Q_1 \times Q_2)$, the pairs $(post[\rho], \widetilde{pre}[\rho])$ and $(pre[\rho], \widetilde{post}[\rho])$ are connections.*

Now, we define a notion of simulation and bisimulation parameterized by connections relating the lattices of properties of two transition systems.

Definition 11. Let $S_1 = (Q_1, R_1)$ and $S_2 = (Q_2, R_2)$, two transition systems and (φ, ψ) a connection from 2^{Q_1} to 2^{Q_2}.

- $S_1 <\varphi, \psi>$-simulates S_2 if $\varphi \circ pre[R_1] \circ \psi \subseteq pre[R_2]$
- $S_1 <\varphi, \psi>$-bisimulates S_2 if $S_1 <\varphi, \psi>$-simulates S_2 and $S_2 <\widetilde{\psi}, \widetilde{\varphi}>$-simulates S_1.

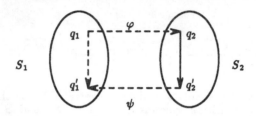

Fig. 1. $<\varphi, \psi>$-simulation

Notice that the definition above implies that for any $<\varphi, \psi>$-simulation, we have necessarily $\varphi(\emptyset) = \emptyset$ since $pre[R_2](\emptyset) = \emptyset$ and φ is monotonic. In that case, as φ is distributive for $\cup$, it can be shown that there exists a relation $\rho \subseteq Q_1 \times Q_2$ such that $\varphi = post[\rho]$ [Sif82b]. Indeed, we have for any $q_1 \in Q_1$ and $q_2 \in Q_2$, $q_1 \rho q_2$ if and only if $q_2 \in \varphi(q_1)$.

We show below that the notion of $<\varphi, \psi>$-simulation is equivalent to the standard notion of simulation [Mil71]: S_1 simulates S_2 if there exists some relation $\rho \subseteq Q_1 \times Q_2$ such that $R_1^{-1}\rho \subseteq \rho R_2^{-1}$. That is, if $q_1 \rho q_2$ then for any q_1' such that $q_1 R_1 q_1'$ there exists q_2' such that $q_2 R_2 q_2'$ and $q_1' \rho q_2'$.

Suppose that for some relation $\rho \subseteq Q_1 \times Q_2$, $S_1 <post[\rho], \widetilde{pre}[\rho]>$-simulates S_2, i.e.

$$post[\rho] \circ pre[R_1] \circ \widetilde{pre}[\rho] \subseteq pre[R_2].$$

Then, as $post[\rho]$ is monotonic and $Id_{Q_1} \subseteq \widetilde{pre}[\rho] \circ post[\rho]$, we obtain,

$$post[\rho] \circ pre[R_1] \circ \widetilde{pre}[\rho] \circ post[\rho] \subseteq pre[R_2] \circ post[\rho] \text{ which implies}$$
$$post[\rho] \circ pre[R_1] \subseteq pre[R_2] \circ post[\rho] \text{ which is equivalent to } R_1^{-1}\rho \subseteq \rho R_2^{-1}.$$

Thus, if $S_1 <post[\rho], \widetilde{pre}[\rho]>$-simulates S_2, then S_1 simulates S_2 in the sense of [Mil71]. It can be shown in a similar way that the converse also holds. A direct consequence of this is that $S_1 <post[\rho], \widetilde{pre}[\rho]>$-bisimulates S_2 for some ρ iff S_1 bisimulates S_2.

Notice also that $<\varphi, \psi>$-simulations define abstract interpretations in the sense of [CC79,CC90]. So, they should allow to establish relationships between on one hand, theories based on behavioral equivalences expressed in term of simulations and on the other hand, existing powerful results on program analysis using abstract interpretation.

The following proposition gives a useful dual condition for the definition of $<\varphi, \psi>$-simulation:

Proposition 12. *For $S_1 = (Q_1, R_1)$ and $S_2 = (Q_2, R_2)$ two transition systems and (φ, ψ) a connection from 2^{Q_1} to 2^{Q_2},*
$$\varphi \circ pre[R_1] \circ \psi \subseteq pre[R_2] \quad iff \quad pre[R_1] \subseteq \psi \circ pre[R_2] \circ \varphi$$

Proof. From $\varphi \circ pre[R_1] \circ \psi \subseteq pre[R_2]$ and monotonicity of φ and ψ one can deduce that $\psi \circ \varphi \circ pre[R_1] \circ \psi \circ \varphi \subseteq \psi \circ pre[R_2] \circ \varphi$. As $Id_{Q_1} \subseteq \psi \circ \varphi$ one obtains $pre[R_1] \subseteq \psi \circ pre[R_2] \circ \varphi$. It is easy to show that the latter implies $\varphi \circ pre[R_1] \circ \psi \subseteq pre[R_2]$. Thus, the two conditions are equivalent.

4 Preservation of the μ-calculus

We consider the problem of preservation of the properties expressible in the branching-time propositional μ-calculus L_μ [Koz83]. We recall that this logic subsumes in expressiveness all the commonly used specification logics as the branching-time temporal logics CTL [CES83] and CTL^* [EH83] and also the linear-time temporal logics as PTL [Pnu77] and ETL [Wol83]. We define two fragments of the μ-calculus called $\Box\mu$-calculus ($\Box L_\mu$) and $\Diamond\mu$-calculus ($\Diamond L_\mu$) and we show that when a system $S_1 <\varphi, \psi>$-simulates another system S_2, the function φ (resp. $\tilde{\psi}$) preserves $\Diamond L_\mu$ (resp. $\Box L_\mu$). We obtain strong preservation of these fragments in case of a simulation equivalence, i.e., existence of simulations in both directions. Furthermore, we show that in the case of $<\varphi, \psi>$-bisimulation, the two functions mentioned above preserve the whole L_μ and that under some conditions they strongly preserve it.

4.1 Fragments of the propositional μ-calculus

We recall the syntax and the semantics of the propositional μ-calculus L_μ [Koz83]. Let $\mathcal{P}$ be a set of atomic propositions, $\mathcal{X}$ a set of variables. The set of the formulas of the μ-calculus is defined by the following grammar:

$f ::= \top \mid P \in \mathcal{P} \mid X \in \mathcal{X} \mid \Diamond f \mid f \vee f \mid \neg f \mid \mu X.f$ where f is syntactically monotonic on X, i.e. any occurrence of X in f is under an even number of negations.

The notion of free occurrences of variables in a formula is defined as in the first-order predicate calculus by considering the operator μ as a quantifier. As usually, a formula is *closed* if there are no variables occurring free in it.

The semantics of the formulas is defined for a given transition system $S = (Q, R)$ and an interpretation function for the atomic propositions $\mathcal{I} \in [\mathcal{P} \to 2^Q]$. A formula with n free variables is interpreted as a function of $[(2^Q)^n \to 2^Q]$. In particular, a closed formula is interpreted as a set of states. The interpretation function is inductively defined as follows, for a *valuation* $V = (V_1, ..., V_n) \in (2^Q)^n$ of the variables occurring free.

$$
\begin{aligned}
|\top|_{\mathcal{I}} &= Q, \\
|P|_{\mathcal{I}} &= \mathcal{I}(P), \\
|X_j|_{\mathcal{I}}(V) &= V_j, \\
|f_1 \vee f_2|_{\mathcal{I}}(V) &= |f_1|_{\mathcal{I}}(V) \cup |f_2|_{\mathcal{I}}(V), \\
|\neg f|_{\mathcal{I}}(V) &= Q - |f|_{\mathcal{I}}(V), \\
|\Diamond f|_{\mathcal{I}}(V) &= \{q \in Q : \exists q' \in Q, qRq' \text{ and } q' \in |f|_{\mathcal{I}}(V)\} = pre[R](|f|_{\mathcal{I}}(V)), \\
|\mu X.f|_{\mathcal{I}}(V) &= \bigcap\{Q' \subseteq Q : |f|_{\mathcal{I}}(Q', V) \subseteq Q'\}.
\end{aligned}
$$

We extend the language of L_μ by adding the formulas $\bot$, $f \wedge g$, $f \Rightarrow g$, $\nu X.f(X)$, $\Box f$ which are respectively abbreviations for $\neg\top$, $\neg(\neg f \vee \neg g)$, $\neg f \vee g$, $\neg\mu X.\neg f(\neg X)$, $\neg\Diamond\neg f$.

A formula of this extended language is in *positive normal form* if and only if all the negations occurring in it are applied on atomic propositions. It can be shown that any formula of L_μ has an equivalent formula which is in positive normal form.

We define two fragments of L_μ called $\Box L_\mu$ and $\Diamond L_\mu$. Their sets of formulas are given respectively by the two following grammars.

$$g ::= \top \mid \bot \mid P \mid \neg P \mid X \mid \Box g \mid g \vee g \mid g \wedge g \mid \mu X.g \mid \nu X.g$$

$$h ::= \top \mid \bot \mid P \mid \neg P \mid X \mid \Diamond h \mid h \vee h \mid h \wedge h \mid \mu X.h \mid \nu X.h$$

Notice that properties expressible in the $\Box L_\mu$ involve only universal quantification on computation sequences (due to the use of the $\Box$ operator) whereas those expressible in $\Diamond L_\mu$ involve only existential quantification.

We consider the *positive* fragments $\Box L_\mu^+$ and $\Diamond L_\mu^+$ obtained from the above languages by forbidding the use of the negation. We consider also the logic L_μ^+ corresponding to the subset of L_μ formulas in positive normal form without negations. We can translate any formula of L_μ which is in positive normal form into an equivalent formula in L_μ^+ by replacing negations of atomic propositions, i.e, formulas in the form $\neg P$, by new atomic propositions. Thus, since any formula of L_μ has an equivalent formula in positive normal form, we can express in L_μ^+ any property expressible in L_μ, modulo this encoding of the formulas $\neg P$. Obviously, the same translation can be done from $*L_\mu$ to $*L_\mu^+$ for $* \in \{\Box, \Diamond\}$.

We can express in $\Box L_\mu$ branching-time properties as for instance, the *safety* properties w.r.t. the simulation preorder [BFG*91]. The class of these properties corresponds to the fragment of $\Box L_\mu$ without the least fixpoint operator μ.

Furthermore, it can be shown that any ω-regular linear-time property, i.e., expressible by a nondeterministic Büchi automaton [Buc62], can be expressed in $\Box L_\mu$ [Bou89]. For example, the *safety* property [Lam77,LPZ85,MP90] *"always P"* can be expressed by the formula $\nu X.(P \wedge \Box X)$. Moreover, the *guarantee* property (according to [MP90]) *"eventually P in any infinite computation sequence"* can be expressed by the formula $\mu X.(P \vee \Box X)$. Properties in the other classes in the hierarchy given in [MP90] are obtained by using alternations of the μ and the ν operators. The formulas of $\Diamond L_\mu$ are equivalent to negations of the $\Box L_\mu$ formulas and conversely. However, the formulas of $\Diamond L_\mu^+$ are equivalent to the duals of $\Box L_\mu^+$ formulas and conversely.

4.2 Preservation results

In the sequel we consider only finite branching transition systems, i.e., transition systems where any state has a finite number of successors. This condition guaranties that the formulas can be interpreted as continuous functions on sets of states.

When we consider any interpretation function of the atomic propositions the preservation and strong preservation results concerns the positive fragments of the μ-calculus. To deal with the fragments where negations of atomic propositions are allowed, we need the following *consistency* condition.

Definition 13. Let $S_1 = (Q_1, R_1)$ and $S_2 = (Q_2, R_2)$ be two transition systems, $\mathcal{I} \in [\mathcal{P} \to 2^{Q_1}]$ be an interpretation and a function $\varphi \in [2^{Q_1} \to 2^{Q_2}]$. We say that φ is *consistent* with $\mathcal{I}$ if and only if $\forall P \in \mathcal{P}.\ \varphi(|\neg P|_{s_1,\mathcal{I}}) \cap \varphi(|P|_{s_1,\mathcal{I}}) = \emptyset$.

We give hereafter the theorems concerning the preservation and strong preservation of $\Box L_\mu$, $\Diamond L_\mu$ and L_μ in presence of $<\varphi, \psi>$-simulations or bisimulations. We consider in the sequel that the functions $\varphi \in [2^{Q_1} \to 2^{Q_2}]$ and $\psi \in [2^{Q_2} \to 2^{Q_1}]$ forming the $<\varphi, \psi>$ simulations and bisimulations satisfy the following conditions: $\varphi(\emptyset) = \emptyset$, $\varphi(Q_1) = Q_2$, $\widetilde{\psi}(\emptyset) = \emptyset$ and $\widetilde{\psi}(Q_2) = Q_1$.

We start with two theorems concerning the preservation of $\Box L_\mu$ and $\Diamond L_\mu$ respectively by $\widetilde{\psi}$ and φ when $<\varphi, \psi>$ is a simulation. Their proofs are given in the appendix.

Theorem 14. *Let $S_1 = (Q_1, R_1)$ and $S_2 = (Q_2, R_2)$ be two transition systems. If $S_1 <\varphi, \psi>$-simulates S_2 then $\widetilde{\psi}$ preserves the formulas of $\Box L_\mu^+$ for any interpretation function $\mathcal{I} \in [\mathcal{P} \to 2^{Q_2}]$. Furthermore, if $\widetilde{\psi}$ is consistent with $\mathcal{I}$ then $\widetilde{\psi}$ preserves $\Box L_\mu$ for $\mathcal{I}$.*

Theorem 15. *Let $S_1 = (Q_1, R_1)$ and $S_2 = (Q_2, R_2)$ be two transition systems. If $S_1 <\varphi, \psi>$-simulates S_2 then φ preserves the formulas of $\Diamond L_\mu^+$ for any interpretation function $\mathcal{I} \in [\mathcal{P} \to 2^{Q_1}]$. Furthermore, if φ is consistent with $\mathcal{I}$, then φ preserves $\Diamond L_\mu$ for $\mathcal{I}$.*

Now, we give a theorem about strong preservation of $\Box L_\mu$ and $\Diamond L_\mu$ in case of a simulation equivalence.

Theorem 16. *Let $S_1 = (Q_1, R_1)$ and $S_2 = (Q_2, R_2)$ be two transition systems. If $S_1 <\varphi, \psi>$-simulates S_2 and $S_2 <\varphi', \psi'>$-simulates S_1 then*

1. *For any set $\Pi \subseteq Q_1$, if $\varphi' \circ \varphi \circ \varphi' = \varphi'$ and $Id_\Pi \subseteq \varphi' \circ \varphi$, then φ strongly preserves $\Diamond L_\mu^+$ on Π for any interpretation $\mathcal{I} \in [\mathcal{P} \to Im(\varphi')]$. Furthermore, if φ (resp. φ') is consistent with $\mathcal{I}$ (resp. $\varphi \circ \mathcal{I}$) then φ strongly preserves $\Diamond L_\mu$ for $\mathcal{I}$ on Π.*

2. *For any set $\Pi \subseteq Q_2$, if $\widetilde{\psi}' \circ \widetilde{\psi} \circ \widetilde{\psi}' = \widetilde{\psi}'$ and $Id_\Pi \subseteq \widetilde{\psi}' \circ \widetilde{\psi}$, then $\widetilde{\psi}$ strongly preserves $\Box L_\mu^+$ on Π for any interpretation $\mathcal{I} \in [\mathcal{P} \to Im(\widetilde{\psi}')]$. Furthermore, if $\widetilde{\psi}$ (resp. $\widetilde{\psi}'$) is consistent with $\mathcal{I}$ (resp. $\widetilde{\psi} \circ \mathcal{I}$) then $\widetilde{\psi}$ strongly preserves $\Box L_\mu$ for $\mathcal{I}$ on Π.*

Proof. Direct application of the theorem 5 using the theorems 14 and 15.

We consider now the case of bisimulation connections. The following theorems concerns the preservation and the strong preservation of the whole μ-calculus in presence of such connections.

Theorem 17. *Let $S_1 = (Q_1, R_1)$ and $S_2 = (Q_2, R_2)$ be two transition systems. If $S_1 <\varphi, \psi>$-bisimulates S_2 then φ (resp. $\widetilde{\psi}$) preserves L_μ^+ for any interpretation function $\mathcal{I}_1 \in [\mathcal{P} \to 2^{Q_1}]$ (resp. $\mathcal{I}_2 \in [\mathcal{P} \to 2^{Q_2}]$).*
Furthermore, if φ (resp. $\widetilde{\psi}$) is consistent with $\mathcal{I}_1$ (resp. $\mathcal{I}_2$) then φ (resp. $\widetilde{\psi}$) preserves L_μ for $\mathcal{I}_1$ (resp. $\mathcal{I}_2$).

Proof. The proof is a combination of the proofs of the theorems 14, 15 and the definition of the bisimulation (see definition 8).

Theorem 18. *Let $S_1 = (Q_1, R_1)$ and $S_2 = (Q_2, R_2)$ be two transition systems. If $S_1 <\varphi, \psi>$-bisimulates S_2 then*

1. If $Id_{Q_1} \subseteq \tilde{\psi} \circ \varphi$ and $\tilde{\psi} \circ \varphi \circ \tilde{\psi} = \tilde{\psi}$ then φ strongly preserves L_μ^+ for any interpretation $\mathcal{I}_1 \in [\mathcal{P} \rightarrow Im(\tilde{\psi})]$. Furthermore, if φ and $\tilde{\psi}$ are respectively consistent with $\mathcal{I}_1$ and $\varphi \circ \mathcal{I}_1$, then φ strongly preserves L_μ for $\mathcal{I}_1$.

2. If $Id_{Q_1} \subseteq \tilde{\psi} \circ \varphi$ and $Id_{Q_2} \subseteq \varphi \circ \tilde{\psi}$ then for any interpretation $\mathcal{I}_1 \in [\mathcal{P} \rightarrow Im(\tilde{\psi})]$, φ (resp. $\tilde{\psi}$) strongly preserve L_μ^+ for $\mathcal{I}_1$ (resp. $\varphi \circ \mathcal{I}_1$).

   Furthermore, if φ (resp. $\tilde{\psi}$) is consistent with $\mathcal{I}_1$ (resp. $\varphi \circ \mathcal{I}_1$) then φ (resp. $\tilde{\psi}$) strongly preserves L_μ for $\mathcal{I}_1$ (resp. $\varphi \circ \mathcal{I}_1$).

Proof. The first point is obtained by direct application of theorem 5 and using the proof of theorem 17 showing actually semi-commutativity which is stronger than preservation. The second point is also obtained by direct application of theorem 5, given that $Id_{Q_1} \subseteq \tilde{\psi} \circ \varphi$ and $Id_{Q_2} \subseteq \varphi \circ \tilde{\psi}$ implies that $\tilde{\psi} \circ \varphi \circ \tilde{\psi} = \tilde{\psi}$ and $\varphi \circ \tilde{\psi} \circ \varphi = \varphi$.

5 Applications

In this section we consider that the functions φ and ψ are defined in terms of a relation $\rho \subseteq Q_1 \times Q_2$ relating states of two transition systems $S_1 = (Q_1, R_1)$ and $S_2 = (Q_2, R_2)$.

As the pair $(post[\rho], \widetilde{pre}[\rho])$ is a connection from 2^{Q_1} to 2^{Q_2}, it is natural to consider $< post[\rho], \widetilde{pre}[\rho] >$-simulations from S_1 to S_2. In this context the results presented can be applied to tackle two problems: the implementation problem and the abstraction problem.

5.1 Implementation

Problem: given a transition system $S_2 = (Q_2, R_2)$, a set of states Q_1 and a relation $\rho \subseteq Q_1 \times Q_2$, find a transition system $S_1 = (Q_1, R_1)$ *implementing* S_2 via ρ that is, a system S_1 such that $S_1 < post[\rho], \widetilde{pre}[\rho] >$-simulates S_2.

From the relation $pre[R_1] \subseteq \widetilde{pre}[\rho] \circ pre[R_2] \circ post[\rho]$, one gets that in general there may be many solutions (relations R_1). However, there exists a largest relation. It is obtained by computing the largest function F such that $F \subseteq \widetilde{pre}[\rho] \circ pre[R_2] \circ post[\rho]$ which is distributive with respect to union and strict ($\overline{F}(\emptyset) = \emptyset$). As it is shown in [Sif82b], for any such function there exists a unique relation $pre[R_1]$ such that $pre[R_1] = F$. This function is defined by taking $F(\emptyset) = \emptyset$, $F(P) = \bigvee_{q \in P} H(q)$, where $H = \widetilde{pre}[\rho] \circ pre[R_2] \circ post[\rho]$.

5.2 Abstraction

Problem: given a transition system $S_1 = (Q_1, R_1)$, a set of state Q_2 and a relation $\rho \subseteq Q_1 \times Q_2$, find a transition system $S_2 = (Q_2, R_2)$ which is an *abstraction* of S_1 via ρ. That is, a transition system S_2 such that $S_1 < post[\rho], \widetilde{pre}[\rho] >$-simulates S_2.

Obviously, the relation $post[\rho] \circ pre[R_1] \circ \widetilde{pre}[\rho] \subseteq pre[R_2]$ may have several solutions (i.e., relations R_2). We are interested in solutions which are sufficiently faithful to S_1. In general, a least solution does not exists ; however, if ρ is total on Q_2, we have $\widetilde{pre}[\rho] \subseteq pre[\rho]$ and taking $post[\rho] \circ pre[R_1] \circ pre[\rho] = pre[R_2]$ defines an acceptable abstraction of S_1. The least abstraction exists if ρ is taken to be a total function. Then, $\widetilde{pre}[\rho] = pre[\rho]$ and $post[\rho] \circ pre[R_1] \circ pre[\rho] = pre[R_2]$.

We compute the abstraction of a program w.r.t. to a relation ρ using symbolic representations for both the program and its abstraction.

Consider a program S_1 defined on a tuple of variables $\mathbf{X} = (X_1, X_2, \dots, X_n)$ ranging on a domain $\mathbf{D} = D_1 \times D_2 \times \cdots \times D_n$, represented by guarded commands:

$$do \; \{C_1 \to \alpha_1 [\!] \dots C_i \to \alpha_i [\!] \dots C_k \to \alpha_k\} \; od$$

where the C_i's are predicates on $\mathbf{X}$ and the α_i's are assignements defining functions of $[\mathbf{D} \to \mathbf{D}]$.

Symbolically, sets of states of S_1 are represented by predicates on $\mathbf{X}$ and the transitions between these sets are given by the function $pre[R_1]$ which, for any predicate $P(\mathbf{X})$ (representing a set of states), is defined by:

$$pre[R_1](P(\mathbf{X})) = \bigvee_{i=1}^{k} C_i \wedge P[\alpha_i(\mathbf{X})/\mathbf{X}].$$

The abstraction S_2 is a program on a tuple of variables $\mathbf{Y} = (Y_1, Y_2, \dots, Y_m)$ ranging on an *abstract* domain $\mathbf{D}' = D_1' \times D_2' \times \cdots \times D_m'$.

Given a relation ρ between the domains $\mathbf{D}$ ans $\mathbf{D}'$ expressed by a predicate on $\mathbf{X}$ and $\mathbf{Y}$, the symbolic representation of S_2 is defined by :

$$pre[R_2] = \bigvee_{i=1}^{k} post[\rho](C_i \wedge pre[\rho](P[\alpha_i(\mathbf{X})/\mathbf{X}])).$$

In [CGL92] a construction of a program abstraction is described. Given a system S_1 and a function h from the domain of the program variables to an abstract domain, a system S_2 is constructed in such a manner that h induces a *homomorphism* from S_1 to S_2. The notion of homomorphism corresponds in our approach to a $<\varphi, \psi>$-simulation where $\varphi = post[\rho]$ and $\psi = \widetilde{pre}[\rho]$ for ρ a total function and φ and $\widetilde{\psi}$ are respectively consistent with the interpretation functions of the atomic propositions $\mathcal{I}$ and $\varphi \circ \mathcal{I}$. In that case, it is shown that the logic $\forall CTL^*$ is preserved from S_2 to S_1. This result is generalized by the theorem 14 since $\Box L_\mu$ is more expressive than $\forall CTL^*$.

Furthermore, the notion of *exact homomorphism* considered in this paper corresponds to a $<\varphi, \psi>$-bisimulation where $\varphi = post[\rho]$ and $\psi = \widetilde{pre}[\rho]$ for ρ a total function, φ and $\widetilde{\psi}$ are consistent respectively with the interpretation functions $\mathcal{I}$ and $\varphi \circ \mathcal{I}$. If S_1 and S_2 are related by an exact homomorphism, the logic CTL^* is strongly preserved. This result is generalized by the theorem 18 since L_μ is more expressive than CTL^* (notice that this theorem can be applied as ρ is a total relation and this implies $Id_{Q_1} \subseteq pre[\rho] \circ post[\rho]$ and $Id_{Q_2} \subseteq post[\rho] \circ pre[\rho]$).

5.3 Example

The motion of a mobile on a grid is controlled so as to visit cyclically the points $CDACDA....$ Initially the mobile is within the rectangle defined by the points (A, B, C, D).

The following program describes the mobile's motion where $Ctrl$ is a control variable with domain $\{A, C, D\}$ recording the most recently visited point and X, Y are its discrete coordinates with respective domains $[0, .., X_0]$ and $[0, .., Y_0]$.

do

$(Ctrl = A) \wedge (0 \le X < X_0)$	$\to (X, Y, Ctrl) := (X+1, Y, Ctrl)$
$\mid (Ctrl = A) \wedge (0 \le Y < Y_0)$	$\to (X, Y, Ctrl) := (X, Y+1, Ctrl)$
$\mid (Ctrl = A) \wedge (X = X_0) \wedge (Y = Y_0)$	$\to (X, Y, Ctrl) := (X-1, Y, C)$
$\mid (Ctrl = C) \wedge (X > 0)$	$\to (X, Y, Ctrl) := (X-1, Y, Ctrl)$
$\mid (Ctrl = C) \wedge (X = 0)$	$\to (X, Y, Ctrl) := (X, Y-1, D)$
$\mid (Ctrl = D) \wedge (Y > 0)$	$\to (X, Y, Ctrl) := (X, Y-1, Ctrl)$
$\mid (Ctrl = D) \wedge (Y = 0)$	$\to (X, Y, Ctrl) := (X, Y, A)$

od

An abstraction of this system with two three-valued variables h and v of domains respectively $\{h_0, h_1, h_2\}$ and $\{v_0, v_1, v_2\}$, is defined via the relation ρ:

$(X, Y, Ctrl) \, \rho \, (h, v, Ctrl)$ iff

$[(X = 0 \wedge h = h_0) \vee (0 < X < X_0 \wedge h = h_1) \vee (X = X_0 \wedge h = h_2)] \wedge$

$[(Y = 0 \wedge v = v_0) \vee (0 < Y < Y_0 \wedge v = v_1) \vee (Y = Y_0 \wedge v = v_2)]$

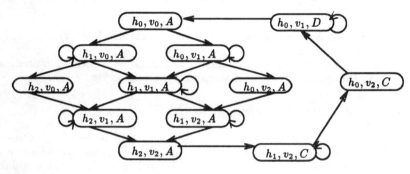

Fig. 2. Abstract mobile system

This abstraction is represented by the finite transition system given in figure 2. Consider the formula,

$f = not \, (Ctrl = A) \, to \, (Ctrl = D) \, unless \, (Ctrl = C) \wedge$
$\qquad not \, (Ctrl = C) \, to \, (Ctrl = A) \, unless \, (Ctrl = D) \wedge$
$\qquad not \, (Ctrl = D) \, to \, (Ctrl = C) \, unless \, (Ctrl = A)$

where $not \, P_1 \, to \, P_2 \, unless \, P_3$ is an abbreviation of the $\Box L_\mu$ formula $P_1 \Rightarrow \nu X.(\neg P_2 \wedge (P_3 \vee \Box X))$.

It can be seen that the function $pre[\rho]$ is consistent with the interpretation of the atomic propositions used in f on the abstract mobile system. We verify that f is true on the abstract system and by theorem 14, we deduce that it is true for the initial mobile system.

6 Conclusion

The paper studies property preserving transformations for reactive systems. A key idea is the use of $< \varphi, \psi >$-simulations which are compatible with the standard notion of simulation (structure homomorphism) often used to define implementations. Furthermore, $< \varphi, \psi >$-simulations induce abstract interpretations à la Cousot and this allows to apply an existing powerful theory for program analysis.

The theory is developed on transition systems but it can be trivially extended to labeled transition systems by requiring $<\varphi, \psi>$-simulation of the corresponding labeled relations. Also this theory can be adapted so as to be applied to preorders and equivalences that can be expressed in terms of simulations or bisimulations by adopting some abstraction criterion. For instance, one can define a $<\varphi, \psi>$-observational equivalence by considering as models, labeled transition systems with silent actions and using the well-known fact that observational equivalence is strong bisimulation equivalence on a modified transition relation.

As a continuation of this work, we intend to focus on the applicability of the results for the verification of properties of reactive systems described as the composition of simple programs with guarded commands.

Acknowledgements

We thank Susanne Graf for many helpful discussions and judicious remarks.

References

[AL88]   M. Abadi and L. Lamport. *The existence of Refinement Mappings.* SRC 29, Digital Equipment Corporation, Systems Research Center, August 1988.

[BFG*91] A. Bouajjani, J.C. Fernandez, S. Graf, C. Rodriguez, and J. Sifakis. Safety for branching time semantics. In J.L. Albert, B. Monein, and M.R. Artalejo, editors, *18th ICALP*, pages 76–92, LNCS 510, Springer-Verlag, October 1991.

[Bou89]   A. Bouajjani. *From Linear-Time Propositional Temporal Logics to a Branching-Time μ-calculus.* RTC 15, LGI-IMAG, Grenoble, 1989.

[Bra78]   D. Brand. *Algebraic simulation between parallel programs.* RC 7206 30923, IBM, Yorktown Heights, 1978.

[Buc62]   J.R. Büchi. On a decision method in restricted second order arithmetic. In *Intern. Cong. Logic, Method and Philos. Sci.*, Stantford Univ. Press, 1962.

[CC79]   P. Cousot and R. Cousot. Systematic design of program analysis framework. In *Proc. 6th ACM Symp. on Principle of Programming Languages*, 1979.

[CC90]   P. Cousot and R. Cousot. *Comparing the Galois Connection and Widening/Narrowing Approaches to Abstract Interpretation.* Technical Report, LIX, Ecole Polytechnique, May 1990.

[CES83]   E. M. Clarke, E. A. Emerson, and E. Sistla. Automatic Verification of Finite State Concurrent Systems using Temporal Logic Specifications: A Practical Approach. In *10th Symposium on Principles of Programming Languages (POPL 83)*, ACM, 1983. Complete version published in ACM TOPLAS, 8(2):244–263, April 1986.

[CGL92]   E.M. Clarke, O. Grumberg, and D.E. Long. Model checking and abstraction. In *Symposium on Principles of Programming Languages (POPL 92)*, ACM, October 1992.

[EH83]   E.A. Emerson and J. Y. Halpern. 'sometimes' and 'not never' revisited: on branching versus linear time logic. In *10th. Annual Symp. on Principles of Programming Languages*, 1983.

[GS86a]   S. Graf and J. Sifakis. A logic for the specification and proof of regular controllable processes of CCS. *Acta Informatica*, 23, 1986.

[GS86b]   S. Graf and J. Sifakis. A modal characterization of observational congruence on finite terms of CCS. *Information and Control*, 68, 1986.

[HM85]   M. Hennessy and R. Milner. Algebraic laws for nondeterminism and concurrency. *Journal of the Association for Computing Machinery*, 32:137–161, 1985.

[KM79]   T. Kasai and R.E. Miller. *Homomorphisms between models of parallel computation.* RC 7796 33742, IBM, Yorktown Heights, 1979.

[Koz83] D. Kozen. Results on the propositional μ-calculus. In *Theoretical Computer Science*, North-Holland, 1983.

[Kur89] R.P. Kurshan.   *Analysis of Discrete Event Coordination.   LNCS 430*, Springer-Verlag, May 1989.

[Lam77] L. Lamport. Proving the correctness of multiprocess programs. *IEEE Transactions on Software Engineering*, SE-3(2):125–143, 1977.

[LPZ85] O. Lichtenstein, A. Pnueli, and L. Zuck. The glory of the past. In *Conference on Logics of Programs, LNCS 194*, Springer Verlag, 1985.

[LT88]   N.A. Lynch and M.R. Tuttle. *An introduction to Input/Ouput Automata.* MIT/LCS/TM 373, MIT, Cambridge, Massachussetts, November 1988.

[Mil71] R. Milner. An algebraic definition of simulation between programs. In *Proc. Second Int. Joint Conf. on Artificial Intelligence*, pages 481–489, BCS, 1971.

[MP90]   Z. Manna and A. Pnueli. A hierarchy of temporal properties. In *Proc. 9th ACM Symp. on Princ. of Dist. Comp.*, 1990.

[NV90]   R. De Nicola and F. Vaandrager. Three logics for branching bisimulation. In *Proc. of Fifth Symp. on Logic in Computer Science*, Computer Society Press, 1990.

[Ore44] O. Ore. Galois connexions. *Trans. Amer. Math. Soc*, 55:493–513, February 1944.

[Pnu77] A. Pnueli. The Temporal Logic of Programs. In *18th Symposium on Foundations of Computer Science (FOCS 77)*, IEEE, 1977. Revised version published in Theoretical Computer Science, 13:45–60, 1981.

[San77] Luis E. Sanchis. Data types as lattices: retractions, projection and projection. In *RAIRO Theorical computer science, vol 11, nomber 4*, pages 339–344, 1977.

[Sif82a] J. Sifakis. *Property preserving homomorphisms and a notion of simulation of transition systems.* RR IMAG 332, IMAG, November 1982.

[Sif82b] J. Sifakis. A unified approach for studying the properties of transition systems. *Theorical Computer Science*, 18, 1982.

[Sif83] J. Sifakis. Property preserving homomorphisms of transition systems. In E. Clarke and D. Kozen, editors, *Workshop on logics of programs*, LNCS 164, Springer-Verlag, 1983.

[Wol83] P. Wolper. Temporal logic can be more expreessive. *Inform. Contr.*, 56, 1983.

Appendix

We give hereafter the proofs of the theorems 14 and 15. These proofs are based on an induction argument using a well-founded ordering on L_μ formulas defined below. We suppose that the formulas are in positive normal form. Consider the binary relation defined for any formulas f and g by : $f \triangleright g$ if and only if either

- f is a subformula of g or
- $g = \mu X.h$ (resp. $g = \nu X.h$) and $\exists k \geq 0.$ $f = h^k[\bot/X]$ (resp. $f = h^k[\top/X]$).

Now, we consider the order $\preceq$ defined as the transitive closure of the relation $\triangleright$.

Proof of Theorem 14 Let us prove the first part of the theorem. Consider an interpretation function $\mathcal{I} \in [\mathcal{P} \rightarrow 2^{Q_2}]$. By lemma 4, it is sufficient to prove that for any formula f in $\Box L_\mu^+$ and for any valuation V, we have $\widetilde{\psi}(|f|_{s_2,\mathcal{I}}(V)) \subseteq |f|_{s_1,\widetilde{\psi}\circ\mathcal{I}}(\widetilde{\psi}(V))$. The proof is by induction on the order $\preceq$ defined above. To simplify the notations, we omit the valuation V whenever it is not relevant in a proof.

- $\widetilde{\psi}(|\bot|_{s_2,\mathcal{I}}) = |\bot|_{s_1,\widetilde{\psi}\circ\mathcal{I}}$ and $\widetilde{\psi}(|\top|_{s_2,\mathcal{I}}) = |\top|_{s_1,\widetilde{\psi}\circ\mathcal{I}}$ as $\widetilde{\psi}(\emptyset) = \emptyset$ and $\widetilde{\psi}(Q_2) = Q_1$.

- $\widetilde{\psi}(|P|_{s_2,\mathcal{I}}) = |P|_{s_1,\widetilde{\psi}\circ\mathcal{I}}$ by definition of the interpretation function.

- $\widetilde{\psi}(|X_j|_{s_2,\mathcal{I}}(V)) = \widetilde{\psi}(V_j) = |X_j|_{s_1,\widetilde{\psi}\circ\mathcal{I}}(\widetilde{\psi}(V))$

- $\widetilde{\psi}(|\Box f|_{s_2,\mathcal{I}}) = \widetilde{\psi} \circ \widetilde{pre}[R_2](|f|_{s_2,\mathcal{I}})$ since $\widetilde{\psi}$ is monotonic and by definition of the interpretation function. The dual of the $<\varphi,\psi>$-simulation condition is $\widetilde{pre}[R_2] \subseteq \widetilde{\varphi} \circ \widetilde{pre}[R_1] \circ \widetilde{\psi}$. We get, $\widetilde{\psi}(|\Box f|_{s_2,\mathcal{I}}) \subseteq \widetilde{\psi} \circ \widetilde{\varphi} \circ \widetilde{pre}[R_1] \circ \widetilde{\psi}(|f|_{s_2,\mathcal{I}})$. As $\widetilde{\psi} \circ \widetilde{\varphi} \subseteq Id_{Q_1}$, we obtain $\widetilde{\psi}(|\Box f|_{s_2,\mathcal{I}}) \subseteq \widetilde{pre}[R_1] \circ \widetilde{\psi}(|f|_{s_2,\mathcal{I}})$. By induction hypothesis, we have $\widetilde{\psi}(|f|_{s_2,\mathcal{I}}) \subseteq |f|_{s_1,\widetilde{\psi}\circ\mathcal{I}}$. Thus, we have
  $\widetilde{\psi}(|\Box f|_{s_2,\mathcal{I}}) \subseteq \widetilde{pre}[R_1](|f|_{s_1,\widetilde{\psi}\circ\mathcal{I}})$ equivalent to $\widetilde{\psi}(|\Box f|_{s_2,\mathcal{I}}) \subseteq |\Box f|_{s_1,\widetilde{\psi}\circ\mathcal{I}}$.

- $\widetilde{\psi}(|f_1 \vee f_2|_{s_2,\mathcal{I}}) = \widetilde{\psi}(|f_1|_{s_2,\mathcal{I}} \cup |f_2|_{s_2,\mathcal{I}})$ by definition of the interpretation function. As $\widetilde{\psi}$ is distributive with respect to $\cup$, we have $\widetilde{\psi}(|f_1 \vee f_2|_{s_2,\mathcal{I}}) = \widetilde{\psi}(|f_1|_{s_2,\mathcal{I}}) \cup \widetilde{\psi}(|f_2|_{s_2,\mathcal{I}})$. By induction hypothesis, we obtain
  $\widetilde{\psi}(|f_1 \vee f_2|_{s_2,\mathcal{I}}) \subseteq |f_1|_{s_1,\widetilde{\psi}\circ\mathcal{I}} \cup |f_2|_{s_1,\widetilde{\psi}\circ\mathcal{I}} = |f_1 \vee f_2|_{s_1,\widetilde{\psi}\circ\mathcal{I}}$.

- $\widetilde{\psi}(|f_1 \wedge f_2|_{s_2,\mathcal{I}}) \subseteq \widetilde{\psi}(|f_1|_{s_2,\mathcal{I}}) \cap \widetilde{\psi}(|f_2|_{s_2,\mathcal{I}})$ and
  $\widetilde{\psi}(|f_1|_{s_2,\mathcal{I}}) \cap \widetilde{\psi}(|f_2|_{s_2,\mathcal{I}}) = |f_1|_{s_1,\widetilde{\psi}\circ\mathcal{I}} \cap |f_2|_{s_1,\widetilde{\psi}\circ\mathcal{I}} = |f_1 \wedge f_2|_{s_1,\widetilde{\psi}\circ\mathcal{I}}$.

- The proof for $\mu X.f$ and $\nu X.f$ is based on the fact that, since the formulas can be interpreted as continuous functions on sets of states we have $|\mu X.f|_{s_2,\mathcal{I}} = \bigcup_{k\geq 0} |f^k|_{s_2,\mathcal{I}}(\emptyset)$ and $|\nu X.f|_{s_2,\mathcal{I}} = \bigcap_{k\geq 0} |f^k|_{s_2,\mathcal{I}}(Q_2)$, $\widetilde{\psi}(\emptyset) = \emptyset$, $\widetilde{\psi}(Q_2) = Q_1$, $\widetilde{\psi}$ is monotonic and that the formulas $f^k[\bot/X]$ and $f^k[\top/X]$ are strictly inferior w.r.t. $\preceq$ to $\mu X.f$ and $\nu X.f$ respectively.

Now, if $\widetilde{\psi}$ is consistent with $\mathcal{I}$, it is straightforward to deduce that $\widetilde{\psi}(|\neg P|_{s_2,\mathcal{I}}) \subseteq |\neg P|_{s_1,\widetilde{\psi}\circ\mathcal{I}}$.

Proof of Theorem 15 Similar to the proof of theorem 14.
The semi-commutativity with the $\Diamond$ operator is proved in the following manner. Let $\mathcal{I} \in [\mathcal{P} \rightarrow 2^{Q_1}]$. By definition of the interpretation function of the formulas, we have $\varphi(|\Diamond f|_{s_1,\mathcal{I}}) = \varphi \circ pre[R_1](|f|_{s_1,\mathcal{I}})$. As $Id_{Q_1} \subseteq \psi \circ \varphi$, we get $\varphi(|\Diamond f|_{s_1,\mathcal{I}}) \subseteq \varphi \circ pre[R_1] \circ \psi \circ \varphi(|f|_{s_1,\mathcal{I}})$. Since $<\varphi,\psi>$ is a simulation, $\varphi \circ pre[R_1] \circ \psi \subseteq pre[R_2]$. Thus, we get $\varphi(|\Diamond f|_{s_1,\mathcal{I}}) \subseteq pre[R_2] \circ \varphi(|f|_{s_1,\mathcal{I}})$. Furthermore, by induction hypothesis, $\varphi(|f|_{s_1,\mathcal{I}}) \subseteq |f|_{s_2,\varphi\circ\mathcal{I}}$. Thus, we have $\varphi(|\Diamond f|_{s_1,\mathcal{I}}) \subseteq pre[R_2](|f|_{s_2,\varphi\circ\mathcal{I}}) = |\Diamond f|_{s_2,\varphi\circ\mathcal{I}}$.

Verification with Real-Time COSPAN[*]

C. Courcoubetis[1]   D. Dill[2]   M. Chatzaki[1]   P. Tzounakis[1]

[1]Department of Computer Science, University of Crete
and Institute of Computer Science, FORTH.

Department of Computer Science, Stanford University.

Abstract. We describe some examples using an extension of Kurshan's COSPAN system to verify bounded delay constraints in a dense time model, based on the method proposed by Dill for adding timing constraints to Büchi automata. The S/R model and COSPAN are reviewed as background, then we describe how timing can be incorporated into S/R processes, and briefly describe the modified verification algorithm. The examples consist of several time-dependent versions of the Alternating Bit Protocol and the Fiber Distributed Data Interface (FDDI).

1   Introduction

It is widely recognized that the design of protocols and concurrent algorithms is a subtle art. Human designers seem to have difficulty anticipating all the possible interactions among processes operating in parallel. The result is that many or perhaps most protocols and algorithms in use contain bugs resulting from unforseen interactions among their components. These design errors are extremely difficult to detect and debug by simulation or even by running an implementation of the system, because such systems are nondeterministic; problems are likely to be intermittent and non-repeatable.

A partial solution to this problem is to use an automatic protocol verification program to assure the correctness of the system. Such programs take advantage of the finite-state nature of many of these problems to enumerate all of the states of the system, which checking for violations of a user-provided specification. When a violation of the specification is discovered, the verifier can report an execution history that shows how the violation could occur.

Currently, one of the most sophisticated verification programs is COSPAN, developed by R. Kurshan and others at AT&T Bell Laboratories. COSPAN has been used to verify many protocols and hardware designs. COSPAN [HK89, KK86, ZH90] is based on a model which specifies the system in terms of finite-state machines coupled with a powerful communication mechanism. The model is powerful enough so that COSPAN can express and validate any finite-state property (more precisely, any property that corresponds to an ω-regular language).

---

[*] This work supported in part by the BRA ESPRIT project REACT, and by the Office of the Chief of Naval Research, Grant number N00014-91-J-1901-P00001. This publication does not necessarily reflect the position or policy of the U.S. Government.

In general, the models used by protocol verifiers abstract away from time — they model the *orderings* of events, but not their times of occurrence. However, this is not adequate for verifying protocols or algorithms that depend on timing constraints crucially for their correct operation, or that must satisfy timing requirements imposed by the external environment. As computers and networks interact more with physical devices and processes, it will become increasingly difficult to hide or ignore timing properties. But obtaining correct real-time systems is especially difficult, because timing constraints amplify the complexity of the interactions that can occur. Hence, automatic verifiers for real-time systems would be very valuable.

The nature of time is a central question that must be addressed in any system for reasoning about time. There have been many proposals for frameworks for verifying timing properties. These can be grouped into three major categories according to their underlying models of time, which we call *discrete time* [JM86, HPOG89], which considers time to be isomorphic to the integers; *fictitious clock* [AK83, AH90, Bur89, Ost90] which measures time by comparing system events with a fictitious *tick* event that occurs at regular intervals; and *dense time*, which allows an unbounded number of events to occur between two different times [AD90, Alu91, ACD90, ACD91a, ACD91b].

Each model has its adherents, and space does not permit a comparative analysis. Suffice it to say that the model used here is *dense time*, because (in the authors' opinion) it is easier to justify in terms of physical processes.

Real-time COSPAN is an extension of the COSPAN verifier to support reasoning about systems with timing constraints, where the constraints are unknown but bounded delays. A detailed description of real-time COSPAN, along with some examples, appears elsewhere [CDT]. The focus in this paper is on more significant examples that have been done with the verifier. Our extension of COSPAN uses a method similar to those proposed by Berthomieu and Menasche [BM83], time-constrained Büchi automata [Dil89], and asynchronous circuits with interval-bounded delays [Lew89]. The method uses a collection of real-valued variables that keep track of the difference between the current time and the time at which certain future events will occur. The analysis algorithm uses systems of linear inequalities to represent sets of assignments to these variables. Since there happen to be a finite number of such systems of inequalities an analysis algorithm is possible.

The basic approach is to augment the description of the system with an automatically-generated "monitor" that excludes event orderings that are inconsistent with a set of given timing constraints. The monitor works by keeping track of systems of linear inequalities. We have implemented the above ideas as an independent module *without changing* the COSPAN code. In general, we believe that the same approach can be used to splice timing analysis into other finite-state verification tools without making major changes to other parts of the system.

The paper is organized as follows. In order to make the paper self-contained we first describe the finite-state machine model and the COSPAN system. Then we explain how timing constraints are added, and give several nontrivial example verifications of systems with timing constraints.

2   The S/R Model and the COSPAN System

2.1   The Selection/Resolution Model

The *selection/resolution* (S/R) model [AKS83, AC85, GK80, Kur90, ABM86] provides a method of describing a complex system as a set of coordinating finite state machines. S/R facilitates concise and understandable specifications by using logical predicates to describe coordination between machines. The model is described here only intuitively. More details are available in the above references.

In the S/R model, a system is decomposed into a set of simple components called *processes*; each process is an edge-labeled directed graph, (see Figure 1). The vertices of the graph are *states* of the process. Each process has a name and a *selection variable*, whose name is the process name followed by $\#$. Each directed edge describes a state transition that is possible in one computation step; it is labeled with a *predicate* on selection variables. To make the examples easier to read, we adopt the convention that a "self-loop" transition with the label "else" is labeled with the negation of the sum of the labels of the outgoing transition.

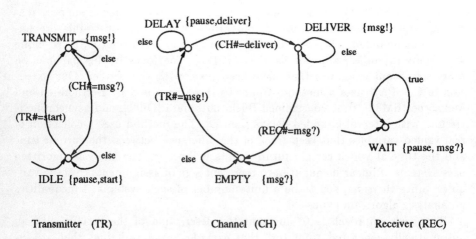

Transmitter (TR)   Channel (CH)   Receiver (REC)

Fig. 1. A Delay Channel Example. The channel process delays the message by selecting pause.

A collection of processes characterizes a set of infinite linear histories, called *chains*. Formally, a chain is an infinite sequence of state/selection pairs $c(0) = (v(0), s(0))$, $c(1) = (v(1), s(1)), \ldots$. The chains of a collection of several processes $P_1, \ldots, P_n$ running in parallel are generated as follows. A *product state* is a vector of states of the individual processes, which summarizes the state of the entire system. Every chain starts with the product state which consists of the initial states of the individual processes. Thereafter, each process chooses a value from among the possible selections in its current state to assign to its selection variable (this step is called *selection*). Then, each process chooses an edge label that is true for the *combined* values of all the selection variables (this step is called *resolution*). Resolution causes the processes to enter simultaneously the next states corresponding to their chosen edges.

Coordination between processes occurs because processes usually refer to the selection variables of other processes in their edge predicates. For example, in figure 1, the transmitter may select "msg!", in which case the resolution will involve the edge from state DELAY to state EMPTY in process CH.

As a convenience feature, COSPAN also allows edge labels to refer to the state variables of the processes as well as their selections.

The product just described models processes running in lock-step, so it is called the *synchronous product*. It is easy to model *asynchronous* processes by adding a selection called *pause* to each process and arranging the edge labels so that selecting pause causes a self-loop. This has the desired effect of allowing one process to take arbitrarily many steps while other processes are pausing. This feature is used in figure 1 in several places, for example to allow the transmitter TR to wait for an arbitrary amount of time in state IDLE before deciding to start transmitting.

One of the features of COSPAN is that a collection of processes can be combined into a single process with the same behavior, using the operation $\otimes$. The resulting process has states which are vectors of the individual states, selections which combine the individual selection, etc. The chains of a composite process are exactly those described above.

2.2 Monitor Processes and Proving Correctness

A *monitor* is a process whose selections are not used by other processes; it is a task that observes, but does not participate in, the execution of the system. Monitors can be used to constrain the behavior of other processes. If M does not accept all of the chains of a process P, $P \otimes M$ will contain only the chains contained by both P and M. For example, we use this feature to incorporate timing constraints into a process.

To verify correctness of a system, we need a formal specification of its desired properties. In COSPAN, these properties are called the *task*. As in other systems based on a *linear-time* models of behavior, a process satisfies a property if all of its chains satisfy the property, so the task represents the set of all desirable chains.

When verifying in COSPAN, the implementation is usually a product of processes $P = \otimes_{i=1}^{n} P_i$. Verification is especially simple if the monitor (call it TC) actually describes the *undesirable* chains[2]. Then, instead of checking that

---

2 COSPAN can also deal with tasks that are given in uncomplemented form. We don't use this feature here, so we will not discuss it further.

278

every chain of P is desirable, we can check whether *there exists* an undesirable chain; in other words, check whether the set of chains accepted by $P \otimes TC$ is empty. Emptiness can be checked in time proportional to the product of the sizes of the implementation processes and TC.

Frequently, a task is expressed as a product of several smaller tasks, $T = T_1 \otimes T_2 \otimes \cdots \otimes T_k$. In this case, we can independently check if $P \otimes TC_i$ is empty for $i = 1, \ldots, k$ for each complemented task TC_i. This is more efficient than checking for the emptiness of $P \otimes TC$, since it reduces the size of the sets of global states that must be constructed. Furthermore, constructing each TC_i is much easier than constructing TC.

2.3 Liveness Conditions

A liveness condition specifies that an event happens "eventually" without putting a specific finite bound on it. An example is a channel that is guaranteed to deliver a message eventually, but may delay arbitrary before doing so. Liveness properties cannot be specified with processes as defined above, because allowing an arbitrary finite delay necessarily entails allowing an infinite delay, also.

Liveness properties in COSPAN are handled using two additional components of a process: a finite set of *cysets* (for "cycling sets") $CY_i, i = 1, \ldots, m$, and a set of *recur edges RE*. Cysets and recur edges are used to restrict the infinite behaviors of chains: a chain c of P is *accepted* iff its state component satisfies the following conditions: (a) it does not eventually stay in some cyset CY_i, $i = 1, \ldots, m$, and (b) it does not perform infinitely often transitions from the set RE.

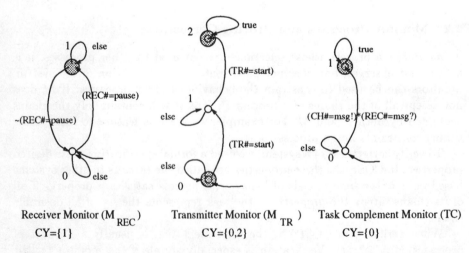

Fig. 2. The Liveness Conditions for the Specification of the Delay Channel. M_{REC} accepts all chains in which not eventually always $REC\# = pause$. M_{TR} accepts all chains in which the transmitter eventually sends a message and then stops. M_{TC} accepts all chains in which the message is never received by the receiver.

Figure 2 shows an example of how to verify some liveness properties for the delay channel example in figure 1. The specification of the system assumes that (a) the receiver always eventually checks for incoming messages, (b) the transmitter eventually transmits a unique message, and (c) the channel does not delay a message forever. These conditions are specified using the monitors M_{REC}, M_{TR} in Figure 2, and by associating the cyset {DELAY} with the channel process CH (we follow the convention of eliminating one set of braces when CY contains only a single set). The task is that the message will be eventually received. This is encoded by the task complement monitor M_{TC}.

3 The Timing Extension

The approach we use to incorporate timing into COSPAN adds to the system description a set of monitor processes which accept only the chains that are consistent with the specified timing constraints.

The specifications of a *timed process* consist of two parts: the *time-independent part* and the *time-dependent part*. The time-independent part specifies a superset of the possible chains that can occur in the actual system, which includes some chains that are not consistent with the timing constraints.

The time-dependent part is represented by a set of constraints of the form "if $c(i)$ satisfies property Q and $c(j)$, $i < j$, satisfies property R, then $l \leq t(j) - t(i) \leq u$", where $c(i)$ and $c(j)$ are elements of the chain of the timing-independent process and l and u are constants. For example, to model a traffic light for which the duration of the green light is between 2 and 3 seconds, Q and R can be defined respectively as "in $c(i)$ the light turns green", "$c(j)$ is the first chain state after $c(i)$ in which the light is red", we get a timing constraint of the form mentioned above with $l = 2, u = 3$.

Each timing constraint is encoded by a *logical timer* T. T has a *set condition* which is property Q, an *expire condition* which is property R, and an *interval specification* which (in the above example) corresponds to the interval $[2, 3]$. The interpretation is that when T is set, it will expire at some arbitrary time in the interval $[2, 3]$ from the time it was set. If needed, we associate with a logical timer a *cancel condition*; when such condition is satisfied after the timer is set, it deactivates the timer (no expiration will take place in the future).

The semantics we give to chains is the following. We assume that a chain corresponds to the sampling of the history of the real-time system at the transition epochs (i.e., immediately after a transition). We also allow an arbitrary number of transitions to occur in zero time.

This time-dependent part of the specification is translated automatically by our extension of the original COSPAN software into a monitor process M_T by using the approach in [Dil89]. This monitor does not accept the chains of the untimed part of the specification which violate the real-time constraints. One can prove by using the results in [Dil89] that the set of timing-consistent chains is the intersection of the timing-independent and timing-dependent processes, in other words, the chains of $P \otimes M_T$. A timed process has no accepted timed behavior (real-time history) iff there is no timing-consistent chain in $P \otimes M_T$, hence iff $P \otimes M_T$ is the empty process.

The monitor works by inferring timing information for the history of timer events in the chains. It stores the timing information in its states and uses it to decide which timing events are allowed next. If a transition on a particular set of timing events is allowed, the monitor updates the state to reflect its inferred changes in timing state. If the events are not allowed, the monitor enters and remains in a "dead" state in which the chain is not accepted (a cyset).

For example, in the case of the traffic light, while the snapshots of the system satisfy the property that the traffic light is green, the time can not progress by more than three seconds. This excludes the occurrence of some other events before the light turns red, if the timing information inferred from the occurrence of these events contradicts the above information.

M_T not only keeps track of the time, but also enforces some timing-independent properties of timers: A timer cannot expire unless it is set, and a timer that is set will eventually expire (a liveness condition).

A product of timed processes can be defined by doing the usual product operation on the untimed parts (to give a new untimed part) and taking the *union* of the timers, to give the set of timers of the product.

Once M_T has been constructed and added to the system description, time-independent properties, which specify only orderings of system events but not time of occurrence, can be verified immediately, using COSPAN as described in the previous section.

A more interesting problem is to verify timed properties, for example, "the time between any two consecutive receptions of a message by the receiver is always less than 2 seconds", or "no two interrupts are sent within less than 1 ms".

Complementing timed processes is very difficult, so we finesse this issue by providing the task complement *directly* by specifying undesirable timed behavior in terms of some timed process, and then checking the emptiness of the composition of the timed processes corresponding to the specification of the system and the task complement. This approach is valid since if there is some "bad" timed behavior, it must satisfy both the timed specification of the system and the timed specification of the complement of the task. Of course our approach is applicable only when the task complement can be expressed as a timed process. In most cases generating a timed task complement is straightforward.

4 Examples

In this section we present S/R specifications and verification results for two well known communication protocols in which real-time is important. Timing information has been included in the S/R models for the Fiber Distributed Data Interface (FDDI) and the Alternating Bit (ABP) Protocols. There is insufficient space to include the full COSPAN specifications, so we summarize here the time related modeling details and the verification objectives.

4.1 FDDI Communication Protocol

Verification of the timing properties of the FDDI timed token access protocol is a challenging task. Our effort is to model FDDI and prove the timing requirements of the protocol with COSPAN. A brief description of FDDI is given below.

A station that wishes to transmit waits until a token frame is released by the previous station on the ring. After seizing the token the station may transmit frames until it has no more data to send or until a token-holding timer expires. This timer was set at the previous time at which the station received a token, and expires after some constant amount of time (which is the same for all the stations on the ring) denoted by TTRT. (This corresponds to the operation of the station for sending "asynchronous" traffic. The FDDI standard is more complex and allows the transmission of "synchronous" traffic as well. A station can always send synchronous traffic at the expense of the asynchronous one. We do not model this for reasons of simplicity, and because to our knowledge, all current FDDI implementations do not support synchronous traffic.) An important property of this protocol is (a) *fairness*, i.e., each station always eventually gets the opportunity to transmit for some positive amount of time and (b) *bounded medium access time*, i.e., the time needed for a station to access the medium is bounded above by some constant, uniformly for all the stations. We have used our method to prove that FDDI satisfies the above properties for a large choice of parameters. Of course our method can not verify the correctness of the protocol in the general case, since we cannot verify parametric specifications.

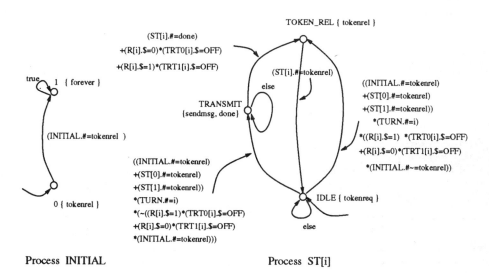

Fig. 3. S/R specification of the initialization process and stations' process.

We have modeled the protocol as follows. The processes of the specification are described in figures 3, 4, 5, 6, 7, and 8. A process called ST is used to model

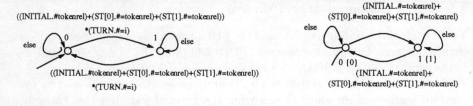

Process R[i]   Process TURN

Fig. 4. R[i] keeps track of the timer that is going to be set with the next token arrival at station i. TURN keeps track of the station that will have the token next time.

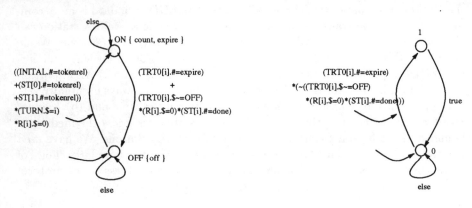

Process TRT0[i]   Monitor MTRT0[i]

Fig. 5. Actual timer process TRT0[i]. MTRT0[i] is a monitor that provides the information about the time TRT0[i] switches state to OFF.

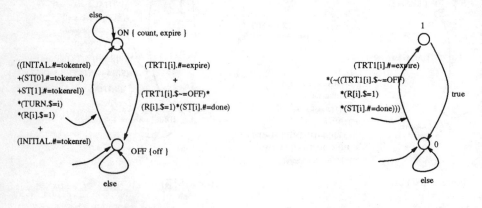

Process TRT1[i]   Monitor MTRT1[i]

Fig. 6. Actual timer process TRT1[i]. MTRT1[i] is a monitor that provides the information about the time TRT1[i] switches state to OFF.

283

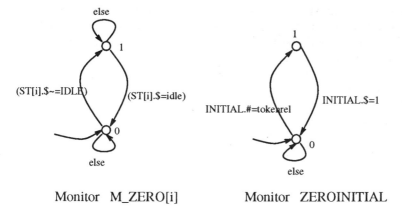

Monitor M_ZERO[i]   Monitor ZEROINITIAL

Fig. 7. Monitor process M_ZERO[i] that provides the information about the first time ST[i] goes to IDLE state. Monitor process ZEROINITIAL that provides the information about the first time INITIAL goes to state 1.

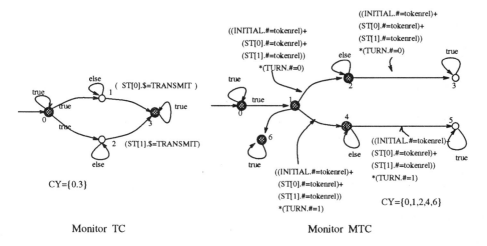

Monitor TC   Monitor MTC

Fig. 8. Task Complement. TC accepts all chains in which some station will transmit finitely many times. MTC is . monitor which tags two consecutive token reception by a station.

stations on the ring. A station can be either in an idle state where it requests for the token, in a transmitting state where it can transmit frames, or in a token-releasing state where it passes the token to the next station. A process called TURN keeps track of which station is going to receive the token next time (for modeling the ring topology). The most interesting part of our specification is the modeling of the timers which are a combination of actual and logical timers. This combination is explained below. Each station has two actual timers which are modeled by the processes TRT0, TRT1. Whenever a token arrives to station i, either TRT0 or TRT1 is set, depending on which state process R is in; R keeps track on the timer that is going to be set by the next token arrival, and there is one such process per station. In our specification TRT0 (TRT1) is set at every odd (even) numbered token arrival at the station. For initialization, TRT1 is set at time 0 for all stations in the ring.

After receiving the token for the k-th time, a station has permission to transmit until the relevant timer expires: if k is odd (even) the relevant timer is TRT1 (TRT0). If this timer has already expired, when the token arrives, the station must immediately release the token without going through the TRANSMIT state. Attached to each actual timer is a logical timer called L_TR_TIMER0, L_TR_TIMER1 respectively, which is set whenever the respective actual timer is set, expires when the respective timer expires, and counts exactly TTRT time units.

An other assumption in our model is that our ring has negligible propagation delays (small with respect to TTRT; this is a valid assumption for most practical cases). We model this by associating logical timers of zero duration with the transitions modeling the exchange of the token by two stations. We also add such a logical timer to model the fact that when the corresponding timer has expired and the station must release the token, this occurs within zero time (fast hardware).

We prove the two tasks mentioned above by using the task–complement monitor processes TC and MTC respectively. The first, TC, guarantees that our protocol is fair, which means that always eventually all the stations have the opportunity to transmit frames (i.e., go to the TRANSMIT state), while the second is a timed task which verifies that 2*TTRT is an upper bound of the token rotation time, that is between any two consecutive token receptions by a station. TC accepts all histories in which for some station state TRANSMIT appears finitely many times. MTC "tags" nondeterministically two consecutive token receptions by some station. We use the logical timers L_TIMER_MTC (one per station) with interval specification $(2*TTRT, \infty]$ to count the time between the above events. Hence MTC accepts all histories for which there is a station which receives the token in two consecutive times in more than $2*TTRT$ time units apart.

The reader will notice that in order to model set and expire conditions for logical timers of the form "process X enters state Y", we need to add monitors which capture the first such time in the chain that process X finds itself in state Y, for each different sojourn of the process in this state. As a final remark, for simplicity our specification is given in terms of a ring consisting of two station. This can be easily upgraded to an arbitrary number of stations.

4.2 Alternating–Bit Communication Protocol

Our model of the alternating–bit protocol is essentially based on the one presented in [ACW90]. Upper layers of this protocol are modeled by two processes called S and R, that generate and receive messages respectively. Two groups of processes model the transmitting and receiving part of the protocol in a peer to peer level. Finally, the lower layers consisting of two half–duplex communication channels that may lose messages and acknowledgements, are modeled by two corresponding channel processes.

Several logical timers have been introduced in order to add timing constraints. These include:

1. The resetable logical timer TICLK. This logical timer is used to supply the real-time information to the retransmission timer TI of the protocol. Its set condition is the same as the set condition of TI, and its expire condition is the expiration of TI, i.e. (TI.# = to). Its interval specification is $[TIME, TIME]$, which implies that the expiration event will occur exactly $TIME$ time units after the set event. Finally, if the correct acknowledgement is received before TI expired (and hence before TICLK expired), then TICLK is canceled.

2. The logical timer CHO_TIMER. This logical timer models the transmission delay of the outgoing channel where messages are sent. CHO_TIMER is set whenever the outgoing channel is handed a message and expires when the outgoing channel delivers or looses the message.

3. The logical timer CHI_TIMER. This logical timer models the transmission delay of the incoming channel where acknowledgements are sent. It is set when the incoming channel is handed an acknowledgement and expires when this acknowledgement is delivered or lost.

These three timers suffice to proof correctness of the protocol, e.g. in-order message delivery. The task complement used in this case is TC as in [ACW90]. However to prove that a message is delivered within specific time bounds, we have to use another logical timer DELIV_TIME, and a new task complement monitor DELIVERY_TIME. This timer is set when the sender decides to send a tagged message, and expires when the message reaches the receiver. Another property to check is whether duplicate copies of a message are ever sent through the outgoing channel under the assumption that the incoming channel does not loose acknowledgements. We have showed that presence of duplicate messages depends on the relation of the timeout value TIME to the sum of the communication channels delays. To prove this we added a new logical timer ZERORECDELAY which ensures that the receiving protocol processes messages in zero time, and we used the monitor DUPLICATES for the task complement. This monitor goes to an error state when a duplicate of a message arrives at the receiving end.

Next we used an extension of the ABP to include the upper protocol layers, in order to study buffer occupancy at the interface above ABP. We added an external message producer PROD, an external message buffer BUF, and we have changed sender S to send messages that PROD generates (this version of the sender process is in the appendix). In this model a message coming from PROD is either temporarily held in BUF in case communication channels are busy, or is directly handed to the transmission protocol using a cut-through mechanism. An logical timer PROD_TIMER controls the rate at which PROD generates messages and a new task complement BUFTHRESHOLD checks whether the buffer occupancy ever exceeds a certain threshold under the assumption that no messages or acknowledgements are lost (this version of the communication channels are in the appendix). Clearly, this depends on the rate at which the producer process generates messages and on the delay characteristics of the channels. We have checked the buffer occupancy for a large range of system parameters.

References

[ABM86] S. Aggarwal, D. Barbara, and K. Z. Meth. Spanner - a tool for the specification, analysis, and evaluation of protocols. *IEEE Trans. on Software Engineering*, 1986.

[AC85] S. Aggarwal and C. Courcoubetis. Distributed implementation of a model of communication and computation. In *Proceedings of the 18th Hawaii Intl. Conference on System Sciences*, pages 206–218, January 1985.

[ACD90] R. Alur, C. Courcoubetis, and D. Dill. Model-checking for real-time systems. In *Proceedings of the 5th Symposium on Logic in Computer Science*, pages 414–425, Philadelphia, June 1990.

[ACD91a] R. Alur, C. Courcoubetis, and D. Dill. Model-checking for probabilistic real-time systems. In *Proceedings of the 18th ICALP*, pages 115–126, Madrid, July 1991.

[ACD91b] R. Alur, C. Courcoubetis, and D. Dill. Verifying automata specifications of probabilistic real-time systems. In *Proceedings of the REX Workshop*, Plasmolen, June 1991.

[ACW90] S. Aggarwal, C. Courcoubetis, and P. Wolper. Adding liveness properties to coupled finite-state machines. *ACM Transactions on Programming Languages and Systems*, 12(2):303–339, 1990.

[AD90] Rajeev Alur and David Dill. Automata for Modeling Real-Time Systems. In *Automata, Languages and Programming : 17th Annual Colloquium*, volume 443 of *Lecture Notes in Computer Science*, pages 322–335, 1990. Warwick University, July 16-20.

[AH90] R. Alur and T. Henzinger. Real-time logics: complexity and expressiveness. In *Proceedings of the 5th Symposium on Logic in Computer Science*, Philadelphia, June 1990.

[AK83] S. Aggarwal and R.P. Kurshan. Modelling elapsed time in protocol specification. In H. Rudin and C.H. West, editors, *Protocol Specification, Testing and Verification, III*, pages 51–62. Elsevier Science Publisers B.V., 1983.

[AKS83] S. Aggarwal, R. P. Kurshan, and K. K. Sabnani. A calculus for protocol specification and validation. In *Protocol Specification, Testing and Verification, III*. North-Holland, 1983.

[Alu91] Rajeev Alur. Techniques for automatic verification of real-time systems. Technical Report STAN-CS-91-1378, Department of Computer Science, Stanford University, August 1991. Ph.D. Thesis.

[BM83] B. Berthomieu and M. Menasche. An enumerative approach for analyzing time petri nets. In *Information Processing*, pages 41–46. Elsevier Scinece Publishers B.V. (North-Holland), 1983.

[Bur89] J. R. Burch. Combining CTL, Trace Theory, and Timing Models. In J. Sifakis, editor, *Automatic Verification Methods for Finite State Systems*, volume 407 of *Lecture Notes in Computer Science*, pages 334–348. Springer-Verlag, 1989.

[CDT]   Costas Courcoubetis, David L. Dill, and Panagiotis Tzounakis. Adding Dense Time Properties to Finite-State Machines: the Tool Cospan. Submitted to a journal.

[Dil89]   D. Dill. Timing assumptions and verification of finite-state concurrent systems. In *Proc. Workshop on Computer Aided Verification*, Grenoble, June 1989. Lecture Notes in Computer Science, Springer-Verlag.

[GK80]   B. Gopinath and B. Kurshan. The selection/resolution model for coordinating concurrent processes. In *AT&T Bell Laboratories Technical Report*, 1980.

[HK89]   Z. Har'El and R. Kurshan. Automatic verification of coordinating systems. In *Proceedings of Workshop on Automatic Verification Methods for Finite-State Systems*, Grenoble, June 1989. Springer Verlag.

[HPOG89]   N. Halbwachs, D. Pilaud, F. Ouabodessalam, and A-C. Glory. Specifying, programming and verifying real-time systems using a synchronous declarative language. In J. Sifakis, editor, *Automatic Verification Methods for Finite State Systems*, volume 407 of *Lecture Notes in Computer Science*. Springer–Verlag, 1989.

[JM86]   F. Jahanian and A. K-L. Mok. Safety analysis of timing properties in real-time systems. *IEEE Transactions on Software Engineering*, 12(9), September 1986.

[KK86]   J. Katzenelson and B. Kurshan. S/R: A language for specifying protocols and other coordinating processes. In *Proc. 5th Ann. Int'l Phoenix Conf. Comput. Commun., IEEE*, 1986.

[Kur90]   R. Kurshan. Analysis of discrete event coordination. *Lecture Notes in Computer Science*, 480, 1990.

[Lew89]   H. R. Lewis. Finite-state analysis of asynchronous circuits with bounded temporal uncertainty. Technical Report TR-15-89, Aiken Computation Laboratory, Harvard University, July 1989.

[Ost90]   J. Ostroff. *Temporal Logic of Real-Time Systems*. Research Studies Press, 1990.

[ZH90]   R. P Kurshan Z. Har'El. Software for analytical development of communication protocols. *AT&T Technical Journal*, 1990.

Model-checking for real-time systems specified in Lotos [*]

N. Rico [†], G.v. Bochmann [†] and O. Cherkaoui [‡]

[†] Département d'informatique et de recherche opérationnelle
Université de Montréal
[‡] Département d'informatique et de mathématiques
Université du Québec à Montréal

Abstract. This paper aims at describing and analyzing concurrent systems whose behavior is dependent on explicit time delays. The formal description technique Lotos [Loto 89] is extended with time intervals in the following way: actions in Lotos must occur at a time t within a given interval $[t_{min}, t_{max}]$ relative to the previous action executed by the process. The syntax and semantics of Time Interval Lotos is given. The model is defined as a labelled transition systems with clocks associated with states and timing conditions associated with transitions. The labelled transition system derived corresponds to a timed graph model [Alur 90]. The logic TCTL (Computation Tree Logic with time) which allows quantitative operators in the formulas can be used to specify assertions. Model-checking is used to determine the truth of a TCTL-formula with respect to a labelled transition system derived from the Time Interval Lotos specification. We illustrate the approach by a simple example. We also present an alternative approach for verifying timing properties. A labelled transition system with time intervals is derived. This graph does not represent the precise evolution of the system in time. Each transition is labelled with an action and a time interval showing the range of possible time occurrences for the action.

1 Introduction

With the proliferation of computer-communication networks and the increasing importance of distributed processing, researchers have worked intensively on the modelling of distributed systems. Formal description techniques such as Lotos [Loto 89, Bolo 87], Estelle [Budk 87] and SDL [SDL 87] have been developed to describe OSI (Open Systems Interconnection) communication protocols and services as well as other kind of distributed systems. Those specification formalisms and the verification methods, however, make abstraction from the quantitative aspect. But for certain type of systems such as real-time systems, the specification methods and verification techniques should incorporate time

[*] Work supported by Bell Northern Research, the Ministry of Education of Quebec and the IDACOM-NSERC-CWARC Industrial Research Chair on Communication Protocols at the University of Montreal

values since the correctness of the system depends not only on the logical result of the computation but also on the time at which the results are produced.

This paper addresses the issue of correctness of a system which is specified with a formal description technique and where actual time values are included in the specification. The idea is to check whether the specified system satisfies a number of desirable properties that include time. Properties can be formulated in a temporal logic formalism augmented with quantitative time. If the system has a finite number of states, then we can use a model-checking approach which is an algorithmic method for verifying automatically those properties. It consists of checking that a given state graph derived from the formal description of the system satisfies a given temporal formula.

The formal description technique we consider in this paper is a variant of Lotos defined in Section 2, called Time Interval Lotos, which adds time intervals of the form $[t_{min}, t_{max}]$ to Lotos actions. An action a, once enabled, cannot occur before time t_{min} and must occur before t_{max} time has elapsed since its enabling, unless it is disabled by the occurrence of another action. The semantics is defined in terms of a labelled transition system which includes clocks associated to states and timing enabling conditions associated to transitions. Temporal formulas are expressed in the logic TCTL [Alur 90], which is an extension of CTL with continuous time. The time assertions written in TCTL are checked against the labelled transition system with clocks and timing conditions generated from the Timed Interval Lotos specification. We also present in Section 5 an alternative approach for verifying timing properties. A labelled transition system with time intervals is derived. This graph shows all the possible paths of timed actions but does not represent the precise evolution of the system in time. Each transition is labelled with an action and a time interval showing the range of possible time occurrences for the action. The contribution of the paper is hence, on the first hand, the definition of an extension of Lotos with Time Intervals and the derivation of a labelled transition system on which model-checking can be performed, and, on the second hand, the presentation of an alternative approach to verify timing properties.

Related work: Process algebras such as CCS [Miln 80], CSP [Hoar 85] and ACP [Berg 84] have been extended with timing characteristics. Nicollin and Sifakis [Nico 91] presented an overview of existing results about timed process algebras. Quemada et al. [Quem 89] proposed a time extension of Lotos where an occurrence time is associated with each action: this time indicates the global time when the action must occur. Bolognesi et al. [Bolo 90b] define a time extension of Lotos which offers operators for specifying the urgency of a specified action. Their model is similar to the Time Petri Net of Merlin and Farber [Merl 76]. In [Rico 91], the model considered is an extension of Lotos with actions that have an associated specific time of occurrence and weights associated in the case of a probabilistic choice. The goal was to predict the performance of distributed systems. The model proposed in this paper considers an extension of Lotos with time intervals associated with actions: time intervals are better suited for the verification of timing assertions. Emerson et al. [Emer 89] defined an extension of

CTL (RTCTL) with discrete time which can be used to specify and verify hard deadlines. Hansson [Hans 91] also extended CTL with time and probability. His temporal logic formulas are interpreted over a labelled transition system derived from a modification of CCS which includes discrete time and probabilities. Alur, Courcoubetis, and Dill [Alur 90] also proposed an extension to CTL, but in their logic (TCTL) formulas are interpreted over models with continuous time. They introduce the concept of a timed graph to model a finite-state real-time system: the system is equipped with a finite set of clocks which record the time elapsed since they were reset. They developed a model checking algorithm for determining the truth of a TCTL formula with respect to a timed graph. Lewis [Lewi 90] presented a variation of CTL with continuous time that is interpreted over a finite-state model in which the time delays between events are constrainted to fall between upper and lower integer time bounds.

The paper is organized as follows. In the next section, we describe a semantics for Time Interval Lotos. In Section 3, the branching time logic with time TCTL is presented as well as the model-checking method for checking TCTL-formulas in respect to a given Time Interval Lotos specification. In Section 4, a small example is given. In Section 5, a method for enumerating all possible timed paths is described. Finally, we discuss the modelling approach in the conclusion.

2 Lotos with Time Intervals

Time Interval Lotos is a variant of Lotos (Language Of Temporal Ordering Specification) [Loto 89, Bolo 87], which adds time intervals to Lotos actions. In this section, we will present Lotos and define our timing interval extension.

2.1 Lotos

Lotos [Loto 89, Bolo 87] is an algebraic specification language based on CCS [Miln 80]. Lotos is defined in terms of processes and uses rendez-vous interactions. The rendez-vous may involve two or more processes and occurs at an interaction point called a gate: it happens when all Lotos processes coupled to the gate are ready for that interaction.Interaction and process parameters are described by ACT ONE [Ehri 85] abstract datatype definitions. We are interested in the basic Lotos language which does not include the interaction and process parameters. The operations of basic Lotos are the following, where B, B_1, B_2 are behavior expressions, a is an action and $g_1, \ldots, g_n$ are gate identifiers:

Inaction	stop	Process instantiation	$p[g_1, \ldots, g_n]$
Action prefix	$a; B$	Parallel composition	$B_1 |[g_1, \ldots, g_n]| B_2$
Choice	$B_1 [] B_2$	Pure Interleaving	$B_1 ||| B_2$
Termination	exit	Relabeling	$p[g_1/g_1', \ldots, g_n/g_n']$
Enabling	$B_1 >> B_2$	Hiding	hide $g_1, \ldots, g_n$ in B
Disabling	$B_1 [> B_2$		

2.2 Time Interval Lotos: Presentation of the Model

This section describes LOTOS which has been enhanced with time intervals of the form $[t_{min}, t_{max}]$ where t_{min} and t_{max} are natural numbers. Those intervals are associated with each action a and are relative to the moment at which the previous action within the same process was executed. When the previous action is executed, we say that action a is "locally" enabled or that action a is enabled due to the execution of a previous "local" action of the process. An implicit global clock exists in the transition system. Assuming that the previous local action has been executed at a global time g_t, action a cannot fire before time $g_t + t_{min}$ and must fire before or at time $g_t + t_{max}$ unless it is disabled by the occurrence of another action. The time domain is represented as real numbers.

Time Interval Lotos assumes that the time intervals associated with the actions have a local meaning. This is the same in Quemada's model [Quem 89]: every action is assigned a single time stamp which indicates the exact time at which the action shall happen relative to the previous local action. A time choice construct also exists for representing the occurrence of an event at an unspecified instant of time out of a given set. The difference between Time Interval Lotos and Quemada's model resides in the definition of the labelled transition system (LTS): the LTS derived in Quemada's model contains transitions with their time of occurrence whereas the LTS derived for Time Interval Lotos has clocks and timing conditions and can therefore deal with time intervals. The other main difference between the two models is that in Quemada's model, some transitions may not be derived due to the timing relation between the different components whereas the LST derived for our model is the same LTS derived by the usual Lotos inference rules with additional timing constraints.

In the model of Bolognesi et al. [Bolo 90b], the time intervals associated with actions have a global meaning, which makes the model semantically very different from ours. An action is enabled when all the processes participating in the action are ready to interact. The model of Bolognesi expresses the urgency of actions, i.e. the fact that something happens as soon as all the processes are ready for it. Bolognesi's model has more expressive power since it can simulate a Turing machine [Bolo 90b]. It can easily model the situation where two processes must synchronize after each one independently executes an action with unbounded delay (i.e. with interval $[0, \infty]$). This situation is not modeled adequately by models in which actions have a local meaning. However, in the case where two processes must synchronize after only one of them executes an action with unbounded delay, then the two types of models are as expressive. This second case occurs more frequently in real examples hence the limitation mentionned in the case of symmetric unbounded delay is not often encountered. One disavantage of the approach of Bolognesi is that there are more properties which are undecidable whereas our model can be more easily analyzed.

2.3 Time Interval Lotos Semantics

The syntax of Time Interval Lotos is the same as standard Lotos except for the action prefix: instead of writing $a; B$ for an action followed by behavior B, we write $a[t_{min}, t_{max}]; B$ which means that action a must occur at a time t in the interval $[t_{min}, t_{max}]$.

The model of Time Interval Lotos is a labelled transition system as defined by the Lotos operational semantics. Each system has a finite set of clocks Cks. We associate with every behavior expression a subset C of Cks. C is a set of clock identifiers corresponding to the clocks which are reset to 0. We associate with each interaction offer a clock which is a fictitious component that keeps track of the possible time at which the event can occur. For example, in the expression $a; b; stop|[b]|b; c; stop$, we associate a clock with a, with c, with offer b in the left side of the parallel expression and with offer b in the right side of the parallel expression. There are as many clock identifiers as there are interaction offers in the system. We use the following notation for the clock identifier: c_{ai} is the clock identifier of offer a where i is a natural number. In the case of an action that is not involved in a rendez-vous, the clock identifier is simply noted c_a. Transitions are labelled with actions and with an enabling condition which is built using the boolean connectives over the formulas of the form $x[t_{min}, t_{max}]$, where $x \in Cks$, and $t_{min}, t_{max} \in N$. An action a with enabling condition $\tau(a) = x[t_{min}, t_{max}]$ is possible if the value of clock identifier x is in the interval $[t_{min}, t_{max}]$.

Definition (Model of Time Interval Lotos behavior: Timed graph)
For a given behavior B_0, the model of Time Interval Lotos behavior is a labelled transition system $< Cks, S, A, TR, s_0 >$, where :

- Cks is a finite set of clocks.
- $S = \{B_C\}$ is the set of all possible states, represented by behaviors, to which we associate a set of clocks that are reset to 0 when the state is entered.
- $A = \{a \ \tau(a)|a \in L(B) \cup \{i\}\}$ is the set of all possible actions. $L(B)$ is the alphabet of actions and i is the internal action. $\tau(a)$ is a function that associates with each edge an enabling condition built using the boolean connectives over the formulas of the form $x[t_{min}, t_{max}]$, where $x \in Cks$, and $t_{min}, t_{max} \in N$.
- $TR \subset S \times S$ is a set of relations $-a\tau(a) \rightarrow$ defining the pairs of states associated with action a. We write $B_1 - a \ \tau(a) \rightarrow B_2$ iff $< B1, B2 >\in TR$.
- $s_0 = B_{0 \ C_0}$ is the initial state where C_0 is the set of clocks corresponding to actions initially enabled.

The timed graph obtained resembles the timed graph of Alur et al. [Alur 90] except that it does not include the proposition truth value assignments to states. The semantic rules of Lotos operators [Loto 89] have to be redefined in order to associate timing conditions with transitions and a set of clocks with behavior expressions. The rules for some of the operators are the following:

Action with Time Interval: The timing condition associated with interaction offer ai for gate a states that the value of clock c_{ai} must be in $[t_{min}, t_{max}]$.

$$(a[t_{min}, t_{max}]; B)_C - a \ c_{ai}[t_{min}, t_{max}] \rightarrow B_{C'}$$
$$where \ C' = \{c_{bj} \mid \exists B' \ such \ that \ B_{C'} - b \ \tau(b) \rightarrow B'_{C''}\}$$

Choice $B_1 [] B_2$:

$$\mathbf{C1.} \quad \frac{B_{1C_1} - a_1 \ \tau(a_1) \to B'_{1C'_1}}{(B_1 [] B_2)_C - a_1 \ \tau(a_1) \to B'_{1C'_1}}$$

C2. *symmetric of rule C1*

Parallelism $B_1 |[G]| B_2$:

$$\mathbf{P1.} \quad \frac{B_{1C_1} - a \ \tau_1(a) \to B'_{1C'_1} \quad B_{2C_2} - a \ \tau_2(a) \to B'_{2C'_2}}{(B_1 |[G]| B_2)_C - a \ (\tau_1(a) \ and \ \tau_2(a)) \to (B'_1 |[G]| B'_2)_{C'_1 \cup C'_2}} \quad a \in G$$

$$\mathbf{P2.} \quad \frac{B_{1C_1} - a \ \tau(a) \to B'_{1C'_1}}{(B_1 |[G]| B_2)_C - a \ \tau(a) \to (B'_1 |[G]| B_2)_{C'_1}} \quad a \notin G$$

P3. *symmetric of rule P2*

Process instantiation $B = p[g_1, g_2, \ldots, g_n]$:

$$\frac{B_p[g_1/h_1, \ldots, g_n/h_n]_C - a \ \tau(a) \to B'_{C'}}{B_C - a\tau(a) \to B'_{C'}}$$

where B_P represents the body of the definition of process p, $(g_1, \ldots, g_n)$ is a list of formal gates, $(h_1, \ldots, h_n)$ is a list of actual gates, $[g_1/h_1, \ldots, g_n/h_n]$ is the relabeling postfix operator, (gate g_i becomes gate h_i for $i = 1, \ldots, n$). The semantic rules of the other operators are defined in [Rico 92].

2.4   Example

The following example illustrates a timeout situation. This example is semantically the same as the one described in [Bolo 90a].
$$P[a, b, c] = Q[a, b] |[b]| R[b, c]$$
$$Q[a, b] = a[0, \infty]; b[0, 0]; Q[a, b]$$
$$R[b, c] = b[0, \infty]; R[b, c][]c[10, 10]; stop$$

Let the clock identifier for actions a, c, b (in process Q) and b (in process R) be respectively c_a, c_c, c_{b1}, c_{b2}. C is the subset of the clocks reset to 0. The labelled transition system for this example is the following:

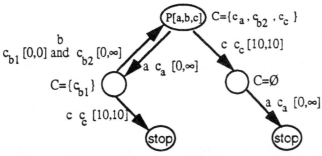

Figure 1. Labelled transition system of P[a.b,c]

3 Model Checking using Time Computation Tree Logic

In this section, we will describe the temporal logic TCTL [Alur 90] and explain how to perform model checking for Time Interval Lotos specifications.

3.1 Time Computation Tree Logic (TCTL)

Computation Tree Logic (CTL) is a branching time logic that was introduced by Emerson and Clarke [Clar 83] as a specification language for finite-state systems. Alur, Courcoubetis and Dill [Alur 90] proposed an extension of CTL with continuous time. The resulting logic is called TCTL and is interpreted over continuous computation trees, i.e. trees in which paths are maps from the set of nonnegative reals to system states. The syntax of TCTL is the following:

Definition [TCTL Syntax]

Let P be the set of atomic propositions. The TCTL formulas are inductively defined as follows: $\phi := p \mid \text{false} \mid \phi_1 \rightarrow \phi_2 \mid \exists\, \phi_1 U_{\sim c}\, \phi_2 \mid \forall\, \phi_1 U_{\sim c}\, \phi_2$

where $p \in P, c \in N, \phi, \phi_1$ and ϕ_2 are TCTL-formulas, and $\sim$ stands for one of the binary relation $<, \leq, =, \geq$ or $>$.

Intuitively $\exists \phi_1 U_{<c}\phi_2$ ($\forall \phi_1 U_{<c}\phi_2$) means that for some (all) path(s), there exists an initial prefix of time length less than c such that ϕ_2 holds at the last state of the prefix and ϕ_1 holds at all the intermediate states.

The semantics is defined with respect to a structure $M = (S, \mu, f)$, where S is a set of states, $\mu \colon S \rightarrow 2^P$ gives an assignment of truth values to propositions in each state, and f is a map giving for each $s \in S$ a set of dense paths starting at that state. f satisfies: $\forall s \in S, \forall \rho \in f(s), \forall t \in R, \rho_t f[\rho(t)] \subseteq f(s)$ where ρ_t is the prefix of path ρ upto time t and $\rho(t)$ is a state corresponding to time t.

Definition [TCTL Semantics].

Let $p \in P$, $c \in N$ and $\sim$ stands for one of the binary relation $<, \leq, =, \geq$ or $>$. For a structure $M = (S, \mu, f)$, a state $s \in S$ and a formula ϕ, the satisfaction relation $(M, s) \models \phi$ is defined inductively as follows:

$(M, s) \not\models \text{false}$

$(M, s) \models p$ iff $p \in \mu(s)$

$(M, s) \models (\phi_1 \rightarrow \phi_2)$ iff $s \not\models \phi_1$ or $s \models \phi_2$

$(M, s) \models \exists \phi_1 U_{\sim c}\phi_2$ iff for some $\rho \in f(s)$, for some $t \sim c$, $\rho(t) \models \phi_2$, and for all $0 \leq t' < t, \rho(t') \models \phi_1$.

$(M, s) \models \forall \phi_1 U_{\sim c}\phi_2$ iff for all $\rho \in f(s)$, for some $t \sim c$, $\rho(t) \models \phi_2$, and for all $0 \leq t' < t, \rho(t') \models \phi_1$.

A TCTL-formula f is called satisfiable iff there is a structure M and a state s such that $(M, s) \models \phi$.

3.2 Model-Checking

Model-checking is a method for verifying concurrent systems in which a given state graph of the system behavior is compared with a given temporal logic formula. It is one of the most successful techniques for automatically checking that a given temporal formula, written in propositional temporal logic, is satisfied by a state-transition graph that represents the actual behavior of the system. One of the advantages of the method is its efficiency. Model-checking is linear in the product of the size of the structure and the size of the formula when the logic is the branching-time temporal logic CTL. With time values, the complexity of the model checking algorithm using TCTL is exponential in the number of clocks and the length of the timing constraints, but linear in the size of the state-transition graph and the length of the formula [Alur 90].

In the model-checking approach for Time Interval Lotos, the idea is to construct the timed graph from the Lotos specification and to add the proposition truth value assignments to the states of this timed graph. The generation of this timed graph is explained in Section 2. We add to this timed graph a labeling function $\mu : S \to 2^P$ which assigns to each state the set of atomic propositions true in that state. The resulting structure is a timed graph in the sense of [Alur 90] and is the structure used for model-checking. Properties to be verified are written in TCTL. User-defined TCTL-formulas are checked against this structure using the algorithm of Alur et al. [Alur 90].

4 Example: Stop and Wait Protocol

4.1 Specification of the Protocol

In this section, we demonstrate the modeling approach described above by presenting the stop-and-wait protocol, which is a simplified version of the alternating bit protocol. This protocol uses two types of messages : information (info) frames and acknowledgement (ack) frames. The transmitter sends an info frame and waits for an ack frame from the receiver. The medium is unreliable in both directions. The specification of the protocol is the following:

```
specification stop-and-wait [get, give] : noexit
behaviour
hide sendinfo, recinfo, sendack, recack in
     ((transmitter[get,sendinfo,recack] |[]| receiver[give,sendack,recinfo])
     |[sendinfo,recinfo,sendack,recack]|
     medium[sendinfo,recinfo,sendack recack] )
where process transmitter[get,sendinfo recack]: noexit :=
     get [0, 1]; sendinfo [0, 1]; sending[get,sendinfo,recack]
where process sending[get,sendinfo,recack] : noexit :=
     recack [0, 2];transmitter[get,sendinfo,recack]
     []i[10, 10];sendinfo[0, 1];sending[get,sendinfo,recack] (*timeout*)
     endproc (*sending*)
endproc (*transmitter*)
process receiver[give,sendack,recinfo]: noexit :=
     recinfo[0, ∞];(give[0, 1];(sendack[0, 1][]i[0, 1]); receiver[give,sendack,recinfo]
               []i[0, 1] receiver[give,sendack,recinfo])
```

296

endproc (*receiver*)
process medium[sendinfo,recinfo,sendack,recack] : noexit :=
    sendinfo[0, ∞]; (recinfo [0, 2];medium[sendinfo,recinfo,sendack,recack])
              [](*i*[0, 2];medium[sendinfo,recinfo,sendack,recack]))
[]   sendack[0, ∞]; (recack [0, 2];medium[sendinfo,recinfo,sendack,recack])
              [](*i*[0, 2];medium[sendinfo,recinfo,sendack,recack]))
endproc (*medium*)
endspec (*stop-and-wait*)

The global behavior is determined by applying the inference rules described in Section 2. The following graph shows the labelled transition system with clocks and timing conditions, where $i(s)$, $i(m)$ and $i(r)$ denote the internal action associated with process sending, medium and receiver, respectively. For readability, we did not indicate the timing condition associated with the internal actions: they are $ci(s)[10, 10]$, $ci(r)[0, 1]$, $ci(m)[0, 2]$.

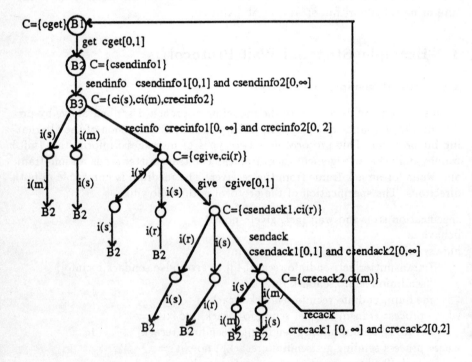

Figure 2. Timed graph of the stop-and-wait protocol

4.2 Model-Checking

One property that may be of interest is that for each *sendinfo* action there is always a subsequent *recack*. For an open system where we do not make any assumptions about the environment, this property does not hold since there is a possibility that the environment will never attempt to communicate a *get* or a *give*. On the other hand, in a closed system, we can verify the following hard deadline that specifies that a *recack* will appear within 10 time units. The closed system is obtained by the following specification, where the user is always prepared to engage in the actions *get* or *give*:

hide |[get,give]| in stop-and-wait [get, give] |[get,give]| user[get, give]

where process user[get,give]: noexit :=

get[0,1]; user[get,give] [] give[0,1]; user[get give]

endproc (*user*)

The property to be verified is the following (the silent action i is parametrized by the action to which the hide operator was applied):

for all paths, $[i(sendinfo) \rightarrow$ true $U_{\leq 10}\ i(recack)]\ U_{<\infty}\ false$

The labelling starts from the subformulas $i(sendinfo)$, $i(recack)$, true and false. It then proceeds to the modal formulas $U_{\leq 10}$. The formula ϕ is not verified for the labelled transition system of the stop and wait protocol since the process *sending* may execute the internal action several times and the *recack* may appear after 10 time units.

5 Path Enumeration for Time Interval Lotos

We assume that we have a Time Interval Lotos specification where a time interval is associated with each action. An alternative approach to the verification of timing properties is to derive a graph that captures all the allowed sequences of actions as well as certain constraints on the time interval in which the allowed actions are to take place. This approach enumerates the possible paths composed of timed actions. Hence we can determine from the path enumeration graph if the system contains livelocks or deadlocks. This approach is similar to the one proposed in [Bert 91].

The timed graph described in Section 2 shows paths which are not possible due to the timing constraints associated with the transitions. For example, in the timed graph of the stop-and-wait protocol shown in figure 3, the paths where action $i(s)$ is followed by action $i(m)$ are not valid since the timing conditions associated with those actions cannot be satisfied. On the opposite, the paths shown in the path enumeration graph are all possible.

We will present informally how the path enumeration graph can be constructed. This graph is composed of nodes and transitions. Each node corresponds to a state augmented with time constraints $< B, T >$ where T is the system of inequalities showing the time constraints of the offers enabled. The time constraints T are the following (we will explain below why the constraints have this specific form):

$tmin_{ai} \leq t_{ai} \leq tmax_{ai}$ for all interaction offer ai enabled

$t_{ai} - t_{bj} \leq d_{ai,bj}$ for all ai and bj, $a \neq b$

Each transition is labelled with an action and a time interval: the time interval indicates the range of possible time when the action may occur.

It is assumed that the times are relative to the moment at which a previous local action has been executed. When first enabled, the times of the offers must satisfy the following inequalities: $imin_{ai} \leq t_{ai} \leq imax_{ai}$ where $imin_{ai}$ and $imax_{ai}$ correspond to the upper and lower bounds of the interval associated with offer ai and t_{ai} is the time of occurrence of a.

Let us consider a transition corresponding to the execution of action f. When f is executed at time t_f, the inequalities of the remaining interaction offers enabled must be updated to eliminate the variable t_f from the system of inequalities. The modified system of inequalities is associated to the next state. Those inequalities become: $tmin'_{ai} \leq t'_{ai} \leq tmax'_{ai}$ for all $a \neq f$ where the new bounds for the action a are $tmin'_{ai}$ and $tmax'_{ai}$ and where $t_{ai} = t_f + t'_{ai}$.

When the variable t_f is eliminated from the system T, this may introduce a relationship between two other variables t_{ai} and t_{bj} that remain enabled. This relationship can be expressed by the following constraint: $t'_{ai} - t'_{bj} \leq d'_{ai,bj}$ where $d'_{ai,bj}$ is the maximal difference between the two variables t'_{ai} and t'_{bj}. This additionnal constraint may narrow the possible occurrence times of future actions, resulting in a time interval for future actions with tigher bounds.

In the initial state or for any new offer a enabled, we can take the following default values for $tmin_{ai}, tmax_{ai}, d_{ai,bj}$:
$tmin_{ai} = imin_{ai}$ and $tmax_{ai} = imax_{ai}$ for all interaction offer ai
$d_{ai,bj} = tmax_{bj} - tmin_{ai}$ for all pair of offers ai, bj with $a \neq b$.

The path enumeration graph is derived from a Time Interval Lotos behavior expression. Given a state $< B, T >$, we determine all the possible transitions that can be derived. We label the transitions of the graph with one of the possible offer f enabled. Action f can occur in the following interval: $[max_i(tmin_{f_i}), min_{a,j}(tmax_{aj})]$. The new state reached is $< B', T' >$ where B' is a new behavior expression derived and T' is the new set of constraints having the same form as T.

The new time region T' is computed from T in the following way:
Step 1. Eliminate from the system the time variables that corresponds to the offers disabled by the occurrence of action f. Each elimination of a variable t_{ej} transforms the system of inequalities in the following way:
$tmin'_{ai} = max(tmin_{ai}, tmin_{ej} - d_{ej,ai})$
$tmax'_{ai} = min(tmax_{ai}, tmax_{ej} + d_{ai,ej})$
$d'_{ai,bk} = min(d_{ai,bk}, d_{ai,ej} + d_{ej,bk})$
Step 2. Express all remaining times t_{ai} of all actions a where $f \neq a$ as the sum of t_f and a new variable t'_{ai}, and eliminate from T all old variables, including t_f.
$tmin'_{ai} = max(0, -d_{fj,ai}, tmin_{ai} - tmax_{fj})$
$tmax'_{ai} = min(d_{ai,fj}, tmax_{ai} - tmin_{fj})$
$d'_{ai,bj} = min(d_{ai,bj}, tmax_{ai} - tmin_{bj})$
Step 3. Add the time interval constraints corresponding to the new actions enabled. The time intervals are the one associated with the interaction offer in the specification.

$tmin'_{ai} = imin_{ai}$ and $tmax'_{ai} = imax_{ai}$ for all new offers ai enabled
$d'_{ai,bj} = imax_{bj} - imin_{ai}$ for all offers bj enabled ($b \neq a$)

Consider the following example. The corresponding graph is shown in figure 3.
$B = B_1|[a_3, a_4]|B_2|[a_3, a_4]|B_3$
$B_1 = a_1[1, 6]; (a_2[1, 6] ||| a_3[2, 3] ||| a_4[1, 4]); B_1$
$B_2 = a_4[1, 4]; B_2$
$B_3 = a_3[2, 3]; B_3$

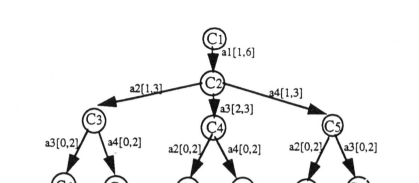

Figure 3. Graph enumarating all possible paths of B

The set of time constraints associated with each state is the following:

State	T	State	T	State	T
C_1	$1 \leq t_{a1} \leq 6$	C_2	$1 \leq t_{a2} \leq 6$ $2 \leq t_{a3} \leq 3$ $1 \leq t_{a4} \leq 4$	C_3	$0 \leq t_{a3} \leq 2$ $0 \leq t_{a4} \leq 3$ $t_{a4} - t_{a3} \leq 2$ $t_{a3} - t_{a4} \leq 2$
C_4	$0 \leq t_{a2} \leq 4$ $0 \leq t_{a4} \leq 2$ $t_{a4} - t_{a2} \leq 3$ $t_{a2} - t_{a4} \leq 5$	C_5	$0 \leq t_{a2} \leq 5$ $0 \leq t_{a3} \leq 2$ $t_{a2} - t_{a3} \leq 4$ $t_{a3} - t_{a2} \leq 2$	C_6	$0 \leq t_{a4} \leq 2$
C_7	$0 \leq t_{a3} \leq 2$	C_8	$0 \leq t_{a4} \leq 2$	C_9	$0 \leq t_{a2} \leq 4$
C_{10}	$0 \leq t_{a3} \leq 2$	C_{11}	$0 \leq t_{a2} \leq 5$		

In the graph enumerating all paths, each state has only a finite number of successor states, at most one for each action enabled. In deriving the states of this graph, a state $< B', T' >$ is equal to a previously defined state $< B, T >$, if the behavior reached is the same ($B = B'$) and if the time constraints are the same $(T = T')$. At each new state, if the behavior reached equals a behavior already generated $(B = B')$, the system of inequalities associated with B' is solved and compared with the solution of a system of inequalities associated with B. This can be done in polynomial time because the system of inequalities have only at most two variables per inequality [Aspv 79]. When the two systems yield the same solution, the new state is the same as the one already derived. The derivation of the graph stops when processes come into a deadlock state or if the states have all been generated. Hence the same behavior can be associated with two different states if the time regions are different for the two states.

6 Summary and Conclusions

Lotos and other formalisms abstract away from time, retaining only the sequencing of events in a system. But for a large class of systems including real-time systems, we need to be able to specify time values and to verify that the system meets certain hard real-time constraints. This paper presents an extension of Lotos with Time Intervals. Its semantics is defined in terms of a labelled transition system augmented with clocks and timing conditions associated with transitions. In the model of Time Interval Lotos presented, time is continuous and not discrete and represented in the form of an interval associated with actions.

Model-checking can be applied to the timed graph obtained from the Time Interval Lotos specification. The formalism we use to express timing assertions about the system is an extension of the branching time logic CTL called TCTL. TCTL is a temporal logic formalism defined by Alur et al. [Alur 90] which handles continuous time. A model-checking approach developed by Alur et al. [Alur 90] is used for verifying that properties expressed in TCTL are verified by the model of Time Interval Lotos.

Another approach to the verification of timing properties is the derivation of all the possible sequences of actions and associated time. The graph generated shows sequences of actions and indicates in what interval the actions can occur. It does not give the evolution for particuliar time values but shows all the possible occurrence times for each action in the path. With this graph, one can determine if the system contains livelock and deadlocks since all the possible execution times are generated.

7 References

[Alur 90] Alur, R., Courcoubetis, C. and Dill, D., "Model-checking for real-time systems", Proc. of 5th IEEE Symp. on Logic in Computer Science, June 90.
[Aspv 79] Aspvall, B and Shiloach, "A polynomial time algorithm for solving systems of inequalities with two variables per inequality", in Proc. 20th Annu. Symp. Foundations of Computer Sciences, Oct. 1979, pp.205-217.
[Berg 84] Bergstra, J.A. and Klop, J.W., "Process Algebra for Synchronous Communication", Information and Control, 60 (1-3), 1984.

[Bert 91] Berthomieu, B. and Diaz, M., "Modeling and Verification of Time Dependent Systems Using Time Petri Nets", IEEE Trans. on SE,17,3, March 1991, pp.259-273.

[Bolo 87] Bolognesi, T. and Brinskma, E., "Introduction to the ISO specification language LOTOS", Computer Networks and ISDN Systems,14,1, 1987.

[Bolo 90a] Bolognesi, T., Lucidi, F. and Trigila, S., "From Timed Petri Nets to Timed LOTOS", Proceedings of 10th IFIP WG6.1 PSTV, June 1990.

[Bolo 90b] Bolognesi, T. and Lucidi F., "LOTOS-like process algebras with urgent or timed interactions", FORTE 90, 1990.

[Budk 87] Budkowski, S. and Dembinski, P., "An introduction to Estelle: a specification language for distributed systems", Computer Networks and ISDN Systems,14,1, 1987, pp.3-23.

[Clar 83] Clarke, E., Emerson, E. and Sistla, A., "Automatic verification of finite-state concurrent systems using temporal logic specifications: A practical approach", in Proc.10th ACM Symp. on Principles of Programming Languages, pp.117-126, 1983.

[Ehri 85] Ehrig, H. and Mahr, B., "Fundamentals of Algebraic Specification 1", Springer Verlag, 1985.

[Emer89] Emerson, E.A., Mok, A.K., Sistla, A.P. and Srinivasan, J., "Quantitative temporal reasoning",in Proceedings of workshop on Automatic Verif. Methods for Finite State Systems, June 1989.

[Hans 91] Hansson, H., "Time and Probability in Formal Design of Distributed Systems", Ph.D. Thesis, Uppsala University, September 1991.

[Hoar 85] Hoare, C., "Communicating sequential processes", Prentice Hall, 1985.

[Hulz 90] van Hulzen, W., Tilanus, P., Zuidweg, H., "LOTOS extended with clocks", Proceedings of FORTE'89, Noth-Holland 1990.

[Lewi 90] Lewis, H.R., "A logic of concrete time intervals", 5th IEEE Symnposium on Logic in Computer Science, June 1990.

[Loto 89] ISO/TC97/SC21, "LOTOS: A Formal Description Technique based on the temporal ordering of observational behavior", Tech. Report IS8807, 1989.

[Merl 76] Merlin, P. and Farber, D., "Recoverability of communication protocols-Implication of a theoretical study", IEEE Trans. on Comm.,24,6, Sept.1976.

[Miln 80] Milner, R., "A Calculus of Communicating Systems", LNCS 92, Springer Verlag, 1980, 171p.

[Nico 91] Nicollin, X. and Sifakis, J., "An overview and synthesis on timed process algebras", CAV'91, Aalborg, Denmark, July 1991.

[Quem 89] Quemada, J., Azcorra, A. and Frutos, D., "A Timed Calculus for LOTOS", Proceedings of FORTE'89, Vancouver, June 1989.

[Rico 91] Rico, N., and Bochmann, G.v., "Performance description and analysis for distributed systems using a variant of Lotos", Proceedings 11th PSTV,1991.

[Rico 92] Rico, N., and Bochmann, G.v., "Time Interval Lotos", Technical Report, University of Montreal, 1992.

[SDL 87] CCITT SG XI, Recommendation Z.100 (1987).

Decidability of Bisimulation Equivalences for Parallel Timer Processes

Kārlis Čerāns
Institute of Mathematics and Computer Science,
University of Latvia
Riga, Rainis blvd. 29, Latvia LV-1050
E-mail: karlis%cs.lu.riga.lv@ussr.eu.net

Abstract. In this paper an abstract model of parallel timer processes (PTPs), allowing specification of temporal quantitative constraints on the behaviour of real time systems, is introduced. The parallel timer processes are defined in a dense time domain and are able to model both concurrent (with delay intervals overlapping on the time axis) and infinite behaviour. Both the strong and weak (abstracted from internal actions) bisimulation equivalence problems for PTPs are proved *decidable*. It is proved also that, if one provides the PTP model additionally with memory cells for moving timer value information along the time axis, the bisimulation equivalence (and even the vertex reachability) problems become undecidable.

1 Introduction

The problem of specification of quantitative timed aspects of real time systems has been widely studied over the last years. This research has resulted in a number of timed specification formalisms covering various aspects of real time system specification process, for some impression of what has been done one can see, for example, [MF76, GMMP89, CC88, AD90, ABBCK91, RR86, Wan91]. There are also a lot of interesting results devoted to the *analysis* of quantitative timed behaviour of real time systems. One can recall here at first the enumerative approach to the Time Petri net [MF76] analysis in [BM83] (actually showing the decidability of the reachability problem for bounded Time Petri Nets). In [AD90] it is showed that for Timed Büchi automata the language emptiness problem is decidable whilst the language inclusion problem is not (it is easy to extend this result also to show the undecidability of the language equivalence problem). A model checking algorithm for branching time temporal logic formulae over Timed Graphs is given in [ACD90].

In [ABBCK91, Cer92a] the analysis automation possibilities (decidability of reachability, complete branch covering, finite and infinite path feasibility problems) are investigated for r.t.s. with dependencies on both quantitative timing constraints and external (integer-valued) data.

All the abovementioned timed specification formalisms are based on the assumption of the *density* of the used space of time moments (time domain) when the action or transition firing is allowed. In this paper we also consider real time systems over dense time domains; in particular the obtained results apply to the domain of *rational* numbers (the discrete-time constraints can often be handled by standard FSM analysis techniques due to the finiteness of the generated "state space").

The abovementioned positive analysis results can be considered as dealing with some kind of "extended reachability" problems for the timed system specifications. The intention of this paper is to find whether decidable can be showed any nontrivial algorithmic problem concerning the *equivalence* properties of r.t.s.. One can mention some already existing work on deciding *bisimulation* equivalence for timed processes, however, the obtained results apply only to rather simple cases (in [HLW91] the bisimulation equivalence has been shown decidable for *regular* (in fact, one-timer) real timed processes and in [Che91] the decidability is obtained for *recursion-free* processes).

The main point of this paper is to prove the *decidability* of both strong and weak (abstracted from internal actions) bisimulation equivalence problems for a class of timed processes with both possibly infinite behaviour and time constraints naturally representing overlapping delays in process components (it seems that these requirements altogether provide the minimum level of specification power needed in more or less practical examples (the specification language SDL [CC88], which is widely used in the practical specification of telecommunication systems, also contain means for quantitative time constraint specification of exactly this kind)). We study the deciding of the bisimulation equivalences in the formalism of Parallel Timer Processes (PTPs), see Section 2 for definitions. The PTP formalism is similar to already considered model of Timed Graphs [ACD90] (or, rather, Action Timed Graphs [NSY91]), however, it differs in some design decisions (use of decreasing timers vs. increasing clocks, well-defined (time-stop free) labelled transition system semantics for all the class of PTPs, explicit firing enforcement of transitions along some edges) borrowed to some extent both from the calculi Timed CCS [Wan90] and the specification language SDL.

We obtain also some *undecidability* results (see Section 4) for PTPs provided additionaly with memory cells for moving the timer value information along the time axis, so showing also the difficulties in analysis of processes in Timed CCS with the expansion theorem [Wan91]. In the conclusions some brief points about the compositionality and possible enrichments of PTPs are given.

This paper is a generalisation of a previous author's work [Cer91], where only the strong bisimulation equivalence for an analogical (slightly weaker) specification model was considered and proved decidable. For a more detailed treatment of the problems addressed here the reader can see [Cer92b] (with the reported decidability results slightly weaker) and [Cer92c].

2 Parallel Timer Processes

Let $G = \langle V, E, L, lab \rangle$ be a finite edge-labelled graph with the set of *vertexes* V, the set of *edges* E, the set of *labels* L and the edge labelling function $lab : E \to L$. For every $e \in E$ let $start(e) \in V$ and $end(e) \in V$ denote the *source* and *target* vertexes of e respectively. Let every edge $e \in E$ be coloured either *red* (instantaneous) or *black* (possibly waiting).

Given such a graph G and a finite set of timers (time variables) $\mathcal{T}$, we define a *timer automaton* by associating with every $e \in E$:

- a set $\gamma(e) \subseteq \mathcal{T}$ of timers, called the edge *condition* (on what timers the transitions along e depend) and
- a *timer setting function* $\phi(e) : \mathcal{T} \to \mathcal{T} \cup Q^{+0}$.

For $\Phi = \langle V, E, L, lab, \mathcal{T}, \gamma, \phi \rangle$ being a timer automaton we define the set of its *states* to be

$$S^{\Phi} = \{\langle v, \delta \rangle \mid v \in V, \ \delta : \mathcal{T} \to Q^{+0}\}.$$

The *Parallel Timer Process* (PTP, for short, called also *timed process*) is defined as a pair $P = \langle \Phi, s \rangle$ for the timer automaton Φ and $s \in S^{\Phi}$ defined to be the P *initial state*. We denote the set of all PTPs by $\mathcal{P}$, let P, Q range over $\mathcal{P}$ and let σ range over L.

The semantics of PTPs is given by labelled transition systems, based on the relations $\xrightarrow{\sigma}$ and $\xrightarrow{\epsilon(d)}$ with $d \in Q^{+0}$ between processes (the label σ is interpreted as the action, performed by the process; the interpretation of $P \xrightarrow{\epsilon(d)} Q$ is, as in [Wan90], that the process P can become Q just by letting time to pass for d units).

For the timer automaton $\Phi = \langle V, E, L, lab, \mathcal{T}, \gamma, \phi \rangle$ define $\langle \Phi, \langle v, \delta \rangle \rangle \xrightarrow{\sigma} \langle \Phi, \langle v', \delta' \rangle \rangle$ iff there exists an edge $e \in E$ leading from v to v', labelled with $lab(e) = \sigma$, such that

- $\delta(t_i) = 0$ for every $t_i \in \gamma(e)$ (a transition along an edge is enabled when all timers this edge depends on have reached 0 values) and
- for every timer $t \in \mathcal{T}$ its new value $\delta'(t)$ is computed via the setting $\phi(e)$ in a way:
  - if $\phi(e)(t) = c \in Q^{+0}$, then $\delta'(t) = c$,
  - if $\phi(e)(t) = t' \in \mathcal{T}$, then $\delta'(t) = \delta(t')$.

For delay transitions, $\quad \langle \Phi, \langle v, \delta \rangle \rangle \xrightarrow{\epsilon(d)} \langle \Phi, \langle v, \delta' \rangle \rangle \quad$ iff

- for every red edge e with $start(e) = v$ there exists $t_i \in \gamma(e)$ with $\delta(t_i) \geq d$ (no red edge will be enabled during the waiting of d seconds) and
- for every $t \in \mathcal{T}$ $\delta'(t) = \delta(t) \ominus d$, where $x \ominus y \stackrel{def}{=} max\{0, x - y\}$ for every x, y (all timer values are synchronously decreasing downto 0).

The Parallel Timer Processes obey the following useful semantical properties:

- *time determinacy* ([Wan90]) meaning that, if $P \xrightarrow{\epsilon(d)} P'$ and $P \xrightarrow{\epsilon(d)} P''$, then $P' = P''$;
- *time continuity* ([Wan90]) meaning that $P \xrightarrow{\epsilon(d+e)} P'$ if and only if $P \xrightarrow{\epsilon(d)} P'' \xrightarrow{\epsilon(e)} P'$ for some P'';

- *time-stop freeness* (this property is similar to the deadlock-freeness considered in [NSY91]) meaning that for every PTP P always either

$$P \xrightarrow{\epsilon(d)} P(d) \text{ for all } d' \in Q^{+0}, \text{ or } P \xrightarrow{\epsilon(d)} P' \xrightarrow{\sigma} P'' \text{ for some } d \in Q^{+0}, \sigma \in L.$$

2.1 Example: Dialling Timing Control

We describe as a PTP a toy version of a process controlling in telephone exchanges the timing aspects of phone number dialling by subscribers. We assume that a phone number can be any nonempty sequence of digits, dialled by the subscriber with some time intervals in between. The duty of the timing control process is to interrupt the number dialling in any of the following three cases:

- the first digit of the number does not arrive in 30 seconds after the beginning of the dialling (picking up the receiver);
- the current digit which is not the first does not arrive in 20 seconds after the arrival of the previous digit; or
- the total time delay from the beginning of the number dialling reaches 60 seconds.

In the process the edge label "Call" denotes the beginning of the number dialling, "Digit" denotes the reception of the current digit, "Tim" stands for the dialling interruption and "Connect" initiates the connection seeking process between two subscribers, the process itself is depicted, as follows (we show the black edges of the process as dashed):

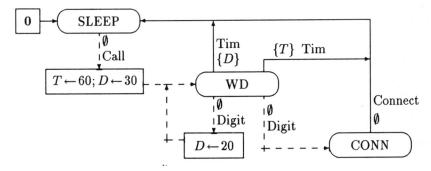

2.2 Bisimulations

Let $\Lambda \stackrel{def}{=} L \cup \{\epsilon(d) | d \in Q^{+0}\}$ be the set of all actions ranged over by ν.

We define the strong *timed bisimulation equivalence* in the set $\mathcal{P}$ of timed processes following [HLW91]:

Definition 2.1 *Let $F(R)$ be the set of all $\langle P, Q \rangle \in \mathcal{P} \times \mathcal{P}$ satisfying*

i) *whenever $P \xrightarrow{\nu} P'$ then $Q \xrightarrow{\nu} Q'$ with $\langle P', Q' \rangle \in R$ for some Q',*
ii) *whenever $Q \xrightarrow{\nu} Q'$ then $P \xrightarrow{\nu} P'$ with $\langle P', Q' \rangle \in R$ for some P'.*

Then R is a timed bisimulation, if $R \subseteq F(R)$. We define the timed bisimulation equivalence, written $\sim$, to be the greatest fixpoint of F.

Theorem 2.2 *There is an algorithm which, given two Parallel Timer Processes A and B, decides whether $A \sim B$ or not.*

We consider also the possibility to abstract from internal actions when observing a system modelled by a PTP. For this purpose we assume that every process can have a special (internal, invisible) action (label) $\tau \in L$, let $Vis = L \setminus \{\tau\}$ be ranged over by α.

Let $P \stackrel{\epsilon}{\Longrightarrow} Q$ if and only if $P(\stackrel{\tau}{\longrightarrow})^* Q$. Define $P \stackrel{\alpha}{\Longrightarrow} Q$ as $P \stackrel{\epsilon}{\Longrightarrow} \stackrel{\alpha}{\longrightarrow} \stackrel{\epsilon}{\Longrightarrow} Q$.
Following [Wan90], for delay transitions let $P \stackrel{\epsilon(d)}{\Longrightarrow} Q$ whenever

$$P \stackrel{\epsilon}{\Longrightarrow} \stackrel{\epsilon(d_1)}{\longrightarrow} \stackrel{\epsilon}{\Longrightarrow} \cdots \stackrel{\epsilon(d_k)}{\longrightarrow} \stackrel{\epsilon}{\Longrightarrow} Q$$

for some $d_1, d_2, \ldots, d_k$ with $d_1 + d_2 + \cdots d_k = d$.

Letting ν to range over $Vis \cup \{\epsilon(d) | d \in Q^{+0}\}$ we define the weak timed bisimulation for PTPs (observe that $P \stackrel{\epsilon}{\Longrightarrow} Q$ iff $P \stackrel{\epsilon(0)}{\Longrightarrow} Q$):

Definition 2.3 *Let $F(R)$ be the set of all $\langle P, Q \rangle \in \mathcal{P} \times \mathcal{P}$ satisfying*

    i) *whenever $P \stackrel{\nu}{\Longrightarrow} P'$ then $Q \stackrel{\nu}{\Longrightarrow} Q'$ with $\langle P', Q' \rangle \in R$ for some Q',*
    ii) *whenever $Q \stackrel{\nu}{\Longrightarrow} Q'$ then $P \stackrel{\nu}{\Longrightarrow} P'$ with $\langle P', Q' \rangle \in R$ for some P'.*

Then R is a weak timed bisimulation, if $R \subseteq F(R)$. We define the weak timed bisimulation equivalence, written $\approx$, to be the greatest fixpoint of F.

Theorem 2.4 *There is an algorithm which, given two Parallel Timer Processes A and B, decides whether $A \approx B$ or not.*

Theorem 2.2 follows from Theorem 2.4 in the case of no edges labelled with the τ action.

Let for arbitrary timed process $P = \langle \Phi, \langle v, \delta \rangle \rangle$ $\tilde{d}(P)$ be the set of processes $\langle \Phi, \langle v', \delta' \rangle \rangle$ with v' being a vertex in Φ graph and $\delta'(t) \leq c^P$ for every P timer t, where c^P is defined to exceed both all timer values from δ and all constants used in Φ edge timer settings. It is easy to see that every P derivative (i.e. every process which can be reached during the execution of P) falls into the set $\tilde{d}(P)$ (the converse might not be true).

Without loosing generality in deciding whether $A \sim B$, $A \approx B$ one can consider $\sim$ and $\approx$ to be the maximal bisimulations in the set $\tilde{d}(A) \times \tilde{d}(B) \subseteq \mathcal{P} \times \mathcal{P}$ (observe that a process does not change its graph when executed).

In this paper we do not consider yet another interesting equivalence which is based on the abstraction from the actual time interval length in the semantical transition relation between the processes. In fact, the deciding procedure for this "time-abstracted equivalence" appears to be even simpler than the algorithms for the "time-sensitive" equivalences considered here, this procedure can be based on a rather direct comparing of "region graphs" (see [ACD90]) of the processes under the test.

3 Deciding of Bisimulations

Without the loss of generality we assume that all the explicit constants $c \in Q^{+0}$, used in the edge timer settings $\phi(e)$ in the graphs of A and B, are *integers* (were it not so one could change the scale of the number line to ensure it; easy to see that the behaviour of the processes is not affected by the scale change).

In order to decide whether $A \sim B$, $A \approx B$ we give an effective characteristic (via a finite partitioning) of all bisimilar process pairs within $\tilde{d}(A) \times \tilde{d}(B)$ (it turns out to be too rough for the proof to consider partitionings of $\tilde{d}(A)$ and $\tilde{d}(B)$ independently: the analogue of the proof cornerstone Lemma 3.7 does not hold for any nontrivial partitioning of $\tilde{d}(A) \times \tilde{d}(B)$ obtained as the product of independent partitionings of $\tilde{d}(A)$ and $\tilde{d}(B)$).

For $\mathcal{T} = \{t_1, t_2, \ldots, t_m\}$ being a finite set of timers, let us represent every $\mathcal{T}$ timer value assignment $\delta : \mathcal{T} \to Q^{+0}$ as the vector $\langle \delta(t_1), \ldots, \delta(t_m) \rangle \in (Q^{+0})^m$. Let $\cong$ be an equivalence relation in the set $\Delta_{\mathcal{T}}$ of $\mathcal{T}$ timer value assignments s.t. $\delta^1 \cong \delta^2$ iff

- $\lfloor \delta^1(t_i) \rfloor = \lfloor \delta^2(t_i) \rfloor$ for every $i = 1, \ldots, n$ and
- for every i, j $\{\delta^1(t_i)\} \geq \{\delta^1(t_j)\}$ if and only if $\{\delta^2(t_i)\} \geq \{\delta^2(t_j)\}$, and
  $\{\delta^1(t_i)\} = 0$ if and only if $\{\delta^2(t_i)\} = 0$

(here $\lfloor x \rfloor$ denotes the "integral part" of x, i.e. the largest integer, which is not greater than x, and $\{x\}$ stands for the fractional part of x (i.e. $\{x\} = x - \lfloor x \rfloor$)).

Given $\delta \in \Delta_{\mathcal{T}}$, let us denote the equivalence class $C \subseteq \Delta_{\mathcal{T}}$ w.r.t. $\cong$ with $\delta \in C$ by $C(\delta)$ and call it the *time region* of $\mathcal{T}$, corresponding to δ. Given a timer value assignment one can easily compute its corresponding time region (one can use the time region representations, say, by linear inequality systems in order to make all computations with them effective).

Example 3.1 *If* $\mathcal{T} = \{t_1, t_2, \ldots, t_7\}$ *and* $\delta = \langle 0.7, 1, 1.23, 4, 17.23, 17.75, 17.75 \rangle$, *then the time region* $C(\delta)$ *can be described as the inequality system*
$$C(\delta) = (0 < t_1 < 1 = t_2 < t_3 < 2 < 4 = t_4 < 17 < t_5 < t_6 = t_7 < 18,$$
$$0 = \{t_2\} = \{t_4\} < \{t_3\} = \{t_5\} < \{t_1\} < \{t_6\} = \{t_7\}).$$

Clearly, if for every $t \in \mathcal{T}$ and every timer value assignment $\delta \in \Delta \subseteq \Delta_{\mathcal{T}}$ always $\delta(t) \in [0, c] \subseteq Q^{+0}$, then the set of the corresponding time regions $\{C(\delta) \mid \delta \in \Delta\}$ is *finite*.

The presented time region construction is actually the same, as used in [ACD90] for demonstrating the effectivity of the model checking procedure over Timed Graphs. One may see also [ABBCK91] for a survey, how similar ideas of variable value space partitioning have worked in deciding reachability for various classes of data-dependent programs.

Definition 3.2 *Let* $P_i = \langle \Phi_A, \langle v^{P_i}, \delta^{P_i} \rangle \rangle \in \tilde{d}(A)$, $Q_i = \langle \Phi_B, \langle v^{Q_i}, \delta^{Q_i} \rangle \rangle \in \tilde{d}(B)$ *for* $i = 1, 2$, *we say that* $\langle P_1, Q_1 \rangle \cong \langle P_2, Q_2 \rangle$ *iff*

- $v^{P_1} = v^{P_2}$ *and* $v^{Q_1} = v^{Q_2}$ *(i.e. the vertexes of corresponding processes coincide) and*

− $\delta^{P_1} :: \delta^{Q_1} \cong \delta^{P_2} :: \delta^{Q_2}$, where :: denotes the concatenation of two vectors (i.e. the "concatenated" vectors belong to the same "time region").

It is important to notice that for $\langle P_1, Q_1 \rangle \cong \langle P_2, Q_2 \rangle$ it is not enough that $v^{P_1} = v^{P_2}$, $v^{Q_1} = v^{Q_2}$ and $\delta^{P_1} \cong \delta^{P_2}$, $\delta^{Q_1} \cong \delta^{Q_2}$, also the timer values in P_1 have to be ordered w.r.t. the timer values in Q_1 the same way as the timer values in P_2 are ordered w.r.t. those in Q_2. In order to show the relations between $\cong$ and the defined transition relations $\xrightarrow{\sigma}, \xRightarrow{\alpha}, \xrightarrow{\epsilon(d)}, \xRightarrow{\epsilon(d)}$ between the processes (see Proposition 3.6 and Lemma 3.7) we use an "invariant relation" technique, characterizing first every $\cong$-equivalence class via the following notion of a uniform mapping:

Definition 3.3 We call a strongly monotone mapping $\rho : Q^{+0} \to Q^{+0}$ uniform if $\rho(0) = 0$ and $\rho(x) + c = \rho(x + c)$ for every natural c.

We extend any mapping $\rho : Q^{+0} \to Q^{+0}$ in a polymorphic manner to any structures containing nonnegative rationals as elements in a way by applying ρ to every component $a \in Q^{+0}$ and not changing any component of other type, e.g.

$$\rho(\delta_1, \delta_2, \ldots, \delta_m) = (\rho(\delta_1), \rho(\delta_2), \ldots, \rho(\delta_m)),$$

as well as for $P \in \tilde{d}(A)$, $Q \in \tilde{d}(B)$ $\rho(P, Q) = \langle P', Q' \rangle$, where P' and Q' have the same vertices as P and Q respectively, but the corresponding timer value vector $\delta^{P'} :: \delta^{Q'} = \rho(\delta^P :: \delta^Q)$, etc. The proofs of the following two facts easily follow from definitions:

Fact 3.4 $\langle P_1, Q_1 \rangle \cong \langle P_2, Q_2 \rangle$ if and only if there exists a uniform mapping ρ, such that $\langle P_1, Q_1 \rangle = \rho(\langle P_2, Q_2 \rangle)$.

Fact 3.5 Whenever $\rho : Q^{+0} \to Q^{+0}$ is a uniform mapping, then for every $d \in Q^{+0}$ the mapping ρ_d, defined $\rho_d(x) = \rho(x + d) - \rho(d)$ for every x, is also uniform.

Proposition 3.6 Whenever $P_2 = \rho(P_1)$ for the processes $P_1, P_2 \in \tilde{d}(A) \cup \tilde{d}(B)$ and some uniform mapping ρ, we have,

if $P_1 \xRightarrow{\alpha} P_1'$, then $P_2 \xRightarrow{\alpha} \rho(P_1')$, and, if $P_1 \xrightarrow{\epsilon(d)} P_1'$, then $P_2 \xrightarrow{\epsilon(\rho(d))} \rho_d(P_1')$.

Proof: Consider first the untimed transitions. Since P_1 and P_2 have the same vertex, and the same timers with 0 values and, so, the transitions along the same edges enabled, the result follows by observing that for every possible newly appearing timer value $c \in N$ $\rho(c) = c$, use induction along the $(\xrightarrow{})^*$ derivation for the transition $\xRightarrow{\alpha}$.

As to the timed transitions, consider first the case $P_1 \xrightarrow{\epsilon(d)} P_1'$. Let P_1 have a state $\langle v, \delta \rangle$, then the state of P_2 is $\langle v, \rho(\delta) \rangle$. By the definition of $\xrightarrow{\epsilon(d)}$ for every red edge e, outgoing from v, there exists $t_i \in \gamma(e)$, such that $\delta(t_i) \geq d$. By the monotonicity of ρ for every such t_i $\rho(\delta(t_i)) \geq \rho(d)$, so $P_2 \xrightarrow{\epsilon(\rho(d))} P_2'$ for some P_2'.

In order to prove that $P_2' = \rho_d(P_1')$ it remains to consult the definitions of the transition relation $\xrightarrow{\epsilon(d)}$ and the mapping ρ_d (consider 2 cases whether $\delta(t_i) \leq d$ or $\delta(t_i) > d$).

As to the general case of $P_1 \xrightarrow{\epsilon(d)} P_1'$, it remains to notice that

$$(\rho_d)_{d'}(x) = \rho_d(x+d') - \rho_d(d') = \rho(x+d+d') - \rho(d) - (\rho(d+d') - \rho(d)) = \rho_{d+d'}(x)$$

and to use the induction along the elementary transition chain in the derivation $\xrightarrow{\epsilon(d)}$. □

Lemma 3.7 *Let $P_1, P_2 \in \tilde{d}(A)$, $Q_1, Q_2 \in \tilde{d}(B)$, such that $\langle P_1, Q_1 \rangle \cong \langle P_2, Q_2 \rangle$. Then $P_1 \approx Q_1$ if and only if $P_2 \approx Q_2$.*

Proof: Define the relation $\approx' \subseteq \tilde{d}(A) \times \tilde{d}(B)$ in a way $P \approx' Q$ iff $P_1 \approx Q_1$ for some $\langle P_1, Q_1 \rangle \cong \langle P, Q \rangle$. We obtain the proof by showing that $\approx'$ is a weak bisimulation.

Take some $P \approx' Q$, let $P_1 \approx Q_1$ and $\langle P_1, Q_1 \rangle \cong \langle P, Q \rangle$, then $\langle P_1, Q_1 \rangle = \rho(\langle P, Q \rangle)$ for some uniform ρ (Fact 3.4). By Proposition 3.6 whenever $P \xRightarrow{\alpha} P'$ then $P_1 \xRightarrow{\alpha} \rho(P')$. Since $P_1 \approx Q_1$, then also $Q_1 \xRightarrow{\alpha} Q_1'$ for some Q_1' with $\rho(P') \approx Q_1'$. Since the inverse of a uniform mapping is also uniform, Proposition 3.6 gives $Q \xRightarrow{\alpha} \rho^{-1}(Q_1')$, easy to see that $\langle P', \rho^{-1}(Q_1') \rangle \cong \langle \rho(P'), Q_1' \rangle$ and, so, $P' \approx' \rho^{-1}(Q_1')$, as requested.

All the other cases (including the timed ones) are very similar to the considered one, their detailed analysis is omitted. □

Consider a partitioning $\mathcal{X}_{A,B}$ of the set $\tilde{d}(A) \times \tilde{d}(B)$, generated by $\cong$, easy to see that it is finite (for every $P \in \tilde{d}(A) \cup \tilde{d}(B)$ any its timer value does not exceed $max\{c^A, c^B\}$). For arbitrary $P \in \tilde{d}(A)$, $Q \in \tilde{d}(B)$ let us denote by $X(P, Q)$ the element in this partitioning to which the pair $\langle P, Q \rangle$ belongs to and call it a *region process*, corresponding to $\langle P, Q \rangle$.

3.1 Deciding Strong Equivalence

We consider first the decidability of the strong (i.e. non-abstracted) bisimulation equivalence. We begin with some results, characterizing the "waiting behaviour" of the processes.

Let for $P \in \mathcal{P}$ $P(d)$ be the process which is obtained from the process P by letting time to pass for d units ($P \xrightarrow{\epsilon(d)} P(d)$) provided P can perform such a waiting. We let $\mu(P)$ for $P \in \mathcal{P}$ to denote the minimal nonzero P timer value fractional part (if all timer values in P are integers, let $\mu(P) = 1$), let $\mu(P, Q) = min\{\mu(P), \mu(Q)\}$. We call a process P is stable, written $P \xrightarrow{WT}$, if and only if there exists $d > 0$, such that $P \xrightarrow{\epsilon(d)} P(d)$.

Fact 3.8 *For $P \in \mathcal{P}$, if $P \xrightarrow{WT}$, then for all $d \leq \mu(P)$ $P \xrightarrow{\epsilon(d)} P(d)$.*
For $P \in \tilde{d}(A)$ and $Q \in \tilde{d}(B)$, if $P \xrightarrow{WT}$ and $Q \xrightarrow{WT}$, then for all $d, d' \in]0, \mu(P, Q)[$ always $P(d), Q(d), P(d'), Q(d')$ exist and $X(P(d), Q(d)) = X(P(d'), Q(d'))$.

Definition 3.9 *Let for* $X = X(P,Q) \in \mathcal{X}_{A,B}$ *such that* $P \xrightarrow{WT}$ *and* $Q \xrightarrow{WT}$, $next_0(X) = X(P(\mu/2), Q(\mu/2))$ *and* $next_1(X) = X(P(\mu), Q(\mu))$, *where* $\mu = \mu(P,Q)$.

Clearly, the operations $next_i$ for region processes are well-defined and effective.
Let for $X, X' \in \mathcal{X}_{A,B}$ $X \xrightarrow{\sigma} X'$ iff there exist $\langle P, Q \rangle \in X$ and $\langle P', Q' \rangle \in X'$ such that $P \xrightarrow{\sigma} P'$ and $Q \xrightarrow{\sigma} Q'$.

Definition 3.10 *The set* $\mathcal{X} \in \mathcal{X}_{A,B}$ *is a strong symbolic bisimulation if and only if for all* $X = X(P,Q) \in \mathcal{X}$

- *whenever* $P \xrightarrow{\sigma} P'$ *then* $X \xrightarrow{\sigma} X(P', Q') \in \mathcal{X}$ *for some* Q';
- *whenever* $Q \xrightarrow{\sigma} Q'$ *then* $X \xrightarrow{\sigma} X(P', Q') \in \mathcal{X}$ *for some* P';
- *whenever* $P \xrightarrow{WT}$, *or* $Q \xrightarrow{WT}$, *then both* $next_0(X) \in \mathcal{X}$ *and* $next_1(X) \in \mathcal{X}$.

Due to the finiteness of $\mathcal{X}_{A,B}$ and according to Lemma 3.7 the following two results complete the proof of Theorem 2.2 (see [Cer92c] for the proof details omitted here).

Lemma 3.11 *The set* $R_{\mathcal{X}} = \{\langle P, Q \rangle \mid X(P,Q) \in \mathcal{X}\}$ *is a strong timed bisimulation if and only if the set* $\mathcal{X}$ *is a strong symbolic bisimulation.*

Proof: See Lemma 3.15.□

Lemma 3.12 *It is decidable whether given set* $\mathcal{X} \subseteq \mathcal{X}_{A,B}$ *is a strong symbolic bisimulation.*

Proof: Follows from the definitions of $\xrightarrow{\sigma}$, $next_0$ and $next_1$. Proposition 3.6 and Fact 3.8 guarantee the independence on the choice of the representants.□

3.2 Deciding Weak Equivalence

In the general case of the deciding weak bisimulation we follow the same lines, as in the case of the strong bisimulation. Let for $P \in \tilde{d}(A)$, $Q \in \tilde{d}(B)$ and $\mu = \mu(P,Q)$:
whenever $P \xrightarrow{WT}$ then $\mathcal{N}_0^A(P,Q) = \{X(P(d), Q_d) \mid Q \xRightarrow{\epsilon(d)} Q_d \ \& \ 0 < d < \mu\}$ and $\mathcal{N}_1^A(P,Q) = \{X(P(\mu), Q') \mid Q \xRightarrow{\epsilon(\mu)} Q'\}$ (the sets $\mathcal{N}_0^B(P,Q)$ and $\mathcal{N}_1^B(P,Q)$ are defined in a similar way).

Fact 3.13 *For every* $X \in \mathcal{N}_0^A(P,Q)$ *and for every* $d \in]0, \mu(P,Q)[$ *there exists* Q_d *with both* $Q \xRightarrow{\epsilon(d)} Q_d$ *and* $\langle P(d), Q_d \rangle \in X$.

We introduce for $\nu \in Vis \cup \{\epsilon\}$ in the set $\mathcal{X}_{A,B}$ of region processes the relations $X \xRightarrow{\nu} X'$ iff there exist $\langle P, Q \rangle \in X$ and $\langle P', Q' \rangle \in X'$ such that $P \xRightarrow{\nu} P'$ and $Q \xRightarrow{\nu} Q'$.

Definition 3.14 *Let for any* $\mathcal{X} \subseteq \mathcal{X}_{A,B}$ $F^*(\mathcal{X})$ *be the set of all* $X(P,Q)$ *satisfying*

- *if* $P \stackrel{\nu}{\Longrightarrow} P'$, *then* $X(P,Q) \stackrel{\nu}{\Longrightarrow} X(P',Q') \in \mathcal{X}$ *for some* Q';
- *if* $Q \stackrel{\nu}{\Longrightarrow} Q'$, *then* $X(P,Q) \stackrel{\nu}{\Longrightarrow} X(P',Q') \in \mathcal{X}$ *for some* P';
- *if* $P \stackrel{WT}{\longrightarrow}$ *then both* $X' \in \mathcal{N}_0^A(P,Q) \cap \mathcal{X}$ *and* $X'' \in \mathcal{N}_1^A(P,Q) \cap \mathcal{X}$ *for some* X', X''; *and*
- *if* $Q \stackrel{WT}{\longrightarrow}$ *then both* $X' \in \mathcal{N}_0^B(P,Q) \cap \mathcal{X}$ *and* $X'' \in \mathcal{N}_1^B(P,Q) \cap \mathcal{X}$ *for some* X', X''.

Then $\mathcal{X}$ *is a weak symbolic bisimulation, if* $\mathcal{X} \subseteq F^*(\mathcal{X})$.

The proof of Theorem 2.4 is obtained by showing the following two lemmas:

Lemma 3.15 *For* $\mathcal{X} \in \mathcal{X}_{A,B}$ *and* $R_{\mathcal{X}} = \{\langle P,Q \rangle \mid X(P,Q) \in \mathcal{X}_{A,B}\}$ $\mathcal{X}$ *is a weak symbolic bisimulation if and only if* $R_{\mathcal{X}}$ *is a weak (timed) bisimulation.*

Lemma 3.16 *It is decidable, whether a given set* $\mathcal{X} \subseteq \mathcal{X}_{A,B}$ *is a weak symbolic bisimulation.*

Proof of Lemma 3.15 (outline): Let $\mathcal{X}$ be a weak symbolic bisimulation. In order to prove that $R_{\mathcal{X}}$ is a weak (timed) bisimulation, take $\langle P,Q \rangle \in R_{\mathcal{X}}$. All α- and ϵ- moves of P can be matched by corresponding moves of Q (and vice versa) due to Proposition 3.6.

Consider the timed cases. Given that for every $X(P,Q) \in \mathcal{X}$ whenever $P \stackrel{WT}{\longrightarrow}$ then also $\mathcal{N}_0^A \cap \mathcal{X}$ and $\mathcal{N}_1^A \cap \mathcal{X}$ are nonempty, we prove first that for every $\langle P,Q \rangle \in R_{\mathcal{X}}$ and every $d > 0$, if $P \stackrel{\epsilon(d)}{\longrightarrow} P(d)$, then also $Q \stackrel{\epsilon(d)}{\Longrightarrow} Q_d$ for some Q_d with $\langle P(d), Q_d \rangle \in R_{\mathcal{X}}$. For this purpose we, given $\langle P,Q \rangle \in R_{\mathcal{X}}$, consider a sequence of process pairs $\langle P_i, Q_i \rangle$ such that

- $P_0 = P$ and $Q_0 = Q$,
- $P_{i+1} = P_i(\mu_i)$ and $Q_i \stackrel{\epsilon(\mu_i)}{\Longrightarrow} Q_{i+1}$ (we abbreviate $\mu_i = \mu(P_i, Q_i)$), and
- $\langle P_i, Q_i \rangle \in R_{\mathcal{X}}$ (we can require this due to the definition of $\mathcal{N}_1^A$).

One can show that $\mu_0 + \mu_1 + \ldots + \mu_k \geq d$ for some k, the result follows.

In the case of $P \stackrel{\epsilon(d)}{\Longrightarrow} P'$, the matching Q' with $\langle P', Q' \rangle \in R_{\mathcal{X}}$ is found inductively along the derivation of P' from P.

The proof that for every weak timed bisimulation $R_{\mathcal{X}}$ the corresponding set $\mathcal{X}$ is a weak symbolic bisimulation can be obtained from the definitions and Fact 3.8.□

Proof of Lemma 3.16: Since for every pair of timed processes $\langle P,Q \rangle \in \tilde{d}(A) \times \tilde{d}(B)$ the set of process pairs $\langle P', Q' \rangle$ with $P \stackrel{\nu}{\Longrightarrow} P'$ and $Q \stackrel{\nu}{\Longrightarrow} Q'$ for any $\nu \in Vis \cup \{\epsilon\}$ is finite and effectively computable from $\langle P,Q \rangle$ (the set of all $\stackrel{\nu}{\Longrightarrow}$ derivations can be infinite due to the repeating τ-loops; all newly appearing timer values in the processes in these derivations are integers from a bounded interval), Proposition 3.6 guarantees the decidability of untimed match existence for all processes $X(P, Q)$ with either $P \overset{\nu}{\Longrightarrow}$, or $Q \overset{\nu}{\Longrightarrow}$.

Let us demonstrate the effectivity of the check, whether for given $X \in \mathcal{X}$ with $P \overset{WT}{\longrightarrow}$ for some $\langle P, Q \rangle \in X$ both the sets $\mathcal{N}_0^A(P, Q) \cap \mathcal{X}$ and $\mathcal{N}_1^A(P, Q) \cap \mathcal{X}$ are not empty. For this purpose we show the algorithms, generating the sets $\mathcal{N}_0^A(P, Q)$ and $\mathcal{N}_1^A(P, Q)$ from the given processes $P \in \tilde{d}(A)$ and $Q \in \tilde{d}(B)$. For the sake of simplicity assume that there exist a timer in P with the value fractional part being $\mu(P, Q)$ (the general case is dealt with in [Cer92c] by a slight refinement of the region processes).

We define for region processes $X \in \mathcal{X}$ the transitions $X \overset{*}{\longrightarrow} next_0(X)$, $X \overset{**}{\longrightarrow} next_1(X)$ and $X(P', Q') \overset{\tau}{\longrightarrow} X(P', Q'')$ whenever $Q' \overset{\tau}{\longrightarrow} Q''$.

Let $R_{P,Q}^0$ be the set of region processes which are reachable from $X(P, Q)$ using the transitions $\overset{*}{\longrightarrow}$ and $\overset{\tau}{\longrightarrow}$. Let $R_{P,Q} \subseteq R_{P,Q}^0$ be the set of processes with a derivation containing at least one $\overset{*}{\longrightarrow}$ transition. Let $R_{P,Q}'$ be the set of region processes, reachable from those in $R_{P,Q}^0$ by one $\overset{**}{\longrightarrow}$ transition, followed by a number of $\overset{\tau}{\longrightarrow}$ transitions.

Observing the effectivity of the set $R_{P,Q}$ and $R_{P,Q}'$ computation, the following result completes the proof of Lemma 3.16, so completing also the proof of Theorem 2.4:

Proposition 3.17 $\mathcal{N}_A^0(P, Q) = R_{P,Q}$ and $\mathcal{N}_A^1(P, Q) = R_{P,Q}'$.

Proof: Rather technical, see [Cer92c].□□

Note: The weak bisimulation deciding algorithm can be simplified in the case, if both the processes A and B satisfy the *maximal progress* assumption, stating that τ-labels in the processes can be ascribed only to red (instantaneous) edges. For instance, we could have $\mathcal{N}_A^0(P, Q) = \{X(P(d), Q_d) \mid Q \overset{\epsilon}{\Longrightarrow} Q' \overset{\epsilon(d)}{\longrightarrow} Q_d \ \& \ 0 < d < \mu\}$, what clearly simplifies the bisimulation deciding procedure in Lemma 3.16.

4 Timed Processes with Memory

We consider an enrichment of PTPs with memory for moving timer value information along the time axis (storing timer value at one moment and retrieving it afterwards).

A parallel timer process with memory (PTPM) is obtained by adding to a given PTP $A = \langle \langle V, E, L, lab, \mathcal{T}, \gamma, \phi \rangle, \langle v, \delta \rangle \rangle$ a finite set $\mathcal{M}$ of *memory cells* and extending every edge timer setting $\phi(e)$ for $e \in E$ with some "remember" operations $m_i \leftarrow t_j$ and some "retrieve" operations $t_j \leftarrow m_i$ for $t_j \in \mathcal{T}, m_i \in \mathcal{M}$ (formally, $\phi(e) : (\mathcal{T} \cup \mathcal{M}) \rightarrow (\mathcal{T} \cup \mathcal{M}) \cup Q^{+0}$).

The semantics (labelled transition system) of PTPMs is easily obtained as a generalization of that of PTPs: every state for a PTPM A consists of its graph's vertex and a value assignment both for timers and memory cells. Every time a transition along an edge e fires, the timer and memory cell setting $\phi(e)$ defines the new values $\delta'(u)$ for $u \in \mathcal{T} \cup \mathcal{M}$ from the old ones, $\delta(u)$, as for PTPs: $\delta'(u) = \delta(\phi(e)(u))$ (here $\delta(c) \stackrel{def}{=} c$ for $c \in Q^{+0}$).

The main difference of the memory cells from the timers is that the values of the memory cells *do not decrease during the passage of time* as the timer values do (whenever $\langle \Phi, \langle v, \delta \rangle \rangle \xrightarrow{\epsilon(d)} \langle \Phi, \langle v, \delta' \rangle \rangle$, then $\delta'(m) = \delta(m)$ for every $m \in \mathcal{M}$).

Let for any PTPM A $d(A)$ denote the set of *derivatives* of A (the least set containing A and closed under the transition relation). We call a vertex v in a given PTPM $A = \langle \Phi, s_0 \rangle$ reachable if $\langle \Phi, \langle v, \delta \rangle \rangle \in d(A)$ for some timer and memory cell value assignment δ.

Theorem 4.1 *The vertex reachability problem for parallel timer processes with 5 timers and 1 memory cell is undecidable.*

Corollary 4.2 *The bisimulation equivalence problem for parallel timer processes with 5 timers and 1 memory cell is undecidable.*

For a proof of Theorem 4.1 the reader may consult [Cer92b]. We just point out here that it is based on the modelling of two 2-way counter machine. One timer in the modelling is used to generate regular "ticks", the values of counters are modeled as ratious $\delta(t_2)/\delta(t_1)$ and $\delta(t_3)/\delta(t_1)$ of timer t_1, t_2 and t_3 values at the appropriate "tick" moments. One can easily implement in a PTPM both the timer addition/subtraction and timer halving, all what is needed to model the counter machine's instructions simultaneously not letting the timers to grow bigger than the largest constant used in the timer settings.

It can be pointed out that the undecidability results of Theorem 4.1 and Corollary 4.2 still retain in force also, if one forbids the assignment operations between the timers, as well as replaces the assignments between timers and memory cells by simply holding and releasing operations over the timers (see [Cer92b] or [Cer92c] for some details).

Both the decidability results, obtained in the previous sections of the paper (see Theorem 2.2 and Theorem 2.4), and the undecidability results, expressed by Theorem 4.1 and Corollary 4.2 have noteworthy implications regarding the possibilities to decide the bisimulation equivalences for various classes of Timed CCS processes (see [Wan90, Wan91]). First, we can model a class of TCCS processes, reasonably called "TCCS-nets", into the PTP formalism, so showing the decidability of the bisimulation equivalence for these net processes (see [Cer91] and [Cer92c] for two different possible modelling strategies). On the other hand, if one considers the version of Timed CCS with the expansion theorem, as presented in [Wan91], it becomes easy to encode every PTPM as a term in these generalised calculi (in fact, rather simple subcalculi of interleaving TCCS are sufficient to have this encoding possibility), so showing that all nontrivial interesting algorithmic problems for this kind of processes are undecidable. It can be an interesting question, whether one can come up with another timed specification formalism which would combine both the interleaving nature of the specifications and the decidability of the bisimulation equivalence problems.

5 Conclusions

This paper does not contain any discussion on the *compositional* properties of Parallel Timer processes because its main aim is to discuss the *decidability* issues. However, the definition of parallel composition (and other static process algebra combinators) for PTPs can be done in a quite straightforward way (in [Cer92c] one can find the rules for combining PTPs in parallel both according to CCS and CSP kinds of inter-process communication).

Despite some design differences of PTPs from Action Timed Graphs [NSY91], the presented algorithms for the bisimulation deciding for PTPs with slight modifications can be applied also for ATGs with "linear" predicates over the clock values, see [Cer92c] for details.

The complexity issues of the obtained bisimulation deciding algorithms are not explicitly discussed here, however, as these algorithms are in fact presented as computing some simple symbolic greatest fixpoint relations, the techniques from [Lar92] are hopefully to be applicable to obtain efficient computations of these relations.

It is possible to consider also various more or less principal enrichments of the PTP model which, unlike the PTPMs, have decidable at least the vertex reachability problem, and in some cases also the bisimulation equivalence problem. One such class is so-called PTPs with Nondeterministic timer settings (PTPNs) which are obtained from PTPs be redefining the timer setting functions in a way $\phi(e) : \mathcal{T} \to \mathcal{T} \cup I(Q^{+0})$, where $I(Q^{+0})$ denotes the set of all intervals over Q^{+0} and defining the early choice semantics of the nondeterminism in the timer value settings. One can show that for PTPNs the vertex reachability problem is decidable; the decidability of the strong and weak bisimulation equivalence problems for PTPNs can be shown provided all the intervals in process edge timer setting functions are *finite*, see [Cer92c] for details. In [Cer92c] also some enrichments of PTPs with external data (both integer- and rational-valued, simple tests on being less or greater for the values of data variables are allowed) are considered, the decidability of the bisimulation equivalences for PTPs with dependencies on rational-valued data is showed.

6 Acknowledgements

I want to thank K.V.S Prasad, Alan Jeffrey, Wang Yi and Uno Holmer in Göteborg as well as Kim G. Larsen and Jens Chr. Godskesen in Aalborg for a lot of very interesting and constructive discussions on process algebras, real time and decidability.

My thanks are also to the anonymous referees of this paper for providing a number of useful comments on an earlier version of it.

The final version of this paper was processed using LaTeX macro package with LLNCS style and printed at Chalmers University of Technology, Göteborg, Sweden.

References

[AD90] R. Alur and D.Dill, *Automata for Modelling Real-Time Systems*, LNCS No. 443, 1990.

[ACD90] R. Alur, C.Courcoubetis and D.Dill, *Model-Checking for Real-Time Systems*, Proceedings from LICS'90 pp. 414-425, 1990.

[ABBCK91] A. Auziņš, J. Bārzdiņš, J. Bičevskis, K. Čerāns and A. Kalniņš, *Automatic Construction of Test Sets: Theoretical Approach*, Baltic Computer Science, LNCS, No. 502, 1991.

[BM83] B. Berthomieu and M.Menasche, *An Enumerative Approach for Analyzing Time Petri Nets*, Proc. IFIP Congress, 1983, North-Holland, 1983.

[CC88] **CCITT Specification and Description Language (SDL)**, Recomendations Z.100, 1988.

[Cer91] K. Čerāns, *Decidability of Bisimulation Equivalence for Parallel Timed Processes*, in Proc. of Chalmers Workshop on Concurrency, Göteborg, Report PMG-R63, Chalmers University of Technology, 1992.

[Cer92a] K. Čerāns, *Feasibility of Finite and Infinite Paths in Data Dependent Programs*, in Proc. for LFCS'92, Russia, Tver, LNCS No. 620, 1992.

[Cer92b] K. Čerāns, **Decidability of Bisimulation Equivalences for Processes with Parallel Timers**, Technical report, Institute of Mathematics and Computer Science, University of Latvia, Riga, 1992.

[Cer92c] K. Čerāns, **Algorithmic Problems in Analysis of Real Time System Specifications**, Dr.Sc.comp theses, University of Latvia, Riga, 1992.

[Che91] L. Chen, *Decidability and Completeness in Real Time Processes*, LFCS, Edinburgh University, 1991.

[GMMP89] C.Ghezzi, D.Mandrioli, S.Morasca and M.Pezze *A General Way To Put Time in Petri Nets*, ACM SIGSOFT Eng. Notes, Vol. 14, No. 3, 1989.

[HLW91] U. Holmer, K.Larsen and Yi Wang, *Deciding Properties for Regular Real Timed Processes*, CAV'91, 1991.

[Lar92] K.G.Larsen, *Efficient Local Correctness Checking*, this Workshop, 1992.

[MF76] P. Merlin and D.J. Farber, *Recoverability of Communication Protocols*, IEEE Trans. on Communication Protocols, Vol. COM-24, No. 9, 1976.

[NSY91] X.Nicollin, J.Sifakis and S.Yovine, *From ATP to Timed Graphs and Hybrid Systems*, in Proc. of REX Workshop "Real-Time: Theory in Practice", 1991.

[RR86] G.M. Reed and A.W. Roscoe, *A Timed Model for Communicating Sequential Processes*, LNCS No. 226, 1986.

[Wan90] Yi Wang, *Real Time Behaviour of Asynchronous Agents*, LNCS No. 458, 1990.

[Wan91] Yi Wang, *CCS + Time = an Interleaving Model for Real Time Systems*, ICALP'91, Madrid, 1991.

A Proof Assistant for Symbolic Model-Checking

J. C. Bradfield

Laboratory for Foundations of Computer Science
University of Edinburgh
The King's Buildings
EDINBURGH
U.K.   EH9 3JZ

email: jcb@dcs.ed.ac.uk

Abstract: We describe a prototype of a tool to assist in the model-checking of infinite systems by a tableau-based method. The tool automatically applies those tableau rules that require no user intervention, and checks the correctness of user-applied rules. It also provides help with checking the well-foundedness conditions required to prove liveness properties. The tool has a general tableau-manager module, and may use different reasoning modules for different models of systems; a module for Petri nets has been implemented.

1 Introduction

Many approaches to the verification of systems have been developed in recent years; model-checking is one to which both theoretical effort and implementation effort have been devoted. The principle of model-checking as it was first studied ([ClE81], [CES86]) is that one expresses a desirable property in some suitable temporal logic, and then checks this property algorithmically. However, there are drawbacks to model-checking. The first is that typically model-checking algorithms traverse the global state-space of the system under investigation, whereas often this may not be necessary. To address this problem, Stirling and Walker [StW89] introduced a tableau-based technique for local model-checking, in which parts of the system are not explored until information on their local structure is required. The second problem follows from the first, and is that traditional model-checking cannot deal with infinite-state systems, although many interesting systems are infinite or potentially infinite. Clearly, model-checking arbitrary infinite systems can no longer be algorithmic, so Stirling and the present author extended tableau-based model-checking to provide a general technique for infinite systems; knowledge about the system may be used where necessary to supplement the model-independent rules. (See [BrS90], [Bra91a], [Bra91b], [BrS92].)

Our infinite-state model-checking technique is well suited to computer-aided verification: although in general one may need powerful reasoning, there is a large part of the technique that is more or less automatic. Moreover, some form of computer assistance is essential in practice, since only very simple formulae and systems can be done by hand. This paper describes a prototype of a proof assistant for our system; the prototype has a module for reasoning with Petri nets, but other models may also be used. The implementation is closely tied to the theoretical basis, and even in prototype has given useful feedback on topics such as how finitely to represent infinite systems and how to represent the information needed to prove well-foundedness (which we require for the proof of liveness properties (in general, least fixed-points in the modal mu-calculus)). The tool provides the user with a reasonably simple X Window System interface for constructing tableaux, and, more importantly, checks the correctness of all rules used in the tableau—this is not a trivial operation, since we are dealing with infinite sets of system states. It can also build a tableau automatically up to the point where user intervention is required to resolve a choice. Moreover, the tool also provides some help with proving the required well-foundedness relations. These relations are defined by the tableau, and are typically complex; however, there is often a simpler relation, apparent to the intelligent observer or designer, the well-foundedness of which implies the well-foundedness of the tableau relations. In such cases the tool can verify that this implication is valid, so that the user only has to check the well-foundedness of the simple relation.

2 The modal mu-calculus

The temporal logic we use is the propositional modal mu-calculus, introduced by Kozen [Koz83]. This is a very rich logic which is now increasingly popular, both as an object of study ([KoP83], [EmL86], [StE89]) and as a logic for use in verification problems and tools such as the Concurrency Workbench ([CPS89], [BrA91], [Bra91b]).

The formulae have the form

$$\Phi ::= Z \mid \neg\Phi_1 \mid \Phi_1 \wedge \Phi_2 \mid [K]\Phi_1 \mid \nu Z.\Phi_1$$

where Z ranges over a countable set Var of variables, K ranges over subsets of a label set $\mathscr{L}$, and $\nu Z.\Phi_1$ is subject to the restriction that any free occurrence of Z in Φ_1 must be within the scope of an even number of negation symbols. The usual boolean and modal dual connectives are employed ($\langle K \rangle \Phi \stackrel{\text{def}}{=} \neg[K]\neg\Phi$), and a dual to ν is defined by

$$\mu Z.\Phi \stackrel{\text{def}}{=} \neg\nu Z.\neg\Phi[\neg Z/Z]$$

where $\Phi[\Psi/Z]$ denotes the syntactic substitution of Ψ for free occurrences of Z in Φ. The symbol σ is used to range over ν and μ. The following abbreviations are used: $[-K]\Phi \stackrel{\text{def}}{=} [\mathscr{L} - K]\Phi$; $[a_1, \ldots, a_n]\Phi \stackrel{\text{def}}{=} [\{a_1, \ldots, a_n\}]\Phi$; $[-]\Phi \stackrel{\text{def}}{=} [\mathscr{L}]\Phi$; and similarly for $\langle K \rangle$.

A model for this logic is a labelled transition system $\mathcal{T} = (\mathcal{S}, \{ \xrightarrow{a} \mid a \in \mathcal{L} \})$ (where $\mathcal{S}$ is a set of states) together with a valuation $\mathcal{V} : \text{Var} \to 2^{\mathcal{S}}$. The denotation $\|\Phi\|_{\mathcal{V}}^{\mathcal{T}}$ (or $\|\Phi\|_{\mathcal{V}}$ when $\mathcal{T}$ is understood) of a formula is a set of states given by the usual rules for variables and booleans together with the modal and fix-point rules

$$\|\nu Z.\Phi\|_{\mathcal{V}} = \bigcup \{ S \subseteq \mathcal{S} \mid \|\Phi\|_{\mathcal{V}[Z:=S]} \supseteq S \}$$

$$\|[K]\Phi\|_{\mathcal{V}} = \{ s \in \mathcal{S} \mid \forall s' \in \mathcal{S} . \forall a \in K . s \xrightarrow{a} s' \Rightarrow s' \in \|\Phi\|_{\mathcal{V}} \}$$

where $\mathcal{V}[Z := S]$ is the valuation $\mathcal{V}'$ which agrees with $\mathcal{V}$ save that $\mathcal{V}'(Z) = S$.

3 The tableau system

We now describe the tableau system for model-checking. This description is necessarily brief; see [BrS90] or [Bra91a] for more information, and [Bra91b] or [BrS92] for a full account.

In order to deal with the fix-point formulae, we extend the mu-calculus by constants $U, V, \ldots$, and introduce definition lists of the form $\Delta = (U_1 = \Phi_1, \ldots, U_n = \Phi_n)$ which assign formulae to constants (subject to the constraint that the only constants appearing in Φ_i are those in $\{U_1, \ldots, U_{i-1}\}$), and write $\Delta(U)$ for the formula assigned to U in Δ. The denotation $\|\Phi_\Delta\|_{\mathcal{V}}$ of a formula with respect to Δ is given in the natural way by

$$\|\Phi_{\Delta \cdot (U = \Psi)}\|_{\mathcal{V}} = \|\Phi_\Delta\|_{\mathcal{V}[U := \|\Psi_\Delta\|_{\mathcal{V}}]}.$$

The sequents of our tableaux have the form $S \vdash_\Delta \Phi$ where S is a set of states, Φ is a formula of the extended mu-calculus in positive normal form (that is, using the dual operators and De Morgan laws to move negations inwards so that they only apply to variables), and Δ is a definition list. These sequents are treated as goals to be proved—$S \vdash_\Delta \Phi$ means we want to prove that $S \subseteq \|\Phi_\Delta\|_{\mathcal{V}}$— and tableaux are built up by means of the following goal-directed rules (where $s \xrightarrow{K} s'$ means $\exists a \in K . s \xrightarrow{a} s'$).

$$\wedge \qquad \frac{S \vdash_\Delta \Phi_1 \wedge \Phi_2}{S \vdash_\Delta \Phi_1 \qquad S \vdash_\Delta \Phi_2}$$

$$\vee \qquad \frac{S \vdash_\Delta \Phi_1 \vee \Phi_2}{S_1 \vdash_\Delta \Phi_1 \qquad S_2 \vdash_\Delta \Phi_2} \qquad S = S_1 \cup S_2$$

$$[K] \qquad \frac{S \vdash_\Delta [K]\Phi}{S' \vdash_\Delta \Phi} \qquad S' = \{ s' \mid \exists s \in S . s \xrightarrow{K} s' \}$$

$$\langle K \rangle \qquad \frac{S \vdash_\Delta \langle K \rangle \Phi}{f(S) \vdash_\Delta \Phi} \qquad f : S \to f(S) \text{ s.t. } \forall s \in S . s \xrightarrow{K} f(s)$$

$\sigma Z.$ $\qquad \dfrac{S \vdash_\Delta \sigma Z.\Phi}{S \vdash_{\Delta'} U} \qquad\qquad U$ not in Δ and $\Delta' = \Delta \cdot (U = \sigma Z.\Phi)$

Un $\qquad \dfrac{S \vdash_\Delta U}{S \vdash_\Delta \Phi[U/Z]} \qquad\qquad \Delta(U) = \sigma Z.\Phi$

Thin $\qquad \dfrac{S \vdash_\Delta \Phi}{S' \vdash_\Delta \Phi} \qquad\qquad S' \supseteq S$

The function f in the $\langle K \rangle$ rule is a choice function whose purpose is to choose the successor state that most quickly leads towards 'termination', in a sense made precise shortly.

One keeps applying rules to the leaves of the tableau (starting with a root sequent for the property one wishes to prove), until all leaves are *terminal*. A leaf is terminal if no rule other than Thin applies, that is

(i) $\Phi = Z$ or $\Phi = \neg Z$, or

(ii) $\Phi = \langle K \rangle \Psi$ and $\exists s \in S . \forall s' \in \mathscr{S} .$ not $s \xrightarrow{K} s'$,

or the state set is trivial

(iii) $S = \varnothing$

or finally

(iv) $\Phi = U$ and $\Delta(U) = \sigma Z.\Psi$ and $\mathbf{n}$ has an ancestor node $\mathbf{n}' = S' \vdash_{\Delta'} U$ such that $S' \supseteq S$ (in which case we call $\mathbf{n}$ a σ-terminal and $\mathbf{n}'$ its companion).

A terminal node is deemed to be *successful* iff

- it is in class (i) and is true, i.e. if $\Phi = Z$ then $S \subseteq \mathscr{V}(Z)$ and if $\Phi = \neg Z$ then $S \cap \mathscr{V}(Z) = \varnothing$; or
- it is in class (iii); or
- it is in class (iv) with $\sigma = \nu$; or
- it is in class (iv) with $\sigma = \mu$ and satisfies the **mu-success** conditions defined below.

A tableau is successful if it is finite and all its terminals are successful.

For the correctness of least fix-points, we define a relation on the states at companion nodes, which corresponds to the dependency of truth of a least fix-point at one state on the truth at other states; then we need to ensure that there are no infinite dependency chains for least fix-points. Since we must take account of nested fix-points, this relation is quite complicated. We start by defining paths and extended paths in the tableau:

In a tableau, a *path* from a state s at a node $\mathbf{n}$ to a state s' at a node $\mathbf{n}'$ is a sequence $(s, \mathbf{n}) = (s_0, \mathbf{n}_0), (s_1, \mathbf{n}_1), \ldots, (s_k, \mathbf{n}_k) = (s', \mathbf{n}')$ of states and nodes such that

- $\mathbf{n}_{i+1}$ is a child of $\mathbf{n}_i$;
- if $\mathbf{n}_i = S_i \vdash_{\Delta_i} \Phi_i$ then $s_i \in S_i$;
- if the rule applied to $\mathbf{n}_i$ is $[K]$ then $s_i \xrightarrow{K} s_{i+1}$, if the rule is $\langle K \rangle$ then $s_{i+1} = f(s_i)$, and otherwise $s_{i+1} = s_i$.

We write $s@\mathbf{n} \longrightarrow s'@\mathbf{n}'$ if there is a path from s at $\mathbf{n}$ to s' at $\mathbf{n}'$.

Now there is an *extended path* from s at $\mathbf{n}$ to s' at $\mathbf{n}'$, written $s@\mathbf{n} \dashrightarrow s'@\mathbf{n}'$, if either

(i) $s@\mathbf{n} \longrightarrow s'@\mathbf{n}'$, or

(ii) there is a node $\mathbf{n}'' = S'' \vdash_{\Delta''} U$ and a finite sequence of states $s_0, s_1, \ldots, s_k$ and nodes $\mathbf{n}_1, \ldots, \mathbf{n}_k$ for $k \geq 0$, where each $\mathbf{n}_i$ is a terminal with companion $\mathbf{n}''$, such that $s@\mathbf{n} \longrightarrow s_0@\mathbf{n}''$ and $s_i@\mathbf{n}'' \dashrightarrow s_{i+1}@\mathbf{n}_{i+1}$ for $0 \leq i < k$, and $s_k@\mathbf{n}'' \dashrightarrow s'@\mathbf{n}'$.

Finally, we can define the relation on states, and the well-foundedness condition:

Let $\mathbf{n} = S \vdash_{\Delta} U$ be a μ-terminal with companion node $\mathbf{n}' = S' \vdash_{\Delta'} U$. Define a relation $\sqsupset_{\mathbf{n}'}$ on S' by $s \sqsupset_{\mathbf{n}'} s'$ iff $s@\mathbf{n}' \dashrightarrow s'@\mathbf{n}''$ for any terminal $\mathbf{n}''$ whose companion is $\mathbf{n}'$. The condition **mu-success** is that $\sqsubset_{\mathbf{n}'}$ should be well-founded, that is, there should be no infinite chains $s_0 \sqsupset_{\mathbf{n}'} s_1 \sqsupset_{\mathbf{n}'} \cdots$.

If now we have a successful tableau, then the root sequent is true, and if the root sequent is true, then a successful tableau exists (see [Bra91b] or [BrS92] for the proofs).

For the purposes of our prototype, two small modifications are made to the tableau rules. The first is that we do not have a Thin rule, but instead allow implicit thinning in every rule, so that, for example, the $\vee$ rule side-condition is $S \subseteq S_1 \cup S_2$. Implicit thinning saves space and time in the tableau; explicit thinning will be added when convenient. The second change is specific to the Petri net model class: in the choice function at a $\langle K \rangle$ rule; rather than specifying the successor marking of M, we specify the transition to fire. This is both more natural and easier to represent.

4 Petri nets

For our purposes, a Petri net is a place/transition net, so that formally a net $\mathcal{N} = (\mathbf{S}, \mathbf{T}; \mathbf{F})$ comprises two disjoint sets $\mathbf{S}$ (the *places*) and $\mathbf{T}$ (the *transitions*) together with a map $\mathbf{F} : (\mathbf{S} \times \mathbf{T}) \uplus (\mathbf{T} \times \mathbf{S}) \to \mathbf{N}$ (where $\uplus$ is disjoint union). $\mathbf{F}$ gives the weight w of an arc connecting a place and a transition: if $\mathbf{F}(s, t) = w$ then when t fires it removes w tokens from place s, and if $\mathbf{F}(t, s) = w$ it adds w tokens to s. A *marking* of $\mathcal{N}$ is a map $M : \mathbf{S} \to \mathbf{N}$, giving the number of tokens in each place. As usual, $^{\bullet}x$ is the map $\mathbf{S} \cup \mathbf{T} \to \mathbf{N}$ given by $^{\bullet}x(y) = \mathbf{F}(y, x)$, and similarly $x^{\bullet}(y) = \mathbf{F}(x, y)$. The behaviour of the net viewed as a transition system with markings as states and transitions (of the net) as labels is given by the normal token game rules: $M \xrightarrow{t} M'$ iff $^{\bullet}t \leq M$ and $M' = M - {}^{\bullet}t + t^{\bullet}$.

To apply the tableau system to nets, we need to make several decisions. Firstly, we must decide what our 'atomic propositions' are, that is, what predefined variables we want in order to express properties of nets. An obvious choice is to take linear (in)equalities on places, so that for places s_i and integers a_i and b, the expression $a_1 s_1 + \cdots + a_n s_n \leq b$ is deemed to be a variable whose denotation is those markings M satisfying the inequality $a_1 M(s_1) + \cdots + a_n M(s_n) \leq b$.

Secondly, we need a means of representing the (infinite) sets of markings on the left of sequents. As considered by [Bra91b], here again (boolean combinations of) linear (in)equalities are often sufficient, and since they are also not too difficult to reason with, they were adopted in our tool.

For example, we could consider the net

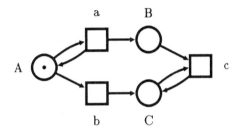

Figure 1

and the formulae $\nu Z.(\text{A} = 1) \wedge \langle - \rangle Z$ (some infinite execution exists on which A is always 1) and $\mu Y.\nu Z.[\text{c}]Y \wedge [-\text{c}]Z$ (event c happens only finitely often). The first of these formulae will demonstrate the basic use of the tool without least fix-points; the second will demonstrate the tool's facilities for checking well-foundedness.

5 Tableau construction with the tool

To construct a tableau using our tool, one starts up the tool, specifying the model being investigated. The model is specified as an ML data structure; in the case of Petri nets, a simple encoding of the definition. A window is created in which the tableau will be displayed, and above which there are some command buttons. One then clicks the 'Make Root' button, and types the initial state set and formula. The choice of state set is the first implicit thinning; typically one is interested in one initial state, but one must thin to a larger set to build a tableau. The logical notation is adapted slightly for the ASCII character set and ease of parsing: **&** and **|** are used for $\wedge$ and $\vee$, μ and ν are written as **mu** and **nu**, and 'atomic propositions' are enclosed in braces, thus: **{A + C = 1}**.

Figure 2 shows the main window of the tool just after the initial sequent has been typed in, using the net and the first formula given above, with an initial set **{ A = 1 }**. The reverse video indicates that the node is selected; the border of the sequent is grey, which indicates that this node is not valid. By valid we mean that either it is the premise of a validly applied rule, or that it is a successful terminal, or that it is a μ-terminal. Thus, when all nodes in a tableau are valid, the only remaining task is to check the well-foundedness conditions.

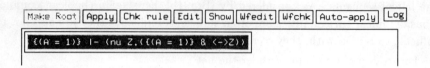

Figure 2

There are eight active command buttons: 'Log' brings up a log of all informational messages issued by the tool in this session; 'Wfedit', 'Wfchk' and 'Auto-apply' will be described later.

The 'Show' button describes the current node, giving information associated with it. For this particular node, there is no information other than the sequent set and formula.

The 'Edit' button can be used to edit the state set on the left of the sequent; this, of course, renders invalid both the edited node and its parent. After editing (or after anything else that invalidates a node), the 'Chk rule' button can be pressed to check the validity of the node. This invokes functions associated with the particular model class and representation of state sets (in this case, Petri nets and linear inequalities) to determine whether the rule applied to the node is a correct instantion of a tableau rule. For example, in the case of an $\wedge$ rule, it is necessary to check that both consequent sets contain the premise set.

The 'Apply' rule applies whatever rule is appropriate—since we do not have an explicit Thin, the rule is entirely determined by the formula. If the rule is anything other than $\vee$ or $\langle K \rangle$, no user input is required: if the node is a leaf, the new children nodes are created and their state sets calculated, and if the node is not a leaf, then the consequent sets are recalculated from the premise. (So if one edits the state set at a node, 'Apply' is used to effect the necessary changes further down the tableau.) In either case, the current node is marked valid.

Figure 3 shows the same tableau after as much as possible has been done without making any choices. Note that the border of the left-hand leaf is black; 'Chk Rule' has been used to check that this terminal is successful, which means simply checking that the state set satisfies the atomic proposition.

To apply the diamond rule to the right-hand leaf, the user must specify a choice function. As mentioned above, we specify for each marking the transition to be fired. This again raises the question of how to represent such functions. For this prototype, we use a simple method: we just give a list $(\mathbf{M}_1, t_1), \ldots, (\mathbf{M}_n, t_n)$

```
Make Root  Apply  Chk rule  Edit  Show  Wfedit  Wfchk  Auto-apply   Log

  ┌──────────────────────────────────────────────────────┐
  │ {(A = 1)} |- (nu Z.({(A = 1)} & <->Z))                │
  │ ┌──────────────────────────────────────────┐         │
  │ │ {(A = 1)} |- Z_1                           │         │
  │ │ ┌──────────────────────────────────────┐  │         │
  │ │ │ {(A = 1)} |- ({(A = 1)} & <->Z_1)    │  │         │
  │ │ │ ┌────────────────────┐ ┌──────────────────┐       │
  │ │ │ │ {(A = 1)} |- {(A = 1)}││ {(A = 1)} |- <->Z_1│     │
  │ │ │ └────────────────────┘ └──────────────────┘       │
  │ │ └──────────────────────────────────────┘  │         │
  │ └──────────────────────────────────────────┘         │
  └──────────────────────────────────────────────────────┘
```

Figure 3

of marking sets (expressed in the same notation used throughout) and transitions, and for a marking M, we fire the first t_i such that $M \in \mathbf{M}_i$. The notation used in the tool is $\mathbf{M}_1$ -> t_1 --- ... --- $\mathbf{M}_n$ -> t_n. For this particular tableau, all we need do is fire the a transition all the time, so the choice function is tt -> a. The tool then calculates the successor set and creates the child node. Figure 4 shows the tableau after applying the diamond rule and 'Show'ing the diamond node.

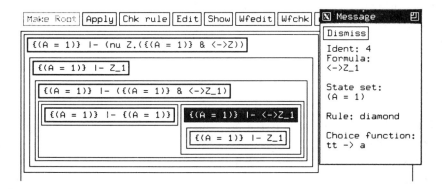

Figure 4

The only remaining task for this tableau is to verify that the new leaf is a successful terminal. 'Chk rule' does this by searching up the tableau to find a companion; in this case it finds the first Z_1 node $\mathbf{n}'$, and finds indeed that the state set at the terminal is a subset of the state set at $\mathbf{n}'$.

So far we have assumed that the user is actually getting everything right; what happens when a rule application is incorrect? The answer to this depends on the reasoning power of the module that handles rule checking for the particular class of models. In the present implementation, a (set of) marking(s) that illustrates the bad rule application is given. For example, suppose that we

324

specified a choice function that always chose event c. This would be bad, since c cannot always fire from markings in { A = 1 }. On trying to apply the diamond rule, the message in Figure 5 would be given, and similar messages are given for other incorrect rule applications.

```
Dismiss
```
Can't apply choice function: chosen transition is blocked for marking:
{A = 1, B = 0}

Figure 5

Finally, we should mention ∨ rules, and the 'Auto-apply' button. When an ∨ rule is applied to a leaf, the user is asked to specify the state set for the left disjunct, and the right state set is calculated from that—it is generally a good idea to have non-intersecting state sets in a disjunction, and sets calculated by the tool have this property. The user can change this by hand-editing the sets, but even then the tool will always take the left disjunct if possible when it calculates the tableau ⊐ relations.

The 'Auto-apply' button is simply a convenience; it builds the tableau as far as can be done without user intervention. It is particularly useful when one realizes some set high up in the tableau is wrong; after editing it, 'Auto-apply' will propagate the change everywhere below, using existing left disjuncts and choice functions if these still give valid rules.

6 Implementation

We have described the tool as the user sees it; we now say a little about the implementation.

The main body of the tool is written in Standard ML, and deals with the maintenance of tableau data-structures, parsing mu-calculus formulae, etc. (All parsers are written using the ML-Yacc parser generator.) It receives commands from the user, and gives information to the user (e.g. displaying tableaux) via a separate front end.

The X Window System front end is a C program which communicates via a pipe with the main program. This is just a matter of convenience: the main body, of course, neither knows nor cares how its user-interface functions are actually implemented. The front end is the bare minimum necessary for sensible use of the tool and would have to be improved in a production version.

The other significant part of the tool is the module for dealing specifically with Petri nets. Not surprisingly, this is the largest part in lines of code. This module is called by the main module to do all manipulations on sets of markings, so it must be able to handle intersection, union and complementation of marking sets. Since our representation of marking sets is by boolean combinations of linear inequalities, these operations are straightforward. It must also calculate successor sets for the modal rules; these are given by the Petri net firing rules. An important practical point is that during the construction of a tableau, many such operations are performed, and by the time one reaches a leaf, a formula obtained just by applying the rules probably has many copies of each atomic proposition in many positions, most of them redundant. This is highly undesirable, both because it will baffle the user with unnecessary complexity, and because it will increase the time required to manipulate sets. Therefore, considerable effort is devoted to simplifying formulae, using various manipulations to remove redundant subformulae. This is by no means complete—we do not use any exponential algorithms in simplification—but we achieve sufficient simplification to avoid irritating the user excessively!

The other task that the reasoning module has to perform, is to determine whether sets of markings are empty. (More often, it is asked whether one set is contained in another, but since we can complement and intersect sets, this is the same problem.) The technique for doing this is first to reduce the formula representing the set to disjunctive normal form, and then to check that each disjunct is empty. This amounts to showing that a set of linear inequalities has no non-negative integer solution. To do this, we use the symbolic manipulation language Maple; we use a branch and bound integer programming algorithm built around the simplex package supplied with Maple. This has the advantage of giving a minimal counter-example if the set is not empty, and it is this counter-example that is displayed in the error message for invalid rules.

7 Well-foundedness

The most difficult part of a tableau proof is proving the well-foundedness of the $\sqsupset$ relations. Although the house-keeping and rule-checking provided by the tool is already useful, assistance with well-foundedness checking would be very welcome. This, even more so than the rest of the implementation, requires careful consideration of representation problems. It is quite possible to have a tableau and net that are easily represented in our tool, but whose well-foundedness proofs require reasoning power far beyond that available to any tool (or indeed, beyond that so far available to human mathematicians—see [Bra91b]). On the other hand, such pathological cases are, we hope, unlikely to occur in practical verification, where if a liveness property holds, it probably holds for some fairly simple reason. The theoretical question of finding classes of models for which a given reasoning power suffices, is of great interest, but also of considerable difficulty. Therefore, the well-foundedness checking assistance in the current implementation is designed to be both sufficient for many of our toy examples and relatively simple to implement; only experience will show how much more power is required in real applications.

The technique used in our prototype rests on the following easy result:

Assume the notation used in the definition of extended path. Suppose that we have a measure $\xi: \mathscr{S} \to X$ which maps each state to an element of a well-ordered set X. If the following condition holds, then $s@\mathbf{n} \dashrightarrow s'@\mathbf{n}'$ implies $\xi(s') < \xi(s)$ (and therefore $\sqsubset_\mathbf{n}$ is well-founded):

- if $\forall s, s'' \in \mathscr{S} . s@\mathbf{n} \longrightarrow s''@\mathbf{n}'' \Rightarrow \xi(s'') < \xi(s)$
  then $\forall s'', s' \in \mathscr{S}, 1 \le i \le k . (s''@\mathbf{n}'' \dashrightarrow s'@\mathbf{n}_i \vee s''@\mathbf{n}'' \dashrightarrow s'@\mathbf{n}') \Rightarrow \xi(s') \le \xi(s'')$; otherwise

- $\forall s, s'' \in \mathscr{S} . s@\mathbf{n} \longrightarrow s''@\mathbf{n}'' \Rightarrow \xi(s'') \le \xi(s)$
  and $\forall s'', s' \in \mathscr{S}, 1 \le i \le k . s''@\mathbf{n}'' \dashrightarrow s'@\mathbf{n}_i \Rightarrow \xi(s') \le \xi(s'')$
  and $\forall s'', s' \in \mathscr{S} . s''@\mathbf{n}'' \dashrightarrow s'@\mathbf{n}' \Rightarrow \xi(s') < \xi(s'')$.

That is, we are requiring that traversing the extended path decreases the measure, either by decreasing it along the top part and not increasing it in any subsidiary extended path, or by not increasing it in the top part or in any subsidiary loop and then decreasing it in the final part. The advantage is that we need only calculate with path relations: although the proposition refers to subsidiary extended paths, these can be checked by applying the proposition recursively (if $<$ is everywhere replaced by $\le$, we have a result that deals with the $\le$ clauses similarly). So the only calculation we need to do is to calculate a path relation R and then determine whether $s \, R \, s' \Rightarrow \xi(s') < \xi(s)$. The disadvantage is that we are requiring a much stronger property than the original tableau well-foundedness; it is possible, for example, for there to be a measure such that the subsidiary extended paths increase it, but the final path down to $\mathbf{n}'$ always compensates for this increases; this situation is not covered by this technique.

To implement this in our tool, we need a representation of binary relations on markings. Since we have a representation of sets (by linear (in)equalities), we represent relations in the same way, using primes to distinguish places in codomain markings from places in domain markings: e.g. $(A = A') \wedge (B' = B + 1)$ represents the relation R such that $M \, R \, M'$ iff $(M(A) = M'(A)) \wedge (M'(B) = M(B) + 1)$. Composition of such relations is handled by letting places with more than one dash represent existentially quantified variables, so that $(A' = A'' + 1) \wedge (A'' = A + 1)$ (which is the composition of $A' = A + 1$ with itself) should be read as R such that $M \, R \, M'$ iff $\exists M'' . (M'(A) = M''(A) + 1) \wedge M''(A) = M(A) + 1$. This interpretation of multiple primes does not require any work, since when such a relation is given to the emptiness checker, all variables are treated existentially anyway. It does mean that relations with multiple primes cannot be complemented; however, we never need to do so.

The calculation of path relations is straightforward: the individual steps are subrelations of the identity for non-modal rules, and are giving by the net firing rules and the choice functions for the modal rules. These steps are then composed to give the path relation.

There remains the question of how to represent the measure: this is done by representing not the measure itself, but rather the relation R such that $M \, R \, M'$ iff $\xi(M) > \xi(M')$; it is the user's responsibility to determine that R is such a relation, and then the tool checks the implications in the above proposition.

For an example, consider the net of Figure 1 and the 'finitely often' formula mentioned earlier: $\mu Y.\nu Z.[c]Y \wedge [-c]Z$. A suitable set for the root sequent is $\{ A + C = 1 \}$.

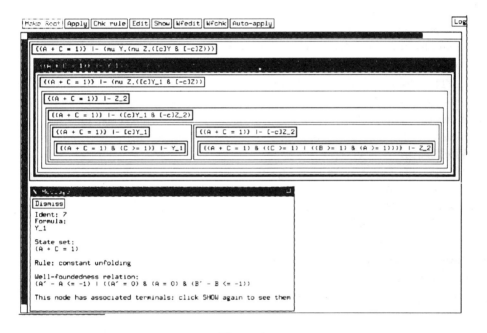

Figure 6

In Figure 6 the tableau for this has been developed to the point where all nodes are valid (using just one click of 'Auto-apply', since there are no $\vee$ or $\langle K \rangle$ rules). The grey background to the selected node shows that well-foundedness must be proved, and in fact a suitable relation has been typed in, as shown by the 'Show' message. The relation says that either A decreases or A remains at zero and B decreases—this corresponds to a measure ξ mapping markings to the set $\omega \cdot 2$, with $\xi(M) = \omega + (M(A) - 1)$ if $M(A) > 0$, and $\xi(M) = M(B)$ otherwise. (Of course, in the net, $M(A)$ is never more than 1.)

Clicking on the 'Wfchk' button will perform all the implication checking required by the proposition, and the grey background turns black to indicate success; if any implication fails, a counter-example is presented just as for rule-checking.

8 Conclusions and further work

We have described a window-based tool which assists in the construction of tableaux for proving temporal properties of arbitrary systems. The tableau management is independent of the model, and relieves the user of the burden of organizing tableau, keeping track of constants, etc. Model-dependent modules deal with representing infinite sets of states and calculating sets required by tableau rules, such as successor sets under certain transitions. Furthermore, the tool provides assistance in checking the complex well-foundedness relations in tableau, and indeed the user never sees these relations, but only has to provide a simpler relation. Here again there are both general and model-dependent components.

There is much scope for further work on this tool. Firstly, the interfaces between the different modules should be frozen and documented in order to move the tool out of the prototype stage. A reasoning module for CCS is a high priority, and will make the tool a useful companion to the Concurrency Workbench.

The representation of states for Petri nets needs further consideration; early experiments show that using linear inequalities to represent the whole state of non-trivial nets results in far too much work for the well-foundedness checker (owing mostly to the exponential blowup when already large relations are converted to disjunctive normal form). A suitable technique is probably to combine finite-state descriptions for parts of the net with infinite-state descriptions for others, and then to calculate successor sets etc. by simple exploration of the finite-state portion together with manipulation of the infinite-state representations.

Much work could be done on well-foundedness checking; this will be influenced both by theoretical investigation and by the results of experience.

The tool should be used in real cases; so far only toy examples have been used. The addition of a CCS module will make this easier, since the MPSS project already has several case studies to draw on.

9 Acknowledgements

This work was supported by the SERC grants 'Mathematically Proven Safety Systems' (GR/F 38808) and 'Verification of Infinite State Systems—Theory, Method and Applications' (GR/H 16056).

'X Window System' is a trademark of the Massachusetts Institute of Technology.

'Maple' is a registered trademark of Waterloo Maple Software.

10 References

[Bra91a] J. C. Bradfield, Proving temporal properties of Petri nets. *Advances in Petri Nets 1991* 29–47. LNCS 524 (1991).

[Bra91b] J. C. Bradfield, *Verifying Temporal Properties of Systems.* Birkhäuser, Boston, Mass. ISBN 0-8176-3625-0 (1991).

[BrS90] J. C. Bradfield and C. P. Stirling, Verifying temporal properties of processes. *Proc. CONCUR '90* 115–125. LNCS 458 (1990).

[BrS92] J. C. Bradfield and C. P. Stirling, Local model checking for infinite state spaces. To appear in *Theoret. Comput. Sci.* (1992).

[BrA91] G. Bruns and S. Anderson, The Formalization and Analysis of a Communications Protocol. In J. F. Lindeberg (ed.) *Proc. SAFECOMP '91* 7–12. IFAC Symposia Series (1991).

[ClE81] E. M. Clarke and E. A. Emerson, Design and synthesis of synchronization skeletons using branching time temporal logic. LNCS 131 52–71 (1981).

[CES86] E. M. Clarke, E. A. Emerson and A. P. Sistla, Automatic verification of finite-state concurrent systems using temporal logic specifications. *ACM Trans. on Programming Languages and Systems* 8 244–263 (1986).

[CPS89] R. Cleaveland, J. Parrow and B. Steffen, A semantics-based verification tool for finite state systems. *Proc. 9th IFIP Symp. on Protocol Specification, Testing and Verification.* North-Holland (1989).

[EmL86] E. A. Emerson and C.-L. Lei, Efficient model checking in fragments of the propositional mu-calculus. *Proc. First IEEE Symp. on Logic in Computer Science* 267–278 (1986).

[Koz83] D. Kozen, Results on the propositional mu-calculus. *Theoret. Comput. Sci.* 27 333–354 (1983).

[KoP83] D. Kozen and R. Parikh, A decision procedure for the propositional mu-calculus. *Second Workshop on Logics of Programs* (1983).

[StW89] C. P. Stirling and D. J. Walker, Local model checking in the modal mu-calculus. *Proc. International Joint Conference on Theory and Practice of Software Development* 369–382. LNCS 351 (1989).

[StE89] R. S. Streett and E. A. Emerson, An automata theoretic decision procedure for the propositional mu-calculus. *Information and Computation* 81 249–264 (1989).

Tableau Recycling

Angelika Mader *
Technische Universität München
Arcisstr. 21
W - 8000 München 2
Germany
e-mail: mader@informatik.tu-muenchen.de

Abstract

In this paper we improve a model checking algorithm based on the tableau method of Stirling and Walker. The algorithm proves whether a property expressed in the modal mu-calculus holds for a state in a finite transition system. It makes subsequent use of subtableaux which were calculated earlier in the proof run. These subtableaux are reduced to expressions. Examples show that both size of tableaux and execution time of the algorithm are reduced.

1 Introduction

The modal mu-calculus is an active area of research. It stands in the tradition of Hoare logic, Dynamic logic, Process logic, and linear and branching time logics [S]. Model checking in the modal mu-calculus plays a part in verification of parallel processes with both finite [CS1] and infinite state spaces [BS], and finds application in preorder models [CS2] and in Petri nets [B].

The main approaches are symbolic model checking [BC] [EFT], model checkers based on the fixpoint induction principle [EL], and tableau based model checkers as in [SW] [C]. An advantage of the latter is its ability to deal also with infinite state spaces. In comparison to the approximation techniques they work locally, i.e. they do not determine the set of all states satisfying a property, but prove a modal formula only for one state. Unfortunately the attractiveness of tableau methods suffers by their complexity. A main reason for this is that these model checkers do not make subsequent use of subresults.

This paper presents a method whereby a tableau based model checker for the full modal mu-calculus can recycle subtableaux, which have been calculated earlier in the model checking algorithm. An implementation of these ideas has confirmed an impressive improvement in execution speed in a variety of examples.

The following section introduces briefly the modal mu-calculus and its semantics. In section 3 the underlying standard tableau model checker is described. The motivating

---

*supported by Siemens AG, Corporate Research and Development

ideas of tableau recycling and the necessary notions are contained in section 4. Sections 5 and 6 present the algorithm and the proofs of its correctness and completeness. Some surprising examples can be found in section 7. Section 8 concludes this paper.

2   The Modal Mu-Calculus

This section gives a brief introduction to the modal mu-calculus. For more details see [S].

The syntax of the modal mu-calculus is defined with respect to a set $\mathcal{Q}$ of atomic propositions including *true* and *false*, a finite set $\mathcal{L}$ of action labels and a denumerable set $\mathcal{Z}$ of propositional variables. A formula of the modal mu-calculus is an expression of the form:

$$A ::= Z \mid Q \mid \neg A \mid A \wedge A \mid [a]A \mid \nu Z.A$$

where $Z \in \mathcal{Z}$, $Q \in \mathcal{Q}$ and $a \in \mathcal{L}$, and where in $\nu Z.A$ every free occurence of Z in A falls under an even number of negations. The standard conventions for the derived operators are:

$$A_1 \vee A_2 := \neg(\neg A_1 \wedge \neg A_2)$$
$$\langle a \rangle A \quad := \neg[a]\neg A$$
$$\mu Z.A \quad := \neg \nu Z.\neg A[\neg Z/Z].$$

Formulae of the modal mu-calculus with the set $\mathcal{L}$ of action labels are interpreted relative to a *labelled transition system* $\mathcal{T} = (\mathcal{S}, \{\xrightarrow{a} \mid a \in \mathcal{L}\})$, where $\mathcal{S}$ is a finite set of states and $\xrightarrow{a} \subseteq \mathcal{S} \times \mathcal{L} \times \mathcal{S}$ for every $a \in \mathcal{L}$ a binary relation on states. A *valuation function* $\mathcal{V}$ assigns to every atomic proposition Q in $\mathcal{Q}$ (and propositional variable Z in $\mathcal{Z}$) a set of states $\mathcal{V}(Q) \subseteq \mathcal{S}$ ($\mathcal{V}(Z) \subseteq \mathcal{S}$) meaning that the proposition Q (variable Z) holds for every state in $\mathcal{V}(Q)$ ($\mathcal{V}(Z)$). The pair $\mathcal{T}$ and $\mathcal{V}$ is called a *model* of the mu-calculus. The semantics of each mu-calculus formula A is the set of states $\|A\|_{\mathcal{V}}^{\mathcal{T}}$ defined inductively as follows:

$$\|Z\|_{\mathcal{V}}^{\mathcal{T}} \quad = \mathcal{V}(Z)$$
$$\|Q\|_{\mathcal{V}}^{\mathcal{T}} \quad = \mathcal{V}(Q)$$
$$\|\neg A\|_{\mathcal{V}}^{\mathcal{T}} \quad = \mathcal{S} - \|A\|_{\mathcal{V}}^{\mathcal{T}}$$
$$\|A_1 \wedge A_2\|_{\mathcal{V}}^{\mathcal{T}} = \|A_1\|_{\mathcal{V}}^{\mathcal{T}} \cap \|A_2\|_{\mathcal{V}}^{\mathcal{T}}$$
$$\|[a]A\|_{\mathcal{V}}^{\mathcal{T}} \quad = \{s \in \mathcal{S} \mid \forall s'. \ if \ s \xrightarrow{a} s' \ then \ s' \in \|A\|_{\mathcal{V}}^{\mathcal{T}}\}$$
$$\|\nu Z.A\|_{\mathcal{V}}^{\mathcal{T}} \quad = \bigcup\{\mathcal{S}' \subseteq \mathcal{S} \mid \mathcal{S}' \subseteq \|A\|_{\mathcal{V}[\mathcal{S}'/Z]}^{\mathcal{T}}\}$$

3   A Standard Tableau Model Checker

This section sketches a standard tableau method based on the model checker of Stirling & Walker [SW]. The notation used here is a mixture of the notations of Cleaveland [C] and Stirling & Walker [SW]. Some additional notions are necessary.
The modal mu-calculus is extended by a set of propositional constant symbols. Let

$U, U_1\ldots$ range over these symbols. A *definition* is a declaration $U = A$, where U is a constant symbol and A a formula of the modal mu-calculus which may contain constant symbols. A *definition list* Δ consists of a sequence of definitions $(U_1 = A_1)\ldots(U_n = A_n)$. It fulfills the requirement that every U_j appearing in A_i is defined before U_i, i.e. $j \leq i$, and that $U_i \neq U_j$ for $i \neq j$. For Δ being such a definition list the function $\Delta(U_i) = A_i$ is declared. A *hypothesis* is an expression of the form $s \in U$, where s is a state of a transition system and U a constant symbol. Hypotheses are collected in a *hypothesis set* H. A *sequent* $H \vdash_\Delta s \in A$ expresses that the formula A is valid at the state s with respect to the hypotheses of H. We drop empty Δs and Hs.

The model checker here is tableau based. This corresponds to a top-down proof method, starting with the intended conclusion and reducing it stepwise to (atomic) premisses. The rules for a tableau method are inverse to the usual rules of natural deduction. Here we take the conclusions and premisses to be sequents. The root sequent $\vdash s \in A$ contains the state s and the modal property A, which we want to prove for this state. The root sequent has an empty hypothesis set and an empty definition list. The rules of the tableau system are:

$$1)\frac{H \vdash_\Delta s \in \neg\neg A}{H \vdash_\Delta s \in A} \qquad 2)\frac{H \vdash_\Delta s \in A \wedge B}{H \vdash_\Delta s \in A \quad H \vdash_\Delta s \in B}$$

$$3)\frac{H \vdash_\Delta s \in \neg(A \wedge B)}{H \vdash_\Delta s \in \neg A} \qquad 4)\frac{H \vdash_\Delta s \in \neg(A \wedge B)}{H \vdash_\Delta s \in \neg B}$$

$$5)\frac{H \vdash_\Delta s \in [a]A}{H \vdash_\Delta s_1 \in A \ldots H \vdash_\Delta s_n \in A} \quad \{s_1,\ldots,s_n\} = \{s' \mid s \xrightarrow{a} s'\}$$

$$6)\frac{H \vdash_\Delta s \in \neg[a]A}{H \vdash_\Delta s' \in \neg A} \quad s \xrightarrow{a} s'$$

$$7)\frac{H \vdash_\Delta s \in \nu Z.A}{H \vdash_{\Delta'} s \in U} \quad \Delta' = \Delta \cdot (U = \nu Z.A)$$

$$8)\frac{H \vdash_\Delta s \in \neg\nu Z.A}{H \vdash_{\Delta'} s \in U} \quad \Delta' = \Delta \cdot (U = \neg\nu Z.A)$$

$$9)\frac{H \vdash_\Delta s \in U}{H' \vdash_\Delta s \in A[Z := U]} \quad (s \in U) \notin H, \ \Delta(U) = \nu Z.A, \ H' = H \cup \{s \in U\}$$

$$10)\frac{H \vdash_\Delta s \in U}{H' \vdash_\Delta s \in \neg A[Z := \neg U]} \quad (s \in U) \notin H, \ \Delta(U) = \neg\nu Z.A, \ H' = H \cup \{s \in U\}$$

A *proof tree* is constructed by applying the rules to the root sequent, and then to its successors etc. The proof tree is *maximal* if no rule is applicable to a leaf sequent. Such a maximal proof tree is called a *tableau*. A tableau is *successful*, if all its leaves are successful. A leaf sequent $H \vdash_\Delta s \in B$ is successful, if it satisfies one of the properties (i)-(iv):

(i) $B = Q$ and $s \in \mathcal{V}(Q)$

(i') $B = Q$ and $s \notin \mathcal{V}(Q)$

(ii) $B = \neg Q$ and $s \notin \mathcal{V}(Q)$

(ii') $B = \neg Q$ and $s \in \mathcal{V}(Q)$

(iii) $B = [a]C$

(iii') $B = \langle a \rangle C$

(iv) $B = U$ and $\Delta(U) = \nu Z.C$
and $(s \in U) \in H$

(iv') $B = U$ and $\Delta(U) = \neg \nu Z.C$
and $(s \in U) \in H$

If one of the dual forms (i')-(iv') of these requirements holds for a leaf sequent, then it is not successful. In an *unsuccessful* tableau there is at least one leaf, which is not successful.

For later considerations the definition of a *computation tree* is also neccessary. A *model checker algorithm* based on the tableau rules builds a tree starting with $\vdash s \in A$ as root sequent and applying nondeterministically the rules. When a leaf fails the algorithm has to use backtracking techniques to try other paths. It will build up this tree until it is sure that a sequent has a successful subtableau or not. In the first case the tree includes a successful tableau, in the second case it is not necessary that the tree contains any maximal proof tree. We call a tree created by such a model checker algorithm a *computation tree*, if it sufficient to decide, whether there exists a successful tableau or not.

Note that such a computation tree determines an "and-or-tree", if the successful leaves are identified with *true*, the unsuccessful ones with *false*, the nondeterministic branching as disjunction and the deterministic branching as conjunction. It can be evaluated to *true*, iff the computation tree contains a successful tableau.

For simplicity of notation in this paper the definition lists Δ, Δ' are considered to be *global* for all different subtrees of one computation tree, i.e. there are no two different definition lists (in two different subtrees) Δ_1, Δ_2 and for any U, $\Delta_1(U) \neq \Delta_2(U)$.

4   Tableau Recycling

This section starts by describing a *basic source of inefficiency* in the standard model checker. Then it considers *how the efficiency might be improved*, and finally *means for an algorithm* are presented that gives a significant gain in efficiency.

The basic problem with the standard model checker is that it does not store any intermediate results (subresults). It is possible that it proves the same formula for the same state arbitrarily often, as the following example will show:

$\vdash s_1 \in \Phi$

$\Phi = \nu X.[a]\langle b \rangle X$

informal meaning: "every a-successor
has a b-successor for which

this property holds,recursively."

Fig. 1.   model with tableau of exponentional size

Here the formula Φ is proved n times for the state s_2, n^2 times for the state s_3, ..., n^{k-1} times for the state s_k. The number of nodes in the computation tree is exponential with respect to the length k of this transition system.

Moreover, a look at computation trees shows that in many cases, different subtableaux of a state and a formula are very *similar*.

The most obvious way to improve efficiency would be just to store the information *"the sequent $H \vdash s \in \Phi$ has a successful (or no successful) subtableau"* , and use it whenever the same state and formula appear again in the computation tree. Unfortunately this idea is too simple:

- The first obstacle is that the constants used in different subtableaus have different names. It therefore does not happen that exactly the same sequent appears twice. A notion of equivalence will help to solve this problem.

- Secondly the hypothesis sets can differ, even when formulae and states are identical. It is obvious that the shapes of the computation subtrees differ accordingly, since they depend on the hypothesis sets. Therefore in order to recycle a computation subtree of a similar sequent with even a slightly different hypothesis set, one has to store also the shape of the computation subtree. It turns out that the shape of such a subtree can be reduced to an expression which is sufficient for the derivation of all useful information.

A cornerstone of the tableau recycling algorithm is a notion of equivalence, which allows different sequents in a computation tree to be compared. The basis for this is the definition of equivalent constants, which have different names but identify syntactically the same formula. In the following let for $Z_1, \ldots, Z_n$ being the free variables in Φ, denote $\Phi(U_{j_1}, \ldots U_{j_n}) = \Phi[U_{j_1}/Z_1, \ldots U_{j_n}/Z_n]$, meaning that every occurence of Z_i in Φ is substituted by U_{j_i}.

DEFINITION 1 (Equivalence)

(1) *A formula* $\Phi(U_{j_1}, \ldots U_{j_n})$ *is equivalent to the formula* $\Phi(U_{k_1}, \ldots U_{k_n})$, *denoted* $\Phi(U_{j_1}, \ldots U_{j_n}) \sim \Phi(U_{k_1}, \ldots U_{k_n})$, *iff* *for* $1 \leq i \leq n$ *all constants* $U_{j_i} \sim U_{k_i}$.

(2) *A constant* U_1 *is equivalent to the constant* U_2, *denoted* $U_1 \sim U_2$, *iff* $U_1 = U_2$ *or* $\Delta(U_1) \sim \Delta(U_2)$.

Note that this equivalence is essentially alpha-conversion with respect to constants. The main insight now is that equivalent sequents can have identical computation subtrees.

We will now show how the shape of a computation tree can be reduced to an expression.

DEFINITION 2 (Hypothesis Tree)
A hypothesis tree is an expression of the form:

$$HT ::= true \mid false \mid unknown \mid Y \mid Y; HT \mid \bigvee_{i \in I} HT_i \mid \bigwedge_{i \in I} HT_i$$

where I is a finite index set and Y is a hypothesis, e.g. $s \in U$.

If the termination behavior of all paths of the computation tree is known, it is determined whether there is a successful subtableau or not. Some of the paths terminate with the rules (i)-(iii) and their dual forms. This kind of termination is independent of the hypothesis sets. The other paths terminate with rule (iv) and its dual form. In this case the kind of termination depends on the hypothesis set and whether for the terminal sequent $H' \vdash_\Delta s \in U$ the constant U stands for a maximal or negated maximal (minimal) fixpoint formula.

The reduction of a computation tree to a hypothesis tree reflects this idea:
transform the computation tree to an "and-or tree", but leave all hypotheses in it.

DEFINITION 3 (Reduction to a Hypothesis Tree)
Reduce a computation tree to a hypothesis tree in the following way:

- *Replace every leaf terminating with rules (i)-(iii) or their dual forms by true or false respectively.*

- *Replace every leaf terminating with a hypothesis which is not contained in the root hypothesis set by true if the leaf is successful or false otherwise.*

- *Replace every nondeterministic branching by a disjunction. If not all of the nondeterministic rules were applied, extend this disjunction by a leaf unknown. The number of all possible nondeterministic rules is called the arity of the disjunction.*

- *Replace every deterministic branching by a conjunction. If not all of the deterministic rules were applied, extend this conjunction by a leaf unknown. The number of all possible deterministic rules is called the arity of the conjunction.*

- *Drop all sequents which are not of the form $H \vdash_\Delta s \in U$, and drop all hypothesis sets.*

DEFINITION 4 (Evaluation of a Hypothesis Tree)
The function eval evaluates a hypothesis tree HT together with a hypothesis set H to $eval(HT, H) \in \{true, false, unknown\}$ in the following way:

- *substitute every hypothesis $s \in U$ in HT which is contained in H by true if $\Delta(U) = \nu X.A$, else by false .*

- *substitute every hypothesis which is not contained in H by unknown.*

- *Evaluate this tree with the following rules which are extended in the obvious way for indexed conjunction and disjunction:*

∨	*true*	*false*	*unknown*
true	*true*	*true*	*true*
false	*true*	*false*	*unknown*
unknown	*true*	*unknown*	*unknown*

∧	*true*	*false*	*unknown*
true	*true*	*false*	*unknown*
false	*false*	*false*	*false*
unknown	*unknown*	*false*	*unknown*

The operator "*;*" is treated as follows:

$$eval(\ unknown\ ;\ HT\ ,\ H\ ) = eval(HT\ ,\ H)$$
$$eval(\ true\qquad ;\ HT\ ,\ H\ ) = true$$
$$eval(\ false\qquad ;\ HT\ ,\ H\ ) = false$$

The following definition reflects the idea that hypothesis trees with equivalent roots particulary have a common structure. Combining two hypothesis trees then means that the common structure is identified and extended by both non common structures parts.

DEFINITION 5 (Combination of Hypothesis Trees)
Consider two sequents $H_1 \vdash_\triangle s \in U_1$ and $H_2 \vdash_\triangle s \in U_2$, $U_1 \sim U_2$. τ_1 is the hypothesis tree constructed from a computation tree of the first sequent, τ_2 from the second one. Let $\tau_3 = \tau_1 \circ \tau_2$ be the combination of τ_1 and τ_2 such that

- *The root of τ_3 is the root of τ_1.*

- *If $t \in U_1'$ is a successor of $s \in U_1$ with the subtree τ_1' and $t \in U_2'$ is a successor of $s \in U_2$ with the subtree τ_2' such that $U_1' \sim U_2'$,*
  then $\tau_1' \circ \tau_2'$ is a direct subtree of the root of τ_3.

- *If $t \in U_1'$ is a successor of $s \in U_1$ with the subtree τ_1' and there is no successor $t \in U_2'$ of $s \in U_2$ such that $U_1' \sim U_2'$,*
  then τ_1' is a direct subtree of the root of τ_3. (symmetrically for $t \in U_2'$)

- *If the successors of $s \in U_1$ and $s \in U_2$ are disjunctions (neccessarily with the same arity) then the successor of the root of τ_3 is also a disjunction with the same arity and those branches are combined pairwise which correspond to the same rule applied at this place in the computation tree. Branches of one disjunction which have no corresponding branch of the other disjunction appear directly in the combined disjunction. If the arity of the disjunction and the number of branches are equal all leaves unknown in this disjunction are dropped. (analogously for conjunction)*

5   The Tableau Recycling Model Checker

The standard tableau model checker is extended by a set of hypothesis trees $\mathcal{HT}$. In the beginning $\mathcal{HT}$ is initialized with the empty set.

Every time, when a computation tree is built up for a sequent $H \vdash_\Delta s \in U$, the hypothesis tree τ is derived and inserted in $\mathcal{HT}$. If there already exists a hypothesis tree τ_1 in $\mathcal{HT}$ with a equivalent root $s \in U'$, $U \sim U'$, the combined hypothesis tree $\tau \circ \tau_1$ is added to $\mathcal{HT}$ replacing τ_1.

The tableau rules 9) and 10) are extended by a further requirement:

9')

$$\frac{H \vdash_\Delta s \in U}{H' \vdash_\Delta s \in A[Z := U]} \quad (s \in U) \notin H, \ \Delta(U) = \nu Z.A, \ H' = H \cup \{s \in U\}$$

and there is no $\tau \in \mathcal{HT}$ such that the root $s \in U'$, $U \sim U'$ and $eval(\tau, H) \in \{true, false\}$;

10')

$$\frac{H \vdash_\Delta s \in U}{H' \vdash_\Delta s \in \neg A[Z := \neg U]} \quad (s \in U) \notin H, \ \Delta(U) = \neg \nu Z.A, \ H' = H \cup \{s \in U\}$$

and there is no $\tau \in \mathcal{HT}$ such that the root $s \in U'$, $U \sim U'$ and $eval(\tau, H) \in \{true, false\}$;

In addition to the conditions (i)-(iv) stated in section 3 a leaf sequent $H \vdash_\Delta s \in U$ of a tableau constructed by by rules 1)-8), 9') and 10') is also successful if it fulfills the following property:

(v) There exists a $\tau \in \mathcal{HT}$ such that the root $s \in U'$, $U \sim U'$ and $eval(\tau, H) = true$.

The number of elements in the set $\mathcal{HT}$ is bounded: for every state in the transition system $\mathcal{T}$ and every fixpoint operator in the root formula there is at most one hypothesis tree contained in $\mathcal{HT}$.

The example on the next page should clarify the algorithm.

6 Correctness and Completeness

In this section it will be shown that the recycling model checker produces the same results as the model checker from Stirling & Walker [SW]. Then correctness and completeness of the model checker presented here follow from the correctness and completeness proved in [SW].

The way of argumentation is as follows: the propositions here are valid for both versions, the standard tableau model checker and the recycling one. First some properties of tableaux and computation trees with similar root sequents are stated. In the remainder it is shown that the evaluation of a hypothesis tree corresponds to the result derived from a computation tree.

As a first step the notion of equivalence given in definition 1 must be extended to hypothesis sets and sequents.

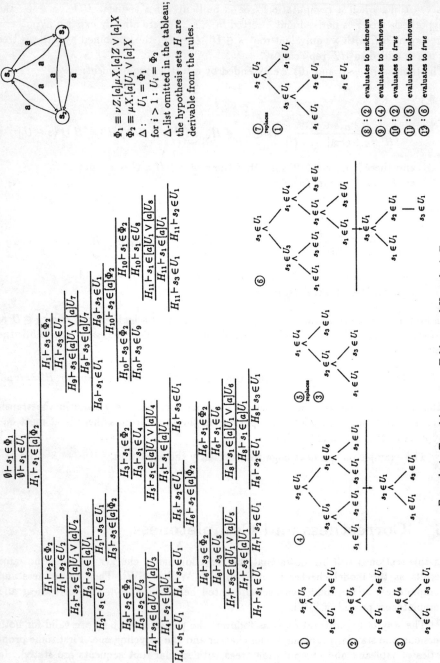

$$\Phi_1 \equiv \nu Z.[a]\mu X.[a]Z \vee [a]X$$
$$\Phi_2 \equiv \mu X.[a]U_1 \vee [a]X$$
$$\Delta: \quad U_1 = \Phi_1$$
$$\text{for } i > 1: U_i = \Phi_2$$

Δ-list omitted in the tableau;
the hypothesis sets H are
derivable from the rules.

Example 1: Transitionsystem, Tableau and Hypothesis Trees

DEFINITION 6 (Equivalence)

(3) A hypothesis set H_1 is smaller than a hypotheses set H_2 with respect to the equivalent constants U_1, U_2, denoted $H_1 \leq_{U_1, U_2} H_2$, iff

- *for every hypothesis $(s \in U_1) \in H_1$ the hypothesis $(s \in U_2)$ is contained in H_2, and*

- *with $\Delta(U_1) = \Phi(U_{j_1}, \ldots U_{j_n})$ and $\Delta(U_2) = \Phi(U_{k_1}, \ldots U_{k_n})$ for every $1 \leq i \leq n$ holds $H_1 \leq_{U_{j_i}, U_{k_i}} H_2$.*

(4) Two hypothesis sets H_1 and H_2 are equivalent with respect to the equivalent constants U_1, U_2, denoted $H_1 \sim_{U_1, U_2} H_2$, iff $H_1 \leq_{U_1, U_2} H_2$ and $H_2 \leq_{U_1, U_2} H_1$.

(5) Two sequents $H_1 \vdash_\Delta s \in \Phi(U_{j_1}, \ldots U_{j_n})$ and $H_2 \vdash_\Delta s \in \Phi(U_{k_1}, \ldots U_{k_n})$ are equivalent, iff for $1 \leq i \leq n$ $U_{j_i} \sim U_{k_i}$, and $H_1 \sim_{U_{j_i}, U_{k_i}} H_2$.

PROPOSITION 1 (Equivalent Sequents have the same Subtableaux)

Suppose τ_1 is a computation tree with the root sequent $H_1 \vdash_{\Delta_1} s \in \Phi_1$, and $H_2 \vdash_{\Delta_2} s \in \Phi_2$ is an equivalent sequent. Then there exists a computation tree τ_2 of $H_2 \vdash s \in \Phi_2$ with the same branching structure as τ_1 such that every node of τ_2 is labelled by a sequent which is equivalent to the sequent of corresponding node of τ_1.

Proof: by induction in the structure of τ_1

Induction hypothesis: $seq_1 \equiv H_i \vdash_{\Delta_i} t \in \Phi_i$ in τ_1 and $seq_2 \equiv H_j \vdash_{\Delta_j} t \in \Phi_j$ in τ_2 are equivalent sequents.

Base case: the induction hypothesis is true for the root sequents of τ_1 and τ_2 by assumption.

Induction step: argumentation about the applicable rules

- leaf sequents
  If seq_1 is a leaf sequent and fulfills one of the requirements (i) - (iii) or their dual forms, then $\Phi_i = \Phi_j$ and there is no rule applicable to seq_2.
  The more interesting case is if the leaf sequent seq_1 fulfills (iv) or its dual form. Here for $\Phi_i = U_i$ the hypothesis $t \in U_i$ is contained in H_i. Since for $\Phi_j = U_j$ $U_i \sim U_j$ and $H_i \sim_{U_i, U_j} H_j$ the hypothesis $t \in U_j$ must be contained in H_j. Therefore also seq_2 is also a leaf sequent.

- One of the rules 1) - 4) is applicable to the sequent seq_1.
  As equivalent formulae have equivalent structure, the same rule can be applied to seq_2. As equivalent formulae have also equivalent subformulae the successor seq_2' of seq_2 is equivalent to the successor seq_1' of seq_1.

- Rule 5) or 6) is applicable to seq_1.
  $\Phi_i = [a]\Phi_i'$ (or $\Phi_i = \neg[a]\Phi_i'$), hence also $\Phi_j = [a]\Phi_j'$ (or $\Phi_j = \neg[a]\Phi_j'$) and $\Phi_i' \sim \Phi_j'$. All a-successors of the state s depend only on the transition system. Therefore the same rule can be applied to seq_2 and the successor sequents of seq_2 contain the same states, equivalent hypothesis sets and equivalent formulae as the sequent successors of seq_1.

- One of the rules 7) or 8) is applicable to seq_1.
  A new constant U'_i is generated in τ_1. As the same rule must be applicable to seq_2, also a new constant U'_j is generated in τ_2 with $\Delta'_i(U'_i) \sim \Delta'_j(U'_j)$. Therefore the successor sequent $H_i \vdash_{\Delta'_i} t \in U'_i$ is equivalent to $H_j \vdash_{\Delta'_j} t \in U'_j$.

- Rule 9) or 10) is applied to seq_1.
  Here $H_i \vdash_{\Delta_i} t \in U_i$ and $(t \in U_i) \notin H_i$. For $H_j \vdash_{\Delta_j} t \in U_j$ holds by induction hypothesis $U_i \sim U_j$ and $H_i \sim H_j$. Therefore $(t \in U_j) \notin H_j$. For the successor sequent holds
  $H_i \cup \{t \in U_i\} = H'_i \sim H'_j = H_j \cup \{t \in U_j\}$ and as
  $\sigma X.A(X, U_{i_1}, \ldots, U_{i_n}) = \Delta_i(U_i) \sim \Delta_j(U_j) = \sigma X.A(X, U_{j_1}, \ldots, U_{j_n})$ the successor sequents are equal.

$\square$

PROPOSITION 2 (Size of the Computation Trees)

Consider a sequent $H_1 \vdash_{\Delta_1} s \in \Phi(U_1, \ldots U_n)$ having τ_1 as computation tree , and a sequent $H_2 \vdash_{\Delta_1} s \in \Phi(U_1, \ldots U_n)$ with $H_1 \leq_{U_i, U_i} H_2$ for all $1 \leq i \leq n$. Then $H_2 \vdash_{\Delta_2} s \in \Phi(U_1, \ldots U_n)$ has a computation tree τ_2 which s contained in τ_1 as subtree, such that (up to the hypothesis sets).

Proof: by induction in the structure of τ_1
omitted in this version $\square$

PROPOSITION 3 (Combination of Hypothesis Trees)

Let τ_1 be the hypothesis tree derived from a computation tree of $H_1 \vdash_\Delta s \in U$ and τ_2 be the hypothesis tree derived from a computation tree of $H_2 \vdash_\Delta s \in U$. Then there exists a hypothesis set H_3 with $H_1 \cap H_2 \subseteq H_3 \subset H_1 \cup H_2$, and $\tau_1 \circ \tau_2$ as in definition 5 is the hypothesis tree derived from a computation tree of $H_3 \vdash_\Delta s \in U$.

Proof: by induction in the structure of τ_1 and τ_2
omitted in this version $\square$

PROPOSITION 4 (Correctness I)

Let τ_1 be a computation tree of $H \vdash_\Delta s \in U$ and HB its hypothesis tree. The hypothesis tree HB is evaluated with the hypothesis set H to true, iff $H \vdash_\Delta s \in U$ has a successful subtableau. The hypothesis tree HB is evaluated with the hypothesis set H to false, iff $H \vdash_\Delta s \in U$ has no successful subtableau.

Proof: omitted in this version $\square$

PROPOSITION 5 (Correctness II)

Let HB be the hypothesis tree of a sequent $H_1 \vdash_\Delta s \in U$, and H_2 a hypothesis set. If HB together with H_2 evaluates to true, then the sequent $H_2 \vdash_\Delta s \in U$ has a successful subtableau. If HB together with H_2 evaluates to false, then the sequent $H_2 \vdash_\Delta s \in U$ has no successful subtableau.

Proof: omitted in this version $\square$

7   Benchmarks

The presented algorithm is implemented in *QUINTUS-PROLOG* on a *SUN/SPARC* system.

In the following examples the standard tableau model checker is compared to the tableau recycling model checker. As units of measurement we took the number of nodes in the computation tree and the system time which the model checker took to solve the task.

Examples 2 to 5 from section 4, *Fig.1*:

	standard tableau model checker		tableau recycling model checker	
	number of nodes	time	number of nodes	time
n=3, k=3	105	< 1s	25	< 1s
n=4, k=3	211	1s	31	< 1s
n=3, k=4	321	1s	33	< 1s
n=4, k=4	851	2s	41	< 1s

Example 6 $: \vdash 1 \in \nu Z.\langle a\rangle \mu X.\langle a\rangle\langle a\rangle X \wedge \langle a\rangle\langle a\rangle Z$

standard tableau model checker		tableau recycling model checker	
number of nodes	time	number of nodes	time
32766	74s	139	4s

Example 7 $: \vdash 1 \in \nu Z.\langle a\rangle \mu X.\langle a\rangle\langle a\rangle X \wedge \langle a\rangle\langle a\rangle Z$

standard tableau model checker		tableau recycling model checker	
number of nodes	time	number of nodes	time
> 22100000	> 1.5h	218	1326s

8   Conclusion

A tableau based model checker for the full modal mu-calculus was presented, which profits from the idea to recycle subtableaux which have been calculated earlier in the model checker algorithm. The information contained in a subtableau is reduced to a much smaller expression. An implementation of this algorithm showed in several examples an impressive acceleration.

Future work will include the following aspects:

We continue to get more experience with real world transition systems and relevant modal properties when verified with the tableau recycling model checker and different model checking approaches.

Secondly in this paper an idea was worked out how the maximal information can be preserved during a proof run. Heuristic methods could help to do it without *maximal* information in order to reduce memory expense.

Finally we will continue in investigating the complexity of the model checker algorithm.

Acknowledgement I thank Dirk Taubner for many motivating discussions. Florian Mengedoht implemented the algorithm.

9 References

[B] Julian Bradfield, Verifying Temporal Properties of Systems, Birkhäuser,1992.

[BC] J.R.Burch, E.M.Clarke, K.L.McMillan, D.L.Dill and L.J.Hwang, Symbolic model checking: 10^{20} states and beyond, in: *Information and Computation*, Vol 98, Num 2, June 1992, (141-170).

[BS] Julian Bradfield and Colin Stirling, Verifying Temporal Properties of Processes, CONCUR 1990, in: LNCS 458, Springer Verlag, Berlin, 1991, (115-125).

[C] Rance Cleaveland, Tableau Based Model Checking in the Propositional Mu-Calculus, in: *Acta Informatica*,1990,(725-747).

[CS1] Rance Cleaveland and Bernhard Steffen, A Linear-Time Model-Checking Algorithm for the Alternation-Free Modal Mu-Calculus, in: *Proc. of the Third Workshop on Computer Aided Verification* ,LNCS 575, 1992,(48-58).

[CS2] Rance Cleaveland and Bernhard Steffen, Computing Behavourial Relations, Logically, in: *Proc. ICALP '91*, 1991.

[EFT] Reinhard Enders, Thomas Filkorn, Dirk Taubner, Generating BDDs for Symbolic Model Checking in CCS, in: *Proc. of the Third Workshop on Computer Aided Verification* ,LNCS 575, 1992, (203-213).

[EL] E.Allen Emerson and Ching-Luang Lei, Efficient model checking in fragments of the propositional mu-calculus, in: *Proc. of Symposium on Logic in Computer Science*,IEEE, 1986, (267-278).

[S] Colin Stirling, Modal and Temporal Logics, in: S.Abramsky, D.Gabbay, and T.Maibaum, editors, *Handbook of Logic in Computer Science*, Oxford University Press.

[SW] Colin Stirling and David Walker, Local model checking in the modal mu-calculus, in: *Proc. International Conference on Theory and Practice of Software Development*, LNCS 351, Springer Verlag, Berlin,1989,(369-382).

CROCOS*: AN INTEGRATED ENVIRONMENT FOR INTERACTIVE VERIFICATION OF SDL SPECIFICATIONS

Dominique Méry[1] and Abdelillah Mokkedem[2]

[1] CRIN-CNRS & INRIA Lorraine
[2] CRIN-INPL & INRIA Lorraine
BP 239, 54506 Vandœuvre-lès-Nancy Cedex, France
email:{mery,mokkedem}@loria.fr

Abstract. We are interested by proofs of concurrent programs properties, such as *invariance* and *eventuality*. They are connected with execution of a program, and, in order to discuss them, we introduce an operational model of the language and show that the deductive system is consistent with respect to it. The studied language is a selected subset of the SDL language. A system for computer-aided reasoning on programs is derived as follows: we implement the deductive system in Isabelle [24] and then integrate it into a programming environment developed under Concerto namely Crocos [19]. The prover proceeds in an interactive way in which the user's intervention may be required at several stages of the proof derivation.

1 Introduction

The need to specify reactive and concurrent systems in a formal manner and to verify their correctness is well perceived. A number of approaches have been developed to tackle the specification problem for such systems and now there are many Formal Description Techniques (FDTs), some of which are international standards, namely, LOTOS [13], SDL [2] and Estelle [5, 12].

Our work is related to the concurrent program verification aided by computer. Recently, many investigations have been aimed in this direction [4, 16, 17].Two main approaches deal with our topics. A first one is based on an analysis of automaton such as *model checking* [4]. It has been applied in the protocol analysis area , for instance, by the Xesar Tool [27] and others [1, 30], but it is restricted to automaton with a reasonable number of states (finite state machines, local finiteness of states, ...). In the second approach, work has concerned formal studies of proof systems such as extended Hoare's logic [14, 22] and temporal logic [16, 26], but little work tries to integrate these formal systems into tools based on theorem proving. Moreover, implementation aspects have not been taken into account. In the current work, we aim to develop a deductive system for proving concurrent programs. This system deals with an intermediate language able to support semantics of a sublanguage of SDL called Crocos and is based on *Wp*-calculus [6] and temporal logic [26]. It is, more precisely, derived from the FEPS system developed by D. Méry [18] and it proceeds by interaction

---
* This work is partially supported by the CNET under grant number 89-58 00 790 92 45/PAA and CNRS National Action C³.

with the user in order to prove properties on SDL programs like *invariance* or *eventuality*. Our system can be used as follows: the user annotates the SDL program by local assertions and tries to prove a given property using axioms and inference rules by the application of tactics or strategies of *Isabelle's logic* in which our deductive system is implemented. This approach is made easier by the genericity of the Isabelle theorem prover [24] which provides us a good implementation framework.

The main functionality of our prover is to provide a computer-aided reasoning which allows the user to build formal proofs for properties that will verify on his program. It is an interactive system, the user being always in control. He is assumed to be familiar with the formalism and corresponding logic. The system is not an *automatic theorem prover*. It is actually a *proof assistant*, but we take the liberty of calling it a *prover*. However, some proof steps can be systematically performed using *proof schemes* and *strategies*.

The whole Crocos system is built as follows. First, a programming environment for SDL is developed into Concerto [29], then we integrate the prover in this environment via an interface which communicates between Concerto and Isabelle.

In this paper we then give some SDL concepts in Section 2 and a brief description of formal tools needed to introduce our logic for reasoning about SDL programs in Section 3. Section 4 gives a brief introduction to Isabelle and we show how SDL's logic is coded into it in Section 5. Working examples are discussed in Section 6. Future tools and concluding remarks are given in Section 7.

2   SDL Concepts

SDL [2] is an international standard language, powerful enough to cope with the dynamic needs of real-time applications. It is, especially, widely used for the formal specification and implementation of telecommunications protocols [28]. SDL is based on the concept of finite state machines. In fact, the SDL processes may exhibit (at least theoretically) infinite data spaces. However, their control state space is finite. Hence, systems are described by extended finite (control) state machines with signals as input and output.

2.1   Syntactic view

SDL provides the means to give a system description at any level of detail, and from several viewpoints. It is, thus, possible to abstract and to represent only those aspects of a system that matter in a given context. The three main class names it gives are SYSTEM, BLOCK and PROCESS, where BLOCK may be partitioned many times. Moreover, SDL provides the means to describe a system using a sequence of levels, each tied to the previous one and providing more details. In this sense, SDL supports both top-down design and representation of virtual system. This is achieved through structuring, partitioning, and refinement and through channel structuring. All these features make a specification in SDL easy to describe and to understand. However, SDL has no mathematical foundations, and in order to improve its verification ability we introduce labelling and annotation on its syntax (*à la Floyd* [7]). A full description of the syntax of the SDL-subset we have selected is given in [21]. The main restrictions are the consideration of one level of concurrency, the elimination of timers, and the number of process instances should be static.

2.2 Semantic view

Our formal semantics of SDL is operational, it is fully described in [19]. We define the meaning of a specification by a set of evaluation rules (*à la Plotkin* [25]). As stated in [8], often the approach is compositional in the sense that the evaluation of an element of a syntactic category is defined relatively to the evaluation of the elements from which it is composed. Intuitively one may think of this set of evaluation rules as an abstract machine that may execute the specified system and formally the semantics of a specification is represented by a labelled transition system. We emphasize that the motivation for defining an operational semantics for SDL is the need for an appropriate interpretation structure in which formulae in temporal logic can be interpreted. Such formulae can be regarded as properties of the temporal behaviour of SDL systems. Finally, we point out that concurrency is modelled by interleaving and fairness requirement since we hope the linear temporal logic we propose will be sufficient to reason about SDL specifications and, therefore, we obtain a deductive system which is consistent with respect to the suggested operational model.

3 Formal tools

To maximize the reusability of our proof system, we want to develop a generic theory for concurrent programs for which communication is modeled by asynchronous exchange of messages and concurrency by interleaving. Our proof system is designed to reason about a more abstract intermediate language able to support semantics of all languages endowing with these features (SDL should be one of such languages). To apply our proof method to a language from this class, it is enough to write a translator from this language to the intermediate language. For instance, the verification of an SDL specification is done in two consecutive steps. The first one consists of mechanically translating the given SDL specification to another one expressed in the intermediate language, namely, E-FCS. In the second step our prover acts on the resulting E-FCS specification. We illustrate this idea with the following scheme:

$$\text{SDL} \xrightarrow{translate} \text{E-FCS} \xrightarrow{wp} \boxed{\text{proof system}} \longrightarrow theorems$$

Here we will discuss the generic logic for E-FCS and we do not focus on the translation of SDL (or other) language to E-FCS. We first briefly present the formal tools needed to introduce our verification methodology.

3.1 E-FCS : an intermediate language

Transition systems are generally considered adequate to represent concurrent programs, and their semantics are clear and well-known [3, 9, 17]. They provide, for instance, a good support for both control and memory features of SDL programs. In fact, the language we use to specify concurrent programs is an extension of the formalism of formal concurrent systems, as studied in [9]. This language is expressive enough to ensure that any SDL program can be translated to it.

An extended formal concurrent system, or an E-FCS, is a set of (concurrent) processes, where a process is a set of (formal) transitions. A transition is a triple $(l, c \rightarrow \alpha, m)$ which intuitively means that when the condition (guard) c holds, execution may proceed from l to m while interpreting the atomic action α. The action α may belong to SDL-like atomic actions. Here is an excerpt of the BNF-representation of the E-FCS syntax.

$$
\begin{aligned}
program &::= nil \mid process :: program \\
process &::= \{transition\}^+ \\
transition &::= (label, guard \rightarrow action, label) \\
action &::= skip \mid task \mid export \mid output \mid input
\end{aligned}
$$

3.2 *Wp*-formulation of the operational model

Our verification method is based on theorem proving, so that an axiomatization of the operational semantics is needed. We adapt Dijkstra's *wp*-calculus [6] to E-FCS language, so we can always derive a sound relationship between the operational semantics of a given SDL specification and the axiomatic one from which theorems in our logic will be derived.

$wpctl:$ $wp((P, (l, C \rightarrow A, m)), q) \equiv at(P, l) \land C \land wp((P, A), inst(q, m, P))$

$task:$ $wp((P, TASK\ x := e), \varphi) \equiv subst(\varphi, e, x)$

$comp\_task:$ $wp((P, TASK\ a_1, a_2), \varphi) \equiv wp((P, TASK\ a1), wp((P, TASK\ a2), \varphi))$

$skip:$ $wp((P, skip), \varphi) \equiv \varphi$

$output1:$ $wp((P, OUTPUT\ S), \varphi) \equiv map\_append(\varphi, S, E(P, S))$

$output2:$ $wp((P, OUTPUT\ S\ TO\ Q), \varphi) \equiv subst(\varphi, append(queue(Q), S), queue(Q))$

$output3:$ $wp((P, OUTPUT\ S\ TO\ SELF), \varphi) \equiv subst(\varphi, append(queue(P), S), queue(P$

$output4:$ $wp((P, OUTPUT\ S\ VIA\ R), \varphi) \equiv subst(\varphi, append(queue(extrem(R, P)), S),$
     $queue(extrem(R, P)))$

$export:$ $wp((P, EXPORT\ lvar), \varphi) \equiv subst(\varphi, lvar, aux(lvar))$

$input0:$ $wp((P, INPUT\ S), \varphi) \equiv first(queue(P), S) = S \land$
     $subst(\varphi, supp(queue(P), S), queue(P))$

$input1:$ $wp((P, INPUT\ S(x)), \varphi) \equiv first(queue(P), S(x)) = S(e) \land$
     $subst(subst(\varphi, supp(queue(P), S(e)), queue(P)), e, x)$

$wp\_ctl:$ $wp((P, (l, c \rightarrow a, m)), at(Q, l')) \equiv (P \neq Q \land at(Q, l')) \lor (P = Q \land l' = m \land at(P$

Intuitively,

- $at(P, l)$ stands for *"the current control in the process P is l"* and *wp* is the Dijkstra's predicate transformer of which definition will be given below.
- $subst(\varphi, e, x)$ is equivalent to φ where free occurrences of x are replaced by e.
- $inst(q, m, P)$ replaces, in q, $at(P, m)$ by *true* and, for all $l \neq m$, $at(P, l)$ by *false*.
- $map\_append(\varphi, S, list)$ replaces, for each process P_i in *list*, $queue(P_i)$ by $append(queue(P_i), S)$.

347

- *aux(lvar)* denotes the list of auxiliary variables representing implicit copies associated with the exported variables in *lvar*.
- *extrem(R, P)* is the process that communicates with P in the other extremities of R.
- $E(P, S)$ is the set of processes located in others extremity of routes originating at P on which S will be in transit.
- $first(queue(P), S(x))$ is the value of the first signal that matches $S(x)$ in the input port of P.

Remark. The introduction of process identifiers in the *wp* definition is linked with the fact that in our interleaving-based approach we need to express the context of some actions, for instance, communication ones, in order to know which control variables or queues will be modified.

3.3 A linear temporal logic

The use of temporal logics to reason about the behaviour of concurrent systems has been widely studied [15, 26, 31]. In our approach, the goal is to be able to show semi-automatically that the temporal logic formula expressing a program's correctness is a logical consequence of some set of formulae immediately derivable from the program itself. One obvious way is to construct an automatic theorem prover for the temporal logic in question. We have, indeed, constructed a linear temporal logic for SDL in [19]. This logic is adapted from FEPS logic [18] and E-FCS's *wp*-calculus sketched below, and it is shown correct and semantically complete in [18, 19].

In short, the language of our logic is defined in an incremental way. First, we define a basic language, denoted by $\mathcal{F}$, which contains *variables formulae* for expressing assertions on variables of programs using the classical predicates such as "$x = 3$", "$y > z$", "$x * 2 \leq y + z$", and *control formulae* for expressing assertions on the control of programs using control predicates like "$at(P, \alpha)$" where P denotes a process name and α is an E-FCS action (or its origine label). Formulae in $\mathcal{F}$ are combined by the classical connectives of the first-order logic $\wedge$, $\vee$, $\Rightarrow$, $\neg$, $\forall$, $\exists$ for composing large formulae in $\mathcal{F}$; for instance, "$at(P1, \alpha_1) \wedge at(P2, \alpha_2) \wedge x = 0 \Rightarrow (at(P1, \beta_1) \vee at(P2, \alpha_2)) \wedge z > y + 1$". Second, we extend the basic language $\mathcal{F}$ with the *predicate transformer wp* which can be introduced as follows. Let us consider a formula φ in $\mathcal{F}$, called "*postcondition*" in this context, and an E-FCS command α, $wp(P, \alpha)(\varphi)$ represents the weakest pre-condition that must be satisfied by variables and control of the process P such that execution of α will eventually terminate leading to a state (or a set of states) satisfying[3] φ. Thereafter, we define the *property language* which contains correctness formulae for expressing some properties of programs. Let p, q be formulae in $\mathcal{F}$, a correctness formula may be either a transition formula, denoted by $p \longrightarrow q$, or an invariance formula, denoted by $Inv(p, q)$, or a strong eventuality formula, denoted by $p \overset{\square}{\rightsquigarrow} q$, or a weak eventuality formula,

---

[3] Formulae are interpreted in the model defined by the set of configurations (also called states) Σ and the classical interpretation functions associated with the connectives. A state σ satisfies a formula φ if and only if φ is true at the state σ what we denoted by $\sigma \models \varphi$, or $\varphi(\sigma)$.

denoted by $p \rightsquigarrow q$. In comparison with UNITY logic [3], eventuality properties are built using the *ensure* operator. Our logic is based on the *Strong Eventuality* operator. Let us remark that, contrary to the programming language of UNITY, our system is not control free and explicit references to control are required by the programming language SDL.

4 Isabelle

Isabelle is a general purpose interactive theorem prover developed by Paulson [23, 24]. It provides a framework in which the user can define his own logic to reason about objects for which this logic is defined. Several first-order logics, Martin-Löf Type Theory, and Zermelo-Fraenkel set theory are implemented in Isabelle. Each new logic is formalised within Isabelle's meta-logic. New types and constants express the syntax of the logic, while new axioms express its inference rules. Isabelle provides the higher-order logic and goal-directed proof is supported. Internally, axioms (or rules) are represented as Horn clauses. Proof construction corresponds to rule composition which is achieved by unification (*à la Prolog*). Since unification used in Isabelle is derived from Huet's higher-order unification procedure [11], it can return multiple or infinitely many results. While the general problem is undecidable, the procedure works well in Isabelle. Proofs are constructed using *tactics* such as *'apply an inference rule to a subgoal, producing some new subgoals'*, or *'solve a goal by assumption under Isabelle's framework for natural deduction'*, etc. Complex tactics typically apply other basic tactics repeatedly to certain goals, possibly using search strategies. In order to conduct proofs the user needs to know more details about Isabelle which can be consulted in [24]. The Isabelle version we use is the one (March 1991) which was still without user interface. We have, in fact, used a window system in our workstation in order to develop a menu manager providing a user interface for Isabelle. A description of this interface is given in [21]. We use Isabelle's framework as follows. We start from an Isabelle's first-order logic, which is *cla_thy*, and successively, we enrich it by a set of layers representing the *wp*-calculus and the temporal logic designed to reason about E-FCS programs.

We give a brief description of the E-FCS's logic in the next section, a theoretical study of this logic was given in [19].

5 E-FCS's logic

5.1 Structure

Among other things, a description may concern the structure of this prover, the different theories we use and the form of proofs we can develop in each theory. The prover is designed according to the *enrichment principle*. A basic layer represents the first-order logic with natural deduction of Isabelle. This one is successively enriched with other theories for reasoning on E-FCS programs. *Arith_bool_thy* adds, to *cla_thy*, rules defining arithmetic and boolean theories which permit deduction of theorems over basic types in SDL (now, Integer, Boolean and Signal lists are considered). *Assertion_thy* codes over *Arith_bool_thy*

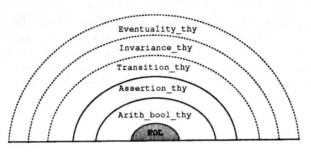

Fig. 1. E-FCS's logic structure

the *wp*-calculus that supports an axiomatization of the E-FCS semantics. In *Transition_thy*, we introduce the basic operator ($\longrightarrow$) of the temporal logic we propose. It allows us to derive transition properties as '*if p holds in the current state of the program, q will hold in the next state*'. To *Transition_thy*, we have supplied two another layers for deriving invariance and eventuality properties which we denote by *Invariance_thy* and *Eventuality_thy*. An upper layer (*Simplify_thy*) enriches the E-FCS's logic with a set of rules that provides a more powerful calculus for simplification of formulae in order to perform complete proofs. Also, we plan to extend our prover in order to include a formal analysis of the static semantics for E-FCS programs based on Hoare's logic [10] and Dijkstra's programming calculus [6]. The logical structure of our prover is described in figure 1.

5.2 Proofs format

Proofs are carried out in a backward (goal-directed) manner. When a goal matches the conclusion of a rule, the premisses can be inserted as new subgoals. The user works at the highest possible level for as long as possible. He has at his disposal axioms and rules of the E-FCS's logic [19], and several kinds of tactics in the built-in logic. The basic tactics are *rewrite-tactics, resolve-tactics* and *assume-tactics*. Tactics are operations on the proof state, such as, '*apply the following rules to these subgoals*', they describe the mechanism whereby a rule (or rules) is invoked to yield subgoals. Strategies are formed from tactics by means of the standard combining operators (tacticals) that describe the control on the form in which a sequence of tactics is applied.

Proofs can be long and complicated, even with much trivial detail. The system is designed to take responsability for much of the detail, and allow the user to interact at critical points in the proof. The generation of a proof involves instantiation of scheme variables. New scheme variables are often introduced by introduction rules like $\wedge\_intr$, $\vee\_intr$, $\longrightarrow\_intr$, $\leadsto\_intr$, etc.

6 A small example

In this section we show how *invariance* (partial correctness, deadlock freedom, mutual exclusion, etc) and *eventuality* (total correctness, accessibility, reachability, etc) properties of a concurrent program can be mechanically deduced using our theorem prover. Our current objective is to get sound SDL specifications with respect to submitted informal properties. It means that only a part of the global correctness is ensured, namely correctness with respect to invariance and eventuality properties. The purpose here is to yield an overall view on the application of the proof system. The example we present is the computation of the greatest common divisor of two natural numbers (GCD). The algorithm consists of reading two values x_0 and y_0 that are assumed to be strictly positive naturals. The SDL specification is made up of a unique bloc, which contains two concurrent processes, namely P1 and P2. P1 (resp. P2) decreases the value of x_1 (resp. y_2), if x_1 (resp. y_2) is strictly greater than y_1 (resp. x_2), and it sends the value of x_1 (resp. y_2) to P2 (resp. P1). Here we only give the equivalent E-FCS program and the interesting part of the annotation which are obtained by the translator (SDL $\rightarrow$ E-FCS) we have integrated into Concerto. Our theorem prover deals with this program and takes the annotation as assumption of the proof.

$$P1 ::= \{ (l_1, True \rightarrow TASK\ x_1 := x_0,\ y_1 := y_0; , l_2),$$
$$(l_2, True \rightarrow OUTPUT\ V(y_1)\ TO\ SELF; , l_3),$$
$$(l_3, \tilde{}(queue(P1) = qempty) \rightarrow INPUT\ V(y_1), l_4),$$
$$(l_4, x_1 = y_1 \rightarrow skip, l_e),$$
$$(l_4, \tilde{}(x_1 = y_1)\&\tilde{}(x_1 > y_1) \rightarrow OUTPUT\ V(x_1)\ TO\ P2; , l_3),$$
$$(l_4, \tilde{}(x_1 = y_1)\&(x_1 > y_1) \rightarrow TASK\ x_1 := x_1 - y_1; , l_5),$$
$$(l_5, True \rightarrow OUTPUT\ V(x_1)\ TO\ P2; , l_3)\}$$

$$P2 ::= \{ (m_1, True \rightarrow TASK\ x_2 := x_0, y_2 := y_0; , m_2),$$
$$(m_2, True \rightarrow OUTPUT\ V(x_2)\ TO\ SELF; , m_3),$$
$$(m_3, \tilde{}(queue(P2) = qempty) \rightarrow INPUT\ V(x_2), m_4),$$
$$(m_4, x_2 = y_2 \rightarrow skip, m_e),$$
$$(m_4, \tilde{}(x_2 = y_2)\&\tilde{}(x_2 < y_2) \rightarrow OUTPUT\ V(y_2)\ TO\ P1; , m_3),$$
$$(m_4, \tilde{}(x_2 = y_2)\&(x_2 < y_2) \rightarrow TASK\ y_2 := y_2 - x_2; , m_5),$$
$$(m_5, True \rightarrow OUTPUT\ V(y_2)\ TO\ P1; , m_3)\}$$

$Annot \equiv at(P1, l_3) \Rightarrow (first(queue(P1), V(y_1)) = V(y_1) \vee first(queue(P1), V(y_1)) = V(y_2) \vee queue(P1) = qempty)\ \wedge\ at(P2, m_3) \Rightarrow (first(queue(P2), V(x_2)) = V(x_2) \vee first(queue(P2), V(x_2)) = V(x_1) \vee queue(P2) = qempty)$

A. *Proof of an invariance property:*

We shall denote by I_0 the following assertion, which holds at any point of the two processes. This is, indeed, a trivial invariant of our program.

$$I_0 \equiv (0 < x_1 \leq x_0) \wedge (0 < x_2 \leq x_0) \wedge (0 < y_1 \leq y_0) \wedge (0 < y_2 \leq y_0) \wedge nat(x_0) \wedge nat(x_1) \wedge nat(x_2) \wedge nat(y_0) \wedge nat(y_1) \wedge nat(y_2)$$

The effectively interesting computation starts from the control point l_2 in P1 and m_2 in P2. In fact, the first action of each process permit to initiate x_1, x_2 with the value of x_0 and y_1, y_2 with the value of y_0. Therefore, we omit these two actions and we assume that the initial condition, denoted by $Init$, is $at(P1, l_2) \wedge at(P2, m_2) \wedge 0 < x_0 \wedge 0 < y_0 \wedge nat(x_0) \wedge nat(y_0) \wedge (x_1 = x_2 = x_0) \wedge (y_1 = y_2 = y_0)$. The main motivation of this part is to construct, by means of our interactive proof assistant, a proof for the following invariance property : $Inv(Init, I_0)$ and to point out the methodology of proof. Since the proof trace and formulae are too long in the prover generated text, we only sketch here with the formal text the main steps of the proof construction and we assume that the property $\bigwedge_{i=0}^{i=2} nat(x_i) \wedge nat(y_i)$ is implicitly induced from the context. We give the more complete proof in appendix A and complete presentation of the same example can be also found in [21].

We want to prove $Annot \vdash_{Prog=\{P_1,P_2\}} Inv(Init, I_0)$?

$$
level1 \cfrac{level2 \cfrac{level3 \cfrac{\{at(P_1,l_i) \wedge I_0 \longrightarrow (at(P_1,l_i') \Rightarrow I_0)/(l_i, c_i \rightarrow a_i, l_i') \in P_1\},}{\{at(P_2,l_j) \wedge I_0 \longrightarrow (at(P_2,l_j') \Rightarrow I_0)/(l_j, c_j \rightarrow a_j, l_j') \in P_2\}} (comp\_actions)}{\cfrac{Init \Rightarrow I_0}{}(STRATEGY1) \quad \cfrac{I_0 \longrightarrow I_0}{I_0 \Rightarrow I_0}(assume\_tac)}}{Inv(Init,I_0)} (InvI)
$$

From $level3$ each subgoal "$at(P_i,l_j) \wedge I_0 \longrightarrow (at(P_i,l_k) \Rightarrow I_0)$" will be proved using the wp of the corresponding action $(l_j, c_j \rightarrow a_j, l_k)$. Such proofs may be made in an independent way. For instance, we show how a complete proof is developed for the first subgoal, associated with $(l_2, True \rightarrow OUTPUT\ V(y_1)\ TO\ SELF, l_3)$, independently from the other ones. Note the use of STRATEGY1 to prove an arithmetic theorem in $level2$, this strategy is defined in the Appendix.

$$
\cfrac{\cfrac{\cfrac{\cfrac{\cfrac{at(P_1,l_2) \wedge I_0 \Rightarrow at(P_1,l_2) \wedge True \wedge I_0}{at(P_1,l_2) \wedge I_0 \Rightarrow at(P_1,l_2) \wedge True \wedge subst(I_0, append(queue(P_1), V(y_1)), queue(P_1))}}{at(P_1,l_2) \wedge I_0 \Rightarrow at(P_1,l_2) \wedge True \wedge wp((P_1, OUTPUT\ V(y_1)\ TO\ SELF), I_0)}}{at(P_1,l_2) \wedge I_0 \Rightarrow wp((P_1,(l_2, True \rightarrow OUTPUT\ V(y_1)\ TO\ SELF, l_3)), I_0)}}{at(P_1,l_2) \wedge I_0 \longrightarrow at(P_1,l_3) \Rightarrow I_0}
$$

$$
\begin{array}{l}(assume\_tac)\\(subst\_tac)\\(output3)\\(wp\_ctl)\\(definition)\end{array}
$$

Proofs of the other subgoals, except for those corresponding to the input actions, are developed in the same way. We summarize the proof of such subgoals using strategies WP_Transition, OUTPUT, SKIP, TASK as shown in the Appendix and we focus on the proof of the last two subgoals associated with the input actions which are $at(P_1,l_3) \wedge I_0 \longrightarrow (at(P_1,l_4) \Rightarrow I_0)$ and $at(P_2,m_3) \wedge I_0 \longrightarrow (at(P_2,m_4) \Rightarrow I_0)$. These proofs are crucial because they require most information about queues of processes P_1 and P_2. Such information are given in the annotation $Annot$ and are used as hypothesis in the proof. Let $c_3 \equiv queue(P1) \neq qempty$,

$$
\cfrac{\cfrac{\cfrac{\cfrac{Annot \quad \cfrac{at(P_1,l_3) \wedge c_3 \wedge I_0 \Rightarrow I_0[y_2/y_1]}{at(P_1,l_3) \wedge c_3 \wedge I_0 \Rightarrow subst(I_0, y_2, y_1)}}{at(P_1,l_3) \wedge c_3 \wedge I_0 \Rightarrow subst(subst(I_0, supp(queue(P_1), V(y_2)), queue(P_1)), y_2, y_1)}}{at(P_1,l_3) \wedge c_3 \wedge I_0 \Rightarrow at(P_1,l_3) \wedge c_3 \wedge first(queue(P1), V(y_1)) = V(y_2) \wedge subst(subst(I_0, supp(queue(P_1), V(y_2)), queue(P_1)), y_2, y_1)}}{at(P_1,l_3) \wedge c_3 \wedge I_0 \Rightarrow at(P_1,l_3) \wedge c_3 \wedge wp((P_1, INPUT\ V(y_1)), I_0)}}{at(P_1,l_3) \wedge c_3 \wedge I_0 \Rightarrow wp((P_1,(l_3, c_3 \rightarrow INPUT\ V(y_1), l_4)), I_0)}
$$
$$
at(P_1,l_3) \wedge I_0 \longrightarrow at(P_1,l_4) \Rightarrow I_0
$$

$$
\begin{array}{l}(assume\_tac)\\(subst\_tac)\\(subst\_tac,\\ assume\_tac)\\(conjI)\\[4pt](input\_wp)\\(wp\_ctl)\end{array}
$$

One of the two subgoals is solved. The same proof scheme is replayed to solve the second subgoal that ends the proof of the invariance property (see INPUT strategy in Appendix). Replay proof scheme to solve subgoals associated with some kind of actions is very promising to develop specific strategies according to these actions.

To construct this proof we have used rules of the Isabelle's FOL ($conjI, impI, \ldots$), rules and axioms of our system [19] ($output\_wp$, $input\_wp$, $definition$, $comp\_actions$, $InvI$, ...), and a concrete substitution we have implemented by a new tactic $subst\_tac$. All such rules are applied using tactics ($assume\_tac$, $resolve\_tac$, $rewrite\_tac$, ...) and are combined using tacticals (REPEAT, SOMEGOAL, THEN, ...) which permit strategies definition. We show in the next part that proofs may became more complicated when we deal with eventuality properties.

B. *Proof of an eventuality property*:

We try to derive a proof for the following eventuality property : $Init \rightsquigarrow at(P1, l_e) \land at(P2, m_e) \land x_2 = y_2 = gcd(x_0, y_0)$ which means that the program must terminate with a correct calculus reaching $x_2 = y_2 = gcd(x_0, y_0)$. The problem here is to transform higher-level operators such as $\rightsquigarrow$ into lower-level ones ($\overset{\square}{\rightsquigarrow}, Inv, \ldots$) in order to reuse theorems (or lemmas) proved in inner layers. The choice of a suitable invariant is crucial to guarantee a complete proof construction. It is clear that a program is something difficult to understand and the strongest (or just sufficient) invariant is therefore difficult to discover. In the full version of this paper [20], we give a first solution based on the invariance of I_0 proved in the previous part and we show that this solution should not complete at the first go and that more intermediate lemmae shall be introduced. To discover such lemmae, an interesting idea could be to take one's inspiration from the proof history focusing on the facts that have provoked the proof obstruction and to suggest some possible strengthenings of the invariant. That will help the user to discover the sufficient invariant and permit the continuation of the proof construction. This is one of the future improvements of our prover in order to make it more intelligent. So, we can derive a more interesting property in our system. It requires to find a well ordering and a sequence of assertions as $P(n)$ (intermediate lemmae). But, it uses the invariance of some formula.

Finally, this example shows that the main problems are to compute variables substitution in the assertions and to identify what is the next rule to introduce. Our implementation helps the user to master the complexity due to these aspects. However, strategies are to study in order to improve and to automate some combinations of different steps.

7 Conclusion

Using our system, the construction of a proof for a given property consists of several steps that are intended to transform a proof into a more elementary one which may be performed in an inner layer (see figure 1). For instance, to develop a proof for a *general eventuality* property, we start at the external layer and use its rules to go down in the lower *"stronger-eventuality"* layer, then in the *"invariance"* layer and so on until we obtain all subgoals in the FOL layer. We can then continue the proof in the Isabelle's FOL-logic that requires less creative effort from the user.

Our approach is intended to be general and it is very easy to quickly obtain a theorem prover for some langages. But, it may be heavy-handed if we use it alone. In order to reach a compromise between genericity and practicality, our method · might be combined with a more specific method for deriving basic properties (such as transition) which are directly linked with the operational model of the considered language. The more abstract properties such as invariance and eventuality should be proved using our system.

The powerful logical framework (typed λ-calculus, higher-order schema variables, ...) which provides Isabelle has motivated us to implement our higher-order logic with it. This was been easy except the absence of concrete substitution to model the actions of programs in Isabelle. To make this possible we have supplied a new tactic for concrete substitution. The higher-order schema variables enable to introduce short-hands and are very useful in constructive proofs. In fact, our longer term purpose was to make our logic more constructive in order to be able to identify proofs with programs providing a more general method to develop concurrent programs together with their proofs. Finally we note the inefficiency drawback like in any theorem prover when we want to verify realistic programs using a purely theorem-proving based method.

Throughout this discussion, we have described a pedagogic example in order to show how our system can be used. To deal with more realistic system specifications, more complex strategies will be needed to summarize intermediate proof steps which may be very large. In the example communication actions have been invoked and rules that cope with such actions exist in our system. However, properties on communication ports used in the SDL program are required to make a proof construction possible. These properties may be either specified in the invariant of the program or introduced as new assumptions during the proof construction.

Based on our experience, desirable features for future tools are suggested. For instance, the emphasis of E-FCS program refinement from temporal specifications in a systematic way is an important result of this experience. New rules may be added to our proof system which will be as powerful as creativity can support. We have also emphasized that no operator in E-FCS's logic supports the hierarchical paradigm of SDL methodology. We hope to study this aspect and to introduce like operators. In this way, our system is a laboratory for experimentation of SDL specifications. It can be used as a tool for stepwise development of correct SDL specifications. However, new concepts of SDL must be added in the current environment. Finally, we hope, for efficiency ends, to use a partial order semantics as a computational model in order to reduce the explosion generated by the interleaving semantics. Thereafter, some extensions should be needed in the temporal logic we propose.

References

1. G. V. Bochmann and C. A. Sunshine. Formal methods in communication protocol design. In *IEEE Transactions on Communications*, pages 362–372. IEEE, April 1980. COM-28.

2. CCITT. Recommendation z.100 Specification and Description Language SDL. Note, 1988.

3. K. M. Chandy and J. Misra. *Parallel Program Design: A Foundation.* Addison-Wesley Publishing Company, 1988. ISBN 0-201-05866-9.

4. E.M. Clarke, E.A Emerson, and A.P Sistla. Automatic verification of finite-state concurrent systems using temporal logic specifications: A practical approach. *Tenth ACM Symposium on Principles of Programming Languages,* pages 117–126, 1983.

5. M. Diaz, J.P. Ansard, J.P Courtiat, P. Azema, and V. Chari, editors. *The formal description technique ESTELLE.* North-Holland, 1989.

6. E. W. Dijkstra. *A Discipline of Programming.* Prentice-Hall, 1976.

7. R. W. Floyd. Assigning meanings to programs. In J.T. Schwartz, editor, *Proc. Symp. Appl. Math. 19, Mathematical Aspects of Computer Science,* pages 19 – 32. American Mathematical Society, 1967.

8. J. C. Godskesen. An operational Semantic Model for Basic SDL - Extended abstract. In O. Faergemand and R. Reed, editors, *Fifth SDL Forum Evolving methods.* North-Holland, 1991.

9. E.P. Gribomont. Stepwise refinement and concurrency: The finite-state case. In Jan L.A van de Snepscheut, editor, *Science of Computer Programming, Mathematics of Program Construction,* volume 14, pages 185–228. North-Holland, october 1990.

10. C. A. R. Hoare, S. D. Brookes, and A. W. Roscoe. A theory of communicating sequential processes. Technical Report PRG-16, Oxford University Programming Research Group, 1981. Technical Monograph.

11. G.P. Huet. A unification algorithm for typed λ-calculus. *Theoretical Computer Science,* 1:27–57, 1975.

12. ISO. Information processing systems, open systems interconnection, est elle (formal description techniques based on an extended state transition model). Technical Report ISO/IS 9074, ISO, 1988.

13. ISO. *Information processing systems - Open Systems Interconnection - LOTOS - A formal description technique based on the temporal ordering of observ ational behaviour,* 1989-02-15 edition, 1989. ISO 8807:1989 (E).

14. L. Lamport. The 'Hoare Logic' of concurrent programs. *Acta Informatica,* 14:21–37, 1980.

15. L. Lamport. What good is temporal logic? pages 657–677. IFIP, 1983.

16. Z. Manna and A. Pnueli. Verification of concurrent programs: temporal proof principles. In *Proceedings of the Workshop on Logics of programs,* pages 200–252, New York, 1981. Spinger Verlag. LNCS 131.

17. Z. Manna and A. Pnueli. Adequate proof principles for invariance and liveness properties of concurrent programms. *Science of Computer Programming,* 4:257–290, december 1984.

18. D. Méry. Méthode axiomatique pour les propriétés de fatalité des programmes parallèles. *RAIRO Informatique Théorique et Application,* 21(3):287–322, 1987.

19. D. Méry and A. Mokkedem. A proof environment for a subset of SDL. In O. Faergemand and R. Reed, editors, *Fifth SDL Forum Evolving methods.* North-Holland, 1991.

20. D. Méry and A. Mokkedem. CROCOS: An Integrated Environment for Interactive Verification of SDL Specifications. In Participant's Proceedings of the Fourth Workshop on Computer-Aided Verification (CAV '92). Montreal, 1992.

21. D. Méry, A. Mokkedem, and D. Roegel. Crocos : Un environnement de preuve interactive de specifications SDL. Technical Report 92-r-001, Université de Nancy I, CRIN, 1991.

22. S. Owicki and D. Gries. An axiomatic proof technique for parallel programs I. *Acta Informatica*, 6:319–340, 1976.
23. L. Paulson. Natural deduction as higher-order resolution. *The Journal of Logic Programming*, 3:237–258, 1986.
24. L. Paulson and T. Nipkow. Isabelle tutorial and users's manual. Technical report, University of Cambridge, Computer Laboratory, 1990.
25. G.D. Plotkin. A structural approach to operational semantics. Technical report, Aarhus University, Denmark, DAIMI, 1981. FN-19.
26. A. Pnueli. The temporal logics of programs. In *Proceedings of 18th Symposium on Foundations of Computer Science*, pages 46 – 57. IEEE, 1977.
27. J.L. Richier, C. Rodriguez, J. Sifakis, and J. Voiron. *Xesar A Tool for Protocol Validation*. CAP Sogeti Innovation and LGI-IMAG, 1987. Version 1.2.
28. R. Saracco, J. R. W. Smith, and R. Reed. *Telecommunications Systems Engineering using SDL*. North Holland.
29. SEMA Group. *CONCERTO Manuel de Référence*, July 1990.
30. C. A. Sunshine. Formal methods for protocol specification and verification. *Computer*, 12:20–27, Sept. 1979.
31. P. Wolper. Temporal logic can be more expressive. *Information and Control*, 56(1-2):72–99, 1983.

Appendix

We give here the more complete proof for the part A. of the example.

```
(* ================== %% The staring up of the proof %% ============== *)
The Crocos Theory (in FOL)
val it = () : unit
- val prems = goal Crocos_thy "[|at (P1,13) ==> first(queue(P1),V(y1))=V(y1)
| first(queue(P1),V(y1))=V(y2) | queue(P1)=qempty; at(P2,m3) ==> first(queue(P2),
V(x2))=V(x2) | first(queue(P2),V(x2))=V(x1) | queue(P2)=qempty|] ==>Inv(at(P1,12)
& at(P2,m2) & 0<x0 & x0=x1 & x0=x2 & 0<y0 & y0=y1 & y2=y0, 0<x1 &x1<=x0 & 0<x2 &
x2<=x0 & 0<y1 & y1<=y0 & 0<y2 & y2<=y0)";


(* ================== %% A strategy for arithmetic proofs %% ============= *)
fun STRATEGY1 i = let
    fun str0 i = (pc_tac i)
  and   str1 i = (rewrite_goal_tac [leq_def] i)
  and   str2 i = (resolve_tac [disjI2] i)
  and   str3 i = (resolve_tac [sym] i)
  and   str4 i = (resolve_tac [sym RS subst] i)
  and   str5 i = (str0 i) ORELSE ((str3 1) THEN (str0 i))
  and   str6 i = (resolve_tac [impI] i) THEN (REPEAT (SOMEGOAL (resolve_tac [conjI])))
  and   STR1 i = EVERY [(str1 i),(str2 i),(str5 i)]
  and   STR2 i = EVERY [(str4 i),(str5 i),(str5 i)]
                in (str6 i) THEN (REPEAT ((str0 i) ORELSE (STR1 i) ORELSE (STR2 i)))
                end;


(* ================== %% A strategy for interleaving %% ============== *)
fun INTERLEAV i = (res_inst_tac [("Prog",Prog)] comp_actions i)
   THEN (rewrite_goal_tac [trans1,trans2,trans3] i)
   THEN (rewrite_goal_tac [biget2,biget3,abs_et1,abs_et2] i)
   THEN (REPEAT (SOMEGOAL (resolve_tac [conjI])));
```

```
(* ================= %% A strategy for WP_Transition %% =============== *)
fun WP_Transition i = let fun TAC7 i = (res_inst_tac [("Prog",Prog)]
          definition0 i) ORELSE (res_inst_tac [("Prog",Prog)] definition1 i)
          and TAC8 i = (rewrite_goal_tac [take1,take2,take3,take4,condact] i)
          and TAC9 i = (rewrite_goal_tac [wpct1] i)
          and TAC10 i = (rewrite_goal_tac [inst5] i)
              in EVERY [(TAC7 i),(TAC8 i),(TAC9 i), (TAC10 i)]  end;

(* ============== %% A strategy for sequence resolution %% ============ *)
fun SEQUENCE tac i max = if i>max then all_tac
                         else ((tac i) THEN (SEQUENCE tac (i+1) max));

(* ================= %% A strategy for list resolution %% ============== *)
fun LISTE tac i list = case list of
                [] => all_tac
              | j::rest => ((tac (j-i)) THEN (LISTE tac (i+1) rest));

(* ================= %% A strategy for ouput actions %% =============== *)
fun OUTPUT i = (rewrite_goal_tac [output1,output2,output3,output4] i)
               THEN (subst_ab_tac i) THEN (pc_tac i);

(* ================= %% A strategy for skip actions %% =============== *)
fun SKIP i = (rewrite_goal_tac [skip] i) THEN (pc_tac i);

(* ================= %% A strategy for task actions %% =============== *)
fun TASK i = (rewrite_goal_tac [task] i) THEN (subst_ab_tac i) THEN
   (rewrite_goal_tac [ass_et,inf_pr1,inf_pr2,inf_pr3,add_def0]  i) THEN
   (resolve_tac [impI] i) THEN (REPEAT (SOMEGOAL (resolve_tac [conjI])))
   THEN  (REPEAT (SOMEGOAL pc_tac)) THEN (TRY ((resolve_tac [inf_pr4] i)
   THEN (pc_tac i)));

(* ================= %% A strategy for input actions %% =============== *)
fun elt 1 l = hd l
 | elt i l = elt (i-1) (tl l);

fun INPUT th i = REPEAT ((SOMEGOAL pc_tac) ORELSE (SOMEGOAL (resolve_tac
  [impI,conjI]))) THEN (forwards_tac conjunct1 i) THEN (forwards_tac th i)
  THEN (REPEAT ((forwards_tac disjE i) THEN  (assume_tac i) THEN
  (rewrite_goal_tac [input1] i) THEN ((subst_ab_tac i) THEN
  (subst_ab_tac i) THEN (REPEAT (pc_tac i)))));

(* ================= %% An invariance proof %% =============== *)
by (resolve_tac [invI] 1);
by ((resolve_tac [impI] 3) THEN (assume_tac 3));
by (STRATEGY1 1);
by (INTERLEAV 1);
by (SEQUENCE WP_Transition 1 12);
by (LISTE OUTPUT 0 [1,4,6,7,10,12]);
by (LISTE SKIP 0 [2,5]);
by (LISTE TASK 0 [2,4]);
by ((INPUT (elt 1 prems) 1) THEN (INPUT (elt 2 prems) 1));
```

Verifying General Safety and Liveness Properties With Integer Programming*

James C. Corbett

Information and Computer Science Department
University of Hawaii at Manoa

Abstract. Analysis of concurrent systems is plagued by the state explosion problem. The *constrained expression* analysis technique uses necessary conditions, in the form of linear inequalities, to verify certain properties of concurrent systems, thus avoiding the enumeration of the potentially explosive number of reachable states of the system. This technique has been shown to be capable of verifying simple safety properties, like freedom from deadlock, that can be expressed in terms of the number of certain events occurring in a finite execution, and has been successfully used to analyze a variety of concurrent software systems. We extend this technique to the verification of more complex safety properties that involve the order of events and to the verification of liveness properties, which involve infinite executions.

1 Introduction

Many concurrent systems can be modeled as a set of communicating finite state machines. Analysis of such systems is generally difficult, however, since the number of system states grows exponentially with the number of state machines. Many techniques have been proposed to cope with this state explosion problem, including symbolic model checking [3], partial order techniques [6, 10], and compositional techniques [4]. Last year at the Third Workshop on Computer Aided Verification, another technique was presented [1] that involves the use of necessary conditions to answer certain types of questions about a system without enumerating the system's states. The technique has been automated as part of the *constrained expression toolset* and has been applied to some concurrent systems having as many as 10^{47} reachable states [2]. Unfortunately, the types of questions that can be answered by this technique are somewhat limited. For example, it can determine if a system could deadlock, but it cannot address liveness questions, which involve infinite traces, nor can it directly address questions like mutual exclusion, which involve the relative order of events. This paper extends the technique to handle both infinite traces and questions about the relative order of events. A further extension of these ideas in [5] enables the technique to verify properties expressible in linear time temporal logic, thus allowing a very general class of questions about a system to be answered while avoiding the construction of an exponentially-sized state graph.

---

* The research described here was partially supported by National Science Foundation grant CCR-9106645 and Office of Naval Research grant N00014-89-J-1064.

2 Model and Basic Technique

As in [1], we model a concurrent system as a collection of coupled finite state automata (FSAs) with additional restrictions expressed as a set of recursive languages on the alphabets of the FSAs. The acceptance of a symbol by an automaton represents the occurrence of an event in the concurrent system. An event may represent a normal action of a component, such as initiating a communication with another component, or an error, such as waiting forever for a communication that never takes place. An execution of the concurrent program is thus modeled by a string of event symbols.

Formally, a concurrent system is a triple (M, R, T) where M is a set of FSAs $M_1, \ldots, M_n$ with alphabets $\Sigma_1, \ldots, \Sigma_n$, $\Sigma = \bigcup_i \Sigma_i$, R is a set of recursive *restriction* languages $R_1, \ldots, R_m$ with alphabets $A_1, \ldots, A_m$, where $A_i \subseteq \Sigma$ for all i, and $T \subseteq \Sigma$ is a terminal alphabet. Let $\rho_A(s)$ denote the projection of string s onto alphabet A (i.e., symbols of s not in A are removed). Then a string $t \in T^*$ represents a legal behavior or *trace* of the concurrent system if there exists a string $s \in \Sigma^*$ with $\rho_T(s) = t$ where $\rho_{\Sigma_i}(s) \in L(M_i)$ for all i and $\rho_{A_j}(s) \in R_j$ for all j.

This model is general enough to represent many common communication mechanisms, including asynchronous message passing [1], but in this paper we will focus on the case where pairs of processes communicate synchronously over named channels that connect them. We model such a communication using the channel name as an event symbol that appears in the alphabets of the FSAs of both processes. The possibility that the task becomes permanently blocked waiting for the communication is represented by the choice to accept a *hang symbol* for that channel rather than engage in the communication. The hang symbols for channel a are denoted $>a$ and $<a$ (there is one hang symbol for each of the two tasks connected by the channel). For each channel a, the restriction language $\{>a, <a, \lambda\}$ forbids hang symbols from both ends of the channel from occurring. A small example is shown in Fig. 1. In all our examples, we shall take the set of event symbols appearing in an FSA or restriction language as its alphabet.

The basic technique, detailed in [1], uses necessary conditions, in the form of linear inequalities, to either help find a trace with certain properties or prove that no such trace could exist. A trace can be viewed as a path in each FSA from the starting state to an accepting state such that the interactions between the FSAs represented by the paths are consistent. Our technique finds a flow in each FSA from the starting state to an accepting state such that the flows satisfy a weaker consistency criterion. Specifically, we require that for each communication channel, the FSAs connected by that channel agree on the number of times that they communicated over that channel.

To produce the inequalities, we assign a variable, x_i, called a *transition variable*, to each transition i in the FSAs that represents the number of times transition i is taken. We also assign an *accept variable*, f_i, to each accepting state i that will be one if the FSA containing state i is in that state at the end of the trace, otherwise it will be zero. We then produce a *flow equation* for each state,

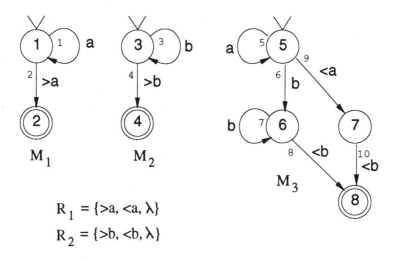

$$R_1 = \{>a, <a, \lambda\}$$
$$R_2 = \{>b, <b, \lambda\}$$

Fig. 1. Small example

equating the flow into the state with the flow out of the state (i.e., the number of times the state is entered equals the number of times it is exited). There is an implicit flow in of one at the start state and accept variables are counted as flow out. We also produce a *communication equation* for each channel, equating the number of times the processes connected by the channel communicated over that channel. Finally, we produce *restriction inequalities* to enforce the restriction languages which, in this case, simply forbid more than one hang symbol for each channel from occurring. The inequalities produced for the example of Fig. 1 are shown in Fig. 2.

These inequalities represent necessary conditions for an assignment of values to the transition variables to correspond to a trace. Clearly every set of paths corresponding to a trace will yield flows through the FSAs satisfying the communication and restriction inequalities, however, not every set of flows satisfying the communication and restriction inequalities will correspond to a trace. There are two reasons for this. First, the communication equations do not guarantee that there is a consistent ordering of the communication events (e.g., one FSA could synchronously communicate with another over channel A and then channel B, while the other communicated over channel B and then channel A). Secondly, the presence of cycles in the FSAs can allow cyclic flows that are not connected to the path found within the FSA. For example, there can be a cyclic flow on arc 7 in M_3 of Fig. 1 even if the flow from the start state passes through arcs 9 and 10; the flow equation for state 6 does not constrain the transition variable for arc 7. For these reasons, a solution to the inequality system may not correspond to a trace of the concurrent system. If such a solution arises, the analysis is inconclusive since the presence of that solution implies nothing about the existence of

$$\textbf{Flow:} \qquad\qquad \text{(state)}$$

$$1 + x_1 = x_1 + x_2 \qquad (1)$$
$$x_2 = f_2 \qquad (2)$$
$$1 + x_3 = x_3 + x_4 \qquad (3)$$
$$x_4 = f_4 \qquad (4)$$
$$1 + x_5 = x_5 + x_6 + x_9 \qquad (5)$$
$$x_6 + x_7 = x_7 + x_8 \qquad (6)$$
$$x_9 = x_{10} \qquad (7)$$
$$x_8 + x_{10} = f_8 \qquad (8)$$

$$\textbf{Communication:} \qquad \text{(channel)}$$
$$x_1 = x_5 \qquad (a)$$
$$x_3 = x_6 + x_7 \qquad (b)$$

$$\textbf{Restriction:} \qquad \text{(number)}$$
$$x_2 + x_9 \le 1 \qquad (1)$$
$$x_4 + x_8 + x_{10} \le 1 \qquad (2)$$

Fig. 2. Inequality System for Finite Trace

another solution that does correspond to a trace. In our experience [2], however, such spurious solutions are uncommon. Also, we can sometimes add additional inequalities to remove such solutions.

Similar techniques have been used to prove structural properties of Petri nets (e.g., boundedness, repetitiveness) using transition matrices. Space limitations preclude a detailed comparison with this work, which is reviewed in [8].

3 Extended Techniques

In this paper, we extend the basic technique presented in the last section to the verification of properties specified by an ω-regular expression [9] of the form:

$$\bigcup_{i=1}^{m} S_{i,0}^* e_{i,1} S_{i,1}^* e_{i,2} \ldots S_{i,n_i-1}^* e_{i,n_i} S_{i,n_i}^* T_i^\omega$$

where $S_{i,j} \subseteq \Sigma$, $e_{i,j} \in \Sigma$, $T_i \subseteq \Sigma$. We call such an expression an ω-*star-less* expression[2]. Specifically, given an ω-star-less expression, the extended technique produces necessary conditions for the existence of a trace lying in the language of infinite strings generated by the expression. This extended technique relies on two key ideas. The first idea allows the technique to test for properties in which events occur in a specific order and is described in Sect. 4. The second idea allows the technique to deal with infinite traces and is described in Sect. 5.

---

[2] Not to be confused with *star-free* expressions. We call these expressions star-less since they specify patterns of the $e_{i,j}$ events using only concatenation and union (allowing the intervening symbols specified by the $S_{i,j}$). Star-free expressions allow concatenation, union, and negation, but not Kleene star.

In [5], these ideas are carried further to allow the verification of properties specified by a Büchi automaton. It is well known that Büchi automata are more expressive than first order logic [9]. This implies that this further extension suffices to handle any property expressible in linear temporal logic. We do not present this further extension here for two reasons. First, although it relies on the same two ideas, it is significantly more complicated to describe. Second, unlike the first extension, it has not been implemented and tried on sample systems; hence the quality of the necessary conditions it produces, and thus its practical significance, is not known.

Using the extended technique presented here, we can verify that a system has any property whose negation is expressible as an ω-star-less expression. To accomplish this, we use the extended technique to produce necessary conditions, in the form of linear inequalities, for the existence of a trace of the system generated by the ω-star-less expression. If these conditions are unsatisfiable (i.e., the inequality system has no integral solution), then there are no traces of the system violating the property, so the property must hold. If the conditions are satisfiable (i.e., the inequality system does have an integral solution), then the property may or may not hold. If the necessary conditions are strong, however, the property will usually not hold when the conditions are satisfiable (i.e., a solution to the inequality system usually corresponds to a trace violating the property). Our experience is that our necessary conditions are strong. Furthermore, if the property does not hold, a solution satisfying our necessary conditions can often be used to find a trace violating the property.

4 Queries Involving Order

The technique presented in Sect. 2 can easily find traces in which certain event symbols occur a specified number of times, but it cannot find traces in which these symbols occur in a specific order. For example, to find a trace with one a event and one b event in the system of Fig. 1, we would add $x_1 = 1$ and $x_3 = 1$ to the inequality system in Fig. 2. There does not appear to be any way, however, to add equations that require the events to occur in a specific order. This is a serious limitation since many safety properties (e.g., mutual exclusion) constrain only the order of events and not their number. To produce necessary conditions for a trace containing a specific sequence of events, we conceptually divide the trace into *intervals* using those events, produce a different inequality system for each interval, and connect these inequality systems together.

We will explain the technique using the example of Fig. 1. Suppose we want to verify that there are no a events after any b event. The negation of this property can be expressed by the ω-star-less expression $\Sigma^* b(\Sigma - \{a, b\})^* a \Sigma^\omega$. We produce necessary conditions for the existence of a prefix of a trace containing a b followed by an a, as generated by the finite part of the expression (since the above is a safety property, the infinite suffix after the violation, generated by Σ^ω, can be ignored). We divide the prefix into two intervals. The first interval is from the initial state of the system to the state of the system after the b event (generated by $\Sigma^* b$). The second interval is from the state of the system after the b event to the state of the system after the a event (generated by $(\Sigma - \{a, b\})^* a$). For each interval, we produce an inequality system similar to the one in Fig. 2, but with the following differences. We want the inequality system for the first interval to find flows ending after a b event rather than at accepting states. To achieve this, we assign to each state i having an incoming b transition a *connection variable* $c_{1,i}$ that will be one if the FSA containing state i is in state i at the end of the first interval, and will be zero otherwise. In FSAs not containing b events, we assign connection variables to all states. Note that requiring the interval to end in an FSA at a state with an incoming b transition does not guarantee that a b event occurred in that FSA during the interval. Therefore, we add a *requirement equation* stating that at least one b event occurs. Since we are seeking only a prefix of a trace, we do not assign accept variables. If the connection variables are counted as flow out in the flow equations, rather than having accept variables, then the resulting inequality system will find a flow in each FSA from a starting state to a state in which the FSA could be immediately after a b event. Furthermore, in FSAs with b events, the flow must pass through at least one such event.

The inequality system for the second interval must find a flow in each FSA from the state the FSA was in at the end of the first interval to a state the FSA could be in after an a event. We assign connection variables $c_{2,i}$, representing the number of times the second interval ends at state i, to states that the FSAs could be in following an a event. In this interval, there can be no b events and only one a event (at the end), so we produce requirement equations setting the number of occurrences of a to one and the number of occurrences of b to zero. We then count the connection variables from the first interval as flow in, rather than having an implicit flow in of one at the start states, and count the connection variables from the second interval as flow out, rather than having accept variables. Finally, the restriction inequalities are produced as before and involve the number of hang symbols from both intervals.

The inequality system produced for this example is shown in Fig. 3. The transition variable for transition j of interval i is denoted $x_{i,j}$. The whole system finds a flow in each FSA starting at the start state, proceeding through the first interval to a state with a connection variable for b, and then continuing through the second interval to a state with a connection variable for a.

Note that this inequality system, which represents necessary conditions for a prefix of a trace containing a b and then an a to exist, has no integral solution. This proves that no trace generated by the expression $\Sigma^* b(\Sigma - \{a, b\})^* a\Sigma^\omega$ exists. For this trivial example, an appropriate kind of intersection between M_3 and the automaton for ba could have shown this; however, the above technique will work even if the events a and b are in different FSAs, as shown by an example in Sect. 6.

We have shown how to produce necessary conditions for the existence of a trace containing a specific sequence of events. We can produce necessary conditions for a trace generated by the union of such sequences as follows. We assign a

Flow (interval 1): (state)

$$1 + x_{1,1} = x_{1,1} + x_{1,2} + c_{1,1} \qquad (1)$$
$$x_{1,2} = c_{1,2} \qquad (2)$$
$$1 + x_{1,3} = x_{1,3} + x_{1,4} + c_{1,3} \qquad (3)$$
$$x_{1,4} = 0 \qquad (4)$$
$$1 + x_{1,5} = x_{1,5} + x_{1,6} + x_{1,9} \qquad (5)$$
$$x_{1,6} + x_{1,7} = x_{1,7} + x_{1,8} + c_{1,6} \qquad (6)$$
$$x_{1,9} = x_{1,10} \qquad (7)$$
$$x_{1,8} + x_{1,10} = 0 \qquad (8)$$

Communication (interval 1): (channel)

$$x_{1,1} = x_{1,5} \qquad (a)$$
$$x_{1,3} = x_{1,6} + x_{1,7} \qquad (b)$$

Requirement (interval 1): (symbol)

$$x_{1,3} \geq 1 \qquad (b)$$

Flow (interval 2): (state)

$$c_{1,1} + x_{2,1} = x_{2,1} + x_{2,2} + c_{2,1} \qquad (1)$$
$$c_{1,2} + x_{2,2} = 0 \qquad (2)$$
$$c_{1,3} + x_{2,3} = x_{2,3} + x_{2,4} + c_{2,3} \qquad (3)$$
$$x_{2,4} = c_{2,4} \qquad (4)$$
$$x_{2,5} = x_{2,5} + x_{2,6} + x_{2,9} + c_{2,5} \qquad (5)$$
$$c_{1,6} + x_{2,6} + x_{2,7} = x_{2,7} + x_{2,8} \qquad (6)$$
$$x_{2,9} = x_{2,10} \qquad (7)$$
$$x_{2,8} + x_{2,10} = 0 \qquad (8)$$

Communication (interval 2): (channel)

$$x_{2,1} = x_{2,5} \qquad (a)$$
$$x_{2,3} = x_{2,6} + x_{2,7} \qquad (b)$$

Requirement (interval 2): (symbol)

$$x_{2,1} = 1 \qquad (a)$$
$$x_{2,3} = 0 \qquad (b)$$

Restriction: (number)

$$x_{1,2} + x_{1,9} + x_{2,2} + x_{2,9} \leq 1 \qquad (1)$$
$$x_{1,4} + x_{1,8} + x_{1,10} + x_{2,4} + x_{2,8} + x_{2,10} \leq 1 \qquad (2)$$

Fig. 3. Inequality System for Prefix of Trace Generated by $\Sigma^* b(\Sigma - \{a, b\})^* a$

sequence variable s_i to each sequence that will be one if that sequence is the one found and zero otherwise. We produce an equation summing the sequence variables to one, forcing one sequence to be sought. We produce inequality systems for each sequence as described above and connect them as follows. The implicit flow into the start states of each FSA in the first interval of sequence i is set to s_i rather than to one, thus flows will only be found in the inequality system for one sequence. Also, the requirement equations are changed to require that the events ending the intervals of that sequence occur s_i times (we cannot force an event in a sequence to occur unless the sequence occurs). The resulting inequality system represents necessary conditions for the existence of a trace generated by one of the sequences.

5   Infinite Traces

Another limitation of the technique presented in Sect. 2 is that it does not admit infinite traces, i.e., traces in which one or more FSAs continue engaging in actions forever. Note that the inequality system in Fig. 2 has no integral solution since all of the traces of the concurrent system are infinite (there is no way for all of the FSAs to reach accepting states without violating the restrictions). To test for liveness properties, we must be able to represent infinite traces since the negation of a liveness property will be an expression forbidding some good event(s) from occurring in a potentially infinite execution.

Consider the simplest case where we are seeking any infinite trace of a concurrent system (as opposed to a trace with a specific property). We can always divide such a trace into a *finite interval*, containing all events occurring only finitely many times in the trace, and a *perpetual interval*, containing only events occurring infinitely often in the trace. We use the term interval in the same technical sense as in the last section: each interval has its own transition variables and inequalities. The perpetual interval, however, represents an infinite suffix of a trace using a finite string of the events that are repeated forever in the suffix (this representation loses information about the order in which these events are repeated). The occurrence of an event in this interval represents the event being repeated infinitely often in the trace.

We produce inequalities for the two intervals as we did in the last section, but with the following differences. In each FSA, the set of transitions taken in the perpetual interval must form a strongly connected component (SCC) of the FSA when viewed as a graph[3]. Therefore, when generating inequalities for the perpetual interval, we include only transitions that are part of SCCs (in the example of Fig. 1, this consists of transitions 1, 3, 5, and 7). We assign connection variables to all states that are part of SCCs, allowing the finite part of the FSA's behavior to end at any point at which it could start repeating events. We then add additional *perpetual inequalities* to force a cyclic flow (a flow with no beginning or end) to occur in an SCC of the perpetual interval if that interval is "entered" via a connection variable. Unlike the case described in Sect. 4, the flow through the FSA does not pass from one interval to another through the connection variable; the flow through the finite interval simply ends at some state in the FSA that is part of an SCC and we then force a cyclic flow to occur in the SCC as part of the perpetual interval. The flow equations for the perpetual interval do not contain connection or accept variables; the only possible flows are cyclic. For each state j, let P_j be the set of transitions out of

---

[3] Strictly speaking, SCCs are composed of nodes, not arcs. We say that an arc is part of an SCC if there exists some SCC containing both of the nodes connected by the arc.

j that are part of an SCC. For each state j where $P_j \neq \emptyset$, we add a perpetual inequality $\Sigma_{i \in P_j} x_{2,i} \geq c_{1,j}$. This inequality requires that if the FSA containing state j enters the perpetual interval at state j, then there must be a cyclic flow through state j in the perpetual interval. Of course, a particular FSA may not run forever, even in an infinite trace. Accept variables allow the flow through an FSA in the finite interval to stop without forcing the occurrence of events in the perpetual interval.

Flow (finite):	(state)
$1 + x_{1,1} = x_{1,1} + x_{1,2} + c_{1,1}$	(1)
$x_{1,2} = f_2$	(2)
$1 + x_{1,3} = x_{1,3} + x_{1,4} + c_{1,3}$	(3)
$x_{1,4} = f_4$	(4)
$1 + x_{1,5} = x_{1,5} + x_{1,6} + x_{1,9} + c_{1,5}$	(5)
$x_{1,6} + x_{1,7} = x_{1,7} + x_{1,8} + c_{1,6}$	(6)
$x_{1,9} = x_{1,10}$	(7)
$x_{1,8} + x_{1,10} = f_8$	(8)

Communication (finite):	(channel)
$x_{1,1} = x_{1,5}$	(a)
$x_{1,3} = x_{1,6} + x_{1,7}$	(b)

Flow (perpetual):	(state)
$x_{2,1} = x_{2,1}$	(1)
$x_{2,3} = x_{2,3}$	(3)
$x_{2,5} = x_{2,5}$	(5)
$x_{2,7} = x_{2,7}$	(6)

Communication (perpetual):	(channel)
$x_{2,1} = x_{2,5}$	(a)
$x_{2,3} = x_{2,7}$	(b)

Restriction:	(number)
$x_{1,2} + x_{1,9} \leq 1$	(1)
$x_{1,4} + x_{1,8} + x_{1,10} \leq 1$	(2)

Perpetual:	(state)
$x_{2,1} \geq c_{1,1}$	(1)
$x_{2,3} \geq c_{1,3}$	(3)
$x_{2,5} \geq c_{1,5}$	(5)
$x_{2,7} \geq c_{1,6}$	(6)

Fig. 4. Inequality System for Potentially Infinite Trace

The inequalities described comprise necessary conditions for the existence of a potentially infinite trace. The inequality system for the example of Fig. 1 is shown in Fig. 4. We may test for the possible starvation of M_2 by adding the equation $x_{1,4} = 1$. The resulting inequality system has a solution corresponding to an infinite trace in which transition 4 is taken once and transitions 1 and 5 are taken perpetually ($x_{1,4} = x_{2,1} = x_{2,5} = 1$). This tells us that, in the absence of any fairness properties for selection of communication partners, it is not the case that a b communication must eventually occur. We can enforce certain types of fairness using additional inequalities that might, for example, forbid the starvation of an FSA waiting for a communication (e.g., b) if that communication is enabled infinitely often, which we can tell from the presence of certain events in the perpetual interval (e.g., the a on transition 5, which indicates that M_3 is infinitely often in state 5 in which a transition on b is enabled).

This technique to represent infinite traces can be combined with the technique of Sect. 4, allowing us to produce necessary conditions for the existence of an infinite trace generated by an ω-star-less expression. To accomplish this, we make the last interval of each sequence a perpetual interval and connect it to the preceding interval just as the perpetual interval was connected to the finite interval above. The size of the inequality system generated by these techniques is linear in the size of the automata and linear in the size of the ω-star-less expression. Finally, we note that the conditions produced are also necessary for the existence of a finite trace generated by the finite version of the ω-star-less expression (obtained by replacing all occurrences of ω with Kleene star).

6   Example

The technique described above has been implemented as an extension of the constrained expression toolset [2]. A series of experiments has demonstrated the feasibility of the technique for verifying different kinds of properties on several examples of concurrent systems. In this section, we describe one of the smallest examples and the properties we verified using the technique.

The concurrent system shown in Fig. 5 contains two customer FSAs (a and b), one router FSA, and one guard FSA. Customer a (b) repeats the following forever: communicate with the guard on channel ra (rb) to gain exclusive access to the router, send the header of a packet to the router on channel ha (hb), send the packet to the router on channel pa (pb), and free the router by communicating with the guard on channel fa (fb). The guard guarantees that the router is used in a mutually exclusive fashion. The router simply accepts any packet or header at any time. Present but not shown are restriction languages, like those in the example of Fig. 1, that forbid both hang symbols for a channel from occurring in the same trace.

First we verified the safety property that the router cannot send a header for one customer followed immediately by a packet from the other. This can be expressed in linear temporal logic as $\Box[(ha \rightarrow \neg pb\,Upa) \wedge (hb \rightarrow \neg pa\,Upb)]$. Its negation can be expressed by the ω-star-less expression

$$\Sigma^* \ ha \ (\Sigma - \{pa\})^* pb \ \Sigma^\omega \cup \Sigma^* \ hb \ (\Sigma - \{pb\})^* pa \ \Sigma^\omega$$

Starting with a specification of the concurrent system in an Ada-like design language and the above expression, the toolset produced an inequality system of

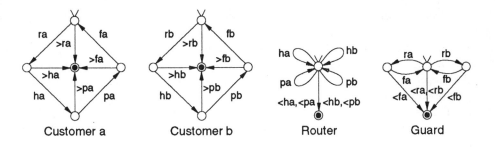

Fig. 5. Packet Router Example

107 inequalities in 128 variables. Our integer programming package determined this inequality system has no integral solution in two seconds on our DECstation 5000. Since the inequality system represents necessary conditions for the existence of a trace generated by the expression, we may conclude that the safety property holds.

The second property we attempted to verify was the liveness property that the first customer would transmit a header infinitely often. This property can be expressed in linear temporal logic as $\Box\Diamond ha$ and its negation by the ω-star-less expression $\Sigma^* (\Sigma - \{ha\})^\omega$. The toolset produced an inequality system of 67 inequalities in 70 variables and the integer programming package found a solution to this system in one second. Examination of the solution reveals that it does correspond to a possible trace of the concurrent system, one in which customer a becomes permanently blocked waiting to acquire the router while customer b repeatedly acquires it forever. Thus we have proved that the the liveness property does not hold by producing a trace violating the property. The problem is that no fairness is enforced when selecting a communication partner. When we instruct the toolset to produce two additional inequalities to enforce fairness in the guard's selection of a communication partner, as described in Sect. 5, the resulting inequality system was determined to have no integral solution in three seconds. This proves that the liveness property does hold, assuming an FSA cannot starve waiting for a communication that is infinitely often possible.

In the absence of such fairness, it is possible to verify a weaker liveness property: once a customer (say a) has acquired access to the router, it must eventually get to transmit a packet. This can be expressed in linear temporal logic by the formula $\Box(ra \rightarrow \Diamond ha)$ and its negation by the ω-star-less expression $\Sigma^* ra(\Sigma - \{ha\})^\omega$. The toolset produced an inequality system of 59 inequalities in 56 variables which was found to have no integral solution in one second, proving this weaker liveness property holds even in the absence of fairness.

368

7 Conclusion

We have presented a technique for verifying many safety and liveness properties of concurrent systems. The technique involves generating linear inequalities that represent necessary conditions for a trace violating the property to exist. The obvious advantage of the approach is that it does not require enumeration of all possible system states. The disadvantages are that spurious solutions to the inequality system can make the analysis inconclusive and the tractability of integer linear programming in practice is not well understood. Nevertheless, our experience [2] suggests that spurious solutions are relatively rare and that our inequality systems, being largely network flow systems, have a special structure that usually makes their solution tractable. Furthermore, a prototype implementation of the technique has demonstrated its feasibility on a range of sample systems [5]. Further experiments in which problem sizes are scaled up, such as those performed in [2] for the original technique, are needed to assess the practicality of this new technique.

Acknowledgements

This work was done as part of the constrained expression project at the University of Massachusetts directed by George Avrunin and Jack Wileden. Special thanks are due to George Avrunin for suggesting the idea of queries involving the order of events and ideas for its solution.

References

1. G. S. Avrunin, U. A. Buy, and J. C. Corbett. Integer programming in the analysis of concurrent systems. In Larsen and Skou [7], pages 92–102.
2. G. S. Avrunin, U. A. Buy, J. C. Corbett, L. K. Dillon, and J. C. Wileden. Automated analysis of concurrent systems with the constrained expression toolset. *IEEE Trans. Softw. Eng.*, 17(11):1204–1222, Nov. 1991.
3. J. Burch, E. Clarke, K. McMillan, D. Dill, and L. Hwang. Symbolic model checking: 10^{20} states and beyond. In *Proceedings of the Fifth Annual IEEE Symposium on Logic in Computer Science*, pages 428–439, 1990.
4. E. Clarke, D. Long, and K. McMillan. Compositional model checking. In *Proceedings of the Fourth Annual IEEE Symposium on Logic in Computer Science*, 1989.
5. J. C. Corbett. *Automated Formal Analysis Methods for Concurrent and Real-Time Software*. PhD thesis, University of Massachusetts at Amherst, 1992.
6. P. Godefroid and P. Wolper. Using partial orders for the efficient verification of deadlock freedom and safety properties. In Larsen and Skou [7], pages 332–242.
7. K. G. Larsen and A. Skou, editors. *Computer Aided Verification, 3rd International Workshop Proceedings*, volume 575 of *Lecture Notes in Computer Science*, Aalborg, Denmark, July 1991. Springer-Verlag.
8. T. Murata. Petri nets: Properties, analysis and applications. *Proceedings of the IEEE*, 77(4):541–580, Apr. 1989.

9. W. Thomas. Automata on infinite objects. In J. van Leeuwen, editor, *Handbook of Theoretical Computer Science*, volume B. MIT Press/Elsevier, 1990.

10. A. Valmari. A stubborn attack on state explosion. In E. M. Clarke and R. P. Kurshan, editors, *Computer-Aided Verification '90*, number 3 in DIMACS Series in Discrete Mathematics and Theoretical Computer Science, pages 25–41, Providence, RI, 1991. American Mathematical Society.

Generating Diagnostic Information for Behavioral Preorders*

Ufuk Celikkan, Rance Cleaveland

Department of Computer Science
N.C. State University
Raleigh, NC 27695-8206
{celikkan,rance}@science.csc.ncsu.edu

Abstract. This paper describes a method for generating diagnostic information for the prebisimulation preorder. This information takes the form of a logical formula explaining why a particular process is not larger than the other in the preorder. Our method relies on modifying an algorithm for computing the prebisimulation preorder to save the information needed for generating these distinguishing formulas. As a number of other behavioral preorders may be characterized in terms of prebisimulation preorder, our technique may be used as a basis for computing diagnostic information for these preorders as well.

1 Introduction

Research in the area of process algebras has sparked interest in *behavioral relations* as tools for verifying processes [15, 18, 20]. In one approach, one uses a *preorder* to relate specifications (formulated as "underspecified" processes) and implementations (given as "fully defined" processes); a system is deemed correct if it is larger than its specification in the preorder, in which case it intuitively provides "at least" the behavior dictated by the specification. These relations have not received as much attention in the literature as behavioral equivalences ([18, 2, 4, 16, 12, 15]) but they are very useful in that the partiality that is allowed in specifications gives system implementors greater flexibility in developing correct implementations. This partiality can also be exploited when developing specifications for components that are to be used in particular network contexts [10, 17, 20], since the constraints that the rest of the network places on the component typically permit many different (and inequivalent) implementations to render the desired behavior of the over-all system. At least two automated tools [8, 13] include algorithms for computing certain preorders over finite-state processes.

Our goal in this paper is to develop an algorithm for generating diagnostic information for a particular preorder, the *prebisimulation preorder* [1, 20]; the algorithm is to be used in conjunction with a method for computing the preorder to generate information explaining why a particular process is *not* larger than another. This information may then be used by system designers to analyze why systems fail to meet their (partial) specifications. The prebisimulation preorder

* Research supported by NSF/DARPA research grant CCR-9014775.

is of interest in its own right; moreover, it may be used as a basis for calculating other behavioral preorders such as trace containment (also known as the *may preorder* [12, 15]), the simulation preorder and the testing/failures preorder [7, 15]. It also has a *logical* characterization: there is a simple modal logic having the property that one process is less than another in the preorder exactly when each formula satisfied by the first process is also satisfied by the second. Thus, when a process is *not* less than another, there exists a formula satisfied by the first and not the second. Our algorithm builds such a formula, and it does so without affecting the complexity of the preorder algorithm.

The remainder of the paper is structured as follows. The next section develops our process model and reviews the definition of the prebisimulation preorder and its logical characterization. Section 3 presents a particular algorithm for computing the preorder, and then Section 4 presents our method for generating diagnostic information. Section 5 gives an example illustrating our technique. Section 6 shows how the method may be used to generate diagnostic information for preorders other than the prebisimulation preorder, while the last section contains our conclusions and directions for future research.

2 Processes, Preorders, and Intuitionistic Hennessy - Milner Logic

2.1 Transition Systems

We use *extended labeled transition systems* to model process behavior. These bear a certain resemblance to nondeterministic finite state automata; to define them, we first introduce the more familiar notion of labeled transition system.

Definition 1. A *Labeled Transition System* (lts) is a triple $\langle P, Act, \rightarrow \rangle$ where

1. P is a set of *states*;
2. Act is set of *actions* containing a distinguished *silent* action τ; and
3. $\rightarrow \subseteq P \times Act \times P$ is the *transition relation*.

The intuitive meaning of these components is as follows. P represents the set of possible computation states, Act contains the actions that computations may consist of, and $\rightarrow$ describes the state transitions that may result from the execution of an action in a state. For convenience we use the notation $p \xrightarrow{a} p'$ in place of $(p, a, p') \in \rightarrow$ and read it as p performs a and becomes p'. When $p \xrightarrow{a} p'$ holds, we often refer to p' as an a-derivative of p. We also write $p \xrightarrow{a}$ if there is a p' such that $p \xrightarrow{a} p'$. The action τ represents an *internal* computation step.

Extended labeled transition systems are then labeled transition systems in which states may be designated as underdefined.

Definition 2. An *Extended Labeled Transition System* (elts) is a quadruple $\langle P, Act, \rightarrow, \uparrow \rangle$ where the triple $\langle P, Act, \rightarrow \rangle$ is a lts and $\uparrow \subseteq P \times Act$ is the undefinedness relation.

The relation $\uparrow$ represents a notion of *underdefinedness* or *incomplete* description. If $(p,a) \in \uparrow$ then the behavior of p in response to action a may not be fully given yet; other a-transitions might be added in later. We shall use $p \uparrow a$ in place of $(p,a) \in \uparrow$ and write $p \downarrow a$ in lieu of $\neg(p \uparrow a)$. For historical reasons, when $p \uparrow a$ holds we sometimes say that p is a-divergent, and when $p \downarrow a$ holds we say p is a-convergent. In the sequel we only consider finite-state *elts*. An *elts* is finite-state if $|P| < \infty$ and $|Act| < \infty$. Note that these imply the finiteness of $|\rightarrow|$ and $|\uparrow|$.

Given an extended labeled transition system, processes may be defined by identifying a distinguished state as the start state. Formally a process is a pair $(\langle P, Act, \rightarrow, \uparrow \rangle, p_0)$ where $\langle P, Act, \rightarrow, \uparrow \rangle$ is an extended labeled transition system and $p_0 \in P$ is the start state. Figure 1 shows such a process.

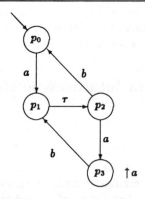

Fig. 1. An extended labeled transition system.

Let $\langle P, Act, \rightarrow \rangle$ be a *lts*. There is a well-known method for generating an *elts* from such a *lts*. The construction is designed to abstract away from the internal computation such a system engages in by introducing a new transition relation $\Rightarrow$ and a divergence relation $\Uparrow$ to support this abstraction. Formally we may define the following:

- $\stackrel{\epsilon}{\Rightarrow}$ if $p_1(\stackrel{\tau}{\rightarrow})^n p_2$, for some $n \geq 0$. (so p_1 may do n τ-steps and evolve to p_2.)
- $p_1 \stackrel{a}{\Rightarrow} p_2$ if there are p_1', p_2' such that $p_1 \stackrel{\epsilon}{\Rightarrow} p_1' \stackrel{a}{\rightarrow} p_2' \stackrel{\epsilon}{\Rightarrow} p_2$.
- $p_1 \Uparrow$ iff there is an infinite sequence $\langle p_i \mid i \geq 1 \rangle$ with $p_i \stackrel{\tau}{\rightarrow} p_{i+1}$ for all $i \geq 1$.
- $p_1 \Uparrow a$ iff either $p \Uparrow$ or for some p', $p \stackrel{a}{\Rightarrow} p'$ and $p' \Uparrow$.

Intuitively, $p \stackrel{a}{\Rightarrow} p'$ holds if from p some internal computation may lead to a state in which an a is performed with additional internal computation then leading to p'. If $p \Uparrow a$ holds, then p may be triggered by means of an a action into an infinite internal computation. $\langle P, (Act-\{\tau\}) \cup \{\epsilon\}, \Rightarrow, \Uparrow \rangle$ is the extended labeled transition system considered, for example, by [20].

Labeled transition systems provide a flexible basis for reasoning in a number of different specification formalisms like CSP [16], CCS [18]and LOTOS [3]. Finite-state concurrent systems specified in those formalisms can be analyzed automatically once they are converted into labeled transition systems as there exists well-known techniques to study them.

2.2 Prebisimulation Preorder

The prebisimulation preorder, $\sqsubseteq$, is a behavioral preorder defined in terms of pre-bisimulations [20]; it is a reflexive and transitive relation that relates processes using transitions and divergence information. Under this relation divergent programs approximate similar convergent ones. Intuitively, a prebisimulation is a "matching" between states of processes $\mathcal{P}$ and $\mathcal{Q}$ that satisfies a couple of conditions. The first stipulates that if state p is matched to state q, then each a-transition of p must be matched by some a-transition of q. The second condition requires that each a-transition of q be matched by some a-transition of p, *provided that* the behavior of p is completely defined with respect to a. In other words, if the behavior of p with respect to a is only partially specified, then p is not required to match the a-transitions of q. Intuitively this is because as a result of "completing" p with respect to a, additional a transitions may be added that could match q's a-transitions. The formal definition may be given as follows.

Definition 3. Let $\mathcal{P} = (\langle P, Act, \to, \uparrow \rangle, p_0)$ and $\mathcal{Q} = (\langle Q, Act, \to, \uparrow \rangle, q_0)$ be processes. A relation $R \subseteq P \times Q$ is a prebisimulation between $\mathcal{P}$ and $\mathcal{Q}$ if pRq implies the following.

1. $p \xrightarrow{a} p' \Rightarrow \exists q'. q \xrightarrow{a} q' \land p'Rq'$.
2. $p \downarrow a \Rightarrow [q \downarrow a \land (q \xrightarrow{a} q' \Rightarrow \exists p'. p \xrightarrow{a} p' \land p'Rq')]$.

We say that $\mathcal{P} \sqsubseteq \mathcal{Q}$ if there is a prebisimulation R with $p_0 R q_0$.

There is a close connection between $\sqsubseteq$ and the relation $\sqsubseteq_W$ studied by Walker [20]. Suppose $\mathcal{P}, \mathcal{Q}$ are of the form $\langle M, p_0 \rangle$ and $\langle N, q_0 \rangle$, where M, N are labeled transition systems. Let $\mathcal{P}', \mathcal{Q}'$ be computed from $\mathcal{P}, \mathcal{Q}$ respectively by replacing $\Rightarrow$ for $\to$ and generating $\Uparrow$ from $\xrightarrow{\tau}$ using the construction specified in Section 1. Then $\mathcal{P}' \sqsubseteq \mathcal{Q}'$ iff $\mathcal{P} \sqsubseteq_W \mathcal{Q}$.

The prebisimulation preorder may also be used as a basis for computing preorders other than $\sqsubseteq_W$. To do so, we slightly refine the usual notion of pre-bisimulation by introducing a "compatibility relation", Π, between states of $\mathcal{P}$ and $\mathcal{Q}$. Sometimes, states contain information in addition to their outgoing transitions that is of interest, and Π determines when this extra information in two states is compatible. Then a relation R is a Π-prebisimulation if $R \subseteq \Pi$ and R is a prebisimulation. So if pRq, then p and q must be related by Π in addition to having their transitions matched appropriately by R.

2.3 Intuitionistic Hennessy-Milner Logic

The prebisimulation preorder also has a logical characterization in terms of Intuitionistic Hennessy-Milner Logic (IHML) [19]. The syntax of formulae in IHML is defined as follows, where $a \in Act$:

$$\Phi ::= tt \mid ff \mid \Phi \wedge \Phi \mid \Phi \vee \Phi \mid \langle a \rangle \Phi \mid [a]_\downarrow \Phi$$

The formal semantics of IHML is given in terms of a satisfaction relation, $\models$, relating states in a process $\mathcal{P} = (\langle P, Act, \rightarrow, \uparrow \rangle, p_0)$ to formulas. Formally $\models$ is defined to be the smallest relation satisfying the following, where $p \in P$:

$p \models tt$

$p \models \Phi_1 \wedge \Phi_2$ if $p \models \Phi_1$ and $p \models \Phi_2$

$p \models \Phi_1 \vee \Phi_2$ if $p \models \Phi_1$ or $p \models \Phi_2$

$p \models \langle a \rangle \Phi$ if $\exists q.\ p \xrightarrow{a} q$ and $q \models \Phi$

$p \models [a]_\downarrow \Phi$ if $p \downarrow a$ and $\forall q$ if $p \xrightarrow{a} q$, then $q \models \Phi$

We say that $\mathcal{P} \models \Phi$ if $p_0 \models \Phi$.

IHML incorporates divergence sensitivity into classical Hennessy-Milner Logic (HML) [14]. The chief difference between IHML and HML is that modal operators $\langle a \rangle$ and $[a]_\downarrow$ are not duals of each other; for p to satisfy $[a]_\downarrow$ it must be completely defined with respect to action a. This requirement reflects the intuition that if $p \uparrow a$, then more a-transitions may be added to p later. Thus we can only make statements about all of p's a-transitions if we know they have all been given.

The logical characterization of $\precsim$ states that if $\mathcal{P} \precsim \mathcal{Q}$ then the set of formulas satisfied by $\mathcal{P}$ is a subset of $\mathcal{Q}$'s, although $\mathcal{Q}$ may satisfy extra formulas [19]. Formally let $H(\mathcal{P})$ be the set of IHML formulas that a process $\mathcal{P}$ satisfies:

$$H(\mathcal{P}) = \{ \Phi \mid \mathcal{P} \models \Phi \}$$

The next theorem is due to Stirling [19].

Theorem 4. $H(\mathcal{P}) \subseteq H(\mathcal{Q})$ iff $\mathcal{P} \precsim \mathcal{Q}$.

This theorem suggests that when $\mathcal{P} \not\precsim \mathcal{Q}$, then there is a formula Φ with $\mathcal{P} \models \Phi$ and $\mathcal{Q} \not\models \Phi$. Thus one way of explaining why $\mathcal{P} \not\precsim \mathcal{Q}$ is to exhibit such a formula.

Definition 5. Let $\mathcal{P} = (\langle P, Act, \rightarrow, \uparrow \rangle, p_0)$ and $\mathcal{Q} = (\langle Q, Act, \rightarrow, \uparrow \rangle, q_0)$ be two processes. IHML formula Φ distinguishes $\mathcal{P}$ from $\mathcal{Q}$ if $\mathcal{P} \models \Phi$ and $\mathcal{Q} \not\models \Phi$.

As an example, consider the two processes $\mathcal{P}$ and $\mathcal{Q}$ given in Figure 2. The formula $\Phi = \langle a \rangle (\langle b \rangle tt \wedge \langle c \rangle tt)$ distinguishes $\mathcal{P}$ from $\mathcal{Q}$; $\mathcal{P} \models \Phi$ but $\mathcal{Q} \not\models \Phi$. Process $\mathcal{Q}$ after performing action a can only do b or c but not both. On the other hand $\mathcal{P}$ can do both b and c after a. Note that the existence of this Φ implies that $\mathcal{P} \not\precsim \mathcal{Q}$.

3 Computing the Preorder

The prebisimulation preorder has an iterative characterization that makes it suitable for algorithmic computation. The algorithm we are about to present is based on this characterization, which is as follows:

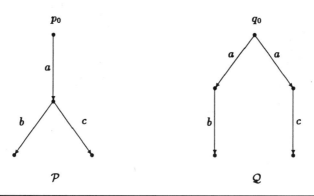

p_0 q_0

a a a

b c b c

$\mathcal{P}$ $\mathcal{Q}$

Fig. 2. Example Processes (with $\uparrow = \emptyset$)

Definition 6. Let $\mathcal{P} = ((\langle P, Act, \rightarrow, \uparrow \rangle), p_0)$ and $\mathcal{Q} = ((\langle Q, Act, \rightarrow, \uparrow \rangle), q_0)$ be processes. Then a family of relations $\precsim_k \subseteq P \times Q$ can be defined as follows:

1. $\precsim_0 = P \times Q$.
2. $\precsim_{k+1} = \mathcal{F}(\precsim_k)$ where $\mathcal{F}(R) = \{\langle p, q \rangle \mid$
   $(p \xrightarrow{a} p' \Rightarrow \exists q'. q \xrightarrow{a} q' \wedge p'Rq') \wedge$
   $(p \downarrow a \Rightarrow [q \downarrow a \wedge (q \xrightarrow{a} q' \Rightarrow \exists p'. p \xrightarrow{a} p' \wedge p'Rq')])\}$.

Note that if R is a prebisimulation then $R \subseteq \mathcal{F}(R)$. We now have the following.

Theorem 7. *Let* $\mathcal{P}, \mathcal{Q}$ *be processes with start states* p_0 *and* q_0 *respectively. Then* $\mathcal{P} \precsim \mathcal{Q}$ *iff* $\forall k \quad p_0 \precsim_k q_0$.

Thus on the basis of this characterization $\precsim$ can be computed by repeatedly applying $\mathcal{F}$ to $\precsim_0$ until $\precsim_{k+1} = \precsim_k$. This suggests the algorithm *PREORDER* (Figure 3) for computing $\precsim$.

4 Generating Diagnostic Information

From the definition $\mathcal{F}$ it follows that if $p \npreceq_k q$ then either $p \npreceq_{k-1} q$ is also true, or one of the three conditions below must hold.

1. $p \xrightarrow{a} p'$ and $\forall q'(q \xrightarrow{a} q'$ implies $p' \npreceq_{k-1} q')$
2. $p \downarrow a$ but $q \uparrow a$
3. $p \downarrow a, q \downarrow a, q \xrightarrow{a} q'$ and $\forall p'(p \xrightarrow{a} p'$ implies $p' \npreceq_{k-1} q')$

This observation leads to a two-step procedure for the computation of diagnostic information. In the first step, when two states are found not to be related by $\precsim_k$ the information as to which condition is violated and why is collected, encoded as tuples and then pushed onto a stack. These tuples have the following format.

```
k := 1 ;
⊑₀ := P × Q;
⊑₁ := F(⊑₀);
while ⊑_k ≠ ⊑_{k-1} do
   ⊑_{k+1} := F(⊑_k);
   k := k + 1 ;
end
if p₀ ⊑_k q₀ then return true
else return false;
```

Fig. 3. Algorithm *PREORDER* for computing preorder.

1) $[1, \langle p, q \rangle, a, p']$
2) $[2, \langle p, q \rangle, a]$
3) $[3, \langle p, q \rangle, a, q']$

The tag in the tuple corresponds to the condition that is violated. For example, if $p \downarrow a$ but $q \uparrow a$ then $[2, \langle p, q \rangle, a]$ will be pushed into stack, and if $p \xrightarrow{a} p'$ but $q \not\xrightarrow{a}$ then $[1, \langle p, q \rangle, a, p']$ will be pushed into the stack. Figure 4 contains a version of *PREORDER* in which these tuples are generated and stacked during the computation of the $\subseteq_k$.

In the second step, using the information pushed onto the stack in the first step, a distinguishing formula is generated which is satisfied by $\mathcal{P}$ but not by $\mathcal{Q}$.

We now remark on some properties that hold of tuples that the modified *PREORDER* pushes into its stack.

Theorem 8.
1. *When* $[1, \langle p, q \rangle, a, p']$ *is pushed onto the stack then it follows that for all* q' *such that* $q \xrightarrow{a} q'$, *a tuple containing* $\langle p', q' \rangle$ *is already in the stack.*
2. *When* $[3, \langle p, q \rangle, a, q']$ *is pushed onto the stack then it follows that for all* p' *such that* $p \xrightarrow{a} p'$, *a tuple containing* $\langle p', q' \rangle$ *is already in the stack.*

Proof. $\subseteq_{k-1}$ is always computed before $\subseteq_k$. So all the pairs which are $\not\subseteq_{k-1}$ are pushed onto the stack before those of $\not\subseteq_k$.

It also follows that if $p \not\subseteq q$ then the tuple containing $\langle p, q \rangle$ is also in the stack when *PREORDER* terminates.

We now remark on the time and space complexity of *PREORDER*.

Theorem 9.
1. *The time complexity of the algorithm PREORDER is* $O(|P|^2 \times |Q|^2 \times max(|\to_P|, |\to_Q|))$
2. *The space complexity of the algorithm PREORDER is* $O(|P| \times |Q| + |\to_P| + |\to_Q|)$

$PREORDER(\mathcal{P} : (\langle P, Act, \rightarrow\rangle, p_0); \mathcal{Q} : (\langle Q, Act, \rightarrow\rangle, q_0)); \rightarrow stack;$
  $k := 1;$
  $\precsim_0 := P \times Q;$
  $\precsim_1 := \mathcal{F}(\precsim_0);$
  while $\precsim_k \neq \precsim_{k-1}$ **do**
    foreach $\langle p, q \rangle$ such that $p\precsim_{k-1}q$ but $p \not\precsim_k q$ **do**
      case *condition* **of**
        1. $p \xrightarrow{a} p'$ and $\forall q'$ $(q \xrightarrow{a} q'$ implies $p' \not\precsim_{k-1}q')$:
          $stack := PUSH([1, \langle p, q\rangle, a, p'], stack)$
        2. $p{\downarrow}a$ but $q{\uparrow}a$:
          $stack := PUSH([2, \langle p, q\rangle, a], stack)$
        3. $p{\downarrow}a$, $q{\downarrow}a$, $q \xrightarrow{a} q'$ and $\forall p'$ $(p \xrightarrow{a} p'$ implies $p' \not\precsim_{k-1}q')$:
          $stack := PUSH([3, \langle p, q\rangle, a, q'], stack)$
      end
    end
    $\precsim_{k+1} := \mathcal{F}(\precsim_k);$
    $k := k + 1;$
  end
  if $p_0 \precsim_k q_0$ **then return** *true*
  else return $(false, stack);$
end $PREORDER;$

Fig. 4. Modified $PREORDER$.

It should be noted that these bounds can be significantly improved; for example, an $O(|\mathcal{P}| \times |\mathcal{Q}|)$ algorithm to compute the preorder is given in [11]. Our procedure for generating diagnostic formulas can also be applied to this more efficient algorithm. In this paper, however, we have elected to consider the less efficient but simpler algorithm in order to highlight the principles underlying the generation of diagnostic information.

The Postprocessing Step

After the $PREORDER$ terminates the second step computes distinguishing formulas using the tuples contained in the stack. The procedure relies on the fact that if $p \not\precsim q$ then the tuple containing $\langle p, q \rangle$ is in the stack with some additional information which explains why this is so. So a postprocessing step can process these tuples to compute formulas. The pseudocode for this step is contained in Figure 5. The intuition is as follows.

1: If the tuple is of type $[1, \langle p, q\rangle a, p']$ then either q does not have an a-derivative and p has one, or a-derivative p' of p is not related by $\precsim$ to any of the a-derivatives of q. In the former case the formula $\langle a \rangle tt$ is satisfied by p but is not satisfied by q. In the latter case one has to recursively build formulas

```
DFG (⟨p, q⟩, stack) → Φ;
    tuple := TOP(stack);
    stack := POP(stack);
    if ⟨p, q⟩ not in tuple then DFG(⟨p, q⟩, stack);
    else
        Γ := ∅;
        case tuple of
            [1, ⟨p, q⟩, a, p']      : R = { s' | q →ᵃ s' };
                                     foreach s' ∈ R do
                                         Φ' = DFG(⟨p', s'⟩, stack);
                                         Γ = Γ ∪ {Φ'};
                                     end do
                                     if Γ = ∅ then return ⟨a⟩tt;
                                     else return ⟨a⟩(∧Γ);
            [2, ⟨p, q⟩, a]          : return [a]↓tt;
            [3, ⟨p, q⟩, a, q']      : R = { s' | p →ᵃ s' };
                                     foreach s' ∈ R do
                                         Φ' = DFG(⟨s', q'⟩, stack);
                                         Γ = Γ ∪ {Φ'};
                                     end do
                                     if Γ = ∅ then return [a]↓ff
                                     else return [a]↓(∨Γ);
        endcase
    endelse
end DFG
```

Fig. 5. Code for computing distinguishing formulas.

that distinguish p' from each a-derivative of q and take the conjunction of them (call it Φ). Then p satisfies the formula $\langle a \rangle \Phi$ but q can not.

2: If the tuple is of type $[2, \langle p, q \rangle, a]$ then p is a-convergent and q is a-divergent. The formula generated then is $[a]_\downarrow tt$. q can not satisfy this because it diverges on action a.

3: If the tuple is of type $[3, \langle p, q \rangle, a, q']$ then the situation is the dual of the one shown in 1. Either p does not have an a-derivative, or one a-derivative q' of q is not related by $\sqsubseteq$ to any of the a-derivatives of p. Note that both p and q are a-convergent. In the former case this implies that p satisfies the formula $[a]_\downarrow ff$, since it does not have any a-derivative, and q can not satisfy it because it does have an a-derivative q' which can not satisfy ff. In the latter case, for each p_i such that $p \xrightarrow{a} p_i$, we may recursively build formulas Φ_i such that $p_i \models \Phi_i$ but $q' \not\models \Phi_i$. This implies that $p \models [a]_\downarrow(\vee\Phi_i)$ but $q \not\models [a]_\downarrow(\vee\Phi_i)$.

Theorem 10. Let $\mathcal{P}$ and $\mathcal{Q}$ be two processes. If $\mathcal{P} \not\sqsubseteq \mathcal{Q}$ then DFG will return a formula Φ such that $\mathcal{P} \models \Phi$ but $\mathcal{Q} \not\models \Phi$.

The formulas generated by DFG may be represented (as sets of propositional equations so that common subformulas may be shared) in space proportional to $|P| \times |Q| \times max(|P|, |Q|)$. This is due to the fact that the number of total recursive calls made by the algorithm is bounded by $|P| \times |Q|$ and each distinguishing formula is of the form $\langle a \rangle \Phi$ or $[a]_{\downarrow} \Phi$ where Φ contains at most $max(|P|, |Q|)$ conjuncts or disjuncts. If the procedure is modified such a way that we save and use this information appropriately then we have the following bound on the amount of computation needed to compute these equations.

Theorem 11. *An equational representation of $DFG(\langle p, q \rangle, stack)$ may be calculated in $O(|P| \times |Q| \times max(|P|, |Q|))$ time, based on the information in the stack.*

5 An Example

Figure 6 gives two labeled transition systems $\mathcal{P}$ and $\mathcal{Q}$ for which $\mathcal{P} \not\sqsubseteq_W \mathcal{Q}$, where $\sqsubseteq_W$ is discussed in Section 2.2. In order to show that $\mathcal{P} \not\sqsubseteq_W \mathcal{Q}$ and generate the corresponding diagnostic formula we apply the method outlined in Section 2.1. First $elts \langle P, Act - \{\tau\} \cup \{\epsilon\}, \Rightarrow, \Uparrow \rangle$ and $\langle Q, Act - \{\tau\} \cup \{\epsilon\}, \Rightarrow, \Uparrow \rangle$ are constructed for $\mathcal{P}$ and $\mathcal{Q}$ and the prebisimulation algorithm is then applied to these. As a result, in the diagnostic information to be generated, $\Downarrow$ will be used in the formulas involving $[]_{\downarrow}$. Note that for all p in $\mathcal{P}$, $p \Downarrow i$ and $p \Downarrow o$, while in $\mathcal{Q}$, $q_0 \Downarrow i$, $q_0 \Downarrow o$ and $q_1 \Downarrow o$, but $q_1 \Uparrow i$, $q_2 \Uparrow i$ and $q_2 \Uparrow o$. The stack is initially empty. After the first iteration the following pairs will be pushed into the stack since they are found to be $\not\sqsubseteq_1$:

$$
\begin{array}{|l|}
\hline
[1, \langle p_2, q_2 \rangle, o, p_1] \\
\hline
[2, \langle p_2, q_1 \rangle, i] \\
\hline
[1, \langle p_2, q_0 \rangle, o, p_1] \\
\hline
[1, \langle p_1, q_2 \rangle, i, p_2] \\
\hline
[2, \langle p_1, q_1 \rangle, i] \\
\hline
[1, \langle p_1, q_0 \rangle, o, p_0] \\
\hline
[1, \langle p_0, q_2 \rangle, i, p_1] \\
\hline
[3, \langle p_0, q_1 \rangle, o, q_0] \\
\hline
\end{array}
$$

After the second iteration $[1, \langle p_0, q_0 \rangle, i, p_1]$ is pushed into stack because $p_0 \overset{i}{\Rightarrow} p_1$, $q_0 \overset{i}{\Rightarrow} q_1$ and $p_1 \not\sqsubseteq_1 q_1$. Since $\langle p_0, q_0 \rangle$ is in the stack process $\mathcal{P}$ is not smaller than process $\mathcal{Q}$. In order to build the formula $DFG(\langle p_0, q_0 \rangle, stack)$, the algorithm first locates the tuple which has the pair $\langle p_0, q_0 \rangle$. In this case the tuple $[1, \langle p_0, q_0 \rangle, i, p_1]$ is in the stack and the action causing this element to be pushed into the stack is i. The formula that will be returned, then, will be

$$\langle i \rangle (DFG(\langle p_1, q_1 \rangle, stack))$$

The algorithm then locates the tuple containing $\langle p_1, q_1 \rangle$; it is $[2, \langle p_1, q_1 \rangle, i]$. The tag 2 indicates the reason why this tuple is in the stack. q_1 is divergent on action

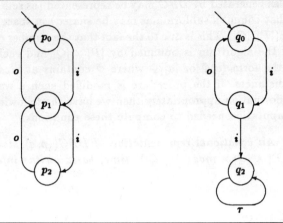

Fig. 6. Processes $\mathcal{P}$ and $\mathcal{Q}$ such that $\mathcal{P} \not\sqsubseteq_w \mathcal{Q}$.

i whereas p_1 is convergent. So the formula returned for $DFG(\langle p_1, q_1 \rangle, stack)$ is

$$[i]_\Downarrow tt$$

This means the formula distinguishing p_0 from q_0 is

$$\langle i \rangle [i]_\Downarrow tt$$

Process $\mathcal{P}$ may engage in an i-transition from its start state p_0 and after that it may evolve to a convergent state on *all* i-transitions. (Note that there is only one such transition in this example.) However process $\mathcal{Q}$ may evolve to an i-divergent state on action i from its start state q_0.

6 Applications of Prebisimulation Preorder

Various other preorders in the literature can be seen to be instances of the prebisimulation preorder applied to special kinds of *elts*. In this section we investigate the form that diagnostic information takes when our methodology is applied to the computation of the preorders. Let $\mathcal{P} = (\langle P, Act, \rightarrow, \uparrow \rangle, p_0)$ and $\mathcal{Q} = (\langle Q, Act, \rightarrow, \uparrow \rangle, q_0)$ be two processes.

Bisimulation Equivalence

Bisimulation equivalence is defined in terms of bisimulations [18].

Definition 12 (Bisimulation Equivalence). A relation $R \subseteq P \times Q$ is a bisimulation between P and Q if pRq implies the following.

1. $p \xrightarrow{a} p' \Rightarrow \exists q'. \, q \xrightarrow{a} q' \wedge p'Rq'$.
2. $q \xrightarrow{a} q' \Rightarrow \exists p'. \, p \xrightarrow{a} p' \wedge p'Rq'$.

$\mathcal{P} \sim \mathcal{Q}$ is defined to hold if there is a bisimulation R with $p_0 R q_0$.

If $\uparrow = \emptyset$ (i.e. all states are completely defined on all actions.) then prebisimulation preorder becomes bisimulation equivalence [18]. The reason is that, in Definition 3, Condition 2 becomes $q \xrightarrow{a} q' \Rightarrow \exists p'. p \xrightarrow{a} p' \wedge p'Rq'$ when $\uparrow$ is $\emptyset$.

Since all states are defined on all actions the convergence requirement in satisfying $[]_{\downarrow}$ is fulfilled trivially. Thus the modal operators $[]_{\downarrow}$ and $\langle \rangle$ become duals of each other. The other consequence of $\uparrow = \emptyset$ is that the formulas do not contain the subformula $[a]_{\downarrow}tt$. This is due to the fact that the tuple $[2, \langle p, q \rangle, a]$ which causes this subformula to be generated can never occur in the stack.

Simulation Preorder

The simulation preorder, $\precsim$, is defined in terms of simulations.

Definition 13 (Simulation Preorder). Let $\mathcal{P}$ and $\mathcal{Q}$ be processes. A relation $R \subseteq P \times Q$ is a simulation between P and Q if pRq implies the following.

1. $p \xrightarrow{a} p' \Rightarrow \exists q'. q \xrightarrow{a} q' \wedge p'Rq'$.

$\mathcal{P} \precsim \mathcal{Q}$ holds if there is a simulation R with $p_0 R q_0$.

If $\uparrow = P \times Act$ (so every state is considered to be *underdefined* or *incomplete* on every action) then $\sqsubseteq$ coincides with the *simulation preorder*. The reason for this is that when $\uparrow = P \times Act$, Condition 2 in Definition 3 of prebisimulation preorder is always true, since it is never the case that $p \downarrow a$ holds.

As an immediate result of the elimination of checking Condition 2 in Definition 3, the diagnostic formulas we generate in this setting do not contain disjunctions or the modal operator $[]_{\downarrow}$, since DFG generates a formula containing $[]_{\downarrow}$ or $\vee$'s only when the second condition in the definition of $\sqsubseteq$ is violated. Then the syntax of the generated formulas turns out to be $\Phi ::= tt \mid \Phi \wedge \Phi \mid \langle a \rangle \Phi$.

Trace Containment

The trace containment preorder is defined in terms of the sequences of actions a process may perform.

Definition 14.
- Let $s = a_1 \ldots a_n$ be in Act^*. Then $p \xrightarrow{s}$ holds if there exists $p_1, \ldots, p_n$ such that $p \xrightarrow{a_1} p_1 \ldots \xrightarrow{a_n} p_n$.
- $\mathcal{P} \sqsubseteq_{trace} \mathcal{Q}$ if for any $s \in Act^*$ such that $p \xrightarrow{s}$, $q \xrightarrow{s}$.

If $\mathcal{P}$ and $\mathcal{Q}$ are deterministic and $\uparrow = P \times Act$ then the relation computed by the preorder checking algorithm turns out to be *trace* or *language* containment. $\mathcal{P} \sqsubseteq_{trace} \mathcal{Q}$ in this sense exactly when $\mathcal{Q}$ is capable of engaging any sequence of actions that $\mathcal{P}$ is capable of. In this setting when $\mathcal{P} \not\sqsubseteq_{trace} \mathcal{Q}$ then $\exists s \in Act^*$ such that $p_0 \xrightarrow{s}$ but $q_0 \not\xrightarrow{s}$.

The formulas generated by DFG have a very simple form when the processes are deterministic and $\uparrow = P \times Act$, and it is straightforward to exhibit a sequence s that $\mathcal{P}$ is capable of but $\mathcal{Q}$ is not when $\mathcal{P} \not\sqsubseteq_{trace} \mathcal{Q}$ based on this formula. In particular the formulas do not contain

- disjunctions,
- conjunctions,
- $[]_\downarrow$,
- ff.

The reason why the formulas have this special form is as follows. Since the processes are deterministic, every state in $\mathcal{P}$ and $\mathcal{Q}$ has at most one a-derivative for any a, and at each stage in DFG we therefore need to distinguish an a-derivative of $p \in P$ from at most one a-derivative of $q \in Q$. This removes the necessity to use conjunction or disjunction. The formulas do not contain $[]_\downarrow$ because Condition 2 of Definition 3 can not be violated.

More precisely the syntax of the formulas is $\Phi ::= tt \mid \langle a \rangle \Phi$. Since the formulas have the following simple form

$$\langle a_1 \rangle ... \langle a_n \rangle tt$$

they can easily be transformed into distinguishing sequences of the form

$$a_1 ... a_n.$$

Testing Preorders and Equivalences

If the compatibility relation Π mentioned in Section 2.2 is initialized correctly and the processes are transformed appropriately then testing preorders and equivalences can also be computed by the preorder checking algorithm. However, this procedure is beyond the scope of this paper, and interested reader should refer [6, 7] for a detailed account.

7 Concluding Remarks

One approach to verifying processes involves the use of behavioral preorder; an implementation may be deemed to satisfy a specification if it is greater than the specification. In this paper we have presented a method for computing diagnostic information for a particular preorder, the *prebisimulation preorder*. This preorder has a logical characterization in terms of a variant of Hennessy-Milner logic that enables us to generate formulas explaining why one process is not greater than the other. The generation of the formulas relies on a postprocessing step that is invoked on a stack-based representation of the information computed by the preorder information. As future work we plan to incorporate this distinguishing formula capability into the Concurrency Workbench [8], a tool for the analysis of finite-state systems. We would also like to investigate applying our techniques to Binary Decision Diagram-based algorithms [5] for computing preorders.

383

References

1. Abramsky, S., "Observation Equivalence as a Testing Equivalence", *Theoretical Computer Science,* vol. 53, (1987), 225-241.
2. Bergstra, J.A., and J.W. Klop, "Process Algebra for Synchronous Communication", *Information and Control 60,* (1984), 109-137.
3. Bolognesi, T. and E. Brinksma, "Introduction to the ISO Specification Language LOTOS", *Computer Networks and ISDN Systems,* vol. 14, (1987), 25-59.
4. Brookes, S.D., C.A.R. Hoare, and A.W. Roscoe, "A Theory of Communicating Sequential Processes", *Journal of the ACM,* vol. 31, no. 3, (1984),560-599.
5. Burch, J.R., E.M. Clarke, K.C McMillan, D.L. Dill, L.J. Hwang. "Symbolic Model Checking: 10^{20} States and Beyond," *In Proceedings LICS'90,* (1990).
6. Celikkan, U., and R. Cleaveland, "Computing Diagnostic Tests for Incorrect Processes" In *Proceedings of the Protocol Specification Testing and Verification, 12, 1992.*
7. Cleaveland, R., and M. Hennessy, "Testing Equivalence as a Bisimulation Equivalence", In *Proceedings of the Workshop on Automatic Verification Methods for Finite-State Systems,* LNCS 407, (1989),11-23. To appear in *Fundamental Aspects of Computing.*
8. Cleaveland, R., J. Parrow, and B. Steffen, " The Concurrency Workbench", *In Proceedings of the Workshop on Automatic Verification Methods for Finite-State Systems,* LNCS 407, (1989),24-37.
9. Cleaveland, R., "On Automatically Distinguishing Inequivalent Processes", *In Proceedings of the Workshop on Computer-Aided Verification, 1990.*
10. Cleaveland, R., and B. Steffen, "When is 'Partial' Adequate? A Logic Based Proof Technique Using Partial Specifications", *In Proceedings LICS'90,* (1990).
11. Cleaveland, R., and B. Steffen, "Computing Behavioral Relations, Logically", *In Proceedings of ICALP'90,* (1991).
12. DeNicola, R., and M.C.B. Hennessy, "Testing Equivalences for Processes", *Theoretical Computer Science,* vol. 24, (1984), 83-113.
13. Godskeen, J.C., K.G. Larsen, and M. Zeeberg, "TAV – Tools for automatic verification", R89-19, Aalborg University, Denmark.
14. Hennessy, M., and R. Milner, "Algebraic Laws for Nondeterminism and Concurrency", *Journal of the Association for Computing Machinery,* vol. 32, no. 1, (January 1985), 147-161.
15. Hennessy, M., *Algebraic Theory of Processes,* MIT Press, Boston, 1988.
16. Hoare, C.A.R., *Communicating Sequential Processes,* Prentice-Hall, London, 1985.
17. Larsen, K.G., and B. Thomsen, "Compositional Proofs by Partial Specification of Processes", Report R 87-20, University of Aalborg, July 1987.
18. Milner, R., *Communication and Concurrency,* Prentice Hall, 1989.
19. Stirling, C., "Modal Logics for Communicating Systems", *Theoretical Computer Science,* vol. 49, (1987), 311-347.
20. Walker, D., "Bisimulations and Divergence", *In Proceedings of the Third Annual Symposium on Logic in Computer Science,* (1988), 186-192.

A Verification Procedure via Invariant for Extended Communicating Finite-State Machines

Masahiro Higuchi* Osamu Shirakawa* Hiroyuki Seki*

Mamoru Fujii** Tadao Kasami***

* Dept. of Information and Computer Sciences, Osaka University
Toyonaka, Osaka 560, Japan

** College of General Education, Osaka University
Toyonaka, Osaka 560, Japan

*** Advanced Institute of Science and Technology, Nara
Ikoma, Nara 630–01, Japan

e-mail: (higuchi, sirakawa, seki, fujii, kasami)@ics.osaka-u.ac.jp

Abstract. This paper presents a method for verifying safety property of a communication protocol modeled as two extended communicating finite-state machines with two unbounded FIFO channels connecting them. In this method, four types of atomic formulae specifying a condition on a machine and a condition on a sequence of messages in a channel are introduced. A human verifier describes a logical formula which expresses conditions expected to be satisfied by all reachable global states, and a verification system proves that the formula is indeed satisfied by such states (i.e. the formula is an invariant) by induction. If the invariant is never satisfied in any unsafe state, it can be concluded that the protocol is safe. To show the effectiveness of this method, a sample protocol extracted from the data transfer phase of the OSI session protocol was verified by using the verification system.

1 Introduction

For implementing reliable communication software, it is important to verify the communication protocol formally. Communicating finite-state machines (CFSMs) are used as a model for verifying communication protocols. If the boundedness of the communication channels is guaranteed, many important properties for CFSMs are decidable[1] in principle, and some decision procedures have been proposed[2][3]. However, even though channel boundedness is guaranteed, the decision procedures based on channel boundedness are not feasible for most practical protocols because of state space explosion.

Furthermore, for practical protocols, protocol machines are usually defined as extended communicating finite-state machine(ECFSM)s whose state is represented by a state of finite control and values of context variables. In fact, two formal description techniques Estelle[4] and SDL[5] for communication protocols are based on extended finite-state machine model. In this paper, a verification method for a class of ECFSMs in which the channel boundedness is not guaranteed is proposed.

For such a class of protocols, the set of global states reachable from the initial global state is potentially infinite and therefore traditional state exploration techniques which enumerate reachable global states cannot be used. Instead, we propose a method based on a verification via invariant using similar techniques to those adopted by such systems as theorem provers[6].

The proposed method is summarized as the following (1) and (2):

(1) Find a logical formula on global states, say F, which is expected to satisfy (a) $RS \subseteq GS(F)$ and (b) $GS(F) \subseteq SAFE$, where RS is the set of reachable global states, $GS(F)$ is the set of those global states which satisfy F and $SAFE$ is the set of safe global states. Although only safety property is considered in this paper, the proposed method can be extended to verify liveness property. F is written as a propositional formula which consists of the following atomic formulae,

  (i) conditions on states of finite controls of ECFSM,
  (ii) regular expressions which specify message type sequences in the channels,

  (iii) conditions on sequences of integers (parameters of messages in the channel) such as 'monotonically increasing', and
  (iv) linear inequalities on integers which specify the relations to hold for the values of context variables of ECFSMs and parameters of messages in the channels.
(2) Verify that the above (a) and (b) hold. Verification of (b) is easy. The above (a) is verified by structural induction on event sequences. Verification in the inductive step is reduced to the inclusion problem for given two regular expressions (for (ii) above), the problem to find the normal form of a given term in the term rewriting system which represents the definition of protocol machines, inductive hypothesis and properties of sequences of integers (for (iii)), and the problem to decide whether a given ordered pair of expressions belongs to the transitive closure of given inequalities (for (iv)).

A verification system which implements the proposed procedure and a verification example of OSI session protocol are also described in this paper.

As related works, a verification method is proposed for ECFSMs with queues of length one[7]. For a protocol for which channel boundedness is not guaranteed, Finkel[8] studies a class of protocols in which the set of message sequences in the channels is exactly expressed by regular expressions, and gives decidable results on some verification problems. However, protocol machines considered in [8] are assumed to be finite. The protocol model discussed in this paper assumes neither finiteness of protocol machines nor channel boundedness. Systematic verification methods for such a class of protocols have been scarcely reported.

2 Basic Definitions

2.1 Protocol Model

Two-extended communicating finite-state machines(2-ECFSMs) are a protocol model which consists of two protocol machines modeled as extended communicating finite-state machines and two unbounded FIFO channels connecting them. Formally, it is defined as below.

A **protocol machine** PM is a 4-tuple (S, Σ, δ, si), where

(M1) $S = \langle SF, r \rangle$ defines a set of **states**, where SF is the state set of finite control part of the machine and r is the number of registers(context variables) which store nonnegative integers. Let $\mathcal{N}$ denote the set of nonnegative integers. The state space of the protocol machine is $SF \times \mathcal{N}^r$.

(M2) $\Sigma = \Sigma_- \cup \Sigma_+$: a finite set of **message types**. Σ_- is a set of message types which PM can send and Σ_+ is a set of message types which PM can receive. Σ_- and Σ_+ are supposed to be disjoint. For $d \in \Sigma$ and $n \in \mathcal{N}$, $\langle d, n \rangle$ is called a **message** and n is called the parameter of the message. The number of parameters of a message is assumed to be exactly one only for simplicity. In the following, for a message sequence u, $type(u)$ and $parameter(u)$ denote the message type sequence of u and the parameter sequence of u respectively. The set of events EV of the protocol machine is defined in connection with the set of messages sent or received by the machine, i.e. $EV = \{-\langle d, n \rangle | d \in \Sigma_-, n \in \mathcal{N}\} \cup \{+\langle d, n \rangle | d \in \Sigma_+, n \in \mathcal{N}\}$. The former subset is the set of **sending events** and the latter one is the set of **receiving events**.

(M3) δ : a partial **state transition function** from $SF \times \mathcal{N}^r \times EV$ to $SF \times \mathcal{N}^r$. For $s \in SF \times \mathcal{N}^r$ and $e \in EV$, if $\delta(s, e)$ is defined, then an event e is said to be **executable** in the state s.

(M4) $si \in SF \times \mathcal{N}^r$: an **initial state**.

For $PM_A = (\langle SF_A, r_A \rangle, \Sigma_A, \delta_A, si_A)$ and $PM_B = (\langle SF_B, r_B \rangle, \Sigma_B, \delta_B, si_B)$, if $\Sigma_{B-} = \Sigma_{A+}$ (denoted Σ_{BA}) and $\Sigma_{A-} = \Sigma_{B+}$ (denoted Σ_{AB}), then $\Pi = (PM_A, PM_B)$ is called a **protocol**. A 4-tuple $(s_A, s_B, ch_{BA}, ch_{AB}) \in (SF_A \times \mathcal{N}^{r_A}, SF_B \times \mathcal{N}^{r_B}, \langle \Sigma_{BA}, \mathcal{N} \rangle^*, \langle \Sigma_{AB}, \mathcal{N} \rangle^*)$ is called a **global state** of protocol Π. s_A and s_B denote states of PM_A and PM_B respectively. ch_{BA} and ch_{AB} denote message sequences in the channel from PM_B to PM_A and that from PM_A to PM_B respectively. $gs_I = (si_A, si_B, \varepsilon, \varepsilon)$ (ε is the empty sequence) is called the **initial global state** of Π.

A global state $gs' = (s'_A, s'_B, ch'_{BA}, ch'_{AB})$ is said to be **transitable** from $gs = (s_A, s_B, ch_{BA}, ch_{AB})$(denoted by $gs \to gs'$) iff one of the following conditions is satisfied for some $d \in \Sigma_{BA} \cup \Sigma_{AB}$ and $n \in \mathcal{N}$:

(TA1) $s'_A = \delta_A(s_A, -\langle d, n \rangle)$, $s'_B = s_B$, $ch'_{BA} = ch_{BA}$, $ch'_{AB} = ch_{AB} \cdot \langle d, n \rangle$;

(TA2) $s'_A = \delta_A(s_A, +\langle d, n \rangle)$, $s'_B = s_B$, $\langle d, n \rangle \cdot ch'_{BA} = ch_{BA}$, $ch'_{AB} = ch_{AB}$;

(TA3) $s'_A = s_A$, $s'_B = \delta_B(s_B, -\langle d, n \rangle)$, $ch'_{BA} = ch_{BA} \cdot \langle d, n \rangle$, $ch'_{AB} = ch_{AB}$;

(TA4) $s'_A = s_A$, $s'_B = \delta_B(s_B, +\langle d, n \rangle)$, $ch'_{BA} = ch_{BA}$, $\langle d, n \rangle \cdot ch'_{AB} = ch_{AB}$.

If (TA1) holds, the relation is also denoted $gs - (- \langle d, n \rangle, A) \rightarrow gs'$. This extended notation is also used for (TA2), (TA3) and (TA4). The transitive reflexive closure of the relation "$\rightarrow$" is denoted by "$\xrightarrow{*}$". If $gs \xrightarrow{*} gs'$, then the global state gs' is said to be **reachable** from gs.

2.2 Safety Property

For a protocol $\Pi = (PM_A, PM_B)$, the set of reachable global states from the initial global state is called the **reachability set** of Π. If the reachability set of Π does not contain following unsafe states, Π is said to be **safe**.

Deadlock state: A global state $gs = (s_A, s_B, ch_{BA}, ch_{AB})$ is said to be a deadlock state if $ch_{BA} = ch_{AB} = \varepsilon$ and any sending event is not executable in s_A and s_B respectively.

Unspecified reception state: A global state $gs = (s_A, s_B, ch_{BA}, ch_{AB})$ is said to be an unspecified reception state if either $ch_{BA} \neq \varepsilon$ and $\delta_A(s_A, +head(ch_{BA}))$ is not defined or $ch_{AB} \neq \varepsilon$ and $\delta_B(s_B, +head(ch_{AB}))$ is not defined, where $head(\alpha)$ denotes the first element of a nonempty sequence α.

3 Verification Method

If a logical formula F on global state on Π is satisfied by all global states in the reachability set of a protocol Π, F is called an **invariant** in Π. If an invariant F in Π is not satisfied by any deadlock state or unspecified reception state, then Π is safe. We present a method for verifying a given formula in a disjunctive normal form $F = P_1 \vee P_2 \vee \ldots \vee P_n$ to be an invariant in Π. In the following, for a formula F, $GS(F)$ denotes the set of global states which satisfy F.

3.1 Description of a Logical Formula

Every disjunct P_i of formula F is a conjunction of **atomic formulae** (or simply **atoms**) of the following four types. Figure 1-A (a) shows an example of P_i.

(AF1) A formula $\langle SSF_A, SSF_B \rangle$, where $SSF_A \subseteq SF_A$ and $SSF_B \subseteq SF_B$, is an atom which holds for a global state $(s_A, s_B, ch_{BA}, ch_{AB})$ iff the finite control part of s_A and s_B belong to SSF_A and SSF_B respectively.

(AF2) A class of regular expression to express an infinite set of message type sequences in a communication channel is introduced as below. The regular expression is restricted to be ε (the empty sequence) or a concatenation of subexpressions of the following types:

R1: A choice of Σ_{BA} (or Σ_{AB}), i.e. $m_1 + m_2 + \ldots + m_n$ for $m_k (1 \leq k \leq n)$ in Σ_{BA} (or Σ_{AB});

R2: Positive closure t^+ of a choice t of Σ_{BA} or Σ_{AB}.

For two restricted regular expressions r_{BA} and r_{AB}, a formula $\langle r_{BA}, r_{AB} \rangle$ is an atom which holds for a global state $(s_A, s_B, ch_{BA}, ch_{AB})$ iff $type(ch_{BA}) \in L(r_{BA})$ and $type(ch_{AB}) \in L(r_{AB})$, where $L(r)$ is the set of sequences denoted by the regular expression r. We assume that exactly one AF2 type atom appears in every P_i. In the following, if a global state $(s_A, s_B, ch_{BA}, ch_{AB})$ satisfies an AF2 type atom "$\langle u_1 \cdot u_2 \cdot \ldots \cdot u_n, \ v_1 \cdot v_2 \cdot \ldots \cdot v_m \rangle$", $BA[k](1 \leq k \leq n)$ denotes a message sequence such that $BA[1] \cdot BA[2] \cdot \ldots \cdot BA[n] = ch_{BA}$ and $type(BA[j]) \in L(u_j)(1 \leq j \leq n)$ and, $AB[k](1 \leq k \leq m)$ denotes the message sequence such that $AB[1] \cdot AB[2] \cdot \ldots \cdot AB[m] = ch_{AB}$ and $type(AB[j]) \in L(v_j)(1 \leq j \leq m)$.

(AF3) A predicate on a message sequence on a communication channel is also an atom. For instance, "$step1(AB[1])$" (in Figure 1-A (a)) states that the parameter sequence $parameter(AB[1])$ satisfies the predicate "$step1$". "$step1$" means that the parameter sequence is an increasing sequence such that the difference of every adjacent elements is one. Predicates which appear in an AF3 type atom are defined in terms of rewrite rules and inequalities. For example, a conditional rewrite rule in Figure 1-A (b) "$|seq| \geq 1, step1(seq), t = last(seq)+1 : step1(seq \cdot \langle type, t \rangle) \Rightarrow true$" asserts that if a message sequence seq of length 1 or more satisfies the predicate $step1$ and t is equal to the parameter of the last message of seq plus 1, then the parameter sequence $parameter(seq) \cdot t$ of the message sequence $seq \cdot \langle type, t \rangle$ also satisfies the predicate $step1$. The conditions of conditional rewrite rules and inequalities are also assumed to be written in the form of an AF3 or AF4 type atom.

(AF4) A linear inequality which represents the relation on the values of registers of protocol machines and the parameter values of messages in a channel. The expressions appearing on the both sides of inequalities are restricted to the form of "$v + C$" where v is a term which denotes either the value of a register of a protocol machine or a parameter value of a message in a channel and C is a constant value of integer. For instance, "$Vm(A) = last(AB[1]) + 1$" in Figure 1-A (a) is an AF4 type atom which states that the value of the register Vm of PM_A is equal to the parameter of the last message in the channel from PM_A to PM_B plus 1 at the global state under consideration.

3.2 Verification Procedure

A given logical formula $F = P_1 \vee P_2 \vee \ldots \vee P_n$ is shown to be an invariant in Π by structural induction on event sequences of Π as follows.

Inductive basis: Prove that the initial global state of Π satisfies F.

Inductive step: Prove that

$$\forall_{gs \in GS(F)} \forall_{gs \to gs'} \{gs' \in GS(F)\}. \tag{$*$ 1}$$

Observe that $GS(F) = GS(P_1) \cup GS(P_2) \cup \ldots \cup GS(P_n)$. Therefore, ($*$ 1) is equivalent to

$$\forall_{i(1 \leq i \leq n)} \forall_{gs \in GS(P_i)} \forall_{gs \to gs'} \exists_{j(1 \leq j \leq n)} \{gs' \in GS(P_j)\}. \tag{$*$ 2}$$

Thus ($*$ 1) is proved by executing the following IS1 and IS2 for each $P_i(1 \leq i \leq n)$.

IS1 Identify all events(pairs of a local event ($\pm\langle d, n\rangle$) and a machine) executable in global states in $GS(P_i)$.

IS2 For every executable event ($\pm\langle d, n\rangle, X$) obtained by IS1, show

$$\forall_{gs\in GS(P_i)}\forall_{gs-(\pm\langle d,n\rangle,X)\to gs'}\exists_{j(1\leq j\leq n)}\{gs' \in GS(P_j)\}. \qquad (*\,3)$$

The inductive basis and IS1 are easily examined from the form of each P_i. To explain the procedure for examining IS2, we consider the following example $EX1$.

> $\underline{EX1}$: • Let P_i in (*3) be shown in Figure 1-A (a).
> • Let ($\pm\langle d, n\rangle, X$) in (*3) be ($-\langle\mathrm{MIP}, Vm(A)\rangle, A$). $\square$

The definition of state transition on the event is shown in Figure 1-A (b). In the following and in Figures 1-A and 1-B, all terms with primes denote the values of the corresponding terms without primes after the transition. The definition of the state transition tells the followings:

(1) If the state of finite control of the machine is STA713, the machine can send MIP with parameter value equal to the value of register Vm;
(2) The finite control still stays at STA713 after sending $\langle\mathrm{MIP}, Vm(A)\rangle$;
(3) The value of register Vm is incremented by one;
(4) The value of register Va is not changed.

Let $P_j = PF_j \wedge PI_j(1 \leq j \leq n)$, where PF_j is the conjunction of AF1 and AF2 type atoms and PI_j is the conjunction of AF3 and AF4 type atoms. Since $GS(P_j) = GS(PF_j) \cap GS(PI_j)$, IS2 is refined as the following (I) and (II) for each i.

(I) Identify all PF_j such that

$$\forall_{gs\in GS(PF_i),gs-(\pm\langle d,n\rangle,X)\to gs'}\{gs' \in GS(PF_j)\}. \qquad (*\,4)$$

In general, it can be checked for gs' to satisfy an AF1 type atom from the definition of δ directly, and to satisfy an AF2 type atom by reducing the satisfaction problem to the inclusion problem for two regular sets. The restrictions **R1** and **R2** simplify the decision procedure for this inclusion problem. Consider the case $P_j = P_i$ in $EX1$. As the message type sequence in the channel from PM_B to PM_A and that from PM_A to PM_B at gs' are required to be in $L(\varepsilon)$ and $L(\mathrm{MIP}^+ \cdot \mathrm{MIP})$ respectively, the problem to decide whether every gs' satisfies $\langle\varepsilon, \mathrm{MIP}^+\rangle$ is reduced to the inclusion problems $L(\varepsilon) \subseteq L(\varepsilon)$ and $L(\mathrm{MIP}^+ \cdot \mathrm{MIP}) \subseteq L(\mathrm{MIP}^+)$.

Then the next step is as follows:

(II) Show that $gs' \in GS(PI_j)$ for some j which satisfies (*4).

To show (II),at first, the rewrite rules to express the message sequences in gs' in terms of the message sequences in gs and the message sent by executing the event are generated.

For example, suppose that the event is $-(\langle d, p \rangle, A)$. The rewrite rules are generated as follows. Let $\langle r_{BA,i}, r_{AB,i} \rangle$ and $\langle r_{BA,j}, r_{AB,j} \rangle$ be AF2 type atoms in P_i and P_j respectively. Let $r_{AB,i} = u_1 \cdot u_2 \cdot \ldots \cdot u_n$ and $r_{AB,j} = u_1' \cdot u_2' \cdot \ldots \cdot u_m'$, where u_k and u_l' are choices of Σ_{AB} or positive closures of choices of Σ_{AB}, for $1 \leq k \leq n$ and $1 \leq l \leq m$. Since the atom $\langle r_{BA,j}, r_{AB,j} \rangle$ holds for every gs' by (I), i.e. $L(r_{AB,i} \cdot d) \subseteq L(r_{AB,j})$, it follows from the restrictions **R1** and **R2** that there exists a mapping φ such that $L(u_1 \cdot \ldots \cdot u_{\varphi(l)}) \subseteq L(u_1' \cdot \ldots \cdot u_l')$ and $\varphi(l-1) \leq \varphi(l)$ for every $1 \leq l \leq m-1$, and $\varphi(0) = 0$. Then the rewrite rule "$AB[l]' \Rightarrow AB[\varphi(l-1)+1] \cdot \ldots \cdot AB[\varphi(l)]$" is generated for $1 \leq l \leq m-1$ and the rewrite rule "$AB[m]' \Rightarrow AB[\varphi(m-1)+1] \cdot \ldots \cdot AB[n] \cdot \langle d, p \rangle$" is generated. In our example, "$AB[1]' \Rightarrow AB[1] \cdot \langle \text{MIP}, Vm(A) \rangle$" is generated. If the mapping φ is not uniquely determined, then for every possible φ, the rewrite rules for φ are generated and the procedure to check (II) is executed. If (II) holds for some φ, it can be concluded that IS2 for given $(-\langle d, n \rangle, A)$ holds.

To check (II), the condition parts of all conditional rewrite rules and conditional inequalities are evaluated with assigning the values in gs to the free variables in the condition. If the condition of a conditional rewrite rule (or inequality) is shown to be true for the assignment, then the rewrite rule (or inequality) instantiated by the assignment is added to the assumption. In our example, $|AB[1]| \geq 1$, $step1(AB[1])$, and $Vm(A) = last(AB[1]) + 1$ are shown to be true, and the rewrite rule
"$step1(AB[1] \cdot \langle \text{MIP}, Vm(A) \rangle) \Rightarrow true$" are added as (5'). The procedures for evaluating AF3 and AF4 type atoms (and the conditions of conditional rewrite rules and conditional inequalities) are described below.

- (AF3) Show that the atom can be rewritten as constant term "true" under the term rewriting system[9] consisting of assumed relations. Figure 1-A (b) shows the example. Figure 1-B (d) shows a process in which "$step1(AB[1]')$" is rewritten to "true".
- (AF4) For an atom "a rel b" ($rel \in \{=, \geq\}$), find the normal forms of a and b under the rewriting system described above, i.e. rewrite a and b to $norm(a)$ and $norm(b)$ respectively until $norm(a)$ and $norm(b)$ can not be rewritten to any terms. In Figure 1-B (e), "$Vm'(A) \geq Va'(A)$" is rewritten to "$Vm(A)+1 \geq Va(A)$". And decide whether $norm(a)$ rel $norm(b)$ belongs to the transitive closure (over the set of expressions of the form "$v + C$") of the assumed inequalities (Figure 1-B (c)). In our example, let $GE = \{(a, b) \mid a \geq b \text{ is an assumed inequality}\}$, then $(Vm(A)+1, Vm(A))$ and $(Vm(A), Va(A))$ belong to GE. The transitive closure of GE contains $(Vm(A) + 1, Va(A))$. We can conclude that "$Vm(A) + 1 \geq Va(A)$"(Figure 1-B (f)).

4 A Verification System

We implemented a verification system based on the verification method described in Section 3. The verification system provides the procedures for executing a state transition, deciding the inclusion problem on given two regular sets, rewriting a term under the given term rewriting system, and deciding whether a given pair of expressions belong to the transitive closure of given relations. The system executes the inductive step of the proposed verification method by conducting the above procedures.

An input to the verification system consists of the definition of protocol machines, properties of predicates on sequences of integers such as *step1* explained in the example in Section 3, and a logical formula F to be shown an invariant. The system constructs a state transition table, unfolds an input formula to obtain a disjunctive normal form, and executes the verification procedure described in Section 3. If there exists a pair of global states gs and gs' such that $gs \to gs'$, $gs \in GS(F)$ and $gs' \notin GS(F)$, then the system always detects the fact and reports relevant information on such global states and a transition. If there exists a deadlock or unspecified reception state which satisfies F, then the system also detects that and reports it.

The verification system was implemented by using C, lex, and yacc on the UNIX environment. The size of the source code of the system is about 10,000 lines.

5 An Experimental Result

To show the usefulness of the proposed verification method, we performed an experiment on a part of OSI session protocol[10].

5.1 Extracting a Sample Protocol

We extract the protocol for *data transfer* phase of *kernel, duplex, minor synchronize* and *major synchronize* functional units from OSI session protocol. For simplification, we omit some PDU(message)s which have no effect on any registers and we assume that the rights to send $MIP(MINOR\ SYNC\ POINT)$ and $MAP(MAJOR\ SYNC\ POINT)$ are transferred simultaneously from a protocol machine to the other machine by sending a token named *ma-mi* token instead of using two tokens *ma* and *mi*. For the extracted protocol $\Pi_{ses} = (PM_{ses_A}, PM_{ses_B})$, PM_{ses_A} and PM_{ses_B} are the same protocol machines except their initial states, i.e. PM_{ses_A} owns *ma-mi* token while PM_{ses_B} does not at the initial states. The size of the states of finite control and the number of registers of the protocol machine are 10 and 2 respectively. And the number of message types used in the protocol is 10.

5.2 Verification Result

For the protocol Π_{ses}, the set of global states expected to be reachable has been divided into 60 subsets by considering the possible combinations of the states of finite control parts of two protocol machines. We have described a logical formula based on these subsets of global states. The numbers of AF1 through AF4 type atoms in the described formula are 180, 60 46, and 297 respectively.

The properties on sequences of integers used for verification were provided in terms of 10 conditional rewrite rules and 7 conditional inequalities.

In the process of describing a formula, a human verifier often misses some reachable global state and describes an incorrect formula, i.e. a described formula is not an invariant in Π_{ses}. In such a case, the verification system detects a global state which does not satisfy the described formula and reports relevant information about the global state. A human verifier revised the formula using the information reported by the verification system.

The described formula was verified to be an invariant and the protocol was verified to be safe by the verification system on a UNIX workstation (Solbourne Series 5/600, 2CPU 48MB). The CPU time and memory storage used in the execution are 12.0 seconds and 816 KBytes respectively. The input formula was expanded to a disjunctive normal form consisting of 170 conjunctive terms. The number of considered state transitions was 428, and the number of AF3 and AF4 type atoms checked to hold in some global states were 222 and 1600 respectively.

6 Discussion

It seems that in a verification procedure via invariant for extended communicating finite-state machines, how to cope with integral registers dominates its verification power and efficiency. In this paper, by restricting the expressions appearing on both sides of inequalities to the form of "$v + C$", the problem whether a given inequality is implied by a given set of inequalities can be decided by an efficient procedure. In most of practical protocols, the operations on integral registers in the definition of a state transition function of a protocol machine are limited to simple types, e.g. "store some value", "add a constant number to the current value", or "clear to 0", and the restriction on the form of inequalities does not affect the verification power on such protocols. If more general operations on integral registers e.g. "summation of register values" are used in a protocol, then a more general procedure, e.g. the decision procedure for Presburger formula which is known to be intractable in general, may be required to deal with such a protocol.

In this paper, we put a restriction on regular expression. This greatly simplifies the procedure for deciding whether a given regular set includes another regular set. We are extending the verification system to allow the following interleaving operator " $\|$ " on regular expressions without loss of simplicity. For regular expressions r_1 and r_2,
$$L(r_1 \parallel r_2) = \{w_1 x_1 w_2 x_2 ... w_k x_k \mid w_1 w_2 ... w_k \in L(r_1) \text{ and } x_1 x_2 ... x_k \in L(r_2)\}.$$

As a practical protocol such as OSI session protocol provides many kinds of services, the definitions of protocols tend to be enormous and any verification method suffers from state space explosion. To facilitate the design and analysis of such a protocol, the authors have proposed a method for composing a safe protocol from a safe protocol defining a priority service and that defining an ordinary service[11]. Furthermore, several composition techniques have been proposed within the framework of CFSM[12]$^-$[14]. It is desirable to fit these techniques to the protocol model discussed in this paper. Currently, we are conducting an experiment to show the safety property of OSI session protocol using these techniques.

References

1. Brand D., and Zafiropulo P.: "On Communicating Finite-State Machines", Journal of ACM, vol.30, pp.323-342, 1983-04.
2. Kakuda Y., Wakahara Y., and Norigoe M.: "A New Algorithm for Fast Protocol Validation", Proc. of Compsac-86, pp.228-236, 1986.
3. Yuang M.C., and Kershebaum A.: "Parallel Protocol Verification: The Two-Phase Algorithm", Proc. 9th Intern. Symp. on PSTV, pp.339-353, 1989.
4. ISO: "Information Processing Systems-Open Systems Interconnection-Estelle: A Formal Description Technique Based on an Extended State Transition Model", ISO/DIS 9074, 1987.
5. CCITT: "Specification and Description Language(SDL)", Recommendation Z100, 1989.
6. Gordon M.J.C.: "A Proof Generating System for Higher-Order Logic" in "VLSI Specification, Verification and Synthesis", Kluwer Academic Publishers, pp.73-128, 1987-01.
7. Sarikaya B., Bochmann G.V., and Koukoulidis V.: "Method of Analysing Extended Finite-State Machine Specifications", Computer Communications, vol.13, no.2, pp.83-92, 1990-03.
8. Finkel A.: "A New Class of Analyzable CFSMs with Unbounded FIFO Channels", Proc. 8th Intern. Symp. on PSTV, pp.283-294, 1988.
9. Huet G., and Oppen D.:"Equations and Rewrite Rules A Survey" in "Formal Language: Perspectives and Open Problems", R. Book eds., Academic Press, pp.349-405, 1980.
10. ISO: "Basic Connection Oriented Session Protocol Specification", ISO 8327.
11. Higuchi M., Seki H., and Kasami T.: "A Method of Composing Communication Protocols with Priority Service", to appear in IEICE Trans. Commun., 1992-10.
12. Choi T.Y., and Miller R.E.: "A Decomposition Method for the Analysis and Design of Finite State Protocols", Proc. of 8th ACM/IEEE Data Comm. Symp., pp.167-176, 1983.
13. Lin H.: "Constructing Protocols with Alternative Functions", IEEE Trans. Comput., vol.40, pp.376-386, 1991-04.
14. Chow C., Gouda M.G., and Lam S.S.: "A Discipline for Constructing Multiphase Communication Protocols", ACM Trans. on Computer Systems, vol.3, pp.315-343, 1985-11.

394

(a) a conjunctive formula

$$P_i = \langle\ \{STA713\}, \{STA713\}\ \rangle \quad \textbf{(AF1)}$$
$$\wedge\ \langle\quad \varepsilon,\ \mathrm{MIP}^+\ \rangle \quad\qquad \textbf{(AF2)}$$
$$\wedge\ step1(AB[1]) \quad\qquad \textbf{(AF3)}$$
$$\wedge\ Vm(A) = last(AB[1]) + 1\ \textbf{(AF4)}$$
$$\wedge\ Vm(B) = head(AB[1])$$
$$\wedge\ Va(A) = Va(B)$$
$$\wedge\ Vm(A) \geq Va(A)$$
$$\wedge\ Vm(B) \geq Va(B)$$

(b) term rewriting system

definition of δ_A:

event: $-\langle \mathrm{MIP}, Vm(A)\rangle$

$$\langle STA713 \Rightarrow STA713\rangle$$
$$Vm'(A) \Rightarrow Vm(A) + 1 \qquad (1)$$
$$Va'(A) \Rightarrow Va(A) \qquad (2)$$

$$\vdots$$

properties of defined predicates:

$$last(seq \cdot \langle type, n\rangle) \Rightarrow n \qquad (3)$$

$|seq| \geq 1:$

$$head(seq \cdot \langle type, n\rangle) \Rightarrow head(seq)\ (4)$$

$|seq| \geq 1, step1(seq), t = last(seq) + 1:$

$$step1(seq \cdot \langle type, t\rangle) \Rightarrow true \qquad (5)$$

$$\vdots$$

added rules by evaluating
     the conditions of conditional rewrite rules:

$$step1(AB[1] \cdot \langle type, Vm(A)\rangle) \Rightarrow true \qquad (5')$$

inductive hypotheses:

$$step1(AB[1]) \Rightarrow true \qquad (6)$$

$$\vdots$$

relation between message sequences:

$$AB[1]' \Rightarrow AB[1] \cdot \langle \mathrm{MIP}, Vm(A)\rangle\ (7)$$

Figure 1-A. A formula and a process of verification of $EX1$
(All terms with primes denote the values after transition.)

(c) assumed inequalities

inductive hypothesis
$$Vm(A) = last(AB[1]) + 1$$
$$Vm(B) = head(AB[1])$$
$$Va(A) = Va(B)$$
$$Vm(A) \geq Va(A)$$
$$Vm(B) \geq Va(B)$$

properties of defined functions

$$\vdots$$

(d) a process of rewriting a predicate

$$step1(AB[1]')$$
$$\rightarrow step1(AB[1] \cdot \langle MIP, Vm(A) \rangle) \text{ by (7)}$$
$$\rightarrow true \qquad\qquad\qquad\qquad \text{by (5')}$$

(e) a process of rewriting an inequality

$$Vm'(A) \geq Va'(A)$$
$$\overset{*}{\rightarrow} Vm(A) + 1 \geq Va(A) \qquad\qquad \text{by (1),(2)}$$

(f) the transitive closure

$$\underline{Vm(A) + 1} \quad \geq \quad Vm(A) \quad \geq \quad \underline{Va(A)}$$

Figure 1-B. A formula and a process of verification of $EX1$
(All terms with primes denote the values after transition.)

Efficient ω-Regular Language Containment

Ramin Hojati (UC Berkeley)[1]
Herve Touati (DEC PRL)
Robert P. Kurshan (AT&T Bell Laboratories)
Robert K. Brayton (UC Berkeley)

Abstract

One method for proving properties about a design is by using L-automata [Kur90]. The main computation involves building the product machine of the system and specification, and then checking for cycles not contained in any of the cycle sets (these are sets of states specified by the user). In [Tou91] two methods were introduced for performing the above task; one involves computing the transitive closure of the product machine, and the other is an application of a method due to Emerson-Lei ([Eme86]). We have implemented both methods and extended them. We introduce a few general-purpose operators on graphs and use them to construct efficient algorithms for the above task. Fast special checks are applied to find bad cycles early on. Initial experimental results are encouraging and are presented here.

1 Introduction

Implementation verification involves checking whether two different representations of a system are equivalent. An example is checking whether a logic implementation faithfully implements a register-transfer language description. *Design verification* is the process of verifying whether a system has a set of desired properties. An example is checking that a communication protocol does not fall in a deadlock state. Presently, design verification is done by extensive simulation.

Design verification is the more challenging and important problem. Two general approaches using formal verification exist. The first employs general theorem-proving techniques to prove a result about some aspect of the design. Verification based on *Boyer-Moore theorem prover* or *HOL verification system* are examples. The second approach uses specialized logics or automata on infinite strings (*w-automata*) to express properties about a set of interacting finite state machines which model the design. Examples are *Computation Tree Logic* ([Cla86]), process calculi ([Bou89]) and *L-automata* ([Kur90]). This work is concerned with the use of L-automata in formal design verification.

1.1 The L-automata Environment

Specification of both systems and properties in this environment is done by the use of ω-automata. [Ch74] provides an introduction to the subject. Here, we briefly cover a few relevant extensions made to the basic theory. For a more detailed explanation of these, see [Kur90]. The system in this environment is modeled by a set of L-processes, which are similar to Moore machines. An *L-process* consists of 6 components.

1) States. The set of states of the L-process.
2) Transition matrix. Specifies the state transitions of the machine. The entries of this matrix are boolean equations, specifying the conditions under which a transition is taken.
3) Initial states. The set of initial states of the machine.

1. During this work, the first author was supported by an SRC grant, under contract number 91-DC-008.

4) Output function. A function of states which specifies a set of outputs for each state. At a given state, each machine chooses one of its outputs non-deterministically. Since the systems are modeled as closed systems, outputs and inputs are the same; they are collectively called *selections*.

5) *Recur edges*. A set of edges in the machine with the interpretation that if the machine follows a recur edge infinitely often, then the resulting sequence is rejected.

6) *Cycle sets*. A set of sets of states with the interpretation that a sequence of states is rejected if the set of states traversed infinitely often is contained in one of the cycle sets.

A string is accepted if one of its runs is not rejected, where a *run* of a string is a path in an L-process which results in that string. The model of concurrent computing used in this environment is know as the *selection/resolution model*, and consists of two basic steps which are repeated indefinitely. During *selection*, all machines simultaneously and non-deterministically choose one of the outputs possible for their respective states. During *resolution*, each machine chooses a new state based on both its current states and the *global selection*, i.e the set of outputs produced by all machines during the previous selection step.

L-automata, which are used for specifying properties or *tasks*, are similar to L-processes with two differences; first L-automata have no outputs, second is the way recur edges and cycle sets are interpreted. In the case of L-automata, a string is accepted either if for one of its runs some recur edge is traversed infinitely often or the infinite portion of the string is contained in some cycle set. Note that this is complementary to the acceptance condition of L-processes.

Verification now consists of modeling a system and its environment as a closed system of L-processes. Non-determinism is used heavily to express concisely all possible behaviors. A property is then represented using an L-automata, which takes inputs from the selections of the L-processes. A complex property is usually broken down into several smaller properties, each one represented by a *deterministic L-automaton*, i.e. an L-automaton which has deterministic transitions but may have multiple initial states. In our environment, all L-automata are deterministic. Verifying whether a system has a property is then reduced to checking whether the language accepted by the system is contained in the language of the L-automata of the property ([Kur90]). The language of the system is the language accepted by the automaton obtained as the product of all of the L-processes with outputs ignored. This acceptance check is sometimes referred to as an ω-regular language containment check.

1.2 Product Machines

At two points in the verification process, we need to form product machines; first, to represent the system of L-processes by their tensor product. Second, to verify that a system has a property, we form the product machine of the L-processes and the L-automaton, and verify that all cycles of this product machine either contain a recur edge or are completely contained in some cycle set. The two products can be performed in one step.

A product machine is formed by taking the tensor product of the transition matrices, taking the Cartesian product of the initial states, and taking the union of the cycle sets and recur edges. Note that the last two unions are in terms of the product machines, i.e. a set of states of a product machine is a cycle set if and only if the set restricted to some component is a cycle set for that component. The case of recur edges is similar.

1.3 Fixpoint Computations

Let Q be a k-ary predicate over $D_1,..., D_k$, where all D_i's are finite. Let $F(X)$ be a k-ary predicate transformer, i.e. a unary function whose first argument is a k-ary predicate and which returns a k-ary predicate. Assume F is **monotone decreasing** (or **monotone increasing**), i.e. $(\forall Q (F(Q) \subseteq Q)) ((\forall Q (Q \subseteq F(Q))))$. A *fixpoint* of F is a predicate Q such that $F(Q) = Q$.

Definition Let F be a k-ary predicate transformer. Define $F^i(X)$ by $F^i(X) = (F(F(...F(X))))$, where F is applied i times to X.

Definition Let F be a k-ary predicate transformer, which is monotone increasing. Define the **greatest fixpoint of F given Q**, denoted by $\mu(X, Q) . FX$, where Q is an k-ary monotone increasing predicate over $D_1,..., D_k$ by the set $F^i(Q)$ such that $F(F^i(Q)) = F^i(Q)$. Similarly, define the **least fixpoint** of a monotone decreasing k-ary predicate transformer F given Q, $v(X, Q) . FX$ by the set $F^i(Q)$ such that $F(F^i(Q)) = F^i(Q)$.

Example Let $T(x, y)$ be the transition function for an unlabeled graph. Let $A(x)$ denote the set of initial states. The fixpoint computation $R^*(A, x) = \mu(X, A) . (X(y) \vee \exists x (X(x) \wedge T(x, y)))$ computes the set of all the states reachable from A.

The computation $R^*(A, y) = \mu(X, A) . (A(y) \vee \exists x (X(x) \wedge T(x, y)))$ is an alternate way to compute the set of reachable states. Note that the two methods compute the same set. However, they perform it differently. Similarly, the fixpoint computation $R^*(x, A) = \mu(X, A) . (X(x) \vee \exists y (X(y) \wedge T(x, y)))$ computes the set of states which can ultimately reach A.

1.4 Our Contribution

The software COSPAN, described in [Har90] performs the language containment check by explicitly building the product machine and then examining the strongly connected components of an altered product machine, where the recur edges removed. If each strongly connected component of this altered machine is contained in a cycle set of the product machine, the check passes. In the case of failure, an error tracing mechanism interacts with the user to help locate the source of error.

[Tou91] presented a method based on Binary Decision Diagrams (BDDs) where explicit enumeration of the states of the product machine is not required. Two algorithms using BDDs were suggested in [Tou91]; one involving a transitive closure computation and one based on an application of the Emerson-Lei method introduced in [Eme86]. After implementing the transitive closure algorithm and noticing that this computation is usually very expensive, we proposed several algorithms based on ideas borrowed from the Emerson-Lei method. Checks for finding simple errors early on were also added. All of our algorithms have been implemented and are compared to each other on a limited set of examples.

The organization of the paper is as follows. Section 2 describes the algorithms for language containment check. Section 3 gives the experimental results. Section 4 defines complexity classes for BDD's. Section 5 is the conclusion. Due to lack of space, most proofs have been omitted.

2 Language Containment Check

In this section, we study several algorithms for checking language containment. In what follows, $P_1,..., P_n$ are a set of L-processes, where $P_i = (Q_i, T_i, I_i, O_i, R_i, C_i)$, and $A = (Q_A, T_A, I_A, O_A, R_A, C_A)$ is an L-automaton, defining a property of the system. Let $P = (Q, T, I, R, C)$ be the product machine $P = P_1 \times ... \times P_n \times A$, where the outputs are ignored. For all the algorithms which follow, we assume that all L-processes, L-automata, and product machines are represented by BDD's. Let γ_j for $j = 1, ..., n$ be the set of cycle sets of P. The language containment check is as follows. All of the algorithms we present, follow the same basic methodology.

Language Containment Algorithm

1) Let $P = P_1 \times ... \times P_n \times A$.

2) **Let Q be the underlying graph of reachable states of P with the recur edges removed.**

3) **If all cycles (or equivalently cyclic strongly connected components) of Q are contained in some cycle set, then the check has passed. Otherwise, it has failed.**

Definition A *bad cycle* is a cycle of the product machine $P = P_1 \times ... \times P_n \times A$, not contained in any of the cycle sets and not containing any recur edge. Equivalently, let Q be P, with recur edges removed from its transition function. Then, a bad cycle in P is a cycle in Q, not contained in any of the cycle sets.

The first algorithm we study involves computing the transitive closure of P. This algorithm is rather expensive because computing the transitive closure of a graph is generally an expensive operation. Iterated squaring, as a possible candidate to speed up the transitive closure operation, is described. Then, we describe three algorithms based on ideas borrowed from [Eme86] and [Tou91]. Methods for finding simple bad cycles early are presented afterwards, which complete all the details needed to present the final algorithm.

2.1 Algorithm Based on Transitive Closure

The first BDD based algorithm for this task appeared in [Tou91]. The algorithm uses transitive closure to represent strongly connected components. Let G be an unlabeled graph, represented by its transition function $T(x, y)$. Let $C(x, y)$ denote the transitive closure of G.

Definition Let G be as above. Define S such that $S(x, y) = 1$ iff x and y are in the same cyclic strongly connected component of G.

Lemma Let G, S, and C be as defined above. Then, $S(x, y) = C(x, y) \wedge C(y, x)$.

Definition Let $P = P_1 \times ... \times P_n \times A$. Define by $B(x)$ the set of all states of P, which are involved in some bad cycle.

The algorithm which follows, uses the transitive closure of Q. For each cycle set, the SCC's of Q, not contained in that cycle set are determined. If the intersection of all such sets is empty, the check passes. Otherwise it fails.

Language Containment Check Using Transitive Closure

1) **Build the product of the component machines and the task. Let $T(x, i, y, r)$ represent the transition function of the product machine.**

2) **Remove the selection variables from the transition function,** $T(x, y, r) = \exists i\, T(x, i, y, r)$.

3) **Compute the set of reachable states,** $R^*(I, y) = \mu(X, I) . (X(y) \vee \exists x (X(x) \wedge T(x, y, r)))$.

4) **Remove the unreachable states and the recur edges from the transition function.**

$$T(x, y, r) = T(x, y, r) \wedge R^*(x) \wedge R^*(y)$$

$$T(x, y) = T(x, y, 0)$$

5) **Compute the transitive closure of the transition function of the product**

machine.

$$C(x, y) = \mu(X, T).(X(x,y) \vee \exists z (X(x,z) \wedge T(z,y)))$$

6) Let γ_j denote the j-th cycle set of the product machine. Then,

$$\hat{B}(x) = \bigcap_j \exists y\, (\overline{\gamma_j(y)} \wedge C(x,y) \wedge C(y,x))$$

7) In the case of failure ($\hat{B} \neq \varnothing$), call the debugger.

Theorem Let $\hat{B}(x)$ be the set calculated by the above algorithm. Then, $\hat{B}(x) = B(x)$.

Building the transitive closure of the product machine has proved to be expensive. In the next section, we discuss algorithms which can speed up this operation.

2.2 Iterated Squaring

In this section, we introduce a technique which can speed up some fixpoint computations on some graphs. Specifically this technique is useful on graphs with long chains of states, such as counters. Consider a fixpoint computation such as computing the set of reachable states of a graph. The usual method of computing this set can take $o(n)$ iterations, where n is the level of the underlying graph. Such computations will be denoted as *linear computations*, where the worst case complexity is $o(n)$, n being the number of vertices of the graph. A method which reduces the time for such computations from $o(n)$ to $O(\log n)$ is *iterated squaring*. [Bur90] introduced one iterated squaring technique for symbolic verification of μ-calculus. We describe iterated squaring techniques for two problems, namely computing reachable states and transitive closure of a graph G. For the first problem, we introduce one iterated squaring method, whereas for the second, we introduce two iterated squaring techniques which perform differently in practice.

Definition Let $T(x,y)$ denote the transition relation of a graph G. Let $T_k(x,y)$ denote the transition relation of a graph where there is an edge between x and y iff there is a path of length exactly k between x and y. Let $C(x,y)$ denote the transitive closure of G. Let $C_k(x,y)$ be the transition relation of a graph, where there is an edge between x and y iff there is a path of length k or less between x and y. Note that $C_n(x,y) = C(x,y)$, where n is the diameter of G.

2.2.1 Computing Reachable States

Recall that the linear computation of reachable states is accomplished by the fixpoint calculation., $R^*(A,y) = \mu(X,A).(X(y) \vee \exists x(X(x) \wedge T(x,y)))$. An iterated squaring form of the above computation is $R^*(A,y) = \mu(X,A).(X(y) \vee \exists x(X(x) \wedge T_{2^{k-1}}(x,y)))$. In order to calculate $T_{2^k}(x,y)$, one has to perform an expensive computation where three sets of variables (x, y, and z) are active at the same time, namely, $T_{2^k}(x,y) = \exists z(T_{2^{k-1}}(x,z) \wedge T_{2^{k-1}}(z,y))$. The above computation is usually time consuming, since the BDD corresponding to $T_{2^{k-1}}(x,y)$ or intermediate BDD's needed to build $T_{2^{k-1}}(x,y)$ can become large (as an aside, note that the number of edges represented by $T_{2^{k-1}}(x,y)$ should be of the same order as those represented by $T(x,y)$). As a rule, computations of the form $\exists z(A(x,z)B(z,y))$, which involve three sets of active variables take much longer than image computations, which involve two sets of active variables.

Our experiments indicate that the use of iterated squaring, as presented above, for computing the reachable states is not recommended. The experimental results were obtained running the dining philosopher examples. With only 6 philosophers, computing the reachable states using iterated squaring takes 60 seconds, where it only takes 1 second using linear computations. Hence, we did not perform further experiments using iterated squaring for computing reached states.

2.2.2 Computing Transitive Closure

Recall the linear computation for transitive closure of a graph G, i.e. $C(x, y) = \mu(X, T) \cdot (X(x, y) \vee \exists z (X(x, z) \wedge T(z, y)))$. We discuss two general methods of using the iterated squaring technique for this computation. Both of these methods compute $C_{2^k}(x, y)$ successively until a fixpoint is reached.

Iterated Squaring by Shifting We calculate $C_{2^k}(x, y)$ by calculating $C_{2^{k-1}}(x, y)$, then shifting it by $T_{2^{k-1}}(x, y)$ and OR-ing it with $C_{2^{k-1}}(x, y)$ (recall from last section how $T_{2^{k-1}}(x, y)$ is computed). The following describes the fixpoint computation

$$C(x, y) = \mu(X, T) \cdot (X(x, y) \vee \exists z (X(x, z) \wedge T_{2^{k-1}}(z, y))).$$

Note that by the above computation every path is added in only once. For example, assume $C_4(x, y)$ and $T_4(x, y)$ have been computed. Let a computation of the form $\exists x (A \wedge B)$ be called a *path extension*. Then, the above path extension adds to C_4 only paths of length 5-8, i.e. an edge is added between x and y iff there is a path of length 5-8 between x and y in the original graph. For example, let *(x1, x2, x3, x4, x5, x6, x7)* be a path of length 6 in the original graph. Then, there is an edge *(x1, x3)* in $C_4(x, y)$, and an edge *(x3, x7)* in $T_4(x, y)$. So *(x1, x7)* is included in $\exists z (C_4(x, z) \wedge T_4(z, y))$. However, there are no edges for *(x1, x3)* and *(x3, x7)* in this path extension. Note that the edge *(x1, x7)* is added only once. We will see that in iterated squaring by folding such an edge can be added many times.

The number of iterations of this method is $\log n$, where n is the diameter of the graph. However, we need to perform two sets of path extensions, each with three sets of active variables at every iteration. On the other hand, we only need to save two functions at every step, namely the current $T_{2^k}(x, y)$ and $C_{2^k}(x, y)$. Based on our experiments, iterated squaring by shifting compared to linear computations, consumes more memory but has about the same running-time.

Iterated Squaring by Folding To calculate $C_{2^k}(x, y)$, we use the fixpoint computation, $C(x, y) = \mu(X, T) \cdot (T(x, y) \vee \exists z (X(x, z) \wedge X(z, y)))$. As an example, assume $C_4(x, y)$ has been calculated. After the above path extension, we get $C_{2-8}(x, y)$, where there is an edge between x and y iff there is a path of length 2-8 between them. To get $C_8(x, y)$, we add $T(x, y)$ to the result. Note that by this computation, an edge for a path may be added many times. For instance, the path *(x1, x2, x3, x4, x5, x6, x7)* creates the edge *(x1, x7)* three times: first, by *(x1, x3)* and *(x3, x7)*; second, by *(x1, x4)* and *(x4, x7)*; and third, by *(x1, x5)* and *(x5, x7)*.

Again, the number of iterations is $\log n$. This computation was faster than the linear computation in the experiments we performed. A main reason is that there is only one path extension with three sets of active variables. It appears that this method is more space consuming compared to linear computations. In the experimental section, we describe the results of our experiments with the transitive closure algorithm for doing language containment, where the transitive closure check was done using iterated squaring. In the next few sections, we describe algorithms which don't need the transitive closure computation.

2.3 The Emerson-Lei Method and Modifications

In this section, we introduce four algorithms for the language containment check. The main idea for these algorithms is a computation introduced in [Eme86] for propositional μ-calculus, and adapted to check language containment by [Tou91]. We first introduce some operators on graphs, which are needed later.

Historical Remark The work in [Eme86] described a method for translating a subset of CTL* ([Cla86]) formulas into a subset of propositional μ-calculus, namely L_{μ_2}, for which polynomial-time algorithms are available. The important point about the model checking algorithm for L_{μ_2} is that it does not involve any transitive closure computation. The works described in [Eme87] and [Cla90] described methods to perform the language containment check for ω-automata using this polynomial subset of CTL*. [Tou91] formulated the language containment check for L-automata in L_{μ_2}. This is the first algorithm we describe. Our contribution was to enhance this algorithm. We view the Emerson-Lei method for performing language containment check as an operator trimming the state space. We introduce several new operators. Moreover, we describe a method for early failure detection.

2.3.1 Some Graph Operators

In what follows, let G be a graph, $V(x)$ the set of its vertices, $A(x) \subseteq V(x)$ a subset of its vertices, and $T(x, y)$ its transition function.

Definition Let G be a graph. A *cyclic strongly connected component (CSCC)* of G is a SCC of G which contains at least one cycle. Hence, all SCC's of G are CSCC's except for single node SCC's which don't have a self-loop, which are called *acyclic strongly connected components (ASCC's)*.

Definition Let $S_1(A, y) = \exists x (A(x) \wedge T(x, y))$ and $S_1(x, A) = \exists y (A(y) \wedge T(x, y))$. Thus, $S_1(A, y)$ are the successors of $A(x)$ and $S_1(x, A)$ are the predecessors of $A(x)$.

Definition Let $R_1(A, y) = A(y) \vee S_1(A, y)$, $R_1(x, A) = A(x) \vee S_1(x, A)$, $R^*(A, y) = \mu(X, A) . (R_1(X, y))$, $R^*(x, A) = \mu(X, A) . (R_1(x, X))$. Note that the first two are "one-step" operators, while the last two compute the least fixed-point containing A. One should read $R^*(A, y)$ as the set of points reachable from A. Similarly $R^*(x, A)$ is the set of vertices that can reach A. $R_1(A, y)$ and $R_1(x, A)$ are the one-step versions of these respectively.

Definition We define two "stable set" operators, $S^*(A, y) = \nu(X, A) . (S_1(X, y))$ and $S^*(x, A) = \nu(X, A) . (S_1(x, X))$. Note these are computing the greatest fixed point contained in A. One can think of the first as calculating the *backward stable set* contained in A (i.e. the set of all vertices which are reached by some vertex involved in some cycle), and the latter as the *forward stable set* of A (i.e. the set of all vertices which can reach some vertex involved in some cycle).

Lemma If A contains a cycle γ, then $S^*(A, y)$ and $S^*(x, A)$ contain γ.

Definition We define one more one-step operator, the *trim operator*.

$$Z_1(c, A) = \begin{cases} \bar{c} \wedge A & \text{if } (A \wedge R_1(c, y) \subseteq c) \text{ or } (A \wedge R_1(x, c) \subseteq c) \\ A & \text{otherwise} \end{cases}$$

where c and A are sets of states. This operator will be used on each cycle set to eliminate cycle sets γ_j that either have no exit from γ_j (*sink cycle sets*) or no incoming edges (*source cycle sets*). Recursive application of this operator, the *recursive trim* operator, defined by $Z^*(x,A) = v(Y,A).Z_1(\gamma_1, Z_1(\gamma_2, ...Z_1(\gamma_n, Y)...))$, where A is some initial set of state, is also useful. The usefulness of recursive trim is because γ_j may be eliminated by Z^* but not by $Z_1(\gamma_j, A)$ as the example below shows.

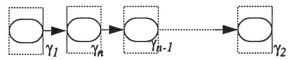

Fig. 1. Each bubble represents a set of states. Each highlighted rectangle represents a set of states which is passed to the recursive trim operator.

In the order tried $\gamma_n, \gamma_{n-1}, ..., \gamma_1$, no eliminations occur until γ_2, where γ_2 and γ_1 are eliminated. Repeated application eliminates all γ_j's. Obviously the order in which the γ_j's are tried is important for efficiency. Also, one can see that the elimination of γ_j's depends on the active set A. As A gets smaller, it becomes more likely that γ_j is a source or sink cycle set.

Remark There are several remarks about the recursive trim operator.

1) In general, the recursive trim operator would not return the same set, if the trim operator deleted only the source cycle sets or only the sink cycle sets.

2) There are situations in which deleting only sinks or sources suffice. For example, consider the following figure. If trim only deleted sources or sinks, all vertices are eliminated. However, applying both tests in trim can sometimes speed up the test. Assume, we are given the sets in the order $(\gamma_1, ..., \gamma_n)$. If trim deleted sinks, the computation takes $O(n^2)$ time, whereas if trim deleted both sinks and sources, the computation would take $O(2n)$. Hence, applying both tests in trim can sometimes speed up the test.

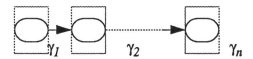

Fig. 2. Each bubble represents a set of states. Each highlighted rectangle represents a set of states which is passed to the recursive trim operator.

3) In our implementation, before calling recursive trim, we sort the cycle sets by the number of states they contain. We start processing the cycle sets from big to small, with the hope that bigger cycle sets will have a better chance of being a source or a sink.

2.3.2 The EL Algorithm

In this section, we will describe the adaptation of the Emerson-Lei method for the language containment check as it first appeared in [Tou91]. We will denote this algorithm by *EL*. This algorithm calculates the set NC^+ as defined below.

Definition Let NC^+ (*NC* stands for not contained) denote the set of states x such that there is a path from x to a bad cycle.

Note that the language containment check passes iff $NC^+ = \varnothing$. All the algorithms presented in this section work on Q, the product of the system and the property with the recur edges removed. The EL method calculates the set $E(x)$ by the fixpoint computation $E(x) = v(X, V) \cdot (\prod_j R_1(x, R^*(x, \bar{\gamma}_j \wedge X)))$ (the language containment check passes iff $E(x) = \varnothing$). Note that $R^*(x, \bar{\gamma}_j \wedge E)$ is the set of all vertices which start a path in E whose end-point is in $\bar{\gamma}_j \wedge E$. We will show that $E(x) = NC^+(x)$. Note that this demonstrates the correctness of the algorithm.

Definition Let x be a vertex of G. Define $SCC(x)$ to be the SCC which contains x. Similarly, if $x \in S$, where S is some CSCC of G, let $CSCC(x) = S$.

Definition Define by SC_G the graph where every SCC of G is replaced by a node. Note that SC_G is acyclic.

Definition Let $x \in V$. Let H be the set of vertices y reachable from x, such that $y \in S$, where S is some ASCC of G. Define by $AS_G(x)$ the graph where G is restricted to H. Again note that $AS_G(x)$ is acyclic.

Lemma Let $H = R_1(x, R^*(x, \bar{\gamma}_j \wedge V))$ for some graph G with vertices V, and some $c \subseteq V$. If $x \in H$, then $SCC(x) \subseteq H$.

Theorem $E(x) = NC^+(x)$.

2.3.3 The EL1 Algorithm

In this section, we describe our first modification of EL. The EL1 method calculates the set $E_1(x)$ by the fixpoint computation

$$E_1(x) = v(X, V) \cdot (R_1(x, \prod_j R^*(x, \bar{\gamma}_j \wedge X))).$$

Theorem $E_1(x) = NC^+(x)$.

2.3.4 The EL2 Algorithm

Although one can present EL2 as a nested fixpoint computation, we choose to present the algorithm in a more sequential manner for two reasons. The first reason is that we would like to think of the operators as deleting irrelevant portions of a graph. Hence, they work like hyper-planes, constraining our current set of possible bad states. The sequential presentation makes this point more clear. The second reason is that such nested computations involve rather long formulas, and may be hard to read (for example, our final algorithm would involve four nested computations).

Definition Define the *forward bad-path operator* by $F(x) = \prod_j R^*(x, \bar{\gamma}_j \wedge A)$, where A is the current active set. Note that if a state can reach a bad cycle, it is not deleted by this operator. So, sink cycle sets are deleted by this operator. Similarly, define the *backward bad-path operator* by $B(x) = \prod_j R^*(\bar{\gamma}_j \wedge V, y)$. Note, if a state is reached by a bad cycle, it is not deleted by this operator. So, source cycle sets are deleted by this operator.

EL2 computes the set $E_2(x)$ as follows.

1) Let $E_2(x) = R(x)$, i.e. the set of all reachable states.

2) **Repeat until convergence is achieved**

    2.1) **Apply forward bad-path operator,** $E_2(x) = \prod_j R^*(x, \overline{\gamma}_j \wedge E_2)$.

    2.2) **Apply forward stable operator,** $E_2(x) = S^*(x, E_2)$.

Theorem $E_2(x) = NC^+(x)$.

Proof Let $H = \overline{E_2 \cap NC^+}$. We will first show $H \subseteq NC^+$, i.e. $H = \emptyset$. Let S be a leaf of SC_H. We will show S is a leaf of SCC_{E_2}. If not, S can reach some vertices in NC^+. Hence, $S \subseteq NC^+$, which is in contradiction to the assumption that S is a subset of H. If S is a ASCC of E_2, then S is deleted by the forward stable operator. This is a contradiction to EL2 having converged. If S is some CSSC of E_2, then it is contained in some γ_j. Since S is a sink cycle set, S is deleted by the forward bad path operator. Again, this is in contradiction to EL2 having converged. We conclude that $H = \emptyset$.

Conversely, assume that $x \in NC^+(x)$. We need to show $x \in E_2(x)$. It suffices to show that if $NC^+(x) \subseteq Y$, then no vertices in Y is deleted by either operator. This is easy to see since every state in Y has a successor and hence is not deleted by the forward stable operator. Moreover, every state of Y can reach a bad cycle, and hence is not deleted by the forward bad-path operator (QED Theorem).

Definition Let NC^- denote the set of states x such that there is a path from a state y, involved in some bad cycle, to x.

Corollary If we replace the forward operators in EL2 with backward operators, EL2 computes NC^-.

2.4) Early Cycle Detection

In practice, it is expected that the algorithm will be applied frequently with properties which fail. Hence, we would like to have special checks to find easily detectable bad cycles early. Let $\Gamma = \bigcup_j \gamma_j$. We classify the cycles of G into three groups:

1) Cycles which lie entirely in $\overline{\Gamma}$, i.e. *cycles of the first kind*. Any cycle of the first kind is a bad cycle.

2) Cycle which intersect both Γ and $\overline{\Gamma}$, *cycle of the second kind*. All such cycles are bad.

3) Cycles which are completely contained in Γ, i.e. *general cycles or cycles of the third kind*. These cycles may be bad or good.

Definition Let $\Gamma = \bigcup_j \gamma_j$. Denote by $FC(x)$ (for first kind) the set of all state in $\overline{\Gamma}$, which can reach some cycle which lies entirely in $\overline{\Gamma}$, i.e. a cycle of the first kind. Let $CS_B(x)$ (for second kind) be the set of all states in $\overline{\Gamma}$, which are involved in some cycle of the second kind, whose length is less than B, where $B \geq 1$. Note that $CS_1(x) = FC(x)$. Similarly, let $CS(x) = \bigcup_n CS_n(x)$ be the set of all states in $\overline{\Gamma}$, which are involved in some cycle of the second kind.

Finding Cycles of the First Kind

1) Let $\Gamma = \bigcup_j \gamma_j$, where each γ_j is a cycle set.

2) Let $\hat{T}(x, y) = \overline{\Gamma(x)} \wedge T(x, y) \wedge \overline{\Gamma(y)}$, i.e. the transition function restricted to $\overline{\Gamma}$.

3) Let $F(x) = S^*(x, \overline{\Gamma})$.

Lemma Let $F(x)$ be the set returned by the above algorithm. Then, $F(x) = FC(x)$.

Remark In section 4, we pose a problem for which we don't have an efficient solution. The problem is finding the set of all states in a graph G which are in some CSCC. In other words, the set of all states which are involved in some cycle. Let this set be $C_G(x)$. If there are no cycles of the first kind, we have

$$CS(x) = \overline{\Gamma(x)} \wedge C_G(x).$$

We present the a method for finding cycles of the second kind after we introduce our final algorithm.

2.5 The Final Algorithm

The final algorithm first checks for cycles of the first kind, and then for short cycles of the second kind. If none is found, then it enters its main computation. First, recursive trim is called to reduce the state space as much as possible. Then, the main loop which consists of a forward and a backward pass is executed. The algorithm computes a set which is no larger than $NC^+(x)$.

Definition Let NC^{+-} denote the set of states x such that there are states y and z, involved in bad cycles, and x can reach y and z can reach x.

Final Algorithm

1) Check for cycles of the first kind. If found, call the debugger.
2) Check for cycles of the second kind. If found, call the debugger.
3) Let $F^*(x) = R(x)$, where $R(x)$ is the set of reachable states.
4)   Apply   recursive   trim   operator,
$$F^*(x) = Z^*(x, R) = \mathsf{v}(Y, R) . Z_1(\gamma_1, Z_1(\gamma_2, ... Z_1(\gamma_n, Y)...)).$$

5) Repeat until convergence

  2.1) Apply forward bad-path operator, $F^*(x) = \prod_j R^*(x, \overline{\gamma}_j \wedge F)$.

  2.2) Apply forward stable operator, $F^*(x) = S^*(x, F^*)$.

  2.1) Apply backward bad-path operator, $F^*(x) = \prod_j R^*(\overline{\gamma}_j \wedge F^*, y)$.

  2.2) Apply backward stable operator, $F^*(x) = S^*(F^*, y)$.

6) If $F^*(x) \neq \varnothing$, call the debugger.

Theorem Let $F^*(x)$ be the set returned by the above algorithm. Then, $F^*(x) = NC^{+-}(x)$.

Remark It is possible that after applying one of the operators in the loop of step 5 of the final algorithm, recursive trim operator can delete some vertices. For example, consider the situation illustrated by the following figure, where each bubble represents a SCC.

Fig. 3. Each bubble represents a
SCC. Each highlighted rectangle
represents a cycle set.

If recursive trim is applied to the above graph, no vertices would be deleted. However, if forward bad path operator is applied to this graph first, vertices in component 3 are removed. If we now apply recursive trim, all vertices are deleted. More experimentation is needed to justify whether recursive trim should be applied inside the loop of step 5.

2.6 Finding Cycles of The Second Kind

The algorithm for finding cycles of the second one returns the following set.

Definition Let CS^+ denote the set of states x such that there are states z and y in $CS(x)$, and there is a path from x to y and from z to x.

Finding Cycles of The Second Kind

1) **Check for cycles of the first kind. If none are found, go to step 2.**
2) **Apply step 4 of the final algorithm on G with the cycle set $\Gamma = \bigcup_j \gamma_j$.**

Remark If the above procedure is used to find cycles of the second kind, we can initialize F to $R \wedge \Gamma$. The reason is that since there are no cycles of the first or second kind, the states in $\bar{\Gamma}$ cannot be involved in any bad cycles.

3 Experimental Results

Up to now, we have performed experiments only on a limited set of examples. Four examples were based on the encyclopedia version of the dining philosophers problem, ranging from 16 to 40 philosophers. We checked for starvation, i.e. if a philosopher becomes hungry s/he is eventually fed. The number of reachable states for an n-philosopher example is about 2^n. Two examples were counters of size 100 and 500 states. In counters, we checked that the edge $(n,0)$ is taken infinitely often. The last example was part of an industrial design.

Seven different algorithms for language containment were compared: using iterated squaring by shifting in our first algorithm to compute transitive closure (iss), iterated squaring by folding in our first algorithm to compute transitive closure (isf), the original algorithm (org), and the algorithms described in section 2 EL, EL1, EL2, and final. The results show that final performs the best on our examples, except for counters where iterated squaring did very well. In general, iterated squaring by folding is faster than iterated squaring by shifting and linear computation, but is more space consuming. Iterated squaring by shifting first ran out of memory on 32 philosophers, where iterated squaring by folding ran out of memory at 48 philosophers. We also experimented with different properties on both the philosopher examples and the counters where the checks fail. On all these examples, the early failure detection algorithms found a bad cycle. Indeed, all bad cycles found were of the first kind. The following table summarizes our results.

	iss	isf	org	EL	EL1	EL2	final
phil16	118	55	114	9.8	6.8	6.7	3.5
phil24	535	290	442	25.9	20	20	9.9
phil32	Mem Out	670	1170	53	42	38	19
phil40	Mem Out	1625	2540	88	73	65	32
cnt100	1.4	1.6	9.7	2.9	2.2	2.2	2.2
cnt500	11.4	15.6	317	48	48	55	55
indus	8.1	7.2	8.5	3.0	4.4	3.5	.2 *

iss: iter sq by shifting in first alg
isf: iter sq by folding in first alg
org: first alg
EL: original Emerson-Lei
EL1: first modification
EL2: second modification
final: final alg

Time: reported in seconds

*: Check fails, and early cycle detection finds the error. Without early cycle detection, the algorithm takes 7.2 seconds.

Table 1

4 BDD Complexity Classes

As we have seen so far, developing efficient general purpose graph manipulation algorithms using BDD's has proven useful in solving our problems. To make the notion of efficiency more concrete when dealing with BDD's, we introduce the following definition. Possibly, this can serve as a guideline for designing efficient algorithms.

BDD Complexity Classes (BCC): Let finite domains $D_1, ..., D_n$ be given. Let ϕ be a formula describing a fixpoint computation involving predicates over the finite domains $D_1, ..., D_n$. Let the *alternation depth* of ϕ be as defined in [Eme86], which is roughly the number of alternations of μ and ν's. Then, the computation described by ϕ is in $BCC_{m, n}$ if the following holds:

1) The maximum arity of predicate variables in ϕ over which fixpoint computations are taken is less than or equal to m.
2) The alternation depth of ϕ is less than or equal to n.

Note that if there are no fixpoint computations in ϕ, then ϕ is in $BCC_{0, 0}$. For example, taking the intersection or union of two sets of vertices is in $BCC_{0, 0}$. Computing the set of reachable states is in $BCC_{1, 1}$; and computing the transitive closure of a graph is in $BCC_{2, 1}$. The EL algorithm of section 2.2.2. is in $BCC_{1, 2}$. Based on our experience, it appears that the algorithms in $BCC_{m, j}$ are more time consuming than algorithms in $BCC_{n, j}$, where $m \geq n$. Also, in general, algorithms in $BCC_{j, m}$ are more time consuming than algorithms in $BCC_{j, n}$, where $m \geq n$. We pose the following problem:

Cycle Problem: Find a $BCC_{1, 2}$ algorithm which finds the set of all vertices in a graph which are involved in some cycle.

Note that the above problem has an efficient (linear time) classical algorithm: find the SCC's and return all states except those in singleton SCC's with no self-loops. However, this algorithm is not efficient when BDD's are used. One application of an efficient solution to this problem is finding cycles of the second kind. Another application of this problem is in finding general cycles. Let $B(x)$ be the set returned by our final algorithm. Running the algorithm for the cycle problem would delete the vertices in $B(x)$ which can reach and are reached by bad cycles but are not themselves involved in any cycle. This can potentially decrease the size of $B(x)$.

5 Conclusion

In this paper, we have presented several ways of speeding up the ω-regular language containment check using BDDs. By introducing five operators which trim the current active space, we are able to obtain very good result on our set of examples. The operators are forward bad-path, backward bad-path, forward stable, backward stable and trim. Special checks are also applied to find easily detectable failures early. On all of our examples, when the check failed, the bad cycles were found with these special checks. It is not clear what fraction of failures in practice will be caught by the early failure detection algorithms. We also introduced iterated squaring by folding as a method to speed up the transitive closure computation, which is needed in the algorithm described in [Tou91] for checking language containment. Finally, an open problem, i.e. a $BCC_{1,2}$ algorithm to find the set of states involved in some cycle in a graph was posed.

References

[Bou91] G. Boudel, V. Roy, R. de Simone, D. Vergamini, *"Process Calculi, from Theory to Practice: Verification Tools"*, in Automatic Verification Methods for Finite State Systems, Joe Sifakis ed., LNCS 407, 1989.

[Bur90] J. R. Burch, E. M. Clarke, K. L. McMillan, D. L. Dill, L. J. Hwang, *"Symbolic Model Checking: 10^{20} states and Beyond"*. Logic in Computer Science, 1990.

[Ch74] Y. Choueka, *"Theories of Automata on ω-Tapes: A Simplified Approach"*, Journal of Computer and System Sciences 8, 117-141, 1974.

[Cla86] E. M. Clarke, E. A. Emerson, A. P. Sistla. *"Automatic Verification of Finite-State Concurrent Systems Using Temporal Logic Specifications"*, ACM Transactions on Programming Languages and Systems. 8(2):244-263, 1986.

[Eme86] E. A. Emerson, C. L. Lei. *"Efficient Model Checking in Fragments of the Prepositional Mu-Calculus"*, In Symp. on Logic in Computer Science. IEEE, June 1986.

[Eme87] E. A. Emerson, C. L. Lei, *"Modalities for Model Checking: Branching Time Logic Strikes Back"*, Science of Computer Programming 8, 275-306, Elsevier Science Publishers, 1987.

[Cla90] E. M. Clarke, I. A. Draghicescu, R. P. Kurshan, *"A Unified Approach for Showing Containment and Equivalence Between Various Types of ω-Automata"*. In Proceedings of Fifteenth Colloquium on Trees in Algebra and Programming, 1990.

[Har90] Z. Har'El, R. Kurshan. *"Software for Analytical Development of Communications Protocols"*, ATT technical journal, 1990.

[Kam91] T. Kam, R. Brayton. *"Multi-valued Decision Diagrams"*, Electronics Research Laboratory, University of California, Berkeley, Memorandum No. UCB/ERL, M90/125, 1990.

[Kur90] R. Kurshan. *"Analysis of Discrete Event Coordination"*, Lecture Notes in Computer Science, 1990.

[Tou90] H. Touati, H. Savoj, B. Lin, R. K. Brayton, A. S. Vincentelli, *"Implicit State Enumeration of Finite State Machines Using BDD's"*, International Conference on Computer-Aided Design, 1990.

[Tou91] H. Touati, R. Kurshan, R. Brayton. *"Testing Language Containment of ω-Automata Using BDDs"*, International Workshop on Formal Methods in VLSI Design, 1991.

Faster Model Checking for the Modal Mu-Calculus

Rance Cleaveland*   Marion Klein†   Bernhard Steffen†

Abstract

In this paper, we develop an algorithm for model checking that handles the full modal mu-calculus including *alternating* fixpoints. Our algorithm has a better worst-case complexity than the best known algorithm for this logic while performing just as well on certain sublogics as other specialized algorithms. Important for the efficiency is an alternative characterization of formulas in terms of equational systems, which enables the sharing and reuse of intermediate results.

1 Introduction

Much work in the field of automated verification has focused on finite-state transition systems (or automata) as models for system behavior [CES, CPS1, CPS2, Fe, MSGS, RRSV, RdS]. The modal mu-calculus [Ko] is a particularly useful logic for reasoning about such models; not only may a number of temporal logics for expressing system properties be translated into it [EL], but it may also be used to encode various behavioral equivalences and preorders [Ste, SI]. Thus, this logic supports algebraic as well as logic-based approaches to verification.

In this paper, we present an algorithm for determining when states in a finite-state transition system possess properties expressed in the modal mu-calculus. Our model-checking algorithm improves on the best existing methods for model checking in this logic [A, EL] while performing just as well on certain sublogics as specialized algorithms (cf. [CS1, CS2]). Important for the efficiency is an alternative characterization of formulas in terms of equational systems, which enables the sharing and reuse of intermediate results.

The remainder of the paper is organized as follows. In the next section we present the syntax and semantics of the mu-calculus, and in the section following we give an alternative, equation-based presentation of this logic. Section 4 presents our model-checking algorithm, while the subsequent section establishes its correctness and complexity. The paper closes with a detailed discussion of an example in Section 6 and some conclusions and directions for future work in Section 7.

2 Syntax and Semantics of the Mu-Calculus

This section first provides a brief overview of *labeled transition systems*, which are used as models for the mu-calculus. Then the syntax and semantics of the logic are developed.

2.1 Transition Systems

Definition 2.1 *A labeled transition system T is a triple $\langle S, Act, \rightarrow \rangle$, where S is a set of states, Act is a set of actions, and $\rightarrow \subseteq S \times Act \times S$ is the transition relation.*

Intuitively, a labeled transition system encodes the operational behavior of a system. The set S represents the set of states the system may enter, and Act contains the set of actions the system may perform. The relation $\rightarrow$ describes the actions available to states and the state transitions that

*Department of Computer Science, North Carolina State University, Raleigh, NC 27695-8206, USA – The author was supported by NSF Grant CCR-9014775.

†Lehrstuhl für Informatik II, RWTH-Aachen, Ahornstraße 55, W-5100 Aachen, GERMANY – Part of the work has been funded by DFG Grant Ste 537/2-1.

Formulas are interpreted with respect to a fixed labeled transition system $\langle S, Act, \rightarrow \rangle$, a valuation $\mathcal{V} : \mathcal{A} \rightarrow 2^S$, and an environment $e : Var \rightarrow 2^S$.

$$
\begin{aligned}
[A]e &= \mathcal{V}(A) \\
[X]e &= e(X) \\
[\neg \Phi]e &= S \setminus [\Phi]e \\
[\Phi_1 \wedge \Phi_2]e &= [\Phi_1]e \cap [\Phi_2]e \\
[[a]\Phi]e &= \{ s \mid \forall s'. \, s \xrightarrow{a} s' \Rightarrow s' \in [\Phi]e \} \\
[\nu X.\Phi]e &= \bigcup \{ S' \subseteq S \mid S' \subseteq [\Phi]e[X \mapsto S'] \}
\end{aligned}
$$

Figure 1: The Semantics of Formulas.

may result upon execution of the actions. In the remainder of the paper we use $s \xrightarrow{a} s'$ in lieu of $\langle s, a, s' \rangle \in \rightarrow$, and if $s \xrightarrow{a} s'$ then we say that s' is an a-derivative of s. Finally, we refer to a labeled transition system as *finite-state* when S and Act are finite.

2.2 Syntax and Semantics of Formulas

The syntax of the modal mu-calculus is parameterized with respect to a (countable) set Var of variables, a set $\mathcal{A}$ of atomic propositions, and a set Act of actions. For technical reasons we assume that $\mathcal{A}$ is closed with respect to negation: for every $A \in \mathcal{A}$ there is a $B \in \mathcal{A}$ that is semantically equivalent to the negation of A. In what follows, X will range over Var, A over $\mathcal{A}$, and a over Act. The syntax of formulas may be given by the following grammar.

$$\Phi ::= A \mid X \mid \neg \Phi \mid \Phi \wedge \Phi \mid [a]\Phi \mid \nu X.\Phi$$

The maximum fixpoint operator ν binds free occurrences of X in Φ in the usual sense. We impose an additional syntactic restriction on formulas of the form $\nu X.\Phi$: each free occurrence of X in Φ must be within the scope of an even number of negations. This requirement ensures the well-definedness of the semantics of the logic.

Let $\Phi[X := \Gamma]$ represent the formula obtained by simultaneously substituting the formula Γ for the free occurrences of the variable X in Φ. Then we may also define the usual dual operators to the ones we have presented.

$$\Phi_1 \vee \Phi_2 = \neg(\neg\Phi_1 \wedge \neg\Phi_2) \qquad \langle a \rangle \Phi = \neg[a](\neg\Phi) \qquad \mu X.\Phi = \neg\nu X.\neg(\Phi[X := \neg X])$$

In what follows we say that Φ' is a *proper* subformula of Φ if it is a subformula of Φ that is not Φ itself. Given a formula, its *top-level* subformulas with a certain property are defined to be those maximal proper subformulas having the property. A formula is said to be a ν-formula (μ-formula) if it has the form $\nu X.\Phi$ ($\mu X.\Phi$) for some X and Φ. We refer to a formula as *closed* if it contains no free variables and *simple* if it is fixpoint-free and contains only variables and atomic propositions as proper subformulas. For example, $X_1 \wedge A_2$ is simple, while $\langle a \rangle (X_3 \vee X_4)$ is not.

The formal semantics of formulas appears in Figure 1. It is given with respect to a finite-state labeled transition system $\langle S, Act, \rightarrow \rangle$, a valuation $\mathcal{V}$ mapping atomic propositions to subsets of S, and an environment e mapping variables to subsets of S. Note that $e[X \mapsto S]$ is the environment that results by updating the binding of X to S in e.

Intuitively, the semantic function maps a formula to the set of states for which the formula is "true". Accordingly, a state s satisfies $A \in \mathcal{A}$ if s is in the valuation of A, while s satisfies X if s is an element of the set bound to X in e. The propositional constructs are interpreted in the usual fashion: s satisfies $\neg\Phi$ if it does not satisfy Φ and s satisfies $\Phi_1 \wedge \Phi_2$ if it satisfies Φ_1 as well as Φ_2. The construct $[a]$ is a *modal operator*; s satisfies $[a]\Phi$ if each a-derivative of s satisfies Φ.

The syntactic restriction on the bodies of ν-formulas and the semantics of the other logical connectives ensures that semantically, the bodies give rise to monotonic functions (on the lattice sets of states) [C]. Accordingly, on the basis of the Knaster-Tarski Fixpoint Theorem [T] the semantics of $\nu X.\Phi$ is given as the greatest fixpoint of the monotonic function corresponding to Φ. In addition, for finite-state labeled transition systems the bodies of ν-formulas are continuous, and Kleene's Fixpoint Theorem then provides the following iterative characterization of the semantics. Define ϕ_i by $\phi_0 = S$ and $\phi_{i+1} = [\![\Phi]\!]e[X \mapsto \phi_i]$ for $i \geq 1$. Then $[\![\nu X.\Phi]\!]e = \bigcap_{i=0}^{\infty} \phi_i$. Formula $\mu X.\Phi$ can be characterized dually as $\bigcup_{i=0}^{\infty} \dot\phi_i$, where $\dot\phi_0 = \emptyset$ and $\dot\phi_{i+1} = [\![\Phi]\!]e[X \mapsto \dot\phi_i]$. The next lemma establishes that the meaning of a closed formula does not depend on its environment.

Lemma 2.2 *Fix a finite-state transition system and valuation, and let Φ be a closed formula. Then for any environments e and e' we have: $[\![\Phi]\!]e = [\![\Phi]\!]e'$.*

The lemma holds because all variables in closed formulas are bound by a fixpoint operator, and this excludes any influence of the initial environment on the semantics of the formula. We therefore omit reference to an environment for closed formulas and write $[\![\Phi]\!]$. Finally, it is also possible to translate formulas into *positive normal form* (PNF), i.e. into a negation-free formula in which no variable is bound more than once. This is a consequence of the following lemma, where $|\Phi|$ represents the number of occurrences of operators and atomic formulas in Φ.

Lemma 2.3 *Let Φ be a closed formula in the modal μ-calculus. Then Φ can be translated into a closed formula Φ' in the logic extended with $\vee$, $\langle a \rangle$ and μ in $O(|\Phi|)$ time such that*

1) *Φ' is negation-free,*   2) *$[\![\Phi]\!] = [\![\Phi']\!]$ and*   3) *$|\Phi'| \leq |\Phi|$.*

The translation is done by "driving" negations inside the subformulas in the standard way following DeMorgans Laws etc, and renaming variables as appropriate. The resulting formula Φ' is not larger than Φ because of our assumptions that all free occurrences of variables in fixpoint formulas must be inside the range of an even number of negations and that the atomic propositions are closed under negation.

For notational simplicity, in what follows we only consider formulas whose top-level operator is a fixpoint operator. This is not a serious restriction, as the semantics of other formulas can be trivially determined in linear time once the semantics of the top-level fixpoint formulas have been computed.

2.3 Alternation Depth of Formulas

The complexity of the algorithm that we present in the following sections will depend on a measure on formulas called *alternation depth*. Intuitively, the alternation depth of a formula is the length of a maximal "chain" of mutually recursive greatest and least fixpoint subformulas (cf. [EL]).

Definition 2.4 (Alternation Depth of Formulas) *Let Φ be in PNF. Then the alternation depth, $ad(\Phi)$, of Φ is defined inductively as follows.*

- *If Φ contains closed top-level fixpoint-subformulas $\Gamma_1, \ldots, \Gamma_n$ then*

$$ad(\Phi) = max(ad(\Phi'), ad(\Gamma_1), \ldots, ad(\Gamma_n))$$

where Φ' is obtained from Φ by substituting new atomic propositions $A_1, \ldots, A_n$ for $\Gamma_1, \ldots, \Gamma_n$.

- *If Φ contains no closed top-level fixpoint-subformulas then $ad(\Phi)$ is defined as follows.*

  - *$ad(A) = ad(X) = 0$, for any atomic proposition A and variable X.*
  - *$ad(\Phi_1 \wedge \Phi_2) = ad(\Phi_1 \vee \Phi_2) = max(ad(\Phi_1), ad(\Phi_2))$.*
  - *$ad([a]\Phi) = ad(\langle a \rangle \Phi) = ad(\Phi)$, for any action a.*

− *Let $\sigma \in \{\mu, \nu\}$, and let $\overline{\sigma}$ be the dual of σ. Then*

$$ad(\sigma X.\Phi) = max(1, ad(\Phi), 1 + ad(\overline{\sigma}X_1.\Phi_1), \ldots, 1 + ad(\overline{\sigma}X_n.\Phi_n))$$

where $\overline{\sigma}X_1.\Phi_1, \ldots, \overline{\sigma}X_n.\Phi_n$ are the top-level $\overline{\sigma}$-subformulas of Φ.

Example 2.5 For $\Phi = \nu X_1.\mu X_2.(X_1 \vee X_2 \vee \nu Y_1.\mu Y_2.\nu Y_3.(Y_1 \wedge Y_2 \wedge Y_3))$ we obtain $ad(\Phi) = 3$.

3 Equational Systems

In order to facilitate the saving and reuse of intermediate results, our model-checking algorithm works on *equational* representations of mu-calculus formulas. This section presents the syntax and semantics of the equational systems and introduces the notions of closed subsystems and alternation depth.

3.1 Syntax of Equational Systems

The systems of mutually recursive equations that we use to represent formulas are lists of the following form[1]: $\langle X_1 \diamond_1 \Phi_1, \ldots, X_n \diamond_n \Phi_n \rangle$ where $\diamond_i \in \{\rightarrow, \leftarrow\}$. The X_i's are distinct variables, and the equation $X_i \rightarrow \Phi_i$ represents a *greatest fixpoint*, while $X_i \leftarrow \Phi_i$ represents a *least fixpoint*. Following [AC, CS1] we restrict our attention to mu-calculus formulas Φ_i that are *negation-free* and *simple*, which guarantees that every *non-atomic* right-hand-side formula has a left-hand-side variable associated with it. This facilitates the saving and reuse of intermediate results. Any equation set E may be transformed in linear time into a simple equational system E' with at most linear blow-up in size. Therefore, the model-checking algorithm presented in this paper has the same complexity for the full logic as for the simple sublogic. In what follows we refer to $X_i \rightarrow \Phi_i$ as a *max equation* with *max variable* X_i and to $X_j \leftarrow \Phi_j$ as a *min equation* with *min variable* X_j, and we associate with each left-hand-side variable a *parity* that is either *max* or *min* depending on the form of the equation. An equational system E is *closed* if all variables in a right-hand side of some equation also appear as left-hand sides in E. It should be pointed out that the order of equations is important in an equational system, owing to the presence of mutually recursive greatest and least fixpoint formulas.

Example 3.1 The following equational system E represents the formula given in Example 2.5. It can be obtained by means of the translation that will be given in Section 3.2.

$$\langle X_1 \rightarrow X_2, X_2 \leftarrow X_1 \vee X_3, X_3 \leftarrow X_2 \vee X_4, X_4 \rightarrow X_5, X_5 \leftarrow X_6, X_6 \rightarrow X_4 \wedge X_7, X_7 \rightarrow X_5 \wedge X_6 \rangle$$

3.2 Semantics of Equational Systems

The semantics for equational systems uses a translation from systems of equations to tuples of closed mu-calculus formulas, one for each equation. An equational system may then be interpreted as a tuple of subsets of states which arises by pointwise application of the semantic function for formulas to the component formulas.

This translation consists of the composition of two functions, B and F (for "backwards" and "forwards"), which repeatedly eliminate occurrences of free variables. Let $E = \langle X_1 \diamond \Phi_1, \ldots, X_n \diamond \Phi_n \rangle$ be a closed, simple equational system, and let $\overline{\Phi} = \langle \Phi_1, \ldots, \Phi_n \rangle$ consist of the right-hand sides of E. Also let $\pi_1, \ldots, \pi_n$ be the obvious projection functions. Given $\overline{\Phi}$, B produces a new tuple $\overline{\Gamma}$ of formulas by setting $\overline{\Gamma}$ to $\overline{\Phi}$ and processing each component in $\overline{\Gamma}$ as follows, beginning with $\pi_n(\overline{\Gamma})$ and working backwards.

- Replace $\pi_i(\overline{\Gamma})$ by $\mu X_i.\pi_i(\overline{\Gamma})$ (if X_i is a min-variable) or $\nu X_i.\pi_i(\overline{\Gamma})$ (if X_i is a max-variable).

---
[1] This form is similar to the one used by Larsen in [La].

414

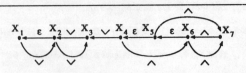

Figure 2: The Dependency Graph for Equational System E in Example 3.1.

- Substitute $\pi_i(\overline{\Gamma})$ for each free occurrence of X_i in $\pi_1(\overline{\Gamma}), \ldots, \pi_{i-1}(\overline{\Gamma})$.

Note that only $X_1, \ldots, X_{i-1}$ can appear free in $\pi_i(B(\overline{\Phi}))$; in particular, $\pi_1(B(\overline{\Phi}))$ is closed. Now F eliminates all remaining free variables: Given a tuple $\overline{\Gamma}$ of formulas, F produces a new tuple $\overline{\Delta}$ by processing each formula in $\overline{\Gamma}$ in the order of the indices as follows: substitute $\pi_i(\overline{\Delta})$ for each free occurrence of X_i in $\pi_{i+1}(\overline{\Delta}), \ldots, \pi_n(\overline{\Delta})$. The semantics of E can now be given as follows.

Definition 3.2 (Semantics of Equational Systems) *Let E be a closed, simple system of n equations, and let $\overline{\Phi}$ be the tuple of right-hand sides of E. Also let $\langle \Delta_1, \ldots, \Delta_n \rangle = F \circ B(\overline{\Phi})$. Then $[\![E]\!] = \langle [\![\Delta_1]\!], \ldots, [\![\Delta_n]\!] \rangle$.*

The connection between equational systems and the mu-calculus can be made explicit by providing translations back and forth. **trans**^{a}, translating equational systems into formulas, is straightforward in terms of F and B: **trans**$^a(E) = \pi_1(F \circ B(\overline{\Phi}))$, where $\overline{\Phi}$ consists of the right-hand sides of E. Given a mu-calculus formula Φ in PNF, the function **trans** builds an equational system by recursing through Φ, adding a new equation at the end of the last of the already generated equations for each subformula of Φ. The parity of a new added left-hand-side variable is determined by the most recently encountered fixpoint operator. As an example, consider the formula and the equational system given in Example 2.5 and 3.1, respectively. Here, the application of **trans** to Φ yields E.

Obviously, **trans** works in linear time as every subformula of Φ is investigated exactly once. Moreover, the number of equations in the resulting simple equational system E_Φ is less than or equal to the size of the formula Φ, because every subformula of Φ is transformed into at most one equation. A detailed account of these translations can be found in [CDS].

Instead of solving the model-checking problem directly for a given formula Φ we solve it on the equational system E_Φ that is gained by the translation given above. The following theorem establishes the correctness of this approach.

Theorem 3.3 *Let Φ be a closed PNF formula and $E_\Phi = $ **trans**(Φ). Then, $[\![\Phi]\!] = \pi_1([\![E_\Phi]\!])$.*

3.3 Graph Representation of Equational Systems

In this section we introduce a graph representation of equational systems that will be used to determine the *closed subsystems* of equational systems and to define the notion of *alternation depth*. Let E be an equational system. Then its dependency graph G_E is an edge-labeled graph with one node for each left-hand-side variable in E and edges defined as follows, where $i \neq j$.

- $X_i \xrightarrow{l} X_j$ if for some Φ either $X_j \Leftrightarrow X_i \, l \, \Phi$ or $X_j \Leftrightarrow \Phi \, l \, X_i$ is an equation in E for $l \in \{\vee, \wedge\}$.

- $X_i \xrightarrow{l} X_j$ if $X_j \Leftrightarrow l \, X_i$ is in E for $l \in \{\langle a \rangle, [a]\}$.

- $X_i \xrightarrow{\varepsilon} X_j$ if $X_j \Leftrightarrow X_i$ is in E.

Intuitively, there is an edge from X_i to X_j if the meaning of X_i directly influences the meaning of X_j. In what follows, we write $X_i \to X_j$ if there is an edge in G_E from X_i to X_j and $X_i \to^* X_j$ if there is a path from X_i to X_j in G_E. As an example, the graph for the equational system in Example 3.1 appears in Figure 2.

415

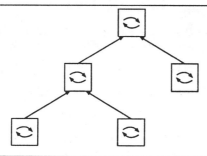

Figure 3: The Dependencies between and within the Closed Subsystems.

Theorem 3.4 *Let $E = \langle X_1 \Leftrightarrow \Phi_1, \ldots, X_n \Leftrightarrow \Phi_n \rangle$ be an equational system. Its dependency graph G_E can be constructed in $O(|E|)$ time, and it contains n vertices and no more than $2n$ edges.*

Let C be a sublist of E. Then we refer to the subgraph of G_E induced by C as G_C. Also, we write $X_i \dashrightarrow_{C,k} X_j$ if $X_i \dashrightarrow X_j$ is an edge in G_C with $i \geq k$ and $j \geq k$. These notions are used in Section 3.5.

3.4 Closed Subsystems of Equational Systems

In analogy with the notion of closed subformulas, we develop the notion of *closed subsystems* of equational systems; these turn out to be essential in order for us to achieve the desired complexity for our model-checking algorithm.

From the definition of the dependency graph G_E, if two variables X_i and X_j are such that $X_i \dashrightarrow^* X_j$ and $X_j \dashrightarrow^* X_i$, it follows that the semantics of X_i affects that of X_j, and vice versa. When this is the case we say that X_i and X_j are *mutually dependent*, since any change to the semantics of one may induce a change in the other. On the other hand, if $X_i \dashrightarrow^* X_j$ but $X_j \not\dashrightarrow^* X_i$, then changes to X_i affect X_j, but not vice versa. In this case we say that there is a *hierarchical* dependency from X_i to X_j, since once the semantics of X_i is computed future changes to X_j cannot affect it.

In graph-theoretic terms, when $X_i \dashrightarrow^* X_j$ and $X_j \dashrightarrow^* X_i$, then X_i and X_j belong to the same *strongly connected component* of G_E.[2] Within a strongly connected component each pair of variables is mutually dependent, while there can exist at most a hierarchical dependence between two variables in distinct strongly connected components. This suggests the following strategy for computing $[\![E]\!]$:

1. Build the condensation graph, G_C, of G_E. (Recall that the condensation graph of G is a graph having the strongly connected components G_i of G as its vertices, with an edge $G_i \rightarrow G_j$ defined if G_i and G_j are distinct and there are nodes $V_i \in G_i$, $V_j \in G_j$, such that $V_i \rightarrow V_j$ is an edge in G.) Note that G_C is acyclic.

2. Topologically sort G_C into $G_m, \ldots, G_1$. (Here G_m is a "source" node in G_C; we have elected to number it m so that, in general, higher-numbered variables belong to higher-numbered components.) Notice that if there is an edge from G_i to G_j then $i > j$.

3. For each G_i, generate a *closed subsystem* C_i containing the equations from E whose left-hand sides are in G_i. These equations are modified by replacing each occurrence of X_j that is not a left-hand side in G_i by a new atomic proposition A_j; this ensures that C_i is closed. Note that if X_j is in component G_k then $k < i$.

---

[2] Recall that a strongly connected component of a graph is a maximal subset $\mathcal{V}$ of vertices having the property that $V_i \dashrightarrow^* V_j$ and $V_j \dashrightarrow^* V_i$ for any $V_i, V_j \in \mathcal{V}$.

4. Beginning with C_m, process each C_i in turn.

As an example, consider E in Example 3.1 with its dependency graph G_E shown in Figure 2. As there are two strongly connected components of G_E we get two closed subsystems:

$$C_1 = \ < X_1 \to X_2 \,,\ X_2 \leftarrow X_1 \vee X_3 \,,\ X_3 \leftarrow X_2 \vee A_4 >$$

$$C_2 = \ < X_4 \to X_5 \,,\ X_5 \leftarrow X_6 \,,\ X_6 \to X_4 \wedge X_7 \,,\ X_7 \to X_5 \wedge X_6 >$$

Note that each C_l is closed and that each left-hand-side variable X_i of E appears as a left-hand side in exactly one of the C_l. Also notice that the construction ensures that if a new atomic proposition A_i appears in a right-hand side in C_j, then X_i must appear as a left-hand side in some C_l with $l > j$. Consequently, we may define the semantics of A_i as follows. Let C_l be the closed subsystem containing X_i as a left-hand side, and let k be the index of X_i in C_l. Then $[\![A_i]\!] = \pi_k([\![C_l]\!])$. The following theorem shows that this transformation of E into $C_1 \ldots C_m$ is, in a certain sense, semantics-preserving.

Theorem 3.5 *The closed subsystems $C_1, \ldots, C_m$ of an equational system E can be determined in $O(|E|)$ time. Furthermore, if X_i is the kth left-hand side in C_l, then $\pi_i([\![E]\!]) = \pi_k([\![C_l]\!])$.*

In our example we have $[\![E]\!] = \langle \pi_1[C_1], \pi_2[C_1], \pi_3[C_1], \pi_1[C_2], \pi_2[C_2], \pi_3[C_2], \pi_4[C_2] \rangle$.

3.5 Alternation Depth of Equational Systems

We close this section by defining the notion of *alternation depth* of an equational system. It will turn out that this notion is consistent with the one given for formulas (cf. Theorem 3.8), and therefore we may use the same notation.

To define the alternation depth we first introduce the notion of *nesting depth* of equations that reflects the length of the chain of mutually depending *min* and *max* equations within a closed subsystem.

Definition 3.6 (Nesting Depth of Equations)
Let $E = \langle X_1 \diamond \Phi_1, \ldots, X_n \diamond \Phi_n \rangle$ be an equational system with its closed subsystems $C_1, \ldots, C_m$. Furthermore, assume $\sigma \in \{max, min\}$ and $\bar{\sigma}$ to be the dual parity. Then the nesting depth of the equation with left-hand side X_i having parity σ and belonging to C_l is given by:

$$nd(X_i, C_l) \ = \ max(1, \ max\{ nd(X_j, C_l) \mid X_j \dot{\to}_{C_l,i} {}^* X_i \text{ and } X_j \text{ has parity } \sigma \},$$
$$max\{ 1 + nd(X_j, C_l) \mid X_j \dot{\to}_{C_l,i} {}^* X_i \text{ and } X_j \text{ has parity } \bar{\sigma} \})$$

The nesting depth of the closed subsystem C_l is defined as $nd(C_l) = max\{nd(X_i, C_l) | X_i \diamond \Phi_i \in C_l\}$.

The alternation depth of an equational system is now defined as the maximal nesting depth of its closed subsystems.

Definition 3.7 (Alternation Depth of Equational Systems)
Let $E = \langle X_1 \diamond \Phi_1, \ldots, X_n \diamond \Phi_n \rangle$ be an equational system with closed subsystems $C_1, \ldots, C_m$. Then the alternation depth of E is given by $\quad ad(E) = max\{nd(C_l) | 1 \le l \le m\}$.

Example: As shown already, the equational system E presented in Example 3.1 has two closed subsystems, and we have: $nd(X_3, C_1) = nd(X_2, C_1) = 1$ and $nd(X_1, C_1) = 2$, thus $nd(C_1) = 2$ and $nd(X_7, C_2) = nd(X_6, C_2) = 1$, $nd(X_5, C_2) = 2$ and $nd(X_4, C_2) = 3$, thus $nd(C_2) = 3$. Therefore $ad(E) = 3$.

We say that an equational system E is *alternation-free* if $ad(E) = 1$. The consistency of the notions of alternation depth for formulas and equational systems is a consequence of the following theorem.

Theorem 3.8 *Let Φ be a closed PNF formula with $ad(\Phi) \geq 1$ and $E_\Phi = \text{trans}(\Phi)$ be the corresponding equational system. Then $ad(\Phi) = ad(E_\Phi)$.*

The left-hand-side variables of a closed subsystem of an equational system can be partitioned into *nesting levels*, which are used to guide the fixpoint computation.

Definition 3.9 (Nesting Levels) *Let $E = \langle X_1 \Leftrightarrow \Phi_1, \ldots, X_n \Leftrightarrow \Phi_n \rangle$ be an equational system with closed subsystems $C_1, \ldots, C_m$. Then the set of variables belonging to a closed subsystem C_l is partitioned into* nesting levels *by $E_{l,i} = \{ X_j \mid nd(X_j, C_l) = i \}$ for $1 \leq i \leq nd(C_l)$.*

Given a nesting level $E_{l,i}$ we call the nesting level $E_{l,j}$ *lower* if $j < i$ and *higher* if $j > i$. Each nesting level consists of at most two *blocks* of equations, where a block consists entirely of min or of max equations.

Theorem 3.10 *Given an equational system E:*

1. Alternation-freedom can be established in $O(|E|)$ time.

2. The nesting levels can be determined in $O(|E|^2)$ time.

4   The Model-Checking Algorithm

In this section we present a model-checking algorithm that, given an equational system E and a transition system $T = \langle S, Act, \to \rangle$, computes $[\![E]\!]$. Due to space limitations, we only sketch an outline of the algorithm; the interested reader is referred to [CDS] for a fuller discussion of the details.

As with the algorithms in [AC, CS1, CS2], our algorithm is bit-vector-based. Each state in S has a bit vector whose i^{th} entry indicates whether or not the state belongs to the set associated with X_i in the current stage of the analysis. These bit-vectors represent the current approximation $\langle S_1, \ldots, S_n \rangle \in (2^S)^n$ to $[\![E]\!]$ during model checking as follows: $s \in S_i$ if and only if $s.X[i]$ is true, for $1 \leq i \leq n$.

Given E, the algorithm works by first determining the closed subsystems $C_1 \ldots C_m$ of E. It then processes each C_l in turn, beginning with C_m and ending with C_1; $[\![C_l]\!]$ is computed and stored in the relevant bit-vector components, and then the atomic predicates whose semantics depend on left-hand sides in C_l have their semantics initialized. The algorithm terminates after C_1 is completed. Given that each $[\![C_l]\!]$ is computed properly, correctness follows from Theorem 3.5.

At the heart of the algorithm is the computation of $[\![C_l]\!]$ for a closed subsystem C_l. This processing proceeds in two phases. During the first phase, bit-vectors are initialized such that components corresponding to *max variables* are set to *true* and components corresponding to *min variables* are set to *false*. In the second phase, the nesting levels of C_l are repeatedly analyzed, beginning with the lowest level, $E_{l,1}$, and proceeding up to $E_{l,nd(C_l)}$. To process a nesting level, the algorithm essentially invokes a variant of the alternation-free model-checking algorithm given in [CS2]. Bit-vector annotations are changed until appropriate fixed points are reached; in addition, if changing a bit-vector component in one variable also causes a change in the semantics of a variable in a lower nesting level, then the lower nesting levels that are affected must be re-initialized and recomputed. The processing of a nesting level is finished when consistency is reached with all lower levels. Then, the next higher level is begun.

In this computation of $[\![C_l]\!]$, one may identify two flows of information.

- **The flow of assumptions:** Our algorithm may be seen as "assumption based": during the computation of a fixpoint for equations in a nesting level, the variables in higher nesting levels are treated essentially as propositional constants in that their meaning is fixed. Thus, the *assumption flow* proceeds from $E_{l,nd(C_l)}$ down to $E_{l,1}$.

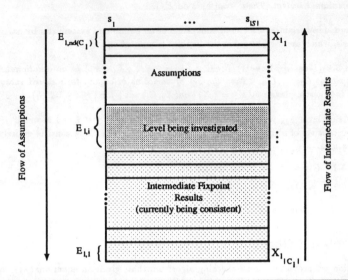

Figure 4: The Flows of Information in a Closed Subsystem C_l.

- **The propagation of intermediate results:** Fixpoints are computed from lower to higher nesting levels. Therefore, the *computation flow* proceeds in the direction opposite to that of the flow of assumptions, as intermediate results computed in one level may affect the results for higher levels.

In this view, the need for recomputing values in lower nesting levels when a higher nesting level changes becomes apparent: the computation of the lower level was based on a wrong assumption.

The two flows of information are illustrated in Figure 4, where the box represents the current approximation of the semantics of C_l with the bit-vectors corresponding to columns through the levels.

Three observations are exploited in order to achieve the complexity stated in the next section.

1. The partitioning of the equational system E into closed subsystems $C_1, \ldots, C_m$ ensures that once $[\![C_l]\!]$ is computed, it cannot be affected by the analysis of subsequent closed subsystems.

2. Within a given closed subsystem C_l the nesting levels are treated exactly as in the (linear-time [CS2]) *alternation-free* case each time their fixpoint is computed.

3. Computing consistency of the lowest, and most often recomputed, nesting level $E_{l,1}$ is less expensive than for the higher levels as $E_{l,1}$ does not give rise to resetting and recomputation of lower levels and also need not account for the new values that resetting and recomputing lower levels can give rise to.

The full structure of the model-checking algorithm is given in [CDS]; Section 6 contains an example illustrating our technique.

5 Correctness and Complexity

The correctness of the algorithm rests on the observation that our algorithm computes $[\![C_l]\!]$ component-wise according to the semantic definition of formulas by representing the environment in the bit vectors. Together with Theorem 3.5 this enables us to prove the following theorem (cf. [CDS]).

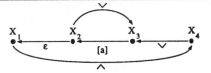

Figure 5: The Dependency Graph.

Theorem 5.1 (Correctness) *Let $T = \langle S, Act, \rightarrow \rangle$ be a labeled finite-state transition system and $E = \langle X_1 \Leftrightarrow \Phi_1, \ldots, X_n \Leftrightarrow \Phi_n \rangle$ be a closed, simple equational system. Then the model-checking algorithm terminates with a bit-vector annotation that represents $[\![E]\!]$.*

The following theorem states our complexity result, where $|T| = |S| + | \rightarrow |$ and $|E|$ is the number of equations in E. A complete proof is given in [CDS].

Theorem 5.2 (Complexity) *Let $E = \langle X_1 \Leftrightarrow \Phi_1, \ldots, X_n \Leftrightarrow \Phi_n \rangle$ be a simple, closed equational system with $ad(E) \geq 1$, and $T = \langle S, Act, \rightarrow \rangle$ be a finite-state transition system. Then the worst-case time complexity of the model-checking algorithm is*

$$O \left(|T| * |E| * \left(|S| * \frac{|E|}{ad(E)} \right)^{ad(E)-1} \right)$$

6 An Example

In this section we illustrate our algorithm with an example taken from [SW]. Consider the formula $\Phi = \nu Z.\mu Y.[a]((A \wedge Z) \vee Y)$ having alternation depth 2. The semantics of Φ with respect to a transition system T is the set of states for which A holds infinitely often on all a-paths. Its corresponding equational system

$$E = \; < X_1 \rightarrow X_2 \,, \;\; X_2 \leftarrow [a]X_3 \,, \;\; X_3 \leftarrow X_4 \vee X_2 \,, \;\; X_4 \leftarrow A \wedge X_1 >$$

only has the trivial closed subsystem consisting of two nesting levels: E_1 holding the last three equations, and E_2 holding the first equation. The dependency graph is shown in Figure 5.

The transition system T we want to investigate is the triple $\langle S, Act, \rightarrow \rangle$, where $S = \{s, t, u, v\}$, $Act = \{a\}$ and the transition relation has six elements: $s \xrightarrow{a} s$, $s \xrightarrow{a} t$, $t \xrightarrow{a} u$, $u \xrightarrow{a} s$, $u \xrightarrow{a} v$ and $v \xrightarrow{a} v$.

The valuation is given by $\mathcal{V}(A) = \{t, u, v\}$; so states t, u and v satisfy A, but s does not. Besides the bit-vectors $s.X[1..4]$, $t.X[1..4]$, $u.X[1..4]$ and $v.X[1..4]$ we need some auxiliary data structures for investigating the levels (cf. [CS2]): the counters $s.C[1..4]$, $t.C[1..4]$, $u.C[1..4]$ and $v.C[1..4]$, where $x.C[i]$ maintains a count of the number of components $y.X[j]$ that may change until $x.X[i]$ must change; and the array of worklists $M[1..4]$, where $M[i]$ holds the states the changes to whose i^{th} bit-vector components have yet to be propagated. The states also contain fields recording whether they satisfy the atomic formula A; so $s.A = ff$, while $t.A = u.A = v.A = tt$. Note that X_1 is a *max* variable initialized with *true* for all states and X_2, X_3 and X_4 are *min* variables accordingly initialized with *false*. In what follows we highlight the changes made to the data structure step by step. Note in particular the change of intermediate results in E_1 because of changing assumptions in E_2.

- Computing a fixpoint over the lowest level E_1 (containing X_2 to X_4) starts with the following initialization of the bit vectors, counters and worklists.

	s	t	u	v		s	t	u	v
X_1	tt	tt	tt	tt	C_1	/	/	/	/
X_2	ff	ff	ff	ff	C_2	2	1	2	1
X_3	ff	ff	ff	ff	C_3	/	/	/	/
X_4	ff	tt	tt	tt	C_4	1	0	0	0

$M[\emptyset, \emptyset, \emptyset, \{t, u, v\}]$

420

The influence of the states in the worklist is determined. First, t, u, v are successively deleted from $M[4]$ and $X_4 \stackrel{\vee}{\to} X_3$ is processed. Second, t, u, v are successively deleted from $M[3]$ and $X_3 \stackrel{[a]}{\to} X_2$ is processed. This provides the following intermediate results:

	s	t	u	v
X_1	tt	tt	tt	tt
X_2	ff	ff	ff	ff
X_3	ff	tt	tt	tt
X_4	ff	tt	tt	tt

	s	t	u	v
C_1	/	/	/	/
C_2	2	1	2	1
C_3	/	/	/	/
C_4	1	0	0	0

and

	s	t	u	v
X_1	tt	tt	tt	tt
X_2	ff	tt	ff	tt
X_3	ff	tt	tt	tt
X_4	ff	tt	tt	tt

	s	t	u	v
C_1	/	/	/	/
C_2	1	0	1	0
C_3	/	/	/	/
C_4	1	0	0	0

$$M[\emptyset,\emptyset,\{t,u,v\},\emptyset] \qquad\qquad M[\emptyset,\{t,v\},\emptyset,\emptyset]$$

Now t and v are successively deleted from $M[2]$ and $X_2 \stackrel{\vee}{\to} X_3$ is processed. As $t.X[3]$ and $v.X[3]$ are already *true* the bit-vectors remain unchanged and the worklists for E_1 are empty.

- On the next nesting level E_2 the fixpoint computation detects an inconsistency for s and an inconsistency for u as $s.X[1] = u.X[1] = tt$ but $s.X[2] = u.X[2] = ff$ and $X_2 \stackrel{s}{\to} X_1$. Thus $s.X[1]$ and $u.X[2]$ are set to *false* and E_1 has to be reset and recomputed accordingly.

- The recomputation of E_1 taking the new assumptions into account starts with the initialization shown on the left and computes the fixpoint shown on the right.

	s	t	u	v
X_1	ff	tt	ff	tt
X_2	ff	ff	ff	ff
X_3	ff	ff	ff	ff
X_4	ff	tt	ff	tt

	s	t	u	v
C_1	/	/	/	/
C_2	2	1	2	1
C_3	/	/	/	/
C_4	2	0	1	0

and

	s	t	u	v
X_1	ff	tt	ff	tt
X_2	ff	ff	ff	tt
X_3	ff	tt	ff	tt
X_4	ff	tt	ff	tt

	s	t	u	v
C_1	/	/	/	/
C_2	1	1	1	0
C_3	/	/	/	/
C_4	2	0	1	0

$$M[\emptyset,\emptyset,\emptyset,\{t,v\}] \qquad\qquad M[\emptyset,\emptyset,\emptyset,\emptyset]$$

- Again computing the fixpoint over E_2 an inconsistency is detected as $t.X[1] = tt$ but $t.X[2] = ff$ and $X_2 \stackrel{s}{\to} X_1$. Thus $t.X[1]$ is set to *false* and E_1 is reset and recomputed, providing the following results for initialization (left) and fixpoint computation (right):

	s	t	u	v
X_1	ff	ff	ff	tt
X_2	ff	ff	ff	ff
X_3	ff	ff	ff	ff
X_4	ff	ff	ff	tt

	s	t	u	v
C_1	/	/	/	/
C_2	2	1	2	1
C_3	/	/	/	/
C_4	2	1	1	0

and

	s	t	u	v
X_1	ff	ff	ff	tt
X_2	ff	ff	ff	tt
X_3	ff	ff	ff	tt
X_4	ff	ff	ff	tt

	s	t	u	v
C_1	/	/	/	/
C_2	2	1	1	0
C_3	/	/	/	/
C_4	2	1	1	0

$$M[\emptyset,\emptyset,\emptyset,\{v\}] \qquad\qquad M[\emptyset,\emptyset,\emptyset,\emptyset]$$

Finally, E_2 is shown to be consistent, the algorithm terminates, and we obtain $[\![\Phi]\!] = \{v\}$, as $v.X[1] = tt$ and the first bit-vector component of all other states is *false*. This reflects one's intuition about the formula, because v is the only state for which A is infinitely often satisfied along all a-paths.

7 Conclusions and Future Work

In this paper, we have presented an algorithm for model checking that handles the full modal mu-calculus including *alternating* fixed points. The algorithm extends the one given in [CS2] for an alternation-free logic. Central is the new complexity result:

$$O\left(|T| * |E| * \left(|S| * \frac{|E|}{ad(E)}\right)^{ad(E)-1}\right)$$

which improves even on our conjecture ([CS2]):

- Instead of being exponential in the full size of the transition system it is only exponential in the number of its states. This saves a quadratic blow-up in the worst case.

- Instead of being exponential in the full size of the formula, it is only exponential in $\frac{|E|}{ad(E)}$, which is important for formulas with high alternation depth.

In [A] Andersen sketches an $O(|S| * |T|^{ad(\Phi)-1} * |\Phi|^{ad(\Phi)})$ algorithm for the full mu-calculus, which improves on Emerson and Lei's result, $O((|T| * |E|)^{ad(E)+1})$. Andersen's algorithm differs from ours in that it is tailored to the mu-calculus structure rather than systems of equations, where properties can be expressed much more concisely. In the worst case, his formalizations are exponentially larger than ours, because equational systems allow to compactly represent common subexpressions. This generality, however, requires a much more involved algorithm. Nevertheless, we were able to prove a stronger complexity result, even with respect to the more compact representations. Our algorithm will be implemented as an extension of the Concurrency Workbench [CPS1, CPS2].

References

[A]   Andersen, H. "Model Checking and Boolean Graphs." *Proc. of ESOP '92*, LNCS 582, 1992.

[AC]   Arnold, A., and P. Crubille. "A Linear Algorithm To Solve Fixed-Point Equations on Transition Systems." *Information Processing Letters*, v. 29, 30 September 1988, pp. 57–66.

[CES]   Clarke, E.M., E.A. Emerson and A.P. Sistla. "Automatic Verification of Finite State Concurrent Systems Using Temporal Logic Specifications." *ACM Transactions on Programming Languages and Systems*, v. 8, n. 2, 1986, pp. 244–263.

[C]   Cleaveland, R. "Tableau-Based Model Checking in the Propositional Mu-Calculus." *Acta Informatica*, v. 27, 1990, pp. 725–747.

[CDS]   Cleaveland, R., M. Klein and B. Steffen. "Faster Model Checking for the Modal Mu-Calculus." In *Technical Report RWTH Aachen Nr. 91-29*, Fachgruppe der Informatik, 1991.

[CPS1]   Cleaveland, R., J. Parrow and B. Steffen. "The Concurrency Workbench." In *Proceedings* CAV'89, LNCS 407, 1989.

[CPS2]   Cleaveland, R., J. Parrow and B. Steffen. "A Semantics-based Verification Tool for Finite-State Systems", In *Proceedings of the Ninth International Symposium on Protocol Specification, Testing, and Verification.* North-Holland, 1989.

[CS1]   Cleaveland, R. and B. Steffen. "Computing Behavioural Relations, Logically." In Proceedings ICALP '91, LNCS 510, 1991.

[CS2]   Cleaveland, R. and B. Steffen. "A Linear-Time Model Checking Algorithm for the Alternation-Free Modal Mu-Calculus." In Proceedings CAV '91, LNCS 575, 1991.

[EL]   Emerson, E.A. and C.-L. Lei. "Efficient Model Checking in Fragments of the Propositional Mu-Calculus." In *Proceedings of LICS*, 1986, pp. 267–278.

[Fe]   Fernandez, J.-C. *Aldébaran: Une Système de Vérification par Réduction de Processus Communicants.* Ph.D. Thesis, Université de Grenoble, 1988.

[K]   Kleene, S. C. "Introduction to Metamathematics", North Holland, 1952.

[Ko]   Kozen, D. "Results on the Propositional μ-Calculus." *TCS*, v. 27, 1983, pp. 333–354.

422

[La]   Larsen, K.G. "Proof Systems for Hennessy-Milner Logic with Recursion." In *Proceedings of CAAP*, 1988.

[MSGS] Malhotra, J., Smolka, S.A., Giacalone, A. and Shapiro, R. "Winston: A Tool for Hierarchical Design and Simulation of Concurrent Systems." In *Proceedings of the Workshop on Specification and Verification of Concurrent Systems*, Univ. of Stirling, Scotland, 1988.

[RRSV] Richier, J., Rodriguez, C., Sifakis, J. and Voiron, J.. "Verification in XESAR of the Sliding Window Protocol." In *Proceedings of the Seventh IFIP Symposium on Protocol Specification, Testing, and Verification*, 1987, North-Holland.

[RdS]   Roy, V. and R. de Simone. "Auto/Autograph." In *Proceedings*, CAV'90, LNCS 531, 1990.

[Ste]   Steffen, B.U. "Characteristic Formulae." In *Proceedings ICALP*, LNCS 372, 1989.

[SI]   Steffen, B.U., and A. Ingólfsdóttir. "Characteristic Formulae for CCS with Divergence." To appear in *Information and Computation*.

[SW]   Stirling, C. and D. Walker. "Local Model Checking in the Modal Mu-Calculus." In *Proceedings of TAPSOFT '89*, LNCS 351, 1989.

[T]   Tarski, A. "A Lattice-Theoretical Fixpoint Theorem and its Applications." *Pacific Journal of Mathematics*, v. 5, 1955.

Springer-Verlag
and the Environment

We at Springer-Verlag firmly believe that an international science publisher has a special obligation to the environment, and our corporate policies consistently reflect this conviction.

We also expect our business partners – paper mills, printers, packaging manufacturers, etc. – to commit themselves to using environmentally friendly materials and production processes.

The paper in this book is made from low- or no-chlorine pulp and is acid free, in conformance with international standards for paper permanency.

Printing: Weihert-Druck GmbH, Darmstadt
Binding: Buchbinderei Schäffer, Grünstadt

Lecture Notes in Computer Science

For information about Vols. 1–587
please contact your bookseller or Springer-Verlag

Vol. 624: A. Voronkov (Ed.), Logic Programming and Automated Reasoning. Proceedings, 1992. XIV, 509 pages. 1992. (Subseries LNAI).

Vol. 625: W. Vogler, Modular Construction and Partial Order Semantics of Petri Nets. IX, 252 pages. 1992.

Vol. 626: E. Börger, G. Jäger, H. Kleine Büning, M. M . Richter (Eds.), Computer Science Logic. Proceedings, 1991. VIII, 428 pages. 1992.

Vol. 628: G. Vosselman, Relational Matching. IX, 190 pages. 1992.

Vol. 629: I. M. Havel, V. Koubek (Eds.), Mathematical Foundations of Computer Science 1992. Proceedings. IX, 521 pages. 1992.

Vol. 630: W. R. Cleaveland (Ed.), CONCUR '92. Proceedings. X, 580 pages. 1992.

Vol. 631: M. Bruynooghe, M. Wirsing (Eds.), Programming Language Implementation and Logic Programming. Proceedings, 1992. XI, 492 pages. 1992.

Vol. 632: H. Kirchner, G. Levi (Eds.), Algebraic and Logic Programming. Proceedings, 1992. IX, 457 pages. 1992.

Vol. 633: D. Pearce, G. Wagner (Eds.), Logics in AI. Proceedings. VIII, 410 pages. 1992. (Subseries LNAI).

Vol. 634: L. Bougé, M. Cosnard, Y. Robert, D. Trystram (Eds.), Parallel Processing: CONPAR 92 – VAPP V. Proceedings. XVII, 853 pages. 1992.

Vol. 635: J. C. Derniame (Ed.), Software Process Technology. Proceedings, 1992. VIII, 253 pages. 1992.

Vol. 636: G. Comyn, N. E. Fuchs, M. J. Ratcliffe (Eds.), Logic Programming in Action. Proceedings, 1992. X, 324 pages. 1992. (Subseries LNAI).

Vol. 637: Y. Bekkers, J. Cohen (Eds.), Memory Management. Proceedings, 1992. XI, 525 pages. 1992.

Vol. 639: A. U. Frank, I. Campari, U. Formentini (Eds.), Theories and Methods of Spatio-Temporal Reasoning in Geographic Space. Proceedings, 1992. XI, 431 pages. 1992.

Vol. 640: C. Sledge (Ed.), Software Engineering Education. Proceedings, 1992. X, 451 pages. 1992.

Vol. 641: U. Kastens, P. Pfahler (Eds.), Compiler Construction. Proceedings, 1992. VIII, 320 pages. 1992.

Vol. 642: K. P. Jantke (Ed.), Analogical and Inductive Inference. Proceedings, 1992. VIII, 319 pages. 1992. (Subseries LNAI).

Vol. 643: A. Habel, Hyperedge Replacement: Grammars and Languages. X, 214 pages. 1992.

Vol. 644: A. Apostolico, M. Crochemore, Z. Galil, U. Manber (Eds.), Combinatorial Pattern Matching. Proceedings, 1992. X, 287 pages. 1992.

Vol. 645: G. Pernul, A M. Tjoa (Eds.), Entity-Relationship Approach – ER '92. Proceedings, 1992. XI, 439 pages, 1992.

Vol. 646: J. Biskup, R. Hull (Eds.), Database Theory – ICDT '92. Proceedings, 1992. IX, 449 pages. 1992.

Vol. 647: A. Segall, S. Zaks (Eds.), Distributed Algorithms. X, 380 pages. 1992.

Vol. 648: Y. Deswarte, G. Eizenberg, J.-J. Quisquater (Eds.), Computer Security – ESORICS 92. Proceedings. XI, 451 pages. 1992.

Vol. 649: A. Pettorossi (Ed.), Meta-Programming in Logic. Proceedings, 1992. XII, 535 pages. 1992.

Vol. 650: T. Ibaraki, Y. Inagaki, K. Iwama, T. Nishizeki, M. Yamashita (Eds.), Algorithms and Computation. Proceedings, 1992. XI, 510 pages. 1992.

Vol. 651: R. Koymans, Specifying Message Passing and Time-Critical Systems with Temporal Logic. IX, 164 pages. 1992.

Vol. 652: R. Shyamasundar (Ed.), Foundations of Software Technology and Theoretical Computer Science. Proceedings, 1992. XIII, 405 pages. 1992.

Vol. 653: A. Bensoussan, J.-P. Verjus (Eds.), Future Tendencies in Computer Science, Control and Applied Mathematics. Proceedings, 1992. XV, 371 pages. 1992.

Vol. 654: A. Nakamura, M. Nivat, A. Saoudi, P. S. P. Wang, K. Inoue (Eds.), Prallel Image Analysis. Proceedings, 1992. VIII, 312 pages. 1992.

Vol. 655: M. Bidoit, C. Choppy (Eds.), Recent Trends in Data Type Specification. X, 344 pages. 1993.

Vol. 656: M. Rusinowitch, J. L. Rémy (Eds.), Conditional Term Rewriting Systems. Proceedings, 1992. XI, 501 pages. 1993.

Vol. 657: E. W. Mayr (Ed.), Graph-Theoretic Concepts in Computer Science. Proceedings, 1992. VIII, 350 pages. 1993.

Vol. 658: R. A. Rueppel (Ed.), Advances in Cryptology – EUROCRYPT '92. Proceedings, 1992. X, 493 pages. 1993.

Vol. 659: G. Brewka, K. P. Jantke, P. H. Schmitt (Eds.), Nonmonotonic and Inductive Logic. Proceedings, 1991. VIII, 332 pages. 1993. (Subseries LNAI).

Vol. 660: E. Lamma, P. Mello (Eds.), Extensions of Logic Programming. Proceedings, 1992. VIII, 417 pages. 1993. (Subseries LNAI).

Vol. 661: S. J. Hanson, W. Remmele, R. L. Rivest (Eds.), Machine Learning: From Theory to Applications. VIII, 271 pages. 1993.

Vol. 662: M. Nitzberg, D. Mumford, T. Shiota, Filtering, Segmentation and Depth. VIII, 143 pages. 1993.

Vol. 663: G. v. Bochmann, D. K. Probst (Eds.), Computer Aided Verification. Proceedings, 1992. IX, 422 pages. 1993.